Oracle GoldenGate 12c

Hands-on Guide to Enterprise Data Integration Solutions

Fawzi Alswaimil

DEDICATION

To my wife, Afrah: *Without her continuous support and understanding of the rough road, this project would never have been started. She is the best there is and the best there will be.*

To my three beautiful daughters, Lujain, Deema, and Nour F. Alswaimil: *Their love, kindness, and motivation is the engine behind my professional success. I admire their talent, values and purity.*

To my parents: *They made me live by example and gave me so much love. May God bless them with mercy. They were such open–minded parents. I'm always honored and proud of them.*

To my sisters and brothers: *Thank you for keeping our small family united. You're my best friends. In memory of my #1 best friend, my brother Seraj (1982-2008): You are always remembered.*

Oracle GoldenGate 12c
Hands-on Guide to Enterprise Data Integration Solutions

By Fawzi Alswaimil

Printed in the United States of America.

Published by Rampant TechPress, Kittrell, North Carolina, USA

Oracle In Focus Series: Book #48

Series Editor: Donald K. Burleson

Editors: Jennifer Kittleson, Donald K. Burleson

Production Editors: Janet Burleson

Cover Design: Janet Burleson

Printing History:

February 2017 for First Edition

ISBN-13: 978-0-9861194-3-9

Table of Contents

Chapter 6:

Comparison of High-Volume In-Flight Data Using Oracle GoldenGate Veridata ... 389

Chapter 8:

Chapter 9:

Chapter 10:

Acknowledgements

This book is a product of a combination of field experience, teaching and research. Imagine sitting on the other end of the globe writing such a book. It's unusual, but believe me it's equally challenging and rewarding. Thanks to virtualization technologies, for without their ability to comprise a large number of interconnected database systems, it would be very difficult to create the working environment to illustrate concepts requiring multiple databases and systems.

Firstly, I want to thank my editor, Jennifer Kittleson. She has been very supportive and understands what it takes to complete such a project using a distinct development approach. Thank you, Jenifer for the tips and techniques you provided me during the writing of this book. Your professional engagement has made its completion a very smooth one. It will be my pleasure to write my next book with you.

Secondly, I extend my appreciation to my reviewer M.D Smith. She is a fun individual who enjoys her profession as a self–employed consultant & teacher. She delivered editing on time and at a great rate. She edited 516 pages and sometimes while being "momentarily health challenged" to meet my deadline. She recommended tips and corrections to make the book more presentable.

Additionally, I would like to thank my daughter "Lujain" who is a pathologist working at Beth Israel Hospital in Boston, MA. She handled all administrative details with Michelle so that I could concentrate on my job and writing. Thank you, honey!

Thanks to Billy who made the first couple of chapters "razor sharp accurate." His feedback and our discussions were very positive. I thank him for keeping in touch, asking about progress, and offering help if needed. Thanks to my daughter "Deema" who is a Computer Science graduate student at Brandeis University in Waltham, MA. She has developed the Java version of GoldenGate Configuration Assistance (GGCA), which includes 1000s of lines of object–oriented programming to produce a well-engineered software.
From the Oracle Data Integration Team, I would like to thank Milomir Vojvodic who is a Senior Business Development Manager for Data Integration. His responses to my inquiries were prompt and 100% accurate.

I'm very fortunate and thankful to friends who consistently kept in touch during this project: Mostafa Ahmed, Khaled Hawahshin, Saeed Alamodi, Sameer Awadallah, Hossam Alhaj, Kashif Meo, the PreciseTrace Management Team (Bassam, Adnan, Johnny and Islam) and the Oracle University Team (Ayman, Moath, Subhi, Carlo, Oana, Supa, Ambreen and Mohamed Issa). Additionally, thank you to all of my friends & associates who supported me throughout this project.

A very special thanks to a talented and motivating Oracle Vice President - Middle East & Africa, Abdul Rahman Al Thehaiban. His continued and strong endorsements have positively influenced me as an Oracle professional. Thank you for years of invaluable support and facilitating my requests and concerns.

A very humble appreciation to the engineers of Oracle GoldenGate software: Eric Fish and Todd Davidson who are the founders of GoldenGate Software Inc. In fact, soon after performing a deep dive into Oracle GoldenGate, you will realize they are geniuses with talented software engineering principles.

With my sincere thanks,

Fawzi Alswaimil

Oracle GoldenGate Fundamentals

CHAPTER

Overview of GoldenGate Topics

The objective of this chapter is to cover Oracle GoldenGate fundamentals, focusing on cases and applications, concepts and architecture, topologies and designs, components and building blocks, and an end-to-end illustrative setup for a head start. For users already knowledgeable in Oracle GoldenGate, this chapter is intended as a refresher; for users new to Oracle GoldenGate, it builds the foundation to continue the remaining chapters. Despite the fact that the illustrative setup and commands are developed on Oracle GoldenGate 12c, they should apply to Oracle GoldenGate supported releases, unless noted otherwise.

The chapter discusses and exemplifies the following topics:

- Oracle database replication evolution and history
- Supported platforms and product set for GoldenGate
- Enterprise applications and use cases
- Network topologies and designs for GoldenGate
- Building blocks, architecture and processes workflow in GoldenGate
- Command-line utilities and obey files
- GoldenGate Parameter files and macros
- GoldenGate Manager process
- Primary and secondary extracts groups for change data capture
- Change data delivery group in GoldenGate
- GoldenGate trails and trail file format
- Commit change number, checkpoint file and checkpoint table
- The GoldenGate data server collector
- Intermediate systems and integrated capture
- Data selection, filtering, transformation and column mapping in GoldenGate
- Data definition file utility
- Built-in functions and tokens
- Call-out to database stored procedures and C programs
- Post deployment configuration options in GoldenGate

- Configure primary extract for Automatic storage environment (ASM)
- Implementing high-performance parallel processing with GoldenGate
- Generate reports and lagging in GoldenGate
- Configure extract and replicate processes for pluggable database environment
- Demonstration of three-step configuration of GoldenGate

The aim of the book is to present an in-depth dive into Oracle GoldenGate 12c applications for area-specific solutions presented in subsequent chapters. Even though Oracle GoldenGate concepts apply across supported platforms, the fundamentals chapter discusses Oracle GoldenGate 12c for Oracle Database 11g, Oracle Database 12c, and Microsoft SQL Server 2008.

For training purposes only, an Oracle VirtualBox and VM player machine are made available and provide a quick setup to practice Oracle GoldenGate 12c.

Oracle GoldenGate, Enterprise Software for Replication

For years, Oracle has been one of the world largest enterprise software company. Today, Oracle software is found globally at fortune companies running core business applications. These companies continue to have real demands for solutions to optimize, consolidate and integrate business functions across the enterprise by running heterogeneous core business applications systems. Oracle GoldenGate is part of Oracle data integration solution (DIS) portfolio, and when deployed as best practices, it becomes the platform for data consolidation and integration delivering best performance, flexible architecture, reliability and extendibility across the enterprise.

As Oracle continues the research and development for the world's leading object relational database management system (ORDBMS), enterprise applications demand more integration between database platforms. When it's for an enterprise, the integration must be *heterogeneous*, and that is a key differentiator to stand out and stay competitive within the data integration market. Oracle GoldenGate is optimized to run on many popular database management systems such as Oracle, MySQL, Microsoft SQL Server, IBM DB2, and others.

Enterprise applications require moving transactional data in real-time between systems hosted globally, and it has been traditionally implemented using in-house developed applications utilizing database links, triggers and materialized views among the enterprise databases.

When it's for the enterprise, data growth maintains a linear pattern and mostly requires instant data replication, without any time lag. Another key differentiator is how Oracle GoldenGate enables real-time data movement with *sub-second latency* using an optimized change data capture and delivery processes, while employing basic-to-complex data transformation and consolidation for data in transit.

Performance and data consistency cannot be compromised at the enterprise level. Oracle GoldenGate uses its proprietary technique to maintain data consistency across systems regardless of databases type. Using in-memory processing, Oracle GoldenGate treats a transaction as a complete logical unit of work. When the transaction is committed, it's assigned an Oracle GoldenGate commit sequence number (CSN) or discarded when the transaction is rolled back. Committed transactions are moved to the next downstream process. At the target system, the transactions are reassembled and applied with the same capture order for maintaining *transaction integrity*. By having Oracle GoldenGate capture committed transactions only, this has a substantial performance enhancement on high-volume transactional systems.

Oracle GoldenGate has *heterogeneous* support, *sub-second latency* for data movement, and transactional data *integrity,* making GoldenGate an ideal enterprise software for powering mission critical applications.

Enterprises running mission critical applications require well engineered software, promoting flexible and extendable architecture. Implementing Oracle GoldenGate is site specific, and based on site business and technical requirements, and a flexible dynamic architecture is developed and deployed for each site. Based on the network topology, capture and delivery groups may be designed loosely or tightly coupled for efficient resource utilization with varying degrees of parallelism and custom development for unlimited extendibility.

Because Oracle GoldenGate uses its own checkpoint sub-system, it's enabled an optimized restart facility to guard against any type of failures. The extract and replicate processes continuously checkpoint their read and write positions. In many systems, data security regulation mandates data availability at all times, and Oracle customers had been using Oracle Data Guard to meet data security requirements for disaster recovery. Oracle GoldenGate extract groups support capture from a Data Guard standby archive log file, and this integration seamlessly promotes data movement from the standby database leaving the source production database dedicated for online transactions, an added advantage for report offloading instance from a standby database environment.

Now, let's look at the evolution of Oracle replication.

Oracle Data Replication Evolution

Data replication has always been a requirement for diverse database applications, and fully transparent data replication is part of the Oracle database framework. Hence, Oracle database replication was developed using PL/SQL database application programmatic interface (API) and enabled from within PL/SQL or Oracle Enterprise Manager (GUI). For high-volume transactions, handling data replication outside of the database contributes to achieving real-time data replication across heterogeneous systems as it's engineered by Oracle GoldenGate.

The following describes the history of Oracle database replication from inception to current; that is, from Oracle 7 to Oracle GoldenGate 12c.

Oracle Replication, June 1992

Oracle replication was first introduced with Oracle 7.0. It was a simple infrastructure, where database triggers associated with database tables, moving data to a remote database using database links. Subsequently, the feature has been completely redeveloped as Oracle advanced replication.

Oracle Advanced Replication, May 1994

Oracle 7.1 introduced Oracle advanced replication. This was a complete data replication framework for creating complex database replication network, such as master-to-master replication. Using PL/SQL API or Oracle Enterprise Manager (GUI), data replication API infrastructure generated and enabled data replication. Basic predefined data conflict resolutions were defined and handled internally.

Oracle Streams, May 2002

Oracle Database 9.2 introduced Oracle Streams. Streams uses advance queuing technology for data capture, propagate and apply workflow. Oracle Streams supports creating complex data replication networks, such as master-to-master by using PL/SQL API or Oracle enterprise manager (GUI). Oracle Streams has superseded Oracle advanced replication.

Oracle GoldenGate, September 2009

This is data replication and beyond. Oracle GoldenGate enables high availability solutions, real-time data integration, transactional change data capture (CDC) and delivery, high-performance data replication, and complex data transformations. Oracle

GoldenGate is engineered for high-performance, real-time heterogeneous data replication, supporting the leading database management systems with three key differentiators: heterogeneous, sub-second latency, and data integrity.

Oracle's strategy for data replication solutions stated Oracle database Streams is superseded by Oracle GoldenGate as quoted on Oracle Statement of Direction, November 2012:

> *"Oracle Streams continues to be supported but will not be enhanced to support any new database features in future releases. This means that Streams will continue to support Exactly what it supports today (11.2) in future releases.*
>
> *It also means that any new database features, data types, or capabilities will not be supported by Streams. Customers who want to take advantage of the new data types and features will need to license Oracle GoldenGate." – Oracle Corporation*

With that said, the direction is definitely strategic and positively reflects the continued research and development efforts for more a comprehensive Oracle GoldenGate product set. It is highly integrated with other related Oracle products, particularly Oracle Data Integrator (ODI) and Oracle Database 12c data guard technology.

What is New for Oracle GoldenGate 12c?

Oracle GoldenGate 12c version 12.1.2.0.0 was made available on October 2013. The following is a brief description of the new features and the enhancements introduced by Oracle GoldenGate 12c.

Database Support

Oracle GoldenGate 12c supports Oracle Database 12c, the database for cloud computing. Oracle GoldenGate continues supporting and enhancing existing non-Oracle database platforms, such as MS SQL Server, Teradata, mainframe and external adapters.

Software Installation

Oracle GoldenGate 12c is shipped with a graphical user interface (GUI) installer, supporting Oracle Database 11g and Oracle Database 12c. The 5-step easy-to-use wizard de-supported the manual installation of previous releases. The GUI installer installs the software, creates the directories' structure, and starts the manager process. The software is bundled for Oracle Database 11g and Oracle Database 12c.

Integrated Capture

For users who want to isolate the Oracle GoldenGate capture process from the production database system, you can rely on integrated capture extracts. With integrated capture, Oracle GoldenGate 12c is installed on a downstream system and continuously receives REDO log files from the source system. Oracle GoldenGate 12c has transparently enhanced the performance of integrated capture and replicate processes. Integrated capture will be the area of enhancements on future releases.

Oracle Multitenant Container Database

Oracle GoldenGate 12c supports capturing from and delivering to an Oracle multitenant container database (CDB). A primary extract captures from a pluggable database (PDB), writes data to a local trail, delivering a remote pluggable database.

Extended TABLE and MAP Statement

Oracle GoldenGate 12c supports a three-part object name for the *table* and *map* statement. The object name includes <container>.<schema>.<table name>.

Enhanced DDL Support

DDL replication does not require that database DDL triggers be created to replicate database structure changes. Oracle GoldenGate 12c performs native DDL replication. This is the default mode, and switching back to capture DDL mode requires Oracle GoldenGate 12c DDL setup.

Character Set

Oracle GoldenGate 12c enhanced the change data delivery by providing automatic character set support, eliminating the need to set the *nls_lang* parameter on the replicate process.

Initial-load Data Types

Oracle GoldenGate 12c initial-load remote task supports all Oracle data types including BLOB, CLOB, NCLOB, LONG, UDT and XML, making the direct initial-load method an excellent technique.

MS SQL Server

Oracle GoldenGate 12c supports compressed backup, in addition to the previously supported uncompressed backup. Compressed backup uses less I/O, thereby increasing the backup speed. Now let's look at the GoldenGate product set.

The Oracle GoldenGate Product Set

Oracle GoldenGate 12c bundles several Oracle software, which are licensed separately. The following is a brief description of Oracle GoldenGate product set. A major software component of Oracle GoldenGate is adapters, used to support legacy systems and site-specific data processing requirements. These are mostly adapted by financial institutes using BASE24 system for payment processing. The IBM mainframe is has always been supported by Oracle GoldenGate for enabling data movement to systems across the enterprise.

The Oracle GoldenGate product set is described next, starting with Oracle GoldenGate core for basic data capture and delivery.

The Oracle GoldenGate Core Features

The core is made of Oracle GoldenGate capture and Oracle GoldenGate apply. Oracle GoldenGate core is classified as:

- Oracle GoldenGate for Oracle database
- Oracle GoldenGate for non-Oracle databases
- Oracle GoldenGate for mainframes (MVS/ESA, System 390)

Oracle GoldenGate core enables real-time change data capture (CDC), moving high volumes of transactional data between databases with very low latency and data integrity using combinations of heterogeneous source and target databases. The separation of capture and apply Oracle GoldenGate core license enables faster return on investment (ROI) and cost-effective integration with non-Oracle data integration software.

An added advantage of Oracle GoldenGate core is support for Oracle Database standard edition, providing high availability solutions for non-enterprise users using Oracle database standard edition. Oracle GoldenGate core includes full use of XStream and Active Data Guard. In a nutshell, XStream is an API for enabling client applications to receive and send real-time data. Active Data Guard enables the physical standby database to be opened for read-only while applying changes from the primary database. Both XStream and Active Data Guard require running Oracle database enterprise edition.

Two essential components of Oracle GoldenGate core are GoldenGate Software Command Interface (GGSCI) and the *logdump* utilities. We use GGSCI to define, configure, create and deploy GoldenGate components from the command-line; use *logdump* utility for reading, searching and managing trail files and troubleshooting. The LOGDUMP opens a trail file and uses the Record Byte Address (RBA) to perform transaction navigation and retrieve statistics.

Management Pack for Oracle GoldenGate

The management pack is composed of a set of Oracle GoldenGate products providing a graphical user interface (GUI) for managing Oracle GoldenGate using the latest Java and Web-based technologies.

Oracle GoldenGate Director

A graphical user interface (GUI) can be used for defining, configuring, managing, monitoring and reporting on Oracle GoldenGate instances through Java client and web-based interfaces. Oracle GoldenGate Director provides a diagramming visual tool for creating diagrams for new or existing Oracle GoldenGate instances. Using drag-and-drop technique, the diagramming tool creates capture and delivery groups, initial load, capture, trial, files and replicates easily and instantly. Figure 1.1 shows the diagramming tool.

Refer to chapter 9 for details regarding Oracle GoldenGate Director.

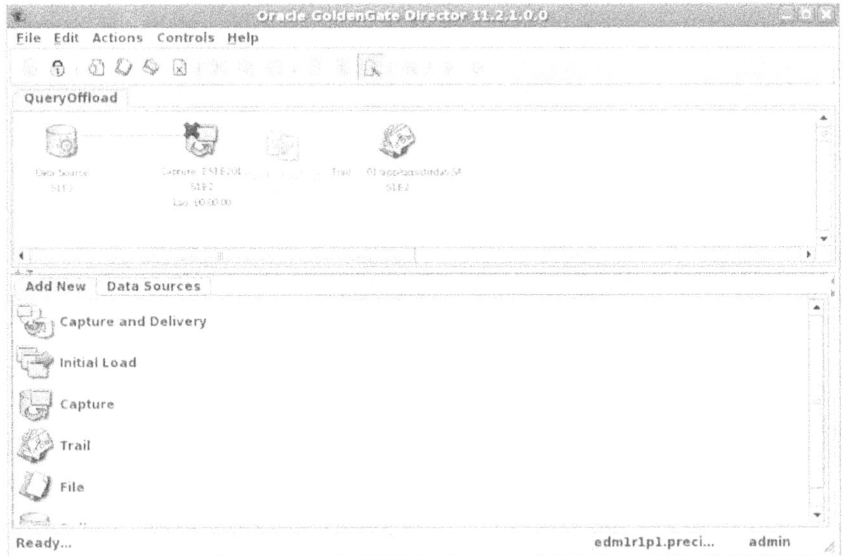

Figure 1.1: **Oracle GoldenGate Director visual diagramming tool**

Oracle GoldenGate Monitor

Oracle GoldenGate monitor is a browser-based tool for viewing purpose only; it does not modify any Oracle GoldenGate configuration files. Rather, it is used to monitor Oracle GoldenGate instance process status, operating and performance statistics, and report runtime events. The major feature of Oracle GoldenGate monitor is external notification using either email or SNMP.

Oracle GoldenGate Plug-in for Oracle Enterprise Manager

Oracle Enterprise Manager Cloud Control 12c management pack for Oracle GoldenGate enables the management of Oracle GoldenGate instances from a centralized integrated console.

Oracle Enterprise Manager Cloud Control 12c management pack for Oracle GoldenGate provides the following functionalities:

- Centralized management of multiple Oracle GoldenGate instances
- General health and performance review

Oracle GoldenGate for Veridata

For sites requiring real-time data monitoring, Oracle GoldenGate Veridata provides an easy-to-use yet powerful solution for identifying out-of-sync data before becoming diverted causing data inconsistency. Deployed together with the Oracle GoldenGate real-time data replication product or separately, Oracle GoldenGate Veridata ensures that data consistency is maintained across two configured databases, playing a major role when performing zero downtime migration and upgrade using Oracle GoldenGate. Figure 1.2 depicts Oracle GoldenGate Veridata.

The major components for configuring Oracle GoldenGate include:

- GoldenGate Veridata server
- Apache Tomcat Web server
- Apache Tomcat Web Server administration tool
- GoldenGate Veridata Web
- GoldenGate Veridata repository
- GoldenGate Veridata agent

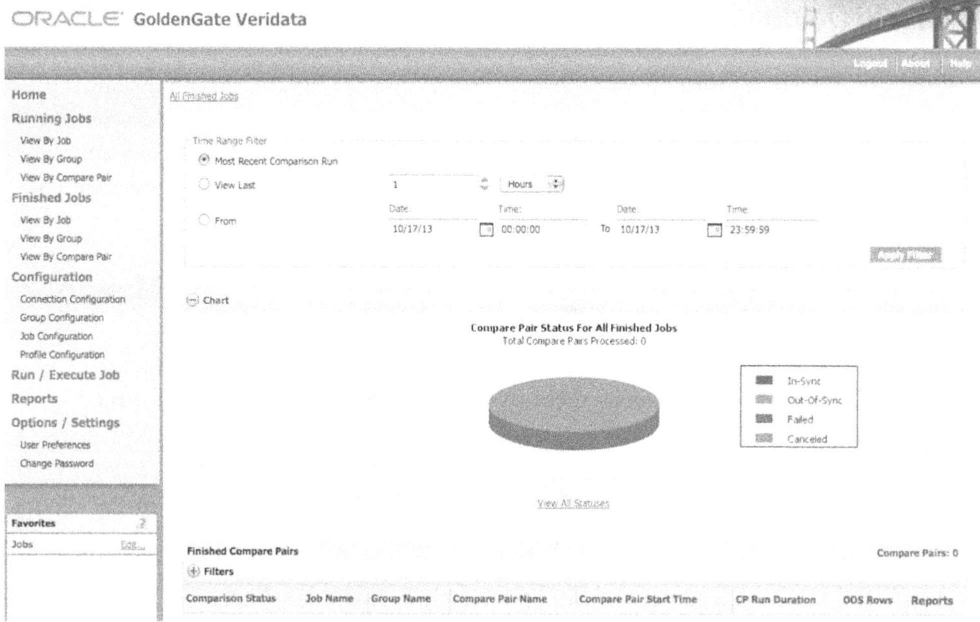

Figure 1.2: **Oracle GoldenGate Veridata**

Refer to chapter 6 for details regarding Oracle GoldenGate Veridata.

Oracle GoldenGate Adapters

Oracle GoldenGate provide support for different types of adapters. These adapters highly promote Oracle GoldenGate integration with legacy systems running legacy applications and ETL-based applications.

Oracle GoldenGate Adapter for Flat File

The GoldenGate flat file adapter enables Oracle GoldenGate to produce a series of sequential flat files data and control files from transactional data capture trail files of a source system. This is widely used for data warehouse applications ETL and proprietary or legacy applications.

Oracle GoldenGate flat file adapter uses a special type of extract, implemented as a user exit, to produce rolling data flat file to be consumed by an interface such as Oracle external tables. The data is formatted by Oracle GoldenGate to the specifications of the target applications either as delimiter separated values or length delimited values. Near real-time data feeds to legacy systems is accomplished by minimizing the window elapsed timeframe for batch file rollover, an advantage for using a flat file adapter.

Refer to chapter 12 to learn more about flat file adapter.

Oracle GoldenGate Adapter for Java

Java Message Service (JMS) messages generated from Java applications are handled by a special type of capture, VAM message capture. Using a source definitions file, a local trail is created and routed to the remote system. The remote system data collector server reassembles the data and creates a remote trail for the replicate process.

Refer to chapter 12 to learn more about Java adapter.

Oracle GoldenGate Application Adapter for BASE24

BASE24 is a series of applications produced by ACI Worldwide, Inc. used by payment processing systems for transaction routing and authorization, mostly found at large financial institutions. Oracle GoldenGate provides adapters to integrate BASE24 components heterogeneously, moving data from ATM networks to the core banking systems for online processing. The adapters are available for BASE24.

D24 Adapter

This adapter enables transactional data to be synchronized bi-directionally in real time with high-availability support while maintaining data consistency and integrity.

N24 Adapter

This adapter performs routing and coordination of the notification message to all BASE24 satellite processes after a file refresh has been completed, thereby providing transparent configuration for bidirectional and uni-directional data flow.

T24 Adapter

This adapter resolves issues when moving data among platforms and databases, and acts on the transaction log of TLF and PTLF tokens for all transaction types, ensuring the correct order and format.

Oracle GoldenGate Logger for Enscribe

This provides the mechanism for change data capture on non-audited Enscribe database platforms. The Logger requires the installation of GGSLIB for binding the Oracle GoldenGate and the user's non-stop application. When an Enscribe operation (such as *write*) executes, GGSLIB intercepts it and sends the record to Logger. The Logger writes the records to the universal format log trail, which can then be processed like any other log-based source.

Supported Database Platforms

Oracle GoldenGate heterogeneity aims to support major database management systems. Depending on the database type, support for capture and apply is determined, and whether the change data capture is log-based. Table 1.1 lists the current supported database platforms by Oracle GoldenGate 11g and higher.

Database Platform	Log-based Capture	Delivery
Oracle Database	☑	☑
Microsoft SQL Server	☑	☑
Oracle MySQL	☑	☑
IBM DB2 for Linux, UNIX and Windows	☑	☑
IBM DB2 for i	☑	☑
IBM DB2 for z/OS	☑	☑
Sybase	☑	☑

SQL/MX	☑	☑
Teradata		☑
Oracle TimesTen		☑
HP Neoview		☑
Netezza		☑
ETL products		☑
JMS message queues		☑

Table 1.1: Oracle GoldenGate supported databases

The vast majority of database capture method are log-based, and translated to low-impact, high-performance on the source database system. The log-based capture technology is a key differentiator of Oracle GoldenGate. By comparison, other extraction tools adapt queuing technology that highly impact the source database system performance. Oracle GoldenGate 12c supports two forms of log-based capture:

1. Classic capture.
2. Integrated capture.

Migration from classic capture to integrated capture is recommended Refer to chapter 8 to learn how to implement Oracle GoldenGate for data warehouse and business intelligence.

Supported Operating Systems

Oracle runs on every conceivable platform from a PC to a mainframe, Oracle GoldenGate offers a foundation for comprehensive integration environments. Oracle GoldenGate 11g and higher supports all of the operating systems, as seen in Table 1.2.

Operating system	Version	Hardware
AIX	5.1, 5.2 and 5.3	IBM PowerPC
HP Nonstop	D46, D47, D48, G06 and H06	NSK
HP-UX	11.11, 11.23 and 11.31	HP Intel IA64 and HP PA-RISC
Oracle Linux	3.0, 4.0, 5.0 and 6.0	AMD/Intel x64, Intel x86 and Intel IA64
RedHat AS	2.1, 3.0, 4.0 and 5.0	AMD/Intel x64, Intel x86 and Intel IA64
Solaris	8, 9 and 10	Sun SPARC
SuSE	9 and 10	Opteron and Intel x86
Tru64	5.1	HP OSF
Windows	2000, 2003, 2008 and XP	AMD/Intel x64, Intel x86 and Intel IA64
z/OS	1.04 and 1.06	Mainframe

Table 1.2: Operating systems support

Oracle GoldenGate Applications

The extendibility, flexibility and adaptability of Oracle GoldenGate enables the implementation of the software across an enterprise to meet the diversity of business objectives. The major areas of applying Oracle GoldenGate listed hereunder are followed by a brief description and diagram.

- Query offloading techniques
- Business continuity solutions
- Zero downtime migration and upgrade
- Operational data warehouse and business intelligence
- Data integration services

Query Offloading Techniques in GoldenGate

Reports are an integral part of any database application system, and the performance overhead associated with running these reports on the production systems sometimes has a negative impact on online users, the real customers. Running standard reports such as end-of-year, month closing, etc. demand more system resources and are normally scheduled during less workload hours. These are usually back-dated reports with a time data gap proportional to the batch window for an online system operating 24/7 using different types for input interfaces.

The solution is implementing Oracle GoldenGate at the enterprise level. This is done for the purpose of query offloading, thereby enabling efficient resource utilization across systems with real-time change data capture (CDC) from OLTP systems acting as data sources, replicating to an adapted database instance that is largely read-only and dedicated for reporting purposes.

For example, cross-platform replication involves heterogeneous change data capture is very common and cost-effective, such as a data source OLTP systems running on Oracle Database 11g on Solaris 11 and a reporting instance running on MySQL 5 on Oracle Enterprise Linux 6.

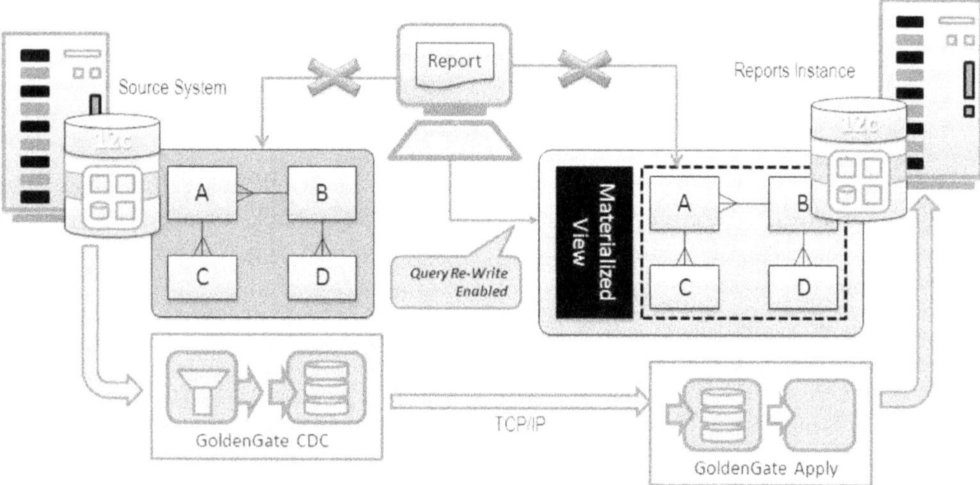

Figure 1-3: **Query offloading technique**

Both Oracle and MS-SQL Server are shipped with features for optimizing out-of-box reporting. Oracle's materialized view enables query rewrite, which greatly enhances report runtime and figure 1.3 depicts a high-level design for query offloading using Oracle GoldenGate.

Refer to Chapter 4 to learn how to implement Oracle GoldenGate for query offloading. Now let's look at GoldenGate business solutions.

GoldenGate Business Continuity Solutions

Oracle GoldenGate is capable of delivering different architectures for business continuity solutions. Each solution is implemented to suit specific high availability needs, and to maximize resource utilization and integration with existing high availability solutions such as Oracle Real Application Clusters (RAC) and Oracle Data Guard (DG).

In general, Oracle GoldenGate high availability solutions are divided into two areas: disaster recovery and high availability.

Disaster Recovery and GoldenGate

The remote database site remains on alert for disaster recovery situation. Oracle GoldenGate unidirectional configuration delivers real-time change data capture (CDC) and change data delivery, ensuring that the gap between the primary (source) and the standby (target) databases is minimized with sub-seconds latency. In the event of primary site failure, the standby database is in read-write mode and ready to accept new connections. The use of Oracle GoldenGate Veridata is recommended for maintaining a consistent view of the two databases for detecting and applying transactions causing data divergence.

Oracle GoldenGate for disaster recovery is a live-standby database. In GoldenGate, the standby database is open for read-write operations, unlike Oracle Data Guard where the database is either in recovery mode or in read-only recovery mode combined.

High Availability with GoldenGate

When using Oracle GoldenGate as a high availability solution, GoldenGate applies the fault tolerance concept system-wide, which includes the database instance and the database files. This is achieved by implementing Oracle Real Application Clusters (RAC) and Oracle Data Guard (DG) combined. Because the local and remote Oracle GoldenGate instances are connected via TCP/IP, constraints related to distance between the two systems are eliminated.

Figure 1.4 shows the high availability architecture that is achieved by implementing Oracle GoldenGate "bi-directional" (two-way) configuration. Users can connect to either system based upon application, location, user type, etc., providing application scalability and best resource utilization.

As with any bi-directional solution, data conflicts are a major concern and should be carefully addressed when using GoldenGate for high availability active-active configuration. GoldenGate's built-in data conflict resolution routines minimize custom development and maintenance of data conflict handling.

However, GoldenGate does not replace RAC or Data Guard; to the contrary, it creates a first-class high availability platform. GoldenGate takes advantage of RAC by registering the manager processes (the application) as a resource in Oracle Clusterware.

This integration ensures that GoldenGate is highly available in the event of a node failure. The GoldenGate instance is transparently migrated to a surviving node.

GoldenGate takes advantage of Data Guard by performing change data capture from the standby database archive log, leaving the primary site intact. This provides the foundation for a near real-time reporting instance, offloading the source database from long running queries and reports.

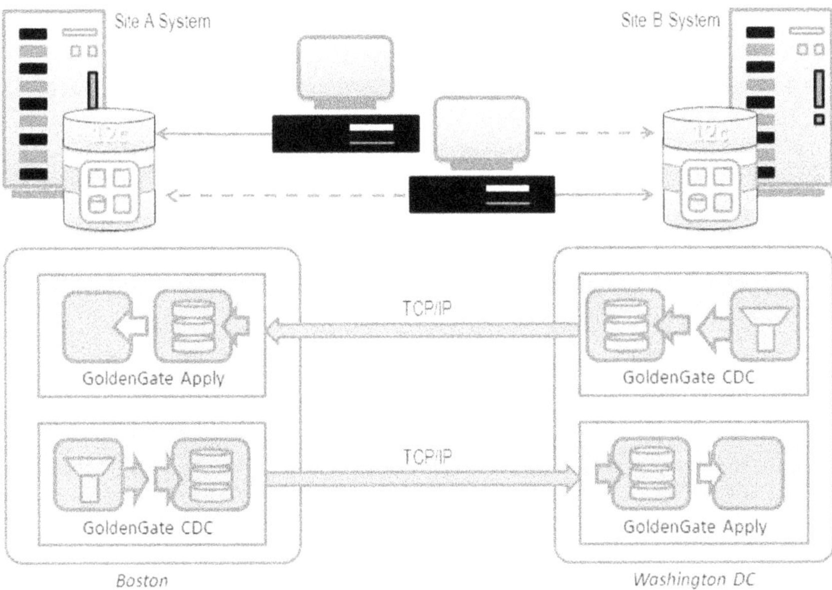

Figure 1.4: **Oracle GoldenGate for high-availability**

Regardless of GoldenGate configurations for high availability, the target database remains open for read-write operations, and it's required by Oracle GoldenGate delivery processes and other applications. Another added value is *heterogeneity*, whereas the source and target systems may have different hardware and software.

Refer to chapter 5 to learn how to implement Oracle GoldenGate for high availability.

Zero Downtime Migration and Upgrade with GoldenGate

Oracle GoldenGate can play a major role in migration and upgrade projects. For systems running mission critical applications, implementing GoldenGate for zero downtime works equally for homogenous and heterogeneous environments. For example, during the migration of Oracle Database 11g on IBM AIX (big endian) to Oracle Database 12c on Oracle Enterprise Linux (small endian), Oracle GoldenGate handles endian differences internally.

When upgrading from 11g to 12c, the Oracle Database Upgrade Assistance (DBUA) requires a database shutdown. The amount of downtime varies, depending on different factors. However, the most obvious benefit when using GoldenGate for migration and upgrade is the provision of solid fail back option. The source database remains intact and active until it's time to be shut down and decommissioned.

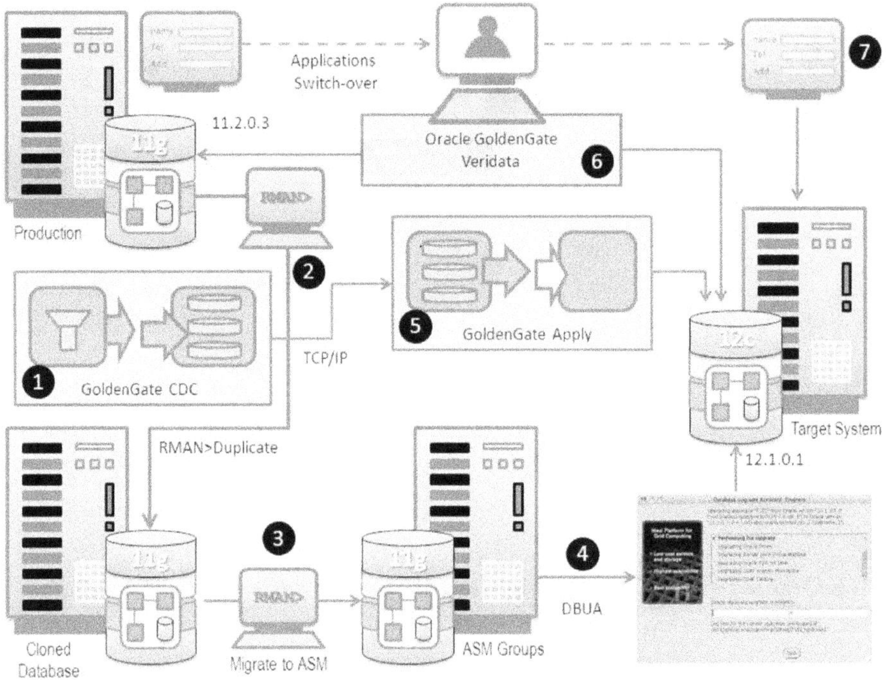

Figure 1.5: **Zero downtime migration and upgrade workflow**

Achieving zero downtime for migration and upgrade requires cloning the current database with GoldenGate. The cloned database is upgraded and synchronized with the existing production database using Oracle GoldenGate. Thr use the Oracle GoldenGate Veridata is highly recommended during the migration and upgrade. Figure 1-5 shows the steps and workflow for performing zero downtime migration and upgrade.

Refer to chapter 7 to learn how to implement Oracle GoldenGate for zero downtime migration and upgrade.

Data warehouse and operational business intelligence with GoldenGate

Very large database (VLDB) for data warehouse and business intelligence needs optimized data feed, are usually delivered using batch windows with ETL using an in-house developed workflow processes. When Oracle GoldenGate is implemented for online data feed to a data warehouse instance, it delivers a high-speed operational repository for data warehouse, and with Oracle GoldenGate data transformation and mapping capabilities, the repository is immediately available for business intelligence applications.

Oracle GoldenGate eliminates the needs for refresh batch windows and customized ETL utilities and Oracle GoldenGate parallel processing feature further enhances the data feed speed for cross-platform heterogeneous systems. The Integration of Oracle GoldenGate with Oracle Data Integrator (ODI) exponentially expedites and optimizes the data feed as an E-LT, promoting highly flexible system. Figure 1-6 shows Oracle GoldenGate for a data warehouse.

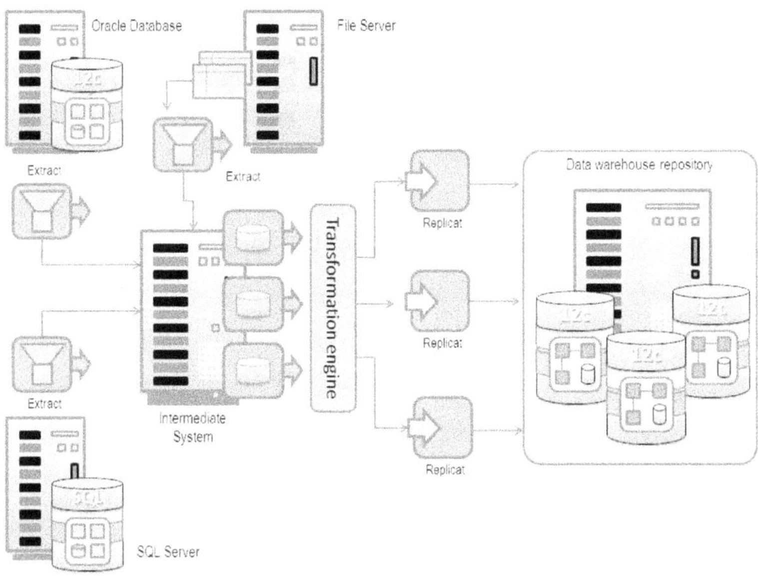

Figure 1-6: Data warehouse feed from heterogamous systems

Refer to Chapter 8 to learn how to implement Oracle GoldenGate on for heterogeneous platforms.

Data integration services in GoldenGate

Oracle GoldenGate provides different types of adapters. These adapters enable integration of modern Java technologies and legacy systems applications with Oracle and non-Oracle databases. A typical example is Oracle GoldenGate BASE24 adapters used by ATM networks for sending data to payment authorization servers. Another example is a smart-phone application sending decoded messages to an application service provider (ASP), where Oracle GoldenGate implemented as a data hub for filtering and routing data across TCP/IP to consumers. Figure 1-7 depicts payment and ATM networks for transactions processing.

Financial institutes processing payments in real-time require access to heterogeneous systems for authorization, validation and reflect changes. With Oracle GoldenGate a unified infrastructure minimizes the complexity for interfacing with foreign systems. Leaving each organization with its own existing databases and platform maximizes the return of investment (ROI) uncompromised.

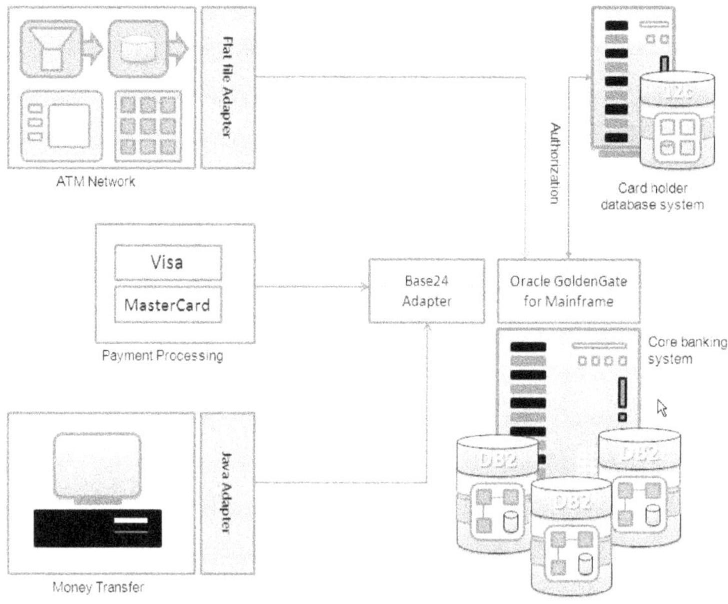

Figure 1-7: payment processing systems

Refer to chapter 12 to learn how to implement Oracle GoldenGate for data integration services.

Oracle GoldenGate Components

The building blocks of Oracle GoldenGate allows high degree for design flexibility for scalable performance, delivering basic-to-complex transactional data replication with transformation capabilities. The basic configuration refer to unidirectional, one-way, data replication from the source to the target database achieving real-time data movement with sub-second latency. However; Oracle GoldenGate commonly deployed to enable integration among heterogeneous systems, moving and consolidating data from various source systems to remote systems with data integrity and consistency. Oracle GoldenGate extract groups can run as either loosely or tightly coupled. The primary extract processes running on source systems for change data capture (CDC), and the secondary extract processes running on an intermediate systems for transformation and routing change data capture to multiple target systems, while the replicate processes are running on target systems (often with parallel processing support for high-performance). Figure 1-8 shows the building blocks found on the source and target systems for configuring an Oracle GoldenGate instance.

An Oracle GoldenGate instance configured for online synchronization consists of the components:

- Source and target databases
- Manager process
- Online extract process
- Local trail files
- Data pump extract process
- TCP/IP Network
- Data server collector
- Remote trail files
- Online replicate process

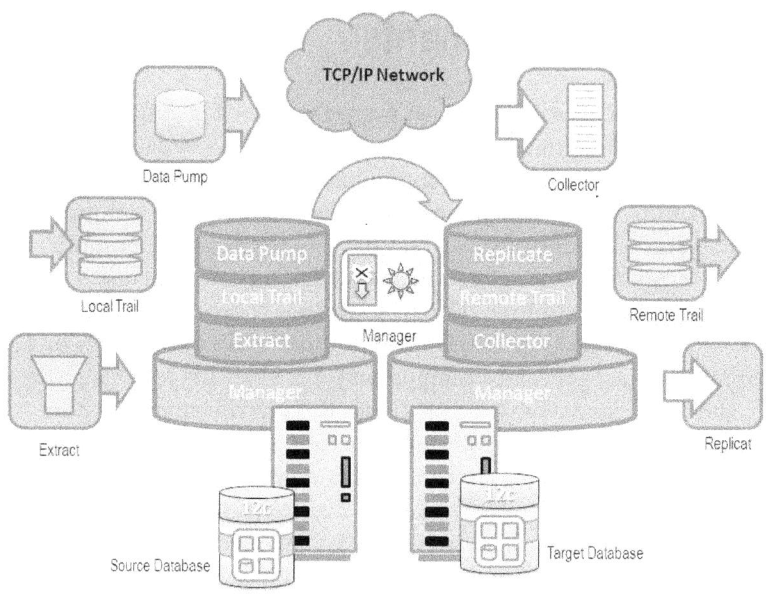

Figure 1-8: Oracle GoldenGate building blocks

The functionality for each of the building block components is described next. Figure 1-9 illustrates a simplified configuration approach, showing the components for performing initial-load and data synchronization. During the initial-load reads from the source database tables, the data synchronization process uses the transaction logs for online data capture and delivery. The use of a Data Pump extract is optional but highly recommend for supporting fault-tolerance and non-interruptible online capture in the event of network failure and avoiding redundant processing by the online extract.

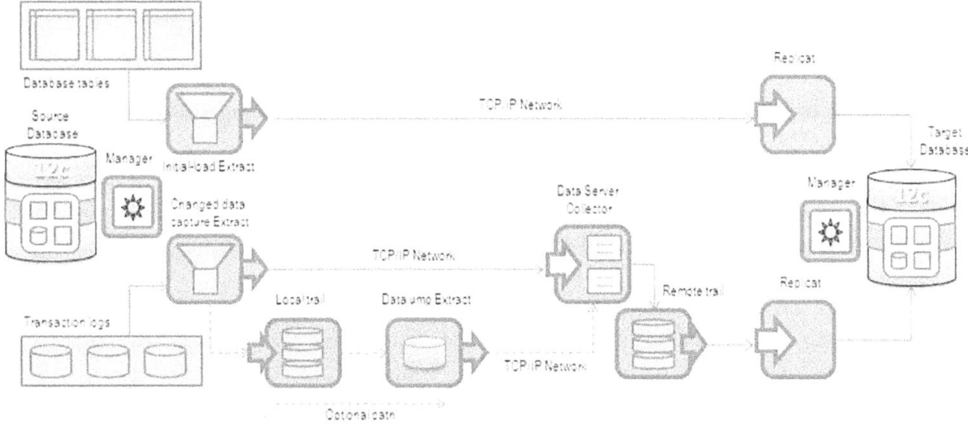

Figure 1-9: Building blocks connected

For initial-load, an initial-load extract read from the source database table and sends insert-type transaction to the remote replicate, which use the database interface to apply the transactions. Refer to chapter 3 to learn how to perform initial-load in GoldenGate.

For change synchronization, a primary extract captures all types of update transactions (both DML and DDL), directly sending the source statements to the data server collector on the remote system, which in turn re-assemble the data and writes to the remote trail in a conical file format. The replicate process in the remote system, reads the trails, creates transaction units, and apply them to the target database in the same commit order occurred in the source database, ensuring data integrity and consistency.

The dotted arrows show the option of using a Data Pump extract, which reads the local trails created by the primary extract process and send them to the data server collector. This configuration avoid redundant processing in case of network failure between the source and target systems. Additionally, it offloads the primary extract from performing non-related task of routing to remote systems.

Inside the GoldenGate source and target databases

Oracle GoldenGate heterogeneous support enables moving data among dissimilar source and target databases. However; the source database must be configured to meet Oracle GoldenGate operating requirements, which is database type specific.

Also, the database platform architecture must be compatible as Oracle GoldenGate 12c is available for 64-bit and 32-bit architecture.

For Linux, to find the platform architecture, use the operating system command:

```
$ uname -a
```

For 64-bit architecture, it will shows x86_64, and x86 for 32-bit architecture.

For MS Windows, use the *systeminfo* command as shown below:

```
C:\>systeminfo | findstr /i TYPE:
```

```
OS Build Type:              Uniprocessor Free
System type:                X86-based PC
```

Oracle database version

For Oracle source database where the change data capture process is running, the database supplemental logging must be enabled. And, the database should be operating on archive log mode. To find the database version, run the following SQL*Plus query.

```
SQL> SELECT banner
  2  FROM   v$version;
```

```
BANNER
--------------------------------------------------------------------------------
Oracle Database 12c Enterprise Edition Release 12.1.0.1.0 - 64bit
Production
PL/SQL Release 12.1.0.1.0 - Production
CORE      12.1.0.1.0    Production
TNS for Linux: Version 12.1.0.1.0 - Production
NLSRTL Version 12.1.0.1.0 - Production
```

MS SQL Server database version

To determine the source MS SQL Server database version, from Microsoft SQL Server Management Studio, execute the query:

```
SELECT @@VERSION
```

The source MS-SQL Server database must be operating on Full Recovery model mode. You right-mouse on database properties and select the *options* page as shown on figure 1-10. However, if the target database is for read-only purpose, it may be operated in *Simple model* mode to avoid growing the log file unnecessarily when performing long running operation such as initial-load.

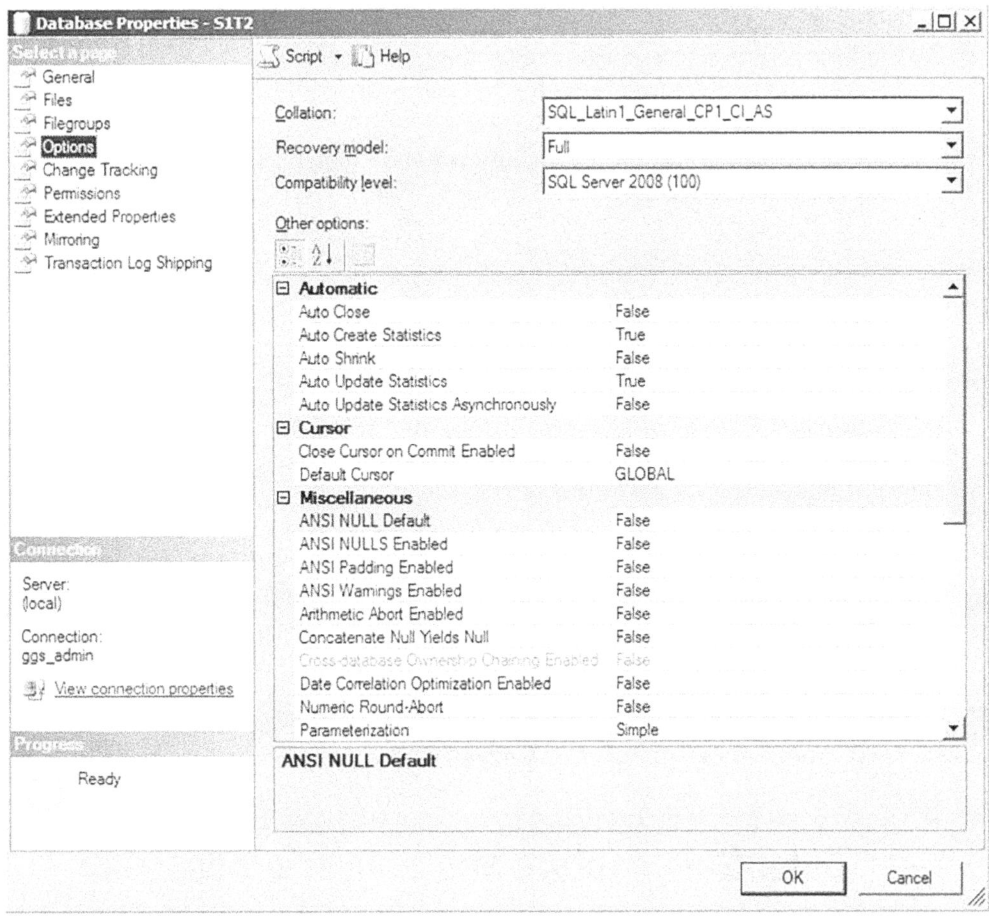

Figure 1-10: MS SQL Server recovery model

The GoldenGate manager process

Each Oracle GoldenGate instance has a dedicated manager process. After successfully installing Oracle GoldenGate, the manager process is the first process configured and started for managing a running Oracle GoldenGate instance. The manager process listen on specific static TCP/IP port and continues running for handling the instances activities. Starting the manager process requires adding the

PORT parameter only to *mgr.prm* file. Refer to chapter 3 to learn more about setting the managers process parameters.

The manager process is responsible for the following activities:

- Response to errors, events and produces reports
- Manages and allocates ports for dynamic processes
- Start Oracle GoldenGate processes
- Start dynamic Oracle GoldenGate processes
- Performs trail files purge management

The status of the manager process is limited to either of the following status:

- STOPPED, manually stopped or unable to start
- RUNNING, started successfully and listening on specific TCP/IP port

The manager process configuration enables automatic start and restart of extract and replicate processes, this provides unattended extract management for enhancing Oracle GoldenGate high availability.

The Oracle GoldenGate manager process on MS-SQL Server runs as a Windows service, with the default services name is GGSMGR. To create multiple Windows Oracle GoldenGate instances, use the GLOBALS parameter *mgrservname* <service name> for defining unique Oracle GoldenGate Windows service for each instance.

While Oracle GoldenGate instance is running, shutdown the manager process, quickly make the modifications to *mgr.prm* and restart it. This technique enhances Oracle GoldenGate availability when re-configuring the manager process.

The GoldenGate capture and deliver processes

There are four types of Oracle GoldenGate processes, depending on the task, the topology adapted, extracts and replicates processes are configured and defined.

GoldenGate Online extract

The online extract process performs change data capture (CDC) for committed transactions. The online extract reads the transaction logs from either of two sources:

- The online log file
- The archive log files

The online redo log files has the advantage of performance for sub-second latency, which cannot be achieved by the archive log file option. These two capture options are mutually exclusive. Figure 1-11 compare the two options. Best practices recommend using online redo log capture with data pump option for fault tolerance and real-time data replication.

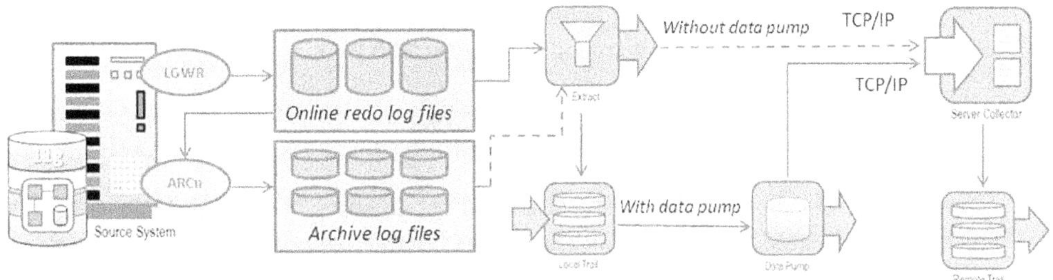

Figure 1-11: Online extract process options

> **Note: Two Data Pump Utilities!** When Oracle acquired GoldenGate, they inherited the utility named data pump, and Oracle Database now has two distinct tools called data pump:
>
> > **Data Pump export/import:** This is a command-line utility used to backup individual tables and schemas into flat files and import from flat files.
> >
> > **Goldengate data pump extract:** This is a process in Goldengate that takes and applies archived redo logs to a remote database.
>
> So there we have it, two separate and distinct utilities named Data Pump. Of course, all references to data pump in this text refer to the GoldenGate data pump process.

Back to Figure 1.1., we see that the online extract either:

1) Writes to local trail files and uses a data pump extract to route data in large block across TCP/IP to a remote dynamic server collector.
2) Alternatively, it routes data to a remote dynamic process on the target system called data server collector.

The status of any GoldenGate online extract is one of the following:

- STOPPED: The extract process stopped using STOP command
- STARTING: The manager invoking the extract process
- RUNNING: The extract process currently running, reading the transaction log
- ABENDED: The extract process terminated abnormally

The online extract performs checkpoints on its reads and writes progress to a checkpoint file. In the event of failure, the extract process is capable to recapturing from the point of failure forward of the transaction logs.

Initial-load extract in GoldenGate

Next, we read the source database tables for establishing the target database tables. When coordinated with an online extract for change data capture, an initial-load extract enables high availability as it does not lock the source database tables.

An initial-load extract has several options:

- Writes to remote initial-load files
- Directly invokes an initial-load replicate process
- Invokes an initial-load replicate process as remote task

The initial-load extract does not maintain a checkpoint, such that in the event of failure the initial-load extract must be restarted after truncating the target tables. Oracle GoldenGate initial-load techniques is suitable for heterogeneous environment, when the source and target database platforms are different. Oracle GoldenGate techniques for initial-load are:

- File to replicate
- Direct load
- File to database utility
- Database utility

Refer to chapter 3 to learn more about initial-load techniques and architecture using GoldenGate and non-GoldenGate methods.

Online replicate in GoldenGate

The online replicate process reads the remote trail files and applies transactions to the target database, thereby ensuring that the transaction committed order of the source database thereby ensuring data consistency and integrity. The online replicate process expects canonical formatted trail files.

The status of the online replicate process is one of the following:

- STOPPED: The extract process stopped using STOP command
- STARTING: The manager invoking the extract process
- RUNNING: The extract process currently running, reading remote trail files
- ABENDED: The extract process terminated abnormally

The online replicate checkpoints it's read and write progress using either of two options:

- Concurrently to checkpoint file and database table, known as a checkpoint table
- Checkpoint file only

It's highly recommended to use checkpoint file and checkpoint table, which is the default. In the event of failure, the replicate process is capable to restart from the point of failure. By repositioning the relative byte address (RBA), the replicate process is capable of re-applying the remote trail transactions to the remote database.

Special run replicate in GoldenGate

Special run replicate is used by the initial-load extract. A special run replicate is started by an initial-load extract and terminated up on completion of the initial-load extract. The special run replicate does not maintain checkpoint; in case of failure the process needs to be restarted.

Remote task replicate in GoldenGate

The mote task replicate is designed for initial-load. This is used when the initial-load extract directly invoking a remote replicate for performing the initial-load replicate. When invoking a replicate as a remote task, the data collector server is not used.

Note, when using these for initial-load methods on heterogeneous environment such as from Oracle database to MS SQL Server, a source definition file is required to be created at the source system, then transferred to the target system as ASCII file.

The Data pump extract in GoldenGate

The GoldenGate data pump is an optional extract process, referred to as *secondary* extract. It reads the local trail files and routes data to the target system. It's highly recommended to use a data pump configuration. The advantages of configuring a data pump extract include:

- In the case of network failure, the primary extract continues writing to the local trail, up on network availability, the data pump process starts sending data to remote system. Without a data pump the primary extract stores change data capture in memory until the network become available. This will cause the primary extract to eventually *abended* due to system resources unavailability.
- Data movement with intensive data transformation occurring at the source system, the data pump extract offloads the primary extract and leaving it dedicated for change data capture only. TCP/IP communication with the data server collector become a function of the data pump extract only.
- For environment composed of multiple target systems, multiple data pumps read the same local trail and route data to the target systems. When one of the connection is not available, only that specific remote system effected. Without data pump it would require using multiple primary extracts each sending data to specific target system data server collector.
- For security and offloading purposes, implementing an intermediate system architecture is an ideal solution. Two data pump extracts must be configured, on source and intermediate system for routing data. Data transformation occurs at the intermediate system entirely offloading the source system.

The data pump extract not to be confused with Oracle database data pump. This is an Oracle GoldenGate process for reading and routing local trail file to remote systems across TCP/IP network.

The data server collector in GoldenGate

The data server collector is a background process, receiving data from either the primary extract (capture) or secondary extract (data pump).

Two types of data server collector are possible, dynamic and statics. Static collector server started manually for the purpose of assigning specific TCP/IP port number to the data collector server, and it can be associated with multiple extract processes. Dynamic collector server is dynamically started, on port allocated by the manager process, and it can be associated with one-only-one extract process.

When using a dynamic mode, starting, stopping and managing the data server collector is fully automatic. The main function is to receive data sent by the extract process, reassemble the data to Oracle GoldenGate universal format (canonical) and write to the remote trail. The data server collector background process is not associated with a checkpoint file, it's either the primary or secondary extract associated with the data collector writing its reads and writes positions to the checkpoint file.

The GoldenGate audit trails

It's a form of advanced queue structure for managing a temporary storage areas used by Oracle GoldenGate online extract and replicates trail. The default trail files are written in canonical format by the primary extract, and read by the online replicate process. In addition, Oracle GoldenGate supports alternative formats for use by other utilities. Some non-default formats include:

- FORMATASCII, required by file to database initial-load utility
- FORMATSQL, generates DML SQL statements
- FORMATXML, generates XML files

None of the non-default trail file formats are not supported by the replicate process.

Local trail files

When implementing the data pump option, the local trail files are created by the online primary extract of the source system. The local trail files are composed of a two characters prefix and defined using the *exttrail* or *extfile* parameters. The local trail file is created by appending 6-digit to the trail name. If the local extract trail name is 'sa', then the local trail files takes the ranged-name from sa000000 to sa999999. The default trail file size is 10MB, customized using the *megabytes* parameter of the *add exttrail* or *add extfile* commands. An extract must be associated with one local trail only.

Remote trail files in GoldenGate

The remote trail files resides on the target system, and it is created by the data collector server. The remote trail files is composed of two characters prefix and defined using the *rmttrail* or *rmtfile* parameters. The remote trail file is created by appending 6-digit to the trail name. For example, if the local extract trail name is 'ta', then the remote trail files takes the ranged-name from ta000000 to ta999999. The default trail file size is 10MB, customized using the MEGABYTES parameter of the *add rmttrail* or *add rmtfile* commands. A replicate must be associated with one extract remote trail only.

Processes grouping in GoldenGate

The real-time data movement from source to target systems handled *by logical groups*. The logical grouping allows an effective allocation and management of physical resource associated with each group. Data down-streaming starts at the capture group, optionally through the secondary group and ends at the replicate group. The number of primary, secondary and replicate groups is effected by the database schemas partitioning. The name of the group is limited to eight characters and created by the *add extract* and *add replicat* commands.

Primary extract group in GoldenGate

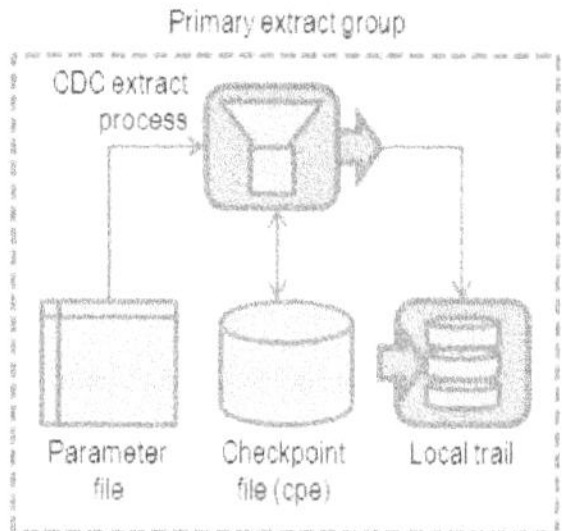

Figure 1-11a: Primary Extract Group

This is the capture group which consists of an extract process for performing change data capture (CDC), a parameter file with the name *<group name.prm>*, a checkpoint file with the name *<group name.cpe>*, and an output local trail (or remote trail) files. The group is also associated with its own discard and report files. The primary process captures committed transaction logs, ensuring transaction integrity and data consistency.

Secondary extract group in GoldenGate

This is the data pump group which consist of an extract process for performing data routing, an input parameter file that has the name *<group name.prm>* and a checkpoint file with the name *<group name.cpe)* and an input local trail. The group is also associated with its own discard and report files. The data pump uses TCP/IP to communicate with a dynamic dedicated data server collector, which re-assemble and write to the remote trail. This group is optional but recommend for fault-tolerance configuration.

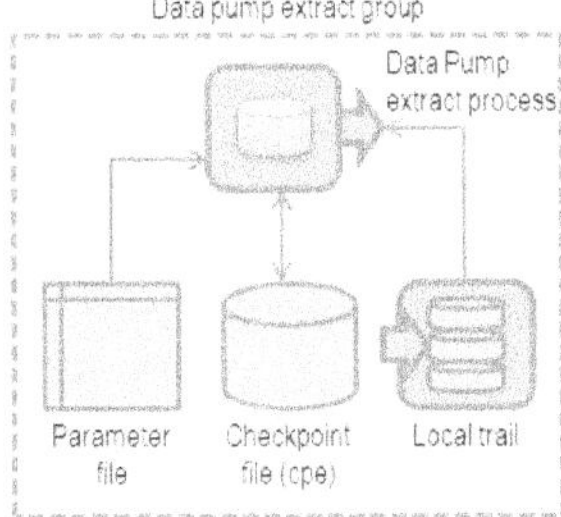

Figure 1-11b: Data Pump Extract

Replicate group in GoldenGate

This the change data delivery group, it consists of a replicate process for performing change data delivery, an input parameter file with the name *<group name.prm>* and a checkpoint table or a checkpoint file with the name *<group name.cpr>*. The group is also associated with its own discard and report files. The replicate process uses the target database SQL native calls to apply changes from the remote trail, maintaining transactional data integrity data consistency.

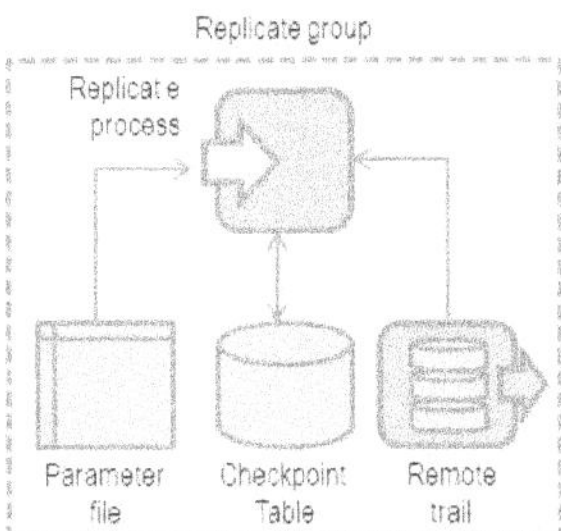

Figure 1-11c: Replicate Group

Figure 1-12 depicts the data streaming and the relationship between the three groups, assuming the optional secondary group is used.

This diagram shows a serialized data streaming without parallel processing, for details on how Oracle GoldenGate implements parallelism, refer to the section implementing parallel processing.

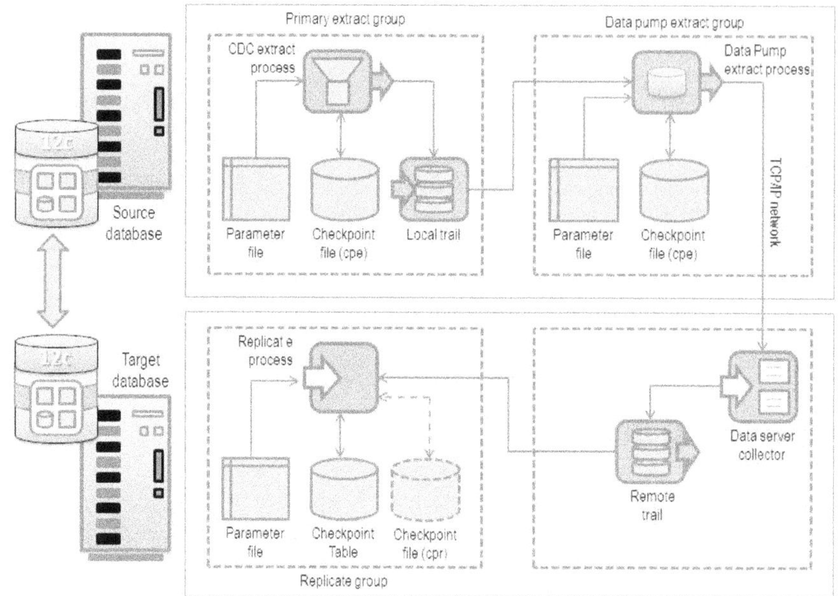

Figure 1-12: Process grouping and workflow

When using intermediate systems, the workflow tends to be loosely coupled, but the concept remains the same. When using integrated capture, the workflow is the same but the change data capture technique is different.

Oracle GoldenGate Architecture explained

The Oracle GoldenGate instance is composed of Oracle GoldenGate software location and an associated manager process. Figure 1-13 depicts Oracle GoldenGate architecture on bi-directional environment.

- The ***manager process***, running on the source and target systems for handling events and starting dynamic extract and replicate processes. It also performs trail file purge management for maintaining an optimized disk utilization.

- The ***primary extract*** is referred to as the *change data capture* (CDC) process, and it reads the transaction logs and write to either a local trail or send data directly to the data sever collector of the remote system (depending weather a data pump is used or not). The recommended practice is to use a data pump process for sending data to the remote data server collector, thereby keeping the primary extract dedicated for change data capture only.

- The ***secondary extract*** is referred to as the *data pump* process, and it reads the local trail file and routes data to remote system. The data is received by a dedicated data collector server.

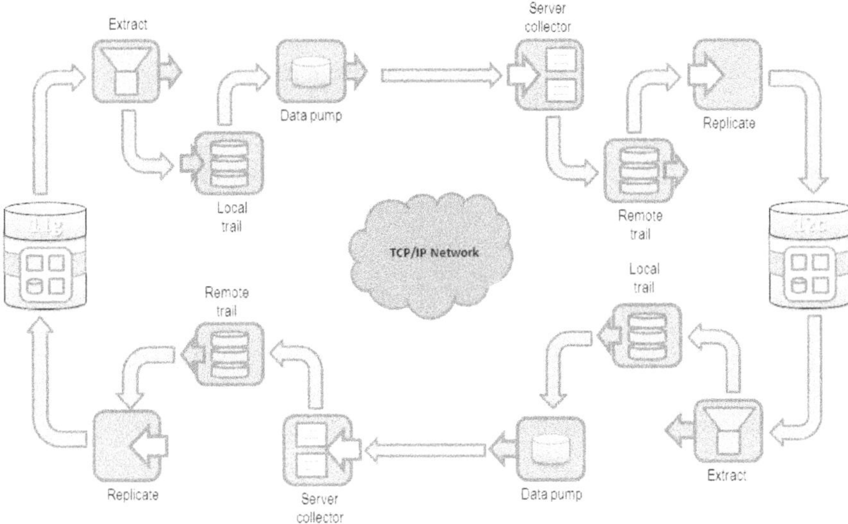

Figure 1-13: GoldenGate processes architecture

- The ***local trail*** is a canonical file format, created by the primary extract, which is read by the database pump process or other Oracle GoldenGate utilities such as LOGDUMP.

- The ***data collector server*** is a background process associated with either a primary extract or a secondary extract. The function of the data collector server the receiving, re-assembling and creating of the remote trail on the target system.

- The ***remote trail*** is a canonical file format, created by the data collector server. Purging of remote trail files is defined by *purgeaoldextracts* parameter.

- The ***replicate process*** (or *replicat* for short) reads the remote trail file and applying the transactions to the remote database, with data integrity and consistency.

GoldenGate Network topologies and GoldenGate Design

The business data acquisition requirements, and the type of Oracle GoldenGate network topology determine the topology and it's very important to be the right topology, because changing the topology at later stage requires changing the configuration as it effects data flow and processes. After the correct topology is selected, the components required to deploy the design are configured, defined, tested and finally deployed. Oracle GoldenGate network topologies listed hereunder followed by description and diagram. These topologies include:

- Unidirectional for query offloading
- Bidirectional for high availability
- Peer-to-peer for load balancing
- Broadcast for data distribution
- Consolidation for data warehouse
- Cascading for scalability

GoldenGate Unidirectional for query offloading

This configuration allows data workflow in one direction, from source to target only. In the source system, Oracle GoldenGate extract groups capture and forward Oracle GoldenGate trails to the remote system. One or more replicate groups apply the transactions to the target database keeping the two databases synchronized.

When using uni-directional setup for query offloading, change data capture (CDC) should limited to the database tables required by the collection of reports, rather than the complete database. Even though offloading to heterogeneous database such as MySQL may be an option, but it's wise to consider an offloading database engine that offer high-performance reporting capabilities. Oracle database OLAP option, materialized views and query rewrite supercharge database SQL drastically. Figure 1-14 depicts Oracle GoldenGate components involve for uni-directional setup.

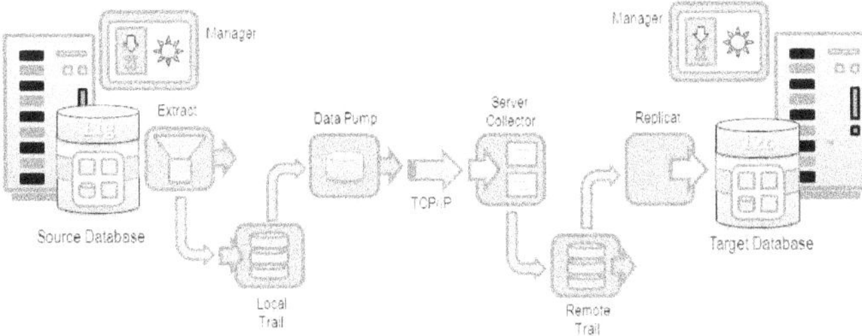

Figure 1-14: Unidirectional Oracle GoldenGate components

GoldenGate Bidirectional network configuration

This configuration enables forward data flow from source to target, and backward data flow from target to source systems. Because Oracle GoldenGate extract and replicate groups are configured on both systems, it's important to handle data conflict as business case scenarios. Oracle GoldenGate supports common data conflict resolutions, for more details regarding data conflict resolutions, refer to chapter 5.

There are two types of bidirectional setup, and it's all depending on the business requirements for implementing either option. Figure 1-15 shows the components and data follow for bi-directional configuration. A major advantage of using Oracle GoldenGate for high availability solution is proximity. Having the source and target systems connected via TCP/IP eliminates many distance restriction. However; network stability and sufficient dedicated bandwidth are key factor to achieve near sub-second latency.

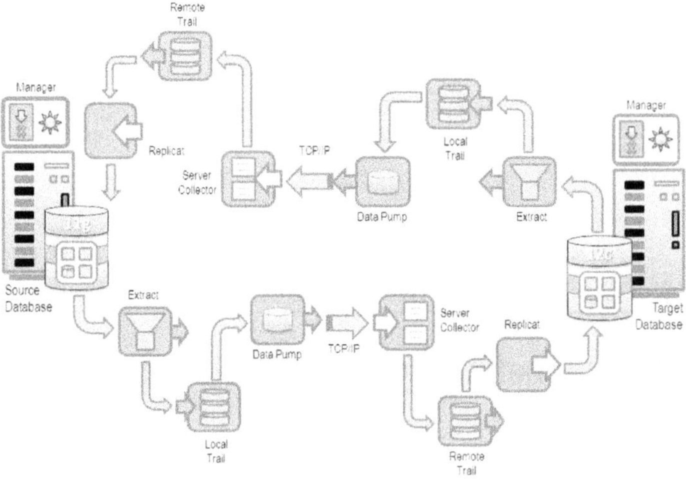

Figure 1-15: Bidirectional configuration

GoldenGate Active-active

Oracle GoldenGate delivers real-time data replication with sub-second latency. Bi-directional active-active setup promotes high availability with customized application scalability, users are able to connect to either system for conducting transactions.

GoldenGate Active-passive

When implementing Oracle GoldenGate for disaster recovery solution, it's configured as active-passive setup. The source and target systems are fully configured to support bidirectional data flow, but at all time, the data flow is active from either directions.

GoldenGate Peer-to-peer configuration

The peer-to-peer configuration commonly used for master-to-master data replication and peer-to-peer is used for load balancing and high availability. The two major distinctive features when using Oracle GoldenGate for such design, it can be deployed in heterogeneous environment.

For example suppose site A is an Oracle Database 12c, site B is MySQL and site C is Microsoft SQL Server. Peer-to-peer replication of subset of the databases has a positive impact on disk storage and network bandwidth.

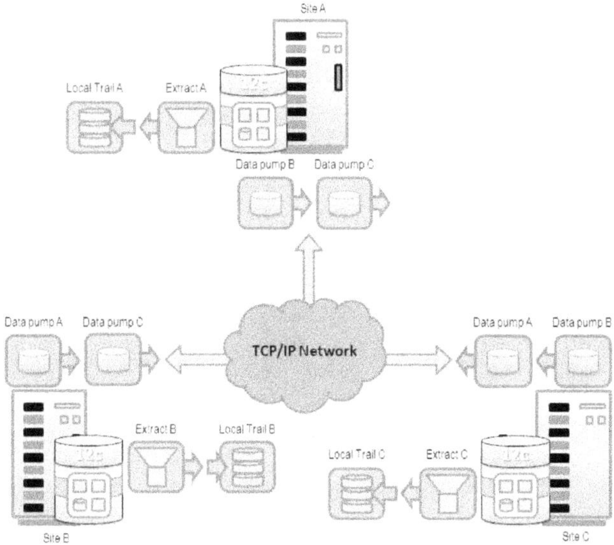

Figure 1-16: Master-to-master replication

Figure 1-16 show master-to-master for three sites. Extending this topology by streaming data from a regional master to a local site achieves efficient transaction processing and higher data availability. The number of sites on peer-to-peer configuration should be limited to 3 sites. Otherwise, the configuration, data collision handling becomes extremely complex to build, and deploy.

GoldenGate Broadcast configuration

We use the broadcast configuration for data distribution from the core business applications database to the enterprise data mart databases. This configuration predominately for read-once, deliver-many, after data is captured from the source transaction logs, it can be routed to any number of destinations (targets), regardless of their of their locations and platform types.

Data streaming is uni-directional from source to targets systems, applying data transformations on the data pump processes (or on the targets replicate processes), and this customizes the target databases to suit application specific data requirements.

Business intelligence applications benefit from real-time data movement and transformation for real-time application support. An important added value from this configuration is security by ensuring physical data separation. The target databases may be small foot-prints of the source, this is very similar to the concept of virtual private database (VPD), but stored remotely. The data is pertaining to subset of related users and/or application for specific region. Figure 1-17 shows the data flow from source to targets.

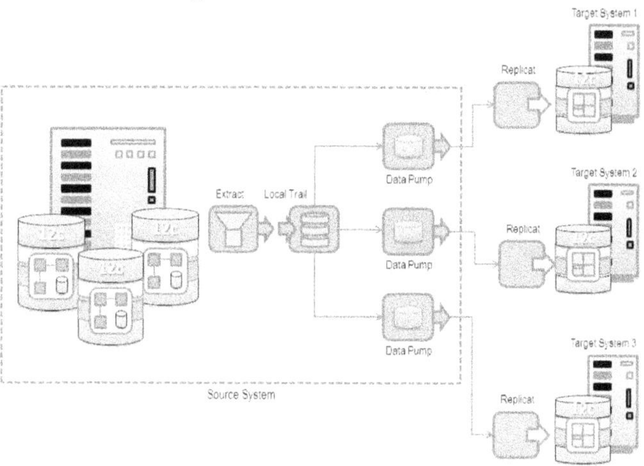

Figure 1-17: Oracle GoldenGate broadcasting topology

GoldenGate Consolidation configuration

We use the consolidation configuration for the data warehouse, the enterprise data warehouse repository receives data from the enterprise online transactional systems, for example, a ETL process using Oracle data integrator (ODI) for enabling real-time population of a star schemas for reporting and business intelligence. Figure 1-18 shows consolidation of three databases into the data warehouse database.

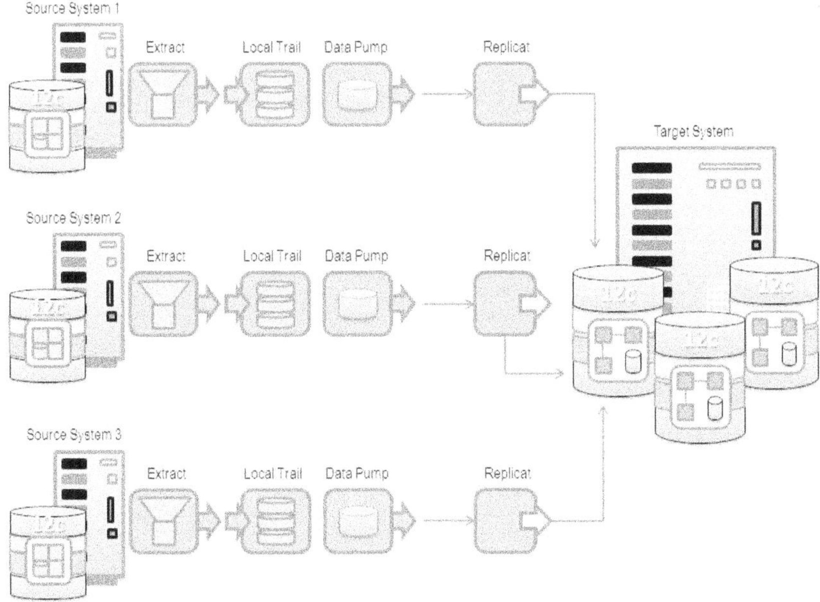

Figure 1-18: Consolidate for data warehouse repository

Cascading configuration

Sites performing intensive data transformation on source and target systems, use an intermediate GoldenGate instance with sufficient processing resources. This enhances scalability by dedicating the source and target systems for capture and deliver functions only, leaving data transformation to occur within the intermediate system. The intermediate system can be with or without a database. Figure 1-19 illustrates an intermediate system without a database, only the client software required for installing Oracle GoldenGate software.

The best practices recommends using multiple data pumps, each dedicated to specific target system, network failure of one system is isolated leaving other systems unaffected by the *abended* data pump process.

In the case of columns mapping or data transformation involving an intermediate system, a source definition file and target definition file must be provided to the intermediate system.

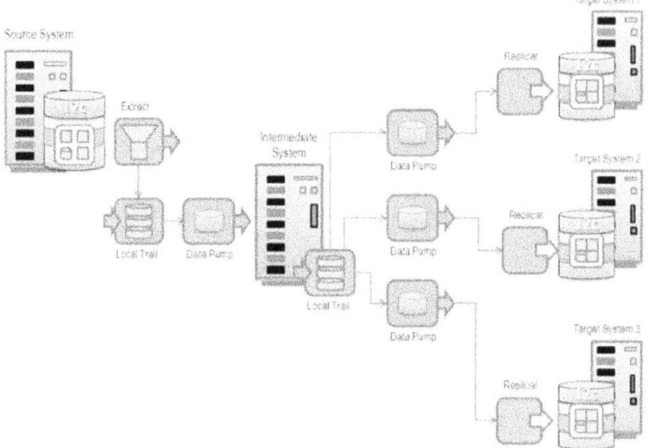

Figure 1-19: Cascade using intermediate system

Oracle GoldenGate command-line interfaces

The Oracle GoldenGate Software command interface, or GGSCI performs administration and management tasks such as adding extracts, adding replicates, trails, login to the database and view reports. On Linux/UNIX operating systems, we must set the environment variable LD_LIBRARY_PATH before starting GGSCI.

```
$export LD_LIBRARY_PATH=$ORACLE_HOME/lib

$cd $GGS_HOME

$./ggsci
```

When using GGSCI for creating and modifying parameter files ensures saving the parameter files on their correct locations. You may also define a non-default preferred text editor. GGSCI is client application tool, it does not require additional software installation, it only uses Oracle database library. Figure 1-20 shows GGSCI on Oracle Enterprise Linux. When using GGSCI for MS SQL Server, run it as Windows administrator user and the manager process runs as a local Windows service.

Examples for using GGSCI interface include:

- Managing the manager process, performing *start, stop* and *info* commands
- Login to the database
- Adding and managing checkpoint table
- Adding and managing extract and replicate processes

- Creating and managing parameter files
- Managing extract and replicate processes
- Generating reports and displaying performance statistics

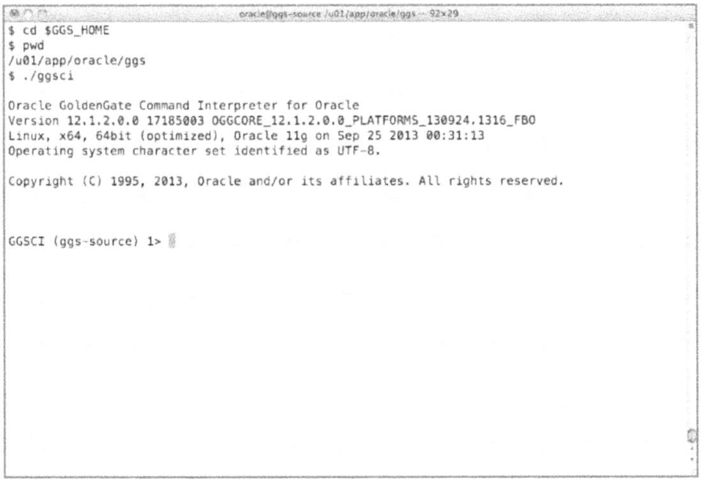
oracle@ggs-source /u01/app/oracle/ggs — 92×29
$ cd $GGS_HOME
$ pwd
/u01/app/oracle/ggs
$ ./ggsci
Oracle GoldenGate Command Interpreter for Oracle
Version 12.1.2.0.0 17185003 OGGCORE_12.1.2.0.0_PLATFORMS_130924.1316_FBO
Linux, x64, 64bit (optimized), Oracle 11g on Sep 25 2013 00:31:13
Operating system character set identified as UTF-8.
Copyright (C) 1995, 2013, Oracle and/or its affiliates. All rights reserved.
GGSCI (ggs-source) 1>

Figure 1-20: Oracle GoldenGate software command interface (GGSCI)

Another important utility for troubleshooting Oracle GoldenGate instance error messages and performing content-search of trail files is the command-line interface LOGDUMP. Figure 1-21 shows the utility, ready to open a trail file.

The command line to run the utility:

```
$export LD_LIBRARY_PATH=$ORACLE_HOME/lib

$cd $GGS_HOME

$./logdump
```

```
$ cd $GGS_HOME
$ pwd
/u01/app/oracle/ggs
$ ./logdump

Oracle GoldenGate Log File Dump Utility for Oracle
Version 12.1.2.0.0 17185003 OGGCORE_12.1.2.0.0_PLATFORMS_130924.1316

Copyright (C) 1995, 2013, Oracle and/or its affiliates. All rights reserved.


Logdump 1 >
```

Figure 1-21: Oracle GoldenGate log file dump utility

For detail regarding the LOGDUMP utility, refer to chapter 13.

Obey files in GoldenGate

The need to run batch job is essential for performing sequence of related tasks, such as running the sequence of commands to deploy an end-to-end Oracle GoldenGate instance. The GGSCI *obey* command reads and execute the commands listed on the text file, known as obey file.

We start by creating a text file, inserting one GGSCI command per line and save the file. The example below creates the file *info_all.oby*, then from GGSCI enter the file name as an input to the GGSCI obey command. The file name is normally has the file extension *oby*, but it's not necessary, hence *info_all.oby* and *info_all.txt* are valid file names.

```
-- File: /home/oracle/oby/info_all.oby
--
start mgr
info all
start extract ES1E201
start extract EPMP01
info all
```

```
GGSCI (ggs-source) 7> OBEY /home/oracle/oby/info_all.oby
```

The GGSCI *obey* command allows nesting of obey files for invoking another obey file from within an obey file. To enable nesting, insert the parameter *allownested* at the beginning of the file before invoking and obey file as illustrated below.

```
-- File: /home/oracle/oby/info_all.oby
--       /home/oracle/oby/add_tran.oby
--
ALLOWNESTED
START mgr
INFO ALL
START EXTRACT es1e201
START EXTRACT epmp01
INFO ALL
OBEY /home/oracle/oby/add_tran.oby

GGSCI (ggs-source) 18> OBEY /home/oracle/oby/info_all.oby

GGSCI (ggs-source) 19> ALLOWNESTED

Nested OBEY scripts allowed.

GGSCI (ggs-source) 20> START mgr

Manager started.

GGSCI (ggs-source) 21> INFO ALL

Program     Status      Group       Lag at Chkpt  Time Since Chkpt

MANAGER     RUNNING
EXTRACT     STOPPED     EPMP01      00:00:00      00:00:29
EXTRACT     STOPPED     ES1E201     00:00:00      00:00:28

GGSCI (ggs-source) 22> START EXTRACT es1e201

Sending START request to MANAGER ...
EXTRACT ES1E201 starting

GGSCI (ggs-source) 23> START EXTRACT epmp01


Sending START request to MANAGER ...
EXTRACT EPMP01 starting

GGSCI (ggs-source) 24> INFO ALL

Program     Status      Group       Lag at Chkpt  Time Since Chkpt

MANAGER     RUNNING
EXTRACT     RUNNING     EPMP01      00:00:00      00:00:32
EXTRACT     RUNNING     ES1E201     00:00:01      00:00:00


GGSCI (ggs-source) 25> OBEY /home/oracle/oby/add_tran.oby

**** Halting script [/home/oracle/oby/info_all.oby], starting script
[/home/oracle/oby/add_tran.oby]...
```

```
GGSCI (ggs-source) 26> dblogin userid ggs_admin, password oracle

Successfully logged into database.

GGSCI (ggs-source) 27> add trandata osm$repapi.customers

Logging of supplemental redo data enabled for table OSM$REPAPI.CUSTOMERS.
TRANDATA for scheduling columns has been added on table
'OSM$REPAPI.CUSTOMERS'.
GGSCI (ggs-source) 28>

GGSCI (ggs-source) 28> **** Terminating script
[/home/oracle/oby/add_tran.oby], resuming script
[/home/oracle/oby/info_all.oby]...

GGSCI (ggs-source) 28>
```

However; for executing an SQL*Plus script and operating system commands, use GGSCI SHELL command embedded within an *obey* file followed by the shell script file.

Restart Oracle from GoldenGate

For example, in certain situations we may need to restart the database from within Oracle GoldenGate, which can be developed as follows:

- Create an obey file, *db_shut.oby*, that has the lines:

```
SHELL /home/oracle/oby/db_shut.sh
```

- Prepare the database shutdown script and save it as *db_shut.sh*. Ensure the file has execute permission.

```
#!/bin/bash
export ORACLE_SID=S1E2
export ORACLE_HOME=/u01/app/oracle/product/11.2.0/dbhome_1
sqlplus /nolog <<EOF
conn / as sysdba
startup force
exit
EOF
```

- Invoke the obey file from GGSCI command-line.

```
GGSCI (ggs-source) 1> OBEY /home/oracle/oby/db_shut.oby
```

When using GGSCI *shell* command to execute an operating system shell commands, these commands are executed with the access rights of the Oracle GoldenGate software owner, applying access rights of the database privileges and operating system security.

GoldenGate Parameters files

There are two types of parameter

- Global parameters which apply to all Oracle GoldenGate instance processes
- Runtime parameters which apply to specific process.

When the same parameter specified as both global and runtime, the runtime parameter takes precedence and override the global parameter. Parameter files are ASCII format, with one line per parameter or append the character '&' to create multi-line parameter. The following syntax for the *purgeoldextracts* parameter produces the same results.

```
PURGEOLDEXTRACTS ./dirdat/*, USECHECKPOINTS, MINKEEPHOURS 1

PURGEOLDEXTRACTS ./dirdat/*, &
USECHECKPOINTS, &
MINKEEPHOURS 1
```

The global parameters are defined on the file GLOBALS (upper case without file extension) located at Oracle GoldenGate root directory. Global parameters are relatively static and rarely modified. Table 1-3 list common global parameters.

Parameter	Description
CHECKPOINTTABLE	Specifies instance-wide checkpoint table
ENABLEMONITORING	Required for enabling Oracle GoldenGate monitor
MGRSERVNAME	The name of the manager process when installed as local Windows service
CHARSET	The character set to when reading the parameter files, overriding the default operating system
GGSCHEMA	The name of the schema for supporting DDL replication between two Oracle databases
SYSLOG	We used for filtering the messages types recorded in ggserr.log file to override the default ALL.

Table 1-3: Common global parameters

When changing global parameters on GLOBALS file from within GGSCI, it's required to exit and restart the GGSCI utility for activating all newly added parameters.

Runtime parameters are specific to an extract or replicate process allowing more control for process runtime. The default location for run-time parameter files is *./dirprm/* directory. Using text editor ('vi' on Linux/UNIX, notepad on Windows, or GGSCI) to create a new or edit an existing parameter file, the group name specified at GGSCI command-line, which becomes the parameter file name, must match the name followed the *extract* parameter. The process name, group name and parameter file name are not case sensitive.

The following listing is the parameter file for extract ES1E201, created using GGSCI command-line.

```
GGSCI (ggs-source) 2> EDIT PARAMS es1e201

EXTRACT ES1E201
SETENV (ORACLE_SID=S1E2)
SETENV (ORACLE_HOME="/u01/app/oracle/product/11.2.0/dbhome_1")
SETENV (NLS_LANG=AMERICAN_AMERICA.AL32UTF8)
USERID ggs_admin@S1E2, PASSWORD oracle
EXTTRAIL ./dirdat/sa
TABLE osm$repapi.customers;
TABLE osm$repapi.policies;
```

Configure the GoldenGate instance manager process

A GoldenGate instance can has one-and-only-one manager process, and it always remains running to monitor activities and start dynamic processes. There are few important facts about the manager process.

- The only required parameter is *port*, which specify a static TCP/IP listening port number.
- There can be one-and-only-one manager process per Oracle GoldenGate instance.
- The manager process status either *running* or *stopped.*
- The manager process parameter file name and location must be *./dirprm/mgr.prm* only.
- The manager process supports up to 250 dynamic ports
- Though the manager should remain running at all times, it may be stopped, change the parameter and restart without effecting currently running processes.

The following is an example of some common instance manager process parameters. These parameters' values settings should be carefully determined as they determine how Oracle GoldenGate instance manager process handles important events.

```
-- mgr.prm
--
PORT 7811
DYNAMICPORTLIST 9001-9250
PURGEOLDEXTRACTS ./dirdat/*, USECHECKPOINTS, MINKEEPHOURS 1
AUTORESTART ER *, RETRIES 10, WAITMINUTES 5
LAGREPORTHOURS 2
LAGINFOMINUTES 5
LAGCRITICALMINUTES 10
```

This manager process is listening on TCP/IP port 7811. It searches and allocates ports from the range of ports 9001 to 9250 for dynamically starting processes.

The parameter *puregeoldextracts* allows the manager to perform trail files management. The option *usecheckpoints* to delete trail files after being transferred to the target system and applied. The option *minkeephours* 1 instructs to delete the trail file until there has been no activity for one hour.

The manager will automatically start any extracts and replicates processes at startup and will attempt to restart any extracts and replicates with status ABENDED after waiting for five minutes, but only up to ten attempts.

The parameter *lagreporthours* 2 instructs the manager to report lag statistics every two hours for those processes that have five and ten minutes of latency using the parameters *laginfominutes* 5 and *lagcriticalminutes* 10. The message recorded as informational for lags of five minutes and critical for lag greater than ten minutes.

To find the basic details about the currently running manager, issue the GGSCI command:

```
GGSCI (ggs-source) 8> INFO mgr

Manager is running (IP port ggs-source.7811, Process ID 21649).
```

To view the manager process parameters, issue the GGSCI command:

```
GGSCI (ggs-source) 9> VIEW PARAMS mgr

PORT 7811
DYNAMICPORTLIST 9001-9250
```

```
PURGEOLDEXTRACTS ./dirdat/*, USECHECKPOINTS, MINKEEPHOURS 1
AUTORESTART ER *, RETRIES 10, WAITMINUTES 5
LAGREPORTHOURS 2
LAGINFOMINUTES 5
LAGCRITICALMINUTES 10
```

To issue stop and restart the manager process, enter the GGSCI commands:

```
GGSCI (ggs-source) 12> STOP mgr!

Sending STOP request to MANAGER ...
Request processed.
Manager stopped.

GGSCI (ggs-source) 13> START mgr
Manager started.
```

Even though the manager process may be stopped without effecting the currently running extracts and replicates processes, it should remain running at all time to handle runtime events and activities. A common case is when very quickly changing a specific parameter value in the manager file, stopping and restarting the manager process immediately.

Refer to chapter 3 for more details regarding the GoldenGate parameters descriptions.

Configure GoldenGate change data capture

The change data capture is a function of the primary extract. During the capture operation the transaction and data remains in memory until the transaction is committed or rolled back. Committed transactions are written to the remote trail, or to the local trail in case a secondary extract (data pump) is configured. Best practices states configuring a data pump provides resiliency against network failures.

The configuration below instructs the primary extract to perform change data capture for the database tables *customers* and *policies*.

```
EXTRACT es1e201
SETENV (ORACLE_SID=S1E2)
SETENV (ORACLE_HOME="/u01/app/oracle/product/11.2.0/dbhome_1")
SETENV (NLS_LANG=AMERICAN_AMERICA.AL32UTF8)
USERID ggs_admin@S1E2, PASSWORD oracle
EXTTRAIL ./dirdat/sa
TABLE osm$repapi.customers;
TABLE osm$repapi.policies;
```

The primary extract group name must matches the parameter file name *es1e201.prm*. The *setenv* parameter access environment variable is required for operating the primary extract. The parameter *userid* enables the primary extract to login to the database S1E2. The parameter *exttrail* instructs the primary extract to write to the local trail *./dirdat/sa*. The *table* parameter lists the tables for change data capture.

Oracle GoldenGate adapts its own universal format for exchanging data across heterogeneous systems. The parameter *exttrail* specifies the location and the name of the local trail files. The name is a two character prefix appended with 6 digit starting 000000 and ending with 999999, then recycling begin at 000000.

Creating the GoldenGate primary extract

From GGSCI command-line use the *add extract* command to define the primary extract. The parameter file may not exist when adding the extract, but required to start it. The *add extract* syntax below is used for defining the primary and secondary extracts.

```
ADD EXTRACT <group name>
{, SOURCEISTABLE |
, TRANLOG [<bsds name>] |
, INTEGRATED TRANLOG |
, VAM |
, EXTFILESOURCE <file name> |
, EXTTRAILSOURCE <trail name> |
, VAMTRAILSOURCE <VAM trail name>}
{, BEGIN {NOW | yyyy-mm-dd [:hh:mi:[ss[.cccccc]]]} |
, EXTSEQNO <seqno>, EXTRBA <relative byte address> |
, LOGNUM <log number>, LOGPOS <byte offset> |
, EOF |
, LSN <value> |
, EXTRBA <relative byte address> |
, EOF | LSN <value> |
, PAGE <data page>, ROW <row>}
[, THREADS <n>]
[, PASSIVE]
[, PARAMS <parameter file>]
[, REPORT <report file>]
[, DESC "<description>"]
```

The *add extract* command has three sections as highlighted above: The extract type, the capture begin timestamp or absolute location and the optional control parameters. For defining the primary extract *es1e201*, we will use the basic parameters.

```
GGSCI (ggs-source) 25> ADD EXTRACT es1e201, TRANLOG, BEGIN now, THREADS 1
```

```
EXTRACT added.
```

The above *add extract* command has successfully defined the extract group *es1e201*. This extract performs change data capture from the transaction logs (online redo log files) indicated by the option *tranlog*. The timestamp to begin change data capture is the time of up on successful completion of the command indicated by option *begin now*. The option *threads* 1 indicates the extract captures from a single thread on non-RAC Oracle database instance.

Using a secondary extract requires creating a local trail. The local trail ./dirdat/sa is associated with the primary extract *es1e201*.

```
GGSCI (ggs-source) 26> ADD EXTTRAIL ./dirdat/sa, EXTRACT es1e201, MEGABYTES
32
```

```
EXTTRAIL added.
```

After the GoldenGate change data capture by the primary extract process is written to the local trail, then the role of the secondary extract process (data pump) begins by routing data to one or more of the target systems. The following refers to the data pump process configuration:

```
EXTRACT epmp01
USERID ggs_admin@S1E2, PASSWORD oracle
PASSTHRU
RMTHOST ggs-target, MGRPORT 7812
RMTTRAIL ./dirdat/ta
TABLE osm$repapi.customers;
TABLE osm$repapi.policies;
```

In this example, the data pump process *epmp01* reads the local trail files. The parameter *passthru* indicate the source and target database tables structure are identical. *nopassthru* parameter is used when using the *@range* function to support parallel processing or *colmap* parameter implemented for non-identical tables.

The parameter *rmthost* specifies the target system, the *mgrport* is the target system manager process.

The parameter *rmttrail* specifies the location and name of remote trail on the target system.

Creating the GoldenGate secondary extract

We begin by defining the secondary group using *add extract* GGSCI command. The secondary extract reads the local trail and routes data across TCP/IP to remote data collector server.

```
GGSCI (ggs-source) 27> ADD EXTRACT epmp01, EXTTRAILSOURCE ./dirdat/sa
```

```
EXTRACT added.
```

The above *add extract* command define the secondary extract *EPMP01*, the extract reads the local trail *./dirdat/sa* indicated by the option *exttrailsource*. The remote trail *./dirdat/ta* associated the secondary extract defined using the *add rmttrail* command.

```
GGSCI (ggs-source) 28> ADD RMTTRAIL ./dirdat/ta, EXTRACT epmp01, MEGABYTES
32
```

```
RMTTRAIL added.
```

We use the command *start extract* * for staring all non-started extracts. Then we find the current status of the extracts by issuing *info all* command. This *info all* command shows the process status, and more importantly lagging and checkpoint details.

```
GGSCI (ggs-source) 34> START EXTRACT *
```

```
Sending START request to MANAGER ...
EXTRACT EPMP01 starting

Sending START request to MANAGER ...
EXTRACT ES1E201 starting
```

```
GGSCI (ggs-source) 35> INFO ALL
```

```
Program    Status     Group      Lag at Chkpt  Time Since Chkpt

MANAGER    RUNNING
EXTRACT    RUNNING    EPMP01     00:00:00      00:00:13
EXTRACT    RUNNING    ES1E201    00:00:01      00:00:00
```

Refer to chapter 3 for more details regarding extracts parameters.

Configure GoldenGate change data delivery

The third and last step of the configuration of GoldenGate is the change data delivery, also known as the replicate process. The replicate process uses the target database native SQL calls to apply the transactions found on the remote trail. Reapplying the remote trail transactions is subject to the database constraint definition for primary keys and referential integrity.

The following is the change data delivery group parameter file.

```
REPLICAT rs1e201
SETENV (ORACLE_SID=T1C1)
SETENV (NLS_LANG=AMERICAN_AMERICA.AL32UTF8)
USERID ggs_admin@t2c1, PASSWORD oracle
ASSUMETARGETDEFS
DISCARDFILE ./dirrpt/rs1e201.dsc, PURGE
MAP osm$repapi.customers, TARGET osm$repapi.customers;
MAP osm$repapi.policies, TARGET osm$repapi.policies;
```

The replicate process *rs1e201* connects to Oracle Database 12c, and it references the list of mapped tables for applying transactions to the target database using its associated remote trail files. The *assumetargetdefs* parameter is for homogenous environment when using identical source and target database tables structure. The *map* and the corresponding *target* parameters are used to map the source with target table.

Creating change data delivery process in GoldenGate

The change data delivery is the replicate process reading from remote trail and applying transactions to the remote database using database native SQL calls. The *add replicat* syntax is used to define change data delivery group.

```
ADD REPLICAT <group name>
{, SPECIALRUN |
, EXTFILE <file name> |
, EXTTRAIL <trail name>}
[, BEGIN {NOW | yyyy-mm-dd:hh:mm[:ss[.cccccc]]} |
, EXTSEQNO <seqno>, EXTRBA <rba>]
[, CHECKPOINTTABLE <owner.table> | NODBCHECKPOINT]
[, PARAMS <parameter file>]
[, REPORT <report file>]
[, DESC "<description>"]
```

The *add replicat* command has three sessions: The replicate process type and data source, the apply begin timestamp and the optional control parameters.

We use the basic parameter to create the replicate group *rs1e201*, specifying the data source and the database checkpoint table name. The replicate process requires checkpoint database table, by default. Using the default option requires creating the checkpoint table before defining the replicate process *rs1e201*.

```
GGSCI (ggs-target) 4> ADD CHECKPOINTTABLE ggs_admin.ggchkpttab
```

```
Successfully created checkpoint table ggs_admin.ggchkpttab.
```

```
GGSCI (ggs-target) 16> ADD REPLICAT rs1e201, EXTTRAIL ./dirdat/ta,
CHECKPOINTTABLE ggs_admin.ggchkpttab
```

```
REPLICAT added.
```

We use the command *start replicat* to start the replicate process, then issue the *info all* command to confirm status of the replicate process.

```
GGSCI (ggs-target) 19> START REPLICAT *
```

```
Sending START request to MANAGER ...
REPLICAT RS1E201 starting
```

```
GGSCI (ggs-target) 20> INFO ALL
```

```
Program    Status     Group      Lag at Chkpt  Time Since Chkpt

MANAGER    RUNNING
REPLICAT   RUNNING    RS1E201    00:00:00      00:00:53
```

Refer to chapter 3 for more details regarding parameter description and database checkpoint table options.

Using GoldenGate macros

Macros enable an easier and more efficient method for building Oracle GoldenGate instance parameter files. A macro defines a group of related parameters so that they can be referenced from within the parameter files, simplifying the configuration of large parameter files with repetitive parameters, commands and functions by reusing the group of parameter defined by the macro.

The definition of macros either *local* within the same process parameter file and invoked from within parameter file only, or *global* to Oracle GoldenGate instance by defining macros library and invoking the macros from any extract or replicate processes parameter files.

Prior to invoking macros, they must be defined. The definition of a macro similar to sub-programs, where a macro has a name beginning with # character, optionally followed by zero or more parameters. The macro body placed between the *begin* and *end* statements. The syntax for defining macros follows.

```
MACRO #<macro name>
PARAMS (#<parameter1>, #<parameter2>, #<parameter>)
BEGIN
   <Macro body>
END;
```

After defining a macro, it can be used on the parameter files for:

- Manager process
- Primary and secondary extracts
- Replicate process
- GLOBALS parameter file

The best approach to work with macros is by creating macro libraries. Let's assume the parameters *login* and *passthru* are included for the majority of parameter files. Defining and invoking a macro replaces explicitly adding the those parameters to the parameter files. The parameter *include* at the top of the parameter file enables invoking any of the macros defined within the macro library file.

- We start by defining the macro named #S1E2LOGIN inside the macro library file

```
$ vi /u01/app/oracle/ggs/dirprm/macrosqe2.mac
```

```
MACRO #S1E2LOGIN
BEGIN
   USERID ggs_admin@S1E2, PASSWORD oracle
   PASSTHRU
END;
```

- Next, we invoke the macro from within the secondary extract EPMP01

```
INCLUDE /u01/app/oracle/ggs/dirprm/macrosqe2.mac
EXTRACT epmp01
#S1E2LOGIN()
RMTHOST ggs-target, MGRPORT 7812
RMTTRAIL ./dirdat/ta
TABLE osm$repapi.customers;
```

```
TABLE osm$repapi.policies;
```

The modular architecture of GoldenGate

Regardless of the design choice, the modular building blocks of Oracle GoldenGate are capable of producing a dynamic architecture for achieving real-time data movement with sub-second latency.

The capture-and-apply processes can operate as loosely or tightly coupled, loosely coupled in the sense the capture processes may be cascaded across multiple systems, where the primary extract process (capture) running on the source database system reading the transaction logs, and the secondary extract process (data pump) running on an intermediate system physically networked with the source system using TCP/IP.

These capture-apply processes run outside of the database, hence Oracle GoldenGate delivers safe, high performance and scalable platform with minimum impact on existing system for supporting heterogeneous data movement.

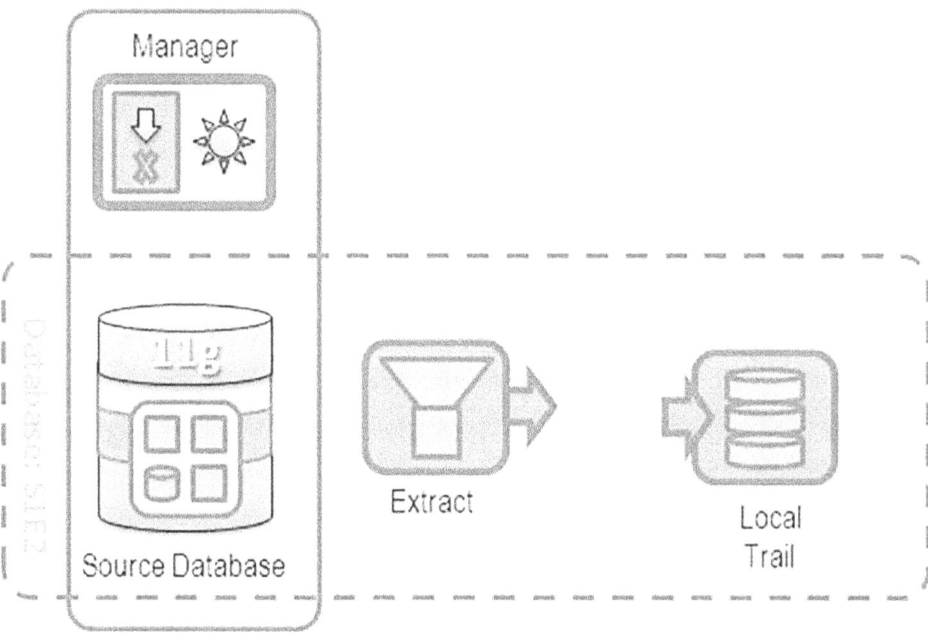

Figure 1-22 illustrates the building block for the three modular blocks:

- Change data capture phase using primary extract group
- Routing phase using secondary extract group
- Apply phase using change data delivery group

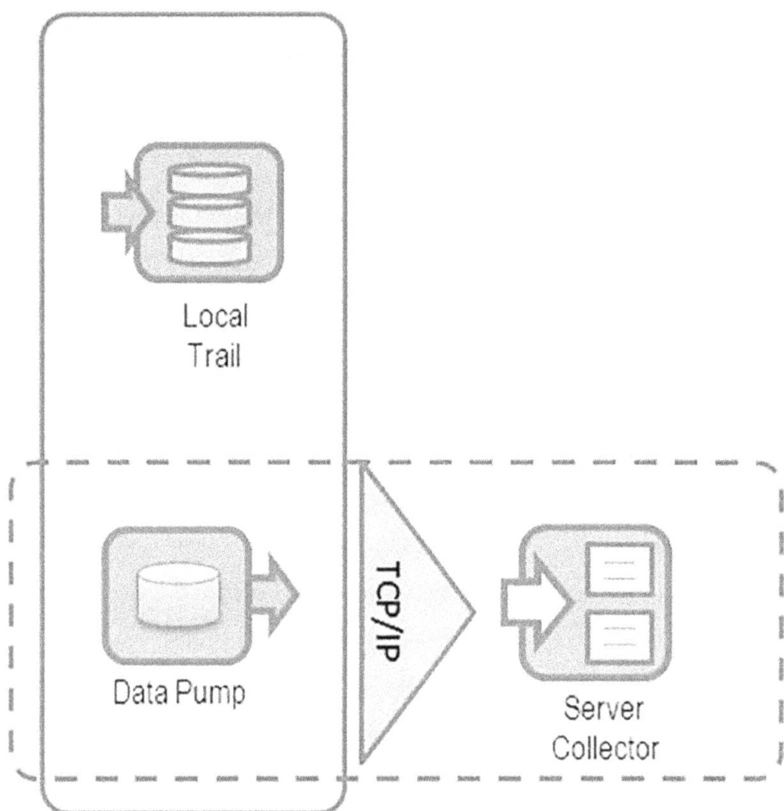

Figure 1-22: Oracle GoldenGate modular architecture

The capture phase involves one or more primary extract capturing *only committed* transactions as soon as they become available on the transaction logs. This is occurring outside of the database, hence minimum impact sustained by the source database. For achieving a fault-tolerance non-interruptible data movement, the primary extract stages captured data in the form of advanced queues composed of local trail files ready for routing to one or more destinations (targets). The target systems could be the final destinations (sources) or an intermediate systems for achieving high-performance broadcasting network topology or intensive data transformation.

The source system manager process normally configured to manage local trail files purge task for sustaining an optimized disk space on the production system. It's also configurable to implement extract processes auto-start during system startup and restart for abnormally terminated extract processes. Trail files purge and extracts auto-start features are implemented for minimizing data movement discontinuity on sites requiring uninterruptable data processing.

The routing phase involves one or more secondary extracts called *data pumps* for routing transactions, *not trail files*, to one or more destinations. Having a data pump within the source system is optional, but very highly recommend to support fault-tolerance as explained on the section – Capture-route options.

The receiving component is the data server collector for re-assembling the data and managing the remote queue. The data server collector is a dynamic server and associated with a data pump. The communication from the data pump extract to the data server collector occurs across TCP/IP network allowing the design for loosely coupled system where the source and target systems are geographically distributed.

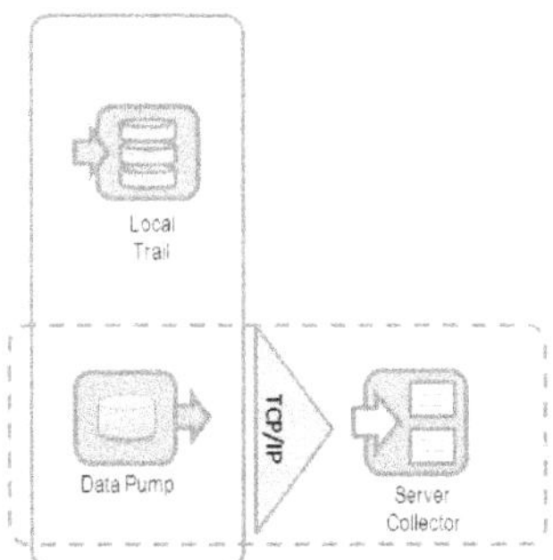

Figure 1-22a: Oracle GoldenGate modular architecture

The third, or last phase involves one or more change data apply, replicate processes know by Replicat. Replicate processes running on the target system use the database interface (SQL calls) for applying the transactions while maintaining transactions ordering for data integrity. The input of the replicate processes is the remote trail files created by the data collector server. High-performance apply is achieved using Oracle

GoldenGate flexible parallelism architecture allowing multiple replicate processes to read from a single trail composed of trail files.

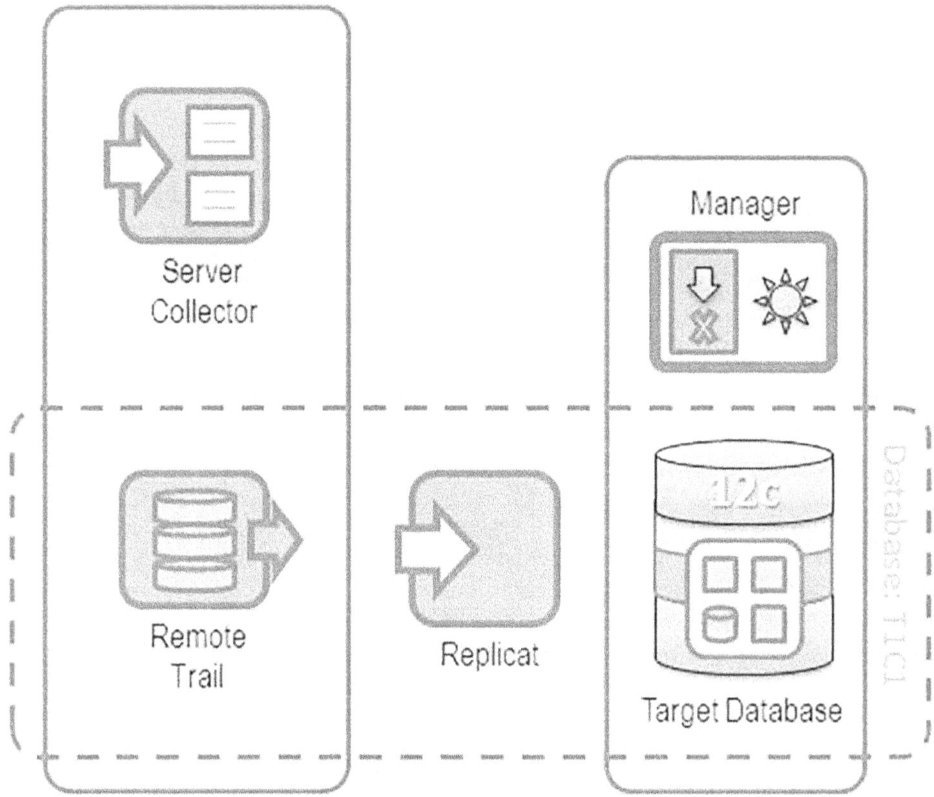

Figure 1-22b: Oracle GoldenGate modular architecture

The manager process on the target system normally configured to manage remote trail files purge task for sustaining an optimized disk space on the target system. It's also configurable to implement replicate processes auto-start during system startup and restart for abnormally terminated replicate processes.

The flexibility of designing an operational Oracle GoldenGate instance is depicted logically on figure 1-23 followed by the interpretation.

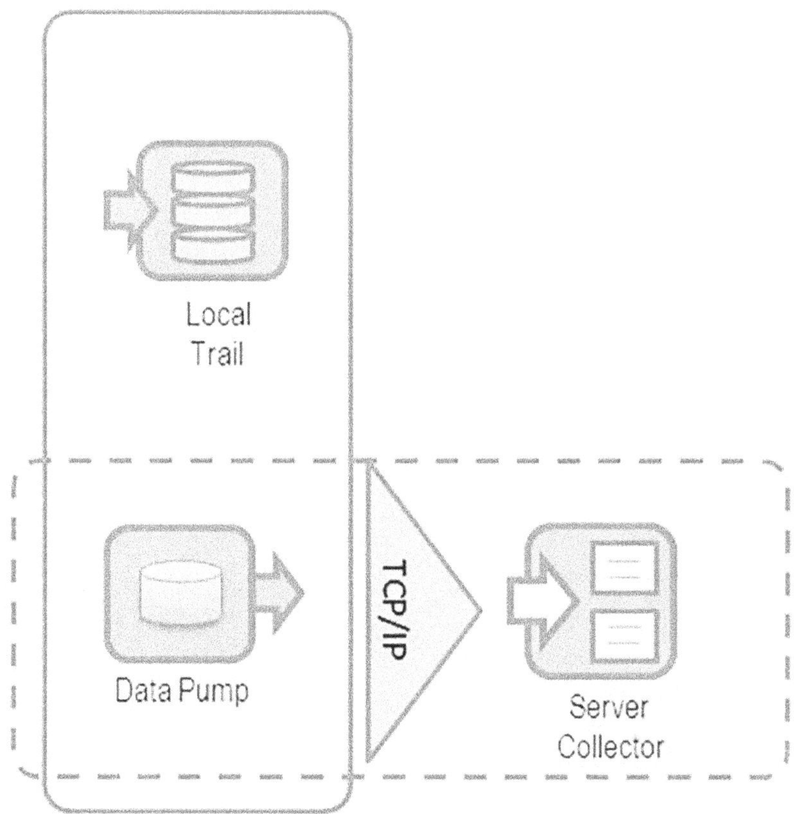

Figure 1-23: GoldenGate components relationship

An Oracle GoldenGate instance must has one-and-only-one manager. An *operational* Oracle GoldenGate instance must be composed of one-or-more primary extract groups (capture), but may has one-or-more secondary extract groups (data pump).

Each primary extract must create one-and-only-one trail, and each trail must be composed of one-or-more local trail files. Each secondary extract (data pump) is associated with one-and-only-one data server collector and each data server collector creates one-and-only-one remote trail. Each remote trail composed of one-or-more remote trail files.

An Oracle GoldenGate instance must be composed of one-or-more replicate processes, and each trail files applied using the target database SQL native interface.

The manager process may manages one-or-more primary extracts, one-or-more secondary extracts and one-or-more trails.

Capture-route options

There are two options available for deploying Oracle GoldenGate as visually compared in figure 1-24. The upper section shows a primary extract (capture) with a data pump extract refers to as option-A and the lower section shows a primary extract (capture) without a data pump extract refers to as option-B. Best practices highly recommends implementing the primary extract with a data pump extract, option-A.

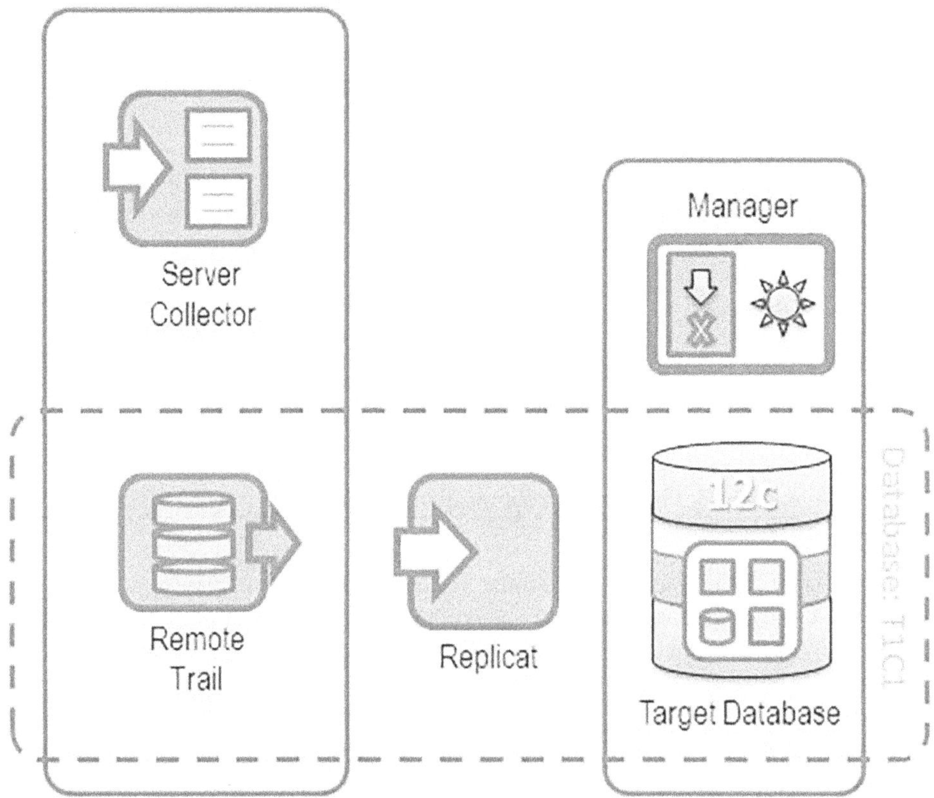

Figure 1-24: End-to-end configuration options

In the event of TCP/IP network disconnection from the source to target systems, option-A supports fault-tolerance because the primary extract continues to deliver change data capture (CDC) by writing to the local trail, only the data pump extract will be terminated temporary. Once TCP/IP network restored, the data pump is restarted and data continue sending data to the data server collector.

Under the same circumstances, option-B will cause the primary extract process to terminate due to system resources unavailability as a result of unable to send data to the remote data server collector. Depending on the downtime timeframe, the transaction logs may not be available after the network is restored and the extract started. This scenario requires manual changes for reading the transaction logs from archived log files.

The storage overhead of writing to local trail files is minimized by the purge task automatically performed by the manager process and the parameters used to configure the purge. In most cases, under normally working extract-route-replicate for option-A the local trail files disk space is negligible and should not cause performance degradation. Option-B is selected in case where the source and target Oracle GoldenGate instances are running on the same host, moving data between two heterogeneous or homogenous databases.

Commit sequence number

The commit sequence number, CSN identifies a particular point in time of the source transaction during the capture. It's constructed from the database, for Oracle database it's the same as the system change number (SCN), for MS SQL Server it's composed of three parts: the virtual log file number, the segment number within the virtual file and the entry number. Oracle GoldenGate uses CSN during apply to identify the point in time at which the transaction is committed for maintaining transaction consistency and data integrity.

Checkpoints in GoldenGate

Primary extract, data pump extract and replicate processes record their reads and writes positions along the data flow. Successfully created extract and replicate groups are associated with a checkpoint file. The checkpoint file name for an extract group is <*group name.cpe*>, the checkpoint file name for a replicate group is <*group name.cpr*>. For primary extracts performing change data capture save their writes and reads positions to a checkpoint file to prevent redundant extraction from the transaction logs.

For data pump extracts performing routing to remote destination across TCP/IP save their reads and writes positions to prevent redundant extraction of the local trail. For replicates processes performing change data apply save their reads and writes positions to a checkpoint table or checkpoint file to prevent redundant extraction from the remote tail files and reapply to the target database.

Oracle GoldenGate checkpoint ensures fault tolerance in case of failure. The recovery process is similar to Oracle database automatic instance recovery.

For primary and data pump extracts checkpoint file is the only option. For replicates, there are two options; checkpoint file or checkpoint database table and checkpoint file combined, the default is the combined option. The name of the table either specified on GLOBALS file for all replicate groups using the parameter *checkpointtable* followed by the schema and the table name, or per replicate group specified when adding the replicate process using GGSCI command *add replicate*. To override the default and use a checkpoint file for the replicate group, use the option *nodbcheckpoint* when adding the replicate process through GGSCI command *add replicate*.

Intermediate systems in GoldenGate

For achieving an enterprise scalability in term of data transformation and routing capabilities, the use of Oracle GoldenGate instance as an intermediate system receiving very active downstream of trail files from multiple source systems, then transforming and routing trail files to multiple remote systems. An intermediate system is configurable as:

- Non-database intermediate system
- Database intermediate system

Figure 1-25 depicts intermediate system, it's composed of an Oracle GoldenGate instance configured with data pump processes for transforming and routing data to target systems.

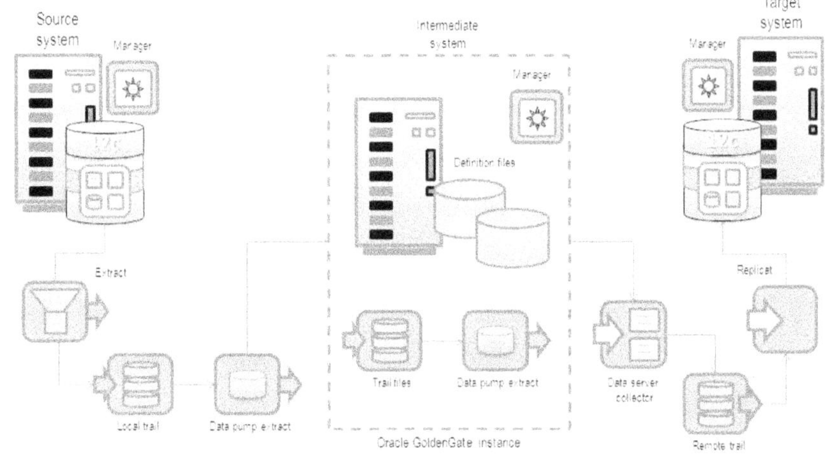

Figure 1-25: Intermediate system for scalability

In addition to achieving best scalability using an intermediate system, it also support enhanced security. Which is true in the case the target system receiving data from non-trusted source systems. With intermediate system in place, prior to routing the data to the target database, the data is verified, transformed then sent over secure channel to the target database.

The intermediate system uses multiple data pump extracts to route data to multiple targets, and has data definition files for each target requiring data transformation before routing to the target database, the advantage of performing transformation within the intermediate system is to offload the target database from the overhead associated with intensive data transformation and filtering.

Integrated capture in GoldenGate

The purpose of the integrated capture is to offload the transaction logs processing by Oracle GoldenGate from the source database (production) to a downstream system. Integrated capture is a specialized form of intermediate system continuously receiving the source database REDO as standby log files, where the integrated capture process on the downstream system performs change database capture (CDC) and forwarding the transaction data to the next downstream process such data pump, which in turn routes data to the target system. Figure 1-26 shows the architecture of the integrated capture environment.

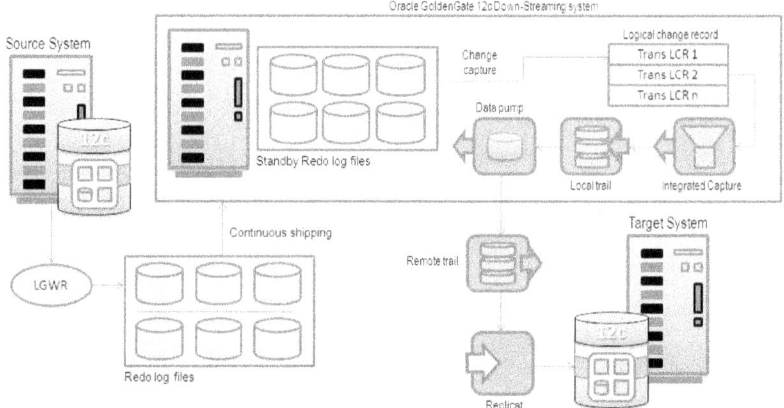

Figure 1-26: Integrated capture architecture

There are three options of integrated capture architecture, available with Oracle Database version 10.2 or higher.

- Option 1: Real-time same system integrated capture
- Option 2: Real-time separate system integrated capture
- Option 3: No-real-time separate system integrated capture

Real-time same system integrated capture requires installing Oracle GoldenGate 12c on source system, the integrated capture delivers remote trails from the source database REDO logs files.

Real-time separate system integrated capture, Oracle GoldenGate is not installed on the source system, but on a downstream system continuously receiving the source database REDO log files, where the integrated capture process delivers the remote trails on real-time.

No-real-time separate system integrated capture, Oracle GoldenGate is not installed on the source system, but on a downstream system continuously receiving the source database REDO log files, but Oracle GoldenGate integrated is operating on archive log only (ALO) mode readings the standby archived log file.

Refer to chapter 10 to learn more about Oracle GoldenGate integrated capture.

GoldenGate Column Mapping

It's the norm having the structure of source database table differs from the target database table requiring handling using columns mapping techniques. This is applicable to tables with different column names, missing column names and different columns ordering. We use the *table* or *map* statement *colmap* option to develop the mapping for each pair of columns.

The key elements of columns mapping are:

- Source definition file, generated using the DEFGEN Oracle GoldenGate utility
- Mapping clause: *colmap* with *usedefaults* or *colmatch*

Let's illustrate columns mapping to handle different column names on the CUSTOMERS table for the two columns *cust_address* and *cust_addr*.

The source database *customers* table

```
S1E2>DESC customers
```

```
 Name                           Null?    Type
 ------------------------------ -------- ---------
 CUST_NO                        NOT NULL NUMBER
 CUST_NAME                      NOT NULL VARCHAR2(128)
 CUST_EMAIL                     NOT NULL VARCHAR2(128)
 CUST_MOBILE                             NUMBER
 CUST_ADDRESS                            VARCHAR2(128)
```

The target database *customers* table

```
T1C1>desc customers
```

```
 Name                           Null?    Type
 ------------------------------ -------- ---------
 CUST_NO                        NOT NULL NUMBER
 CUST_NAME                      NOT NULL VARCHAR2(128)
 CUST_EMAIL                     NOT NULL VARCHAR2(128)
 CUST_MOBILE                    NOT NULL VARCHAR2(16)
 CUST_ADDR                               VARCHAR2(128)
```

GoldenGate Definition file utility

For heterogeneous data replication and replicating dissimilar tables on homogenous environment, a definition file created using Oracle GoldenGate DEFGEN utility is required. The utility generates the a source file describing the structure of the source to enable Oracle GoldenGate handles the internal data type mapping.

The steps to use the DEFGEN utility for generating a source definition file and apply it to the replicate process parameter file follows.

- Prepare the parameter file *defgen.prm*. Save the parameter file on the */dirprm* directory.

```
DEFSFILE ./dirdef/oracle.def, PURGE
USERID ggs_admin, PASSWORD oracle
TABLE osm$repapi.customers;
TABLE osm$repapi.policies;
```

- Run the utility using the parameter file. The utility creates the definition file specified by the parameter DEFSFILE.

```
$cd $GGS_HOME
$ ./defgen PARAMFILE ./dirprm/defgen.prm REPORTFILE ./dirrpt/defgen.rpt
```

- Using ASCII mode, transfer the source definition file oracle.def to the target system into the directory */dirdef*

- Modify the replicate parameter file to include the parameter *sourcedefs*, and remove the parameter *assumetargetdefs*.

```
REPLICAT rs1e201
SETENV (ORACLE_SID=T1C1)
SETENV (NLS_LANG=AMERICAN_AMERICA.AL32UTF8)
USERID ggs_admin@t1c1, PASSWORD oracle
DISCARDFILE ./dirrpt/rs1e201.dsc, PURGE
SOURCEDEFS ./dirdef/oracle.def
MAP osm$repapi.customers, TARGET osm$repapi.customers, &
COLMAP (USEDEFAULTS, cust_addr = cust_address);
MAP osm$repapi.policies, TARGET osm$repapi.policies;
```

When using the DEFGEN utility to produce the source definition file, the character set of the source and target systems presumably matching. However; to guarantee the definition file generated compatible with the target system character set, specify the *charset* parameter.

```
CHARSET UTF-8
```

```
DEFSFILE ./dirdef/oracle.def PURGE CHARSET UTF-8
USERID ggs_admin@S1E2, PASSWORD oracle
TABLE osm$repapi.customers;
TABLE osm$repapi.policies;
```

GoldenGate Columns mapping clauses

There are two techniques for handling columns mapping, using the parameters *colmap* or *colmatch*. Depending on how dissimilar the two tables one would be more preferred to use than the other.

The two methods are illustrated using the replicate process TS1E201.

The COLMAP clause in GoldenGate

We use *colmap* on cases where the columns have completely different names, or where one table has large number of column with only few columns differences. The benefit of *colmap* is using the *usedefault* option which causes implicit mapping of identical columns, followed by explicit column-to-column mapping process as illustrated next.

```
REPLICAT rs1e201
SETENV (ORACLE_SID=T1C1)
SETENV (NLS_LANG=AMERICAN_AMERICA.AL32UTF8)
USERID ggs_admin@t1c1, PASSWORD oracle
DISCARDFILE ./dirrpt/rs1e201.dsc, PURGE
SOURCEDEFS /u01/app/oracle/ggs_2/dirdef/oracle.def
MAP osm$repapi.customers, TARGET osm$repapi.customers, &
COLMAP (USEDEFAULTS, cust_addr = cust_address);
MAP osm$repapi.policies, TARGET osm$repapi.policies;
```

Notice, column mapping syntax allows the target column placed only on the left side of the assignment statement.

The COLMATCH clause in GoldenGate

We use *colmatch* on cases where tables have similar structure with different column names. The *colmatch* clause uses either the *names* or the *suffix/prefix* options.

The *names* option explicitly maps two columns names, while the *suffix/prefix* relies on substring mapping to dynamically determine columns mapping. *suffix* is used for ignoring columns suffix and *prefix* is used for ignoring column prefix.

The clause *colmatch prefix pk_* maps any target column having a PK_ prefix to any source column of similar name. For example, *pk_pol_no* with *pol_no*.

Here we see the *colmatch* using the *names* option illustrated on the replicate parameter file.

```
REPLICAT rs1e201
SETENV (ORACLE_SID=T1C1)
SETENV (NLS_LANG=AMERICAN_AMERICA.AL32UTF8)
USERID ggs_admin@T1E2, PASSWORD oracle
DISCARDFILE ./dirrpt/rs1e201.dsc, PURGE
SOURCEDEFS ./dirdef/oracle.def
COLMATCH NAMES CUST_ADDR = CUST_ADDRESS
MAP osm$repapi.customers, TARGET osm$repapi.customers;
MAP osm$repapi.policies, TARGET osm$repapi.policies;
```

Refer to chapter 8 to learn more about column mapping.

GoldenGate Built-in functions

Functions are mostly used for performing data transformation, required by the target database table structure and applications. Oracle GoldenGate supports categories of functions for characters, numbers, dates and general usages. The same principle of database and user-defined functions applies to Oracle GoldenGate functions in term of:

- Accepting of zero or more input parameters
- Allowing functions nesting
- Returning a value

Oracle GoldenGate functions invoked using the character '@' followed immediately by the function name. Functions are may be found in the parameter file of primary extract (capture), secondary extract (data pump) or replicate process.

Numbers and character functions

Table 1-4 lists number and character built-in functions.

Function Name	Description
@COMPUTE	Returns the result of arithmetic expressions into a target column. The return value is of type string
@NUMBIN	Converts a binary string into number
@NUMSTR	Converts a string to number
@STRCAT	Concatenates sequence of strings
@STRCMP	Compares two strings to determine whether they are equal, or the first string is less or greater than the second string.

@STREQ	Tests two strings to see if they equal or not. Return 1 for equal strings, returns 0 for not equal strings.
@STREXT	Returns substring from a string indicated by a begin and an end positions
@STRFIND	Returns the first occurrence of a substring within a string
@STRLEN	Returns the length of a string
@STRTRIM	Removes the leading spaces from a string
@STRNCAT	Concatenates one or more strings up to the specified number of characters per string
@STRNCMP	Compares two strings up to specific number of characters
@STRRTRIM	Trims the trailing spaces in a string
@STRSUB	Substitutes one string for another within a string
@STRTRIM	Trims both leading and trailing spaces in a string
@STRUP	Converts the string to uppercase

Table 1-4: Number and character built-in functions

Examples of using the character strings functions *@strup*, *@strfind* and *@strcat* follows.

- Converting the customer address to upper case for the target column.

```
MAP osm$repapi.customers, TARGET osm$repapi.customers, &
COLMAP (USEDEFAULTS,
 cust_addr = @STRUP(cust_address));
```

- Validate the email address contains the '@' character:

```
MAP osm$repapi.customers, TARGET osm$repapi.customers, &
COLMAP (USEDEFAULTS,
        cust_addr  = cust_address,
           cust_email = @STRFIND (CUST_EMAIL, "@") > 0);
```

- Construct an upper case email by concatenating the name with specific domain. The upper case email achieved by nesting the two function @STRCAT and @STRUP.

```
MAP osm$repapi.customers, TARGET osm$repapi.customers,
COLMAP (USEDEFAULTS,
           cust_email=@STRUP(@STRCAT(cust_name,
                     '@precisetrace.com')));
```

Date functions in GoldenGate

Table 1-5 lists Oracle GoldenGate date related functions.

Function Name	Description
@DATE	Returns the date from specific input format, and output the date to specific output format
@DATEDIFF	Returns the difference between two dates
@DATENOW	Returns the current date and time value

Table 1-5: Oracle GoldenGate built-in date functions

An example of using the date function *@datenow*:

- We use the current date for the column *cust_name*.

```
MAP osm$repapi.customers, TARGET osm$repapi.customers, &
COLMAP (USEDEFAULTS, &
        cust_addr = cust_address,
        cust_date = @DATENOW());
```

GoldenGate General Purpose Functions

Table 1-6 lists the Oracle GoldenGate general purpose functions.

Function Name	Description
@BINARY	Ensures source binary data remains binary in the target column when the source column is defined as a character column data type.
@BINTOHEX	Converts a binary string to hexadecimal string value
@GETENV	Returns Oracle GoldenGate environment variable value.
@GETVAL	Extracts parameter value from a stored procedure when using SQLEXEC clause, requires the name procedure and parameter name.
@HEXTOBIN	Converts from hexadecimal to binary string value
@RANGE	We used to provide parallel processing for enabling multiple secondary extract or replicate processes read the same trail.
@TOKEN	We used to retrieves environment variable value for column mapping.

Table 1-6: Oracle GoldenGate general purpose built-in functions

Here is an example of using general function @TOKEN:

- First, we retrieve Oracle GoldenGate environment variable for the hostname, operating system user and database name.

```
MAP osm$repapi.customers, TARGET osm$repapi.customers,
COLMAP (USEDEFAULTS, &
           cust_addr = cust_address,
           cust_date = @DATENOW(),
           cust_hostname = @TOKEN ('TK_HOST'),
           cust_osname   = @TOKEN ('TK_OSUSER'),
           cust_dbname   = @TOKEN ('TK_DBNAME'));
```

GoldenGate Data selection and filtering

Data selection and filtering are fundamental to data integration, and Oracle GoldenGate provides the capabilities to perform data selection and filtering to meet applications requirements. There are several advantages for performing data selection and filtering from within GoldenGate, and by far, the most appealing is data security.

GoldenGate Data Replication Security

Implemented as a form of a *physical private database* (PPD), this is a method of data routing to the target databases that may be designed based on application context. A example sophisticated use of PPD is implementing physical private database based on a partitioned source table. Figure 1-27 illustrates limiting data access by implementing physical private database based on the table partitioning design.

The *customers* table is partitioned by range. The partitioning column is *cust_no* created as shown below.

```
SQL> CREATE TABLE customers (
     cust_no      NUMBER NOT NULL PRIMARY KEY,
     cust_name    VARCHAR2(128) NOT NULL,
     cust_email   VARCHAR2(128) NOT NULL,
     cust_mobile  NUMBER,
     cust_address VARCHAR2(128))
     PARTITION BY RANGE (cust_no)
       (PARTITION p100000 VALUES LESS THAN (100001),
        PARTITION p200000 VALUES LESS THAN (200001),
        PARTITION p300000 VALUES LESS THAN (300001),
        PARTITION p999999 VALUES LESS THAN (MAXVALUE));

Table created.
```

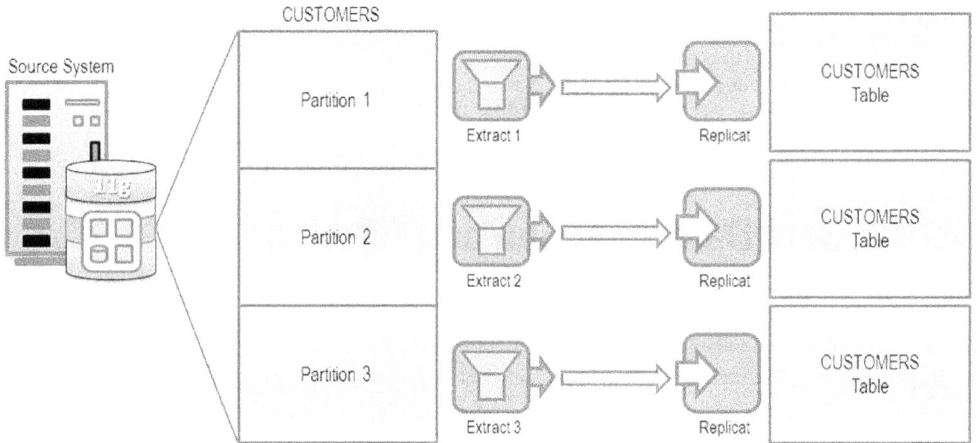

Figure 1-27: Physical private database (PPD)

For each partition, a dedicated primary extract performs change data capture using selection clause, creating its own local trail. Next, a data pump extract routes the data to a data server collector which creates a remote trail. The replicate process then applies the transactions to the target database *customers* table.

The above example is more realistic when implemented using the *interval* or *list partitioning* methods. The combination of Oracle GoldenGate selection, filtering, tokens and application context contribute for building secure data model.

GoldenGate Data selection

Oracle GoldenGate data selection is conceptually similar to the *where* clause found on SQL. The purpose is to limit data replication to a specific criteria. The selection can be developed as part of the primary extract, data pump extract or replicate process. The following illustrates data selection on the *customers* and *policies* tables for customers with policy no greater than 100000 through the primary extract *es1e201*.

```
EXTRACT es1e201
SETENV (ORACLE_SID=S1E2)
SETENV (ORACLE_HOME="/u01/app/oracle/product/11.2.0/dbhome_1")
SETENV (NLS_LANG=AMERICAN_AMERICA.AL32UTF8)
USERID ggs_admin@S1E2, PASSWORD oracle
EXTTRAIL ./dirdat/sa
TABLE osm$repapi.customers, WHERE (cust_no > 100000);
TABLE osm$repapi.policies,  WHERE (cust_no > 100000);
```

The *selection* clause should be defined for all related tables to avoid referential integrity violation when applying the transactions to the target database. Hence, it's necessary to construct the where clause to the *customers* table and *policies* table as well.

Data filtering in GoldenGate

Data filtering is suitable for complex data selection by utilizing Oracle GoldenGate built-in functions. For the replicate process, the *filter* parameter is developed as part of the MAP statement.

The example below illustrates the use of the *filter* parameter with the function *@strfind* to filter out email addresses that does not contains the character '@'.

```
REPLICAT rs1e201
SETENV (ORACLE_SID=T1C1)
SETENV (NLS_LANG=AMERICAN_AMERICA.AL32UTF8)
USERID ggs_admin@T1C1, PASSWORD oracle
DISCARDFILE ./dirrpt/rs1e201.dsc, PURGE
SOURCEDEFS ./dirdef/oracle.def
MAP osm$repapi.customers, TARGET osm$repapi.customers, &
COLMAP (USEDEFAULTS,
        cust_addr = cust_address),
FILTER (@STRFIND (cust_email, "@") > 0);
MAP osm$repapi.policies, TARGET osm$repapi.policies;
```

GoldenGate Data Transformation

The need to transform table columns values is very essentials for implementing an online operational data warehouse repository for business intelligence applications.

GoldenGate data transformation predominately applies to:

- Heterogeneous environment requirements
- The target database application uses rigid data types of different format
- Data warehouse repository summaries

For more complex operational data stores (ODS), (a common form of data warehouse repository), data transformation is essential. The transformation may be configured as part of the primary extract, secondary extract, the delivery process or a combination of any of them. Transformations achieved using Oracle GoldenGate offload the database and enable transparent application support. A simple yet common transformation example is the conversion of number data type to formatted character string data type as shown below:

Source table column data type: NUMBER
Source input value: 5085797993

Target table column data type: VARCHAR2(16)
Target output value: (508) 579-7993

Nesting Oracle GoldenGate built-in functions *@strcat*, *@strext* and *@strnum* convert the number to a formatted string. Starting with *@strnum* to convert the number to string, *@strext* to extract substrings of input string and then use *@strcat* to concatenate the substrings.

This data transformation is developed as part of replicate process configuration. Because of mismatched column names for the customer address, column mapping is also included.

```
REPLICAT rs1e201
SETENV (ORACLE_SID=T1C1)
SETENV (NLS_LANG=AMERICAN_AMERICA.AL32UTF8)
USERID ggs_admin@T1C1, PASSWORD oracle
DISCARDFILE ./dirrpt/rs1e201.dsc, PURGE
SOURCEDEFS ./dirdef/oracle.def
MAP osm$repapi.customers, TARGET osm$repapi.customers, &
COLMAP (USEDEFAULTS,
        cust_addr = cust_address,
        cust_mobile = @STRCAT('(',
        @STREXT(@STRNUM(cust_mobile), 1, 3), ')',
        ' ',
        @STREXT(@STRNUM(cust_mobile), 4, 6),
        '-',
        @STREXT(@STRNUM(cust_mobile), 7, 10)));
MAP osm$repapi.policies, TARGET osm$repapi.policies;
```

GoldenGate Tokens

Oracle GoldenGate tokens are attributes to stores environment variable values, which are available on the header of trail record header. Using Oracle GoldenGate built-in function *@token* within the parameter files retrieves the token value.

Table 1-6 lists pre-defined Oracle GoldenGate tokens.

Token Name	Description
TK_HOST	Stores the host name
TK_GROUP	Stores the operating system group name
TK_OSUSER	Stores the operating system user name
TK_DOMAIN	Stores the hostname domain

TK_COMMIT_TS	Stores the current commit transaction sequence number
TK_POS	Stores the current read position
TK_RBA	Stores the relative byte address (RBA)
TK_TABLE	Stores the table name
TK_OPTYPE	Stores the operation types (INSERT, UPDATE, DELETE or DDL)

Table 1-6: Oracle GoldenGate pre-defined tokens

Another type of tokens are user-token. These are defined on the source system and moved to target system for event handling, providing extendibility for attributes that are not pre-defined by Oracle GoldenGate.

The replicate *rs1e201* parameter file illustrates a basic implementation of token by associating each row with Oracle GoldenGate environment pre-defined tokens values that can be used by other applications, such as auditing.

```
T1C1>DESC customers
```

```
Name                                Null?    Type
----------------------------------- -------- ---------
CUST_NO                             NOT NULL NUMBER
CUST_NAME                           NOT NULL VARCHAR2(128)
CUST_EMAIL                          NOT NULL VARCHAR2(400)
CUST_MOBILE                         NOT NULL VARCHAR2(16)
CUST_ADDR                                    VARCHAR2(128)
HOST                                         VARCHAR2(128)
GG_GROUP                                     VARCHAR2(128)
OSUSER                                       VARCHAR2(128)
DOMAIN                                       VARCHAR2(128)
BA_IND                                       VARCHAR2(128)
COMMIT_TS                                    VARCHAR2(128)
POS                                          VARCHAR2(128)
RBA                                          VARCHAR2(128)
TABLENAME                                    VARCHAR2(128)
OPTYPE                                       VARCHAR2(128)
```

```
REPLICAT rs1e201
SETENV (ORACLE_SID=T1C1)
SETENV (NLS_LANG=AMERICAN_AMERICA.AL32UTF8)
USERID ggs_admin@T1C1, PASSWORD oracle
DISCARDFILE ./dirrpt/rs1e201.dsc, PURGE
SOURCEDEFS ./dirdef/oracle.def
MAP osm$repapi.customers, TARGET osm$repapi.customers, &
COLMAP (USEDEFAULTS,
        cust_addr = cust_address,
        host      = @TOKEN ('TK_HOST'),
        gg_group  = @TOKEN ('TK_GROUP'),
```

```
        osuser     = @TOKEN ('TK_OSUSER'),
        domain     = @TOKEN ('TK_DOMAIN'),
        ba_ind     = @TOKEN ('TK_BA_IND'),
        commit_ts = @TOKEN ('TK_COMMIT_TS'),
        pos        = @TOKEN ('TK_POS'),
        rba        = @TOKEN ('TK_RBA'),
        tablename = @TOKEN ('TK_TABLE'),
        optype     = @TOKEN ('TK_OPTYPE'));
MAP osm$repapi.policies, TARGET osm$repapi.policies;
```

Refer to chapter 5 to learn about embedding SQL queries and invoking database procedures to retrieve and manipulate data.

GoldenGate Programs call-out

Oracle GoldenGate extends its functionalities through call-out to database stored procedures and C programs. For database stored procedures, the call-out enabled through *sqlexec* parameter, call-out to C programs developed using user-exist.

To invoke a database stored procedures, extends the *target* clause to include the *sqlexec* option. The parameter *spname* specifies the <owner>.<procedure name> and *params* specifies the list of formal parameters.

```
MAP osm$repapi.customers, TARGET osm$repapi.customers, &
COLMAP (USEDEFAULTS,
        cust_addr = cust_address),
SQLEXEC (SPNAME osm$repapi.load_cust_pic,
         PARAMS (pcust_no = cust_no));
```

Refer to chapter 5 for an end-to-end demonstration on how to invoke database. The demonstration uses of *dbms_file_transfer* Oracle database built-in package to enable moving an image file of type BFILE from source system to target system. The purpose of the demonstration to show the technique for handling unsupported data types such as BFILE.

Configuration options in GoldenGate

Post-deployment of Oracle GoldenGate instance often requires environment enhancements. This section is limited to the basic enhancements only.

We will discuss enabling the following:

- Secure parameter files
- Data compression

- Scheduler
- Batch SQL

Secure parameter files

Extract and replicate processes parameter files often requires login to the database. Best practices should avoid using clear-text password, instead use encrypted password. Two methods are available: default method and named method.

We will illustrate using the default method to encrypt and use the encrypted password.

- From the GGSCI command-line, run the *encrypt* command using the default algorithm, *blowfish.*

```
GGSCI (ggs-source) 34> ENCRYPT PASSWORD oracle, ENCRYPTKEY default
```

```
Using Blowfish encryption with DEFAULT key.
Encrypted password:  AACAAAAAAAAAAAGAIFAAUDVHCFUGFIYF
Algorithm used:  BLOWFISH

GGSCI (ggs-source) 35>
```

- Test the encrypted password

```
GGSCI (ggs-source) 39> DBLOGIN USERID ggs_admin@S1E2, PASSWORD
AACAAAAAAAAAAAGAIFAAUDVHCFUGFIYF, ENCRYPTKEY DEFAULT
```

```
Successfully logged into database.
```

- Copy the encrypted password into the extract and replicate parameter files.

```
EXTRACT es1e201
SETENV (ORACLE_SID=S1E2)
SETENV (ORACLE_HOME="/u01/app/oracle/product/11.2.0/dbhome_1")
SETENV (NLS_LANG=AMERICAN_AMERICA.AL32UTF8)
USERID ggs_admin@S1E2, PASSWORD AACAAAAAAAAAAAGAIFAAUDVHCFUGFIYF,
ENCRYPTKEY DEFAULT
EXTTRAIL ./dirdat/sa
TABLE osm$repapi.customers, WHERE (cust_no > 100000);
TABLE osm$repapi.policies,  WHERE (cust_no > 100000);
```

GoldenGate Data compression

Moving data between source and target systems highly benefits from trail files compression, the default is non-compressed. Compression is transparent and enabled by adding the compression parameter option to the data pump process.

The following illustrates using Oracle GoldenGate compression option of type zlib. Automatic decompression is performed by the data collector server.

```
EXTRACT epmp01
USERID ggs_admin@S1E2, PASSWORD oracle
PASSTHRU
RMTHOST localhost, MGRPORT 7810, COMPRESS, &
                                 COMPRESSTHRESHOLD 512
RMTTRAIL /u01/app/oracle/ggs_2/dirdat/ta
TABLE osm$repapi.customers;
TABLE osm$repapi.policies;
```

GoldenGate Job scheduler

Oracle GoldenGate has its own job scheduler sub-system. It enables executing SQL statements and PL/SQL stored sub-programs. However, for complex event scheduling, consider using the database scheduler *dbms_scheduler* API. Oracle GoldenGate scheduler uses simplified expression to trigger the jobs.

An application area for using Oracle GoldenGate scheduler is to implement self-monitoring tool by scheduling the replicate processes to send an email every 10 minutes to inform the Oracle GoldenGate administrator it's on *running* status.

```
SQL> CREATE PROCEDURE email_rep_status(p1 VARCHAR2) IS
  2  BEGIN
  3      smtp_send(p1||' IS RUNNING...');
  4  END;
  5  /

Procedure created.
```

Now, we add the parameter *sqlexec* to each replicate process parameter file. Stop and restart replicate processes.

```
REPLICAT rs1e201
SETENV (ORACLE_SID=T1C1                   )
SETENV (NLS_LANG=AMERICAN_AMERICA.AL32UTF8)
USERID ggs_admin@T1C1, PASSWORD oracle
SQLEXEC "CALL email_rep_status('RS1E201')" EVERY 10 MINUTES
DISCARDFILE ./dirrpt/rs1e201.dsc, PURGE
SOURCEDEFS ./dirdef/oracle.def
MAP osm$repapi.customers, TARGET osm$repapi.customers, &
```

```
COLMAP (USEDEFAULTS,
        cust_addr = cust_address),
SQLEXEC (SPNAME osm$repapi.load_cust_pic,
         PARAMS (pcust_no = cust_no));
MAP osm$repapi.policies, TARGET osm$repapi.policies;
```

An informational message is sent to the process report file whenever every time the statement executed. Nice and simple tool!

```
2013-07-14 22:23:25  INFO    OGG-00888  SQL statement
executed successfully on interval.
```

GoldenGate Batch SQL

The replicate process parameter *batchsql* increases the apply throughput by classifying and building in-memory arrays for similar SQL statements to be applied as one database operation.

A typical environment is an OLTP system that applies transactions differing on bind variable values only. Oracle GoldenGate supercharges the replicate processes using batch SQL technique. By default, replicate processes apply transactions one at a time, with *batchsql* the replicate process applies transactions on batch mode.

The replicate process parameter *batchsql* follows.

```
REPLICAT rs1e201
SETENV (ORACLE_SID=T1C1)
SETENV (NLS_LANG=AMERICAN_AMERICA.AL32UTF8)
USERID ggs_admin@T1C1, PASSWORD oracle
BATCHSQL
DISCARDFILE ./dirrpt/rs1e201.dsc, PURGE
SOURCEDEFS ./dirdef/oracle.def
MAP osm$repapi.customers, TARGET osm$repapi.customers, &
COLMAP (USEDEFAULTS,
        cust_addr = cust_address);
MAP osm$repapi.policies, TARGET osm$repapi.policies;
```

The BATCHSQL parameter enhances the target database Replicat by arranging the individual SQL statement into arrays using memory caching and variable binding.

Automatic storage management (ASM) support for

GoldenGate

Oracle Database 10g release 2 introduced Oracle automatic storage management (ASM). Since then, Oracle Corporation has been enhancing ASM to provide high-performance file system management supporting all Oracle database file types. Figure 1-28 depicts Oracle ASM instance showing the data flow from Oracle GoldenGate extract on an ASM environment. Oracle GoldenGate change data capture requires ASM authentication for accessing the transaction logs. The extract parameter *tranlogoptions* handles authentication to the ASM instance.

```
TRANLOGOPTIONS ASMUSER SYS@<ASM_instance>, ASMPASSWORD
<password> [<algorithm> ENCRYPTKEY {<keyname> | DEFAULT}]
```

The parameter *tranlogoptions* is database type dependent, and may appear several times within the same parameter file.

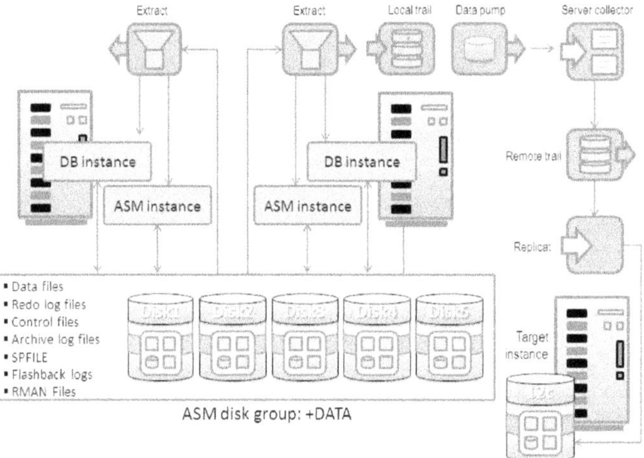

Figure 1-28: Oracle ASM for GoldenGate

To enable Oracle GoldenGate capture from an ASM instance transaction logs, it requires configuring the network for the ASM instance. The steps to prepare Oracle GoldenGate for an ASM instance follows.

Step 1: Ensure the database listener is configured to handle connection, and the TNS alias is configured. The network configuration is for the grid infrastructure network.

```
SID_LIST_LISTENER =
  (SID_LIST =
    (SID_DESC =
      (GLOBAL_DBNAME = S2E2.precisetrace.com)
      (ORACLE_HOME = /u01/app/oracle/product/11.2.0/dbhome_1)
      (SID_NAME = S2E2)
    )
    (SID_DESC =
      (ORACLE_HOME = /u01/app/oracle/product/11.2.0/grid)
      (SID = +ASM)
    )
  )

LISTENER =
  (DESCRIPTION =
    (ADDRESS = (PROTOCOL = TCP)(HOST = ggs-source)(PORT = 1521))
  )

ADR_BASE_LISTENER = /u01/app/oracle

ASM =
  (DESCRIPTION =
    (ADDRESS_LIST =
      (ADDRESS = (PROTOCOL = TCP)(HOST = ggs-source)(PORT = 1521))
    )
    (CONNECT_DATA =
      (SID = +ASM)
    )
  )
```

Step 2: Test connectivity using SQL*Plus as SYSASM users. The test must be successful before proceeding to step 3.

```
$ . oraenv
ORACLE_SID = [S2E2] ? +ASM
The Oracle base remains unchanged with value /u01/app/oracle
$ sqlplus /nolog

SQL*Plus: Release 11.2.0.3.0 Production on Fri May 31 11:08:35 2013
Copyright (c) 1982, 2011, Oracle.  All rights reserved.

SQL> conn / as SYSASM
Connected.
```

Step 3: Modify the primary extract parameter file to include the *translogoptions* parameter.

```
EXTRACT es1e201
SETENV (ORACLE_SID=S1E2)
SETENV (ORACLE_HOME="/u01/app/oracle/product/11.2.0/dbhome_1")
SETENV (NLS_LANG=AMERICAN_AMERICA.AL32UTF8)
USERID ggs_admin@S1E2, PASSWORD AACAAAAAAAAAAAGAIFAAUDVHCFUGFIYF, ENCRYPTKEY
DEFAULT
TRANLOGOPTIONS ASMUSER sys@ASM, ASMPASSWORD oracle_4U
EXTTRAIL ./dirdat/sa
TABLE osm$repapi.customers, WHERE (cust_no > 100000);
TABLE osm$repapi.policies,  WHERE (cust_no > 100000);
```

When using Oracle GoldenGate on an ASM instance, ensure the maximum number of concurrently processes parameter is sufficient to handle the addition of GoldenGate extracts, default value is 50. When using Oracle GoldenGate parallel processing, set the value to support the total number of processes defined by the *@range* function. A typical parameter value setting is 300.

Parallel processing in GoldenGate

Oracle GoldenGate supports high-performance parallel processing. The degree of parallelism controlled using the *@range* function. Figure 1-29 delivers 1-3-6 degree of parallelism. The extract *es1e201* performs change data capture from the list of tables. The data pump extract groups *epmp01*, *epmp02,* and *epmp03* parallelize extracting from the local trail *./dirdat/sa* into degree of 3, each data pump extract has its associated data server collector, which into turn re-assemble the data and write to its own remote trail. Ultimately, using parallel processing maintains stable sub-second latency and lagging.

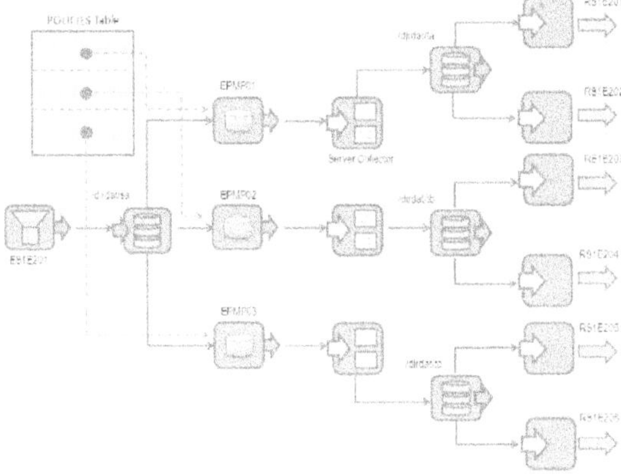

Figure 1-29: Oracle GoldenGate Parallel processing

replicate groups *rs1e201, rs1e202, rs1e203, rs1e204, rs1e205* and *rs1e206* parallelize its associated remote trail extract into degree of 2, hence a total of 6 replicates processes are used to apply the transaction, captured by the extract *es1e201*, to the target database.

Implementing parallelism in GoldenGate Replication

Parallel processing is a key for maximizing system scalability and throughput. Oracle GoldenGate built-in function *@range* implemented to deploy parallel processing for increasing throughput on large volume transaction tables for online synchronization, keeping the lag time to a minimum.

Specify each range in a *filter* clause in a *table* or *map* statement. *@range* function is very similar to hash database partitioning, it's safe and scalable preserving data integrity by guaranteeing that the row is processed by related process groups.

The *@range* computes a hash value of the columns specified in the input. If no columns are specified, the *keycols* clause of the *table* or *map* statement is used to determine the columns to hash, if a *keycols* clause exists. Otherwise, the primary key columns are used, which the default.

The function takes three arguments, the current process number, the degree of parallelism and partitioning column(s), which optional. The general syntax:

```
@RANGE (<range>, <total ranges> [, <column>] [, <column>] [,
...])
```

Memory resource requirements for GoldenGate

Prior to deploying high-degree parallel processing, calculate and provision the memory requirements for all processes. The required memory size is dynamic and depends on the transaction volume processed by each process. Table 1-x shows the calculation for the above parallel processing design using the operating system Linux process status (ps) and process mapping (*pmap*) commands. Table 1-7 illustrates the memory consumption for the above design while the source and target system engaged on real-time data replication for a low volume transaction.

Start by determining the Linux process ID, then use the process for on pmap (process map) operating system command.

```
GGSCI (ggs-target) 28> SHELL ps -edf | grep RS1E201
```

```
oracle    6427  6584  0 05:25 pts/3    00:00:00 sh -c ps -edf |
grep RS1E201
oracle    6429  6427  0 05:25 pts/3    00:00:00 grep RS1E201
oracle    8943  4964  0 04:22 ?        00:00:03
/u01/app/oracle/ggs/replicat PARAMFILE
/u01/app/oracle/ggs/dirprm/rs1e201.prm REPORTFILE
/u01/app/oracle/ggs/dirrpt/RS1E201.rpt PROCESSID RS1E201 USESUBDIRS
```

```
GGSCI (ggs-target) 29> shell pmap -x 6427 | grep total

total kB  204252       -       -       -
```

Follow the above syntax to calculate the memory for all processes as shown in table 1-7.

GoldenGate process Name	GoldenGate process Type	Memory size (KB)
ES1E201	Primary extract	204252
EPMP01	Second extract, data pump	112396
EPMP02	Second extract, data pump	111808
EPMP03	Second extract, data pump	111812
RS1E201	Replicate process	131476
RS1E202	Replicate process	131476
RS1E203	Replicate process	131128
RS1E204	Replicate process	131124
RS1E205	Replicate process	131128
RS1E206	Replicate process	131476
	Total (GB)	**1.27**

Table 1-7: Oracle GoldenGate process memory utilization

Parallel processing implementation in GoldenGate

The following shows the parameter files and the GGSCI *add extract*, *add exttrail* and *add rmttrail* commands executed to deploy the above parallel processing design shown in figure 1-30.

The source system setup creates the primary extract group *es1e201* and the secondary extract groups *epmp01*, *epmp02* and *epmp03*. The parameter files are listed below. Because of the *filter* clause, the parameter *nopassthru* is required.

```
-- es1e201.prm

EXTRACT es1e201
SETENV (ORACLE_SID=S1E2)
SETENV (ORACLE_HOME="/u01/app/oracle/product/11.2.0/dbhome_1")
SETENV (NLS_LANG=AMERICAN_AMERICA.AL32UTF8)
USERID  ggs_admin@S1E2,  PASSWORD  AACAAAAAAAAAAAGAIFAAUDVHCFUGFIYF,
ENCRYPTKEY DEFAULT
EXTTRAIL ./dirdat/sa
TABLE osm$repapi.customers;
TABLE osm$repapi.policies;

-- epmp01.prm
```

```
EXTRACT epmp01
USERID  ggs_admin@S1E2,  PASSWORD  AACAAAAAAAAAAAGAIFAAUDVHCFUGFIYF,
ENCRYPTKEY DEFAULT
NOPASSTHRU
RMTHOST ggs-target, MGRPORT 7812
RMTTRAIL ./dirdat/ta
TABLE osm$repapi.customers, FILTER (@RANGE(1, 3));
TABLE osm$repapi.policies,  FILTER (@RANGE(1, 3));
```

-- epmp02.prm

```
EXTRACT epmp02
USERID  ggs_admin@S1E2,  PASSWORD  AACAAAAAAAAAAAGAIFAAUDVHCFUGFIYF,
ENCRYPTKEY DEFAULT
NOPASSTHRU
RMTHOST ggs-target, MGRPORT 7812
RMTTRAIL ./dirdat/tb
TABLE osm$repapi.customers, FILTER (@RANGE(2, 3));
TABLE osm$repapi.policies,  FILTER (@RANGE(2, 3));
```

-- epmp03.prm

```
EXTRACT epmp03
USERID  ggs_admin@S1E2,  PASSWORD  AACAAAAAAAAAAAGAIFAAUDVHCFUGFIYF,
ENCRYPTKEY DEFAULT
NOPASSTHRU
RMTHOST ggs-target, MGRPORT 7812
RMTTRAIL ./dirdat/tc
TABLE osm$repapi.customers, FILTER (@RANGE(3, 3));
TABLE osm$repapi.policies,  FILTER (@RANGE(3, 3));
```

Now, run the *add extract, add exttrail* and *add rmttrail* commands.

```
GGSCI (ggs-source) 5> ADD EXTRACT es1e201, TRANLOG, BEGIN now, THREADS 1

EXTRACT added.

GGSCI (ggs-source) 6> ADD EXTTRAIL ./dirdat/sa, EXTRACT es1e201, MEGABYTES
32

EXTTRAIL added.

GGSCI (ggs-source) 7> ADD EXTRACT epmp01, EXTTRAILSOURCE ./dirdat/sa

EXTRACT added.

GGSCI (ggs-source) 8> ADD RMTTRAIL ./dirdat/ta, EXTRACT epmp01, MEGABYTES 32

RMTTRAIL added.

GGSCI (ggs-source) 9> ADD EXTRACT epmp02, EXTTRAILSOURCE ./dirdat/sa

EXTRACT added.
```

```
GGSCI (ggs-source) 10> ADD RMTTRAIL ./dirdat/tb, EXTRACT epmp02, MEGABYTES
32

RMTTRAIL added.

GGSCI (ggs-source) 11> ADD EXTRACT epmp03, EXTTRAILSOURCE ./dirdat/sa

EXTRACT added.

GGSCI (ggs-source) 12> ADD RMTTRAIL ./dirdat/tc, EXTRACT epmp03, MEGABYTES
32

RMTTRAIL added.
```

The target system setup creates the replicate process *rs1e201*, *rs1e201*, *rs1e201*, *rs1e201*, *rs1e201* and *rs1e201*. The parameter files prepared to successfully start the replicate processes.

```
-- rs1e201.prm

REPLICAT rs1e201
SETENV (ORACLE_SID=T1C1)
SETENV (NLS_LANG=AMERICAN_AMERICA.AL32UTF8)
USERID ggs_admin@t1c1, PASSWORD oracle
ASSUMETARGETDEFS
DISCARDFILE ./dirrpt/rs1e201.dsc, PURGE
MAP osm$repapi.customers, TARGET osm$repapi.customers,
FILTER (@RANGE(1, 2));
MAP osm$repapi.policies, TARGET osm$repapi.policies,
FILTER (@RANGE(1, 2));
```

```
-- rs1e202.prm

EPLICAT rs1e202
SETENV (ORACLE_SID=T1C1)
SETENV (NLS_LANG=AMERICAN_AMERICA.AL32UTF8)
USERID ggs_admin@t1c1, PASSWORD oracle
ASSUMETARGETDEFS
DISCARDFILE ./dirrpt/rs1e202.dsc, PURGE
MAP osm$repapi.customers, TARGET osm$repapi.customers,
FILTER (@RANGE(2, 2));
MAP osm$repapi.policies, TARGET osm$repapi.policies,
FILTER (@RANGE(2, 2));
```

```
-- rs1e203.prm

REPLICAT rs1e203
SETENV (ORACLE_SID=T1C1)
SETENV (NLS_LANG=AMERICAN_AMERICA.AL32UTF8)
USERID ggs_admin@t1c1, PASSWORD oracle
```

```
ASSUMETARGETDEFS
DISCARDFILE ./dirrpt/rs1e203.dsc, PURGE
MAP osm$repapi.customers, TARGET osm$repapi.customers,
FILTER (@RANGE(1, 2));
MAP osm$repapi.policies, TARGET osm$repapi.policies,
FILTER (@RANGE(1, 2));
```

```
-- rs1e204.prm
```

```
REPLICAT rs1e204
SETENV (ORACLE_SID=T1C1)
SETENV (NLS_LANG=AMERICAN_AMERICA.AL32UTF8)
USERID ggs_admin@t1c1, PASSWORD oracle
ASSUMETARGETDEFS
DISCARDFILE ./dirrpt/rs1e204.dsc, PURGE
MAP osm$repapi.customers, TARGET osm$repapi.customers,
FILTER (@RANGE(2, 2));
MAP osm$repapi.policies, TARGET osm$repapi.policies,
FILTER (@RANGE(2, 2));
```

```
-- rs1e205.prm
```

```
REPLICAT rs1e205
SETENV (ORACLE_SID=T1C1)
SETENV (NLS_LANG=AMERICAN_AMERICA.AL32UTF8)
USERID ggs_admin@t1c1, PASSWORD oracle
ASSUMETARGETDEFS
DISCARDFILE ./dirrpt/rs1e205.dsc, PURGE
MAP osm$repapi.customers, TARGET osm$repapi.customers,
FILTER (@RANGE(1, 2));
MAP osm$repapi.policies, TARGET osm$repapi.policies,
FILTER (@RANGE(1, 2));
```

```
-- rs1e206.prm
```

```
REPLICAT rs1e206
SETENV (ORACLE_SID=T1C1)
SETENV (NLS_LANG=AMERICAN_AMERICA.AL32UTF8)
USERID ggs_admin@t1c1, PASSWORD oracle
ASSUMETARGETDEFS
DISCARDFILE ./dirrpt/rs1e206.dsc, PURGE
MAP osm$repapi.customers, TARGET osm$repapi.customers,
FILTER (@RANGE(2, 2));
MAP osm$repapi.policies, TARGET osm$repapi.policies,
FILTER (@RANGE(2, 2));
```

Let's start by creating the checkpoint table. This is the default checkpoint location for replicate processes. The *add checkpointtable* command requires successful login to the database.

```
GGSCI (ggs-target) 2> DBLOGIN USERID ggs_admin@t1c1,
PASSWORD oracle
Successfully logged into database.

GGSCI (ggs-target) 3> ADD CHECKPOINTTABLE

No checkpoint table specified. Using GLOBALS specification
(ggs_admin.chkpttab)...

Successfully created checkpoint table ggs_admin.chkpttab.
```

Now, creating replicate processes RS1E201, RS1E202, RS1E203, RS1E204, RS1E205 and RS1E206.

```
GGSCI (ggs-target) 6> ADD REPLICAT rs1e201, EXTTRAIL ./dirdat/ta

REPLICAT added.

GGSCI (ggs-target) 7> ADD REPLICAT rs1e202, EXTTRAIL ./dirdat/ta

REPLICAT added.

GGSCI (ggs-target) 8> ADD REPLICAT rs1e203, EXTTRAIL ./dirdat/tb

REPLICAT added.

GGSCI (ggs-target) 9> ADD REPLICAT rs1e204, EXTTRAIL ./dirdat/tb

REPLICAT added.

GGSCI (ggs-target) 10> ADD REPLICAT rs1e205, EXTTRAIL ./dirdat/tc

REPLICAT added.

GGSCI (ggs-target) 11> ADD REPLICAT rs1e206, EXTTRAIL ./dirdat/tc

REPLICAT added.
```

Start and verify the source system processes status

```
GGSCI (ggs-source) 40> START er *

Sending START request to MANAGER ...
EXTRACT EPMP01 starting

Sending START request to MANAGER ...
EXTRACT EPMP02 starting

Sending START request to MANAGER ...
EXTRACT EPMP03 starting
```

```
Sending START request to MANAGER ...
EXTRACT ES1E201 starting

GGSCI (ggs-source) 41> INFO ALL

Program    Status     Group     Lag at Chkpt  Time Since Chkpt

MANAGER    RUNNING
EXTRACT    RUNNING    EPMP01    00:00:00      00:00:12
EXTRACT    RUNNING    EPMP02    00:00:00      00:00:11
EXTRACT    RUNNING    EPMP03    00:00:00      00:00:10
EXTRACT    RUNNING    ES1E201   00:00:00      00:00:09

GGSCI (ggs-source) 43>
```

Now we start and verify the target system processes status.

```
GGSCI (ggs-target) 11> START ER *

Sending START request to MANAGER ...
REPLICAT RS1E201 starting

Sending START request to MANAGER ...
REPLICAT RS1E202 starting

Sending START request to MANAGER ...
REPLICAT RS1E203 starting

Sending START request to MANAGER ...
REPLICAT RS1E204 starting

Sending START request to MANAGER ...
REPLICAT RS1E205 starting

Sending START request to MANAGER ...
REPLICAT RS1E206 starting

GGSCI (ggs-target) 12> INFO ALL

Program     Status      Group       Lag at Chkpt  Time Since Chkpt

MANAGER     RUNNING
REPLICAT    RUNNING     RS1E201     00:00:00      00:00:09
REPLICAT    RUNNING     RS1E202     00:00:00      00:00:09
REPLICAT    RUNNING     RS1E203     00:00:00      00:00:08
REPLICAT    RUNNING     RS1E204     00:00:00      00:00:08
REPLICAT    RUNNING     RS1E205     00:00:00      00:00:08
REPLICAT    RUNNING     RS1E206     00:00:00      00:00:08
```

Now let's look at generating reports in GoldenGate.

Generating Reports in GoldenGate

Oracle GoldenGate generates various types of reports for troubleshooting and monitoring purposes. These report are available from GGSCI command-line.

We use the view GGSCI command to view process report.

```
GGSCI (ggs-target) 13> VIEW REPORT rs1e201
```

GGSCI STATS command reports process statistics. For example, display the @RANGE statistics using wild-card character. The STATS indicates parallel processing has been distributed almost evenly across the replicate processes.

```
GGSCI (ggs-target) 15> STATS REPLICAT rs1e2*
```

```
Sending STATS request to REPLICAT RS1E201 ...

Start of Statistics at 2013-11-05 08:52:00.

Replicating from OSM$REPAPI.CUSTOMERS to OSM$REPAPI.CUSTOMERS:

*** Total statistics since 2013-11-05 08:23:19 ***
    Total inserts                          19494.00
    Total updates                              0.00
    Total deletes                              0.00
    Total discards                             0.00
    Total operations                       19494.00

*** Daily statistics since 2013-11-05 08:23:19 ***
    Total inserts                          19494.00
    Total updates                              0.00
    Total deletes                              0.00
    Total discards                             0.00
    Total operations                       19494.00

*** Hourly statistics since 2013-11-05 08:23:19 ***
    Total inserts                          19494.00
    Total updates                              0.00
    Total deletes                              0.00
    Total discards                             0.00
    Total operations                       19494.00

*** Latest statistics since 2013-11-05 08:23:19 ***
    Total inserts                          19494.00
    Total updates                              0.00
    Total deletes                              0.00
    Total discards                             0.00
    Total operations                       19494.00
```

Monitoring processes lagging in GoldenGate

The difference between the commit and the apply determines the amount of lagging. The following show the lag for replicate process RS1E201.

```
GGSCI (ggs-target) 16> LAG REPLICAT rs1e201
```

```
Sending GETLAG request to REPLICAT RS1E201 ...
Last record lag: 12 seconds.
At EOF, no more records to process.
```

The column *Lag at Chkpt* column of the *info all* command display the lagging of the replicate process.

```
GGSCI (ggs-target) 17> INFO ALL
```

```
Program     Status      Group       Lag at Chkpt  Time Since Chkpt

MANAGER     RUNNING
REPLICAT    RUNNING     RS1E201     00:00:00      00:00:07
REPLICAT    RUNNING     RS1E202     00:00:00      00:00:07
REPLICAT    RUNNING     RS1E203     00:00:00      00:00:06
REPLICAT    RUNNING     RS1E204     00:00:00      00:00:06
REPLICAT    RUNNING     RS1E205     00:00:00      00:00:06
REPLICAT    RUNNING     RS1E206     00:00:00      00:00:06

GGSCI (ggs-target) 18>
```

GoldenGate Events logging system

Oracle GoldenGate is integrated with Linux/UNIX syslog messaging system and Windows Event Viewer for events logging. There are three files for managing runtime errors, namely: *ggserr.log, tcperr* and *ggMessage.dat* all located on Oracle GoldenGate home directory. The file *ggserr.log* is for logging currently running instance activities, tcperr defines rules for handling TCP/IP errors and actions and *ggMessage.dat* is an obfuscated data file for storing Oracle GoldenGate error messages specific to the instance version.

By default Oracle GoldenGate writes all levels of messages to *ggserr.log* file, which is crucial for newly deployed instance for monitoring. After the instance runs operational and highly stable, logging level can be adjusted to filter out less important messages send to the log file. The logging level is determined by Oracle GoldenGate *syslog* parameter.

Setting *syslog* in the GLOBALS parameter file allows Oracle GoldenGate to write and maybe filter out messages for all instance processes, setting *syslog* at *mgr.prm* parameter files allows Oracle GoldenGate to write and maybe filter out the manager process related messages only. Setting *syslog* on both locations causes the manager to override the GLOBALS setting for the manager process, this allows the use of separate settings between the manager and other processes. The *syslog* parameter takes the following arguments for level settings.

ALL

Writes all Oracle GoldenGate messages. This setting is the same as combining INFO, WARN, ERROR arguments. This is the default level of logging messages. This argument cannot be combined with other arguments.

NONE

Suppresses all Oracle GoldenGate messages. This is not a recommended setting and it should be used for non-production environment only. This argument cannot be combined with other arguments.

INFO

Writes messages of type INFO (information) only. This argument can be combined with WARN (warning) and ERROR arguments. Information messages include activities such as stopping and starting extracts and replicates processes.

WARN

Write messages of type WARN (warning). This argument can be combined with INFO (information) and ERROR arguments.

ERROR

Write messages of type ERROR. This argument can be combined with INFO (information) and WARN (warning) arguments.

Because the log file *ggserr.log* is not cyclic, periodically archiving the log file is recommend to avoid the file growing linearly. When *ggserr.log* is deleted, Oracle GoldenGate re-creates the logging file *ggserr.log* once it's trying to write the very next message. The following Linux/UNIX shell program archives *ggserr.log* file to */tmp* directory when *ggserr.log* exceeds 10MB (10485760 bytes).

 **archive_goldengate.bash**

```
#--------------------------------------------------------------
#--     DISCLAIMER:
#--
#--     This script is provided for educational purposes only.
#--     The script has been tested on an Oracle GoldenGate instance
#--     and run as intended. However; prior to using the script on
#--     production systems, a dynamic test should be conducted prior
#--     to deployment.
#--
#--------------------------------------------------------------#
#!/bin/bash
GGS_HOME="/u01/app/ogg/11.2.0"
if [ -f $GGS_HOME/ggserr.log ]; then
   FS=$( stat -c %s $GGS_HOME/ggserr.log)
   if [ $FS -gt 10485760 ]; then
       mv $GGS_HOME/ggserr.log /tmp
       echo "$GGS_HOME/ggserr.log was last archived on:" `date` >>
/tmp/ggserr.txt
   fi
else
   echo "$GGS_HOME/ggserr.log does not exist:" `date` >> /tmp/ggserr.txt
fi
```

For scheduled archiving on Linux/UNIX platforms, save the above shell program to a file, for example *ggserr.sh,* set the execute permission, add the file *ggserr.sh* to */etc/crontab* using the command crontab. However; Adapting Oracle GoldenGate monitor notification system enables immediate response to all types events.

The Syntax for *syslog* parameter is shown next. The default setting is *syslog all*, which writes *info* (information), *warn* (warning) and *error* messages.

```
SYSLOG {[ALL | NONE] | [, INFO] [, WARN] [, ERROR]}
```

Windows Event Viewer with GoldenGate

Oracle GoldenGate on MS Windows for SQL Server writes GoldenGate messages to *ggserr.log* file and to Windows Event Viewer, if enabled. The event levels is controlled by setting the parameter *syslog* as explained above. To sort Oracle GoldenGate related messages, from Administrative Events click on the source column and scroll down to GGS ER.

Oracle GoldenGate is enabled to utilize Windows Event Viewer by running Oracle GoldenGate install program with the *addevents* option, this is normally performed after the installation. Then from Oracle GoldenGate home directory, copy the files *category.dll* and *ggsmsg.dll* libraries to Windows SYSTEM32 directory for more detailed Windows specific messages. Figure 1-30 shows an ERROR level message from Windows Event Viewer, the same message is written to *ggserr.log* file.

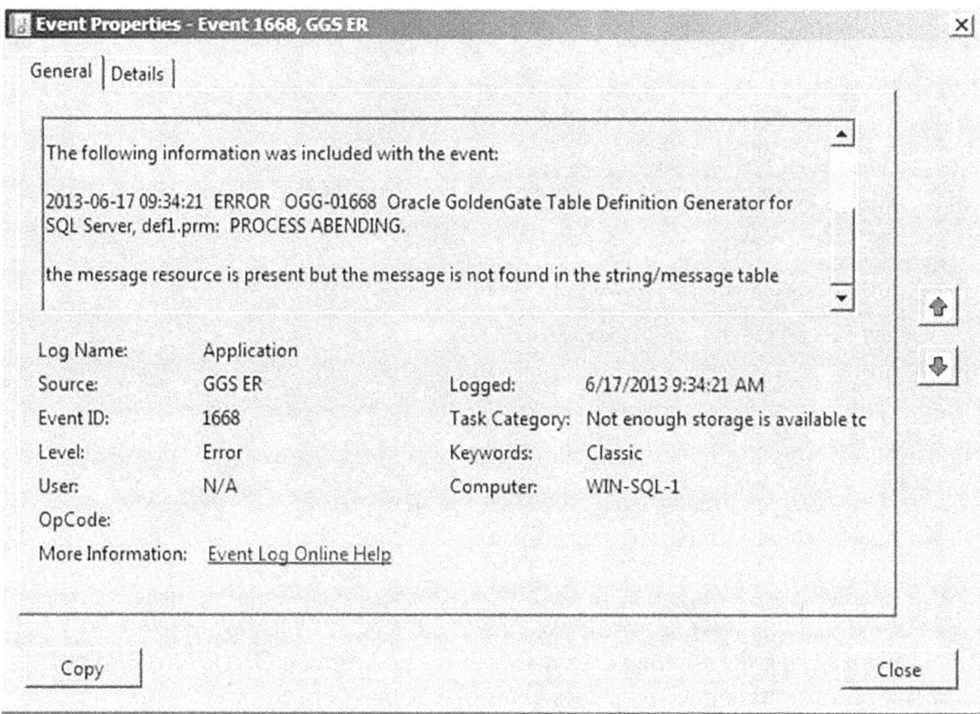

Figure 1-30: MS Windows event viewer for Oracle GoldenGate

Windows events handling in GoldenGate

MS Windows allows you to attach a task to an event level, providing an automated event handling for Oracle GoldenGate log messages. For example, events of level Information and Warning can be regularly cleared out to avoid the Event Viewer from growing quickly, events of level Error are associated with an action for immediate notification and action, as explained next.

Right-clicking on the event to start the Create Basic Task Wizard. Figure 1-31 associate an event of level Error with the action Send an email. Send an E-mail task uses the inputs: From, To, Subject, Text, Attachment, and SMTP server. An alternative to using the Create Basic Task Wizard is to create a customized archiving batch program to run using the Windows scheduler created by the AT command. AT command schedules operating system commands and batch programs (utilities) to run at a specific time and date, the *computername* argument refer to the local host (default) or remote host. Before using the AT command, Windows schedule service must be running.

Failure to manage *ggserr.log* file and Windows Event Viewer may result on:

- Performance related issues for large file size of *ggserr.log*
- Disk storage related issues for excessive events messaging

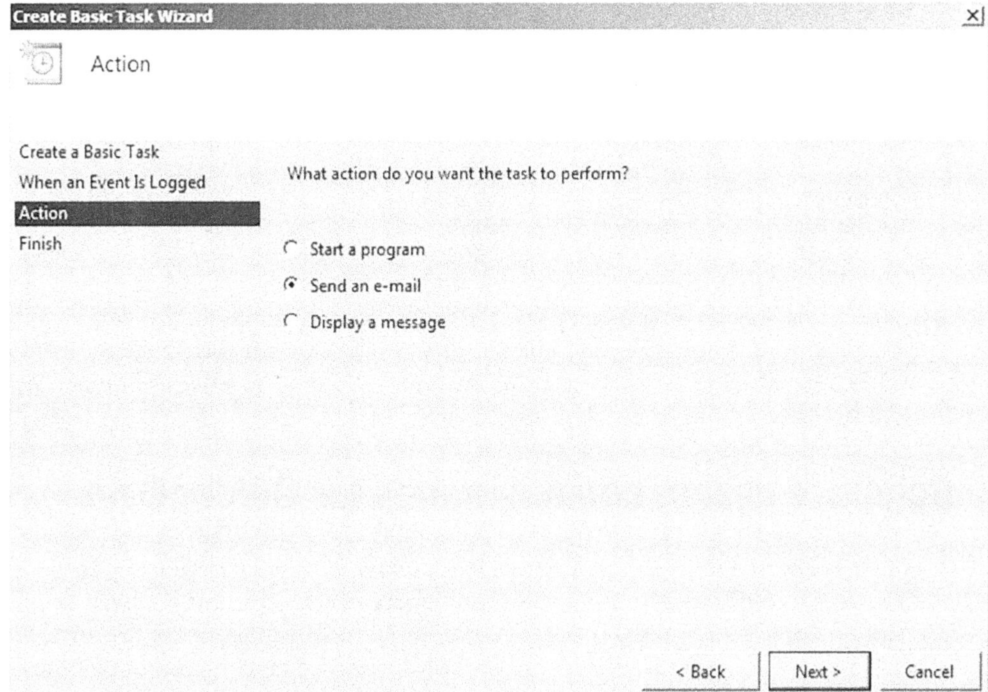

Figure 1-31: Managing and associating an event using an action

TCP/IP network errors and GoldenGate

Because Oracle GoldenGate uses TCP/IP network to communicate between source and target systems processes, TCP/IP network related errors response are adjustable to suite the network throughput. Modify TCP/IP values found at *tcperr* file to customize Oracle GoldenGate TCP/IP related error message, such as time-out interval and dynamic port allocation. The following table shows the default TCP/IP error response settings found at *tcperr* file.

```
#
# TCP/IP error handling parameters
#
# Default error response is abend
```

```
#
# Error          Response    Delay (csecs)    Max Retries

ECONNABORTED      RETRY         1000              10
#ECONNREFUSED     ABEND            0               0
ECONNREFUSED      RETRY         1000              12
ECONNRESET        RETRY          500              10
ENETDOWN          RETRY         3000              50
ENETRESET         RETRY         1000              10
ENOBUFS           RETRY          100              60
ENOTCONN          RETRY          100              10
EPIPE             RETRY          500              10
ESHUTDOWN         RETRY         1000              10
ETIMEDOUT         RETRY         1000              10
NODYNPORTS        RETRY          100              10
```

Carefully modify *tcperr,* and test using the same network throughput before deploying on production. As unexpected behavior may result due to incorrect settings of delay and retires values when moving from intranet for testing to internet for production TCP/IP network with firewall settings.

Database design considerations for GoldenGate

The majority of enterprise applications require data movement originating from heterogeneous databases, from within and outside of the organization. Because Oracle GoldenGate maintains transaction commit order of the source database, the source database layout influences the level of flexibility when implementing Oracle GoldenGate. Data movement is applications transparent eliminating any type of changes. The source system sustains minimum overhead as Oracle GoldenGate is optimized for change data capture from the transaction logs. However; Oracle GoldenGate implementers need to consider the following:

Partitioned schemas in GoldenGate

A partitioned schema is forms data model where the schema is self-contained, mostly found on specialized applications with limited number of related database tables. In such environment Oracle GoldenGate achieves the highest level of flexibility during the implementation and deliver sub-seconds latency for data movement, due to no transformation requirements. Partitioned schema helps eliminates data conflict when deploying Oracle GoldenGate on bidirectional topology for active-active environment. For example, in the case of using Oracle sequence as an artificial primary key value on partitioned schema design, associating the generated sequence number with a unique identifier such as the *instance_name* context attribute value always ensures a unique value across the source and target databases, thus avoiding data conflict on bidirectional replication as illustrated next.

For the source database (S1E2),

```
SQL> conn osm$repapi/oracle@S1E2
Connected.
SQL> CREATE SEQUENCE pol_no_seq;

Sequence created.

SQL> SELECT CONCAT(pol_no_seq.nextval,
  2  CONCAT('-', SYS_CONTEXT('USERENV', 'INSTANCE_NAME'))) POL_NO
  3  FROM dual;

POL_NO
-----------------------------------------------------------------
7-S1E2
```

For the target database (T1C1),

```
SQL> conn osm$repapi/oracle@T1C1
Connected.
SQL> CREATE SEQUENCE pol_no_seq;

Sequence created.
SQL> SELECT CONCAT(pol_no_seq.nextval,
  2  CONCAT('-', SYS_CONTEXT('USERENV', 'INSTANCE_NAME'))) POL_NO
  3  FROM dual;

POL_NO
----------------------------------------------------------------
7-T1C1
```

Data types and GoldenGate

Depending on the database type, certain data types are not supported. It always possible to migrate unsupported data types to similar functionality data types. For Oracle database, the list is of unsupported data type is limited to: *anydata, anydataset, anytype, bfile, binary_integer, mlslabel, orddicom, pls_integer, timezone_abbr, uritype* and *urowid.*

For MS SQL Server, the list of unsupported data types is limited to: SQL_Variant

Referential integrity constraints

Oracle GoldenGate perform transactional change data capture from the transaction logs, preserving the transaction commit order. Even though the ordering of tables found at the extract parameter file is irrelevant. However; the ordering of tables found at the replicate parameter file requires proper listing. When the target database table constraints are enabled, the order of tables must consider referential integrity constraints among tables, otherwise the replicate processes *abended* due to constraint violation. This is a challenging task for complex database schemas definition when replicating the entire database.

Three steps demonstration setup

The objectives of presenting an end-to-end configuration is to demonstrate how Oracle GoldenGate fundamental setup is concise and easy when used for as-is data movement such as homogenous replication, which absolutely true when compared with Oracle Steams configuration. The details of the steps are explained in throughout the book.

This fundamental setup can be used for the purpose of quick demonstration or as a reference for time-to-time GoldenGate users. Figure 1-32 shows the topology and the processes and trail files names used throughout the configuration. The source system is running Oracle Database 11g, while the target system is running Oracle Database 12c. The operating system for source and target systems is Oracle Enterprise Linux 5 update 6.

Refer to chapter 2 for details regarding downloading, installing and database pre-requisite of Oracle GoldenGate.

The components used throughout the configuration of the source and target systems are:

- Source database SID: S1E2
- Primary extract process: ES1E201
- Local trail: ./dirdat/sa
- Secondary extract (data pump) process: EPMP01
- Remote trail: ./dirdat/ta
- Replicate process: RS1E201
- Target database SID: T1C1

The unidirectional setup illustrated is using a data pump extract option in a non-ASM Oracle database environment. The database tables used for the demonstration listed below. These table are identical on both systems since no columns mapping required.

- *osm$repapi.customers*
- *osm$repapi.policies*

Because of referential integrity enabled on the target system, the *customer* is mapped before the *policies* table. Failure to do so results on referential integrity violation returning an Oracle database error code ORA-02291 integrity constraint violation. In case the target database is for read-only database such as data warehouse, referential integrity constraints may remain disabled.

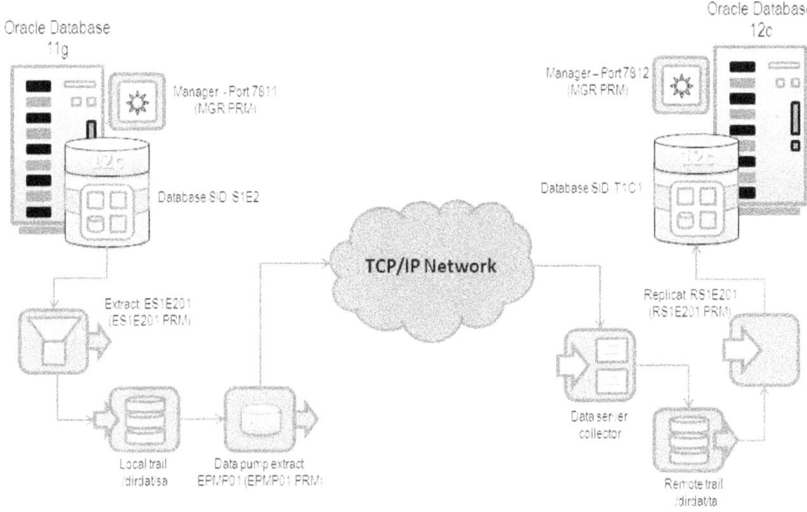

Figure 1-32: Fundamental setup components

Step 1: Primary extract process configuration for GoldenGate

The primary extract ES1E201 performs change data capture (CDC) from the transaction logs to keep the source and the target databases synchronized delivering sub-second latency. It's linked with a local trail 'sa' starting at sa000000 and recycling at sa999999. The runtime parameter file is ES1E201.PRM. The primary extract uses in-memory technique to capture currently running transactions, until it's committed and sent to the trail file, or rolled back and discarded by the primary extract.

While the primary extract is running, a checkpoint process keep records it read and write position to the checkpoint file. In an event of failure, the primary extract avoid redundant capture of transactions already processed. Oracle GoldenGate uses its own commit sequence number (CSN) to guarantee the transaction integrity and data consistency when applied at the target database by the down-streaming replicate.

```
-- Parameter file ES1E201.PRM

EXTRACT es1e201
SETENV (ORACLE_SID=S1E2)
SETENV (ORACLE_HOME="/u01/app/oracle/product/11.2.0/dbhome_1")
SETENV (NLS_LANG=AMERICAN_AMERICA.AL32UTF8)
USERID ggs_admin@S1E2, PASSWORD AACAAAAAAAAAAAGAIFAAUDVHCFUGFIYF,
ENCRYPTKEY DEFAULT
EXTTRAIL ./dirdat/sa
TABLE osm$repapi.customers;
TABLE osm$repapi.policies;
```

```
GGSCI (ggs-source) 7> ADD EXTRACT es1e201, TRANLOG, BEGIN now, THREADS
1

EXTRACT added.

GGSCI (ggs-source) 8> ADD EXTTRAIL ./dirdat/sa, EXTRACT es1e201,
MEGABYTES 32

EXTTRAIL added.
```

Step 2: Secondary extract process configuration (optional)

The secondary extract process is the data pump, *epmp01*. It reads the local trail files then on real-time routes data to the remote data server collector. This data pump uses *passthru* option because source and target tables structure are identical. The runtime parameters *rmthost* and *mgrport* specify the remote system and Oracle GoldenGate manager listening port number. The remote trail files re-assembled by the data server collector are denoted by *rmttrail* with the absolute or relative path followed by the name, a two characters prefix for the trail files name starting with ta000000 and recycling at ta999999.

```
-- Parameter file EPMP01.PRM

EXTRACT epmp01
USERID ggs_admin@S1E2, PASSWORD AACAAAAAAAAAAAGAIFAAUDVHCFUGFIYF,
ENCRYPTKEY DEFAULT
PASSTHRU
RMTHOST ggs-target, MGRPORT 7812
RMTTRAIL ./dirdat/ta
```

```
TABLE osm$repapi.customers;
TABLE osm$repapi.policies;
```

```
GGSCI (ggs-source) 13> ADD EXTRACT epmp01, EXTTRAILSOURCE
./dirdat/sa
EXTRACT added.

GGSCI (ggs-source) 14> ADD RMTTRAIL ./dirdat/ta, EXTRACT
epmp01, MEGABYTES 32
RMTTRAIL added.

GGSCI  (ggs-source) 15> info all

Program     Status      Group       Lag      Time Since
Chkpt

MANAGER     RUNNING
EXTRACT     STOPPED     EPMP01      00:00:00 00:02:27
EXTRACT     STOPPED     ES1E201     00:00:00 00:08:29

GGSCI  (ggs-source) 16> start extract *

Sending START request to MANAGER ...
EXTRACT EPMP01 starting

Sending START request to MANAGER ...
EXTRACT ES1E201 starting

GGSCI (ggs-source) 17> info all

Program     Status      Group       Lag      Time Since Chkpt

MANAGER     RUNNING
EXTRACT     RUNNING     EPMP01      00:00:00 00:02:41
EXTRACT     RUNNING     ES1E201     00:07:55 00:00:02

GGSCI (ggs-source) 18>
```

Step 3: Replicate process configuration

The last down-streaming group of the configuration is the replicate process. The replicate process applies transactions to the target database with data consistency and integrity. The replicate relies on the commit sequence number (CSN) for ensuring transactions commit order of the source database.

When the target database is solely for the purpose of data warehouse repository to support business intelligence application, then it's required to enable the primary key constraints and indexes, the referential integrity constraints should remain disabled for read-only application. However; when the target database is for load-balancing active-active bidirectional environment, referential integrity constraints must be enabled to ensure data consistency, data integrity and data conflict resolutions.

```
-- Parameter file RS1E201.PRM

REPLICAT rs1e201
SETENV (ORACLE_SID=T1C1)
SETENV (NLS_LANG=AMERICAN_AMERICA.AL32UTF8)
USERID ggs_admin@t1c1, PASSWORD oracle
handlecollisions
ASSUMETARGETDEFS
DISCARDFILE ./dirrpt/rs1e201.dsc, PURGE
MAP osm$repapi.customers, TARGET osm$repapi.customers;
MAP osm$repapi.policies, TARGET osm$repapi.policies;
```

```
GGSCI (ggs-target) 6> ADD REPLICAT rs1e201, EXTTRAIL ./dirdat/ta

GGSCI (ggs-target) 7> info all

Program     Status      Group       Lag         Time Since Chkpt

MANAGER     RUNNING
REPLICAT    STOPPED     RS1E201     00:00:00       00:00:05

GGSCI (ggs-target) 9> start replicat *

Sending START request to MANAGER ...
REPLICAT RS1T201 starting

GGSCI (ggs-target) 10> info all

Program     Status      Group       Lag         Time Since Chkpt

MANAGER     RUNNING
REPLICAT    RUNNING     RS1E201     00:00:00 00:00:00
```

Oracle GoldenGate on multitenant container database

Deploying Oracle GoldenGate 12c on an Oracle Database 12c container database (CDB) inherits multitenant database operating requirements for pluggable database (PDB) as source and target databases.

Figure 1-33 depicts Oracle GoldenGate for capture from T2C1PDB01 pluggable database.

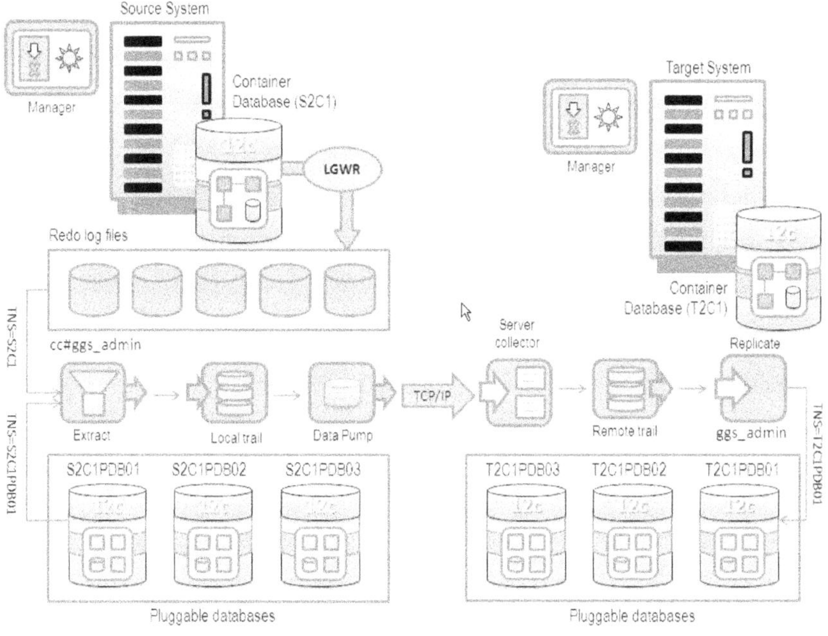

Figure 1-33: Pluggable database Support

TNS Service name for GoldenGate databases

A pluggable database (PDB) has a service name associated with it, the service name matches the pluggable database name. In order to connect from within Oracle GoldenGate to the specific pluggable database, the network configuration is required. The following is portion of the *tnsnames.ora* for connecting to the T2C1PDB01 pluggable database as Oracle GoldenGate target database.

```
# $ORACLE_HOME/network/admin/tnsnames.ora
```

```
#
T1C1PDB01 =
  (DESCRIPTION =
    (ADDRESS_LIST =
      (ADDRESS = (PROTOCOL = TCP)(HOST = ggs-target)(PORT = 1521))
    )
    (CONNECT_DATA =
      (SERVICE_NAME = T1C1PDB01)
    )
  )
```

Test the connection to the pluggable database before creating the local type database user. The built-in function SYS_CONTEXT returns the session current container database name.

```
$ . oraenv
ORACLE_SID = [T2C1] ?
The Oracle base remains unchanged with value /u01/app/oracle
$ sqlplus /nolog

SQL*Plus: Release 12.1.0.1.0 Production on Mon Sep 16 03:36:59 2013

Copyright (c) 1982, 2013, Oracle.  All rights reserved.

SQL> connect system/oracle_4U@t2c1pdb01
Connected.
SQL> SELECT sys_context('USERENV', 'CON_NAME')
  2  FROM   dual;

SYS_CONTEXT('USERENV','CON_NAME')
----------------------------------------------------------------
T2C1PDB01
```

Source database user in GoldenGate

In a multitenant database, the transaction logs (online redo log files) are part of root level database. Oracle GoldenGate capture process must uses a common user for change data capture from the transaction logs.

```
SQL> show con_name

CON_NAME
------------------------------
CDB$ROOT
SQL> create user c##ggs_admin identified by oracle;

We user created.

SQL> grant dba to c##ggs_admin;

Grant succeeded.
```

Target database user in GoldenGate

GoldenGate change data delivery process (replicate) requires a local database user for pluggable database (PDB). The user login to the pluggable database to perform database SQL calls to apply changes.

An error is returned when using common user at the root level database.

```
SQL> show con_name

CON_NAME
------------------------------
T2C1PDB01
SQL> create user ggs_admin identified by oracle;

We user created.

SQL> grant dba to ggs_admin;

Grant succeeded.
```

The above *grant* command grants DBA privilege to the local user *ggs_admin*, which is a highly powerful database access rights and should not the practice on production environment. Refer to chapter 2 to learn more about source and target database privileges required by Oracle GoldenGate extracts and replicate processes.

Checkpoint table for GoldenGate databases

The database schema, *ggs_admin,* for the checkpoint table specified when adding the replicate process via ADD REPLICAT command or globally on GLOBALS parameter file uses the pluggable database local schema, explicitly connecting to the pluggable database using the network alias T2C1PDB01 from GGSCI command line.

```
GGSCI (ggs-target) 1> dblogin userid ggs_admin@t2c1pdb01, password oracle
Successfully logged into database T2C1PDB01.
```

```
GGSCI (ggs-target) 2> add checkpointtable

No checkpoint table specified. Using GLOBALS specification
(ggs_admin.chkpttab)...
Logon catalog name T2C1PDB01 will be used for table specification
T2C1PDB01.ggs_admin.chkpttab.
```

```
Successfully created checkpoint table T2C1PDB01.ggs_admin.chkpttab.
```

Change data delivery in GoldenGate

The pluggable database is determined by the *userid* parameter of the replicate process parameter file. The *userid* parameter resolves the pluggable database service name. Now, there are two replicate processes RS1E201 and RPDB01, both use the same remote trail ./dirdat/ta. RS1E201 applies transactions to non-CDB database T1C1,while RPDB01 applies transactions to the pluggable database T2C1PDB01.

```
-- Parameter file: rpdb01.prm
--

replicat rpdb01
setenv (ORACLE_SID=T2C1)
setenv (NLS_LANG=AMERICAN_AMERICA.AL32UTF8)
userid ggs_admin@t2c1pdb01, password oracle
assumetargetdefs
discardfile ./dirrpt/rpdb01.dsc, purge
map osm$repapi.customers, target osm$repapi.customers;
map osm$repapi.policies, target osm$repapi.policies;

GGSCI (ggs-target) 3> ADD REPLICAT rpdb01, EXTTRAIL ./dirdat/ta
REPLICAT added.

GGSCI (ggs-target) 5> START REPLICAT rpdb01

Sending START request to MANAGER ...
REPLICAT RPDB01 starting

GGSCI (ggs-target) 6> INFO ALL
```

```
Program     Status      Group       Lag at Chkpt  Time Since Chkpt

MANAGER     RUNNING
REPLICAT    RUNNING     RPDB01      00:00:00      00:00:27
REPLICAT    STOPPED     RS1E201     00:00:00      00:13:50

GGSCI (ggs-target) 7>
```

Summary

This chapter has covered Oracle GoldenGate fundamentals. The topics presented provided the basis for applying Oracle GoldenGate to an application area requiring design specific configuration to meet the business requirements. Areas where Oracle GoldenGate commonly deployed are:

- Query offloading to reporting instance
- Business continuity for high-availability solutions
- Zero downtime migration and upgrade
- Data warehouse and operational business intelligence
- Data integration services

Oracle GoldenGate topologies and architecture flexibility extends the deployed application area to suite business requirements. For example, query offloading architecture is deployable as one-to-one or many-to-one configuration, depending on the number of data sources and data consolidation requirements. Chapter 4 discusses the technique from a generic prospective and from applying it to Oracle R12 E-Business suite, an important area for the majority of Oracle customers.

Heterogeneity is a key differentiator for Oracle GoldenGate for supporting an enterprise environment running various database management system. The chapter has covered Oracle GoldenGate 12c for Oracle database MS SQL Server, these platforms commonly found at enterprise data processing environment, moving customer's data from the workgroup computing servers running MS Windows to Exadata machine for data consolidation and business intelligence.

The chapter also discussed very specialized application using Oracle GoldenGate 12c adapters, which are necessary components for extending the capabilities to any form of integration services, and this is a major needs for enterprise customers moving data from the mainframe to Linux/UNIX platforms. With Oracle GoldenGate 12c, it's all about being heterogeneous and real-time data movement.

The next chapter will get you started in preparation for deploying Oracle GoldenGate 12c to meet your business requirements. It covers installation and preparation of Oracle database 11g, Oracle Database 12c and Microsoft MS SQL Server for Oracle GoldenGate 12c.

Good luck, and let's get started with Oracle GoldenGate 12c, *the Oracle bridge.*

Getting started with GoldenGate

CHAPTER

GoldenGate Overview

The objective of this "getting started" chapter is to perform Oracle database, Microsoft SQL Server pre-requisites tasks for Oracle GoldenGate, Oracle GoldenGate installations, Oracle GoldenGate setup and basic instance configuration. Successful completion of this getting started chapter steps is mandatory for users planning to complete any of the remaining chapters.

The Oracle GoldenGate pre-requisites steps are database specific, and this chapter is dedicated for Oracle Database 11g as the source and Oracle Database 12c as the target environment. Oracle GoldenGate 12c setup for Microsoft SQL Server is will also be presented.

In this chapter we will discuss and prepare the components of the source and the target systems running on Oracle Enterprise Linux and Microsoft Windows operating systems. The same steps on Linux are applicable to UNIX operating systems certified by Oracle GoldenGate releases.

In this chapter, we will cover and perform the following tasks:

- Network, Domain Name Services (DNS) configuration and TCP/IP ports validation
- Verify and enable the source and target database archive operating mode
- Prepare the source and target databases for Oracle GoldenGate
- Download and install Oracle GoldenGate on source and target systems
- Discuss and validate Oracle GoldenGate directory structure
- Configure Oracle GoldenGate database user and grant required database privileges
- Working with Oracle GoldenGate Software Command Interface (GGSCI)
- Configure and manage source and target Oracle GoldenGate manager process
- Enable table-level logging using Oracle GoldenGate
- Configure Oracle networking files for remote access to source and target database
- Configure Oracle networking files for ASM instance extracts

- Performing Oracle GoldenGate backup, recovery, upgrade and uninstall

The major three Oracle GoldenGate systems are shown in figure 2-1. Depending on the business requirements, each system has its own configurable components enabling flexible design architecture among the source, the intermediate and the target systems connected via TCP/IP network. These systems can be heterogeneous, use complex topology, or geographically apart, thereby creating a loosely coupled data sources across the enterprise.

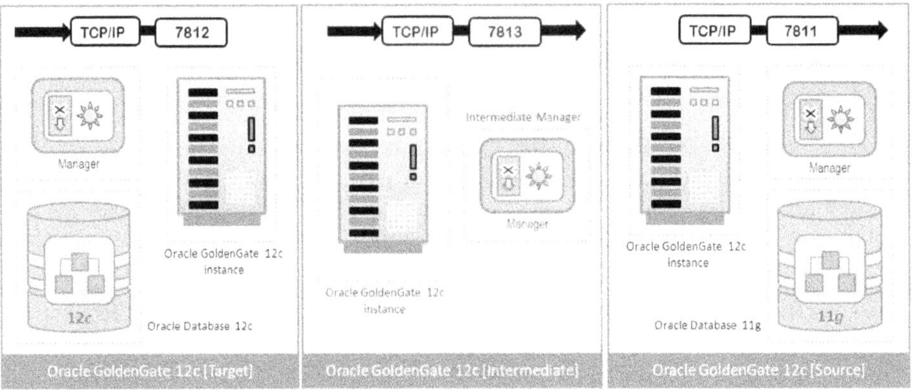

Figure 2-1: Oracle GoldenGate systems

The GoldenGate Source System

The left system of figure 2-1 is the *source* database system running an Oracle Database 11g instance for an on-line transaction processing (OLTP) applications. Oracle GoldenGate 12c for Oracle Database 11g performs continuous change data capture (CDC) from the source database transaction logs for real-time data replication. The Oracle GoldenGate manager and extracts groups are configured and optimized on the source system to meet the application demands for real-time processing.

The source Oracle GoldenGate manager process communicates with the remote Oracle GoldenGate instance through TCP/IP network, the manager process listen on static port. Local trails transactions are transported to the target system with compression and encryption, as required, with sub-second latency for achieving real-time data access.

The GoldenGate Target System

The right-hand system in figure 2-1 is the *target* Oracle GoldenGate instance running Oracle Database 12c. The target Oracle GoldenGate instance receives and reassembles the change data capture routed from the source system and creates remote trails, applying the transactions with data integrity and consistency. The data may be applied as it's or transformed and/or manipulated then applied to the target database maintaining sub-seconds latency between the source and the target systems.

For high-volume transactions, applying the transactions to the target database is enhanced by using Oracle GoldenGate parallel processing capabilities using Oracle GoldenGate @RANGE built-in function, which creates in-parallel transactions data streams while maintaining the transaction integrity and consistency among the ranges created for parallel processing on the target database. Parallelism requires sufficient system resources to support large number of replicate processes.

The GoldenGate Intermediate System

For environment performing complex and massive data transformation, the use of Oracle GoldenGate *intermediate* system is highly recommended. The middle system of figure 2-1 is the intermediate system for offloading the processing of transformations from the source and target systems. Additionally, the intermediate system data pumps ships the source data capture to any number of target systems while managing its own local trails to avoid disk space issue.

The above description is for homogenous Oracle environment. For details regarding setting up Oracle in heterogeneous environment, see chapter 8 – Oracle GoldenGate heterogeneous data replication, where the source database is Oracle Database 11g running on Oracle Enterprise Linux and the target database is Microsoft SQL Server running on Microsoft Windows.

GoldenGate Network and local DNS configuration

Configure */etc/hosts* file for local Domain Name System (DNS). When Oracle GoldenGate instances are running on the same host, the source and target systems maybe referred to as *localhost* when the host name is required by an Oracle GoldenGate parameter such as the RMTHOST. However; when configuring two separate servers, we replace the localhost with TCP/IP address, hostname or the alias configured on */etc/hosts* files.

Before proceeding further, let's configure the source and target systems network connectivity then perform the typical connection diagnostic using the Linux operating system ping command as illustrated below. The command uses TCP/IP addresses 192.168.0.111 for the source system and 192.168.0.112 for the target system.

```
$vi /etc/hosts

127.0.0.1           edmr1s35 localhost.localdomain localhost
::1                 localhost6.localdomain6 localhost6
192.168.0.100       edmr1s35         edmr1s35
192.168.0.111       ggs-source       ggs-source
192.168.0.112       ggs-target       ggs-target
192.168.0.113       ggs-interm       ggs-interm
```

Throughout this book, Oracle GoldenGate source system manager process listens on port 7811, the target system manager process listens on port 7812 and the intermediate system manger listens on port 7813. When conducting the bidirectional network tests, include the port of the remote manager process using the parameter –p followed by the port number. Using the port number parameter ensures the port is available for use and not protected by firewall configuration or closed for any type of network security reason.

The *ping* command, with 3 echo requests, from source to target system for port 7812.

```
$ hostname

ggs-source

$ ping ggs-target -p 7812 -c 3

PATTERN: 0x7812
PING ggs-target (192.168.0.112) 56(84) bytes of data.
64 bytes from ggs-target (192.168.0.112): icmp_seq=1 ttl=64 time=1.28 ms
64 bytes from ggs-target (192.168.0.112): icmp_seq=2 ttl=64 time=0.768 ms
64 bytes from ggs-target (192.168.0.112): icmp_seq=3 ttl=64 time=0.839 ms
```

Perform the reserve test from target to source system for port 7811.

```
$ hostname

ggs-target

$ ping ggs-source -p 7811 -c 3

PATTERN: 0x7811
PING ggs-source (192.168.0.111) 56(84) bytes of data.
64 bytes from ggs-source (192.168.0.111): icmp_seq=1 ttl=64 time=0.328 ms
64 bytes from ggs-source (192.168.0.111): icmp_seq=2 ttl=64 time=0.799 ms
64 bytes from ggs-source (192.168.0.111): icmp_seq=3 ttl=64 time=0.928 ms
```

The TCP/IP Network is a major component for Oracle GoldenGate configuration, the network throughput should be accurately calculated and monitored across interval when the source and target systems are connected across wide-area network (WAN).

For more regarding Oracle GoldenGate TCP/IP handling, see chapter 1 – for configuring Extract and Replicat response to a TCP/IP related errors. Next, let's examine Goldengate database configuration.

Goldengate Database configuration

The source and target Oracle databases must be configured to meet Oracle GoldenGate database requirements. These tasks are normally performed by the Database Administrators as it requires clean database shutdown, mount and then open the database for users. The tasks are mandatory for the source database to enable Oracle GoldenGate change data capture. For bidirectional Oracle GoldenGate setup, the tasks are performed on the target database too.

The database tasks to be performed are listed below. For the majority of the customers, these pre-requisites may have been already enabled.

- Enabling database archiving mode
- Enabling and starting database supplemental logging mode

Enable GoldenGate database archiving mode

Although Oracle GoldenGate does not complain when the source database is not operating on archive log mode, however; it's highly important operating any production database on archive log mode, which enables Oracle GoldenGate to perform change data capture using the archive log files dynamically, in case the online log files are not available temporary. The following SQL*Plus administrative commands enable database archiving.

Let's start by determining the current database operating mode. Connect as SYSDBA user and query *v$database* dictionary view.

```
S1E2> CONN / as sysdba
Connected.

S1E2> SELECT log_mode
   2  FROM   v$database;

LOG_MODE
------------
NOARCHIVELOG
```

When the source database is operating on NOARCHIVELOG, as indicated above, enable the database archive log mode by executing the steps below.

```
S1E2> SHUTDOWN IMMEDIATE
Database closed.
Database dismounted.
ORACLE instance shut down.
SQL> STARTUP MOUNT
ORACLE instance started.

Total System Global Area  535662592 bytes
Fixed Size                  1375792 bytes
Variable Size             352322000 bytes
Database Buffers          176160768 bytes
Redo Buffers                5804032 bytes
Database mounted.
S1E2> ALTER DATABASE ARCHIVELOG;

Database altered.
```

Open the database and verify the source Database is operating on archive log mode. Oracle GoldenGate may uses the archive log files in the event the online files are not available or a log switch has occurs while Oracle GoldenGate extract processes was not running for a period of time.

```
S1E2> ALTER DATABASE OPEN;

Database altered.

S1E2> SELECT log_mode
   2  FROM   v$database;

LOG_MODE
------------
ARCHIVELOG
```

The default location of the archive log files generated by the archive processes is the database fast recovery area (FRA). The database FRA area is managed by two database parameters, as illustrated below.

```
S1E2>show parameters db_recovery

NAME                         TYPE         VALUE
---------------------------  --------    ------------------------------------
db_recovery_file_dest        string      /u01/app/oracle/flash_recovery_area
db_recovery_file_dest_size   big integer 6G
```

In event of disk space shortages, the database instance start purging files from the FRA, which is based on the current Recovery Manager (RMAN) retention policy. To view the current retention policy, start RMAN, connect to the target database and issue the SHOW command.

```
$ rman

Recovery Manager: Release 11.2.0.3.0 - Production on Thu Sep 26 10:38:46
2013

Copyright (c) 1982, 2011, Oracle and/or its affiliates.  All rights
reserved.

RMAN> connect target

connected to target database: S1E2 (DBID=4262461972)

RMAN> show retention policy;

using target database control file instead of recovery catalog
RMAN configuration parameters for database with db_unique_name S1E2 are:
CONFIGURE RETENTION POLICY TO REDUNDANCY 1; # default
```

When the database is operating on archive log mode, the FRA may run out of disk space causing the database to stale and ultimately return an error, which requires manually deleting the archive log files, then synchronizing the physical records existence with the database control file and recovery manager catalog metadata, if in use. After deleting the files, run the command:

```
RMAN> crosscheck archivelog all;
```

Enable GoldenGate database-level supplemental logging

As most of the Oracle Database features, supplemental logging can enabled at the table level or at the Database level. There are two types of database level supplemental logging: minimal logging and identification key logging

We query *v$database* dynamic view to determine the current setting for the database supplemental logging.

```
S1E2> SELECT supplemental_log_data_min "Minimum",
  2          supplemental_log_data_pk  "Primary key",
  3          supplemental_log_data_ui  "Unique Key",
  4          supplemental_log_data_fk  "Foregin Key",
  5          supplemental_log_data_all "All"
  6   FROM   v$database;

Minimum  Pri Uni For All
-------- --- --- --- ---
NO       NO  NO  NO  NO
```

We need to be careful which supplemental logging to enable because it has an impact on the size of the redo logs generated, hence, for highly active transactional database, the volume of the archive log files can linearly increase. Oracle GoldenGate requires the minimum logging which ensures the LogMiner engine will have sufficient information to support the various storage requirements. We use the SQL*Plus command below to enable minimum supplemental logging.

```
S1E2> ALTER DATABASE ADD SUPPLEMENTAL LOG DATA;

Database altered.

S1E2> SELECT supplemental_log_data_min "Minimum"
   2  FROM   v$database;

Minimum
--------
YES
```

The above *alter database* command to add database supplemental logging requires obtaining the appropriate table dictionary locks, and when the applications performing data manipulation at the same time, it causes the command to wait until the application completes and locks are released. Hence, online systems with large number active sessions may prevent the command from executing. The workaround is to start the *alter database add supplemental logging* command, momentarily stop application access to the database, which will cause the *alter database add supplemental* command to proceed.

To enable the various Database-Level logging, below are the commands for each type of supplemental logging.

Enabling all system-generated unconditional supplemental log group.

```
S1E2> ALTER DATABASE ADD SUPPLEMENTAL LOG DATA(ALL) COLUMNS;

Database altered.
```

Enable primary keys system-generated unconditional supplemental log group.

```
S1E2> ALTER DATABASE ADD SUPPLEMENTAL LOG DATA(PRIMARY KEY) COLUMNS;

Database altered.
```

Enable unique keys system-generated unconditional supplemental log group.

```
S1E2> ALTER DATABASE ADD SUPPLEMENTAL LOG DATA(UNIQUE) COLUMNS;

Database altered.
```

Enable foreign keys system-generated unconditional supplemental log group.

```
S1E2> ALTER DATABASE ADD SUPPLEMENTAL LOG DATA(FOREIGN KEY) COLUMNS;

Database altered.
```

Enabling GoldenGate table-level supplemental logging

For installation where Oracle GoldenGate is operating on specific tables, that are small portion of the total transactions, then enabling table-level supplemental logging is extremely suitable to minimize the size of the transaction logs which impact the performance of the LogMiner engine.

```
S1E2> ALTER TABLE OSM$REPAPI.CUSTOMERS ADD SUPPLEMENTAL
    2  LOG DATA(ALL) COLUMNS;

Table altered.

S1E2> ALTER TABLE OSM$REPAPI.POLICIES ADD SUPPLEMENTAL
    2 LOG DATA(ALL) COLUMNS;

Table altered.
```

Now that we understand the basic of replication let's look at the installing of Oracle GoldenGate.

Oracle GoldenGate installation

The installation process of Oracle GoldenGate 12c is easy and fast. For Oracle Enterprise Linux, default kernel parameters settings are sufficient to start using Oracle GoldenGate. The Oracle GoldenGate software must be compatible with the source and target system architecture.

The overall installation task consists of:

- Download Oracle GoldenGate 12g. This bundles the software for Oracle Database 11g and Oracle Database 12c.
- Install Oracle GoldenGate 12c on the source system, Oracle Database 11g
- Install Oracle GoldenGate 12c on the target system, Oracle Database 12g
- Starting Oracle GoldenGate Software Command Interface, GGSCI

Installation of Oracle GoldenGate 12c for intermediate system is covered on chapter 10. Installation of prior release command line oriented, as explain on the section installing Oracle GoldenGate 11g.

Downloading Oracle GoldenGate software

Because Oracle GoldenGate can operate on heterogeneous environment, it's critical to download the correct software media pack. The software is downloadable from Oracle Software Delivery Cloud homepage. Figure 2-2 shows what we need to download. We start by selecting Oracle Fusion Middleware as the Product Pack and Linux x86-64 as the Platform, click on Oracle GoldenGate on Oracle v12.1.2 Media Pack for Linux x86-64 and download Oracle GoldenGate V12.1.2.0.0 for Oracle on Linux x86-64.

To download Oracle GoldenGate 12c for Microsoft SQL Server, click on Oracle GoldenGate for Non Oracle Databases v12.1.2 Media Pack for Microsoft Windows x64 (64-bit), then click download for Oracle GoldenGate V12.1.2.0.0 for SQL Server on Windows (64 bit).

Oracle GoldenGate 12c for Oracle Database 10g is available by creating an Oracle support services request (SR) via *support.oracle.com.* Also, it's highly recommended to obtain the latest Oracle GoldenGate patch set available from *support.oracle.com.* Applying patch sets before starting the configuration eliminates interruptions to Oracle GoldenGate processes and avoid performing upgrade to the different components.

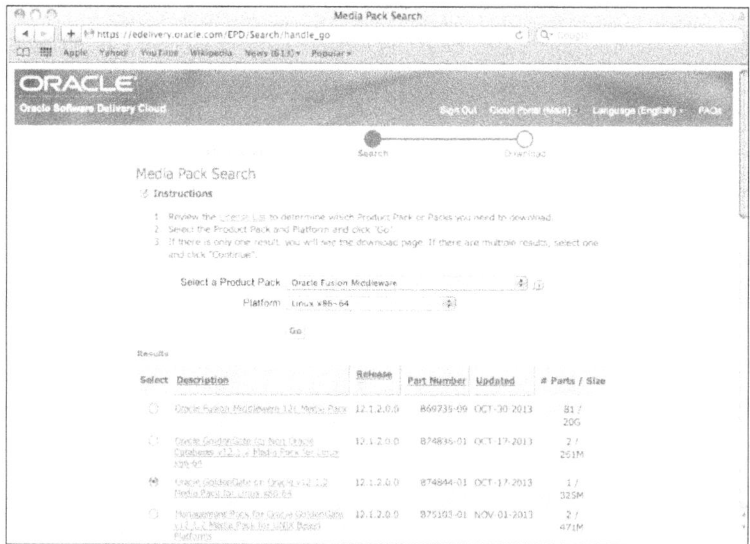

Fig 2-2: Oracle GoldenGate Download

Stage and unzip the software on the directory /stage of source and target systems ready to perform installation for Oracle GoldenGate 12c on the source and target systems.

Running the Oracle GoldenGate Installer

Oracle GoldenGate 12c is shipped with a graphical user interface (GUI) installer. Prior to release 12c, the installation of Oracle GoldenGate performed using the operating system command line only. The installation procedures for the source and target systems are identical as illustrated next.

Before starting the installer, it's important to confirm the software owner and the group. The file system permission are correctly set for the mount point where Oracle GoldenGate 12c will be installed. The file system attributes setting should prevent unauthorized users from modifying Oracle GoldenGate parameters files. The file attributes setting of 740 enables the GoldenGate owner executes programs such as extract and replicate. There are two types of installations:

- Interactive installation using Java graphical user interface (GUI) Installer
- Automated installation using the command-line with response file

The vast majority of Oracle customers prefer using the interactive installation option, for customers deploying large number of GoldenGate instances, it's recommend to use automated installation to apply installation standards. Also, in the absence of X-Windowing system used by GUI installer, the automated installation becomes an option. Oracle GoldenGate 12c is shipped with a response file template for customization to suite environment specific installation.

GoldenGate Interactive installation

Oracle GoldenGate 12c installation program requires X11, Linux/UNIX X-Windowing system. There are two methods to start the installation program using X11.

- Run the installer from the server console, using localhost for display
- Use a remote X-Windowing system for display

The installation screenshots below ran remotely using Apple Mac OS X X11 "The X Windows System". Fig 2-3 shows the steps to lunch the installer remotely from the terminal.

```
oracle@ggs-target:/u01/app/oracle/ggs/121200_fbo_ggs_Linux_x64_shiphome/fb...
bash-3.2$
bash-3.2$
bash-3.2$ xhost +
access control disabled, clients can connect from any host
bash-3.2$ telnet 192.168.2.112
Trying 192.168.2.112...
Connected to 192.168.2.112.
Escape character is '^]'.
Last login: Sat Sep 14 11:54:07 from 192.168.2.171
$
$
$ pwd
/u01/app/oracle/ggs/121200_fbo_ggs_Linux_x64_shiphome/fbo_ggs_Linux_x64_shiphome
/Disk1
$ ./runInstaller
```

Fig 2-3: Staring the installer

The steps for launching Oracle GoldenGate 12c GUI installation program follows.

- The installation program must run as Oracle GoldenGate software owner. Verify this step using the *id* shell command.

```
$ id
uid=500(oracle) gid=501(oinstall) groups=500(dba),501(oinstall)
```

- Then we set the DISPLAY shell environment variable using the export shell command.

```
$export DISPLAY=<IP address of the computer running X11>
```

- Now we change directory to the software staging area, and execute the installation program on the background.

```
$./runInstaller &
```

GoldenGate Installation wizard steps

The installation wizard goes through the following 5 steps:

Step 1 of 5: Select the database for this Oracle GoldenGate instance. The installation supports Oracle Database 11g or Oracle Database 12c only, see figure 2-4.

Step 2 of 5: Specify the location of the software and an existing Oracle database home. To start the manager process up on successful installation, provide an unused TCP/IP port number. The installer validate the port number and must be an unused TCP/IP port number, see figure 2-5.

Step 3 of 5: Summary of the installation, see figure 2-6.

Step 4 of 5: Software installation online progress report, see figure 2-7.

Step 5 of 5: Installation confirmation, see figure 2-8.

Successful installation delivers the following:

- Installation of Oracle GoldenGate 12c software and components
- Create Oracle GoldenGate directory structure
- Start the manager process

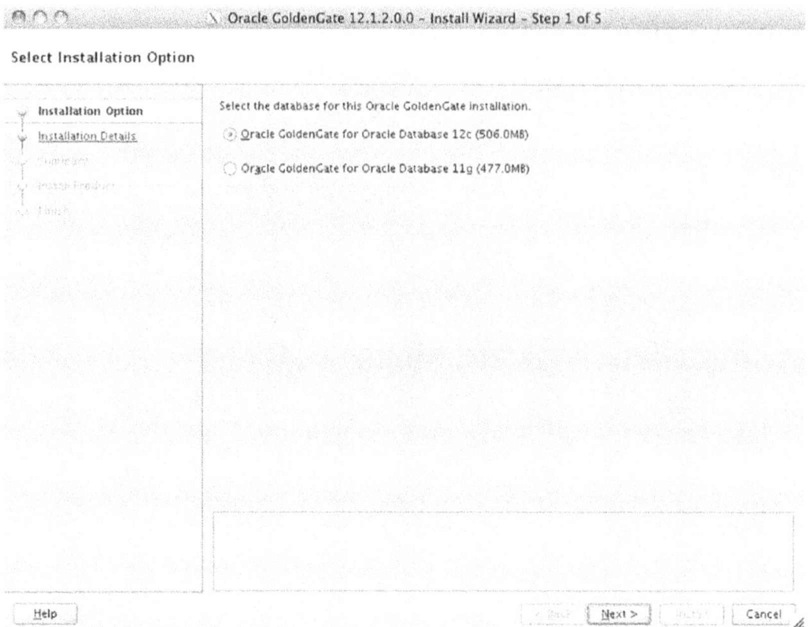

Fig 2-4: Step 1 of 5, the database version

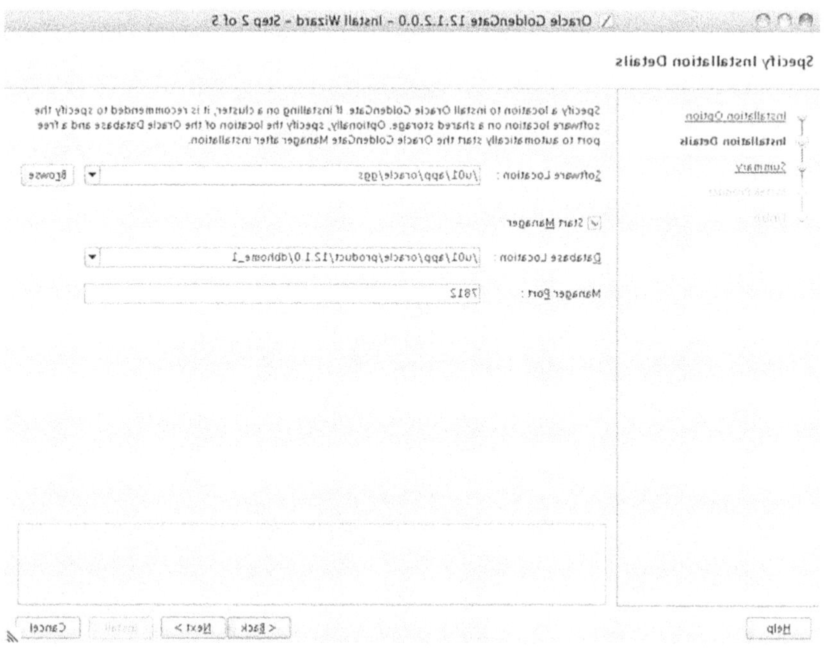

Figure 2-5: Step 2-5, software location

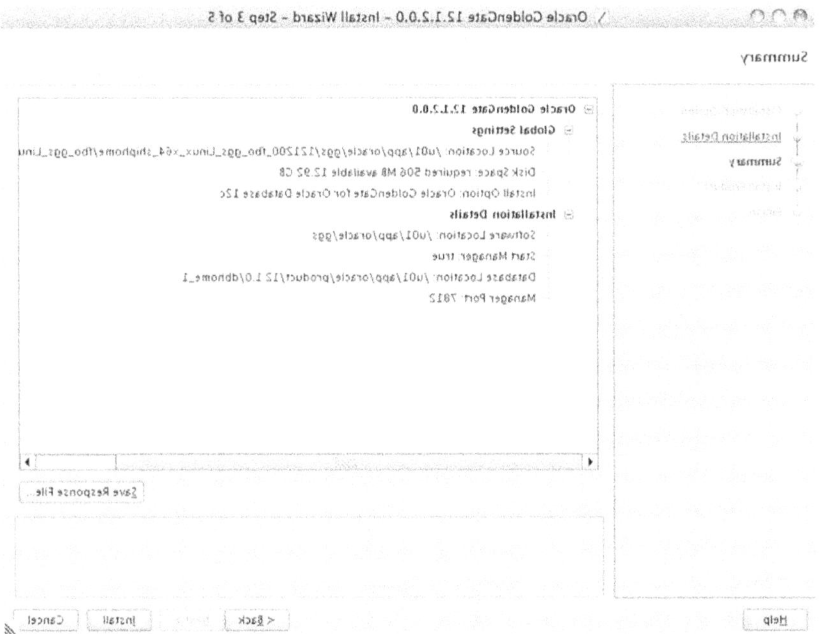

Figure 2-6: Step 3-5, Installation summary

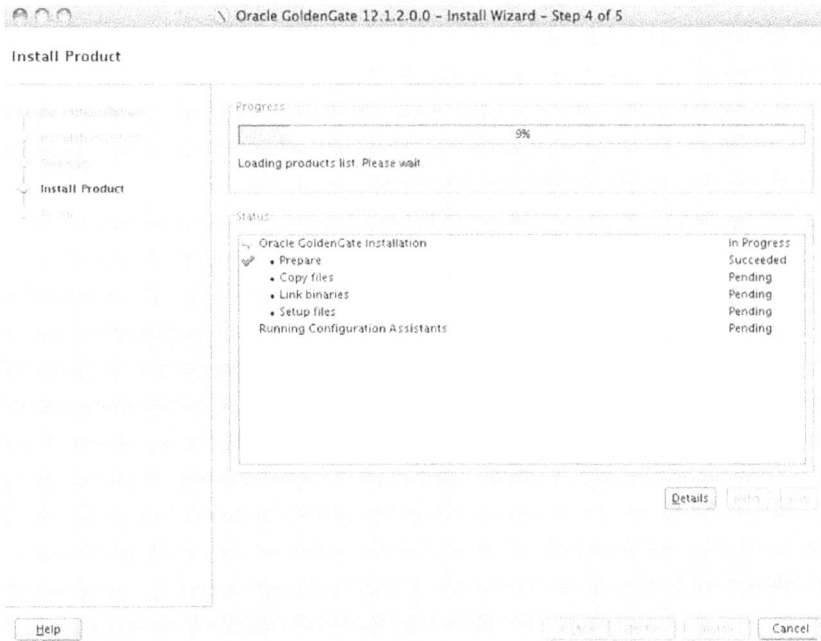

Oracle GoldenGate 12.1.2.0.0 - Install Wizard - Step 4 of 5

Install Product

Install Product

Progress

9%

Loading products list. Please wait.

Status

Oracle GoldenGate Installation	In Progress
• Prepare	Succeeded
• Copy files	Pending
• Link binaries	Pending
• Setup files	Pending
Running Configuration Assistants	Pending

Details

Help

Cancel

Figure 2-7: Step 4 of 5, installation in progress

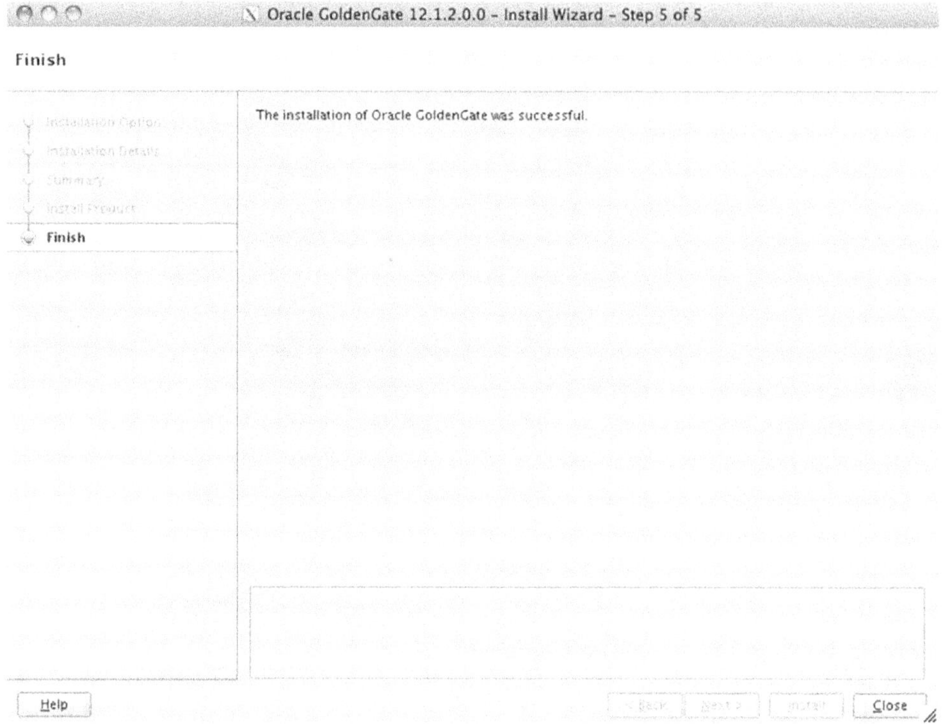

Figure 2-8: Step 5 of 5, installation completed

Now we have completed the installation of Oracle GoldenGate 12c, it's time to start using the software in preparation to configure source and target systems for data replication.

GoldenGate Automated installation

Automated installation uses response file in place of manually supplying the value through an interactive session. The installer program at minimum requires the parameters *–silent* and *–responsefile.* There two steps to run automated installation, preparing the response file and running the installer program from the command line.

Preparing the GoldenGate response file

The response file consists of parameters settings used by the installer program. The following are the list of parameters and their corresponding values. Copy the shipped template file oggcore.rsp to oggcore1.rsp to make the necessary modifications.

```
oracle.install.responseFileVersion=/oracle/install/rspfmt_ogginstall_respons
e_schema_v12_1_2
INSTALL_OPTION=ORA11g
SOFTWARE_LOCATION=/u01/app/oracle/ggs3
START_MANAGER=true
MANAGER_PORT=7822
DATABASE_LOCATION=/u01/app/oracle/product/11.2.0/dbhome_1
#INVENTORY_LOCATION=/u01/app/oraInventory3
#UNIX_GROUP_NAME=oinstall
```

The commented parameters INVENTORY_LOCATION and UNIX_GROUP_NAME are only required for time first installation only of Oracle GoldenGate 12c.

Running the GoldenGate installer

Logged in as software owner (oracle), execute the *runInstaller* program on silent mode as shown below. The automation is provided using the parameters –silent and *–responsefile.*

```
$ . oraenv
ORACLE_SID = [oracle] ? S1E2
The Oracle base remains unchanged with value /u01/app/oracle
$ ./runInstaller -silent -responseFile $HOME/oggcore1.rsp
```

```
Starting Oracle Universal Installer...

Checking Temp space: must be greater than 120 MB.   Actual 6126 MB    Passed
Checking swap space: must be greater than 150 MB.   Actual 10431 MB
Passed
Preparing to launch Oracle Universal Installer from /tmp/OraInstall2013-09-
26_02-05-35PM. Please wait ...$
You can find the log of this install session at:
 /u01/app/oraInventory/logs/installActions2013-09-26_02-05-35PM.log
The installation of Oracle GoldenGate Core was successful.
Please check '/u01/app/oraInventory/logs/silentInstall2013-09-26_02-05-
35PM.log' for more details.
Successfully Setup Software.
```

After Successfully Setup Software message displayed, test the installation by starting GGSCI to confirm the instance manager is running and the directory structure created on the correct location.

```
$ cd /u01/app/oracle/ggs3
$ ./ggsci

Oracle GoldenGate Command Interpreter for Oracle
Version 12.1.2.0.0 17185003 OGGCORE_12.1.2.0.0_PLATFORMS_130924.1316_FBO
Linux, x64, 64bit (optimized), Oracle 11g on Sep 25 2013 00:31:13
Operating system character set identified as UTF-8.

Copyright (C) 1995, 2013, Oracle and/or its affiliates. All rights reserved.
```

```
GGSCI (ggs-source) 1> info all

Program     Status      Group       Lag at Chkpt  Time Since Chkpt

MANAGER     RUNNING

GGSCI (ggs-source) 2> show

Parameter settings:

SET SUBDIRS    ON
SET DEBUG      OFF

Current directory: /u01/app/oracle/ggs3

Using subdirectories for all process files

Editor:  vi

Reports (.rpt)                 /u01/app/oracle/ggs3/dirrpt
Parameters (.prm)              /u01/app/oracle/ggs3/dirprm
Replicat Checkpoints (.cpr)    /u01/app/oracle/ggs3/dirchk
Extract Checkpoints (.cpe)     /u01/app/oracle/ggs3/dirchk
Process Status (.pcs)          /u01/app/oracle/ggs3/dirpcs
SQL Scripts (.sql)             /u01/app/oracle/ggs3/dirsql
Database Definitions (.def)    /u01/app/oracle/ggs3/dirdef
Dump files (.dmp)              /u01/app/oracle/ggs3/dirdmp
Masterkey wallet files (.wlt)  /u01/app/oracle/ggs3/dirwlt
Credential store files (.crd)  /u01/app/oracle/ggs3/dircrd


GGSCI (ggs-source) 3>
```

Now let's look at installing GoldenGate for Windows.

Installation requirements for Oracle GoldenGate on Microsoft Windows

Prior to installing Oracle GoldenGate on Microsoft Windows, the Microsoft Visual C++ 2005 SP1 Redistributable Package must be installed, this is the runtime components of Visual C++ Libraries required to run applications developed with Visual C++ on a computer that does not have Visual C++ 2005 installed. Because Oracle GoldenGate developed using Microsoft Visual C++ 2005 SP1, it requires the package for the same version. Figure 2-9 shows the version specific to Oracle GoldenGate.

When using automated installation for Microsoft Windows, use the below parameters only.

```
oracle.install.responseFileVersion=/oracle/install/rspfmt_ogginstall_respons
e_schema_v12_1_2
INSTALL_OPTION=ORA11g
SOFTWARE_LOCATION=C:\u01\app\oracle\ggs4
START_MANAGER=true
MANAGER_PORT=7823
DATABASE_LOCATION=c:\u01\app\oracle\product\11.2.0\dbhome_1
```

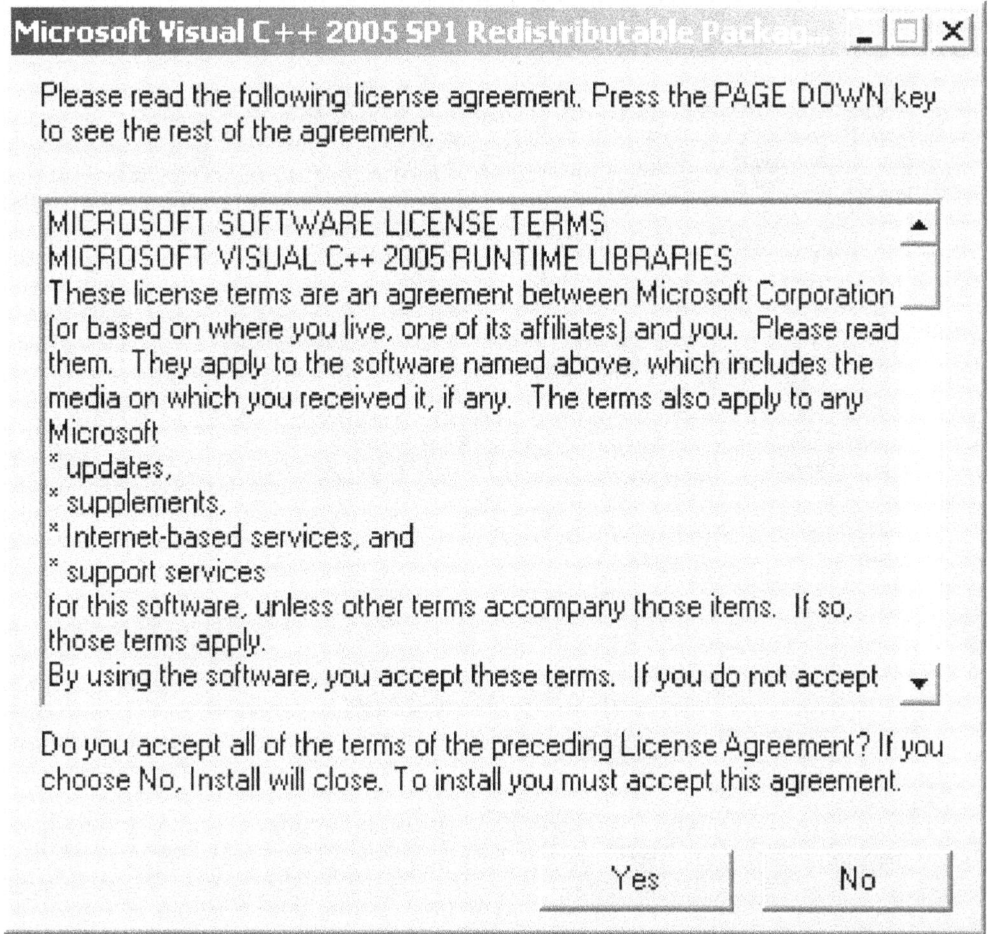

Figure 2-9: Microsoft Visual C++distributable package

The package is downloadable from *http://www.microsoft.com/en-us/*download. Ensure to download the compatible package for your platform, 32-bit or 64-bit.

Installing Oracle GoldenGate manager as Windows Service

When you install Manager as a service, it operates independently of user connections, and you can configure it to start manually or at system start-up. Login as administrator and issue the command from the operating system prompt.

```
C:\GGS>install addevents addservice

Oracle GoldenGate messages installed successfully.
Service 'GGSMGR' created.

Install program terminated normally.
```

The service OGGMGR windows services is created with automatic startup option. Figure 2-10 shows the Window GGSMGR service created. In the case you need to run multiple Oracle GoldenGate instances on the same server, you will need to use the GLOBALS parameter MGRSERVNAME <name>. We repeat this parameter for each instance manager process name.

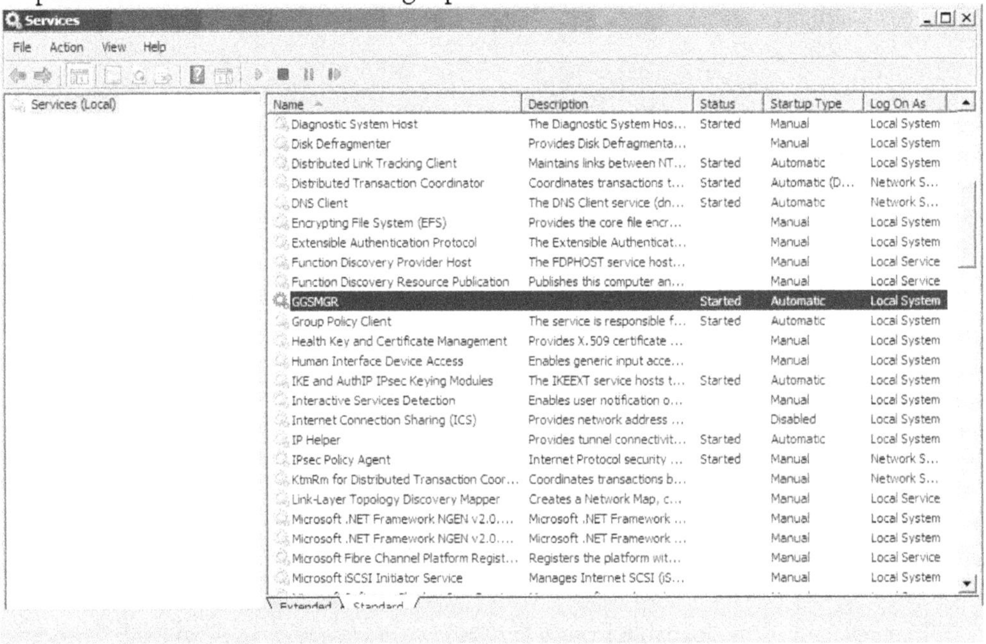

Services

File Action View Help

Services (Local)

Name	Description	Status	Startup Type	Log On As
Diagnostic System Host	The Diagnostic System Hos...	Started	Manual	Local System
Disk Defragmenter	Provides Disk Defragmenta...		Manual	Local System
Distributed Link Tracking Client	Maintains links between NT...	Started	Automatic	Local System
Distributed Transaction Coordinator	Coordinates transactions t...	Started	Automatic (D...	Network S...
DNS Client	The DNS Client service (dn...	Started	Automatic	Network S...
Encrypting File System (EFS)	Provides the core file encr...		Manual	Local System
Extensible Authentication Protocol	The Extensible Authenticat...		Manual	Local System
Function Discovery Provider Host	The FDPHOST service host...		Manual	Local Service
Function Discovery Resource Publication	Publishes this computer an...		Manual	Local Service
GGSMGR		Started	Automatic	Local System
Group Policy Client	The service is responsible f...	Started	Automatic	Local System
Health Key and Certificate Management	Provides X.509 certificate ...		Manual	Local System
Human Interface Device Access	Enables generic input acce...		Manual	Local System
IKE and AuthIP IPsec Keying Modules	The IKEEXT service hosts t...	Started	Automatic	Local System
Interactive Services Detection	Enables user notification o...		Manual	Local System
Internet Connection Sharing (ICS)	Provides network address ...		Disabled	Local System
IP Helper	Provides tunnel connectivit...	Started	Automatic	Local System
IPsec Policy Agent	Internet Protocol security ...	Started	Manual	Network S...
KtmRm for Distributed Transaction Coor...	Coordinates transactions b...		Manual	Network S...
Link-Layer Topology Discovery Mapper	Creates a Network Map, c...		Manual	Local Service
Microsoft .NET Framework NGEN v2.0....	Microsoft .NET Framework ...		Manual	Local System
Microsoft .NET Framework NGEN v2.0....	Microsoft .NET Framework ...		Manual	Local System
Microsoft Fibre Channel Platform Regist...	Registers the platform wit...		Manual	Local Service
Microsoft iSCSI Initiator Service	Manages Internet SCSI (iS...		Manual	Local System

Extended Standard

Figure 2-10: the Windows manager process run as Window service

Install Oracle GoldenGate on 10g and 11*g*

Installing Oracle GoldenGate 10g and 11g is command-line oriented. From the Oracle Software Delivery Cloud homepage, download the media for Oracle Database 10g and Oracle Database 11g as shown in table 2-1.

Extracted Media Pack Name	Database Release	Operating System
fbo_ggs_Linux_x86_ora10g_32bit.tar	Oracle Database 10g	Oracle Enterprise Linux x86
fbo_ggs_Linux_x86_ora11g_32bit.tar	Oracle Database 11g	Oracle Enterprise Linux x86
fbo_ggs_Linux_x64_ora10g_64bit.tar	Oracle Database 10g	Oracle Enterprise Linux x86-64
fbo_ggs_Linux_x64_ora11g_64bit.tar	Oracle Database 11g	Oracle Enterprise Linux x86-64

Table 2-1: Oracle GoldenGate media packs

Create Oracle GoldenGate software location (homes), recursively set the operating system owner to oracle and group to oinstall. Setting the permission to 740 enables read and execute only by the group and others.

```
#mkdir -p /u01/app/oracle/ogg/10.2.0

#mkdir -p /u01/app/oracle/ogg/11.2.0

#cd /u01/app/oracle

#chown -R oracle:oinstall ogg

#chmod -R 740 ogg

#su - oracle
```

We uncompress, then extract the media pack files for the specific platform. The extracted file must matches the database release and operating system architecture.

```
$unzip V32406-01.zip

$tar -xvf fbo_ggs_Linux_x86_ora10g_32bit.tar
```

```
UserExitExamples/
UserExitExamples/ExitDemo_pk_befores/
UserExitExamples/ExitDemo_pk_befores/exitdemo_pk_befores.vcproj
UserExitExamples/ExitDemo_pk_befores/Makefile_pk_befores.AIX
UserExitExamples/ExitDemo_pk_befores/Makefile_pk_befores.LINUX
UserExitExamples/ExitDemo_pk_befores/readme.txt
UserExitExamples/ExitDemo_pk_befores/Makefile_pk_befores.HPUX
```

```
UserExitExamples/ExitDemo_pk_befores/exitdemo_pk_befores.c
UserExitExamples/ExitDemo_pk_befores/Makefile_pk_befores.SOLARIS
UserExitExamples/ExitDemo_lobs/
UserExitExamples/ExitDemo_lobs/Makefile_lob.SOLARIS
UserExitExamples/ExitDemo_lobs/Makefile_lob.LINUX
UserExitExamples/ExitDemo_lobs/Makefile_lob.HPUX
UserExitExamples/ExitDemo_lobs/exitdemo_lob.c
UserExitExamples/ExitDemo_lobs/Makefile_lob.AIX
UserExitExamples/ExitDemo_lobs/readme.txt
UserExitExamples/ExitDemo_lobs/exitdemo_lob.vcproj
UserExitExamples/ExitDemo/
…
notices.txt
params.sql
prvtclkm.plb
pw_agent_util.sh
remove_seq.sql
replicat
retrace
reverse
role_setup.sql
sequence.sql
server
sqlldr.tpl
tcperrs
usrdecs.h
zlib.txt
$
```

Follow that same procedures to install Oracle GoldenGate on target systems. Assuming the target platform is running Oracle Database 11g for Oracle Enterprise Linux x86.

The Goldengate Directory structure

After successfully installing Oracle GoldenGate 11g, you must create the sub-directories structure used by the different components of Oracle GoldenGate. The directories are the default locations when creating objects and parameter files. Now, start GGSCI and run the below commands to create the directory structure.

```
GGSCI (edmrls35) 1> create subdirs

Creating subdirectories under current directory /u01/app/ogg/10.2.0

Parameter files                 /u01/app/ogg/10.2.0/dirprm: created
Report files                    /u01/app/ogg/10.2.0/dirrpt: created
Checkpoint files                /u01/app/ogg/10.2.0/dirchk: created
Process status files            /u01/app/ogg/10.2.0/dirpcs: created
SQL script files                /u01/app/ogg/10.2.0/dirsql: created
Database definitions files      /u01/app/ogg/10.2.0/dirdef: created
Extract data files              /u01/app/ogg/10.2.0/dirdat: created
Temporary files                 /u01/app/ogg/10.2.0/dirtmp: created
Veridata files                  /u01/app/ogg/10.2.0/dirver: created
```

```
Veridata Lock files             /u01/app/ogg/10.2.0/dirver/lock: created
Veridata Out-Of-Sync files      /u01/app/ogg/10.2.0/dirver/oos: created
Veridata Out-Of-Sync XML files /u01/app/ogg/10.2.0/dirver/oosxml: created
Veridata Parameter files        /u01/app/ogg/10.2.0/dirver/params: created
Veridata Report files           /u01/app/ogg/10.2.0/dirver/report: created
Veridata Status files           /u01/app/ogg/10.2.0/dirver/status: created
Veridata Trace files            /u01/app/ogg/10.2.0/dirver/trace: created
Stdout files                    /u01/app/ogg/10.2.0/dirout: created

GGSCI (edmr1s35) 2>
```

In case the directory already exist, the *create subdirs* command do not attempt to create the directory, instead an informational messages already exist are returned. The directories structure used by Oracle GoldenGate core object are explain on the section Directory structure. Veridata directories are used by Oracle GoldenGate Veridata, which is covered in more detail in chapter 6.

The directory */dirdat* is where trails are located by default. Automatic management of this directory is recommended to avoid disk space issues. The purge of trail files is best implemented using the instance manager process, ensuring files are fully consumed before deletion occurred. Refer to chapter 3 for more details.

Other directories are relatively static and managed manually. The directory */dirrpt* is an important for troubleshooting your instance activities.

Starting the Oracle GoldenGate Software Command Interface, (GGSCI)

All administrative, maintenance and operational commands are executed from the Oracle GoldenGate Software Command Interface (GGSCI), Oracle GoldenGate command interpreter.

Depending on the Linux shell used, ensure the shell profile environment variables are correctly set before starting GGSCI. The Oracle database dynamic library, LD_LIBRARY_PATH, must be defined to enable GGSCI execute correctly. To determine the current active Linux Shell, enter the command `$ps -p $$`.

The following is part of *.bash_profile* startup file for Linux operating system running bash Shell, which is the default Shell used by Oracle Enterprise Linux.

```
umask 022
DISPLAY=localhost:0.0;export DISPLAY
EDITOR=vi;export EDITOR
PATH=/bin:/usr/bin:/usr/local/bin:/usr/X11R6/bin:$HOME
```

```
ORACLE_BASE=/u01/app/oracle
ORACLE_HOME=$ORACLE_BASE/product/11.2.0/dbhome_1
LD_LIBRARY_PATH=/usr/lib:/usr/X11R6/lib:$ORACLE_HOME/lib
ORACLE_SID=S1T2
PATH=$ORACLE_HOME/bin:$PATH
TMP=/tmp; export TMP
TMPDIR=/tmp; export TMPDIR

export PATH LD_LIBRARY_PATH
export ORACLE_BASE ORACLE_HOME ORACLE_SID
```

From the shell prompt while logged in as Oracle GoldenGate software owner, start GGSCI as show below. The optimized Oracle GoldenGate command-line is ready for entering GGSCI commands.

```
$ cd $GGS_HOME
$ ./ggsci
```

```
Oracle GoldenGate Command Interpreter for Oracle
Version 12.1.2.0.0 17185003 OGGCORE_12.1.2.0.0_PLATFORMS_130924.1316_FBO
Linux, x64, 64bit (optimized), Oracle 11g on Sep 25 2013 00:31:13
Operating system character set identified as UTF-8.

Copyright (C) 1995, 2013, Oracle and/or its affiliates. All rights reserved.

GGSCI (ggs-source) 1>
```

For every command executed, GGSCI builds a command history, for all successful or unsuccessful commands. Within the same session, each command is tracked by a sequence number, and exiting the session clears the previous command history and start a new history.

Whenever the GGSCI command requires access to the database, the DBLOGIN command must be executed successfully, followed by the GGSCI commands. However; the majority of GGSCI commands does not require database access to execute successfully.

Until the Oracle GoldenGate database user is created, let's explore some of the command that does not require database access, which are categorized as miscellaneous. GGSCI commands are case insensitive and get interpreted after pressing ENTER. GGSCI command are categorized by object types as shown in Table 2-2.

Category	Description	GGSCI Example
MANAGER	Perform action on the manager process	START MGR

EXTRACT	Perform action on Extract processes	START EXTRACT <group name>
REPLICAT	Perform action on Replicat processes	START REPLICAT <group name>
TRAIL	Perform action on Extract Trails	ADD EXTTRAIL <trail name>
PARAMS	Perform action on parameter files	EDIT PARAMS <group name>
DATABASE	Login to the Database	DBLOGIN userid <user name>
TRANDATA	Enable table-level supplemental log	ADD TRANDATA <table name>
CHECKPOINT	Create checkpoint database table	ADD CHECHPOINTTABLE
MISC	Miscellaneous commands	SHOW

Table 2-2: GGSCI command categories

Let's start by exploring the HELP command.

GoldenGate GGSCI HELP command

GGSCI has an extensive help system. Entering HELP from GGSCI command-line displays a summary for all the GGSCI commands. To obtain help for specific command, enter HELP followed by the command name and object type.

```
GGSCI (ggs-source) 1> HELP
```

```
GGSCI Command Summary:

Object:          Command:
SUBDIRS          CREATE
DATASTORE        ALTER, CREATE, DELETE, INFO, REPAIR
ER               INFO, KILL, LAG, SEND, STATUS, START, STATS, STOP
EXTRACT          ADD, ALTER, CLEANUP, DELETE, INFO, KILL,
                 LAG, REGISTER, SEND, START, STATS, STATUS, STOP
                 UNREGISTER
EXTTRAIL         ADD, ALTER, DELETE, INFO
GGSEVT           VIEW
JAGENT           INFO, START, STATUS, STOP
MANAGER          INFO, SEND, START, STOP, STATUS
MARKER           INFO
PARAMS           EDIT, VIEW
REPLICAT         ADD, ALTER, CLEANUP, DELETE, INFO, KILL, LAG, SEND,
                 START, STATS, STATUS, STOP, SYNCHRONIZE
REPORT           VIEW
RMTTRAIL         ADD, ALTER, DELETE, INFO
TRACETABLE       ADD, DELETE, INFO
TRANDATA         ADD, DELETE, INFO
SCHEMATRANDATA   ADD, DELETE, INFO
```

```
CHECKPOINTTABLE  ADD, DELETE, CLEANUP, INFO, UPGRADE
WALLET           CREATE, OPEN, PURGE
MASTERKEY        ADD, INFO, RENEW, DELETE, UNDELETE
CREDENTIALSTORE  ADD, ALTER, INFO, DELETE

Commands without an object:
(Database)       DBLOGIN, LIST TABLES, ENCRYPT PASSWORD, FLUSH SEQUENCE
                 MININGDBLOGIN
(DDL)            DUMPDDL
(Miscellaneous)  DEFAULTJOURNAL, FC, HELP, HISTORY, INFO ALL, OBEY,
                 SET EDITOR, SHELL, SHOW, VERSIONS, !
                 (note: type the word COMMAND after the ! to display the
                 ! help topic, for example: GGSCI (sys1)> help ! command

For help on a specific command, type HELP <command> <object>.

Example: HELP ADD REPLICAT

GGSCI (ggs-source) 2>
```

For example, to find out the help for adding a replicate group, enter the command HELP followed by the ADD as command, followed by REPLICAT as object name.

```
GGSCI (ggs-source) 7> HELP ADD REPLICAT
```

```
ADD REPLICAT

Use ADD REPLICAT to create a Replicat group. Unless SPECIALRUN is specified,
ADD REPLICAT creates checkpoints so that processing continuity is maintained
from run to run.

This command cannot exceed 500 bytes in size for all keywords and input,
including any text that you enter for the DESC option.

The Oracle GoldenGate GGSCI command interface fully supports up to 5,000
concurrent Extract and Replicat groups per instance of Oracle GoldenGate
Manager. At the supported level, all groups can be controlled and viewed in
full with GGSCI commands such as the INFO and STATUS commands. Beyond the
supported level, group information is not displayed and errors can occur.
Oracle GoldenGate recommends keeping
the number of Extract and Replicat groups (combined) at the default level of
300 or below in order to manage your environment effectively.

(Oracle) Unless the INTEGRATED option is used, this command creates a
Replicat group in non-integrated mode.

Syntax:

ADD REPLICAT <group name>
[, INTEGRATED | COORDINATED [MAXTHREADS <number>]]
{
, SPECIALRUN |
, EXTFILE <filename> |
, EXTTRAIL <filename>
}
[, BEGIN {NOW | yyyy-mm-dd:hh:mm[:ss[.cccccc]]} |
 , EXTSEQNO <seqno>, EXTRBA <rba>]
```

```
[, CHECKPOINTTABLE <owner.table> | NODBCHECKPOINT]
[, PARAMS <parameter file>]
[, REPORT <report file>]
[, DESC "<description>"]
```

GoldenGate GGSCI SHELL command

To execute an operating system shell command from within GGSCI, enter the *shell ggsci* command followed by the operating system command.

```
GGSCI (ggs-source) 8> SHELL cp ./dirprm/* /tmp

GGSCI (ggs-source) 10> SHELL ls -al /tmp/*.prm
```

```
-rw-r----- 1 oracle oinstall 268 Sep 26 12:03 /tmp/epmp01.prm
-rw-r----- 1 oracle oinstall 268 Sep 26 12:03 /tmp/epmp02.prm
-rw-r----- 1 oracle oinstall 268 Sep 26 12:03 /tmp/epmp03.prm
-rw-r----- 1 oracle oinstall 310 Sep 26 12:03 /tmp/es1e201.prm
-rwxr-x--- 1 oracle oinstall 103 Sep 26 12:03 /tmp/jagent.prm
-rw-r----- 1 oracle oinstall  10 Sep 26 12:03 /tmp/mgr.prm

GGSCI (ggs-source) 11>
```

To re-execute the previous executed GGSCI command, use the explanation mark "!".

```
GGSCI (ggs-source) 11> !
SHELL ls -al /tmp/*.prm
```

```
-rw-r----- 1 oracle oinstall 268 Sep 26 12:03 /tmp/epmp01.prm
-rw-r----- 1 oracle oinstall 268 Sep 26 12:03 /tmp/epmp02.prm
-rw-r----- 1 oracle oinstall 268 Sep 26 12:03 /tmp/epmp03.prm
-rw-r----- 1 oracle oinstall 310 Sep 26 12:03 /tmp/es1e201.prm
-rwxr-x--- 1 oracle oinstall 103 Sep 26 12:03 /tmp/jagent.prm
-rw-r----- 1 oracle oinstall  10 Sep 26 12:03 /tmp/mgr.prm

GGSCI (ggs-source) 12>
```

The GoldenGate OBEY command

This command is used to execute series of Oracle GoldenGate commands listed in a file. The *obey* command is useful for deploying a production Oracle GoldenGate instance.

After the design, build and testing phases are completed, the commands used for creating Oracle GoldenGate objects are stored on an obey file and executed as batch file from GGSCI command-line. Using ALLOWNESTED parameter enable nested obey files. An *obey* command example illustrated next.

Start by listing the below four series of GGSCI commands in an obey file. Ensure the file is saved at Oracle GoldenGate root directory. The obey command reads the file line-by-line and using the current line as an input to GGSCI. When encountering an invalid command, the message ERROR: Invalid command is displayed and processing continues to the next line.

```
INFO ALL
START MANAGER
START EXTRACT *
INFO ALL
```

```
GGSCI (ggs-source) 13> obey start.oby
```

The GoldenGate HISTORY and FC commands

The *history* command-line lists the last 10 executed GGSCI commands. When passing an argument of positive number such as 15, to the HISTORY command, GGSCI lists the last 15 executed commands. The FC command fetches the command from the history list for re-execution. The example below illustrates using the three commands HISTORY and FC.

```
GGSCI (ggs-source) 1> info all

GGSCI (ggs-source) 2> start mgr

GGSCI (ggs-source) 3> history

GGSCI Command History

    1: info all
    2: start mgr
    3: history

GGSCI (ggs-source) 4> fc 1

GGSCI (ggs-source) 4> info all
```

GoldenGate SET EDITOR command

Oracle GoldenGate GGSCI uses the default Shell editor, vi. To change he default editor when creating parameter files, use the SET EDITOR command. The example below illustrate changing the GGSCI editor from *vi* to *gedit,* an editor commonly used on Linux operating system.

```
GGSCI (ggs-source) 1> SET EDITOR gedit
```

GoldenGate Directory structure

Successful installation of Oracle GoldenGate 12c creates the directory structure. Use the GGSCI SHOW command to display the instance directory structure.

The Goldengate dirprm directory

This directory is the default location for parameter files associated with group names. When an object created such as extract, data pump extract and replicat, a parameter file is looked at for the group name. Using non-default location is referenced by the parameter PARAMS <parameter file>. Regardless of the parameter file location, the parameter file name and the group name must match.

The Goldengate dirrpt directory

This directory is the default location for reports and discarded records. Whenever a process ABENDED, a report file is created on this directory. The report file indicates the reasons for failure, and if the failure is database related, it also indicate the Oracle error code. Using non-default location is referenced by the parameter REPORT <report file>.

The Goldengate dirchk directory

This directory is for storing extract, data pump and replicat checkpoint files. Depending on the object type, a file is created using the group name with proper a relevant extension. For extract process, the checkpoint file name is <group name>.cpe. For replicat process, the checkpoint file name is <group name>.cpr.

The Goldengate dirpcs directory

This directory stores Oracle GoldenGate process identifier (PID). It's the PID assigned by the operating system to running program, which is associated with an Oracle GoldenGate process. To obtain more details, use the operating system command ps –edf | grep <group name>.

The Goldengate dirsql directory

This directory is default location to store SQL Script used by Oracle GoldenGate.

The Goldengate dirdef directory

This directory is used to store definition files. Definition files are required when the source and the target tables are not identical. Mostly used for heterogeneous environment when mapping tables across dissimilar platforms.

The Goldengate dirdat directory

This directory is used to start trail files. The trail files are identified by a two character prefix, followed by 6 digits. An extract or replicat processes trail files are designated by the parameter EXTTRAIL followed by the trial file location and name. For example, EXTTRAIL ./dirdat/sa.

The Goldengate dirtmp directory

This directory is the default location for Oracle GoldenGate temporary files due to capturing large transactions that goes beyond default cache size used by the extract process. The location and size is controlled by the CACHEMGR sub-parameters CACHESIZE, CACHEDIRECTORY and CACHEPAGEOUTSIZE. Also, it's always recommended to dedicate a directory location to host the temporary files, avoiding contention with other type of files.

To confirm the current Oracle GoldenGate environment and subdirectories locations, use the GGSCI SHOW command.

```
GGSCI (ggs-source) 12> show

Parameter settings:

SET SUBDIRS    ON
SET DEBUG      OFF

Current directory: /u01/app/oracle/ggs

Using subdirectories for all process files

Editor:  vi

Reports (.rpt)                 /u01/app/oracle/ggs/dirrpt
Parameters (.prm)              /u01/app/oracle/ggs/dirprm
Replicat Checkpoints (.cpr)    /u01/app/oracle/ggs/dirchk
Extract Checkpoints (.cpe)     /u01/app/oracle/ggs/dirchk
Process Status (.pcs)          /u01/app/oracle/ggs/dirpcs
SQL Scripts (.sql)             /u01/app/oracle/ggs/dirsql
Database Definitions (.def)    /u01/app/oracle/ggs/dirdef
Dump files (.dmp)              /u01/app/oracle/ggs/dirdmp
Masterkey wallet files (.wlt)  /u01/app/oracle/ggs/dirwlt
Credential store files (.crd)  /u01/app/oracle/ggs/dircrd
GGSCI (ggs-source) 13>
```

Now let's look at how to configure the GoldenGate Oracle user.

Configure the Oracle GoldenGate database user

Oracle's Database guidelines highly recommends creating a dedicated database user for Oracle GoldenGate. The approach allows the Database Administrator to manage this database user by applying and enforcing database standards practices. Also, it allows the Database Administrator to perform the following functions:

- Monitor database activities performed the user, to measure database resource utilization
- Avoid conflict of data access with other users and sharing of database users
- Apply auditing practices, for security and compliance
- Separation of database extent allocation for data files

Before creating the user, we create a dedicated tablespace for Oracle GoldenGate database user. The tablespace should relatively small, 50MB-100MB with auto-extend feature enabled. This approach enables the Recovery Manager (RMAN) to create an online data files backup without impacting other applications. The following illustrates creating the tablespace and the database users for Oracle GoldenGate on the source database.

```
S1T2>create tablespace ggs_dat
  2  datafile '/u01/app/oracle/oradata/S1T2/ggs_dat01.dbf'
  3  size 50M autoextend on;

Tablespace created.
```

```
S1T2>grant create session, alter session, resource, connect,
  2  select any dictionary, flashback any table, select
  3  any table to ggs_admin identified by oracle;

Grant succeeded.

S1T2>grant execute on dbms_flashback to ggs_admin;

Grant succeeded.

S1T2>alter user ggs_admin default tablespace ggs_dat
  2  quota unlimited on ggs_dat;

User altered.
```

Repeat the same steps on the target database system, which uses the database to perform database lookup operations on the target database when required. Also, the schema owns Oracle GoldenGate checkpoint tables.

GoldenGate Database privileges

Even though Oracle GoldenGate database user exist on the source and target databases, it has slightly different privileges assigned. Table 1-3 lists the privileges on source and target databases for the user ggs_admin.

Database Privilege	Source Database	Target Database
CREATE SESSION, ALTER SESSION	X	X
RESOURCE	X	X
CONNECT	X	X
SELECT ANY DICTIONARY	X	X
FLASHBACK ANY TABLE or FLASHBACK ON <owner.table>	X	
SELECT ANY TABLE or SELECT ON <owner.table>	X	X
INSERT, UPDATE, DELETE ON <target.table>		X
CREATE TABLE		X
EXECUTE on DBMS_FLASHBACK package	X	

Table 2-3: Oracle GoldenGate database user privileges

Login into Goldengate with GGSCI

Having created the Oracle GoldenGate database user, assigned system and object privileges, it's time now to test the different login methods to the database from GGSCI using the DBLOGIN command.

```
GGSCI (edmr1s35) 1> dblogin userid ggs_admin, password oracle
Successfully logged into database.
```

```
GGSCI (edmr1s35) 1> dblogin userid ggs_admin
Password:
Successfully logged into database.
```

```
GGSCI (edmr1s35) 5> dblogin userid ggs_admin@s1t2, password oracle
Successfully logged into database.
```

```
GGSCI (edmr1s35) 6> dblogin userid ggs_admin, password
AACAAAAAAAAAAAGAIFAAUDVHCFUGFIYF, encryptkey default
```

```
Successfully logged into database.
```

Database login to MS SQL Server database requires configuring an ODBC data source, then issuing the DBLOGIN GGSCI command using the ODBC data source name. Figure 2-11 and 2-12 show ODBC configuration options, followed by database login from Oracle GoldenGate. The username GGS_ADMIN requires grant *sysadmin* to Server role.

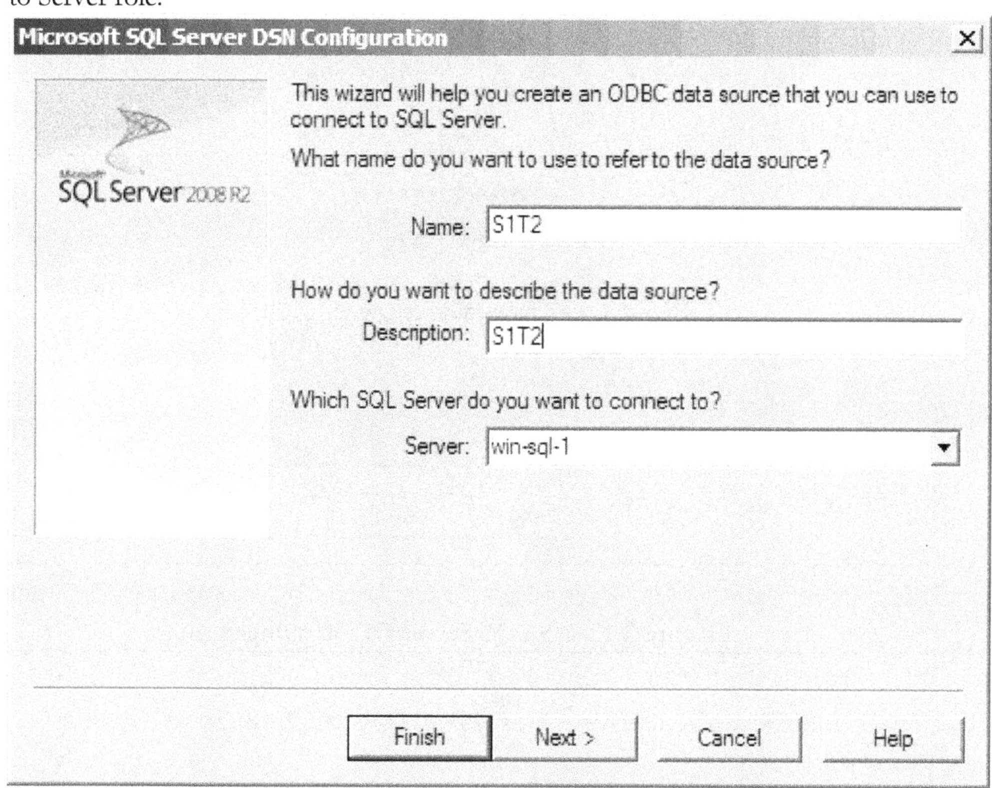

Figure 2-11: MS SQL Server ODBC DSN name

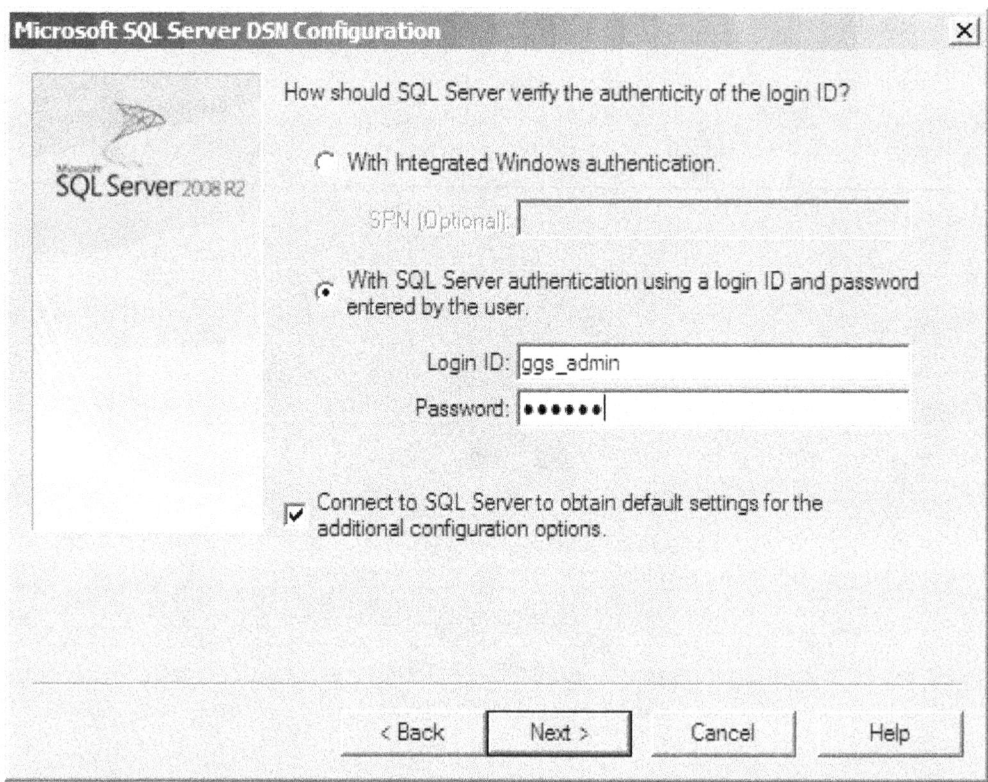

Figure 2-12: MS SQL Server ODBC authentication

```
GGSCI (WIN-SQL-1) 13> dblogin sourcedb S1T2, userid ggs_admin, password
oracle

Successfully logged into database.

GGSCI (WIN-SQL-1) 14>
```

From within GGSCI, database related commands connect to the database to perform each command. Below are examples of GGSCI commands that access the GoldenGate database.

Determine the GoldenGate database version

The GGSCI command is used to determine the operating system details and database version.

```
GGSCI (edmrls35) 7> versions
Operating System:
Linux
Version #1 SMP Thu Sep 3 02:28:20 EDT 2009, Release 2.6.18-164.el5PAE
Node: edmrls35
Machine: i686

Database:
Oracle Database 10g Enterprise Edition Release 10.2.0.5.0 - Prod
PL/SQL Release 10.2.0.5.0 - Production
CORE 10.2.0.5.0      Production
TNS for Linux: Version 10.2.0.5.0 - Production
NLSRTL Version 10.2.0.5.0 - Production
```

List of database table

The GGSCI command below lists all tables for specific schema using GGSCI wild-card character.

```
GGSCI (edmrls35) 10> list table osm$repapi.*
OSM$REPAPI.CUSTOMERS
OSM$REPAPI.DISCOUNT_TYPES
OSM$REPAPI.OSM_DOCUMENTS
OSM$REPAPI.POLICIES
OSM$REPAPI.POLICY_TYPES
OSM$REPAPI.RANDOM_DOMAIN
OSM$REPAPI.RANDOM_FIRST
OSM$REPAPI.RANDOM_LAST
OSM$REPAPI.RANDOM_MIDDLE

Found 9 tables matching list criteria.

GGSCI (edmrls35) 11>
```

Creating a GoldenGate Checkpoint Table

Oracle GoldenGate processes extract and *replicat* processes perform checkpoint operations, in the event of failure, the checkpoint file or database table ensures extract and replicat re-start from the point failure avoiding re-capture and re-apply of transactions. The GGSCI command below create the checkpoint table specifying the database schema and table name.

```
GGSCI (edmrls35) 11> add checkpointtable ggs_admin.ggschkpt

Successfully created checkpoint table GGS_ADMIN.GGSCHKPT.
```

An alternative to the above method is to add the parameter CHECKPOINTTABLE *ggs_admin.ggschkpt* to the GLOBALS parameter file, then execute the command without specifying *ggs_admin.ggschkpt*. To activate new parameters added to GLOBALS file, exit and re-start GGSCI. The example below drop and recreate the checkpoint table.

```
GGSCI (edmrls35) 13> delete checkpointtable ggs_admin.ggschkpt

This checkpoint table may be required for other installations.  Are you sure
you want to delete this checkpoint table? yes

Successfully deleted checkpoint table GGS_ADMIN.GGSCHKPT.
```

```
GGSCI (edmrls35) 1> dblogin userid ggs_admin, password oracle
Successfully logged into database.
```

```
GGSCI (edmrls35) 2> add checkpointtable

No checkpoint table specified, using GLOBALS specification
(ggs_admin.ggschkpt)...

Successfully created checkpoint table GGS_ADMIN.GGSCHKPT.

GGSCI (edmrls35) 3>
```

Configure Oracle GoldenGate manager process

The manager process is a primary process for Oracle GoldenGate, and should always remain running. Each Oracle GoldenGate instance has its own manager process, responsible for managing and overlooking the activities performed by other running processes. The manager process requires an explicit PORT parameter, other parameters are optional but commonly used to perform background administrative tasks.

Before assigning port to the manager process, it wise to find the current used ports and the corresponding services by scan the server using the operating system command *nmap*. You may also search */etc/service* for existing ports to avoid conflict with an already used ports by other applications.

```
# nmap -sS -O localhost
```

```
PORT     STATE SERVICE
22/tcp   open  ssh
23/tcp   open  telnet
25/tcp   open  smtp
111/tcp  open  rpcbind
631/tcp  open  ipp
673/tcp  open  unknown
1521/tcp open  oracle
1522/tcp open  rna-lm
2016/tcp open  bootserver
```

The source Oracle GoldenGate instance manager uses port 7810. The dynamic ports allocated by the manager processes are specified by the parameter DYNAMICPORTLIST. Each manager process can have a range of 250 ports.
The manager process mgr.prm parameter listing and description are illustrated next.

mgr.prm

```
port 7810
dynamicportlist 9001-9250
purgeoldextracts ./dirdat/*, usecheckpoints, minkeephours 1
AUTORESTART ER *, RETRIES 10, WAITMINUTES 5
```

Table 2-4 describes the parameters commonly used with the manager process.

Parameter Name	Parameter Description
DYNAMICPORTLIST	Range of TCP/IP port for process allocation
PURGEOLDEXTRACTS	Purge trail files up on consumed
USECHECKPOINTS	Use checkpoint to purge the trail files
MINKEEPHOURS	The timeframe to keep the trail file after a checkpoint occurs.
AUTOSTART	Automatic start of Extract and Repicat processes, during normal manager start up process.
AUTORESTART	Automatic re-start of Extract and Replicat processes when abnormally ended (ABBEND).
LAGREPROTHOURS	Specifies the interval, in hours, at which the manager check the lag for Extract and replicate processes.
LAGINFOMINUTES	Specifies the interval at which the Extract and Replicat send informational message to the event log.
LAGCRITICALMINUTES	Specifies the interval at which the Extract and Replicat send informational message to the event log.

Table 2-4: Commonly used manager process parameters

When utilizing the parameter AUTORESTART to restart ABBEND extract and replicats, it's highly recommended to specify the sub-parameters RETRIES and WAITMINUTES. The parameter RETIRES refers to The maximum number of times that Manager should try to restart a process before aborting retry attempts, the default number of tries is 2. The parameter WAITMINUTES refers to the amount of time, in minutes, to pause between discovering that a process has terminated abnormally and restarting the process. Use this option to delay restarting until a necessary resource becomes available or some other event occurs, the default delay is 2 minutes. These parameters eliminates consuming unnecessary resources when trying to restart a severely ABBEND process that requires applying manual fix. An example, a Replicat enouncing NO_DATA_FOUND error for INSERT or UPDATE statements, which requires manipulating the target database tables or advancing the Replicat read position.

For Microsoft SQL Server, If an extract with MANAGESECONDARYTRUNCATIONPOINT parameter is ABBEND or offline for an extended period of time, the truncation point in the transaction log is no longer managed and committed transactions will not be free at subsequent log backups. This can cause a transaction log with auto growth enabled to extend to it maximum size on disk, consuming excessive disk space leading to system crash.

In such case, an SQL Server built-in stored procedure SP_REPLDONE must be executed, or scheduled as an SQL Server agent job as shown below.

```
EXEC sp_repldone NULL, NULL, 0, 0, 1
```

However; Under normal condition, where extracts status are RUNNING, SQL Server SP_REPLDONE stored procedure is executed within Oracle GoldenGate making managing the truncation point in the transaction log highly transparent, as long as at least one extract remains running.

Managing the GoldenGate manager process

Management of the manager process performed using GGSCI. Starting, stopping and verifying the status of the manager process using the command line is illustrated next.

```
GGSCI (edmr1s35) 7> info all

Program     Status      Group       Lag       Time Since Chkpt
MANAGER     STOPPED
```

```
GGSCI (edmr1s35) 8> start mgr
Manager started.
```

```
GGSCI (edmr1s35) 9> info all

Program     Status      Group       Lag       Time Since Chkpt
MANAGER     RUNNING
```

```
GGSCI (edmr1s35) 10> stop mgr !
Sending STOP request to MANAGER ...
Request processed.
Manager stopped.
```

```
GGSCI (edmrls35) 11> start mgr
Manager started.
```

After configuring the manager process to run on specific port, while trying to start the manager process, GGSCI returns the message, ERROR OGG-01224 Address already in use. You have two options to resolve the error,

- Use another unreserved TCP/IP port
- Release the port after ensuing it's not currently used by another application

For the second option, use the Linux operating system command fuser to release the port assigned to the PORT parameter in mgr.prm file. The command executed while connected as root user.

```
#/sbin/fuser -k 7812/tcp
```

Enabling Oracle GoldenGate table-level logging

Table-level login is enabled using the ADD TRANDATA GGSCI command. There are two techniques for enabling table-level logging. Using wild-card to enable table-level very common when the database and application are well partitioned and the need to replicate the complete schema.

```
GGSCI (edmrls35) 15> dblogin userid ggs_admin, password oracle
Successfully logged into database.
```

```
GGSCI (edmrls35) 16> add trandata osm$repapi.*
```

```
Logging of supplemental redo log data is already enabled for table
OSM$REPAPI.CUSTOMERS.

Logging of supplemental redo log data is already enabled for table
OSM$REPAPI.DISCOUNT_TYPES.

2013-02-06 11:46:51  WARNING OGG-00869  No unique key is defined for table
OSM_DOCUMENTS. All viable columns will be used to represent the key, but may
not guarantee uniqueness.  KEYCOLS may be used to define the key.

Logging of supplemental redo log data is already enabled for table
OSM$REPAPI.OSM_DOCUMENTS.

Logging of supplemental redo log data is already enabled for table
OSM$REPAPI.POLICIES.

Logging of supplemental redo log data is already enabled for table
OSM$REPAPI.POLICY_TYPES.
```

```
Logging of supplemental redo log data is already enabled for table
OSM$REPAPI.RANDOM_DOMAIN.

Logging of supplemental redo log data is already enabled for table
OSM$REPAPI.RANDOM_FIRST.

Logging of supplemental redo log data is already enabled for table
OSM$REPAPI.RANDOM_LAST.

Logging of supplemental redo log data is already enabled for table
OSM$REPAPI.RANDOM_MIDDLE.

GGSCI (edmr1s35) 17>
```

Notice the absent of a primary key returns WARNING OGG-00869 Note that no unique key is defined for table OSM_DOCUMENTS. In such situation, the row unique identifier is created using all columns which has a negative performance impact, or using the GoldenGate 11g KEYCOLS parameter for extract. The primary key is necessary for update and delete operations applied to the target database to locate the row.

Table-level logging can also be performed on table-by-table basis. Query the data dictionary view to list the tables, then supply the schema and the table name to ADD TRANDATA command as illustrated below.

```
S1T2>select table_name
  2  from   dba_tables
  3  where  owner = 'OSM$REPAPI';
```

```
TABLE_NAME
------------------------------
RANDOM_DOMAIN
RANDOM_FIRST
RANDOM_MIDDLE
RANDOM_LAST
POLICY_TYPES
DISCOUNT_TYPES
CUSTOMERS
POLICIES
OSM_DOCUMENTS

9 rows selected.
```

```
GGSCI (edmr1s35) 4> add trandata osm$repapi.customers
```

```
Logging of supplemental redo data enabled for table OSM$REPAPI.CUSTOMERS.
```

```
GGSCI (edmr1s35) 5> add trandata osm$repapi.policies
```

```
Logging of supplemental redo data enabled for table OSM$REPAPI.POLICIES.
```

An alternative method is to use an obey file and use the OBEY GGSCI command as illustrated next.

```
SQL>spool /tmp/addtran.oby
SQL>select 'add trandata osm$repapi.'||table_name
  2  from   dba_tables
  3  where  owner = 'OSM$REPAPI';
```

```
add trandata osm$repapi.RANDOM_DOMAIN
add trandata osm$repapi.RANDOM_FIRST
add trandata osm$repapi.RANDOM_MIDDLE
add trandata osm$repapi.RANDOM_LAST
add trandata osm$repapi.POLICY_TYPES
add trandata osm$repapi.DISCOUNT_TYPES
add trandata osm$repapi.CUSTOMERS
add trandata osm$repapi.POLICIES
add trandata osm$repapi.OSM_DOCUMENTS

SQL>spool off
```

```
GGSCI (edmr1s35) 1> dblogin userid ggs_admin, password oracle
Successfully logged into database.

GGSCI (edmr1s35) 2> obey /tmp/addtran.oby
```

The GGSCI ADD TRANDATA command requires obtaining the appropriate table dictionary locks, and when the applications performing data manipulation at the same time, it prevent the command from executing and returning an ORA-00054: resource busy and acquire with NOWAIT specified. Online systems with always active sessions may prevent the command from successfully executing. The workaround is to momentarily stop application access to the database to enable successful completion of ADD TRANDATA command.

Configure the Goldengate Oracle networking files

Oracle GoldenGate does not use Oracle Net Service when sending data across the network, it uses TCP/IP network on specific port. However; because of remote connection to the source database, the target database and +ASM instance, the configuration of Oracle network files should be configured to enable GGSCI DBLOGIN command, extract and replicate processes to access the database remotely.

Use Oracle *netmgr* utility, Oracle netca utility or manually to configure Oracle networking files. Figure 2-13 shows Oracle *netmgr* commonly used to configure the database listener and database connection aliases. When the server is running multiple databases, the use of database connect string is necessary on the parameter file and the GGSCI LOGIN command.

```
EXTRACT es1e201
SETENV (ORACLE_SID=S1E2)
SETENV (ORACLE_HOME="/u01/app/oracle/product/11.2.0/dbhome_1")
SETENV (NLS_LANG=AMERICAN_AMERICA.AL32UTF8)
USERID ggs_admin@S1E2, PASSWORD AACAAAAAAAAAAAGAIFAAUDVHCFUGFIYF, ENCRYPTKEY
DEFAULT
EXTTRAIL ./dirdat/sa
TABLE osm$repapi.customers;
TABLE osm$repapi.policies;
```

```
GGSCI (ggs-source) 1> DBLOGIN USERID ggs_admin@S1E2, PASSWORD oracle
Successfully logged into database.
```

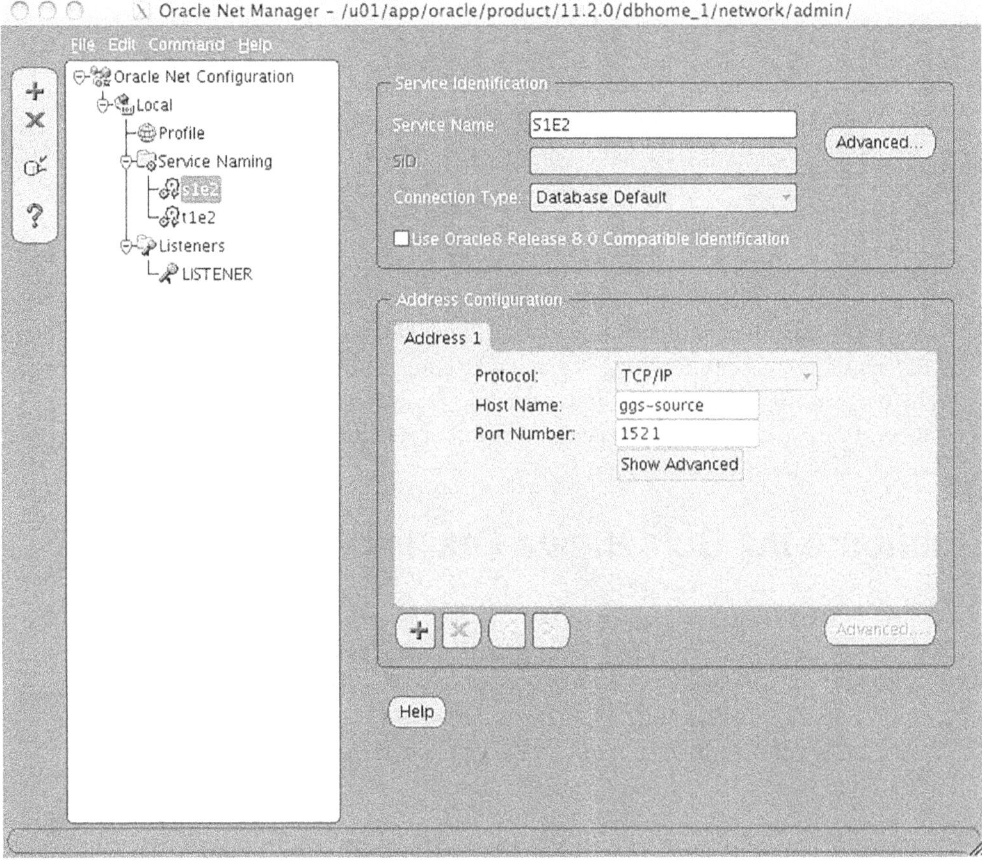

Figure 2-13: Network configuration using netmgr utility

The source database service S1E2 on local host, the listener uses the default port 1521. Adding the parameter (SERVER = DEDICATED) ensures the connection is of type dedicated even when the source database is configured to operate on shared mode.

tnsnames.ora

```
S1T2 =
  (DESCRIPTION =
    (ADDRESS = (PROTOCOL = TCP)(HOST = localhost)(PORT = 1521))
    (CONNECT_DATA =
      (SERVER = DEDICATED)
      (SERVICE_NAME = S1T2.precisetrace.com)
    )
  )
```

The target database service T1E2.precisetrace.com running on local host, the listener uses the default port 1521. Adding the parameter (SERVER = DEDICATED) ensures the connection is of type dedicated even when the target database is configured to operate on shared mode.

```
T1E2 =
  (DESCRIPTION =
    (ADDRESS = (PROTOCOL = TCP)(HOST = localhost)(PORT = 1521))
    (CONNECT_DATA =
      (SERVER = DEDICATED)
      (SERVICE_NAME = T1E2.precisetrace.com)
    )
  )
```

When the source database data files are ASM-based, the extract parameter TRANLOGOPTIONS is used which requires an ASM User authentication using connection alias to the ASM instance, as illustrated next.

```
ASM =
  (DESCRIPTION =
    (ADDRESS_LIST =
      (ADDRESS = (PROTOCOL = TCP)(HOST = localhost)(PORT = 1521))
    )
    (CONNECT_DATA =
      (SID = +ASM)
    )
  )
```

Now we test the connection to the +ASM instance.

```
$ . oraenv
ORACLE_SID = [S1T2] ? +ASM
[oracle@edmr1s35 ~]$ sqlplus /nolog

SQL*Plus: Release 11.2.0.3.0 Production on Wed Feb 6 13:09:06 2013

Copyright (c) 1982, 2011, Oracle.  All rights reserved.

SQL> conn sys/oracle_4U@ASM as sysasm
Connected.
```

Now let's look at GoldenGate backup & recovery issues.

Oracle GoldenGate backup, recovery and upgrade

The GoldenGate backup procedures should be developed to include all components that comprises Oracle GoldenGate. The backup is needed to recover from disk failure and for the purpose of upgrade or downgrade. The following section is an additional section, and used to develop:

1. Backup for Oracle GoldenGate schemas for source and target database
2. Backup Oracle GoldenGate instance
3. Oracle GoldenGate upgrade
4. Oracle GoldenGate de-installation

Source and target GoldenGate schema backup

An Oracle GoldenGate instance may have one or more database schemas. The backup for these schemas should be explicitly performed when for the regularly scheduled database backup excludes them, and these schemas own objects created outside of Oracle GoldenGate commands, or when the schemas are used to support Oracle GoldenGate functionalities, an example, developing database PL/SQL packages to perform advanced data transformation or data manipulation invoked using SQLEXEC parameter.

Also, for data warehouse repository classified as very large database (VLDB), recovering the database in the event of failure is more efficient done by performing an extract, transfer and load (ETL) from the different sources to the target data warehouse repository. For such environments backup of Oracle GoldenGate target schemas is recommended and justified.

Considering what mentioned above, using the database data pump export utility creates the backup file, which can be used to quickly restore the Oracle GoldenGate schema using the database data pump import utility. The database data pump utility requires creating a database directory which reference a file system directory to store the backup file, which must be transported to another server or tape system protecting it from a major disk failures.

```
SQL>create directory dp_dir as '/tmp';
Directory created.
SQL>grant read, write on directory dp_dir to system, ggs_admin;
Grant succeeded.
$ expdp system/oracle directory=dp_dir dumpfile=ggs.dmp schemas=ggs_admin
```

```
Export: Release 10.2.0.5.0 - Production on Friday, 08 February, 2013
12:23:22

Copyright (c) 2003, 2007, Oracle.  All rights reserved.

Connected to: Oracle Database 10g Enterprise Edition Release 10.2.0.5.0 -
Production
With the Partitioning, OLAP, Data Mining and Real Application Testing
options
FLASHBACK automatically enabled to preserve database integrity.
Starting "SYSTEM"."SYS_EXPORT_SCHEMA_01":  system/******** directory=dp_dir
dumpfile=ggs.dmp schemas=ggs_admin
Estimate in progress using BLOCKS method...
Processing object type SCHEMA_EXPORT/TABLE/TABLE_DATA
Total estimation using BLOCKS method: 0 KB
Processing object type SCHEMA_EXPORT/USER
Processing object type SCHEMA_EXPORT/SYSTEM_GRANT
Processing object type SCHEMA_EXPORT/ROLE_GRANT
Processing object type SCHEMA_EXPORT/DEFAULT_ROLE
Processing object type SCHEMA_EXPORT/PRE_SCHEMA/PROCACT_SCHEMA
Master table "SYSTEM"."SYS_EXPORT_SCHEMA_01" successfully loaded/unloaded
******************************************************************************
Dump file set for SYSTEM.SYS_EXPORT_SCHEMA_01 is:
  /tmp/ggs.dmp
Job "SYSTEM"."SYS_EXPORT_SCHEMA_01" successfully completed at 12:23:54
```

The main advantage of using the export and import data pump utility, it quickly backup and restores the database structure related to Oracle GoldenGate schemas. And, if importing across platform, the mapping capabilities for data files, tablespace and schema enables mapping directly to the target operating system environment. An example, is when cloning Oracle GoldenGate instance from Linux to Microsoft Windows platform, or when using different schema and/or tablespace for the new environment.

Performing a GoldenGate instance backup

The backup for Oracle GoldenGate instance simply performed using the operating system cp command. The backup should include the root directory and sub-directories. The sub-directories include the parameter files and other related files. Using the –R option recursively backup the sub-directories. Also, ensure the shell environment variable $OGG_HOME is enabled. Zipping the backup into a single file is recommended for archiving purpose and file transfer.

```
$ echo $GGS_HOME
/u01/app/ogg
$ cp -R $GGS_HOME/* /u01/backup/ggs/
$ zip ggs.zip /u01/backup/ggs/*
```

Now let's look at upgrading GoldenGate.

Oracle GoldenGate upgrade

It's important to consider upgrade is an unavoidable and you must be prepared to upgrade Oracle GoldenGate software. As of the time of writing the book, the current release for Oracle GoldenGate is 12.1.2.0.0. Although the source and target Oracle GoldenGate releases may differ, its highly recommended to use at minimum the same release across all systems so that trail files format compatibility settings is not required when sending data from the source to the target systems.

Upgrading Oracle GoldenGate from release 11.2 to 12.2 involves sequence of steps described below. In case of upgrading large number of source and target systems, plan for rollout upgrade to minimize the database downtime. However; properly designed Oracle GoldenGate environment is upgradable within a timeframe of 30-60 minutes as outlined on table 1-5, steps 1 through 11.

Step No	Step Description	Step Type
1	Open the database on restricted mode	Database
2	Stop Oracle GoldenGate processes	GoldenGate
3	Delete Oracle GoldenGate extract groups	GoldenGate
4	Delete Oracle GoldenGate replicate groups	GoldenGate
5	Drop the target checkpoint table	GoldenGate
6	Delete current Oracle GoldenGate software	OS Command
7	Install the new Oracle GoldenGate release	Installer
8	Verify installation and directory structure	GoldenGate
9	Restore GLOBALS parameters and recreate checkpoint table	GoldenGate
9	Drop and Recreate the target systems database checkpoint table	Database
10	Restore parameter files	GoldenGate
11	Create extract and replicate groups	GoldenGate
12	Start and verify extract replicate processes	GoldenGate
13	Disable database restricted session	Database
14	Gradually apply new features	GoldenGate

Table 2-5: Oracle GoldenGate upgrade steps

Figure 2-14 depicts before and after upgrade, moving from Oracle GoldenGate 11g for Oracle Database 11g to Oracle GoldenGate 12c for Oracle Database 11g.

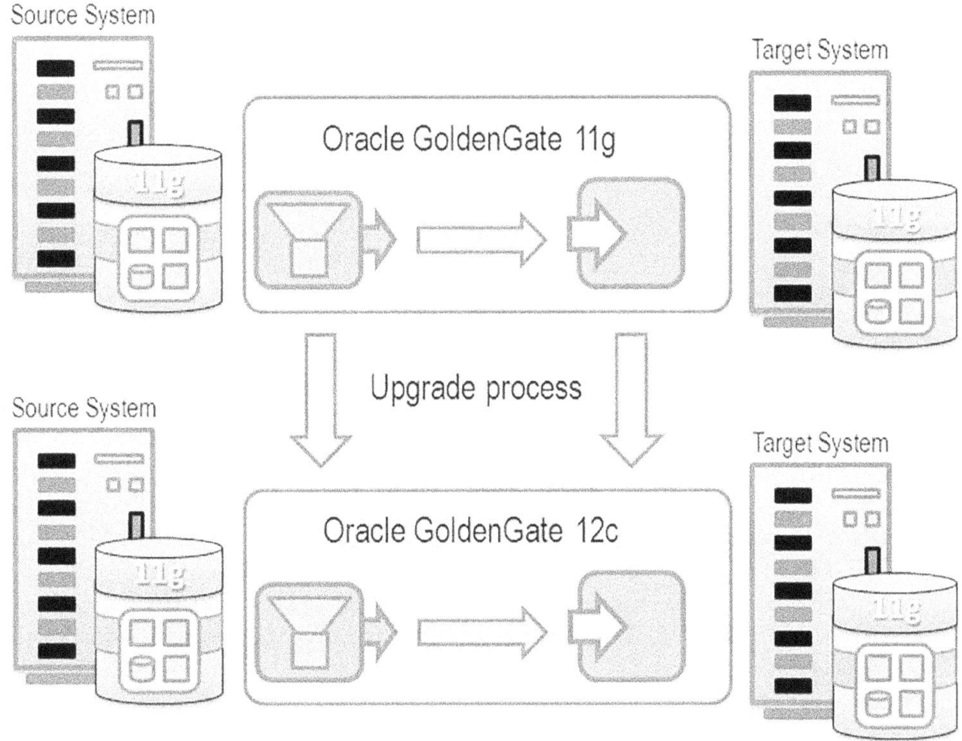

Figure 2-14: Oracle GoldenGate upgrade

For systems running Oracle GoldenGate for Oracle Real Application (RAC) Clusters database, the upgrade is transparent and provide zero-downtime upgrade for the source and target systems.

Step 1: Open the database on restricted mode (Optional)

Placing the source database on restricted mode is optional but recommended during Oracle GoldenGate upgrade timeframe, if business allows it. If the database must remain open, Oracle GoldenGate primary extract may capture from the archived log files following the upgrade which is caused by frequent database online log files switching for high-volume system. A workaround for the database to remain open on unrestricted read/write mode during Oracle GoldenGate upgrade is to add sufficiently large size 1-member online groups so that Oracle GoldenGate can find the transactions log available before overwritten by the next log file sequence after log switch. If the decision is to enable restricted session, then ensure users with restricted session privilege are revoked temporary.

Perform the steps below for source and target systems.

```
SQL> shutdown immediate
Database closed.
Database dismounted.
ORACLE instance shut down.
SQL> startup restrict
ORACLE instance started.

Total System Global Area  535662592 bytes
Fixed Size                  1375792 bytes
Variable Size             352322000 bytes
Database Buffers          176160768 bytes
Redo Buffers                5804032 bytes
Database mounted.
Database opened.
SQL>
```

Now, users without restricted session privilege trying to connect to the database receive the error ORA-01035: ORACLE only available to users with RESTRICTED SESSION privilege. Also, ensure only trusted users have restricted session privilege avoiding unrelated users connecting to the database. Query DBA_SYS_PRIVS to find users with RESTRICTED SESSION privilege and revoke them temporary for the duration of the upgrade.

```
SQL> SELECT *
  2  FROM   dba_sys_privs
  3  WHERE  privilege='RESTRICTED SESSION';

GRANTEE                         PRIVILEGE                          ADM
------------------------------ ------------------------------      ---
DBA                             RESTRICTED SESSION                 YES
HR                              RESTRICTED SESSION                 NO
SYS                             RESTRICTED SESSION                 NO

SQL> REVOKE restricted session FROM hr;

Revoke succeeded.

SQL>
```

Step 2: Stop Oracle GoldenGate processes

Stop Oracle GoldenGate processes in proper sequence to release the operating system process identifier (PID) and to avoid any data loss due to transactions still running on the systems. On the source systems, verify no pending records, stop primary extracts, data pump extracts, then stop the manager process. On the target systems, verify no pending records exist, stop the replicate processes then stop the manager process.

The GGSCI command LAG reports the current lagging. Keep executing the command until the message *no record to process* is returned.

Next, we execute the commands INFO, LAG and STOP on the source system.

```
GGSCI (ggs-source) 44> INFO ALL

Program     Status      Group       Lag at Chkpt  Time Since Chkpt

MANAGER     RUNNING
EXTRACT     RUNNING     EPMP01      00:00:00      00:00:06
EXTRACT     RUNNING     ES1E201     00:00:00      00:00:10
```

```
GGSCI (ggs-source) 45> LAG ES1E201

Sending GETLAG request to EXTRACT ES1E201 ...
Last record lag: 1 seconds.
At EOF, no more records to process.
```

```
GGSCI (ggs-source) 47> STOP EXTRACT *

Sending STOP request to EXTRACT EPMP01 ...
Request processed.

Sending STOP request to EXTRACT ES1E201 ...
Request processed.
```

```
GGSCI (ggs-source) 48> STOP MGR !

Sending STOP request to MANAGER ...
Request processed.
Manager stopped.

GGSCI (ggs-source) 49>
```

Execute the commands INFO, LAG and STOP on the target system.

```
GGSCI (ggs-target) 18> INFO ALL

Program     Status      Group       Lag at Chkpt  Time Since Chkpt

MANAGER     RUNNING
REPLICAT    RUNNING     RS1E201     00:00:00      00:00:02
```

```
GGSCI (ggs-target) 19> LAG RS1E201

Sending GETLAG request to REPLICAT RS1E201 ...
No records yet processed.
At EOF, no more records to process.
```

```
GGSCI (ggs-target) 20> STOP REPLICAT *

Sending STOP request to REPLICAT RS1E201 ...
```

```
Request processed.

GGSCI (ggs-target) 21> STOP MGR !

Sending STOP request to MANAGER ...
Request processed.
Manager stopped.

GGSCI (ggs-target) 22>
```

Step 3: Delete the primary and secondary extract groups

To avoid any form of inconsistency, before removing Oracle GoldenGate software, explicit delete and deregistration of the primary extract must be performed. This is because Oracle database records change data capture in *dba_captures* data dictionary view.

```
GGSCI (ggs-source) 51> DBLOGIN USERID ggs_admin@S1E2, PASSWORD oracle
Successfully logged into database.

GGSCI (ggs-source) 52> DELETE EXTRACT ES1E201
Deleted EXTRACT ES1E201.

GGSCI (ggs-source) 56> UNREGISTER EXTRACT ES1E201 DATABASE

2013-09-29 15:59:08  ERROR   OGG-01759  Cannot unregister EXTRACT ES1E201
from database because this Extract is not currently registered.

GGSCI (ggs-source) 57> DELETE EXTRACT epmp01
Deleted EXTRACT EPMP01.

GGSCI (ggs-source) 58>
```

The UNREGISTER EXTRACT command is only for primary extracts, it does not apply to data pump extracts.

Step 4: Delete the replicate groups

From GGSCI command-line, login to the target database and drop the replicate group.

```
GGSCI (ggs-target) 24> DBLOGIN USERID ggs_admin@T1E2, password oracle
Successfully logged into database.

GGSCI (ggs-target) 25> DELETE REPLICAT rs1e201
Deleted REPLICAT RS1E201.

GGSCI (ggs-target) 26>
```

Step 5: Drop the Checkpoint table

To avoid inconsistencies between Oracle GoldenGate software and the database checkpoint table created by Oracle GoldenGate previous release, dropping and re-creating the checkpoint table ensures consistency with the new Oracle GoldenGate release.

```
GGSCI (ggs-target) 26> DELETE CHECKPOINTTABLE
```

```
No checkpoint table specified, using GLOBALS specification
(ggs_admin.chkpt)...
This checkpoint table may be required for other installations.  Are you sure
you want to delete this checkpoint table? yes

Successfully deleted checkpoint table ggs_admin.chkpt.

GGSCI (ggs-target) 27>
```

Step 6: Delete the old Oracle GoldenGate software

Now we delete the files and sub-directories from the current Oracle GoldenGate software location. If you decided to have multiple Oracle GoldenGate instances and not removing existing release, it would require modifying the parameters files to point to the new software location wherever it's referenced.

Recursively remove the source and target Oracle GoldenGate installations, then optionally create new homes for Oracle GoldenGate 12c on source and target systems.

```
$ cd $GGS_HOME
$ pwd
/u01/app/ogg/11.2.0
$ rm -Rf *
$ mkdir 12.1.0
```

Step 7: Install the new Oracle GoldenGate release on source and target

Unzip and extract the new release. Placing Oracle GoldenGate on the same location as the previous release allows using the parameters files without modifications.

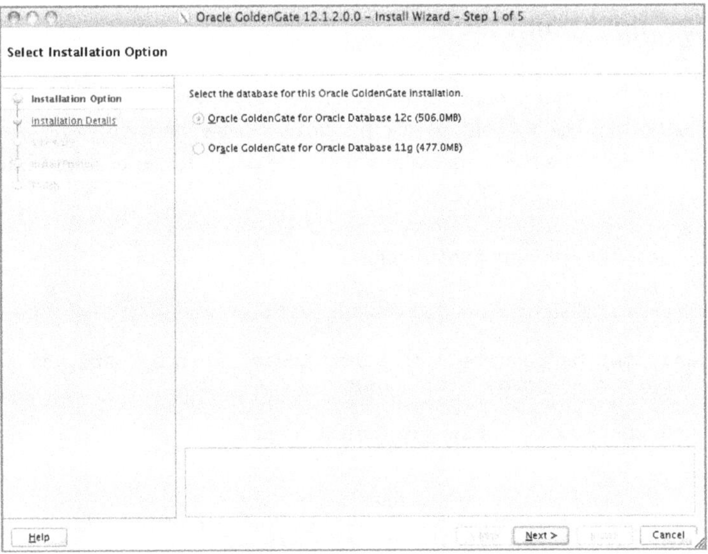

Figure 2 – 14A: Installation Screen

Step 8: Verify directories structure for source and target systems

Before proceeding further, verify the installation completed successfully by starting GGSCI and the directory structure has been created.

```
$ pwd
/u01/app/oracle/ggs/12.1.0
$ ./ggsci
```

```
Oracle GoldenGate Command Interpreter for Oracle
Version 12.1.2.0.0 17185003 OGGCORE_12.1.2.0.0_PLATFORMS_130924.1316_FBO
Linux, x64, 64bit (optimized), Oracle 11g on Sep 25 2013 00:31:13
Operating system character set identified as UTF-8.

Copyright (C) 1995, 2013, Oracle and/or its affiliates. All rights reserved.
```

```
GGSCI (ggs-source) 1> show
```

```
Parameter settings:

SET SUBDIRS    ON
SET DEBUG      OFF

Current directory: /u01/app/oracle/ggs/12.1.0

Using subdirectories for all process files
```

```
Editor:  vi

Reports (.rpt)                 /u01/app/oracle/ggs/12.1.0/dirrpt
Parameters (.prm)              /u01/app/oracle/ggs/12.1.0/dirprm
Replicat Checkpoints (.cpr)    /u01/app/oracle/ggs/12.1.0/dirchk
Extract Checkpoints (.cpe)     /u01/app/oracle/ggs/12.1.0/dirchk
Process Status (.pcs)          /u01/app/oracle/ggs/12.1.0/dirpcs
SQL Scripts (.sql)             /u01/app/oracle/ggs/12.1.0/dirsql
Database Definitions (.def)    /u01/app/oracle/ggs/12.1.0/dirdef
Dump files (.dmp)              /u01/app/oracle/ggs/12.1.0/dirdmp
Masterkey wallet files (.wlt)  /u01/app/oracle/ggs/12.1.0/dirwlt
Credential store files (.crd)  /u01/app/oracle/ggs/12.1.0/dircrd

GGSCI (ggs-source) 2>
```

```
$ pwd
/u01/app/oracle/ggs/12.1.0
$ ./ggsci
```

```
Oracle GoldenGate Command Interpreter for Oracle
Version 12.1.2.0.0 17185003 OGGCORE_12.1.2.0.0_PLATFORMS_130924.1316_FBO
Linux, x64, 64bit (optimized), Oracle 11g on Sep 25 2013 00:31:13
Operating system character set identified as UTF-8.

Copyright (C) 1995, 2013, Oracle and/or its affiliates. All rights reserved.
```

```
GGSCI (ggs-target) 1> show
```

```
Parameter settings:

SET SUBDIRS    ON
SET DEBUG      OFF

Current directory: /u01/app/oracle/ggs/12.1.0

Using subdirectories for all process files

Editor:  vi

Reports (.rpt)                 /u01/app/oracle/ggs/12.1.0/dirrpt
Parameters (.prm)              /u01/app/oracle/ggs/12.1.0/dirprm
Replicat Checkpoints (.cpr)    /u01/app/oracle/ggs/12.1.0/dirchk
Extract Checkpoints (.cpe)     /u01/app/oracle/ggs/12.1.0/dirchk
Process Status (.pcs)          /u01/app/oracle/ggs/12.1.0/dirpcs
SQL Scripts (.sql)             /u01/app/oracle/ggs/12.1.0/dirsql
Database Definitions (.def)    /u01/app/oracle/ggs/12.1.0/dirdef
Dump files (.dmp)              /u01/app/oracle/ggs/12.1.0/dirdmp
Masterkey wallet files (.wlt)  /u01/app/oracle/ggs/12.1.0/dirwlt
Credential store files (.crd)  /u01/app/oracle/ggs/12.1.0/dircrd


GGSCI (ggs-target) 2>
```

Step 9: Restore GLOBALS file and create checkpoint table

Restore the GLOBALS parameter file to Oracle GoldenGate root directory, then using GGSCI command-line, login to the database to create the checkpoint table.

```
GGSCI (ggs-target) 1> DBLOGIN USERID ggs_admin@t1e2, password oracle
Successfully logged into database.
```

```
GGSCI (ggs-target) 2> ADD CHECKPOINTTABLE
```

```
No checkpoint table specified. Using GLOBALS specification
(ggs_admin.chkpttab)...

Successfully created checkpoint table ggs_admin.chkpttab.

GGSCI (ggs-target) 3>
```

Step 10: Restore the parameters files

From the most recent backup, restore the parameters files to the same location of the previous release, or to the default location is $GGS_HOME/dirprm. When using non-default parameters file locations, ensure the restore is available on this non-default location as specified by ADD EXTRACT or ADD REPLICAT parameter PARAM <parameter file>.

Step 11: Create the source and target processes

This step is best performed using an obey file. It includes creating the manager process, extracts on source and replicats on target systems.

On the source Oracle GoldenGate instance, recreate the extract groups.

```
GGSCI (ggs-source) 5> ADD EXTRACT es1e201, TRANLOG, BEGIN now, THREADS 1
EXTRACT added.


GGSCI (ggs-source) 6> ADD EXTTRAIL ./dirdat/sa, EXTRACT es1e201, MEGABYTES
32
EXTTRAIL added.


GGSCI (ggs-source) 7> ADD EXTRACT epmp01, EXTTRAILSOURCE ./dirdat/sa
EXTRACT added.


GGSCI (ggs-source) 8> ADD RMTTRAIL ./dirdat/ta, EXTRACT epmp01, MEGABYTES 32
RMTTRAIL added.


GGSCI (ggs-source) 9>
```

On the target Oracle GoldenGate instance, recreate the replicate groups.

```
GGSCI (ggs-target) 4> ADD REPLICAT rs1e201, EXTTRAIL ./dirdat/ta
REPLICAT added.
```

Step 12: Start Oracle GoldenGate processes and verify status

Start Oracle GoldenGate processes on the proper sequence. Manager, extracts then replicates. The status should be RUNNING for all processes.

Start the source primary and secondary extract groups

```
GGSCI (ggs-source) 9> START EXTRACT *

Sending START request to MANAGER ...
EXTRACT EPMP01 starting

Sending START request to MANAGER ...
EXTRACT ES1E201 starting
```

```
GGSCI (ggs-source) 11> INFO ALL

Program     Status      Group       Lag at Chkpt  Time Since Chkpt

MANAGER     RUNNING
EXTRACT     RUNNING     EPMP01      00:00:00      00:00:00
EXTRACT     RUNNING     ES1E201     00:01:28      00:00:04

GGSCI (ggs-source) 12>
```

Start the target replicate group

```
GGSCI (ggs-target) 12> START REPLICAT *

Sending START request to MANAGER ...
REPLICAT RS1E201 starting
```

```
GGSCI (ggs-target) 13> INFO ALL

Program     Status      Group       Lag at Chkpt  Time Since Chkpt

MANAGER     RUNNING
REPLICAT    RUNNING     RS1E201     00:00:00      00:00:00


GGSCI (ggs-target) 14>
```

Step 13: Disable restricted database access (Optional)

If you have performed step 1, then disable restricted database access to enable database general use. Also, grant restricted session to users revoked in step 1.

Execute disable restricted session on source and target systems.

```
SQL>alter system disable restricted session;
```

```
System altered.
```

Step 14: Verify and monitor local and remote trails

Ensure the new Oracle GoldenGate installation is performing capture, routing and apply by monitoring the local and remote trails.

On the source system, display the current trail files

```
$ ls -al
```

```
total 12
drwxr-x---  2 oracle oinstall 4096 Sep 29 17:08 .
drwxr-xr-x 29 oracle oinstall 4096 Sep 29 17:19 ..
-rw-r-----  1 oracle oinstall 1401 Sep 29 17:08 sa000000
```

```
$ ls -al
```

```
total 464
drwxr-x---  2 oracle oinstall   4096 Sep 29 17:08 .
drwxr-xr-x 29 oracle oinstall   4096 Sep 29 17:19 ..
-rw-r-----  1 oracle oinstall 460374 Sep 29 17:19 sa000000
$
```

On the target system, display the current trail files

```
$ ls -al
```

```
total 8
drwxr-x---  2 oracle oinstall 4096 Oct  8 12:52 .
drwxr-xr-x 28 oracle oinstall 4096 Oct  8 12:24 ..
-rw-r-----  1 oracle oinstall    0 Oct  8 12:52 ta000000
```

```
$ ls -al
```

```
total 1684
drwxr-x---  2 oracle oinstall    4096 Oct  8 12:52 .
drwxr-xr-x 28 oracle oinstall    4096 Oct  8 12:24 ..
-rw-r-----  1 oracle oinstall 1711719 Oct  8 13:03 ta000000
$
```

Steps 1 through 12 to be performed on both source and target systems. However; when the source and target systems having different Oracle GoldenGate releases, for instance the source is running Oracle GoldenGate 10g while the target is running Oracle GoldenGate 11g, it's required to explicitly set the primary extract compatibility level for the RMTTRAIL parameter by indicating the source release format.

Also, in case of Oracle GoldenGate intermediate system is part of the architecture, the intermediate system should be upgraded. Even though the upgrade sequence is not strict, but it should start by upgrading the source systems first, followed by upgrading intermediate systems, and upgrading target systems last.

Step 15: Applying new features

The last step is mostly based on business requirements and should be applied gradually, because a new feature may requires major modification before implementing it. Oracle GoldenGate 12g has improved existing features or introduced totally new features. The key features are listed below without detailed description.

Uninstalling Oracle GoldenGate

Uninstalling Oracle GoldenGate performed using destructive commands from the operating system and the database. The steps are outlined and illustrated next.

- Stop Oracle GoldenGate processes
- Delete the extract and replicates groups
- Unregister the extract and replicate processes
- Delete Oracle GoldenGate home, recursively
- Drop Oracle GoldenGate database schema

Executing the above steps remove not only Oracle GoldenGate software, but also completely remove the instance which include software, the associated processes and the database objects owned by Oracle GoldenGate schema.

Stop Oracle GoldenGate processes on source system.

```
GGSCI (ggs-source) 2> STOP EXTRACT *
```

```
Sending STOP request to EXTRACT EPMP01 ...
Request processed.

Sending STOP request to EXTRACT ES1E201 ...
Request processed.
```

```
GGSCI (ggs-source) 3> STOP MGR!

Sending STOP request to MANAGER ...
Request processed.
Manager stopped.
```

```
GGSCI (ggs-source) 4> INFO ALL

Program     Status      Group       Lag at Chkpt  Time Since Chkpt

MANAGER     STOPPED
EXTRACT     STOPPED     EPMP01      00:00:04      00:00:14
EXTRACT     STOPPED     ES1E201     00:00:00      00:00:12

GGSCI (ggs-source) 5>
```

Stop Oracle GoldenGate processes on target system.

```
GGSCI (ggs-target) 2> STOP REPLICAT *

Sending STOP request to REPLICAT RS1E201 ...
Request processed.
```

```
GGSCI (ggs-target) 3> STOP MGR !

Sending STOP request to MANAGER ...
Request processed.
Manager stopped.
```

```
GGSCI (ggs-target) 4> INFO ALL

Program     Status      Group       Lag at Chkpt  Time Since Chkpt

MANAGER     STOPPED
REPLICAT    STOPPED     RS1E201     00:00:00      00:00:12

GGSCI (ggs-target) 5>
```

For MS SQL Server, unlock Oracle GoldenGate home directory by deleting the manager process Windows services, if installed. Otherwise, the DEL operating system command will fails.

```
C:\GGS>install deleteevents deleteservice

Oracle GoldenGate messages installed successfully.
Service 'GGSMGR' deleted.

Install program terminated normally.

C:\GGS>
```

From GGSCI command-line, login to the database and delete the extract and replicate groups from both system. Also, deregister the primary extract from the source database.

```
GGSCI (ggs-source) 5> DBLOGIN USERID ggs_admin@s1e2, password oracle
```

```
Successfully logged into database.
```

```
GGSCI (ggs-source) 6> delete extract ES1E201
```

```
Deleted EXTRACT ES1E201.
```

```
GGSCI (ggs-source) 7> delete extract EPMP01
```

```
Deleted EXTRACT EPMP01.
```

```
GGSCI (ggs-source) 8> UNREGISTER EXTRACT ES1E201 DATABASE
```

```
ERROR: EXTRACT ES1E201 must be registered with the database to perform this
operation.

GGSCI (ggs-source) 9>
```

Next, the destructive recursive command is executed to remove Oracle GoldenGate software from the source and target systems.

```
$ cd $GGS_HOME
$ pwd
/u01/app/oracle/ggs/11.2.0
```

```
$ rm -Rf *
```

The last step is to drop Oracle GoldenGate schema.

```
SQL>conn / as sysdba
Connected.
```

```
SQL>drop user ggs_admin cascade;
```

```
User dropped.
```

Repeat the above commands on the target systems. When Oracle GoldenGate database schema ggs_admin is using dedicated tablespace, you may need to drop the tablespace using the SQL*Plus command below.

```
SQL>conn / as sysdba
Connected.
SQL>drop tablespace ggs_dat including contents and datafiles;

Tablespace dropped.
```

Summary

This chapter has prepared Oracle GoldenGate instances, the foundation for the remaining chapters. Because the getting started chapter is the pre-requisite, it must complete successfully before proceeding further.

This chapter covered the basics from Oracle GoldenGate best practices.

- Network, Domain Name Services (DNS) configuration and TCP/IP ports validation
- Verify and maybe enable the source and target database archive operating mode
- Prepare the source and target databases for Oracle GoldenGate
- Download and install Oracle GoldenGate on source and target systems
- Creating Oracle GoldenGate directory structure
- Configure Oracle GoldenGate database user and grant required database privileges
- Working with Oracle GoldenGate Software Command Interface (GGSCI)
- Configure and manage source and target Oracle GoldenGate manager process
- Enable table-level logging using Oracle GoldenGate
- Configure Oracle networking files for remote access to source and target database
- Configure Oracle networking files for ASM instance extracts
- Performing Oracle GoldenGate backup, recovery, upgrade and uninstall

Next, using Oracle GoldenGate heterogeneous capability for establishing the target database through initial-load techniques. By configuring the initial-load, the change data capture and apply across different platforms enables establishing the target database without downtime, for maximum business continuity.

Based on the source and target database type, it's critical to select the most suitable method for initial-load as described on chapter 3.

GoldenGate Initial data load techniques

CHAPTER

Overview of GoldenGate Data Loading

An essential part of an enterprise data integration projects is the initial-load phase for transporting and consolidating data across heterogeneous systems to establish the "big data" database. Frequently the case, the data in transit need to be transformed to meet the design of the destination data source environment running on heterogeneous platforms for different purposes.

A common enterprise example is the initial-load for the enterprise data warehouse repository star schema database from several back-end sales Microsoft SQL Server databases to a unified Oracle Exadata database machine running Oracle business intelligence or reporting and analytics instance. Oracle GoldenGate is highly flexible for moving real-time data across databases, however it's always the business requirements that dictate selecting the most optimum methods for initial data load followed by data validation techniques.

This chapter covers initial data loading techniques using Oracle GoldenGate and database methods for GoldenGate. An assessment of these techniques should be performed to qualify the data loading method. The combination of Oracle GoldenGate with other techniques is possible, this is because Oracle GoldenGate techniques has the advantage of heterogeneity, but also certain techniques have the disadvantage of non-supported data types and reliability on very large database environment (VLDB).

The decision of choosing the initial-load technique largely depends on the three factors, which are commonly found within an enterprise environment.

- **Continuous availability:** Database availability for supporting 24/7 business requirements. The source database must remain online during the initial-load.
- **Heterogeneous platforms**: Mismatching architecture of the source and target platforms, requiring data type transformation from source target database.
- **Data volume:** Very large database (VLDB) environments with limited load window and disk storage availability.

Critical mission system running on 24/7 basis requires performing an online initial data loading. OLTP databases that have to remain open for users during the initial-load process requires configuring Oracle GoldenGate change data capture (CDC) first, then use Oracle GoldenGate techniques for initial data load. However; if the database in restricted mode, become temporary unavailable, then configuring change data capture is usually deferred.

Another common use case for using Oracle GoldenGate initial data load is when using Oracle GoldenGate for zero downtime migration and upgrade where the source and target systems have mismatched database endians, for example when migrating Oracle database from IBM AIX to Oracle Enterprise Linux platforms.

Performing an initial data load for very large database (VLDB) is best performed using Oracle Recovery Manager (RMAN), which can be implemented from the existing backup or by cloning the database using RMAN duplicate feature. Another form of initial data load is done by breaking the existing hardware storage mirroring and configuring Oracle GoldenGate change data capture (CDC) to keep the broken storage synchronized with the primary storage. Figure 3-1 depicts the general components for initial-load. However; each method uses and implements the components in the lower part differently.

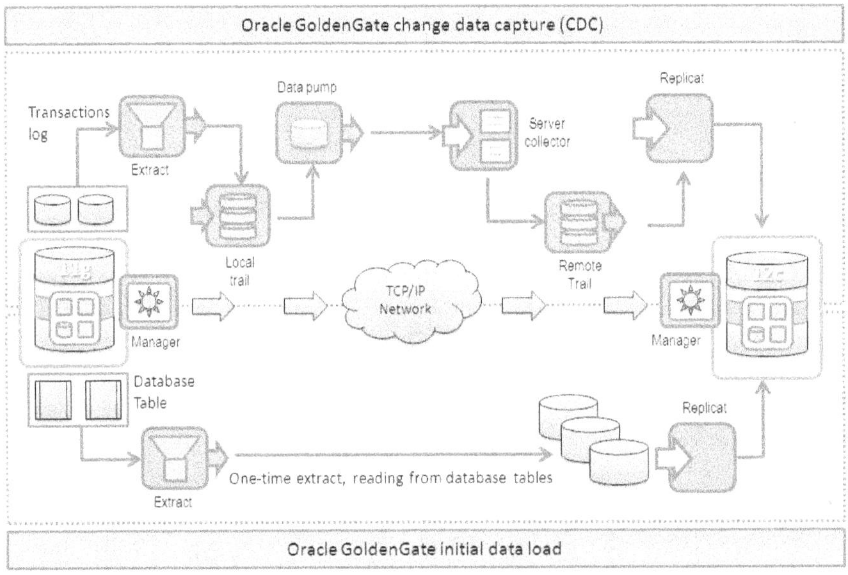

Figure 3-1: Initial-load using Oracle GoldenGate

From within Oracle GoldenGate, number of initial data load methods are available. Each load method will be discussed, developed and implemented to help you make the decision to qualify your initial-load methods. The method components of parameter files, extracts process, replicate process, commands and deployment are explained.

The list of initial-load methods covered in this chapter:

- Method 1: Initial data load using files to replicate
- Method 2: Initial data load using direct load
- Method 3: Initial data load using database utility
- Method 4: Initial data load using files to database utility
- Method 5: Initial data load using Direct bulk SQL*Loader API (Oracle only)

The option for using Oracle recovery manager (RMAN) for establishing the target database, suitable for very large database (VLDB) running on homogenous environment is covered on chapter 7 – Near Zero-Downtime Database Migration and Upgrade.

Using Microsoft SQL Server Integration Services (SSIS) for initial-load is covered under the section Non-Oracle GoldenGate initial load techniques. SSIS connects to the source MS-SQL Server and to the target Oracle database to perform high-performance bulk inserts. We will discuss installation, configuration and usage to establish the target database using MS-SQL Server SSIS.

GoldenGate Initial-load Workflow Options

The workflow of Oracle GoldenGate initial-load techniques is developed from either the following database environments.

- Initial-load from active source database
- Initial-load from inactive source database

It's the enterprise business requirements for non-stop operations that play the rule for deciding which initial-load technique and the workflow to use. The combination of multiple initial-load techniques and workflows is suitable when the vast majority of the database tables are static (e.g. lookup tables) and the remaining are transactional tables that is a situation promoting a combination of options. For example, using direct load method for lookup tables and database utility method such as export data pump for transactional tables achieves consistent target database and business continuity.

The initial-load for an active database is mostly due to either or both of the following situations outlined on figure 3-2.

- Very large source database, an offline initial-load for establishing the target database is beyond the service level agreement (SLA) for downtime.
- The business requirements demand strict operation for 24/7 support, examples of such systems are airlines, medical support, banking, etc. Or the source database is accessed by other 24/7 systems.

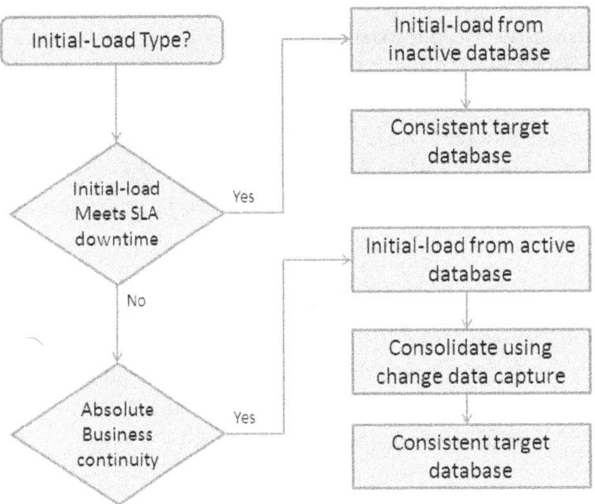

Figure 3-2: Initial-load type

An environment running Oracle Active Data Guard greatly benefits from this configuration. Because the source database (primary) is protected by a physical standby database which is block-to-block copy and open on read-only mode, it's a valid option to use the standby database for initial-load as depicted on figure 3-3.

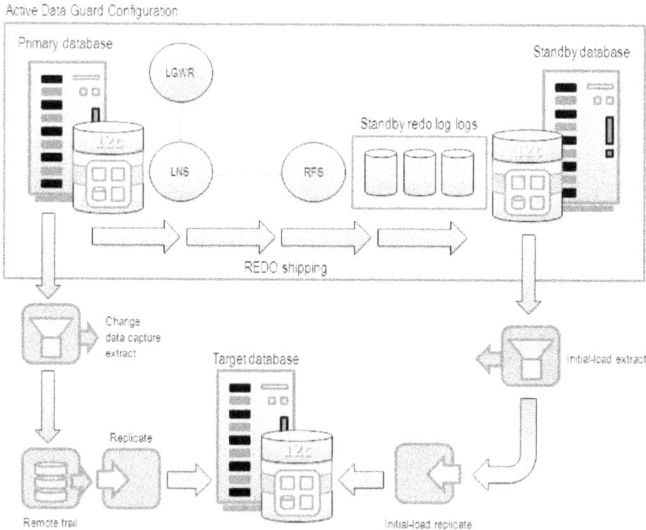

Figure: 3-3: Initial-load from standby database

GoldenGate Initial load from an active database

Oracle GoldenGate initial-load from an active database must be carefully developed to ensure data consistency and integrity, and the configuration steps must consider several factors such as disk space availability, handling collision and performance overhead. After your successful initial-load from an active database, a post configuration is developed on top of the existing running Oracle GoldenGate instance is required to support business requirements for data transformations, columns mapping and data manipulations.

Figure 3-4 depicts the initial-load workflow from an active source database to establish the target database without incurring downtime. The workflow consists of four phases, providing business continuity without impacting the continuity and integrity of online transactions. The workflow starts by configuring Oracle GoldenGate change data capture (CDC) extract groups which creates and manages local, then apply and reconcile transactions after performing initial-load delivery. Handling data collision occurred during the initial-load must be explicitly enabled, and then disabled after data reconciliation.

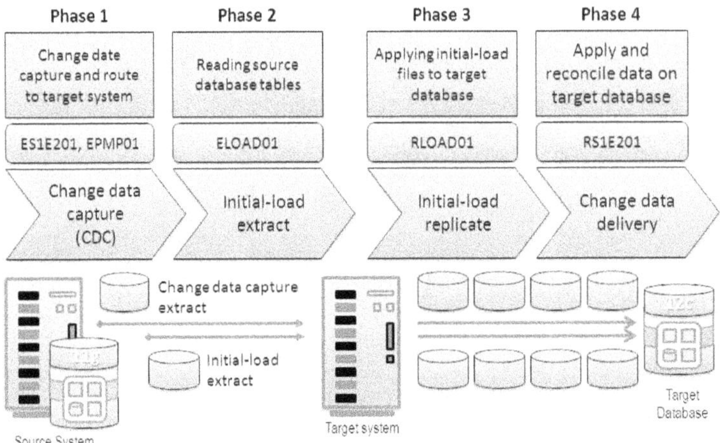

Figure 3-4: Initial load phases from an active database

The workflow within the source system consists of the change data capture ES1E201 extract, and secondary extract EPMP01 and the initial-load extract ELOAD01. The workflow within the target system consists of the initial-load replicate RLOAD01 and the change data delivery RS1E201 replicate.

The following is a description of each phase developed for the initial-load from an active database. The steps explained from the prospective of file to replicate method.

Phase 1: GoldenGate Change data capture from an Active database

To achieve business continuity, the change data capture is configured first when performing initial-load from an active database environment. The change data capture (CDC) phase consists of the following steps.

1. The change data capture (CDC) extract process, configured to read from the transaction logs, and creates the local trail. To avoid disk space issues, local trail files are subject to purge as configured on the source manager process.
2. The data pump extract process, configured to read the local trail, then routes transactions to the target data collector server across TCP/IP network. By routing trail files ensures the source (production environment) maintains its optimized disk space.

3. The data collector server on the target system re-assembles the data and creates the remote trail. The trail files are read and applied to the target database using the replicate process, which is the last phase of the initial-load.

The data pump on step 2 is optional, but highly recommended. It ensures the change data capture process continues capturing from the transaction logs in the event of network failure avoiding abnormal termination due to the luck of resources for long running transactions.

Phase 2: GoldenGate Initial-load extract from an Active database

The initial-load extract directly reads from the database source tables to establish the target database. Online transactions occurred during the initial-load extract are being captured by change data capture extract and sent to the target system. The initial-load extract phase consists of the following steps.

1. An initial-load extract database session is invoked from the operating system command prompt or started from GGSCI command-line. This initial-load extract process does not perform checkpoint.
2. The initial-load extract session uses the database credential specified in the parameter file to login to the database. The database user must have *select* privilege on the source tables. The source tables are available for applications during the extract.
3. The initial-load data is send to the target system over TCP/IP, with compression and encryption options, if required.
4. On the target server, the data collector server re-assemble the received data creating remote files as specified by the parameter *rmtfile*. For very large database (VLDB), multiple remote file option should be configured. Oracle GoldenGate limits the remote files to 2GB in size.

It's important to record the completion timestamp for the initial-load extract, this timestamp is used as a reference for the change data delivery (replicate process) has reconciled all transactions occurred during the initial-load operation, and it is time to disable data collision handling.

Phase 3: GoldenGate Initial-load delivery from an Active database

The initial-load delivery applies the transactions from the remote files to the database using the database interface, SQL native calls. It includes these steps:

1. An initial-load replicate is started from either the operating system or started from GGSCI command-line, this replicate process does not perform checkpoint. Optionally, apply parallelism for multiple remote files.
2. The special run replicate uses the parameter file to login to the target database. The database user must have *insert* privilege on the target database tables.
3. The special run replicate applies the transactions to the target database with collision handling specified by the parameter *handlecollisions*.

Upon completion of the initial-load delivery, verification of static data (lookup tables) can be done using Oracle GoldenGate reports or Veridata. Accurate comparison of transactional tables is postponed until the completion of phase 4.

Phase 4: GoldenGate Change data delivery from an Active database

The change data delivery replicate applies transactions occurred during the initial-data load process and continues applying captured transactions for the configured database tables. The change date delivery replicate should be started only after the initial-load delivery replicate has successfully completed. These steps occur during this phase:

1. The data collector server keeps re-assembling the transactions received from the data pump extract, creating the remote trail during the initial-load delivery.
2. The change data delivery replicate reads the remote trail and applies transactions using the database interface while ensuring transactions consistency. The change data delivery replicate process uses a checkpoint database table thereby providing quick recovery in case of failure.
3. Upon completion and reconciliation of the data occurred during the change data capture, we disable collision handling.

The above four phases are discussed from the prospective of homogenous database environment. In the case of heterogeneous environment, phase 3 and phase 4 require using a source definition file. Refer to chapter 8 for to learn more about configuring and applying source definition file.

Now let's look at the steps for an inactive database.

GoldenGate Initial-load from an inactive database

The purpose of initial-load from an inactive database is to establish the target database from a consistent data source. The source database remains unavailable for users throughout the initial-load elapsed timeframe. The most justified reason for

performing such an initial-load from an inactive database is when the source database size allows the initial-load to complete within the acceptable downtime, meeting the service level agreement (SLA), or when the initial-load from an inactive database is from Oracle snapshot standby database.
Because the primary database is open for users, the snapshot database provides a consistent point-in-time initial-load, sufficiently usable for non-production purposes such development and testing platforms.

Figure 3-5 depicts the general workflow by the initial-load workflow from an inactive database.

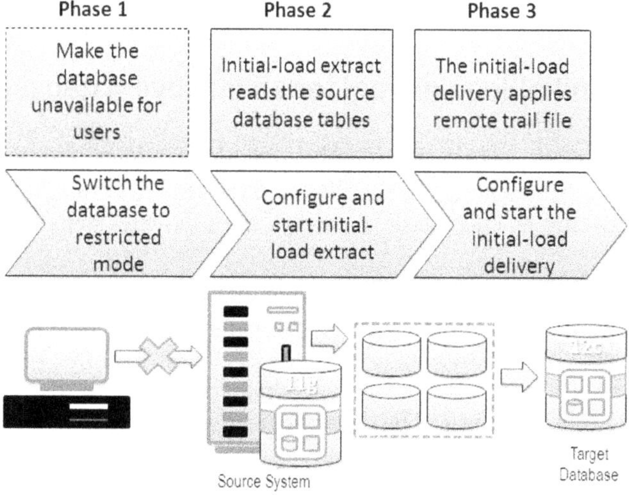

Figure 3-5: Workflow for an inactive database

Using Oracle GoldenGate initial-load techniques for heterogamous environment requires the use of a source definition file. The file is generated on the source and shipped to the target database using an ASCII format.

For Oracle-to-Oracle database initial-load, using tools such as Oracle data integrator (ODI) expedites the delivery by performing bulk-transformation and bulk-load. For MS-SQL Server-to-MS-SQL Server, using tools such as SQL Server Integration Services (SSIS) is an option available for bulk-load and transformations. Both ODI and SSIS support heterogeneous environments.

Phase 1: GoldenGate Restricted mode for an inactive database

This is an optional phase, however making the database unavailable for users during the initial-load extract provides a guaranteed data consistency when the initial-load delivery is completed. This phase consists of two steps:

1. Place the database on restricted mode
2. Terminate all existing active database sessions

Only user with *restricted* mode database privileges are able to connect to the database. This requires temporary granting Oracle GoldenGate database users restricted session privilege.

Phase 2: GoldenGate Initial-load extract for an inactive database

While this database is operating in restricted mode, the initial-load extract reads the database source tables, and either creating remote files or directly performing initial-load delivery to the target database. This phase consists of the following steps.

1. A special one-time run initial-load extract session is invoked from the operating system command prompt, (or from the GGSCI command-line). This type of extract does not perform checkpoint.
2. The initial load extract session uses the database credential specified in the parameter file to login to the database. The database user must have *select* privilege on the source tables.
3. The initial load extract read the source tables, the source tables are available for user with restricted session privilege during the extract.
4. The initial-load extract send data to the target system over TCP/IP, optionally with compression and encryption. The target data collector server is not required when performing direct load technique.

Use Oracle GoldenGate reporting feature to verify the initial-load extract by generating initial-load extract report, this will be compared with the initial-load delivery report.

Phase 3: GoldenGate Initial-load delivery for an inactive database

The steps below for the initial-load delivery depends on the method that you have implemented. For the file to replicate method, before starting the initial-load delivery process, verify the initial-load remote files location on the remote system. For direct load, before you start the initial-load extract, verify that the initial-load delivery group has been created. In general, the initial-load delivery phase consists of the following steps.

1. Ensure that the remote files are available on the target system
2. Start the initial-load delivery to apply the transactions to the target database using the database interface.

Finally, we generate the initial-load delivery report and compare it with the initial-load extract report. The use of Oracle GoldenGate Veridata is an excellent tool to compare table's pairs.

GoldenGate Database restricted mode for an inactive database

Since we are planning to configure an initial-load from an inactive source database, the database should be placed in *restricted* mode prior to starting the initial-load process. A restricted session database allows only users with *restricted session* privilege to access the database, guaranteeing consistent initial-load.

While connected as a privileged database user, place the source database on restricted session, and grant the *restricted session* privileges to the Oracle GoldenGate database user. This ensures the change data capture (CDC) groups are starting from synchronized and consistent state. The command to place the database on restricted mode:

```
SQL> ALTER SYSTEM ENABLE RESTRICTED SESSION;

System altered.

SQL> GRANT RESTRICTED SESSION TO ggs_admin;

Grant succeeded.
```

In the case of very large database (VLDB) and/or databases requiring continuous availability (where the source database must remain open for general use), refer to performing your initial-load from an active database. This provides details regarding the initial-load workflow and setup for keeping the source database available for users during the initial-load process.

Now let's look at the general set-up of GoldenGate.

Oracle GoldenGate general setup

Before proceeding further, ensure the manager process is configured on source and target system, GLOBALS parameter file created on target system and the database checkpoint table created. This general setup is the basis for running Oracle GoldenGate.

GoldenGate Manager Process

The source system manager process listen to port 7811, but also uses a range of dynamic ports for starting extract and replicate processes. Up to 250 ports are available for the manager process.

```
GGSCI (ggs-source) 1> INFO MGR

Manager is running (IP port ggs-source.7811, Process ID 4214).
```

The target system manager process listen to port 7812. If the source and target are on different systems, identical ports may be used.

```
GGSCI (ggs-target) 1> INFO MGR

Manager is running (IP port ggs-target.7812, Process ID 5319).
```

Using the GoldenGate GLOBALS parameter file

You create the GLOBALS parameter files for inheriting Oracle GoldenGate parameters and values across all extract and replicate processes. However; the same parameter are overridden by the run-time parameter of a process. For example, when creating the checkpoint table for replicate process, two options are available: specifying the checkpoint table *owner.table_name* on the GLOBALS parameter file or by specifying the checkpoint table when adding the replicate process as shown below.

```
GGSCI (ggs-target) 2> ADD REPLICAT rs1e201, CHECKPOINTTABLE
ggs_admin.chkpttab, EXTTRAIL ./dirdat/ta
```

Creating a GoldenGate checkpoint table

The default and best-practice checkpoint for the delivery group is a database table, and we use the GGSCI *add checkpointtable* command to create the checkpoint table. An alternative is the use of checkpoint file by specifying *nocheckpointtble* parameter.

Next we issue the command to create the checkpoint table using the option of specifying the checkpoint table on the GLOBALS parameter file. Before executing the GGSCI *add checkpointtable*, you must exist GGSCI and re-start it to activate the added parameters.

```
GGSCI (ggs-target) 2> DBLOGIN USERID ggs_admin, PASSWORD oracle
Successfully logged into database.
```

```
GGSCI (ggs-target) 2> ADD CHECKPOINTTABLE
```

```
No checkpoint table specified. Using GLOBALS specification
(ggs_admin.chkpttab)...

Successfully created checkpoint table ggs_admin.chkpttab.

GGSCI (ggs-target) 3>
```

Method 1: Initial GoldenGate data load using file-to-replicate

Ultimately, the file-to-replicate method uses an initial-load replicate to instantiate the target database. An initial-load extract process reads the source database tables and creates a remote canonical formatted file on the target system. Then, an initial-load replicate process applies the transactions by performing sequential database inserts operations.

This method enables the configuration of multiple remote files of specific size on the target system, which is suitable for performing initial data load on very large database (VLDB) running on heterogeneous environment. For this example, the source is Oracle database and the target is Microsoft SQL Server database.

When creating multiple remote files to support heterogeneous very large database (VLDB), the initial-load delivery should be performed using separate replicate processes for enhancing the performance by applying parallelism using concurrent replicate processes. The use of single replicate process serializes the initial-load due to passing one remote file at a time. For a database of size 100GB, at least 50 remote files will be generated as the maximum remote file size is 2GB.

Figure 3-6 shows the workflow for this method from an active database homogenous environment. For heterogeneous environment such as Oracle database to MS-SQL Server database, a source definition file must be created on the source system, then transferred to the target system using ASCII mode. The four phases of this technique include:

1. Configure and the change data capture groups (CDC)
2. Configure and start the initial-load capture
3. Configure and start the initial-load delivery
4. Configure and start the change data delivery

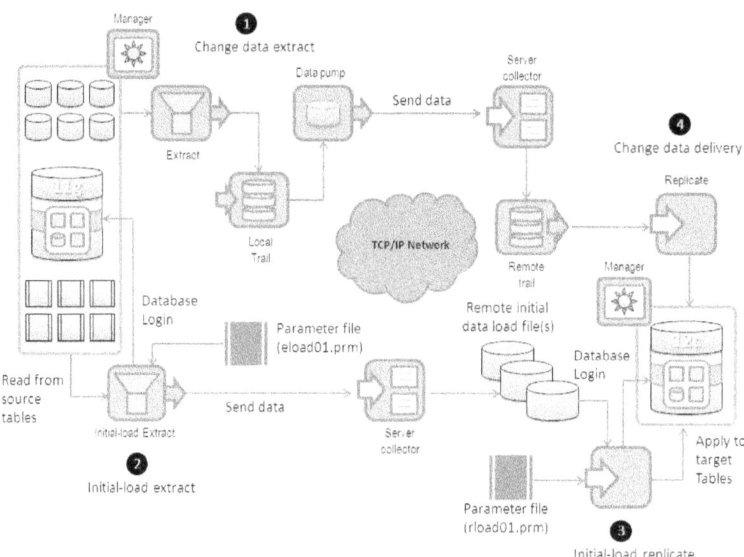

Figure 3-6: File to replicate initial-load method architecture

When performing initial-load from an active database, the change data capture extract and replicate groups are deployed to reconcile data that occurred during the initial-load extract, thereby keeping the source database available for users.

Configure GoldenGate extract groups

Prior to performing initial-load from an active source database, the change data capture (CDC) and the data pump extracts groups components must be configured. This approach enables business continuity by eliminating quiescing the database during the initial-load operations.

The primary and secondary extract groups configurable components consists of the following:

- Change data capture extract process (ES1E201)
- Local trail (sa)
- Data pump extract process (EPMP01)
- Remote trail (ta)

GoldenGate Change data capture extract group

The change data capture extract group is collectively composed of: a parameter file, a checkpoint file and a local trail. Our change data capture extract (ES1E201), referred to by the primary extract, is configured to capture from the transaction logs as depicted in figure 3-6. The option of reading from the archive log files is available as an alternative data source, but should be avoided when performing change data capture during the initial-load extract.

GoldenGate Primary extract parameter file

The primary *extract group* parameter file identifies the run-time parameters, sub-parameters, options and the associated values. These parameters may override globally set parameters on the GLOBALS parameter file. Use one line for each parameter, sub-parameter and value, for multi-line parameters, use the '&' character at the end of the current line.

```
GGSCI (ggs-source) 5> EDIT PARAMS es1e201
```

```
EXTRACT es1e201
SETENV  (ORACLE_SID=S1E2)
SETENV  (ORACLE_HOME="/u01/app/oracle/product/11.2.0/dbhome_1")
SETENV  (NLS_LANG=AMERICAN_AMERICA.AL32UTF8)
USERID  ggs_admin@S1E2, password oracle
EXTTRAIL ./dirdat/sa
TABLE    osm$repapi.customers;
TABLE    osm$repapi.policies;
```

Table 3-1 lists the run-time parameters for the primary extract. The parameters listed are the basic, advanced parameters may be included for additional features and requirements.

Parameter	Description
EXTRACT	Identifying the name of the primary extract group
SETENV	Set environment variable for Oracle GoldenGate, minimizing INFO type messages
USERID, PASSWORD	The source database login credential
EXTTRAIL	The destination and local trail name
TABLE	Mapped tables

Table 3-1: Primary extract parameters

Creating a GoldenGate change data capture extract

We use the GGSCI *add extract* command to create ES1E201 primary extract defined in the parameter file. At this moment, leave ES1E201 primary extract stopped until completing the configuration for the data pump group and the initial-load extracts.

```
GGSCI (ggs-source) 6> ADD EXTRACT es1e201, TRANLOG, BEGIN now, THREADS 1
EXTRACT added.

GGSCI (ggs-source) 7> INFO ALL

Program     Status      Group       Lag at Chkpt  Time Since Chkpt

MANAGER     RUNNING
EXTRACT     STOPPED     ES1E201     00:00:00      00:00:49

GGSCI (ggs-source) 8>
```

Creating a GoldenGate local trail

The local trail identified by the directory specified and a two-character prefix for the parameter named EXTTRAIL. Using this two-character prefix, the primary extract creates the local trail files sequentially starting with sa000000. The default location of the local trail files is Oracle GoldenGate sub-directory *dirdat,* or can be explicitly identified by the parameter EXTTRAIL. The local trail disk storage is best managed using the source manager process parameter PURGEOLDEXTRACTS. Use GGSCI command-line ADD EXTTRAIL to associate the primary extract with the local trail identified by *./dirdat/sa.*

```
GGSCI (ggs-source) 9> ADD EXTTRAIL ./dirdat/sa, EXTRACT es1e201, MEGABYTES
100

EXTTRAIL added.
```

GoldenGate Data pump extract group

An optional but highly recommended component is the data pump extract. It serves two purposes. First, it eliminates the change data capture primary extract from performing dual task, extracting and routing data to remote server. Also, it provides resilience against failure as a result of network disconnection.

GoldenGate Data pump extract parameter file

The main functionality of the data pump approach is to route data to the remote server. It communicates with a collector server running on the remote server. The collector server re-assemble the data and creates the remote trail. Table 3-2 describes the parameters used for the data pump extract.

```
GGSCI (ggs-source) 10> EDIT PARAMS EPMP01
```

```
XTRACT EPMP01
USERID ggs_admin@S1E2, PASSWORD oracle
PASSTHRU
RMTHOST ggs-target, MGRPORT 7812
RMTTRAIL ./dirdat/ta
TABLE osm$repapi.customers;
TABLE osm$repapi.policies;
```

Parameter	Description
EXTRACT	Identifying the name of the data pump extract group
PASSTHRU	Identical tables structure used on source and target databases
RMTHOST	The target server and the manager listening port
RMTTRAIL	The remote trail location and prefix
TABLE	Mapped tables

Table 3-2: Data pump extract parameters

Creating a GoldenGate data pump extract

Use Oracle GoldenGate GGSCI command-line to create EPMP01 data pump extract defined by the parameter file EPMP01.PRM. At this moment, leave EPMP01 extract stopped until completing the configuration for the initial-load replicate process.

```
GGSCI (ggs-source) 12> ADD EXTRACT epmp01, EXTTRAILSOURCE ./dirdat/sa
```

```
EXTRACT added.
```

Verify the secondary extract (data pump) has been created.

```
GGSCI (ggs-source) 14> INFO ALL

Program     Status      Group       Lag at Chkpt  Time Since Chkpt

MANAGER     RUNNING
EXTRACT     STOPPED     EPMP01      00:00:00      00:01:19
EXTRACT     STOPPED     ES1E201     00:00:00      00:09:36

GGSCI (ggs-source) 15>
```

Creating a GoldenGate remote trail

The remote trail serves two purposes, it create the remote trail files for the replicate process, and to signal the local manager process to purge the local trail files, thereby keeping the local (production) disk utilization uniform without space pressure that may impact server performance. The remote trail identified by a two-character prefix such as *ta,* which create remote trail files starting with a name like ta000000.

```
GGSCI (ggs-source) 13> ADD RMTTRAIL ./dirdat/ta, EXTRACT epmp01, MEGABYTES
100
```

```
RMTTRAIL added.
```

Configure and verify a GoldenGate initial-data load extract

We start by preparing the parameter files for the initial-load extract. The parameter files instructs the initial- load extract to connect to the database and read from the source tables directly. Using the target system hostname and the manager process port number, the remote files created as configured, single file or multiple remote files depending on the overall size of the source database. Oracle GoldenGate restrict a maximum remote file size to 2GB.

Configure GoldenGate initial-load extract

Because the initial load extract is of type special run, it's not associated with a checkpoint file, a failure of the initial load extract process requires resubmitting the initial load task. Table 3-3 lists the initial load extract parameter file (eload01.prm).

Parameter	Description
SOURCEISTABLE	Instructs the initial load extract to read from the source database tables
USERID, PASSWORD	The source database login credential
RMTHOST, MGRPORT	The target system identified by the hostname and manager port number
RMTFILE, PURGE	The remote file location and name with the purge option
TABLE	The list of tables read by the initial load extract

Table 3-3: Initial load extract parameters

The RMTFILE parameter uses the options *purge* or *append.* When purge is specified, the initial load extract removes the initial data load file, if exists, before instantiating the data file. When append is specified, the initial data load extract instantiate the file by appending to the file, if exists.

From within GGSCI, use the *edit params* command to create the initial data load extract parameter file. The RMTFILE parameter is used to create one initial data load only. However; If the initial data load file is expected to exceed 2GB, then use the RMTFILE options *maxfiles* and *megabytes* which instruct the initial load extract to create multiple initial data load files.

```
GGSCI (ggs-source) 15> EDIT PARAMS eload01
```

```
EXTRACT eload01
SOURCEISTABLE
USERID ggs_admin@S1E2, PASSWORD oracle
RMTHOST ggs-target, MGRPORT 7812
RMTFILE ./dirdat/initload01.dat, PURGE
TABLE osm$repapi.customers;
TABLE osm$repapi.policies;
```

Let's create the initial-load extract. This extract will be used during the deployment phase.

```
GGSCI (ggs-source) 16> ADD EXTRACT eload01, SOURCEISTABLE
```

```
EXTRACT added.

GGSCI (ggs-source) 17>
```

Next let's look at GoldenGate configuration options

GoldenGate Configuration options

An optimized-advanced initial extract parameter file considers security, compression and multiple initial load remote files settings. Applying such parameters should be used selectively, and they are mostly used for databases that are subject to compliance regulation, such as credit cards and social security numbers.

GoldenGate Security settings

The GoldenGate security settings are suitable for highly sensitive environment by encrypting passwords and remote trails. An encrypted Oracle GoldenGate generated password stored in a flat file protected by file-system read-write permission.

Encrypted data sent across TCP/IP network applies encryption to remote trail files. Oracle GoldenGate data encryption requires the generation of encryption key. When applying trail file encryption, be aware of the performance overhead introduced for encryption on source and decryption on target systems. See chapter 1 – Oracle GoldenGate fundamentals for details encrypting password techniques and generating encryption keys. Performance testing showed encryption slowdown initial-load process by approximately 23%.

GoldenGate Compression settings

Adding the compression parameter COMPRESSION enables default compression algorithm. Additionally, the parameter COMPRESSIONTHRUSHHOLD <size> further optimizes the compression based on the threshold specified, eliminating unnecessary compression. The compression ratio depends on columns data types, an average ratio of 1:4 is highly achievable. Our particular initial load the compression ratio achieved is 1:5. Compression considerably help enhances the performance across low-bandwidth wide-area network.

GoldenGate Multiple remote files settings

This option supports very large database (VLDB) initial-load. Using *maxfiles* and *maxsize* options of RMTFILE parameter creates multiple remote files on the target system. This feature avoids having one initial-load remote file reaching 2GB, which is an enforced upper limit by Oracle GoldenGate. During the initial-load delivery, temporary disabling table constraints improves the performance and avoids referential integrity violations. We deploy parallel delivery groups for high-performance initial-load by mapping one delivery group per one remote file as illustrated in figure 3-7 where multiple delivery groups (replicate processes) are read in parallel remote files.

GoldenGate Range processing

Use the *sqlpredicate* clause of TABLE to partition the rows of large tables among the different Extract processes. This is treated as parallel initial-load extract when running concurrently.

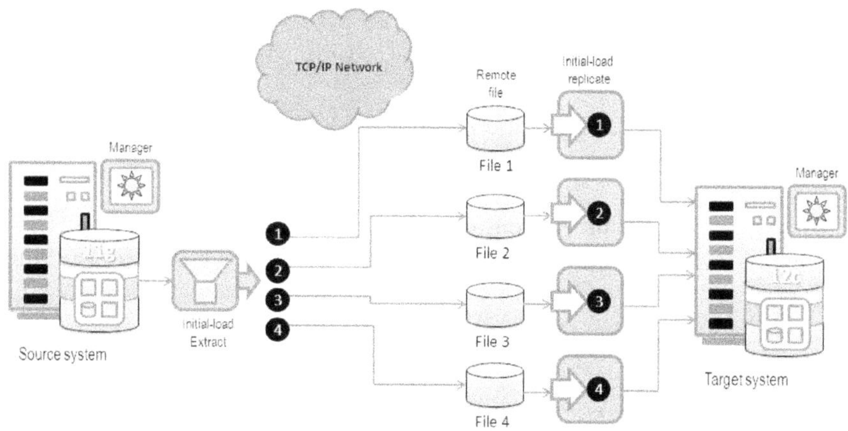

Figure 3-7: File to replicate initial-load using 4-degree parallel delivery groups

The parameter file eload02.prm configures an initial-load extract (ELOAD02) to support the following Oracle GoldenGate features.

- Password encryption
- Remote trail compression
- Remote trail encryption
- Multiple remote files
- Rows splitting for large tables

Password encryption and encryption key must be generated, otherwise the extract process terminates with an error.

```
GGSCI (ggs-source) 20> EDIT PARAMS eload02
```

```
SOURCEISTABLE
USERID ggs_admin@S1E2, &
-- Password encryption
PASSWORD AACAAAAAAAAAAAGAIFAAUDVHCFUGFIYF, ENCRYPTKEY default
RMTHOST ggs-target, MGRPORT 7812, COMPRESS, COMPRESSTHRESHOLD 512  &
-- Message Encryption
ENCRYPT blowfish, KEYNAME key1
-- Remote trail encryption and compression
ENCRYPTTRAIL AES128, KEYNAME key1
RMTFILE ./dirdat/initload, PURGE, &
-- Mutltiple remote file option
MAXFILES 100, MEGABYTES 10
TABLE osm$repapi.customers, &
-- Range processing
SQLPREDICATE "WHERE CUST_NO BETWEEN 100000 and 2000000";
TABLE osm$repapi.policies, &
```

```
SQLPREDICATE "WHERE CUST_NO BETWEEN 100000 and 2000000";
```

```
$ ./extract pf dirprm/eload02.prm rf dirrpt/eload02.rpt
```

Where *pf* stands for PARAMFILE and *rf* stands for REPORTFILE. Note that these can be used interchangeably.

The generated remote files using the RMTFILE options are composed of two parts: the specified file name sub-string appended with numbers staring at 000000. From the target server, list the remote files created from the above initial-load parameters file eload01.prm and extract session.

```
$ ls -al
total 552
drwxr-x---   2 oracle oinstall   4096 Oct 29 23:18 .
drwxr-xr-x 27 oracle oinstall   4096 Oct 29 23:07 ..
-rw-r-----   1 oracle oinstall 129315 Oct 29 23:18 initload000000
-rw-r-----   1 oracle oinstall   1507 Oct 29 22:36 ta000000
-rw-r-----   1 oracle oinstall    865 Oct 29 22:36 ta000001
-rw-r-----   1 oracle oinstall 407897 Oct 29 22:44 ta000002
$
```

Testing a GoldenGate initial-load extract

Now, because the initial-load extract ELOAD01 already created, it will be started from GGSCI command-line of the source system, which will create the initial load remote file on the target system. This will be used for testing purposes only.

```
GGSCI (ggs-source) 23> START eload01

Sending START request to MANAGER ...
EXTRACT ELOAD01 starting

GGSCI (ggs-source) 24>
```

Optionally, you may run the initial-load extract from the operating system prompt.

```
$ cd $GGS_HOME
$ pwd
/u01/app/oracle/ggs
$ ./extract PARAMFILE ./dirprm/eload01.prm REPORTFILE ./dirrpt/eload01.rpt
$
```

Before proceeding to configure and perform the initial-load replicat, we ensure that the remote file has been created on the target system specified by the parameter RMTFILE, which will be used by the initial-load replicate parameter EXTFILE.

```
$ pwd
/u01/app/oracle/ggs/dirdat
$ ls -al
total 101392
drwxr-x---  2 oracle oinstall      4096 Oct 29 22:01 .
drwxr-xr-x 27 oracle oinstall      4096 Oct 29 21:41 ..
-rw-r-----  1 oracle oinstall 103706277 Oct 29 22:01 initload01.dat
-rw-r-----  1 oracle oinstall      1507 Oct 29 21:42 ta000000
$
```

Verify a GoldenGate initial-load extract

Using GGSCI, different reports can be viewed. The following is the run time statistics portion view of the initial data load report. This report captures runtime parameters, runtime messages and runtime statistics. The runtime statistics section shows the transaction types and counts. We use this to investigate further when the discard count shows non-zero value.

```
GGSCI (ggs-source) 1> VIEW REPORT eload01
```

```
Processing table OSM$REPAPI.CUSTOMERS

Processing table OSM$REPAPI.POLICIES

***********************************************************************
*                   ** Run Time Statistics **                         *
***********************************************************************

Report at 2013-10-21 02:10:20 (activity since 2013-10-21 02:10:07)

Output to ./dirdat/initload01.data:

From Table OSM$REPAPI.CUSTOMERS:
       #                   inserts:    268187
       #                   updates:         0
       #                   deletes:         0
       #                  discards:         0
From Table OSM$REPAPI.POLICIES:
       #                   inserts:    267767
       #                   updates:         0
       #                   deletes:         0
       #                  discards:         0

REDO Log Statistics
  Bytes parsed                    0
```

```
  Bytes output           103704910

GGSCI (ggs-source) 2>
```

Configure, create and verify a GoldenGate initial-load delivery

Because the initial load data files created are in canonical format, a special initial load replicate process is created and run to read the remote files and applies to the target database tables. Table 3-4 lists the parameters used for the initial load replicate.

Configure a GoldenGate initial-load delivery

The initial-load replicate is a one-time replicate process. This is indicated by the run-time parameter SPECIALRUN. The parameter END RUNTIME causes the replicate process to stop as soon as it completes applying the current remote files.

Parameter	Description
SPECIALRUN	Designates this a special run process and does not use checkpoint file
END RUNTIME	The type of the extract, it will be on STOPPED status upon completing
USERID, PASSWORD	Database login credentials
ASSUMETARGETDEFS	The source and target uses the same table definition
HANDLECOLISSIONS	Handling collision using Oracle GoldenGate
EXTFILE	The name of the extract file
DISCARDFILE	The generated log file name and location for the initial load replicate
MAP	The mapping of table names between source and target

Table 3-4: Initial-load replicate parameters

```
GGSCI (ggs-target) 8> EDIT PARAMS rload01
```

```
REPLICAT rload01
SPECIALRUN
ASSUMETARGETDEFS
HANDLECOLLISIONS
USERID ggs_admin@T1C1, PASSWORD oracle
EXTFILE ./dirdat/initload01.dat
DISCARDFILE ./dirrpt/rload01.dsc, PURGE
MAP osm$repapi.*, TARGET osm$repapi.*;
END RUNTIME
```

The parameter ASSUMETARGETDEFS must be included, otherwise the extract program will not able to retrieve the table definition.

Create a GoldenGate initial-load replicate process

Before running the replicate program to perform target database instantiation, create the special run replicate. Using GGSCI ADD REPLICAT command and specifying the location of the initial data load file created by the initial load extract.

```
GGSCI (ggs-target) 9> ADD REPLICAT rload01, EXTFILE ./dirdat/initload01.dat
REPLICAT added.

GGSCI (ggs-target) 10>
```

```
GGSCI (ggs-target) 10> INFO ALL

Program     Status      Group       Lag at Chkpt  Time Since Chkpt

MANAGER     RUNNING
REPLICAT    STOPPED     RLOAD01     00:00:00      00:00:20

GGSCI (ggs-target) 11>
```

Testing a GoldenGate initial-load replicate

After configuring and defining the initial-load replicate, it's tested by starting the initial-load replicate process from GGSCI command-line.

```
GGSCI (ggs-target) 4> START REPLICAT rload01
```

```
Sending START request to MANAGER ...
REPLICAT RLOAD01 starting
```

Keep executing INFO ALL command until the status of the replicate process RLOAD01 change to STOPPED.

```
GGSCI (ggs-target) 5> INFO ALL
```

```
Program     Status      Group       Lag at Chkpt  Time Since Chkpt

MANAGER     RUNNING
REPLICAT    RUNNING     RLOAD01     383729:25:10  460:47:21
REPLICAT    STOPPED     RS1E201     00:00:00      460:42:04

GGSCI (ggs-target) 6>
```

Optionally, testing the initial-load replicate the Linux operating system shell prompt by executing the extract Oracle GoldenGate program using the argument PARAMFILE or abbreviation *pf*, and the argument REPORTFILE or abbreviation

```
$ cd $GGS_HOME

$ pwd

/u01/app/oracle/ggs

$ ./replicat PARAMFILE ./dirprm/rload01.prm REPORTFILE ./dirrpt/rload01.rpt
```

Verify a GoldenGate initial-load replicate

Using GGSCI, different reports are viewed with details using the *view report* command. The following is a view of the initial data load report. The report captures runtime parameters, runtime messages and runtime statistics. The runtime statistics section shows the transaction type and count to verify record count. Investigate further when the discard count shows non-zero value.

```
GGSCI (ggs-target) 15> VIEW REPORT rload01
```

```
Reading ./dirdat/initload01.dat, current RBA 103706277, 535954 records

Report at 2013-10-29 22:21:22 (activity since 2013-10-29 22:19:39)

From Table OSM$REPAPI.CUSTOMERS to OSM$REPAPI.CUSTOMERS:
       #                   inserts:    268187
       #                   updates:         0
       #                   deletes:         0
       #                  discards:         0
From Table OSM$REPAPI.POLICIES to OSM$REPAPI.POLICIES:
       #                   inserts:    267767
       #                   updates:         0
       #                   deletes:         0
       #                  discards:         0


Last log location read:
     FILE:      ./dirdat/initload01.dat
     RBA:       103706277
     TIMESTAMP: 2013-10-29 22:01:33.229775
     EOF:       NO
     READERR:   400
```

Another quick test can be performed using SQL*Plus as shown below. Because it's done on inactive database, the row-count result should always match.

Execute on source database

```
SQL> CONN osm$repapi/oracle@S1E2
Connected.
SQL> SELECT count(*)
  2  FROM   customers;
```

```
  COUNT(*)
----------
    268187
```

```
SQL> SELECT count(*)
  2  from   POLICIES;
```

```
  COUNT(*)
----------
    267767
```

Execute on Target database

```
SQL> conn osm$repapi/oracle@T1C1
Connected.
SQL> SELECT count(*)
  2  FROM   customers;
```

```
  COUNT(*)
----------
    268187
```

```
SQL> SELECT count(*)
  2  FROM   policies;
```

```
  COUNT(*)
----------
    267767
```

Configure a GoldenGate change data replicate group

The final step of configuring initial-load environment from an active database is the change data replicate group. The change data replicate group (RS1E201) reads the remote trail as shown in figure 3-6 and applies transactions to the target database. The configurable components for the change data replicate:

- Checkpoint database table
- Replicat group

Change data replicate group

The change data replicate group is composed of a run-time parameter file and a checkpoint table. After the server collector re-assemble the remote trail, the replicate process read the remote trail files and applies the transactions to the target database with data integrity and consistency.

GoldenGate Replicate parameter file

The replicate run-time parameters file lists parameters, sub-parameter and the associate values. Table 3-5 describes the parameters used by the replicate (RS1T201).

```
GGSCI (ggs-target) 12> EDIT PARAMS rs1e201
```

```
REPLICAT rs1e201
SETENV (ORACLE_SID=T1C1)
SETENV (NSL_LANG=AMERICAN_AMERICA.AL32UTF8)
USERID ggs_admin@T1C1, PASSWORD oracle
ASSUMETARGETDEFS
HANDLECOLLISIONS
DISCARDFILE ./dirrpt/rs1e201.dsc, PURGE
MAP osm$repapi.customers, TARGET osm$repapi.customers;
MAP osm$repapi.policies, TARGET osm$repapi.policies;
```

Parameter	Description
REPLICAT	Identifies the replicate group name
SETENV	Set environment for Oracle GoldenGate, avoiding warning messages
ASSUMETARGETDEFS	No transformation, source and target tables are identical
HANDLECOLLISIONS	Oracle GoldenGate handle initial-load data collision
DISCARDFILE	The transaction log file
MAP, TARGET	Mapped tables from source to target database

Table 3-5: change data replicate parameters

Creating a GoldenGate change data delivery

The change data delivery applies transactions to the target database. The data source is the remote trail identified by the parameter EXTTRAIL.

```
GGSCI (ggs-target) 13> ADD REPLICAT rs1e201, EXTTRAIL ./dirdat/ta
REPLICAT added.

GGSCI (ggs-target) 14>
```

```
GGSCI (ggs-target) 14> INFO ALL

Program     Status      Group       Lag at Chkpt  Time Since Chkpt
```

```
MANAGER     RUNNING
REPLICAT    STOPPED     RLOAD01     00:00:00      00:05:46
REPLICAT    STOPPED     RS1E201     00:00:00      00:00:30

GGSCI (ggs-target) 15>
```

We have concluded with the configuration the configuration and deployment of an initial-load from an active source database. The database was available for users while establishing the target database. Reference to the method is made throughout chapter 2. Refer to the section Deploying Oracle GoldenGate instance for details on deploying your instance configuration.

Method 2: GoldenGate Initial-load using direct load

The direct initial-load method uses an initial load extract for reading the source database tables, across TCP/IP sending data directly to the target system initial-load replicate. The special run replicate process applies the data to the target database using the database interface.

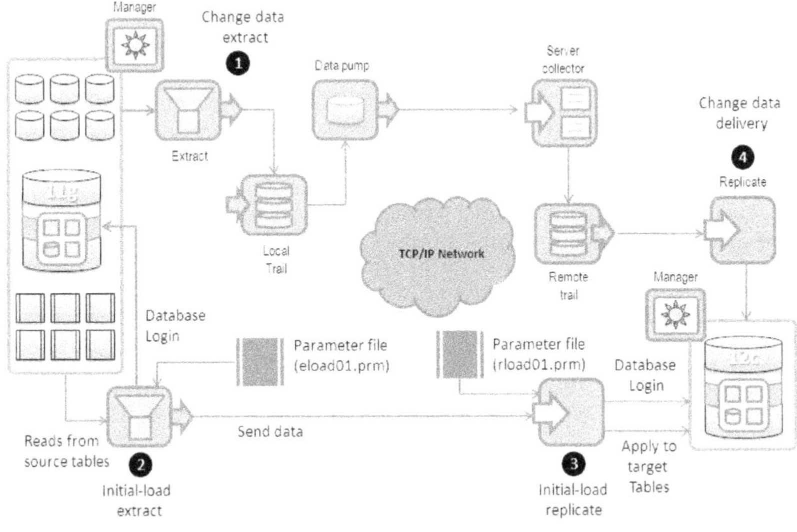

Figure 3-8: initial-load using direct method

This method is suitable for target systems that are already in-place and ready for perfuming initial-load, and it also eliminates the need of staging remote files on the target systems, thereby avoiding issue related to creating and managing remote files. Because this method is relatively slow, considerable timeframe should be allocated for the initial-load phase. Figure 3-8 depicts the configurable components of direct-load method.

Configure, create and perform a GoldenGate initial-load extract

In this example, the database is temporarily inaccessible to the users. The timeframe to perform initial-load extract and replicate depends on the size of the source database, during which the database remains unavailable to end-users due to *restricted* session mode. Because this method performs row-by-row insert operations using the database interface, it tends to be slow for very large database, where other methods are more suitable.

Configure a GoldenGate initial-load extract

The initial-load extract reads the source database table, then ships data across TCP/IP to the target replicate process, where it is ready to be applied to the target database. An advantage of the technique is handling data transformation processing at source, eliminating intensive processing at the target replicate.

```
GGSCI (ggs-source) 1> EDIT PARAMS eload03
```

```
EXTRACT eload03
USERID ggs_admin@S1E2, PASSWORD oracle
RMTHOST ggs-target, MGRPORT 7812
RMTTASK REPLICAT, GROUP rload03
TABLE osm$repapi.customers;
TABLE osm$repapi.policies;
```

Create a GoldenGate initial-load extract

Using GGSCI command, create the initial-load extract. This extract uses *sourceistable* parameter, which instructs the initial-load to read from the source database tables. Because it's a one-time extract, it's not performing checkpoint. Failure of the initial-load requires truncating the target tables and re-running the initial-load gain.

```
GGSCI (ggs-source) 2> ADD EXTRACT eload03, SOURCEISTABLE
EXTRACT added.
```

```
GGSCI (ggs-source) 3>
```

Configure, create and perform a GoldenGate initial-load replicate

The initial-load replicate receives and applies rows directly to the target tables. Even though this technique is relatively slow when used for large tables, the technique eliminates the storage overhead associated with staging data on remote files. Additional data transformations processing may occur prior to applying data by the replicate.

Configure a GoldenGate initial-load replicate

The initial-load replicate parameter file *rload.prm* defines an initial-load replicate. This is replicate is of type task and started by the initial-load extract. The replicate task process is stopped automatically when the initial-load extract and replicate is completed, as shown by the initial-load extract process.

```
GGSCI (ggs-target) 1> EDIT PARAMS rload03
```

```
REPLICAT rload03
USERID ggs_admin@T1C1, password oracle
ASSUMETARGETDEFS
HANDLECOLLISIONS
DISCARDFILE ./dirrpt/initload01.dsc, PURGE
MAP osm$repapi.*, TARGET osm$repapi.*;
```

Create a GoldenGate initial-load replicate

Using GGSCI command-line we can create the initial-load replicate. This replicate is referenced by the initial-load extract using the parameter *task*.

```
GGSCI (ggs-target) 2> ADD REPLICAT rload03, SPECIALRUN
REPLICAT added.

GGSCI (ggs-target) 3>
```

The *specialrun* parameter indicates the replicate process will start as special task, by the initial-load process, and will be terminated upon completing the initial-load replication.

Starting an initial-load extract

You have two options to start the initial-load extract, either from the operating system prompt, or from GGSCI command-line. Since the initial-load extract already created, using GGSCI is more flexible. Both options illustrated next.

```
GGSCI (ggs-source) 5> START EXTRACT eload03

Sending START request to MANAGER ...
EXTRACT ELOAD03 starting

GGSCI (ggs-source) 6>
```

Verify a GoldenGate initial-load operation

The initial-load extract and replicate is run as special task. We use the combination of *view report* command and *ps* operating system to verify successful completion of the load.

From the target system, use the operating system to verify the process is running.

```
GGSCI (ggs-target) 9> sh ps -edf | grep rload03

oracle   11187  4394  1 01:15 ?       00:00:00 ./replicat INITIALDATALOAD -
p 7819-12818 -m 7812 PARAMFILE /u01/app/oracle/ggs/dirprm/rload03.prm
REPORTFILE /u01/app/oracle/ggs/dirrpt/RLOAD03.rpt PROCESSID RLOAD03
USESUBDIRS
oracle   11203 10991  0 01:16 pts/2   00:00:00 sh -c ps -edf | grep rload03
oracle   11205 11203  0 01:16 pts/2   00:00:00 grep rload03
```

Also, using Oracle GoldenGate report show the operation completed on the target database. The output is a portion of the report showing Run Time Statistics details.

```
     GGSCI (ggs-target) 1> VIEW REPORT rload03
```

```
***********************************************************************
*                   ** Run Time Statistics **                         *
***********************************************************************


Report at 2013-10-30 01:26:35 (activity since 2013-10-30 01:25:07)

From Table OSM$REPAPI.CUSTOMERS to OSM$REPAPI.CUSTOMERS:
      #                   inserts:    269000
      #                   updates:         0
      #                   deletes:         0
      #                  discards:         0
From Table OSM$REPAPI.POLICIES to OSM$REPAPI.POLICIES:
      #                   inserts:    268580
```

```
#                        updates:          0
#                        deletes:          0
#                       discards:          0
```

Alternatively, use SQL*Plus for matching record counts.

```
SQL> CONN osm$repapi/oracle@S1E2
Connected.
SQL> SELECT count(*)
  2  FROM   customers;

  COUNT(*)
----------
    269000

SQL>
```

```
SQL> CONN osm$repapi/oracle@T1C1
Connected.
SQL> SELECT count(*)
  2  FROM   customers;

  COUNT(*)
----------
    269000

SQL>
```

This was quick implementation of initial-load from an inactive source database, it delivers consistent data readily available to configure change data capture and delivery for keeping the two database synchronized.

The next method uses Microsoft SQL Server as the source and target databases. It's implemented from an active source database.

Method 3: Initial data load using a GoldenGate database utility

This method is commonly used on homogenous environment where the source and target system running the same database type, the database the utilities used to establish the target database should support operating across different database releases, sometimes with minor restrictions and guidelines. Among the database utilities used for initial-load are: Oracle export and import data pump, Oracle Recovery Manager (RMAN), Microsoft SQL Server bulk copy program (BCP) and IBM LOADUTIL utilities.

In addition, in-house developed copy utilities across database network provides an added flexibility and control. For example, using an Oracle database link to create the remote SCOTT.EMP table, then use the same database link to perform insert operations remotely.

```
SQL> exec dbms_utility.exec_ddl_statement@t1e2('create table scott.emp -
>    as select empno, ename, job, mgr, hiredate from scott.emp where 1=2');

PL/SQL procedure successfully completed.

SQL> insert into scott.emp_target@t1e2(empno, ename, job, mgr, hiredate)
  2  select e.empno, e.ename, e.job, e.mgr, e.hiredate
  3  from   scott.emp e;

14 rows created.

SQL> commit;
```

However; Method 3 will be dedicated to Microsoft SQL Server using BCP utility. It proven to be a very effective tool for the vast majority of Microsoft SQL Server users.

What is Microsoft SQL Server Bulk Copy (BCP)?

Microsoft SQL Server BCP (Bulk Copy Program) is a high-performance command line utility for exporting and importing data between SQL Server instances and data files. Moving data using BCP is a two-phase operation. Data files are generated from the source database tables, then the data files are imported to the target database SQL Server instances. The BCP utility can also be used to generate formatted files which specify the number and type of data columns.
The BCP utility is often used as an Oracle GoldenGate initial-load database utility, because it quickly transfers large amounts of data by using BCP batch commit. This makes it suitable for very large database environment, performing very acceptable export and import performance.

The BCP utility operates on two directions. An OUT direction for performing an export from database tables to data files, and an IN direction for performing an import from data files to database tables. When running BCP utility, the command-line is composed of 4 parts: The table name (owner and table name and optionally database name), the direction either OUT or IN, the data file name and the command-line options. Table 3-6 lists common options, the complete list and detailed description about BCP utility available at Microsoft MSDN library homepage, *http://msdn.microsoft.com*.

option	Description
-e	Used to store any rows bcp is unable to transfer from the file to the database
-m	Maximum errors encountered before aborting current operation
-S	The instance of SQL Server to connect to or TCP/IP address
-T	Trusted authentication using the network user
-U	User login identifier
-P	User login password
-b	Batch size, the number of rows per batch of data copied
-a	Packet size, the number of bytes, per network packet, sent to and from the server
-c	Performs the bulk copy operation using a character data type

Table 3-6: BCP command-line common options

From the command-line, entering bcp.exe displays the options as shown in figure 3-9. When establishing the target database, BCP uses the basic options, however, BCP can also provide some kind of filtering for partial data transportation by using table query.

BCP utility transfer performance is largely controlled by the parameters *packetsize* and *packetsize*. The *packetsize* parameter specifies the number of bytes, per network packet, sent to and from the server using packet size. The *batchsize* parameter specifies the number of rows per batch of imported data. Each batch is imported and logged as a separate transaction that imports the whole batch before being committed. We always consider the proximity and the network bandwidth of the source and target systems when changing the default settings.

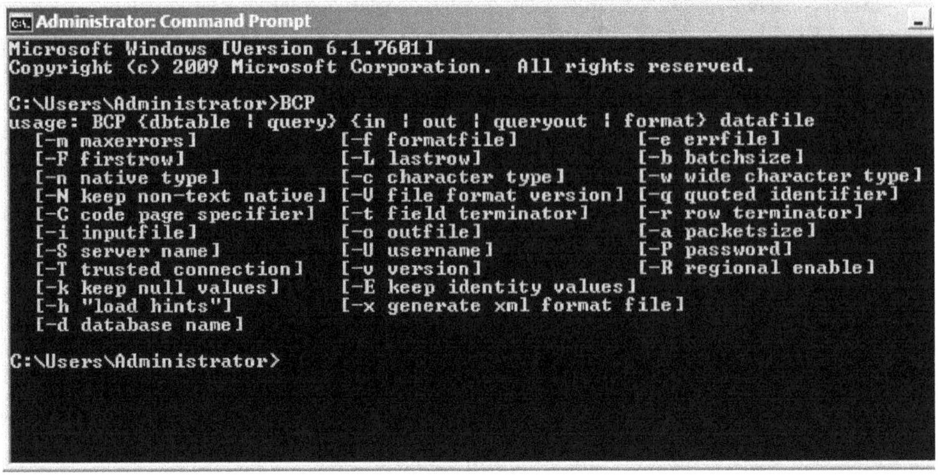

```
Administrator: Command Prompt
Microsoft Windows [Version 6.1.7601]
Copyright (c) 2009 Microsoft Corporation.  All rights reserved.

C:\Users\Administrator>BCP
usage: BCP {dbtable | query} {in | out | queryout | format} datafile
  [-m maxerrors]            [-f formatfile]          [-e errfile]
  [-F firstrow]             [-L lastrow]             [-b batchsize]
  [-n native type]          [-c character type]      [-w wide character type]
  [-N keep non-text native] [-V file format version] [-q quoted identifier]
  [-C code page specifier]  [-t field terminator]    [-r row terminator]
  [-i inputfile]            [-o outfile]             [-a packetsize]
  [-S server name]          [-U username]            [-P password]
  [-T trusted connection]   [-v version]             [-R regional enable]
  [-k keep null values]     [-E keep identity values]
  [-h "load hints"]         [-x generate xml format file]
  [-d database name]

C:\Users\Administrator>
```

Figure 3-9: SQL Server BCP utility command-line options

The process of using BCP to export tables from the source and import to the target systems are illustrated next. For large number of tables, create a batch file (.BAT) for processing the sequence of BCP commands non-interactively. Ensure to include –e for log file review.

Start the export command by running BCP using the *out* parameter. Use the *–e* and *–m* options to verify the export completion status. The BCP command below creates the data file for the table *customers.*

```
C:\>bcp s1t2.dbo.customers OUT c:\cust.bcp -T -c -m 0 -e c:\cust.log -T
```

View the log file to verify the export command successfully completed, then move the data files to the target system. Before starting the import BCP command, the table must exist on the target database and has identical table structure. Figure 3-10 shows MS-SQL Server Management Studio to generate tables *create table* statements. MS-SQL Server Management Studio generated script file includes the *create table* and supporting objects such as index and constraints.

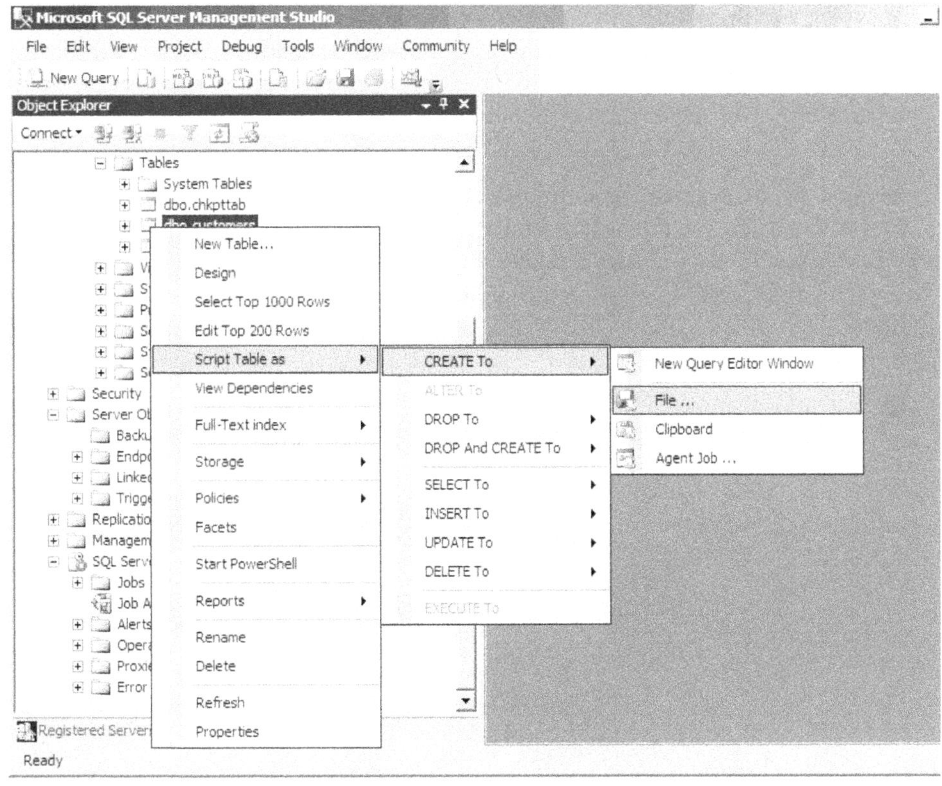

Figure 3-10: SQL Server Management Studio

```
CREATE TABLE [dbo].[customers](
    [cust_no] [int] NOT NULL,
    [cust_name] [varchar](64) NULL,
PRIMARY KEY CLUSTERED
(
    [cust_no] ASC
)WITH (PAD_INDEX  = OFF, STATISTICS_NORECOMPUTE  = OFF, IGNORE_DUP_KEY =
OFF, ALLOW_ROW_LOCKS  = ON, ALLOW_PAGE_LOCKS  = ON) ON [FGDAT01]
) ON [FGDAT01]
```

Start the import command, run BCP using IN parameter. Use the –e and –m options to verify the import completion status. The BCP command below import the CUSTOMERS data file to an MS-SQL Server instance.

```
C:\>bcp tle2.dbo.customers IN c:\cust.bcp -T -c -m 0 -e c:\cust.log
```

View the log file to verify the import command successfully completed. Additionally, use SQL Server Management Studio to run row-count and compare the result with the source database. Also, Oracle GoldenGate Veridata provides advanced data verify features.

Because we are performing an initial-load from an active MS-SQL Server-to-MS-SQL Server databases, the initial-load implemented using the 4-phase approach, supporting business continuity and data integrity. Figure 3-11 depicts the components for implementing initial-load using the source and target MS-SQL Server BCP database utility.

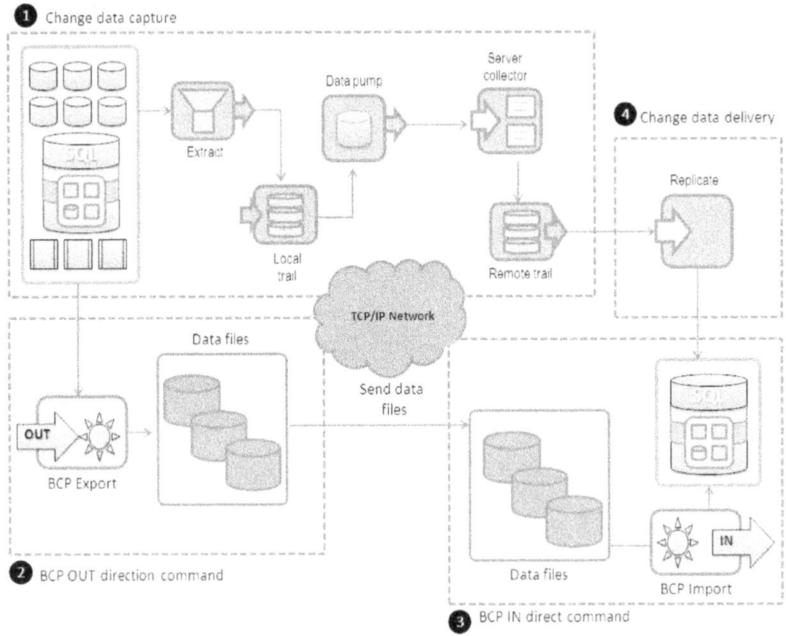

Figure 3-11: Initial data load using database utility

When performing the initial-load (regardless of the database type) the workflow is technically similar. The initial-load using MS-SQL Server BCP database utility 4-phase approach described next.

Phase 1: Configure Oracle GoldenGate change data capture (CDC) for MS-SQL

On the source system, we configure the change data capture (CDC), which composed of the primary extract, data pump extract groups, local trail and remote trail. The primary extract group creates the local trail, the data pump extract group routes to the target system where the server collector creates the remote trail. To maintain an optimized storage on the source system (production), the source manager process is configured to purge local trail files upon successfully routed to the target system, waiting for phase 4 to start applying them to the target database.

Phase 2: Start MS-SQL Server BCP export utility, out direction

While the change data capture is running, the source database BCP utility is started to create the data file for the tables listed on *table* extracts parameter. The data files is transported to the target system ready for tables import. At this point the target database tables must be available with enabled primary and/or unique key only, leave the foreign key disabled until the completion of the initial-load.

Phase 3: Start MS-SQL Server BCP import utility, in direction

While the change data capture extracts continue running, run the target database BCP utility to import the tables. We verify that the initial-load has been completed successfully, and this is considered to be a very crucial step before starting the next phase. Any table import failure should be fixed and re-run the BCP utility before proceeding with the next phase.

Record the completion time for the import phase and the current remote trail file sequence number, the information is needed for disabling collision handling.

Phase 4: Start Oracle GoldenGate change delivery

Now, once the change data capture has been running without interruption, and the initial-load is verified completed and successful y using BCP utility, it is time to start the Replicat process to apply the transactions to the target database using the database interface.

Let's now configure and deploy the different components required to perform initial-load where the source and target database running on MS-SQL Server 2008 Release 2, and MS Windows 2008 Release 2.

Configure GoldenGate extract groups for MS SQL

It's highly recommended to configure primary and data pump extract groups. The configuration of the optional data pump group ensures processing continues in cases of connectivity failure between the source and target systems. In the event of failure, the data pump extract will ABENEND due to disconnection, while the primary extract continues creating local trail files, waiting for the connectivity to be restored.

Before proceeding further, let's verify the TCP/IP communication between the source and the target system and the manager processes are running using GGSCI run as administrator. Figure 3-12 shows GGSCI running PING command from within GGSCI command-line.

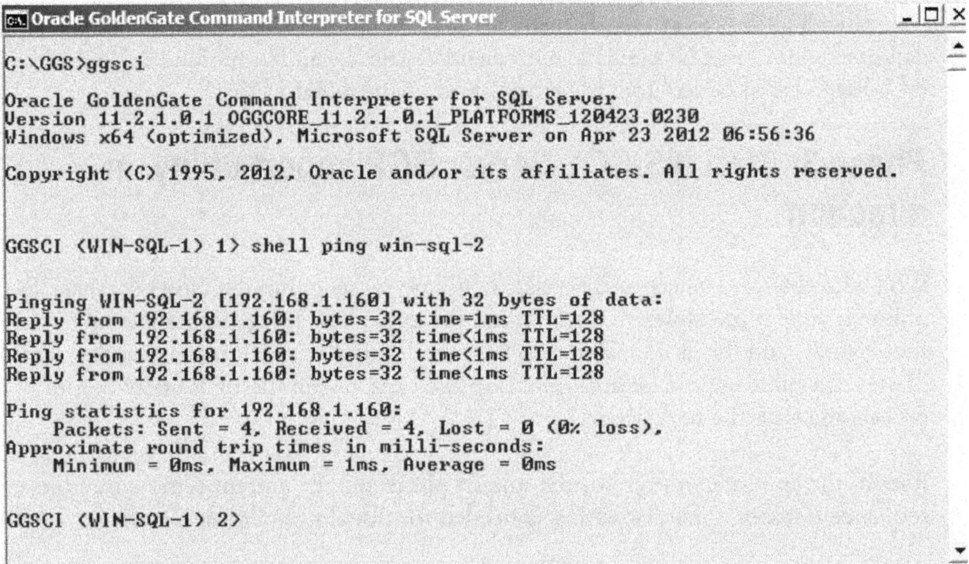

Oracle GoldenGate Command Interpreter for SQL Server
C:\GGS>ggsci
Oracle GoldenGate Command Interpreter for SQL Server
Version 11.2.1.0.1 OGGCORE_11.2.1.0.1_PLATFORMS_120423.0230
Windows x64 (optimized), Microsoft SQL Server on Apr 23 2012 06:56:36
Copyright (C) 1995, 2012, Oracle and/or its affiliates. All rights reserved.
GGSCI (WIN-SQL-1) 1> shell ping win-sql-2
Pinging WIN-SQL-2 [192.168.1.160] with 32 bytes of data:
Reply from 192.168.1.160: bytes=32 time=1ms TTL=128
Reply from 192.168.1.160: bytes=32 time<1ms TTL=128
Reply from 192.168.1.160: bytes=32 time<1ms TTL=128
Reply from 192.168.1.160: bytes=32 time<1ms TTL=128
Ping statistics for 192.168.1.160:
Packets: Sent = 4, Received = 4, Lost = 0 (0% loss),
Approximate round trip times in milli-seconds:
Minimum = 0ms, Maximum = 1ms, Average = 0ms
GGSCI (WIN-SQL-1) 2>

Figure 3-12: GGSCI for MS-SQL Server

```
C:\GGS>ggsci
```

```
Oracle GoldenGate Command Interpreter for SQL Server
Version 11.2.1.0.1 OGGCORE_11.2.1.0.1_PLATFORMS_120423.0230
Windows x64 (optimized), Microsoft SQL Server on Apr 23 2012 06:56:36
```

```
Copyright (C) 1995, 2012, Oracle and/or its affiliates. All rights reserved.

GGSCI (WIN-SQL-1) 1> INFO ALL

Program     Status      Group       Lag at Chkpt  Time Since Chkpt

MANAGER     RUNNING

GGSCI (WIN-SQL-1) 2> INFO MGR

Manager is running (IP port WIN-SQL-1.7810).
```

The source system manager is listening on TCP/IP port 7810. It's run as a default Oracle GoldenGate Windows service, GGSMGR.

```
C:\GGS>ggsci
```

```
Oracle GoldenGate Command Interpreter for SQL Server
Version 11.2.1.0.1 OGGCORE_11.2.1.0.1_PLATFORMS_120423.0230
Windows x64 (optimized), Microsoft SQL Server on Apr 23 2012 06:56:36

Copyright (C) 1995, 2012, Oracle and/or its affiliates. All rights reserved.

GGSCI (WIN-SQL-2) 1> INFO ALL

Program     Status      Group       Lag           Time Since Chkpt

MANAGER     RUNNING

GGSCI (WIN-SQL-2) 2> INFO MGR

Manager is running (IP port WIN-SQL-2.7811).

GGSCI (WIN-SQL-2) 3>
```

The target system manager is listening on TCP/IP port 7811, also using the default MS Windows service GGSMGR.

Both source and target Oracle GoldenGate instance use identical file system structure, use the SHOW ENV command to display the directory structures for Oracle GoldenGate installation.

```
GGSCI (WIN-SQL-1) 4> SHOW ENV
```

```
Parameter settings:

SET SUBDIRS    ON
SET DEBUG      OFF

Current directory: C:\GGS
```

```
Using subdirectories for all process files

Editor:  notepad

Reports (.rpt)                 C:\GGS\dirrpt
Parameters (.prm)              C:\GGS\dirprm
Replicat Checkpoints (.cpr)    C:\GGS\dirchk
Extract Checkpoints (.cpe)     C:\GGS\dirchk
Process Status (.pcs)          C:\GGS\dirpcs
SQL Scripts (.sql)             C:\GGS\dirsql
Database Definitions (.def)    C:\GGS\dirdef

GGSCI (WIN-SQL-1) 5>
```

MS-SQL Change data capture GoldenGate extract group

Now we start the GGSCI command-line as administrator. We create the change data capture (CDC) group named S1T2. The extract then reads the transaction log and writes to the local trail queue. The group composed of parameter files, checkpoint file and local trail.

GoldenGate Primary extract parameter file for MS-SQL

The primary extract requires run-time parameters, the name of the extract must match the parameter and checkpoint file names without the file extension. For the extract ES1T201 the parameter file name is *es1t201.prm* and the checkpoint file name is *es1t201.pce.* The default location of the parameter file is *C:\GGS\dirprm.* Table 3-7 lists the parameters used by the primary extract.

Parameter	Description
EXTRACT	The name of the primary extract
SOURCEDB	The database login details, using the data source name
TRANLOGOPTIONS	The change data capture for supporting platform specific option
EXTTRAIL	The local trail location and name
TABLE	The list of tables

Table 3-7: ES1T01 primary extract parameters

```
GGSCI (WIN-SQL-1) 9> EDIT PARAMS es1t201
```

```
extract es1t201
sourcedb s1t2, userid ggs_admin, password oracle
tranlogoptions managesecondarytruncationpoint
exttrail c:\ggs\dirdat\sa
table dbo.customers;
table dbo.policies;
```

When working with different Oracle GoldenGate releases, you will need to inform the recipient GoldenGate instance the version of the trail file. Use the *format* parameter when the target Oracle GoldenGate instance is version 11.1.

```
exttrail c:\ggs\dirdat\sa, format release 11.1
```

Creating GoldenGate change data capture extract for MS-SQL

Use the GGSCI command line to create the primary extract, ES1T201. The primary extract performs change data capture. The parameter *managesecondarytruncationpoint* is required when Oracle GoldenGate managing MS-SQL Server truncation point. We use the *add extract* command to add the primary extract.

```
GGSCI (WIN-SQL-1) 10> ADD EXTRACT es1t201, TRANLOG, BEGIN now
EXTRACT added.
```

Creating a GoldenGate local trail for MS-SQL

The primary extract writes to the local trail. The following command creates and associates the primary extract with a local trail identified by the prefix '*sa*'. The default size of the trail file is 100MB. We use *add exttrail* to add the local trail.

```
GGSCI (WIN-SQL-1) 12> ADD EXTTRAIL c:\ggs\dirdat\sa, EXTRACT es1t201,
MEGABYTES 10

EXTTRAIL added.
```

GoldenGate Data pump extract group for MS-SQL

For transporting the local trail files, a second group created, it's the data pump extract group. It's composed of a parameter file, a checkpoint file and a remote trail. The data pump reads the local trail and across TCP/IP communicates with a remote dynamic server collector, which in turn creates reassemble the data and creates the remote trail file.

GoldenGate Data pump extract parameter file for MS-SQL

The parameters file controls process runtime. We create the parameter file *epmp01.prm* for the first data pump, the data pump extract name is *epmp01*. Table 3-8 lists the parameters for the data pump extract.

```
GGSCI (WIN-SQL-1) 13> EDIT PARAMS epmp01
```

```
extract epmp01
passthru
rmthost win-sql-2, mgrport 7811
rmttrail c:\ggs\dirdat\ta
table dbo.customers;
table dbo.policies;
```

Parameter	Description
EXTRACT	The name of the data pump extract
PASSTHRU	Tables structure are identical without the use of @RANGE function
RMTHOST	The remote system hostname or IP address
MGRPORT	The port manager of the remote manager
RMTTRAIL	The location and name of the remote trail
TABLE	List of tables

Table 3-8: EPMP01 data pump extract parameters

When using Oracle GoldenGate @RANGE function for implementing multi-processing data pump extracts, you must use the *nopassthru* and *sourcedb* parameters.

```
extract epmp01
nopassthru
sourcedb s1t2, userid ggs_admin, password oracle
rmthost win-sql-2, mgrport 7811
rmttrail c:\ggs\dirdat\ta
table dbo.customers;
table dbo.policies;
```

Creating a data pump extract for GoldenGate for MS-SQL

From GGSCI, create the data pump extract. The data pump reads the transactions from the local and across TCP/IP forward transactions to the target system Server collector, which in turn reassemble data and create remote trail files. Use ADD EXTRACT command to create the data pump extract.

```
GGSCI (WIN-SQL-1) 14> ADD EXTRACT epmp01, EXTTRAILSOURCE c:\ggs\dirdat\sa
EXTRACT added.
```

Creating a remote trail for MS-SQL

Use the *add rmttrail* GGSCI command from the source system, which associate the data pump extract with the remote trail *'ta'*. It's recommended the local and the remote trails are the same size. The *megabytes* parameters specifies the trail file size.

```
GGSCI (WIN-SQL-1) 15> ADD RMTTRAIL c:\ggs\dirdat\ta, EXTRACT epmp01,
MEGABYTES 10

RMTTRAIL added.
```

Starting primary and data pump extracts for GoldenGate with MS-SQL

After starting the primary and data pump extracts, do not proceed further until verifying the remote trail is created and transactions are replicated on real-time. Use the INFO command on source and the LOGDUMP utility. The LOGDUMP utility opens one trail file at a time, perform search, display transaction details, transaction statistics and contents.

On the source system, issue INFO GGSCI command.

```
GGSCI (WIN-SQL-1) 1> INFO ALL

Program     Status      Group       Lag at Chkpt  Time Since Chkpt

MANAGER     RUNNING
EXTRACT     STOPPED     EPMP01      00:00:00      20:05:04
EXTRACT     STOPPED     ES1T201     00:00:00      20:05:04

GGSCI (WIN-SQL-1) 2> START er *

Sending START request to MANAGER ('GGSMGR') ...
EXTRACT EPMP01 starting

Sending START request to MANAGER ('GGSMGR') ...
EXTRACT ES1T201 starting

GGSCI (WIN-SQL-1) 4> INFO ALL

Program     Status      Group       Lag at Chkpt  Time Since Chkpt

MANAGER     RUNNING
EXTRACT     RUNNING     EPMP01      00:00:00      00:00:00
EXTRACT     RUNNING     ES1T201     00:00:00      20:05:17

GGSCI (WIN-SQL-1) 5>
```

On the target system, start LOGDUMP utility. Issue the COUNT command to display transaction details and summary, per table.

```
C:\GGS>logdump
```

```
Oracle GoldenGate Log File Dump Utility
Version 11.1.1.1.2 OGGCORE_11.1.1.1.2_PLATFORMS_111004.2100

Copyright (C) 1995, 2011, Oracle and/or its affiliates. All rights reserved.

Logdump 59 >open c:\ggs\dirdat\ta000003
Current LogTrail is c:\ggs\dirdat\ta000003
Logdump 60 >count detail
LogTrail c:\ggs\dirdat\ta000003 has 26489 records
Total Data Bytes            663388
  Avg Bytes/Record              25
Insert                       26488
Others                           1
After Images                 26488

Average of 26489 Transactions
    Bytes/Trans .....         73
    Records/Trans ...          1
    Files/Trans .....          1


*FileHeader*                                              Partition 0
Total Data Bytes              1188
  Avg Bytes/Record            1188
Others                           1

DBO.CUSTOMERS                                             Partition 4
Total Data Bytes            662200
  Avg Bytes/Record              25
Insert                       26488
After Images                 26488
Logdump 61 >
```

GoldenGate Data copy using MS-SQL BCP utility

Next, while the change data capture is running, we use the SQL Server BCP utility to create the data files for the source database tables. Before executing the BCP utility, we verify the primary extract and data pump extracts are running and remote trail files are generated for all remote trails.

Export database tables

Here we use the OUT direction to export database table using BCP utility. A data file is create for each database table exported.

```
# initial_out_bcp.bat
```

```
C:\>bcp s1t2.dbo.customers OUT c:\customers.bcp -T -c -m 0 -e c:\cust.log -T
C:\>bcp s1t2.dbo.policies OUT c:\policies.bcp -T -c -m 0 -e c:\pol.log -T
```

Import database tables

Now we use the IN direction to import the data files using BCP utility. The table structure should exist prior to importing data.

```
# initial_in_bcp.bat
```

```
C:\>bcp t1e2.dbo.customers IN c:\customers.bcp -T -c -m 0 -e c:\cust.log
C:\>bcp t1e2.dbo.policies IN c:\policies.bcp -T -c -m 0 -e c:\pol.log
```

Upon successful completion of tables import, It's important to know the time and the current remote trail file number, this is needed for disabling collision – see Disable collision handling section.

Configure and create change delivery Replicat groups for MS-SQL

Change delivery is performed by the Replicat processes of the target system. The Replicat group composed of one or more Replicat process, the checkpoint table, checkpoint file and runtime parameter file.

GoldenGate GLOBALS parameter file for MS-SQL

The global parameters globally controls Oracle GoldenGate runtime, these parameters may be overridden by the individual process parameters. For now, we will add the only parameter *checkpointtable*. This parameter used by the *add checkpointtable* command.

```
-- GLOBALS

CHECKPOINTTABLE ggs_admin.chkpttab
```

You must quit GGSCI and start it again for the global parameters to become effective.

Creating GoldenGate checkpoint table for MS-SQL

We use GGSCI command to create the checkpoint table used by the Replicat. Creating the checkpoint table requires us to login to the database using *dblogin* command.

```
GGSCI (WIN-SQL-2) 2> DBLOGIN SOURCEDB t1e2, USERID ggs_admin, PASSWORD
oracle
```

```
Successfully logged into database.
GGSCI (WIN-SQL-2) 3> ADD CHECKPOINTTABLE

No checkpoint table specified, using GLOBALS
specification(dbo.chkpttable)...

Successfully created checkpoint table DBO.CHKPTTABLE.
```

Using the checkpoint table for the Replicat is optional, but highly recommended. If you need want to use a checkpoint file, when creating the Replicat specify *nodbcheckpoint* option.

```
GGSCI (WIN-SQL-2) 4> ADD REPLICAT rs1t201, NODBCHECKPOINT, EXTTRAIL
c:\ggs\dirdat\ta

REPLICAT added.
```

GoldenGate Change data Replicat group for MS-SQL

The initial Replicat group configuration consists of a single Replicat process. Creating multiple Replicat processes to enhance change delivery performance required using Oracle GoldenGate @RANGE function, the @RANGE function takes two parameters: the Replicat process number and the total number of Replicat processes. The following illustrate how to use @RANGE to create degree of 4 replicates: RS1T201, RS1T202, RS1T203 and RS1T204.

```
MAP DBO.CUSTOMERS, TARGET DBO.CUSTOMERS, FILTER (@RANGE (1, 4));
MAP DBO.CUSTOMERS, TARGET DBO.CUSTOMERS, FILTER (@RANGE (2, 4));
MAP DBO.CUSTOMERS, TARGET DBO.CUSTOMERS, FILTER (@RANGE (3, 4));
MAP DBO.CUSTOMERS, TARGET DBO.CUSTOMERS, FILTER (@RANGE (4, 4));
```

GoldenGate Replicat parameter files for MS-SQL

We prepare the parameter file rs1t201.prm for the change delivery Replicat – RS1T201. The parameter file uses by default checkpoint database table. Table 3-9 lists the parameter for the Replicat process.

```
GGSCI (WIN-SQL-2) 5> EDIT PARAMS rs1t201
```

```
replicat rs1t201
targetdb t1e2, userid ggs_admin, password oracle
assumetargetdefs
handlecollisions
discardfile c:\ggs\dirrpt\rs1t201.dsc, purge
map dbo.customers, target dbo.customers;
map dbo.policies, target dbo.policies;
```

Parameter	Description
REPLICAT	The Replicat name
TARGETDB	Login to the database, using the ODBC data source name
ASSUMETARGETDEFS	The source and target tables are identical
HANDLECOLLISIONS	Handel collision during the initial load
DSCARDFILE	Log file for discarded record
MAP	List of mapped tables

Table 3-9: RS1T201 Replicat process parameters

Creating change delivery Replicat for MS-SQL

The last configuration step is to create the Replicat group. RS1T201 Replicat uses the remote trail to perform change delivery using the database interface.

```
GGSCI (WIN-SQL-2) 9> ADD REPLICAT rs1t201, EXTTRAIL c:\ggs\dirdat\ta

REPLICAT added.
```

Starting a GoldenGate replicate process for MS-SQL

Before starting the Replicat process, verify the primary and data pump extracts are running. Use the *send* and *info* commands to confirm the status.

```
GGSCI (WIN-SQL-2) 2> START REPLICAT *
```

```
Sending START request to MANAGER ('GGSMGR') ...
REPLICAT RS1T201 starting

GGSCI (WIN-SQL-2) 3> INFO ALL

Program     Status      Group       Lag           Time Since Chkpt

MANAGER     RUNNING
REPLICAT    RUNNING     RS1T201     00:00:00      00:22:15

GGSCI (WIN-SQL-2) 4>
```

Verify extract and replicate processes status

```
GGSCI (WIN-SQL-1) 1> INFO ALL

Program     Status      Group       Lag at Chkpt  Time Since Chkpt

MANAGER     RUNNING
EXTRACT     RUNNING     EPMP01      00:00:00      00:14:13
EXTRACT     RUNNING     ES1T201     00:00:00      00:00:02
```

```
GGSCI (WIN-SQL-2) 3> INFO ALL

Program     Status      Group       Lag           Time Since Chkpt

MANAGER     RUNNING
REPLICAT    RUNNING     RS1T201     00:00:00      00:22:15

GGSCI (WIN-SQL-2) 4>
```

You have completed a homogenous unidirectional topology of Oracle GoldenGate from MS-SQL Server-to-MS-SQL Server. The configuration is from an active source database requiring 4-phase approach. After the change delivery goes beyond the completion time of establishing the target database, it's necessary to disable collision handling implemented by the target Replicat – RS1T201. For details refer to Post initial-load section, at the end of the chapter. Also, you may need to consider enhancing the configuration for parallel data pump and Replicat processing, DDL replication and error handling.

Method 4: Initial data load using files to GoldenGate database utility using MS-SQL

This method uses database specific supported utility to establish the target database. For Oracle Database, the method uses Oracle SQL*Loader. For Microsoft SQL Server, the method uses one of three utilities BCP, DTS or SQL Server Integration Services (SISS). For IBM DB2 the method uses LOADUTIL. Hence, any kind of limitations are inherited from the database utility and not from Oracle GoldenGate, refer to the database utility documentations for limitations, if any. The initial-load file to database utility technique enables supporting heterogeneous environment by generating extract files in ASCII format that are compatible with the target database utility. For example, when the source database is Oracle database and target database is MS-SQL Server, the extract files in ASCII format generated from the source are compatible with BCP on the target database, and vice versa.

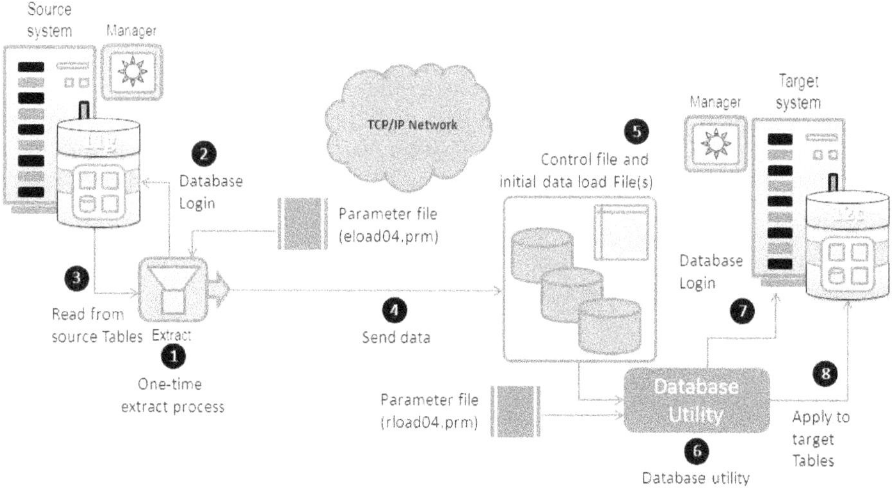

Figure 3-13: File to database utility initial-load method

The method will be illustrated on the basis of inactive source database. For details regarding establishing the target database from active source database, refer to method 1. Figure 3-13 shows the components from the platform of Oracle database-to-Oracle database, hence using Oracle SQL*Loader utility to establish the target database. However; when the method is implemented for very large database, the method should be performed from an active source database, which eliminates the considerable downtime of the source while generating the ASCII format files and establishing the target database using the database utility, SQL*Loader.

For Oracle database specific, the method creates the following components:

- Input data file
- SQL*Loader control file
- Shell command file (run file)

Input data file

The input data file data are delimited based on your Oracle GoldenGate configuration. The input data format is control by the parameter *formatascii* options. Usually, the data input is either space or comma delimited.

SQL*Loader Control file

The control file generated by Oracle GoldenGate initial-load Replicat uses the basic SQL*Loader options, however; this control file may be modified post-generation to suite the site additional requirements. The default SQL*Loader options used by Oracle GoldenGate are part of the template file used with GENLOADFILES parameter.

Shell command file (run file) for MS-SQL

This is the file you run on the target system. It's composed of the arguments required by Oracle SQL*Loader.

The initial-load replicate uses *genloadfiles* parameter, which uses a template file to generate the run and control files. The template file is shipped with Oracle GoldenGate, and need to be modified to suite your requirements, the template file name is sqlldr.tpl.

```
# Sqlldr.tpl

#
# File Names
#
controlfile ?target.ctl
runfile     ?target.run

#
# Run File Template
#
sqlldr userid=osm\$repapi/oracle control=/u01/app/ogg/11.2.0/?target.ctl
log=?target direct=true
```

```
#
# Control File Template
#
unrecoverable
load data
infile ?source.dat
truncate
into table ?target
```

For more details regarding SQL*Loader, refer to Oracle Database Utilities documentation available at *http://otn.oracle.com*

Configure, create input data file and verify initial-load extract for MS-SQL

Because the initial-load is from an inactive database, a 2-phase approach is used. Each phase is configured and implemented next.

Configure the initial-load extract for MS-SQL

Prepare the parameter files for the initial-load extract. The initial-load extract reads the source tables, and creates an ASCII file output designed by RMTHOST and RMTFILE parameters.

```
GGSCI (ggs-source) 1> EDIT PARAMS eload04
```

```
SOURCEISTABLE
USERID ggs_admin@S1E2, PASSWORD oracle
FORMATASCII SQLLOADER, &
            CHARSET UTF8, &
            NOHDRFIELDS, &
            NONAMES, &
            NULLISSPACE, &
            NOQUOTE, &
            DATE, &
            NOTRANSTMTS, &
            PLACEHOLDERS
RMTHOST ggs-target, MGRPORT 7812
RMTFILE ./dirdat/initload04.dat, PURGE
TABLE osm$repapi.customers;
```

Parameter	Description
SOURCEISTABLE	Instruct extract to read from the source table
USERID	Oracle GoldenGate database user, GGS_ADMIN
FORMATASCII	Instruct the extract to generate ASCII text output file
RMTHOST	The remote system IP address or DNS hostname
RMTFILE	The name and location of the data file generated on the remote system
TABLE	List of tables

Table 3-10: initial-load extract file

FORMATASCII parameter

The FORMATASCII parameter, when used an initial-load parameter, creates non-canonical formatted output files. FORMATASCII supports popular database load utilities for Oracle database, MS-SQL Server and IBM DB2.

To produce MS-SQL Server compatible external ASCII files, the extract parameter file uses FORMATASCII for BCP utility.

```
SOURCEISTABLE
TARGETDB S1E2, USERID ggs_admin, PASSWORD oracle
FORMATASCII, bcp
RMTHOST ggs-target, MGRPORT 7812
RMTFILE ./dirdat/initload04.dat, PURGE
TABLE osm$repapi.customers;
```

By default, FORMATASCII produces tab delimited ASCII output files, table 3-11 describes the most common arguments used for the parameter FORMATASCII.

Argument	Description
BCP, SQLLDR	BCP is for MS-SQL Server, SQLLDR for Oracle Database SQL*Loader
DELIMITER	The delimited character
NAMES, NONAMES	Include or exclude the name of the database objects
NOHDRFIELDS, IND, OP	Suppress everything thing, except data. IND include the Before and After image, OP is the transaction type (insert, update, or delete)
NOQUOTE	Excludes the quotation surrounding the values
DATE, TIME, TS	Include the DATE format, TIME format or TS timestamp

Table 3-11: FORMATASCII arguments

To produce '|' character delimited output, use the syntax:

```
FORMATASCII sqlloader, delimiter '|'
```

To produce a suppressed, exclude column names and quote, delimited, use the syntax:

```
formatascii sqlloader, nohdrfields, nonames, noquote, delimiter '|'
```

The placement of the parameter FORMATASCII is very important, it must be read before the effected parameters: RMTHOST, RMTFILE and TABLE.

Create SQL*Loader input data file

From within GGSCI command, use the SHELL command to execute the extract program. It takes the parameters: *pf* (parameter file) and *rf* (report file), using either relative or absolute file location and name. The command below uses *eload04.prm* for extract parameter file and *eload04.rpt* as the report file.

```
$ ./extract PARAMFILE dirprm/eload04.prm REPORTFILE dirrpt/eload04.rpt
```

Verify initial-load extract for MS-SQL

Use the VIEW REPORT command to verify the extract operation. The below partial output shows the Run Time Statistics for the initial-load extract.

```
$ pwd

/u01/app/oracle/ggs

$ cd dirrpt
$ vi eload04.rpt
```

```
Processing table OSM$REPAPI.CUSTOMERS

***********************************************************************
*                   ** Run Time Statistics **                         *
***********************************************************************

Report at 2013-10-26 03:09:29 (activity since 2013-10-26 03:09:11)

Output to ./dirdat/initload04.dat:

From Table OSM$REPAPI.CUSTOMERS:
       #                   inserts:    269000
       #                   updates:         0
       #                   deletes:         0
       #                  discards:         0


REDO Log Statistics
  Bytes parsed                    0
  Bytes output            123202000
```

Configure, create components and verify initial-load replicate

These steps are composed of creating the parameter file, customizing GENLOADFILES template file, generating the control file and run file for SQL*Loader, running SQL*Loader utility and verifying the result.

Configure initial-load replicate

The initial-load replicate (rload04) parameter file used by the replicate program.

```
GGSCI (ggs-target) 1> EDIT PARAMS rload04
```

```
SETENV (ORACLE_SID=T1C1)
SETENV (ORACLE_HOME="/u01/app/oracle/product/12.1.0/dbhome_1")
GENLOADFILES /u01/app/oracle/ggs/dirprm/sqlldr.tpl
USERID ggs_admin@T1C1, PASSWORD oracle
ASSUMETARGETDEFS
HANDLECOLLISIONS
EXTFILE ./dirdat/initload04.dat
DISCARDFILE ./dirrpt/initload04.dsc, PURGE
MAP osm$repapi.customers, TARGET osm$repapi.customers;
```

Parameter	Description
GENLOADFILES	Identify the location of the template file
USERID	Oracle GoldenGate database administrator
ASSUMETARGETDEFS	The source and target tables are identical
HANDLECOLLISIONS	Handle collision during initial-load
EXTFILE	The location and name of the data file
DISCARDFILE	The location and name of the log file for discarded records
MAP	The list of mapped tables

Table 3-12: initial-load replicate file

Create SQL*Loader components for GoldenGate

From within GGSCI, we use the SHELL command to execute replicate program (replicat). The program does not perform the actual initial-load, but generate the required files for running the database utility, SQL*Loader. A customized template file is used to generate the files.

```
#
# File Names
#
controlfile /u01/app/oracle/ggs/dirdat/?target.ctl
runfile     /u01/app/oracle/ggs/dirdat/?target.run
```

```
#
# Run File Template
#
sqlldr userid=osm\$repapi/oracle
control=/u01/app/oracle/ggs/dirdat/?target.ctl
log=/u01/app/oracle/ggs/dirdat/?target direct=true
```

```
#
# Control File Template
#
unrecoverable
load data
```

```
infile '/u01/app/oracle/ggs/dirdat/initload04.dat'
truncate
into table ?target
```

Run the replicat program using the argument pf (parameter file) and rf (report file).

```
$ pwd
/u01/app/oracle/ggs
$ ./replicat PARAMFILE dirprm/rload04.prm REPORTFILE dirrpt/rload04.rpt
```

Verify SQL*Loader components for GoldenGate

Upon completion of the above command, use *view report* command to display the operation details.

```
$ vi rload04.rpt
```

```
Process id: 7925

Description:

***********************************************************************
**           Running with the following parameters                  **
***********************************************************************

2013-11-01 14:44:33  INFO    OGG-03059  Operating system character set
identified as UTF-8.

2013-11-01 14:44:33  INFO    OGG-02695  ANSI SQL parameter syntax is used
for parameter parsing.
SETENV (ORACLE_SID=T1C1)
SETENV (ORACLE_HOME="/u01/app/oracle/product/12.1.0/dbhome_1")
GENLOADFILES /u01/app/oracle/ggs/dirprm/sqlldr.tpl
USERID ggs_admin@T1C1, PASSWORD ******
ASSUMETARGETDEFS
HANDLECOLLISIONS
EXTFILE ./dirdat/initload04.dat
DISCARDFILE ./dirrpt/initload04.dsc, PURGE
MAP osm$repapi.customers, TARGET osm$repapi.customers;

2013-11-01 14:44:33  WARNING OGG-06439  No unique key is defined for table
CUSTOMERS. All viable columns will be used to represent the key, but may not
guarantee uniqueness. KEYCOLS may be used to define the key.
Using following columns in default map by name:
  CUST_NO, CUST_NAME, CUST_EMAIL, CUST_MOBILE, CUST_ADDRESS

File created for loader initiation: /u01/app/oracle/ggs/dirdat/CUSTOMERS.run
File created for loader control:    /u01/app/oracle/ggs/dirdat/CUSTOMERS.ctl


2013-11-01 14:44:33  INFO    OGG-06451  Triggers will be suppressed by
default.
Load files generated successfully.
```

```
$ pwd
/u01/app/oracle/ggs
$ cd dirdat
$ ls -al CUSTOMERS.*
-rw-r----- 1 oracle oinstall 616 Nov  1 14:44 CUSTOMERS.ctl
-rwxr----- 1 oracle oinstall 135 Nov  1 14:44 CUSTOMERS.run
$
```

```
$ vi CUSTOMERS.ctl
```

```
load data
infile '/u01/app/oracle/ggs/dirdat/initload04.dat'
truncate
into table CUSTOMERS
(
  CUST_NO                          position(4:53)
                                   defaultif (3)='Y'
, CUST_NAME                        position(55:182)
                                   defaultif (54)='Y'
, CUST_EMAIL                       position(184:311)
                                   defaultif (183)='Y'
, CUST_MOBILE                      position(313:328)
                                   nullif (312)='Y'
, CUST_ADDRESS                     position(330:457)
                                   nullif (329)='Y'
)
```

```
$ vi CUSTOMERS.run
```

```
sqlldr userid=osm\$repapi/oracle
control=/u01/app/oracle/ggs/dirdat/CUSTOMERS.ctl
log=/u01/app/oracle/ggs/dirdat/CUSTOMERS direct=true
```

Perform GoldenGate initial-load operation

As indicated by the report file, the REPLICAT command generated the control file and the run file only, the command did not perform the actual data loading. Establishing the target database is done by running the run file for each table.

Navigate to the directory where the run file is create, and execute it as shown next.

```
$ pwd
/u01/app/oracle/ggs/dirdat

$ ./CUSTOMERS.run
```

```
SQL*Loader: Release 12.1.0.1.0 - Production on Fri Nov 1 14:51:21 2013

Copyright (c) 1982, 2013, Oracle and/or its affiliates.  All rights
reserved.

Path used:      Direct
```

```
Load completed - logical record count 269000.

Table CUSTOMERS:
  269000 Rows successfully loaded.

Check the log file:
  /u01/app/oracle/ggs/dirdat/CUSTOMERS.log
for more information about the load.
$
```

Verify the initial-load by querying the database, using COUNT(*) function.

```
SQL> CONN osm$repapi/oracle@T1C1
Connected.
SQL> SELECT COUNT(*)
  2  FROM   customers;

  COUNT(*)
----------
    269000

SQL>
```

Method 5: GoldenGate Direct bulk load for Oracle SQL*Loader

This method is exclusive to Oracle Database, and it is a robust technique for performing initial-load for Oracle databases by using bulk data movement from source to target databases.

On the source system, Oracle GoldenGate initial-load extract reads the source database tables, then communicates directly with the target system SQL*Loader direct path API (DPAPI) to establish the remote database, without the involvement of Oracle GoldenGate server collector process for reassembling extract files, making the technique is suitable for very large database (VLDB). Figure 3-14 shows direct bulk load for Oracle SQL*Loader configurable components.

To enable high-performance parallel processing for this method, concurrent processing should be configured at the source database. This is done by grouping tables among separate initial-load extracts, or by using *sqlpredidate* clause in the case of large tables.

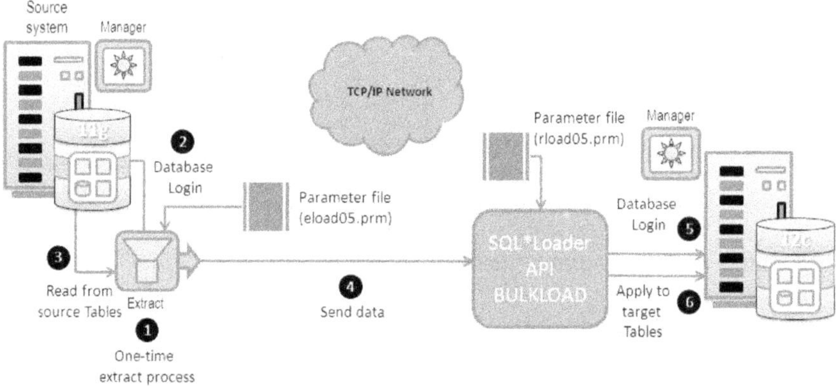

Figure 3-14: Direct-bulk load components

Because Oracle SQL*Loader runs within the target system only, regardless of your source database version, direct bulk load will be supported on target. As an example, when the source system is Oracle Database 11g and the target system is Oracle Database 12c. In this environment, the initial-load extract process on source system transparently communicates with the replicate process running on the target system. This feature nominates the method for upgrade and migration projects, where downtime may be eliminated or minimized.

What is Oracle direct-path load?

The direct-path load is a feature available for different Oracle database utilities such as SQL*Loader. When performing an insert operation using direct-path, the operation perform unconventional database transactions, delivering high-performance because direct-path load bypass the overhead associated with conventional transaction by formatting Oracle data blocks and writing the data blocks *directly* to the data files. Also, direct-path load uses data save to write blocks of data to Oracle data files, making it faster than using COMMIT. Additionally, direct-path load:

- Merge index entries at the end of the load operation
- Do not generate redo log entries under specific conditions
- Enforces primary key, unique and NOT NULL
- Do not fire INSERT triggers
- Prevent other users from making changes to tables
- Writes after beyond the table high water mark (HWM)
- Avoid data conversion

The above contributes to make data operation using direct-path load faster than conventional load. Tests have demonstrated direct-path load is even much faster, when combined with *unreciverable* option. The following configuration developed for an inactive source database, hence the database is placed on restricted session during the timeframe of establishing the target database. For more details regarding configuring from active database, see details presented for method 1.

Configure and create GoldenGate initial-load extract

Using Oracle SQL*Loader API (Application Programmatic Interface) is an out-of-the-box technique for performing Oracle-to-Oracle initial-load for establishing the target database. However; before starting the initial-load, the Oracle GoldenGate database administrator needs the following database system privileges, on the target database.

```
SQL> CONN / AS SYSDBA

Connected.

SQL> GRANT INSERT ANY TABLE TO ggs_admin;

Grant succeeded.

SQL> GRANT LOCK ANY TABLE TO ggs_admin;

Grant succeeded.
```

Configure the initial-load extract

The initial-load extract parameter file uses the basic parameters, necessary to read the source tables. Because this method do not support data transformation on target, in the case of data transformation requirements, it has to be developed on the source system, or on the intermediate system, if used.

Table 3-13 lists and describes the parameters used by the initial-load process runtime.

```
GGSCI (ggs-source) 1> EDIT PARAMS eload05
```

```
EXTRACT eload05
USERID ggs_admin@S1E2, PASSWORD oracle
RMTHOST ggs-target, MGRPORT 7812
RMTTASK REPLICAT, GROUP rload05
TABLE osm$repapi.customers;
TABLE osm$repapi.policies;
```

Parameter	Description
EXTRACT	Identify the name of the extract process, same as the extract group name
USERID	Database username and password
RMTHOST	The target system, IP address or DNS configured hostname
MGRPORT	The target manager TCP/IP
RMTTASK	Communicate with a remote replicate process of type task
GROUP	The remote replicate process name
TABLE	List of tables

Table 3-13: initial-load extract parameter file

Create the initial-load extract

From GGSCI, create the extract group, *eload05*. The parameter *sourceistable* instructs the initial-load extract process to read the source database tables, no checkpoint created for this type of extract process. This source extract process directly communicates with the target replicate process (*rload05*), which in turn uses SQL*Loader API interface.

```
GGSCI (ggs-source) 3> ADD EXTRACT eload05, SOURCEISTABLE
EXTRACT added.

GGSCI (ggs-source) 4>
```

Configure and create the GoldenGate initial-load replicate

When using this method, before starting the initial-extract process, the initial-load replicate group must be defined by preparing the parameter file and created using GGSCI ADD REPLICAT command, as it will be referenced and started by the initial-load extract. Because this replicate is of special run process and treated as a task, it's started automatically by the source extract process.

Configure the initial-load replicate for SQL*Loader

This method designed for Oracle SQL*Loader only, but it works across database versions. Using the replicate parameter BULKLOAD, it internally invokes SQL*Loader API to directly perform a bulk insert operations on the target database.

```
GGSCI (ggs-target) 1> EDIT PARAMS rload05
```

```
REPLICAT rload05
USERID ggs_admin@T1C1, PASSWORD oracle
BULKLOAD
ASSUMETARGETDEFS
HANDLECOLLISIONS
```

```
DISCARDFILES ./dirrpt/initload05.dsc, PURGE
MAP osm$repapi.*, TARGET osm$repapi.*;
```

Parameter	Description
REPLICAT	Identify the name of the extract process, same as the extract group name
USERID	Database username and password
BULKLOAD	SQL*Loader direct interface to the target database
ASSUMETARGETDEFS	The source and target database table definition are identical
HANDLECOLISSIONS	Handle collision during the initial-load
DISCARDFILE	Log file for reject records
MAP	Mapped tables statement

Table 3-14: initial-load replicate parameter file

Create the initial-load replicate

Use GGSCI ADD REPLICAT command to create the initial-load replicate as a special run task. A task is a process that is started dynamically by the manager process and does not require the use of a collector process or file, and terminates upon completion.

```
GGSCI (ggs-target) 2> ADD REPLICAT rload05, SPECIALRUN
REPLICAT added.

GGSCI (ggs-target) 3>
```

Start the initial-load extract

After successfully configuring and creating the initial-load extract and replicate, it's time to start the initial-load process only. Because the initial-load replicate created as a special task, the replicate process (RLOAD05) is started dynamically by starting the extract process, running as a background process.

```
GGSCI (ggs-source) 8> START EXTRACT eload05

Sending START request to MANAGER ...
EXTRACT ELOAD05 starting

GGSCI (ggs-source) 9>
```

Verify the initial-load extract and replicate

During the initial-load extract, tables are read serially as listed on the parameter file. Hence, it's important not to consider referential integrity constraints violation. Because it's run as a background process, using the operating system, Oracle GoldenGate *ggsci send* and *view report* commands, SQL*Plus provide current running status.

- The operating system provide process status details. Additional command can be used to monitor CPU and memory utilization by the initial-load process. Run the operating system '*ps*' command from source and target systems.

```
GGSCI (ggs-source) 15> shell ps -edf | grep ELOAD05
```

```
oracle    4113  4003  2 02:13 ?        00:00:00
/u01/app/oracle/ggs/extract PARAMFILE
/u01/app/oracle/ggs/dirprm/eload05.prm REPORTFILE
/u01/app/oracle/ggs/dirrpt/ELOAD05.rpt PROCESSID ELOAD05 USESUBDIRS
oracle    4126  4055  0 02:13 pts/1    00:00:00 sh -c ps -edf | grep
ELOAD05
oracle    4128  4126  0 02:13 pts/1    00:00:00 grep ELOAD05
```

```
GGSCI (ggs-target) 7> shell ps -edf | grep RLOAD05
```

```
oracle    5286  4975  7 13:05 ?        00:00:05 ./replicat
INITIALDATALOAD -p 7819-12818 -m 7812 PARAMFILE
/u01/app/oracle/ggs/dirprm/rload05.prm REPORTFILE
/u01/app/oracle/ggs/dirrpt/RLOAD05.rpt PROCESSID RLOAD05 USESUBDIRS
oracle    5327  4971  0 13:06 pts/3    00:00:00 sh -c ps -edf | grep
RLOAD05
oracle    5329  5327  0 13:06 pts/3    00:00:00 grep RLOAD05

GGSCI (ggs-target) 8>
```

- Use GGSCI to send a report request, this provides current read/write details. Because it's an initial-load process, INSERT statistics are shown only. The following is the section from the report for *Run Time Statistics*, only.

```
GGSCI (ggs-source) 17> SEND EXTRACT eload05, REPORT
```

```
Sending REPORT request to EXTRACT ELOAD05 ...
Request processed.

GGSCI (ggs-source) 18> VIEW REPORT eload05

Processing table OSM$REPAPI.CUSTOMERS

2013-10-26 02:17:08  INFO    OGG-01021  Command received from GGSCI:
REPORT.
```

```
*************************************************************************
*                   ** Run Time Statistics **                           *
*************************************************************************

Report at 2013-10-26 02:17:08 (activity since 2013-10-26 02:16:48)

Output to rload05:

From Table OSM$REPAPI.CUSTOMERS:
       #                  inserts:        532
       #                  updates:          0
       #                  deletes:          0
       #                 discards:          0


*************************************************************************
**                     Run Time Warnings                               **
*************************************************************************
```

- Iteratively running SQL*Plus COUNT(*) to confirm initial-load is progressing on the target database.

```
SQL> SELECT COUNT(*)
  2  FROM   osm$repapi.customers;

  COUNT(*)
----------
    269000
```

Post successful initial-load operations

Now the initial-load is successfully completed. The change data capture and change delivery keep synchronizing the target database on real-time. Monitoring the lagging time is important for further enhancement of the existing extract-replicat groups.

The following post initial-load are deemed necessary to be completed, and most important is collision handling.

Disable GoldenGate collision handling

When performing initial data load using Oracle GoldenGate, data collision is handled by Oracle GoldenGate. Adding the parameter *handlecolissions* to the initial data load, it internally resolves collision thus avoiding terminating the initial load process due to record duplication, for example. The collision resolution is based on the transaction system change number (SCN) and type. After the initial load completes, collision handling should be disabled using the steps below.

1. Send disable signal to the replicat group

```
GGSCI (ggs-target) 5> SEND REPLICAT rs1e201, NOHANDLECOLLISIONS,
osm$repapi.*
```

```
Sending NOHANDLECOLLISIONS, request to REPLICAT RS1E201 ...
RS1E201 NOHANDLECOLLISIONS set for 0 tables and 2 wildcard entries.

GGSCI (ggs-target) 6>
```

2. Edit the replicat parameter file by commenting or removing the *handlecolissions* parameter. This ensures collision handling feature remains disabled on next startup.

```
GGSCI (ggs-target) 6> EDIT PARAMS rs1e201
```

```
REPLICAT rs1e201
SETENV (ORACLE_SID=T1C1)
SETENV (NSL_LANG=AMERICAN_AMERICA.AL32UTF8)
USERID ggs_admin@T1C1, PASSWORD oracle
ASSUMETARGETDEFS
-- HANDLECOLLISIONS
DISCARDFILE ./dirrpt/rs1e201.dsc, PURGE
MAP osm$repapi.customers, TARGET osm$repapi.customers;
MAP osm$repapi.policies, TARGET osm$repapi.policies;
```

Drop GoldenGate initial-load replicates

The initial-load replicate is a one-time operation, preferably drop the replicat group to avoid applying destructive commands when using wild-card to manage the target's extract and replicat groups. Dropping a group requires logging to the target database, ensure the group status is *stopped*, then issue the GGSCI *delete* command.

```
GGSCI (ggs-target) 7> INFO ALL
```

```
Program     Status      Group       Lag at Chkpt  Time Since Chkpt

MANAGER     RUNNING
REPLICAT    STOPPED     RLOAD01     00:00:00      62:53:04
REPLICAT    RUNNING     RS1E201     00:00:00      00:00:04
```

```
GGSCI (ggs-target) 8> DBLOGIN USERID ggs_admin@T1C1, PASSWORD oracle
Successfully logged into database.
```

```
GGSCI (ggs-target) 9> DELETE REPLICAT rload01
Deleted REPLICAT RLOAD01.
```

Non-Oracle GoldenGate initial load techniques

For homogenous environments, such as Oracle-to-Oracle change data capture and replication, the initial load may be best performed using techniques outside of Oracle GoldenGate. These techniques luck the heterogeneity and transformation features, but normally provides faster initial load process, when compared with native Oracle GoldenGate techniques.

Initial-load using Oracle data pump utility over network database link

A real bonus of Oracle database data pump utility is online import of data across the network. This feature requires creating a database link between source and target databases. This nominates Oracle data pump utility is one of the preferred Oracle database utilities for initial-load using database utility technique – see method 3. Furthermore, when using Oracle data pump utility using database link, it eliminates staging of data dump files on target system or both systems, saving disk storage proportional to the database size.

Additionally, Oracle GoldenGate benefits from the data pump utility export and import table's metadata only feature, using the parameter *content=metadata_only*. The import utility creates database objects initialized, without data, then Oracle GoldenGate initial-load techniques establishes the target database, assuming identical source and target table definitions.

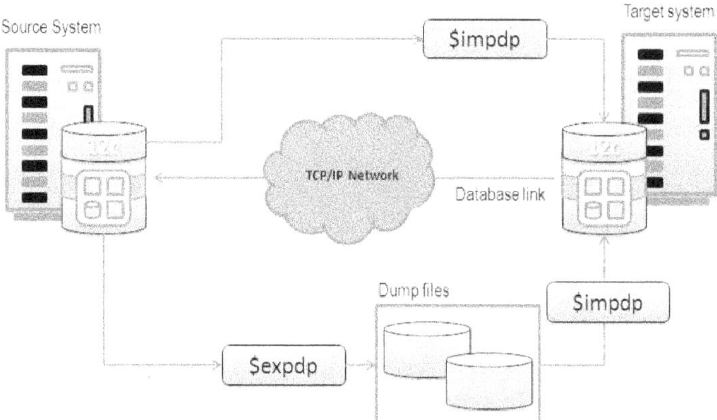

Figure 3-15: Oracle data pump utility over network link

Figure 3-15 depicts Oracle data pump utility components when configured to perform online import over a network link between the source and target databases.

When using Oracle database export and import data pump utility using a database link parameter, two options are available:

- The export utility (*expdp*) from within the target system uses *network_link* parameter to perform data export across the network, this method creates dump files on the target system only, designated by the expdp parameter DIRECTORY.

- The import utility (*impdp*) from within the target system uses *network_link* parameter to establish the target database. This is an online operation from source to target database, eliminating the disk storage for storing the dump files and explicitly performing an import operation on the target database, hence, treated suitable for very large database (VLDB).

The following steps illustrate importing data online into the target database using the impdp utility with *network_link* parameter.

- Create the database directory, where dump and log files are stored.

```
SQL> CREATE DIRECTORY impdir2 as '/home/oracle';

Directory created.

SQL> GRANT ALL ON DIRECTORY impdir2 TO public;

Grant succeeded.
```

- Create the database link from target to source.

```
SQL> CREATE PUBLIC DATABASE LINK s1e2.precisetrace.com
  2  CONNECT TO osm$repapi IDENTIFIED BY oracle
  3  USING 'S1E2';
```

```
Database link created.
```

- Execute the import utility from within the target system to import data online on the target database, using the database link name for the parameter NETWORK_LINK.

```
$ impdp system/oracle_4U@S1E2 TABLES=osm$repapi.customers,
osm$repapi.policies NETWORK_LINK=S1E2.precisetrace.com DIRECTORY=IMPDIR2
LOGFILE=impdir2.log
```

The data pump utility performs compatibility check between source and target database versions. The above import utility is executed between two databases running Oracle Database 11g. Additional impdp utility parameters are applicable when combined with the *network_link* parameter.

Microsoft SQL Server Integration Services

SQL Server Integration Services (SSIS) is an initial-load option for homogenous and heterogeneous database environments. It's one of the best options used when performing initial-load from Oracle database to MS-SQL Server and vice versa.

Installing Oracle database client

SSIS is part of MS-SQL Management studio. However to enable connection to an Oracle database, it requires installing Oracle database client, and configure a database connection using Oracle Network configuration assistant (NETCA). Figure 3-16 shows NETCA wizard.

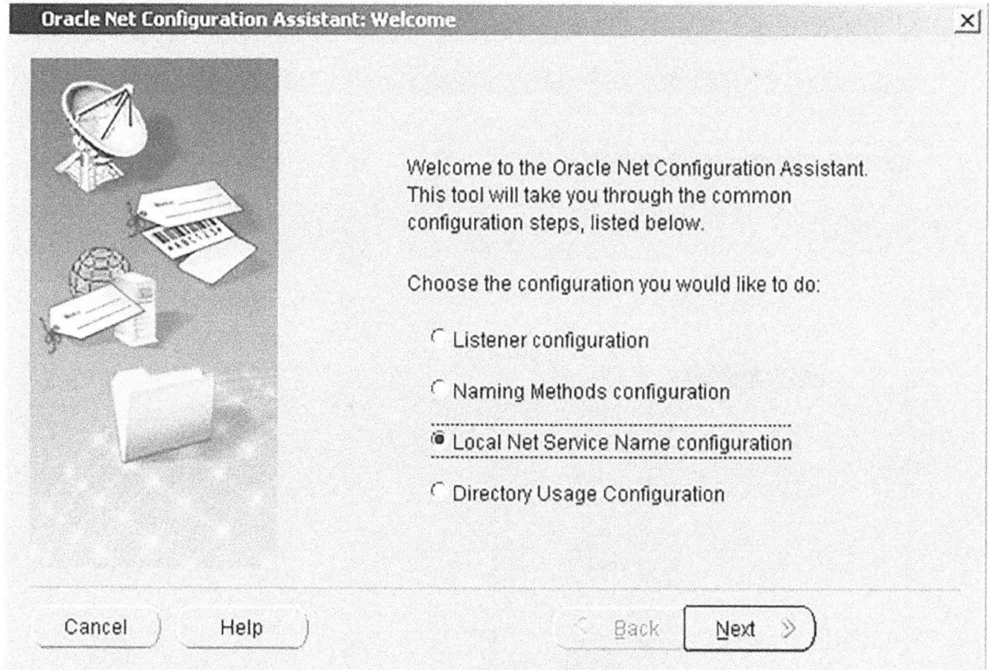

Figure 3-16: Oracle network configuration assistant (NETCA)

After creating the local net service name, start Oracle SQL*Plus for testing the connection to Oracle database before starting SSIS export and import utility.

```
C:\> sqlplus /nolog

SQL*Plus: Release 11.2.0.1.0 Production on Sun Dec 8 12:51:28 2013

Copyright (c) 1982, 2010, Oracle.  All rights reserved.

SQL> CONN system/oracle_4U@T1C1

Connected.
```

Using SSIS for initial-load

From the Task menu, select Export data to start an 8-step wizard for moving data from source to target system. During the process the wizard supports table mapping, column transformation from source to target. The following illustrates running export data wizard to move data from the source MS-SQL Server database to the target Oracle database. As shown on figure 3-17, right-mouse click, select Task then Export Data option, this starts SSIS export and import utility.

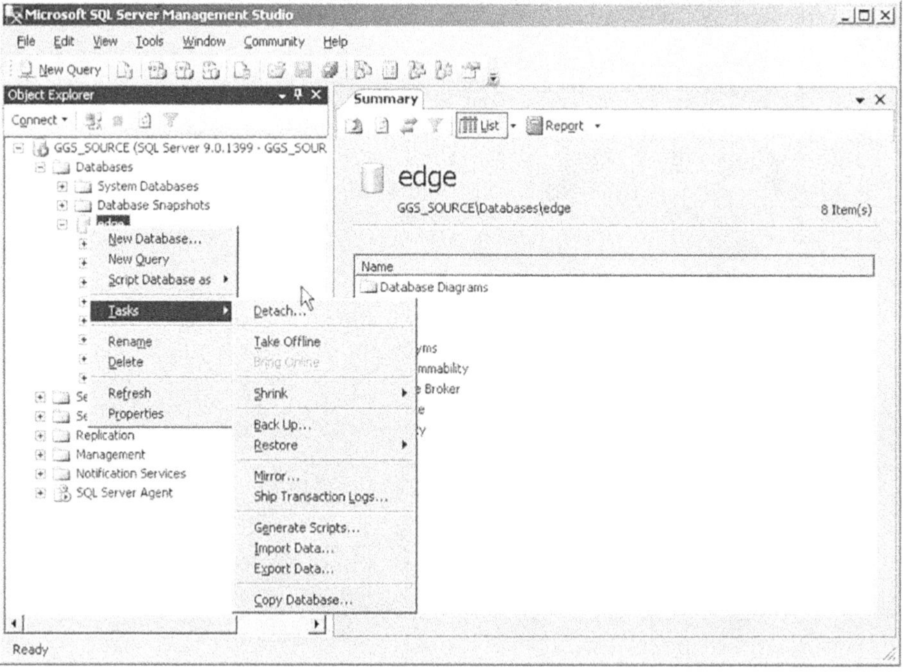

Figure 3-17: SSIS, Export Data wizard

The 8-step wizard runtime is illustrated on figure 3-18 through figure 3-26. We select the source database and the authentication method as shown in figure 3-19. Figure 3-20 defines the target database connection, click on properties to enter the remote Oracle database TNS connection, username and password, before proceeding further ensure the connection test is successful. Figure 3-23 for table selection, de-selection, columns mapping and creation options. Prefix the table name with schema name to create the remote table with a different owner.

On figure 3-24 click finish to start the initial-load process for the selected tables. Monitor the completion status as illustrated on figure 3-26.

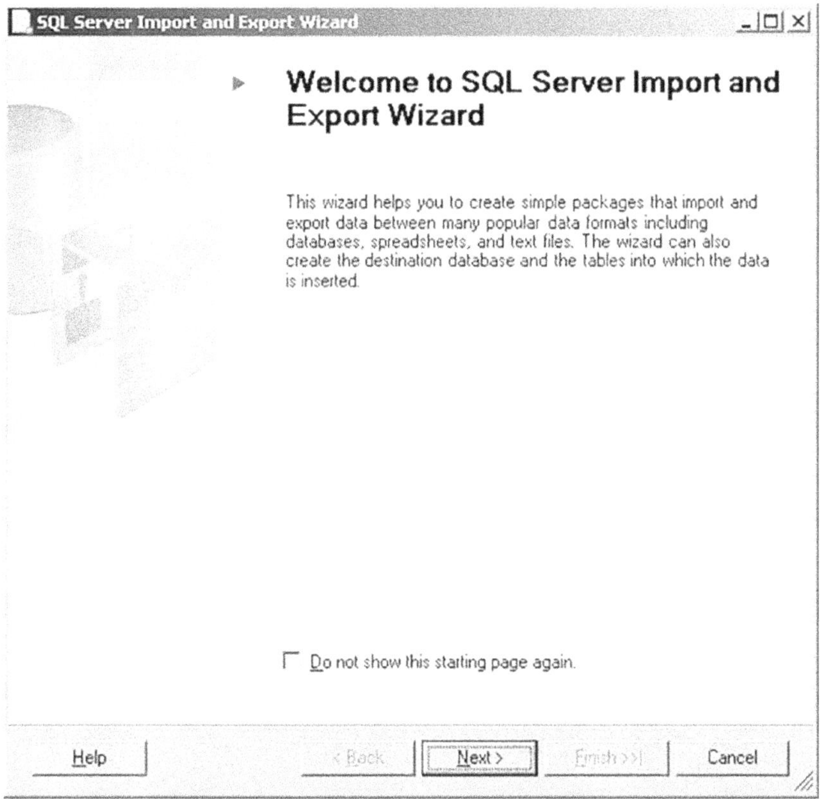

Figure 3-18: Start SQL Server export and import startup

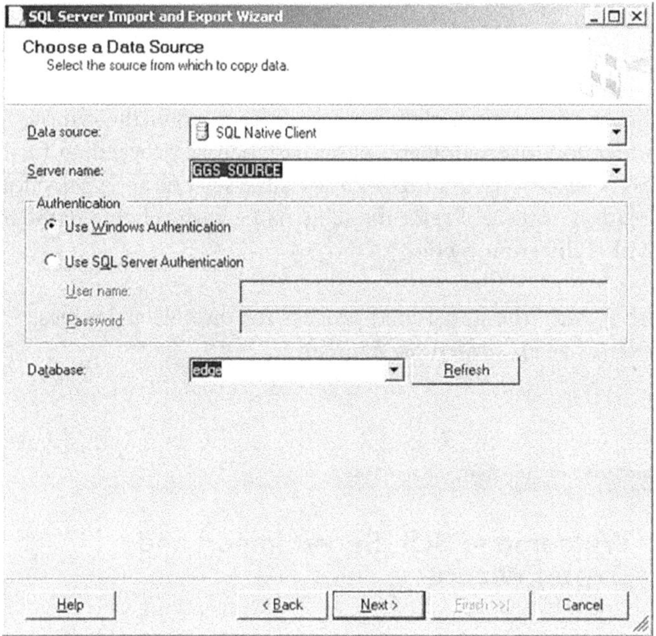

Figure 3-19: Select the source database

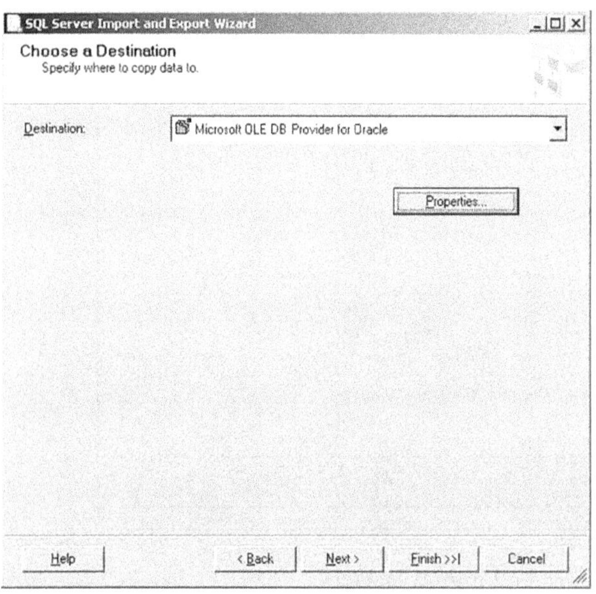

Figure 3-20: Select the destination

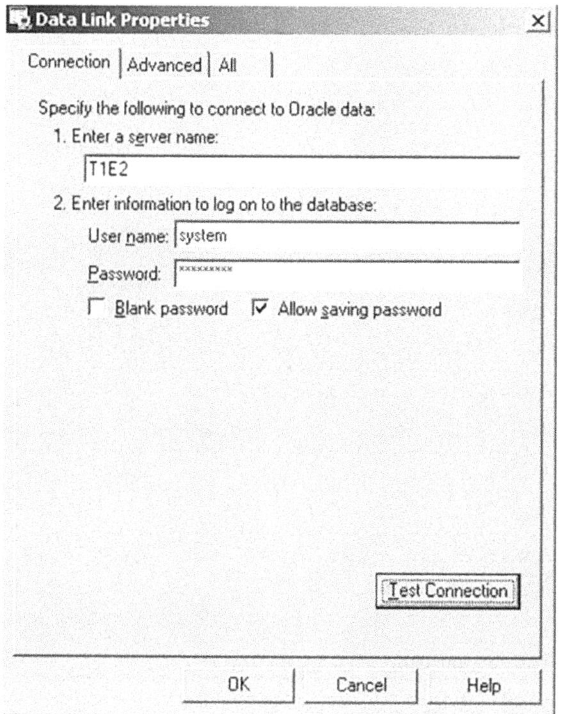

Figure 3-21: Test connection

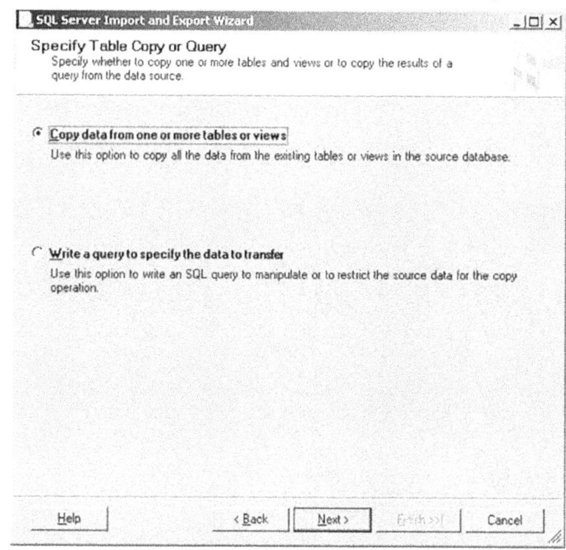

Figure 3-22: Specify the copy option

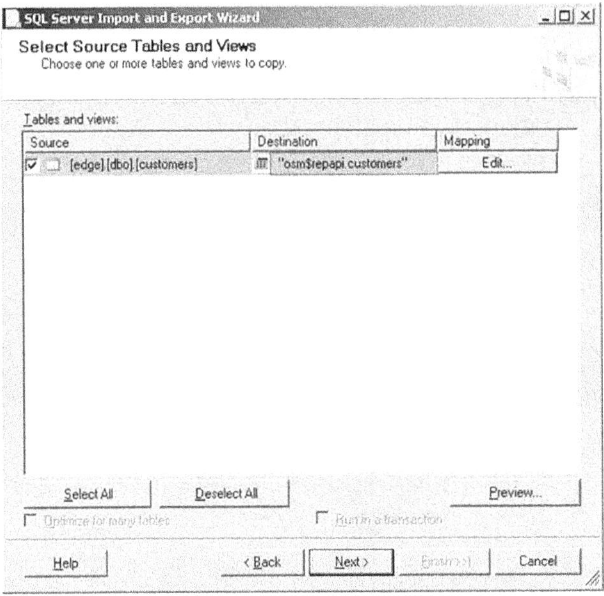

Figure 3-23: Tables selection and columns mapping

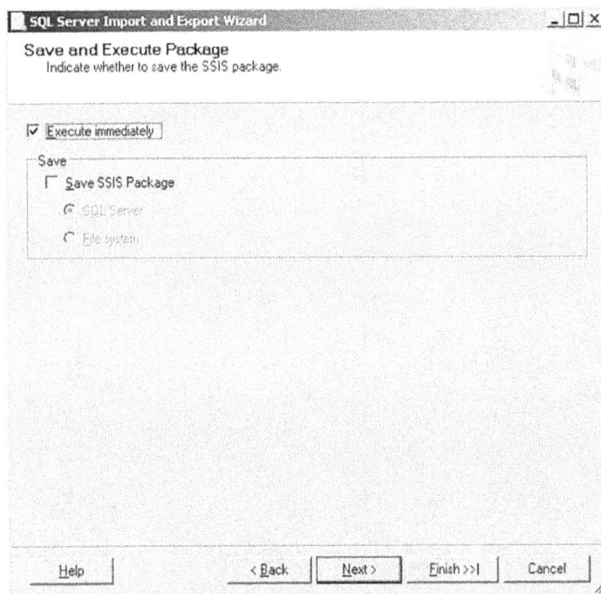

Figure 3-24: Save SSIS package option

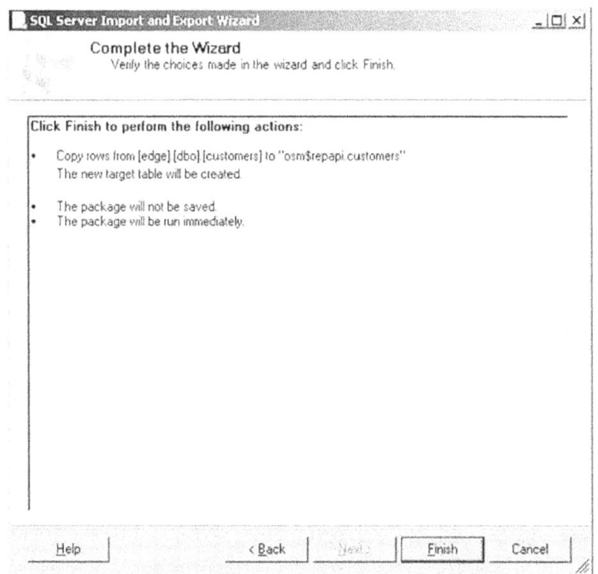

Figure 3-25: Actions list

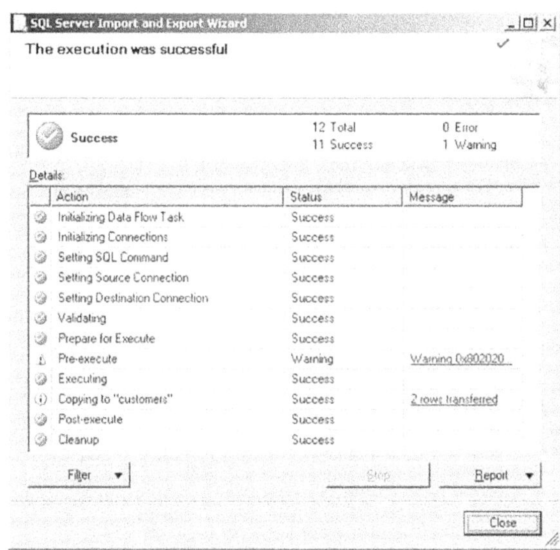

Figure 3-26: Execution results

Oracle database configuration assistant

A graphical user interface option for performing an initial load outside of Oracle GoldenGate is Oracle database configuration assistant (DBCA), suitable for newly created environment. A database created based on either DBCA templates shipped with Oracle software, or based on customized template stored under $ORACLE_HOME/assistants/dbca/templates. The target database established through two separate DBCA source and target sessions.

Source session: Create a template from an existing database (source database)
Target session: Create the target database based on the source session template

Create the target database template

From the source system, we use DBCA template management, step 2 of 5 to create a template based on the source database as shown in figure 3-27. The target database created using this template will be identical to the source database, it includes user defined schemas and data. The template can be created to support different or identical file system structure for the target system. Transfer the template files (.dfb, .ctl and .dbc) to the target system DBCA templates default location. The next step is to use DBCA to create the target database using this template.

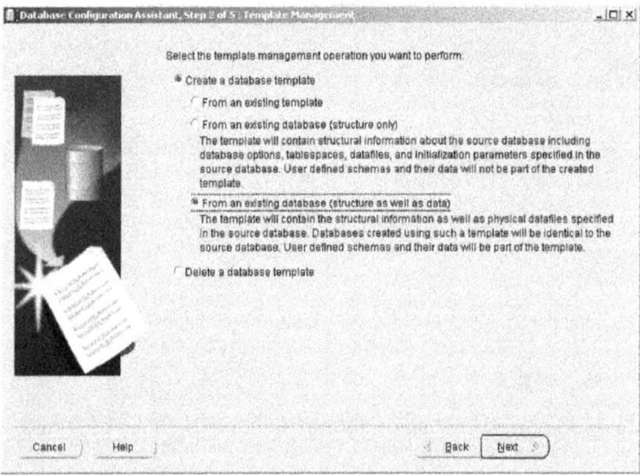

Figure 3-27: Create target database template

Create the target database

From the target session, we create the target database using the template created from the source database by selecting the template name. Figure 3-28 lists Oracle supplied templates, and the customized templates. When creating the target database from a template, provide the database global name, SID for the target database the newly created database contains the user's defined schemas and data. Oracle Database 12c DBCA is backward compatible, it supports templates created from Oracle Database 11g or higher.

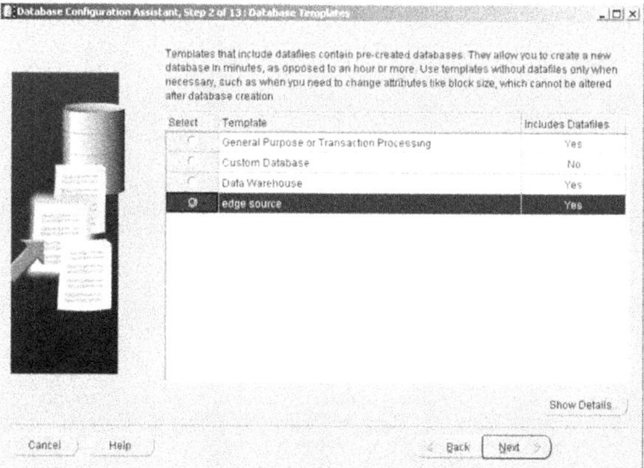

Figure 3-28: Select target database template

Creating remote database tables structure

Several technique are available to create the remote target table's structure, which must be done before starting initial-load extract and Replicat.

For Oracle database, several options are available, such as:

- SQL*Developer
- *dbms_metadata*
- Database export and import data pump utilities
- In-house develop dictionary SQL scripts

For MS-SQL Server, the available option include:

- MS-SQL Server Studio
- In-house develop dictionary SQL scripts

Figure 3-18 depicts CREATE TABLE statement for SCOTT.EMP table. Using SQL Developer, you can reverse engineer database design for:

- Tables
- Indexes
- Constraints

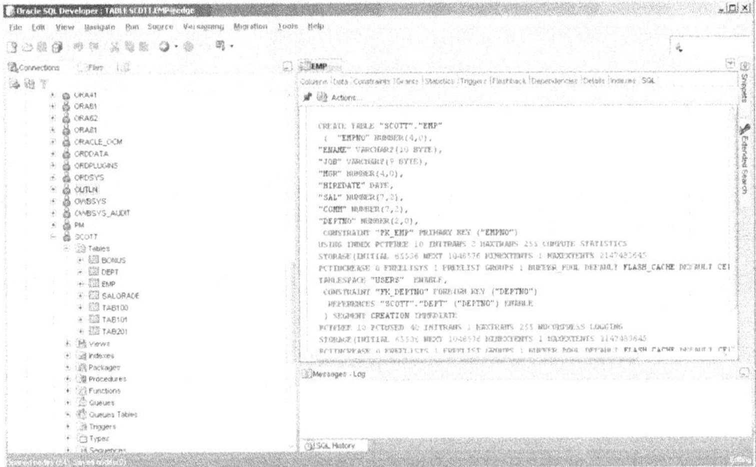

Figure 3-29: Oracle SQL Developer SQL script generator

General GoldenGate guidelines and considerations

- Be aware of common errors when performing initial load operations. Initial load error cause the operation to end abnormally with status ABENDED. These errors may occur when performing other operation, as well.

  - The extract terminates for unable to communicate with the target manager process, and return the error messages below.

    ```
    ERROR   OGG-00303  Could not establish host TCP/IP address
    ERROR   OGG-01668  PROCESS ABENDING.
    ```

    Resolve the error by ensuring the parameter RMTHOST is using the correct target hostname and forwarding to the correct target port manager.

  - Upon starting extract or replicat programs, quickly terminating with the error message:

    ```
    ERROR   OGG-00664  OCI Error beginning session (status = 1017-ORA-
                       01017:  invalid username/password; logon denied).
    ERROR   OGG-01668  PROCESS ABENDING.
    ```

Resolve the error by ensuring the parameter USERID is using the correct database username and password. Test the database connection from GGSCI using the USERID parameter details by specify the database connect string (TNS).

```
GGSCI 2> dblogin userid ggs_admin@s1t2, password oracle
Successfully logged into database.
```

- Prior to performing initial data load, create the table structure on the target database. On source, use Oracle database data pump export utility using the parameter setting *content=metadata_only,* then on target apply the same parameter setting for creating the table structures using Oracle database data pump import utility. An alternative for creating the target table structure is Oracle database supplied PL/SQL package *dbms_metadata.*

- Because the target file is written in canonical format, transformation can occur on the source or the target systems. This features is suitable when feeding targets that has different database structures or operating on heterogeneous environment.

- When the source database has to remain active, first configure the change data capture extract and replicate, then configure and perform initial data load. Oracle GoldenGate reconcile the change data occurred during initial data load.

- Suitable for heterogeneous large database environment (VLDB), by creating multiple target initial data load files, then create multiple replicat groups to instantiate the target database in parallel.

- Because file to replicate method reads record-by-record from a canonical formatted file, the method tends to be a slower compared to other initial data load methods. To enhance the target performance, consider temporary disabling constraints, dropping indexes and database logging.

- Since the file to replicate method is an end-to-end Oracle GoldenGate configuration, it will be inherits the same limitation for supporting data types. Oracle GoldenGate release 2 has non-supported data types list of Abstract data type (ADT), *anydataset, anytype, bfile, mslabel, orddicom, rowid, timezone_abbr, uritype* and *urowid.*

- For initial-load on a quiesced database, by dropping indexes and disabling constraints drastically improve the initial-load performance. The indexes and constraints should be enabled after the initial-load is completed.

- When performing initial-load on homogenous environment, keep DDL replication disabled until the initial-load is completed. Best practice dictates, avoid DDL changes to database tables currently undergoing initial-load.

- Performing initial data load for database with mix tables characteristics, consider the use of two methods such as file-to-replicat method for the smaller size tables, and database utility for the larger size tables. For example, It would take considerable amount of time to perform initial-load for tables of size 50GB with 50 million rows.

- For large number of tables where the majority of the tables are considerably small size, use the wild-card feature with *tableexeclude* parameter as shown below.

```
TABLEEXECLUE osm$repapi.first_name
TABLE osm$repapi.*
```

- Regardless of the initial-load method used to establish the target database, gather statistics to allow the database optimize queries. Using DBMS_STATS to gather schema level statistics illustrated below.

```
begin
  dbms_stats.gather_schema_stats('OSM$REPAPI');
end;
```

Summary

This chapter covered the tasks of establishing the target databases by performing an initial data load from one or more source databases. Several methods available, from within and outside of Oracle GoldenGate. However; the combination of multiple methods such as file-to-replicate and database utility is common for very large database, with tables beyond 5GB and requiring some kinds of data transformations.

Table 3-15 presents a quick reference to help you select the initial-load method(s) based on the source database environment and target system resources. Never the less, realistic data load testing has to be developed for measuring the initial-load performance prior to deploying the method(s) on active database environment, where the database available for online users.

Initial-load Method	Applies to
File-to-replicate	◘ Heterogeneous database environment ◘ Data transformation required, applied on source and/or target ◘ The target instances of database and GoldenGate may not be in place ◘ Large number of tables, but very less large tables size ◘ Database with LOB data types support ◘ Disk storage available on target system for remote files ◘ From hours-days to allows the completion of the initial-load tasks
Direct load	◘ Heterogeneous database environment ◘ Data transformation required, applied on source and/or target ◘ The target instances of database and GoldenGate must be in place ◘ Large number of tables, but very less large tables size ◘ Database with no LOB data types support ◘ Limited disk storage available on the target system ◘ From hours-days to allows the completion of the initial-load tasks
Bulk-direct load	◘ Homogenous, Oracle database environment only ◘ Data transformation is restricted to source only ◘ Large number of very large database tables size, above 5GB ◘ Database with no LOB data types support ◘ Disk storage available on target system for remote files
Files to database utility	◘ Heterogeneous database environment ◘ Data transformation is restricted to source only ◘ Large number of tables with large tables size, above 5GB ◘ Database with LOB data types support ◘ Multi-files support for very large database ◘ Storage available on target system for utility files ◘ Supported tools ◘ SQL Server: BCP, DTS and SISS ◘ Oracle: SQL*Loader ◘ IBM: LOADUTIL
Database utility	◘ Homogenous database environment ◘ No data transformation required ◘ Large number of tables, with large tables size, above 5GB ◘ Database with LOB data types ◘ Disk space available on the target system

Table 3-15: Initial-load quick reference

The successful completion of the initial-load process is crucial for avoiding future data inconsistency related errors. The data verification is important before starting the replicate processes, it avoids Replicat processes terminate and become ABBEND due to unhandled exception such as ORA-01403 NO DATA FOUND for an any sort of DML operations. However; because we're mostly performing initial-load from an active database, data verification is mostly relative to the completion time and the volume of data applied by the change data capture processes occurred during the initial-load timeframe. Among the tools for conducting data verification include:

- Database utility log files
- Oracle GoldenGate report files
- Database table's row-count between source and target
- Oracle GoldenGate Veridata

Next, we are going to configure one of the most common application of Oracle GoldenGate 12c, implementing Oracle GoldenGate for report offloading. The focus will be on the generic approach for report offloading, but we will also discuss the approach for creating e-business suite reporting instance for report offloading.

Real-time query offloading techniques for GoldenGate

CHAPTER

Overview

The objective of this chapter is to cover implementing Oracle GoldenGate for real-time query offloading solutions. Diverting resource intensive queries and reports applications to a dedicated reporting instance enhances the performance of an optimized Online Transaction Processing (OLTP) systems.

This technique is not only applicable to in-house developed applications, but also to packaged CRM and ERP applications. Implementing query offloading speeds up and maximizes the return of investment (ROI) by increasing the scalability of the online OLTP systems by processing short transactions for best throughput and diverting reports applications to a specially-optimized real-time reporting instance. The query offloading technique is transparent, and report applications will run without modifications. This is essentials to packaged applications because the applications source code is not available.

The GoldenGate architecture is built on common foundation delivered by Oracle GoldenGate and remote the database instance. Oracle GoldenGate provides the real-time data feed, and the database internal Online Analytical Processing (OLAP) capabilities provides the infrastructure required to optimize the design.

For example, when the report instance (target) is an Oracle 12c Enterprise Edition, the optimization achieved by using *materialized view, query re-write, advanced compression, partitioning and online redefinition.* These are essentials features for deploying high-performance reporting instance. The heterogeneity of Oracle GoldenGate enables cost-effective platform for the report instance. An example is running the report instance using open source platforms such as Oracle Enterprise Linux and Oracle MySQL.

This chapter covers offloading Oracle R12 EBusiness suite application only, but the technique workflow applicable to non-Oracle applications. We will discuss the real-time query offloading technique from the prospective of:

- General purpose query offloading
- Oracle R12 E-Business suite query offloading

Chapter 3 is the foundation for query offloading solution. The reporting instance and the initial-load should be available prior to implementing query offloading.

The GoldenGate Architecture for query offloading

Before deploying a query offloading instance, let's describe Oracle GoldenGate and the configurable components for query offloading. The vast majority of the database components are optional, but when implemented properly, the resulting infrastructure delivers high-performance report runtime. Even so, Oracle GoldenGate is certified with Oracle standard edition, the database components discussed on this chapter are only available on Oracle enterprise edition. Each of the component listed below is briefly explained, then configured to produce a fully working query offloading instance.

- OLTP instance (source database)
- Report applications
- Real-time changed data capture (CDC)
- Real-time changed data delivery
- Report instance (target database)
- Target report infrastructure

Figure 4-1 depicts Oracle GoldenGate and Oracle components and workflow that will be configured to implement query offloading. This is a form of uni-directional topology for data flow from the source to the target database.

The configuration developed is between Oracle 11g (source) and Oracle 12c (target). Table 4-1 lists the components used by the query offloading implementation.

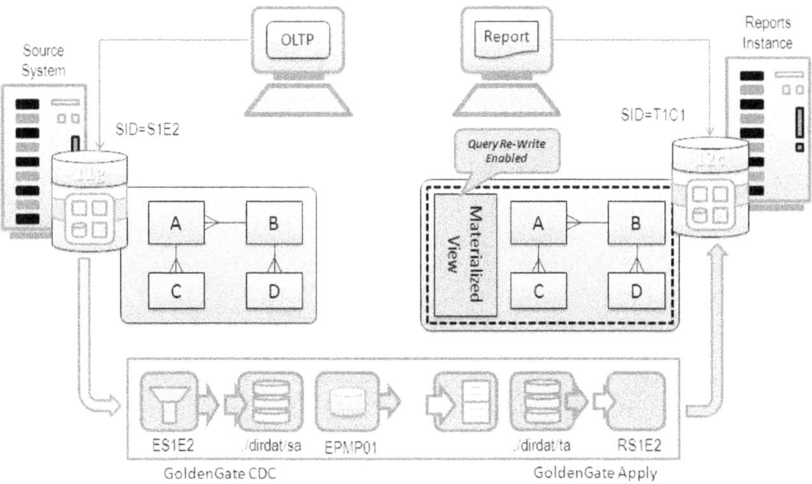

Figure 4-1: Query offloading architecture

The general purpose query offloading is implemented from Oracle 11g to Oracle 12c. However; for R12 Oracle E-Business suite query offloading, it's implemented from Oracle 11g to Oracle 11g running Oracle Enterprise Linux version 5.

Component	Description
S1E2	Source database/instance name
T1C1	Target database/instance name
ES1E202	Primary extract for change data capture group
EPMP02	Secondary extract group for sending data to target system
./dirdat/sb	Local trail
./dirdat/tb	Remote trail
RS1E202	Change data delivery (replicate) group
ggs1	A dedicated service name for report application running on source
ggs2	A dedicated service name for report application running on source

Table 4-1: Query offloading components and description

The OLTP instance with GoldenGate offloading

The online transaction processing (OLTP) component should strictly handle short business transactions. These types of transactions use minimum system resources allowing maximum system scalability. An OLTP database instance are configured with suitable database shared memory requirements, using a mid-range buffer cache size of 8K.

The application server component is an Oracle HTTP server that runs online applications for accessing the database and performs data manipulation language (DML) statements which are captured by Oracle GoldenGate with sub-second delay to be delivered real-time for data synchronization. Figure 4-2 shows an OLTP database accessed by an Oracle HTTP server for running an Oracle portal applications developed using Oracle PL/SQL web toolkit.

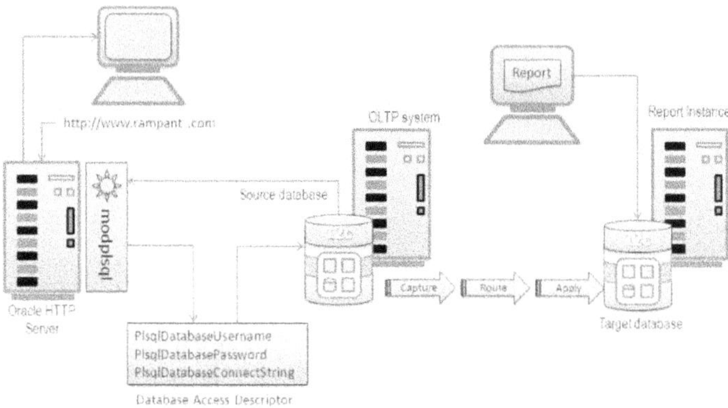

Figure 4-2: Oracle HTTP server running Oracle portal applications

Report applications for GoldenGate

Accessing the database and running report applications is achieved with several techniques. This chapter uses Oracle HTTP server extension *mod_plsql* which through a database access descriptor (DAD) connects to the database, generates Web PL/SQL server pages applications. Oracle *mod_plsql* relies on the configuration file *dads.conf* to implement the authentication method using pre-determined credential parameters. Examples of mod_plsql applications are Oracle Enterprise manager (OEM) and Oracle Application Express (APEX).

The following is the source database access descriptor (DAD) from *dads.conf* configuration file.

```
<Location /osm$dad$112>
  SetHandler pls_handler
  Order deny,allow
  Allow from all
  AllowOverride None
  PlsqlDatabaseWe username                 osm$repapi
  PlsqlDatabasePassword                   oracle
  #ggs1 is dedicated database service
  PlsqlDatabaseConnectString              ggs1
```

```
  PlsqlAuthenticationMode                 Basic
  PlsqlDocumentTableName                  osm$repapi.osm_documents
  PlsqlDefaultPage                        system.pl
  PlsqlNLSLanguage                        AMERICAN_AMERICA.AL32UTF8
  PlsqlTransferMode                       RAW
</location>
```

The database access descriptor *osmdad112* uses the values specified by the parameters: *PlsqlDatabaseWe username, PlsqlDatabasePassword* and *PlsqlDatabaseConnectString* for connecting to the database and executing the online report application shown in figure 4-3. The parameter *PlsqlDatabaseConnectString* uses a dedicated database service, *ggs1* to connect to the target database.

Regardless of the applications development platform and report runtime environment, the techniques explained in this chapter for query offloading should be applied across all environments because they are transparent to the application. Several tools are available to develop query offloading, however; this chapter focuses on tools that are part of the Oracle utilities and PL/SQL API, in particular:

- *dbms_service*
- *dbms_monitor*
- *dbms_system*
- TKPROF

Figure 4-3: Report application ruing on source system - S1E2

As displayed at the top of the report, the screen indicates the hostname and the database instance (SID) against which the report replication is running.

Real-time change data capture (CDC) in GoldenGate

The primary group (*es1e202*) configured to perform change data capture only for the referenced tables by the specific report. Having successfully performed initial-load for establishing the target database, the primary, secondary and delivery groups keep synchronizing the target database ready for real-time reporting. Best practices recommend creating a dedicated primary, secondary and delivery groups for the specific report. This promotes easier management and maintenance of each Oracle GoldenGate configuration.

GoldenGate Report instance for Data Warehouse Applications

The report instance database should be created to sustain intensive queries for business intelligence and data warehouse repository applications. Report applications are redirected to a report instance, with no modifications and fully transparent to the application source code. The database instance for the report applications is configured with two database buffer caches. A primary block size of 8k for the data dictionary and a secondary block size of 32K for long-running query applications. The configuration of multiple Oracle block sizes follows:

- Here we confirm the primary block size, used by the SYSTEM tablespace. The most suitable block size is 8K, to handle OLTP and internal transactions.

```
SQL> SELECT block_size
  2  FROM   dba_tablespaces
  3  WHERE  tablespace_name='SYSTEM';

BLOCK_SIZE
----------
      8192
```

- Next, we configure the cache size for 32K block size to support long-running query applications. In case of real application clusters (RAC), specify the instance SID for the report applications.

```
SQL> ALTER SYSTEM SET db_32k_cache_size=64K scope=both;

System altered.
```

- Now we create tablespaces for 32K block size. Change the file name to the disk group name for automatic storage management (ASM).

```
SQL> CREATE TABLESPACE dwhdat
  2  BLOCKSIZE 32K
  3  DATAFILE '/u01/app/oracle/oradata/S1E2/dwhdat01.dbf' SIZE 1000M
  4  AUTOEXTEND ON;

Tablespace created.
```

- Here we verify the block size for the new tablespace as 32K (32768).

```
SQL> SELECT block_size
  2  FROM   dba_tablespaces
  3  WHERE  tablespace_name='DWHDAT';

BLOCK_SIZE
----------
     32768
```

- Next, we move tables to the newly created tablespace so that I/O is delivered using 32K instead of 8K.

```
SQL> ALTER TABLE osm$repapi.policies MOVE TABLESPACE dwhdat;

Table altered.

SQL> ALTER TABLE osm$repapi.customers MOVE TABLESPACE dwhdat;

Table altered.
```

Notice that a 32K block size I/Os is available on Oracle 11g and 12c 64-bit architecture. For 32-bit architecture platforms, and for Windows, the maximum block size is 16K.

Real-time change data delivery in GoldenGate

The changed data delivery group (*rs1e202*) reads the remote trail and applies the transaction to the target database using native SQL calls. Referential integrity constraints among tables on the target database are not implemented as it's not required for query offloading. For implementing parallel changed data delivery groups, refer to using *@range* Oracle GoldenGate function for parallel processing alter in Chapter 1.

Report instance infrastructure for GoldenGate

There are several components that need to be created and/or configured for deploying high-performance query offloading solution. These components are not required, but they add-value by increasing the report instance I/O throughput and optimize the queries performance.

For highly complex business intelligence using very large database (VLDB) data warehouse repository, Oracle machine Exadata engineered to deliver the highest level of service for meeting the needs for advanced database applications requirements of mixed workloads.

Database services

The database service isolates the report session from using an existing or default instance services. It can be used for enabling session trace and monitoring based on the service name. Oracle supplied package *dbms_service* creates, starts, stops and drop database services. This is not required, but highly recommended and used for clustered database running Oracle real application clusters (RAC).

Materialized views and GoldenGate

A materialized view is a database segment for storing the result of a query, mainly for the purpose of performing dynamic query re-write. It's should be created to support DSS applications with intensive query impacting OLTP application performance. The optimizer decision for using the materialized view instead of original tables is called query re-write and it produces faster response time.

Because it's a real database segment and not a view definition, a refresh option is used to synchronize the materialized view from the tables referenced by the query. A materialized view logs created for efficient refresh (*fast*). Other refresh types are *complete* and *force*.

Advanced compression and GoldenGate

Table compression achieves efficient storage and faster query performance without any impact on DML operations. We use the compression adviser *dbms_compression* to identify tables that are candidate from compression. The advisor estimates the space saving for the different compression methods.

Issue the *alter table* statement to apply compression for candidate tables. The following enables BASIC compression that delivers high compression ratio with minimal CPU overhead designed for DSS type of applications.

```
SQL> ALTER TABLE customers COMPRESS;

Table altered.
```

Oracle GoldenGate classic capture does not support change data capture from compressed tables. When the table is compressed, the extract process ABENDED with the error:

```
OGG-01433  Failed to validate table OSM$REPAPI.CUSTOMERS. The table is
compressed and extract will not be able to extract data from Oracle logs.
```

However; Oracle GoldenGate integrated capture is more compressive and supports compressed database tables. See chapter 10 to learn more about integrated capture.

Partitioning and GoldenGate

Database partitioning provides a management window for very large tables. Instead of managing the table as one single segment, table and index partitioning sub-divides the segment into multiple segments that are managed individually. There are several types of partitioning supported by Oracle and it's important to apply the correct partitioning method for replication to tables and indexes. The following is an example of creating partitioned table using *range* method.

```
SQL> CREATE TABLE osm$repapi.CUST_PART (
       cust_no       NUMBER NOT NULL PRIMARY KEY,
       cust_name     VARCHAR2(128) NOT NULL,
       cust_email    VARCHAR2(128) NOT NULL,
       cust_mobile   VARCHAR2(16),
       cust_address  VARCHAR2(128))
     PARTITION BY RANGE (cust_no)
       (PARTITION p1 VALUES LESS THAN (50000),
        PARTITION p2 VALUES LESS THAN (100000),
        PARTITION p3 VALUES LESS THAN (150000),
        PARTITION p4 VALUES LESS THAN (MAXVALUE));

Table created.
```

Online redefinition and GoldenGate

To support non-stop database operations, Oracle online redefinition *dbms_redefinition* PL/SQL supplied package enables redefining database objects, such as tables without impacting the online users. A good example is migrating a normal table (non-partitioned) to partitioned table. The following *dbms_redefinition* session illustrates an online redefinition of the *customers* table to become partitioned table.

The original *osm$repapi.customers* table is non-partitioned table segment. Currently being accessed by an online applications, while it's being migrated and maybe modified using in-place operations.

```
SQL> conn / as sysdba
Connected.

SQL> DESC osm$repapi.customers

 Name                                      Null?    Type
 ----------------------------------------- -------- ------------------------
 CUST_NO                                   NOT NULL NUMBER
 CUST_NAME                                 NOT NULL VARCHAR2(128)
 CUST_EMAIL                                NOT NULL VARCHAR2(128)
 CUST_MOBILE                                        VARCHAR2(16)
 CUST_ADDRESS                                       VARCHAR2(128)
```

Step 1: We start by confirming the target table can be redefined online. The call to this procedure return an error in case the table cannot be redefined. Example of errors are tables without primary key and table with materialized views.

```
SQL> BEGIN
  2      DBMS_REDEFINITION.CAN_REDEF_TABLE(
  3      uname=>'osm$repapi', tname=>'CUSTOMERS');
  4  END;
  5  /

PL/SQL procedure successfully completed.

SQL>
```

Step 2: Create an interim table, it's used as a template for the redefinition. The interim table become the original database table by the end of the session.

```
SQL> CREATE TABLE osm$repapi.cust_int (
  2    cust_no      NUMBER NOT NULL PRIMARY KEY,
  3    cust_name    VARCHAR2(128) NOT NULL,
  4    cust_email   VARCHAR2(128) NOT NULL,
  5    cust_mobile  VARCHAR2(16),
  6    cust_address VARCHAR2(128))
```

```
PARTITION BY RANGE (cust_no)
  (PARTITION p1 VALUES LESS THAN (50000),
   PARTITION p2 VALUES LESS THAN (100000),
   PARTITION p3 VALUES LESS THAN (150000),
   PARTITION p4 VALUES LESS THAN (MAXVALUE));

Table created.
```

Step 3: Start the redefinition process by specifying the original table and the interim table names. From now onward, data is diverted to the interim table.

```
SQL> BEGIN
       DBMS_REDEFINITION.START_REDEF_TABLE(
          uname=>'osm$repapi',
          orig_table=>'CUSTOMERS',
          int_table=>'CUST_INT');
     END;
     /

PL/SQL procedure successfully completed.
```

Step 4: Synchronize the changes that occurs during the redefinition.

```
SQL> BEGIN
      DBMS_REDEFINITION.SYNC_INTERIM_TABLE (
        uname=>'osm$repapi',
        orig_table=>'CUSTOMERS',
        int_table=>'CUST_INT');
     END;
     /

PL/SQL procedure successfully completed.
```

Step 5: Finish the redefinition. This step performs internal data dictionary updates to swap the tables.

```
SQL> BEGIN
      DBMS_REDEFINITION.FINISH_REDEF_TABLE(
        uname=>'osm$repapi',
        orig_table=>'CUSTOMERS',
        int_table=>'CUST_INT');
     END;
     /

PL/SQL procedure successfully completed.
```

Verify the table is partitioned. Drop the interim table structure as it's not required.

```
SQL> SELECT partitioned
     FROM   dba_tables
     WHERE  table_name='CUSTOMERS' AND
            owner='OSM$REPAPI';

PAR
---
YES
```

Database parameters for GoldenGate Instances

The database parameters settings effect the database performance. When running intensive queries for the data warehouse applications, it's highly important to consider the settings of these parameters to work and support large I/O environment. The list of important parameters discussed next.

query_rewrite_enabled

Oracle enterprise edition has query re-write enabled by default. It causes the database optimizer to fetch from the materialized views when it finds the execution plan is more efficient. Query re-write maybe enabled at the database level, materialized view and SQL application code using hits (directives).

db_32k_cache_size

The main objective of supporting different instance cache sizes is to implement true database consolidation. Before creating the tablespaces using the *blocksize* option, it's required to allocate the cache size corresponding to the block size. This cache size is independent without automatic management.

cursor_sharing

The default setting of this parameter is *exact.* we need to consider changing the value to *similar* when the database handling report requests with parameter forms, such as Oracle R12 E-Business applications. The *similar* setting causes statements that may differ in literal values, but are otherwise identical, to share SQL work areas, unless the literals values affect the optimizer execution plan.

db_file_multiblock_read_count

The parameter *db_file_multiblock_read_count* intended for applications performing frequent full tables scan. By employing 32K block size, at the tablespace level, with this parameter the database minimizes I/Os during table scans by maximizing the number of blocks read in one I/O operation during a sequential scan. This parameter is obsolete in later releases of Oracle.

cpu_count

The *cpu_count* parameter cages the instance to specific number of CPU cores on multi-instance server. The setting can be either designed as partitioned or over-provisioned.

To activate *cpu_count* parameter, enable the CPU resource plan by setting *resource_manager_plan* to 'default_plan'.

parallel_adaptive_multi_user and PARALLEL parameter

When the parameter *parallel_adaptive_multi_user* is set to true, it adjusts the degree of parallelism in a dynamic manner when explicitly set at the table level, by reducing the degree of parallelism based on the current system workload. Consider using the *parallel* and *buffer_pool keep* options of the *create table* statement for look up tables (dimensions) and relatively static tables as shown here.

```
SQL> CREATE TABLE POLICY_TYPES (
       pol_type  VARCHAR2(8)   NOT NULL PRIMARY KEY,
       pol_desc  VARCHAR2(128) NOT NULL)
     PARALLEL 4
     STORAGE (BUFFER_POOL keep);

Table created.
```

RAC cluster_database and GoldenGate

The *cluster_database* parameter is for operating a real application clusters (RAC) database. RAC is an important component to be considered and designed properly to support data warehouse applications as well as any 24x7 system. The RAC environment should be designed to equally promote scalability, high-availability server consolidation and database consolidation. For a mixed workload environment, partitioning applications achieves the best level of scalability. Figure 4-4 depicts a 4-node cluster, dividing them into a set of 2-node environment to support OLTP and OLAP applications.

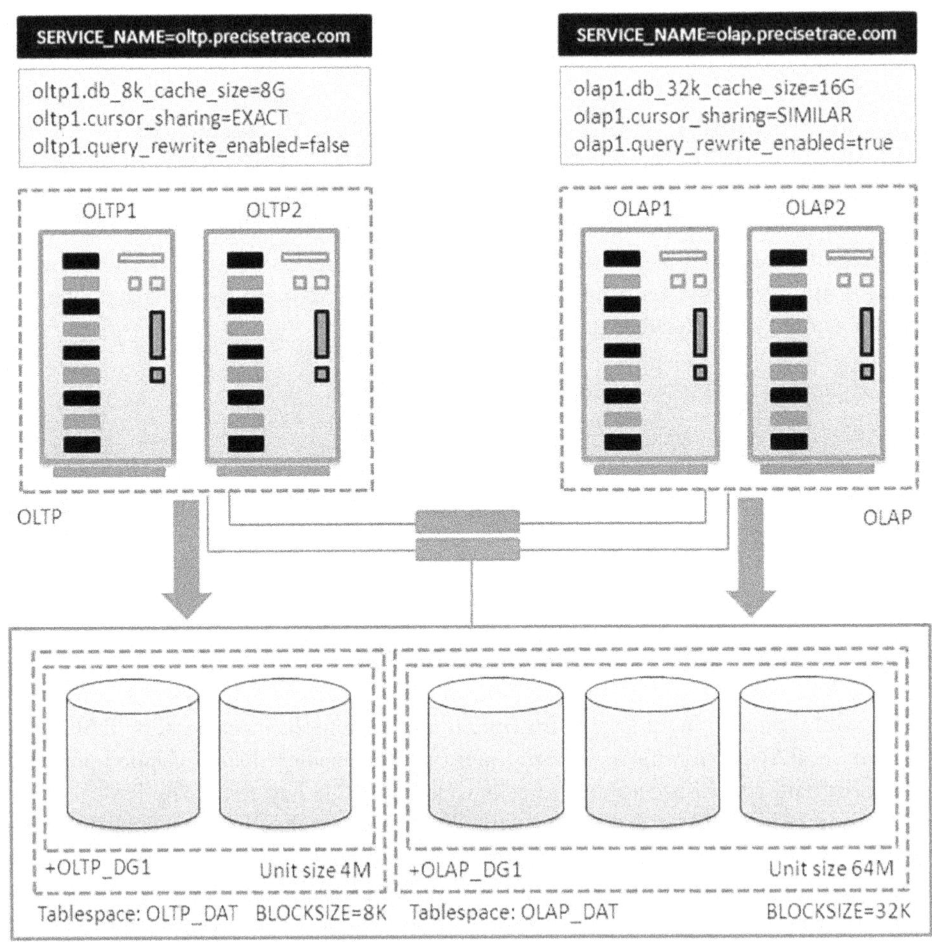

Figure 4-4: Oracle real application clusters (RAC) for mixed workload

For data warehouse sessions, the database connections must be explicitly use dedicated connection when the database is configured for shared sessions. The connect strings defined in *tnsnames.ora* employs the setting *server=dedicated* as shown below.

```
T1C1_OLAP =
  (DESCRIPTION =
    (ADDRESS = (PROTOCOL = TCP)(HOST = ggs-target)(PORT = 1521))
    (CONNECT_DATA =
      (SERVER = DEDICATED)
      (SERVICE_NAME = t1c1.precisetrace.com)
    )
  )
```

Clustered tables and GoldenGate

Table clustering designed to speed up join queries among clustered tables and to optimize the storage by referencing the cluster, so that tables related by referential integrity do not refer to the column on referenced the table, but to share the cluster column. The following SQL DDL statements create the tables *customers* and *policies* as clustered tables. It starts by creating the cluster, the clustered tables, cluster index and finally the referential integrity constraint.

```
SQL> CREATE CLUSTER cust_no_clus (
        cust_no NUMBER);

Cluster created.

SQL> CREATE TABLE customers (
       cust_no      NUMBER NOT NULL PRIMARY KEY,
       cust_name    VARCHAR2(128) NOT NULL,
       cust_email   VARCHAR2(128) NOT NULL,
       cust_mobile  VARCHAR2(16),
       cust_address VARCHAR2(128))
     CLUSTER cust_no_clus(cust_no);

Table created.

SQL> CREATE TABLE policies (
       pol_no NUMBER NOT NULL PRIMARY KEY,
       pol_from DATE NOT NULL,
       pol_to  DATE NOT NULL,
       pol_value NUMBER(8, 2) NOT NULL,
       pol_sub_total NUMBER(8, 2) NOT NULL,
       pt_code       VARCHAR2(8) NOT NULL,
       dt_code       VARCHAR2(8) NOT NULL,
       pol_total     NUMBER(16, 2),
       cust_no       NUMBER NOT NULL)
     CLUSTER cust_no_clus(cust_no);

Table created.

SQL> CREATE INDEX cust_no_idx ON CLUSTER cust_no_clus;

Index created.

SQL> ALTER TABLE policies ADD CONSTRAINT cust_no_fk FOREIGN KEY (cust_no)
     REFERENCES customers (cust_no);

Table altered.
```

The column *cust_no* exists physically on the cluster *cust_no_clus* only, and logically on *customers* and *policies* tables, saving database storage for very large database (VLDB), and minimizes I/Os for queries joining the two tables using the CUST_NO column.

Report database tables for GoldenGate

There are several techniques for determining the tables referenced by a packaged report application. The set of database tables includes the *base* and *look up* tables. For packaged applications such as R12 E-Business suite, the tables are determined using techniques such as:

- Oracle TKPROF utility
- Oracle audit
- Oracle Enterprise Manager (OEM)

Implementing the above three techniques described next. However; this chapter uses TKPROF to identify the query and referenced tables. The objective of determining the query is for enabling query re-write by creating materialized view and materialized view log. Unlike TKPROF and Oracle audit that are part of the Oracle software license, Oracle Enterprise Manager (OEM) SQL Monitor is a licensable software.

TKPROF utility and GoldenGate

The TKPROF utility needs the report's session SQL trace file, which is achieved by activating SQL trace using a designated database service name alone, or a combination of the session ID, serial# and the database service name.

Because using the database service name is more efficient to determine the session's SQL trace, dynamic database service names are created and used by the report's session. The original report uses the database service name '*ggs1*', the report running on the reporting instance uses the database service name '*ggs2*'.

Create dedicated database service name for GoldenGate

To ensure monitoring the specific report, we create a dedicated database *service name* to be used by the report's database session. The Oracle supplied PL/SQL package *dbms_service* creates and manages non-default database service names.

Create service name

We use the *dbms_service.create_service* procedure to create the service name. We provide the service name (ggs1) and the network service name (ggs1.precisetrace.com).

```
SQL> conn / as sysdba
Connected.
SQL> EXEC DBMS_SERVICE.CREATE_SERVICE('ggs1', 'ggs1.precisetrace.com');

PL/SQL procedure successfully completed.
```

Prior to using the service ggs1, it must be started using *dbms_service.start_service*. We verify that the service is registered with the database listener using *lsnrctl* command-line, *lsnrctl services*

```
SQL> EXEC DBMS_SERVICE.START_SERVICE('ggs1');

PL/SQL procedure successfully completed.
```

We verify the service name is listed for the database services. The parameter *service_name* supports multiple service names separated by comma.

```
SQL> SHOW PARAMETERS service

NAME                                 TYPE        VALUE
------------------------------------ ----------- ------------------------------
service_names                        string      ggs1.precisetrace.com
```

Next, we add the service name ggs1 to TNSNAMES.ORA file.

```
ggs1 =
  (DESCRIPTION =
    (ADDRESS = (PROTOCOL = TCP)(HOST = ggs-source)(PORT = 1521))
    (CONNECT_DATA =
      (SERVICE_NAME = ggs1.precisetrace.com)
    )
  )
```

Now we can perform a quick connection test, using the service name.

```
SQL> conn osm$repapi/oracle@ggs1

Connected.
```

We use *dbms_monitor* PL/SQL package to enable SQL trace for the sessions established using the service name, *ggs1*.

```
SQL> EXEC DBMS_MONITOR.SERV_MOD_ACT_TRACE_ENABLE(service_name=>'ggs1');

PL/SQL procedure successfully completed.
```

We run the application using the database connect string *ggs1*, which uses the service name, *ggs1*. Because the application is running with SQL trace enabled, it starts generating trace files.

300000001	PAUL D. HERNANDEZ	Heath Insurance	24-DEC-13	23-DEC-14	116,165.03	5,808.25	Rampant Emplloyee	5,517.84
300000002	FAWZI T. TAYLOR	Life Insurance	24-DEC-13	23-DEC-14	314,300.59	15,715.03	Rampant Emplloyee	14,929.28
300000003	FAWZI S. ALSWAIMIL	Libility Insurance	24-DEC-13	23-DEC-14	332,867.40	16,643.37	Rampant Emplloyee	15,811.20
300000004	ELIZABETH U. MARTIN	Professional Libility	24-DEC-13	23-DEC-14	380,290.86	19,014.54	Senior over 80 years	18,063.82
300000005	EDWARD M. ALLEN	Accident Insurance	24-DEC-13	23-DEC-14	428,315.30	21,415.77	University Student	20,344.98
300000006	DOROTHY T. ANDERSON	Libility Insurance	24-DEC-13	23-DEC-14	233,573.17	11,678.66	University Student	11,094.73
300000007	RUTH E. BROWN	Life Insurance	24-DEC-13	23-DEC-14	267,306.09	13,365.30	Rampant Emplloyee	12,697.04
300000008	JENNIFER L. MARTINEZ	Medicare Supplement	24-DEC-13	23-DEC-14	27,954.17	1,397.71	Senior over 80 years	1,327.82
300000009	JESSICA L. MARTIN	Business Insurance	24-DEC-13	23-DEC-14	468,724.42	23,436.22	Senior over 80 years	22,264.41
300000010	RICHARD C. JOHNSON	Life Insurance	24-DEC-13	23-DEC-14	214,092.49	10,704.62	Rampant Emplloyee	10,169.39
300000011	KEVIN J. THOMPSON	Disability Insurance	24-DEC-13	23-DEC-14	195,438.54	9,771.93	Rampant Emplloyee	9,283.33
300000012	KAREN Y. MARTIN	Heath Insurance	24-DEC-13	23-DEC-14	220,100.82	11,005.04	Rampant Emplloyee	10,454.79
300000013	JESSICA B. MILLER	Heath Insurance	24-DEC-13	23-DEC-14	89,801.35	4,490.07	Rampant Emplloyee	4,265.56
300000014	JOHN T. KING	Home Insurance	24-DEC-13	23-DEC-14	220,409.95	11,020.50	University Student	10,469.47
300000015	BETTY X. THOMPSON	Professional Libility	24-DEC-13	23-DEC-14	212,623.46	10,631.17	University Student	10,099.61
300000016	JENNIFER G. THOMPSON	Disability Insurance	24-DEC-13	23-DEC-14	480,963.87	24,048.19	Senior over 80 years	22,845.78
300000017	JESSICA X. YOUNG	Auto Insurance	24-DEC-13	23-DEC-14	201,186.85	10,059.34	University Student	9,556.38
300000018	MICHELLE H. BROWN	Auto Insurance	24-DEC-13	23-DEC-14	458,076.72	22,903.84	Senior over 80 years	21,758.64
300000019	ANTHONY W. THOMAS	Disability Insurance	24-DEC-13	23-DEC-14	322,509.42	16,125.47	Rampant Emplloyee	15,319.20
300000020	MICHAEL J. DAVIS	Accident Insurance	24-DEC-13	23-DEC-14	413,487.35	20,674.37	Rampant Emplloyee	19,640.65
300000021	THOMAS W. CLARK	Disability Insurance	24-DEC-13	23-DEC-14	493,309.74	24,665.49	Rampant Emplloyee	23,432.21

Figure 4-4a: Miracle Broker

An alternative of *dbms_monitor* is to use *dbms_system* to enable SQL trace for the sessions connected via the service name *ggs1*. The following anonymous PL/SQL block enables SQL trace for sessions connected using *ggs1*.

```
SQL> SET SERVEROUTPUT ON
SQL> DECLARE
       CURSOR c1 IS SELECT sid, serial#
                    FROM   v$session
                    WHERE  service_name='ggs1';
       vsid      NUMBER;
       vserial# NUMBER;
     BEGIN
       OPEN c1;
       LOOP
          FETCH c1 into vsid, vserial#;
          EXIT WHEN c1%NOTFOUND;
          DBMS_SYSTEM.SET_SQL_TRACE_IN_SESSION(vsid, vserial#, true);
          DBMS_OUTPUT.PUT_LINE('SID='||vsid||' '||'SERIAL#='||vserial#);
       END LOOP;
       CLOSE C1;
     END;
     /
SID=17 SERIAL#=285
SID=40 SERIAL#=863

PL/SQL procedure successfully completed.
```

TKPROF output

The TKPROF utility formats the generated trace files for identifying the referenced tables from SQL statements listed on the output file. The directory location of the trace file is at *$ORACLE_BASE/diag/rdbms/s1e2/S1E2/*trace. We sort the files using the UNIX/Linux command *ls –ltr* to display the files sorted by modification time on reverse order. The option *sys=no* ignores complex recursive SQL statements generated by SYS user during report runtime, this makes the output file easier to identify the report runtime SQL *select* statements.

```
$ tkprof S1E2_ora_4222.trc S1E2_ora_4222.txt SYS=NO

TKPROF: Release 11.2.0.3.0 - Development on Mon Dec 16 15:14:35 2013

Copyright (c) 1982, 2011, Oracle and/or its affiliates.  All rights
reserved.

$ vi S1E2_ora_4222.txt
```

The output file is reviewed for identifying the report queries. The report lists the main query, but it is intuitive to return additional sub-queries for supporting bind variables used by the main query. Regardless of the report development technique, TKPROF identifies the base tables for views.

The first SQL statement references the *polcies* table. This returned value may not be relevant to the main query.

```
SQL ID: gkrxkpw4gkx57 Plan Hash: 3563362071

SELECT COUNT(*)
FROM   POLICIES
```

The second SQL statement references *policies* and *customers* tables. This is the report main report query. The main query is used to create the materialized view, which is necessary to speed up report runtime.

```
SQL ID: bwljwbvmp3ua7 Plan Hash: 583893952

SELECT P.CUST_NO, C.CUST_NAME, P.POL_NO, P.POL_FROM, P.POL_TO, P.POL_VALUE,
       P.POL_SUB_TOTAL, P.PT_CODE, P.DT_CODE, P.POL_TOTAL
FROM   POLICIES P, CUSTOMERS C
WHERE  P.CUST_NO=C.CUST_NO
ORDER BY P.POL_NO
```

The third SQL statement references *policy_types* table. This is a look up table used by the main query for referencing the column *pt_code.*

```
SQL ID: d6tvhwxmabarf Plan Hash: 2250350636

SELECT PT_DESC
FROM   POLICY_TYPES
WHERE  PT_CODE = :B1
```

The fourth SQL statement references *discount_types* table. This is a *look up* table used by the main query for referencing the column *dt_code*.

```
SQL ID: gfttngmmwcxzx Plan Hash: 1956721938

SELECT DT_DESC
FROM   DISCOUNT_TYPES
WHERE  DT_CODE = :B1
```

Referenced tables in GoldenGate

The list of *sql id* values shows the report is referencing the database objects listed below. Because Oracle GoldenGate performs change data capture from tables, identify the base tables for views and materialized views. The *sql id* is used for extracting performance related details from *v$session*, *v$sql* and *v$sqltext*.

Table 4-2 lists the tables extracted from TKPROF formatted output.

Table Name	Query Type
POLICIES	Main query
CUSTOMERS	Main query
POLICY_TYPES	Look up query
DISCOUNT_TYPES	Look up query

Table 4-2: Referenced tables by the report application

We verify the objects type using the data dictionary view *dba_objects* or *user_objects*.

```
SQL> COLUMN object_name FORMAT A30
SQL> COLUMN object_type FORMAT A12
SQL> SELECT object_name, object_type
  2  FROM   dba_objects
  3  WHERE  object_name in ('POLICIES', 'CUSTOMERS', 'POLICY_TYPES',
                            'DISCOUNT_TYPES') AND
  4  OWNER = 'OSM$REPAPI';

OBJECT_NAME                        OBJECT_TYPE
------------------------------     ------------
CUSTOMERS                          TABLE
DISCOUNT_TYPES                     TABLE
POLICIES                           TABLE
POLICY_TYPES                       TABLE
```

For objects of type *view* query the data dictionary *dba_views* to identify the view base tables. Furthermore, we identify the type of objects returned as a view so that we may query from a view.

For object of type *materilized view* we query the data dictionary view *dba_mviews* to identify the materialized view base tables.

Database audit for GoldenGate

The database audit is an option that can be used to determine the referenced tables by the report. Follow the steps below to enable database auditing and setting the audit options for SELECT statements only.

Enable database audit

The database audit is enabled by setting the database static parameters *audit_trail=db, extended.* This parameter collect statistics, bind variables, and SQL text. Because this is a static parameter, re-starting the database is necessary.

```
SQL> ALTER SYSTEM SET audit_trail='DB_EXTENDED' SCOPE=SPFILE;

System altered.

SQL> SHUTDOWN IMMEDIATE
Database closed.
Database dismounted.
ORACLE instance shut down.
SQL> STARTUP
ORACLE instance started.

Total System Global Area   542814208 bytes
Fixed Size                 2230152 bytes
Variable Size              448792696 bytes
Database Buffers           88080384 bytes
Redo Buffers               3710976 bytes
Database mounted.
Database opened.
SQL> SHOW PARAMETERS audit_trail

NAME                                 TYPE        VALUE
------------------------------------ ----------- ---------------------------
audit_trail                          string       DB_EXTENDED
```

Now, set the audit option for the user running the report.

```
SQL> CONN / AS SYSDBA
Connected.
SQL> AUDIT SELECT TABLE BY osm$repapi BY ACCESS;

Audit succeeded.
```

Run the report, query the data dictionary view *dba_audit_trail* to determine the SQL text for the running report. Filters out unnecessary SQL text referencing objects owned by SYS and SYSTEM schemas.

```
SQL> SELECT sql_text
     FROM   dba_audit_trail
     WHERE  username='OSM$REPAPI' AND
            sql_text IS NOT NULL  AND
            (sql_text NOT LIKE '%SYSTEM.%' AND
             sql_text NOT LIKE '%SYS.%' AND
             sql_text NOT LIKE '%DUAL%');

SQL_TEXT
----------------------------------------------------------------------------
select * from customers where rownum < 10
select max(cust_no) from customers
select * from policy_types
```

We verify the object type for referenced objects found in the SQL *select* statements. This is necessary to determine the base tables for objects of type *view* and *materialized view*.

Oracle Enterprise Manager and GoldenGate

Oracle Enterprise Manager (OEM) SQL Monitor captures and analyzes SQL statements. SQL Monitor delivers detailed SQL analysis, which is far beyond the requirements for developing query offloading using Oracle GoldenGate.

However; the Search Sessions from within Oracle Enterprise Manager shows the query text from which the referenced tables are identified. Figure 4-4 shows the session from the Search Session.

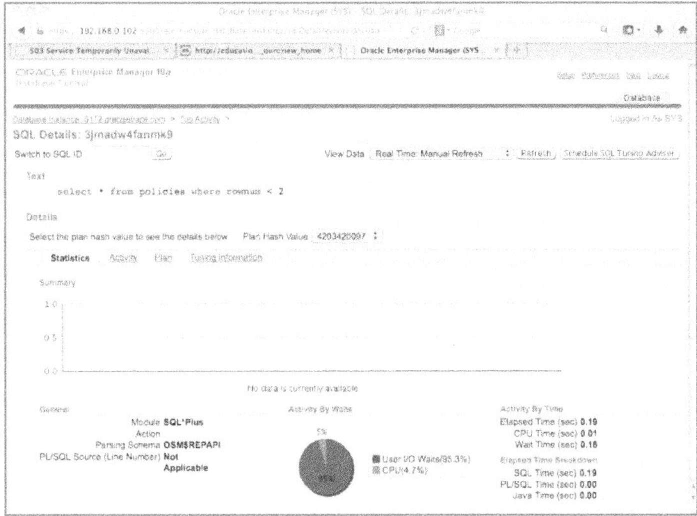

Figure 4-4: Oracle Enterprise Manager Search Sessions

Oracle Real Application Testing (RAT) suite for GoldenGate

Another option for finding packaged report queries is to use SQL Performance Analyzer (SPA) shipped with Oracle Real Application Testing suite. The result return from SPA session include details SQL *select* statements analysis and execution plans.

Oracle SQL Developer

SQL Developer is a graphical user interface (GUI) that is available free-of-charge. SQL Developer also has the option to display the execution plan for ad-hoc queries.

Other non-Oracle graphical user interface tools are available, the majority of these performance analysis tools capture the query and the execution plans.

Prerequisites for GoldenGate

Moving report runtime to the target system for query offloading demands implementing Oracle GoldenGate on both systems. Reports running on the target database need an optimized infrastructure to support higher throughput and scalability. Ultimately, it's the combination of Oracle 12c Enterprise Edition features for data warehouse, very large database (VLDB) and online analytical processing (OLAP), and Oracle GoldenGate 12c for real-time data movement for sub-second delay and data transformations.

To implement query offloading, it's recommend to complete the following chapters, for meeting the requirements, preparing the environment, installing the software and establishing the target database.

Chapter 1: Fundamentals of GoldenGate

This is an optional chapter but highly recommend for new Oracle GoldenGate users. Learn about applying Oracle GoldenGate features to enhance and to optimize the capture and delivery processes.

Chapter 2: Getting started with GoldenGate

This chapter explains the installation and preparing the source and target databases requirements for Oracle GoldenGate. It's important to verify the installation log, directory structure and network TCP/IP port availability.

Chapter 3: Initial-load techniques in GoldenGate

The initial-load establishes the target database, from either active or inactive source database. Different methods are available to support homogenous and heterogeneous environments. The chapter covers Oracle GoldenGate, Oracle, and Microsoft SQL Server database methods.

Configure change data capture group for GoldenGate

The primary group (*es1e202*) performs change data capture (CDC) from the source database (S1E2) transaction logs. Group *es1e201* uses a local trail for configuring a secondary extract group.

The tables referenced by the report are listed in table 4-2 and implemented for change data capture. Limiting the primary extract to only the referenced tables by the report eliminates unnecessary data replication, hence delivering best performance for real-time reporting.

From within GGSCI command-line, prepare the parameter file *es1e202.prm*.

```
GGSCI (ggs-source) 1> EDIT PARAMS es1e202
```

```
EXTRACT es1e202
SETENV  (ORACLE_SID=S1E2)
SETENV  (ORACLE_HOME="/u01/app/oracle/product/11.2.0/dbhome_1")
```

```
SETENV  (NLS_LANG=AMERICAN_AMERICA.AL32UTF8)
USERID  ggs_admin@S1E2, password oracle
EXTTRAIL ./dirdat/sb
TABLE osm$repapi.policy_types;
TABLE osm$repapi.discount_types;
TABLE osm$repapi.customers;
TABLE osm$repapi.policies;
```

Create the primary group for GoldenGate

The primary group extract read from the transaction logs and writes them to the local trail called '*tb*'. The local trail files are created on the default location ./dirdat/ and managed using the manager process. The *add extract* command creates the primary extract, and the *add exttrail* creates the local trail. The size of the local trail files of 32MB is relatively small for highly active environment. For most sites, it's recommended to set the local trail file size equal to the smallest online redo log member or use the value of 128MB.

```
GGSCI (ggs-source) 2> ADD EXTRACT es1e202, TRANLOG, BEGIN now, THREADS 1

EXTRACT added.

GGSCI (ggs-source) 4> ADD EXTTRAIL ./dirdat/sb, EXTRACT es1e202, MEGABYTES
128

EXTTRAIL added.
```

Starting a primary extract in GoldenGate

Now, that the primary group has been configured and created, it's time to start it for change data capture from the source database transaction logs. We use the *start extract* command, then verify the status of the extract using *info extract* command. Do not proceed further until the extract *es1e202* status is *running* and writing to the local trail.

```
GGSCI (ggs-source) 6> START EXTRACT es1e202

Sending START request to MANAGER ...
EXTRACT ES1E202 starting
```

```
GGSCI (ggs-source) 6> INFO EXTRACT es1e202

EXTRACT    ES1E202   Last Started 2013-10-30 19:03   Status RUNNING
Checkpoint Lag       00:10:08 (updated 00:00:08 ago)
Process ID           23959
Log Read Checkpoint  Oracle Redo Logs
                     2013-10-30 18:53:42  Thread 1, Seqno 52, RBA 4247040
                     SCN 0.0 (0)

GGSCI (ggs-source) 7>
```

Handling extracts errors in GoldenGate

The status returned by the *info extract* command is either *abended* or *stopped*, use the following steps to identify, fix and re-attempt starting the extract. A common cause of errors maybe due to a parameter that is misspelled or a missing required definition such as the extract *local trail*. The following illustrates these two specific cause of errors.

We begin by viewing the current extract error report using GGSCI *view* command.

```
GGSCI (ggs-source) 7> VIEW REPORT ES1E202
```

The error shows the parameter *exttrail* is misspelled. We fix this by editing the parameter file by correcting the parameter, then re-attempt starting the extract.

```
2013-12-22 01:43:35  ERROR   OGG-00303  Unrecognized parameter (EXTRAIL).

2013-12-22 01:43:35  ERROR   OGG-01668  PROCESS ABENDING.
```

The next error indicates the local trail is missing. It also suggests the command to define the local trail.

```
2013-12-22 01:46:39  ERROR   OGG-01044  The trail './dirdat/sb' is not
assigned to extract 'ES1E202'

. Assign the trail to the extract with the command "ADD EXTTRAIL/RMTTRAIL

./dirdat/sb, EXTRACT ES1E202".
```

We use the same procedure to identify and fix errors related to the data pump and change data delivery extracts.

Configure data pump group for GoldenGate

To avoid the primary extract failure in case of network disconnections, the secondary group *epmp02* is configured. The data pump extract routes the data to the target system leaving the primary extract dedicated to perform change data capture only. The data pump uses the parameter *passthru* to send data as is, unaltered. *rmttrail* identifies the remote trail name followed by the list of tables.

From within GGSCI command-line prepare parameter file *epmp02.prm*, it's saved on the default location of ./dirprm/ directory.

```
GGSCI (ggs-source) 1> EDIT PARAMS epmp02
EXTRACT EPMP02
```

```
USERID ggs_admin@S1E2, PASSWORD oracle
PASSTHRU
RMTHOST ggs-target, MGRPORT 7812
RMTTRAIL ./dirdat/tb
TABLE osm$repapi.policy_types;
TABLE osm$repapi.discount_types;
TABLE osm$repapi.customers;
TABLE osm$repapi.policies;
```

Create the secondary group in GoldenGate

The *add extract* command creates the secondary group. The data pump extract *epmp02* reads the local trail file identified by the option *exttrailsource.*

```
GGSCI (ggs-source) 2> ADD EXTRACT epmp02, EXTTRAILSOURCE ./dirdat/sb

EXTRACT added.

GGSCI (ggs-source) 3> ADD RMTTRAIL ./dirdat/tb, EXTRACT epmp02, MEGABYTES
128

RMTTRAIL added.
```

Starting the secondary extract in GoldenGate

Upon successful startup of the data pump group, local trail transaction are shipped over TCP/IP to the designated server by *rmtrail* and manager port, *mgrport.*

```
GGSCI (ggs-source) 9> START EXTRACT epmp02

Sending START request to MANAGER ...
EXTRACT EPMP02 starting
```

Before proceeding to configure the change data delivery group, we verify the data pump status is *running*, remote trail is created, and remote trail files are receiving transactional data. In case of errors, we correct the cause of the error and re-attempt restarting the database pump.

```
GGSCI (ggs-source) 10> INFO EXTRACT epmp02

EXTRACT    EPMP02    Last Started 2013-10-30 19:14   Status RUNNING
Checkpoint Lag       00:00:00 (updated 00:00:05 ago)
Process ID           24022
Log Read Checkpoint  File ./dirdat/sb000000
                     First Record  RBA 0
```

Configure change data delivery group for GoldenGate

The delivery group *rs1e202* reads the remote trail files and uses the database native interface to apply the transactions to the target database. The replicate process *rs1e202* is configured to operate only on the referenced table by the report. The parameter *assumetargetdefs* indicates that the receiving remote trail is from identical tables structures, and therefore no transformation is required.

```
GGSCI (ggs-target) 1> EDIT PARAMS rs1e202
```

```
REPLICAT rs1e202
SETENV (ORACLE_SID=T1C1)
SETENV (NSL_LANG=AMERICAN_AMERICA.AL32UTF8)
USERID ggs_admin@T1C1, PASSWORD oracle
ASSUMETARGETDEFS
DISCARDFILE ./dirrpt/rs1e202.dsc, PURGE
MAP osm$repapi.policy_types, TARGET osm$repapi.policy_types;
MAP osm$repapi.discount_types, TARGET osm$repapi.discount_types;
MAP osm$repapi.customers, TARGET osm$repapi.customers;
MAP osm$repapi.policies, TARGET osm$repapi.policies;
```

Create the change data delivery group in GoldenGate

We use the *add replicat* GGSCI command to create the delivery group *rs1e202*. The replicate process *rs1e202* reads and applies the remote trail *./dirdat/tb* using the target database native SQL interface.

```
GGSCI (ggs-target) 3> ADD REPLICAT rs1e202, EXTTRAIL ./dirdat/tb
REPLICAT added.

GGSCI (ggs-target) 4>
```

Starting the change data delivery process for GoldenGate

We start by verifying the status of the delivery process. The delivery process must remain running to provide real-time data movement. In the case of an error, view the report file using *view report rs1e202*.

```
GGSCI (ggs-target) 4> START REPLICAT rs1e202

Sending START request to MANAGER ...
REPLICAT RS1E202 starting
```

```
GGSCI (ggs-target) 5> INFO REPLICAT rs1e202

REPLICAT   RS1E202   Last Started 2013-11-06 08:06   Status RUNNING
Checkpoint Lag       00:00:00 (updated 00:00:06 ago)
Process ID           7325
Log Read Checkpoint  File ./dirdat/tb000000
                     First Record  RBA 0
```

Materialized view support in GoldenGate

The following DDL statements are executed on the target database only. They are optional, but highly recommended for data warehouse applications.

Oracle enterprise edition supports creating materialized views for automatic query re-write. The database optimizer re-writes the query to retrieve data from the materialized view when it matches the report original SQL statement and deliver better execution plan. To ensure the materialized view performs query re-write, the materialized view should be created using the *create materialized view* statement.

```
SQL> CREATE MATERIALIZED VIEW cust_pol
  2     BUILD IMMEDIATE
  3     REFRESH FORCE
  4     ENABLE QUERY REWRITE AS
  5  SELECT P.CUST_NO, C.CUST_NAME, P.POL_NO, P.POL_FROM, P.POL_TO,
  6         P.POL_VALUE, P.POL_SUB_TOTAL, P.PT_CODE, P.DT_CODE, P.POL_TOTAL
  7  FROM   POLICIES P, CUSTOMERS C
  8  WHERE  P.CUST_NO=C.CUST_NO
  9  ORDER BY P.POL_NO;

Materialized view created.

SQL>
```

Materialized view log

A materialized view is refreshed using three refresh options. To support *fast* refresh, a materialized view log is created.

Enable and verify query rewrite

The following steps is to force query re-write, so that the execution plan attempt to employ the materialized view.

```
SQL> ALTER MATERIALIZED VIEW osm$repapi.cust_pol ENABLE QUERY REWRITE;

Materialized view altered.
```

Refresh the materialize view using *dbms_mview.refresh* procedure.

```
SQL> EXEC DBMS_MVIEW.REFRESH('osm$repapi.cust_pol');

PL/SQL procedure successfully completed.
```

For the optimizer to make better execution plan, refresh the schema statistics using *dbms_stats.gather_schema_stats* procedure.

```
SQL> EXEC DBMS_STATS.GATHER_SCHEMA_STATS('osm$repapi');

PL/SQL procedure successfully completed.
```

We run the report application on the modified target database environment using the database service ggs2, created using *dbms_service.create_service* procedure.

```
SQL> EXEC DBMS_SERVICE.CREATE_SERVICE('ggs2', 'ggs2.precisetrace.com');

PL/SQL procedure successfully completed.
```

```
SQL> EXEC DBMS_SERVICE.START_SERVICE('ggs2');

PL/SQL procedure successfully completed.
```

The target database is accessed using the below database access descriptor (DAD) *osmdad121*, which uses the connect string ggs2 for the service named *ggs2*.

```
<Location /osm$dad$121>
  SetHandler pls_handler
  Order deny,allow
  Allow from all
  AllowOverride None
  PlsqlDatabaseWe username                 osm$repapi
  PlsqlDatabasePassword                 oracle
  PlsqlDatabaseConnectString            ggs2
  PlsqlAuthenticationMode               Basic
  PlsqlDocumentTableName                osm$repapi.osm_documents
  PlsqlDefaultPage                      system.pl
  PlsqlNLSLanguage                      AMERICAN_AMERICA.AL32UTF8
  PlsqlTransferMode                     RAW
</location>
```

Figure 4-5a: Miracle Broker

Target database execution plan with a materialized view

This report is using a better execution plan to fetch data from the database tables and we verify the query re-write is part of the execution plan.

We then enable SQL trace for connection using the service name, *ggs2*.

```
SQL> EXEC DBMS_MONITOR.SERV_MOD_ACT_TRACE_ENABLE(service_name=>'ggs2');

PL/SQL procedure successfully completed.
```

To confirm the report is retrieving from the materialized view, create *plan_table* for the *osm$repapi* schema.

```
SQL> conn osm$repapi/oracle

Connected.

SQL> @$ORACLE_HOME/rdbms/admin/utlxplan.sql

Table created.

SQL> exit
```

We can run TKPROF to format the trace file for confirming the database optimizer is performing query re-write using the materialized view and not executing the report by joining the *customers* and *policies* tables.

```
$ tkprof T1C1_ora_9388.trc T1C1_ora_9388.txt SYS=NO
table=osm\$repapi.plan_table explain=osm\$repapi/oracle
```

Viewing the execution indicate the report is now retrieving data from the materialized view, *cust_pol*.

```
Rows     Execution Plan
-------  ---------------------------------------------------
      0  SELECT STATEMENT   MODE: ALL_ROWS
  10000   SORT (ORDER BY)
  10000    MAT_VIEW REWRITE ACCESS   MODE: ANALYZED (FULL) OF 'CUST_POL'
               (MAT_VIEW REWRITE)
```

Disable SQL trace

It's necessary to disable SQL trace to avoid trace files keep building up. This action should be executed on the source and target databases.

```
SQL> EXEC DBMS_MONITOR.SERV_MOD_ACT_TRACE_DISABLE(service_name=>'ggs2');

PL/SQL procedure successfully completed.
```

This concludes the implementation of Oracle GoldenGate 12c for real-time query offloading. Applying Oracle features to the target database environment is optional and may requires additional software licenses.

Oracle GoldenGate for R12 Oracle E-Business suite

Packaged applications such as R12 Oracle E-Business suite benefits from Oracle GoldenGate 12c query offloading. By submitting reports to an star schema instance dedicated and designed for intensive reports increases the throughput of R12 Oracle E-Business suite database server by handling online transaction processing (OLTP) only.

For the purpose of demonstrating Oracle GoldenGate query offloading, the default R12 Oracle E-Business suite vision database is used. This section uses a cloned R12 Oracle E-Business suite instance. The server names, IP addresses and DNS server shown on tables 4-2 and 4-3.

Component	Description/Value
Server name	apps-srv1
TCP/IP address	192.168.1.205
Oracle home	/d01/app/oracle/product/11.2.0/dbhome_1
Oracle version	11.2
Oracle GoldenGate home	/d01/oracle/ggs
Database user	ggs_admin
Database password	oracle

Table 4-2: Source R12 Oracle E-Business suite instance

Component	Description/Value
Server name	apps-srv2
TCP/IP address	192.168.1.206
Oracle home	/d01/app/oracle/product/11.2.0/dbhome_1
Oracle version	11.2
Oracle GoldenGate home	/d01/oracle/ggs
Database user	ggs_admin
Database password	oracle

Table 4-3: Target R12 Oracle E-Business suite instance

Vision database for GoldenGate

Figure 4-5 shows the login page for Oracle vision R12 E-Business suite database. The reports demonstrated in this section are from the vision database instance. The same workflow applies to production R12 E-Business suite instance. Because Oracle R12 E-Business report always uses parameter files, this may prevent the use of materialized views for query re-write.

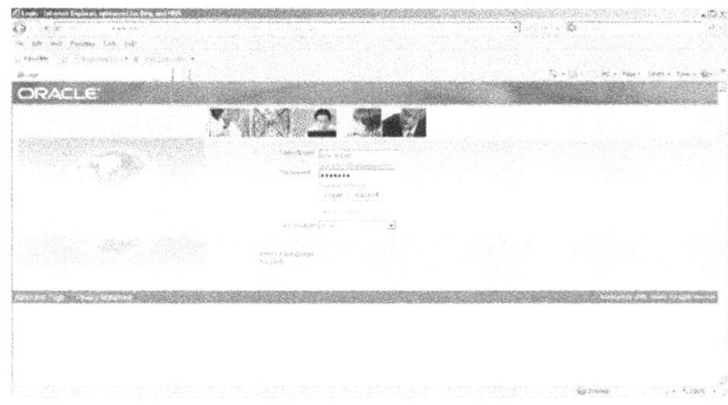

Figure 4-5: Oracle R12 E-Business suite login

This section covers the following topics.

- Submitting reports requests
- Viewing reports requests
- View submitted reports referenced tables
- Configure Oracle GoldenGate for real-time R12 E-Business reports

It's recommended to install a new home for Oracle 11g R2 to support Oracle GoldenGate 12c. There is no need to create a database as Oracle GoldenGate requires the shared library only.

Submit new request in GoldenGate

From the source database system, we use the *Submit Request* function to enter the report request. As shown in figure 4-6, select the report name from the list of reports, the remaining fields are optional. Because our objective is to identify the referenced tables only, the process does not require enabling SQL trace of the report session. However; to retrieve the report session ID and serial# for further monitoring, use the performance tab by navigating to system administrator, dashboard links.

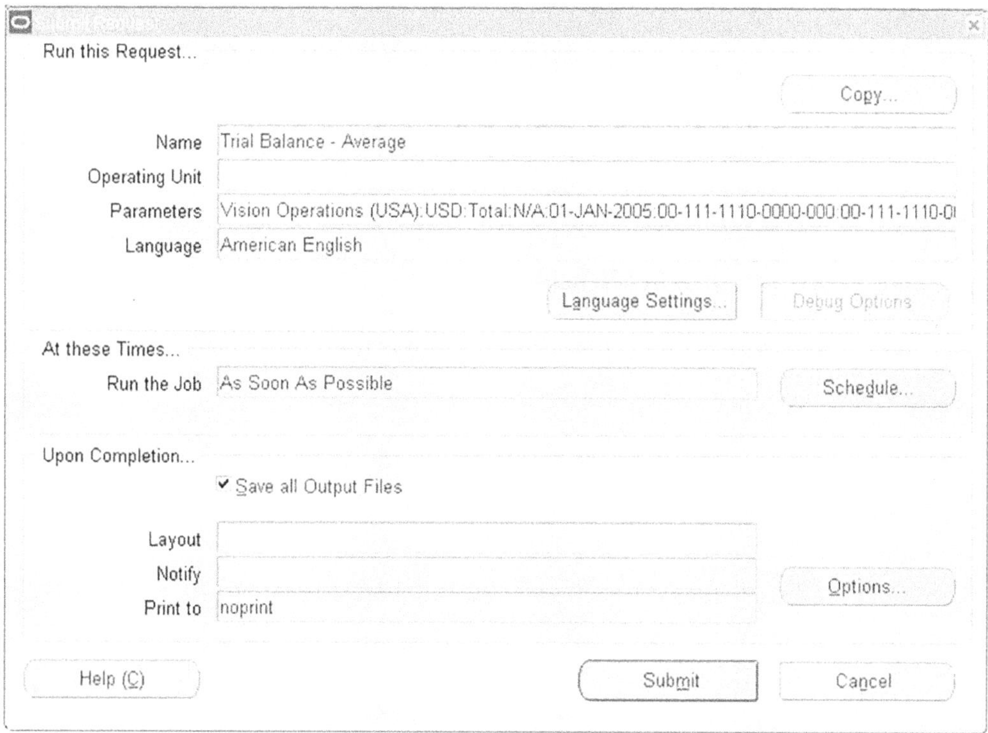

Figure 4-6: Submit report request

A request ID is generated for managing the report request and monitoring the report completion status.

Request status in GoldenGate

The requests generated are viewable from the request function as shown in figure 4-7. The query offloading is developed for the report: Actual/Budget Income Statement (Financial Statement Generator). Oracle GoldenGate requires the list of tables referenced by the report. We use the following functions from Request function.

Submit a New Request

Quickly submits new report request.

Refresh Data

By clicking on *Refresh Data*, the list of report updated with the current status.

View Output

Display the report on the new browser window.

The View log in GoldenGate

The view log displays the report details including the report *select* statement, which is used to determine the referenced tables by the report.

Refresh Data | Find Requests | Submit a New Request...

Request ID	Name	Parent	Phase	Status	Parameters
5798513	Chart of Accounts - Detail l		Completed	Normal	101, 00-000-0000-0000-000, 9
5798512	Journals - Voucher		**Completed**	**Warning**	1017, A, 1, P, USD, , 2007/01
5798511	Trial Balance - Detail		Completed	Normal	1017, Vision Operations, 1, 10
5798510	Trial Balance - Detail		Completed	Normal	1017, Vision Operations, 1, 10
5798502	DBI Annual Comparison (Fi		Completed	Normal	1017, 101, FSG-ADHOC-, C, (
5798501	Actual/Budget Income Stat		Completed	Normal	1017, 101, FSG-ADHOC-, C, (
5798500	Company Balance Sheet (F		Completed	Normal	1017, 101, FSG-ADHOC-, C, (
5798499	Actual/Budget Income Stat		Completed	Normal	1017, 101, FSG-ADHOC-, C, (
5798498	Company Balance Sheet (F		Completed	Normal	1017, 101, FSG-ADHOC-, C, (
5798497	Actual/Budget Income Stat		Completed	Normal	1017, 101, FSG-ADHOC-, C, (

Hold Request | View Details... | View Output

Cancel Request | Diagnostics | View Log...

Figure 4-7: Submitted requests

Report query

Upon successful completion of the report, select the report and click on the *View Log*. We then review the *select* statement to determine the referenced tables by the report.

```
SELECT
nvl(bal.PERIOD_TYPE, ''),
```

```
    nvl(bal.PERIOD_YEAR, -1),
    bal.PERIOD_NAME,
    nvl(bal.PERIOD_NUM, -1),
    nvl(bal.PERIOD_NUM, -1),
    bal.ACTUAL_FLAG,
    decode(cc.TEMPLATE_ID, NULL, 'N', 'Y'),
    -1,
    nvl(bal.BUDGET_VERSION_ID, -1),
    -1,
    nvl(bal.ENCUMBRANCE_TYPE_ID, -1),
    bal.CURRENCY_CODE,
    bal.LEDGER_ID,
    nvl(bal.TRANSLATED_FLAG, ''),
    nvl(bal.PERIOD_NET_DR, 0) - nvl(bal.PERIOD_NET_CR, 0),
    nvl(bal.PERIOD_NET_DR, 0),
    nvl(bal.PERIOD_NET_CR, 0),
    nvl(bal.QUARTER_TO_DATE_DR,0)-nvl(bal.QUARTER_TO_DATE_CR, 0),
    nvl(bal.QUARTER_TO_DATE_DR, 0),
    nvl(bal.QUARTER_TO_DATE_CR, 0),
    nvl(bal.BEGIN_BALANCE_DR, 0) - nvl(bal.BEGIN_BALANCE_CR, 0),
    nvl(bal.BEGIN_BALANCE_DR, 0),
    nvl(bal.BEGIN_BALANCE_CR, 0),
    nvl(bal.PROJECT_TO_DATE_DR, 0) - nvl(bal.PROJECT_TO_DATE_CR, 0),
    nvl(bal.PROJECT_TO_DATE_DR, 0),
    nvl(bal.PROJECT_TO_DATE_CR, 0),
    nvl(bal.PERIOD_NET_DR_BEQ, 0) - nvl(bal.PERIOD_NET_CR_BEQ, 0),
    nvl(bal.PERIOD_NET_DR_BEQ, 0),
    nvl(bal.PERIOD_NET_CR_BEQ, 0),
    nvl(bal.QUARTER_TO_DATE_DR_BEQ,0)-nvl(bal.QUARTER_TO_DATE_CR_BEQ, 0),
    nvl(bal.QUARTER_TO_DATE_DR_BEQ, 0),
    nvl(bal.QUARTER_TO_DATE_CR_BEQ, 0),
    nvl(bal.BEGIN_BALANCE_DR_BEQ, 0) - nvl(bal.BEGIN_BALANCE_CR_BEQ, 0),
    nvl(bal.BEGIN_BALANCE_DR_BEQ, 0),
    nvl(bal.BEGIN_BALANCE_CR_BEQ, 0),
    nvl(bal.PROJECT_TO_DATE_DR_BEQ, 0) - nvl(bal.PROJECT_TO_DATE_CR_BEQ,
0),
    nvl(bal.PROJECT_TO_DATE_DR_BEQ, 0),
    nvl(bal.PROJECT_TO_DATE_CR_BEQ, 0),
    nvl(gl.SHORT_NAME, ''),
    nvl(gl.NAME, '') DESCRIPTION,
    nvl(gl.CURRENCY_CODE, ''),
    nvl(SEGMENT3,''),
    nvl(SEGMENT1,''),
    nvl(SEGMENT2,''),
    nvl(SEGMENT4,''),
    nvl(SEGMENT5,''),
    nvl(gl.SHORT_NAME,'') LEDGER_SEGMENT
FROM
    GL_BALANCES bal,
    GL_CODE_COMBINATIONS cc,
    GL_LEDGERS gl
WHERE bal.CODE_COMBINATION_ID = cc.CODE_COMBINATION_ID
AND bal.LEDGER_ID = gl.LEDGER_ID
AND   cc.CHART_OF_ACCOUNTS_ID = 101
AND ( bal.CURRENCY_CODE in ('ANY','USD')  )
AND ( bal.LEDGER_ID = 1 )
AND   nvl(bal.TRANSLATED_FLAG, 'x')in ('Y','N','x')
AND   cc.TEMPLATE_ID is NULL
AND ( (nvl(SEGMENT3,'') >= '4001' AND  nvl(SEGMENT3,'') <= '4999')
```

```
OR (nvl(SEGMENT3,'') >= '5001' AND  nvl(SEGMENT3,'') <= '5999')
OR (nvl(SEGMENT3,'') >= '6001' AND  nvl(SEGMENT3,'') <= '6999')
OR (nvl(SEGMENT3,'') >= '7001' AND  nvl(SEGMENT3,'') <= '7299')
OR (nvl(SEGMENT3,'') >= '7301' AND  nvl(SEGMENT3,'') <= '7399')
OR (nvl(SEGMENT3,'') >= '7401' AND  nvl(SEGMENT3,'') <= '7599')
OR (nvl(SEGMENT3,'') >= '7601' AND  nvl(SEGMENT3,'') <= '7758')
OR (nvl(SEGMENT3,'') >= '7760' AND  nvl(SEGMENT3,'') <= '7799')
OR (nvl(SEGMENT3,'') >= '7801' AND  nvl(SEGMENT3,'') <= '7899')
OR (nvl(SEGMENT3,'') >= '7901' AND  nvl(SEGMENT3,'') <= '7998')
OR (nvl(SEGMENT3,'') >= '8300' AND  nvl(SEGMENT3,'') <= '8519')
)
AND (
(bal.period_name in ('Mar-00')
AND (       (nvl(bal.period_name,'') = 'Mar-00'
AND (       (bal.CURRENCY_CODE = 'USD'
            AND     bal.ACTUAL_FLAG = 'B'
            AND     bal.BUDGET_VERSION_ID = 3625
)
 OR
 (   (bal.CURRENCY_CODE = 'USD'
            AND     bal.ACTUAL_FLAG = 'A'
)
 OR
 (   (bal.CURRENCY_CODE = 'USD'
            AND     bal.ACTUAL_FLAG = 'B'
            AND     bal.BUDGET_VERSION_ID = 3625
            AND     ((nvl(bal.PERIOD_NET_DR,0) != 0) or
(nvl(bal.PERIOD_NET_CR,0) != 0)))
 OR
 (   (bal.CURRENCY_CODE = 'USD'
            AND     bal.ACTUAL_FLAG = 'A'
            AND     ((nvl(bal.PERIOD_NET_DR,0) != 0) or
(nvl(bal.PERIOD_NET_CR,0) != 0)))))))))))
```

Referenced tables

The tables referenced by the report are listed below. Oracle GoldenGate instance configured to perform change data capture (CDC) and delivery for real-time data movement.

- *gl_balances*
- *gl_code_combinations*
- *gl_ledgers*

These table is owned by the database schema 'GL'. Refer to chapter 2 for granting object database privileges *to ggs_admin* database user.

Manager process in GoldenGate

The manager process should be configured on the source and target Oracle R12 E-Business systems. As indicated below, the source Oracle GoldenGate instance uses port 7805 and the target Oracle GoldenGate instance uses port 7806. Refer to chapters 1 and 2 for more details regarding the preparation steps.

Start GGSCI and verify the status using *info mgr* command.

```
[oracle@apps-srv1 ~]$ cd /d01/oracle/ggs
[oracle@apps-srv1 ggs]$ ./ggsci

Oracle GoldenGate Command Interpreter for Oracle
Version 12.1.2.0.0 17185003 OGGCORE_12.1.2.0.0_PLATFORMS_130924.1316_FBO
Linux, x64, 64bit (optimized), Oracle 11g on Sep 25 2013 00:31:13
Operating system character set identified as UTF-8.

Copyright (C) 1995, 2013, Oracle and/or its affiliates. All rights reserved.


GGSCI (apps-srv1) 1> INFO MGR

Manager is running (IP port apps-srv1.7805, Process ID 10750).
```

Then we configure and verify status the manager process on source and target systems.

Database login for GoldenGate

To ensure that you are able to login to the database from within GGSCI command-line we use the following steps for successful database login, executing *oraenv*.

```
[oracle@apps-srv1 ggs]$ . oraenv

ORACLE_SID = [oracle] ? VIS
ORACLE_HOME = [/home/oracle] ? /d01/oracle/VIS/db/tech_st/11.1.0
The Oracle base has been set to /d01/oracle/VIS/db/tech_st/11.1.0
[oracle@apps-srv1 ggs]$ ./ggsci

Oracle GoldenGate Command Interpreter for Oracle
Version 12.1.2.0.0 17185003 OGGCORE_12.1.2.0.0_PLATFORMS_130924.1316_FBO
Linux, x64, 64bit (optimized), Oracle 11g on Sep 25 2013 00:31:13
Operating system character set identified as UTF-8.

Copyright (C) 1995, 2013, Oracle and/or its affiliates. All rights reserved.


GGSCI (apps-srv1) 1> dblogin userid ggs_admin, password oracle
Successfully logged into database.
```

We then verify successful database login from within Oracle GoldenGate for the source and target systems.

Table level supplemental logging in GoldenGate

Here we add supplemental logging to the database tables. This is to be executed on the source database only.

```
GGSCI (apps-srvl) 1> DBLOGIN USERID ggs_admin, PASSWORD oracle
Successfully logged into database.

GGSCI (apps-srvl) 2> ADD TRANDATA GL.GL_BALANCES

2013-12-29 09:06:36  WARNING OGG-06439  No unique key is defined for table
GL_BALANCES. All viable columns will be used to represent the key, but may
not guarantee uniqueness. KEYCOLS may be used to define the key.

2013-12-29 09:06:36  WARNING OGG-01387  Table GL.GL_BALANCES has no valid
key columns, added unconditional supplemental log group for all table
columns.

Logging of supplemental redo data enabled for table GL.GL_BALANCES.
TRANDATA for scheduling columns has been added on table 'GL.GL_BALANCES'.

GGSCI (apps-srvl) 3> ADD TRANDATA GL.GL_CODE_COMBINATIONS

Logging of supplemental redo data enabled for table GL.GL_CODE_COMBINATIONS.
TRANDATA for scheduling columns has been added on table
'GL.GL_CODE_COMBINATIONS'.

GGSCI (apps-srvl) 4> ADD TRANDATA GL.GL_LEDGERS

Logging of supplemental redo data enabled for table GL.GL_LEDGERS.
TRANDATA for scheduling columns has been added on table 'GL.GL_LEDGERS'.
```

Deploying the primary group in GoldenGate

The primary group manages the change data capture (CDC). The group is composed of configuration file, primary extract, the local trail and checkpoint file. The source database is expected to run on ARCHIVELOG mode, the primary extract EVIS01 uses the transaction logs to provide real-time data movement.

Configure the primary extract

The primary extract is configured to perform change data capture from the table reference by the report. Even though, an Oracle 11g is installed for Oracle GoldenGate, the ORACLE_HOME attribute value is Oracle R12 E-Business suite database home.

```
GGSCI (apps-srv1) 4> EDIT PARAMS EVIS01
```

```
EXTRACT EVIS01
SETENV  (ORACLE_SID=VIS)
SETENV  (ORACLE_HOME="/d01/oracle/VIS/db/tech_st/11.1.0")
SETENV  (NLS_LANG=AMERICAN_AMERICA.AL32UTF8)
USERID  ggs_admin, password oracle
EXTTRAIL ./dirdat/sd
TABLE GL.GL_BALANCES;
TABLE GL.GL_CODE_COMBINATIONS;
TABLE GL.GL_LEDGERS;
```

Create the primary extract

From GGSCI command-line, we execute *add extract* command with the options to read from the transaction logs (TRANLOG). The *add exttrail* defines the local trail '*sd*' for the primary extract (*evis01*). Consider sizing the local trail appropriately, which should equal the size of the online redo log files or 128MB, otherwise.

```
GGSCI (apps-srv1) 2> ADD EXTRACT EVIS01, TRANLOG, BEGIN now, THREADS 1
EXTRACT added.

GGSCI (apps-srv1) 3> ADD EXTTRAIL ./dirdat/sd, EXTRACT EVIS01, MEGABYTES 128
EXTTRAIL added.
```

Start the primary extract

From GGSCI command-line, start and verify the status for the primary extract. We then monitor the status while the application is running and primary extract is writing to the local trail continuously starting at file sd000000.

```
GGSCI (apps-srv1) 44> START EXTRACT evis01

Sending START request to MANAGER ...
EXTRACT EVIS01 starting

GGSCI (apps-srv1) 45> INFO ALL

Program     Status      Group       Lag at Chkpt  Time Since Chkpt

MANAGER     RUNNING
EXTRACT     RUNNING     EVIS01      00:00:00      00:00:00

GGSCI (apps-srv1) 46>
```

Deploying the secondary group in GoldenGate

Because the primary extract (EVIS01) is creating a local trail, a secondary extract reads the local trail files and routes data across TCP/IP to the remote system. The deployment of the secondary group is optional, but highly recommended to protect the primary extract from failure.

For example, in the event of remote system disconnection, the primary extract continues operating without considering the network status. In such situation, the data pump extract status will soon become *abended*, waiting for remote system to become available. To enable the data pump extract to restart automatically, we configure the source system Oracle GoldenGate instance manager process to reattempt starting *abended* processes.

Configure the secondary extract

We prepare the configuration for the secondary extract named (*pvis01*). The data pump extract ships data to remote system indicated by the parameter *rmthost* and *mgrport*. The data pump extract uses the parameters *passthru* and *table* for shipping data without transformation.

```
GGSCI (apps-srv1) 46> EDIT PARAMS PVIS01
```

```
EXTRACT pvis01
USERID ggs_admin, PASSWORD oracle
PASSTHRU
RMTHOST apps-srv2, MGRPORT 7806
RMTTRAIL ./dirdat/td
TABLE GL.GL_BALANCES;
TABLE GL.GL_CODE_COMBINATIONS;
TABLE GL.GL_LEDGERS;
```

Create the secondary extract

The data pump extract (PVIS01) reads the local trail created by the primary extract, this is indicated by the option *exttrailsource* of the *add extract* command. The *add rmttrail* command defines the remote trail created by the dynamic server collector, receiving data from the data pump extract.

```
GGSCI (apps-srv1) 48> ADD EXTRACT pvis01, EXTTRAILSOURCE ./dirdat/sd
EXTRACT added.

GGSCI (apps-srv1) 49> ADD RMTTRAIL ./dirdat/td, EXTRACT pvis01, MEGABYTES
128
RMTTRAIL added.

GGSCI (apps-srv1) 50>
```

Starting the secondary extract

The secondary extract (PVIS01) should remain running at all times. This guarantees the disk space is optimized by purging consumed local trail files from the source system.

```
GGSCI (apps-srv1) 51> START EXTRACT PVIS01

Sending START request to MANAGER ...
EXTRACT PVIS01 starting

GGSCI (apps-srv1) 52> INFO ALL

Program     Status      Group       Lag at Chkpt  Time Since Chkpt

MANAGER     RUNNING
EXTRACT     RUNNING     EVIS01      00:00:00      00:00:06
EXTRACT     RUNNING     PVIS01      00:00:00      00:01:11
```

Deploying the delivery group in GoldenGate

On the target Oracle R12 E-Business suite instance, we prepare the parameter file, define the replicate process and ensure it's starting successfully.

Checkpoint table in GoldenGate

The replicate process default checkpoint is a database table. We create the global parameter file *globals*, add the parameter *checkpointtable* followed by the schema and table name. The table name is subject to Oracle naming rules and convention.

```
CHECKPOINTTABLE.GGS_ADMIN.CHKPTTAB
```

```
GGSCI (apps-srv2) 1> DBLOGIN USERID ggs_admin, PASSWORD oracle
Successfully logged into database.

GGSCI (apps-srv2) 2> ADD CHECKPOINTTABLE

No checkpoint table specified. Using GLOBALS specification
(ggs_admin.chkpttab)...

Successfully created checkpoint table ggs_admin.chkpttab.

GGSCI (apps-srv2) 3>
```

To avoid using database table for checkpoint, use the option *nodbcheckpoint* when defining the replicate group using the *add replicat* GGSCI command.

Configure delivery group for GoldenGate

The parameter file for the delivery group (*rvis01*) maps the list of tables referenced by the report. The target database is kept continuously synchronized using the remote trail files, providing real-time data movement with sub-second delay. For high volume transactional system, Oracle GoldenGate supports parallel processing. Refer to chapter 1 to learn more about using Oracle GoldenGate built-in @RANGE function to enable parallel processing for the delivery groups. The parameter *assumetargetdefs* indicates the source and target tables on the map statements have identical structure, otherwise, a source definition file is required.

```
GGSCI (apps-srv2) 3> EDIT PARAMS rvis01
```

```
REPLICAT rvis01
SETENV (ORACLE_SID=VIS)
SETENV (NSL_LANG=AMERICAN_AMERICA.AL32UTF8)
USERID ggs_admin, PASSWORD oracle
ASSUMETARGETDEFS
DISCARDFILE ./dirrpt/rvis01.dsc, PURGE
MAP GL.GL_BALANCES, TARGET GL.GL_BALANCES;
MAP GL.GL_CODE_COMBINATIONS, TARGET GL.GL_CODE_COMBINATIONS;
MAP GL.GL_LEDGERS, TARGET GL.GL_LEDGERS;
```

Create the delivery group

We use the *add replicat* GGSCI command to define the delivery group, which includes the delivery extract. Before creating the delivery group, ascertain the remote trail '*td*' is created successfully and checkpoints are applied, i.e. the remote files size is increasing.

```
GGSCI (apps-srv2) 4> ADD REPLICAT rvis01, EXTTRAIL ./dirdat/td
REPLICAT added.

GGSCI (apps-srv2) 5>
```

Start the delivery process

The last step is to start the delivery process (*rvis01*). While the process checkpoint is changing, monitor the replicate process using the command, GGSCI (apps-srv2) 18> *info replciat rvis01, details.*

```
GGSCI (apps-srv2) 13> START REPLICAT RVIS01

Sending START request to MANAGER ...
REPLICAT RVIS01 starting

GGSCI (apps-srv2) 14> INFO ALL
```

```
Program     Status      Group       Lag at Chkpt  Time Since Chkpt

MANAGER     RUNNING
REPLICAT    RUNNING     RVIS01      00:00:00      00:01:46
```

The target Oracle GoldenGate instance manager process should be configured to handle remote trail files after being consumed and applied to the target database by the replicate process.

Run a GoldenGate report against report E-Business Suite instance

Now, Oracle GoldenGate is performing real-time change data capture and delivery from source to the target R12 E-Business suite database. Running reports on this instance leaves the source database dedicated to online transactions only.

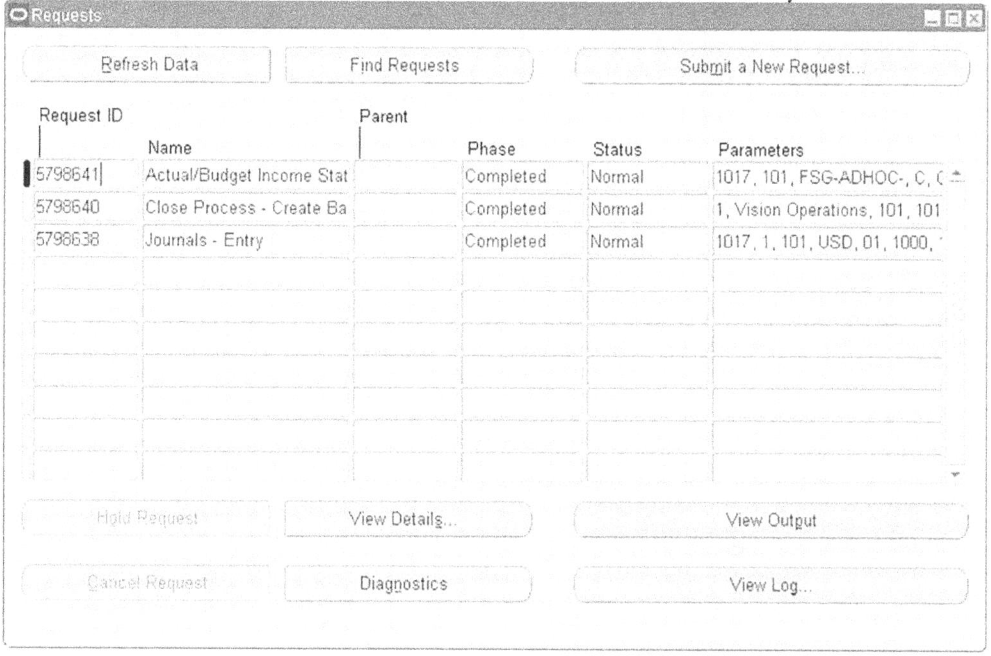

Requests

Refresh Data | Find Requests | Submit a New Request...

Request ID	Name	Parent	Phase	Status	Parameters
5798641	Actual/Budget Income Stat		Completed	Normal	1017, 101, FSG-ADHOC-, C, (
5798640	Close Process - Create Ba		Completed	Normal	1, Vision Operations, 101, 101
5798638	Journals - Entry		Completed	Normal	1017, 1, 101, USD, 01, 1000,

Hold Request | View Details... | View Output

Cancel Request | Diagnostics | View Log...

Figure 4-7a: Requests Screen

Applying advanced database compression to referenced tables enhances report runtime. The list of referenced tables by the report are altered to become compressed as illustrated below.

```
SQL> ALTER TABLE gl.gl_balances COMPRESS;

SQL> ALTER TABLE gl.gl_code_combinations COMPRESS;

SQL> ALTER TABLE gl.gl_ledgers COMPRESS;
```

However; creating database materialized views to enable query re-write may not be fully effective, this is because Oracle R12 E-Business suite reports rely on a parameter form to supply runtime values which are embedded on the report SQL SELECT statement. This is a form of dynamic SQL determined at runtime.

Summary

This chapter has explained applying Oracle GoldenGate 12c for real-time query offloading. When Oracle GoldenGate real-time data movement coupled with Oracle built-in capabilities, the report instance delivers high performance report runtime for in-house developed and packaged applications.

The essential Oracle features for enhancing the runtime of long running reports are transparent, hence access to packaged application source code is not required. The target database takes advantage of the following features:

- Materialized view and materialized view logs
- Query re-write
- Advanced compression
- Online redefinition
- Database table and index partitioning

The query offloading is also covered from the prospective of Oracle R12 E-Business suite. However; because the techniques applied is mostly database related, it should be also applicable to other packaged ERP and CRM systems such as SAP, Oracle Seibel and Oracle PeopleSoft.

The next chapter implements Oracle GoldenGate for active-active environment, proving high availability for the instance and database. By applying Oracle GoldenGate and Oracle built-in features for handling and resolving conflict more manageable.

Bi-Directional Topology for Business Continuity

CHAPTER

Overview of HA for GoldenGate

The objective of this chapter is to use Oracle GoldenGate 12c two-node configuration for building high availability infrastructure to support business applications maximum availability by minimizing disruption due to system failure. Oracle customers have been implementing Oracle real application clusters (RAC) for high availability and Oracle Data Guard (DG) for disaster recovery.

The two solutions co-exist for the best continuity. RAC and DG require an advanced level of skills to implement and manage together. RAC and DG are the major components of Oracle Maximum Availability Architecture (MAA) for sites running mission critical systems and requiring a maximum level of scalability, data availability and data protection. For applications that may compromise RAC embedded scalability and DG fast start failover, Oracle GoldenGate achieves the requirements for business continuity with a sustainable budget, operational cost, and reasonable infrastructure complexity.

The flexibility of Oracle GoldenGate advanced configuration enables the software to provide business continuity similar to RAC and DG combined using active-passive and active-active bi-directional topology architecture. However, this specific implementation is not out-of-the-box and requires a considerable level of Oracle GoldenGate and database experience in respect to the database design and application coding.

This chapter implements Oracle GoldenGate for business continuity using similarly designed architecture for deploying:

- Active-Passive Model for Disaster Recovery (DR)
- Active-Active Model for High Availability (HA)

Unlike Oracle Real Application Clusters (RAC) in terms of scalability, Oracle GoldenGate does not promote the built-in scalability provided by RAC, which is the core function of RAC to support linearly increasing transactions volume. When scalability is an important element of the application, sufficient evaluation is necessary before deploying Oracle GoldenGate for high availability. Also, with Oracle Real Application Clusters (RAC), increasing the number of nodes delivers higher scalability. However, Oracle GoldenGate encourages the use of two-node architecture only for high-availability. This is recommended to avoid complex data conflict detection and resolutions in an active-active bi-directional topology.

For an enterprise, Oracle GoldenGate does not replace RAC or DG, rather it is implemented to complement and integrate with the Oracle clusterware and Oracle physical standby database. Refer to Chapter 10 to learn more about integrating Oracle GoldenGate with DG.

For sites running the Oracle Database Standard Edition, Oracle GoldenGate is an attractive option for implementing high availability (HA) and disaster recovery (DR). The option is cost-effective and highly suitable for in-house developed applications, but needs to be developed from the group-up so that the applications are replication-aware. In deploying Oracle GoldenGate on bi-directional active-active topology, the challenge is to handle data conflicts which are discussed using the following:

- Data and Applications Segmentation
- Oracle GoldenGate Built-In Conflict Detection and Resolution (CDR)
- Custom Conflict Detection and Resolution using PL/SQL Sub-Programs Development
- Oracle Virtual Private Database (VPD)

GoldenGate Business Continuity Architecture

The Oracle GoldenGate bi-directional architecture achieves better performance by splitting the load across two instances. This sustains fault tolerance when one of the two instances fail by moving all processing to the surviving system. However, the top advantage of using Oracle GoldenGate bi-directional architecture is the geographically separated data centers that enable cost-effective business continuity.

Figure 5-1 depicts bi-directional topology components needed for business continuity. The data flow is from the primary system (the source) to the live standby system (the target) and vice versa. The primary system database S1E2 is on Oracle Database 11g and the live standby system database T1E2 is on Oracle Database 11g. The Oracle GoldenGate building blocks of extract groups, delivery groups, and related components for data movement are outlined below.

The Primary System (The Source) Components for bi-directional replication

- Extract groups, the primary extract ES1E203, the local trail ./dirdat/sc and the secondary extract PS1E203.

- The delivery group, the dynamic collector server, the remote trail ./dirdat/tc and the delivery process RS1E203.

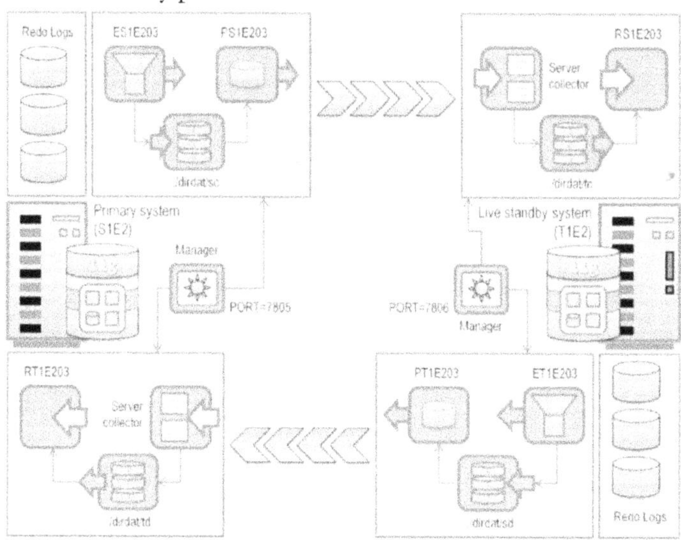

Figure 5-1: Bi-Directional Topology Building Blocks

The Live Standby System (The Target) Components for bi-directional replication

- Extract groups, the primary extract ET1E203, the local trail ./dirdat/sd and the secondary extract PT1E203.

- The delivery group, the dynamic collector server, the remote trail ./dirdat/td and the delivery process RT1E203.

GoldenGate Database Configuration for bi-directional replication

The primary system database and live standby database are operating in ARCHIVELOG mode, and the transaction logs (online redo log files) structure of both databases are identical. Each has 3 groups used by the primary extract for performing change data capture (CDC). Online redo log files are archived and stored in the fast recovery area (FRA) for a recovery window of (7) days in case of being required by the primary extract or the recovery manager (RMAN) recover operation.

The below RUN command backup the archived log files while maintaining a recovery window of (7) days of archived files in the FRA. Deleting files that are not required by the recovery window of (7) days.

```
RMAN> RUN {
2> BACKUP ARCHIVELOG ALL;

3> DELETE COPY OF ARCHIVELOG ALL COMPLETED BEFORE 'SYSDATE-7';
4> }
```

At minimum, we set the size of the recovery window equal to or greater than the value of the database parameter *control_file_record_keep_time*. The default is (7) days, unless a recovery catalog is configured. Also, ensuring FRA storage capacity allows retaining (7) days of archived log files by setting the database parameter *db_recovery_file_dest_size* as needed.

Extending Oracle GoldenGate for High Availability

When using Oracle GoldenGate for business continuity, the task of migrating users from the primary system to standby system and vice versa requires the database administrator (DBA) intervention and users reconnect to the surviving instance.

However, for an active-active environment, the application needs the load balancing technique for connecting sessions to the database with minimal workload. Figure 5-2 shows the load balancer workflow that dynamically routes the application to the database with minimal workload.

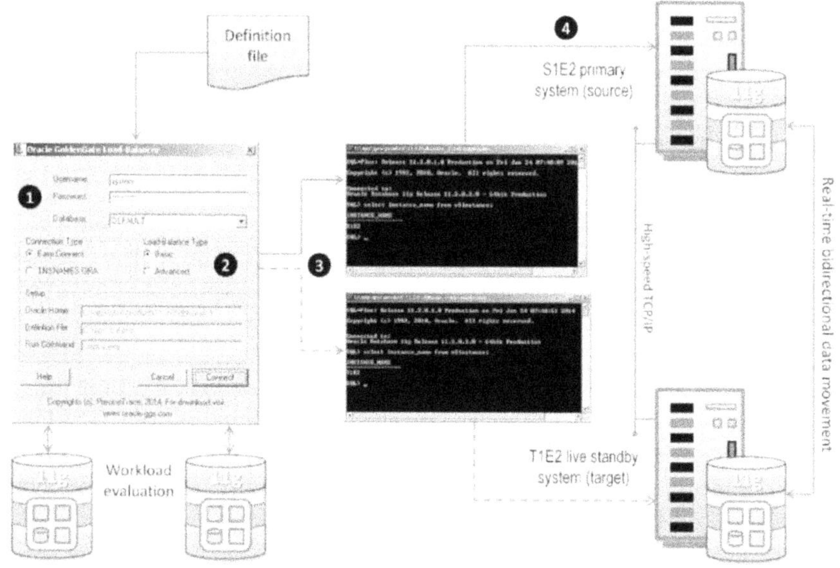

Figure 5-2: GoldenGate High Availability Load Balancer

The load balancer negotiates the primary and standby database to determine the preferred instance based on current workload. Then, it uses the selected connection type to establish the connection to the primary or standby systems – the database with lesser workload. The load balancer uses a definition file that defines the primary and standby systems. Each line is composed of the host name or IP address, the listener port, the database service name, and the run command. The definition file c:\ggs-bal.prm is mandatory and the database credential must be identical for the primary system and live standby system database. The following lines define the primary and live standby systems configuration.

```
ggs-source   1521   s1e2.precisetrace.com    sqlplus.exe
ggs-target   1521   t1e2.precisetrace.com    sqlplus.exe
```

The above load balancer maintains the workload between the primary and the live-standby systems by performing the following:

1. Connecting to the primary and standby systems for evaluating the current database workload.
2. Comparing the two workloads to determine the preferred database instance – the one with lesser workload.
3. Using the selected connection type to compose the database connect string.
4. Routing and spawning the application to the preferred system.

When using Oracle GoldenGate for high-availability (active-active), the number of Oracle GoldenGate database instances should be limited to a maximum of (3) database instances to avoid complex conflicts resolution and configuration.

GoldenGate Disaster Recovery

When using Oracle GoldenGate to implement a disaster recovery (DR) site, it is developed as *active-passive*, bi-directional topology architecture. The source database is designated as the primary system and the target database is designated as the live-standby system.

The live-standby system database remains on read-write mode. Applications users are connected to either the primary or the live-standby system, but not both. The live-standby system remains ready for the failover and switchover situations. Routing connection to one-and-only-one system is mostly handled from within the application servers as depicted on Figure 5-3 where sessions are established from either the primary or the live-standby system database.

The tremendous advanced features, configurable components flexibility, communication robustness and extendibility of Oracle GoldenGate have technically established a distinctive architecture for designing an enterprise heterogeneous platform suitable for protection and integration the enterprise data.

Having a live-standby database continuously synchronized in real-time, maximizes the usability of the database for other applications. Another distinctive advantage of Oracle GoldenGate is heterogeneity.

The capability of the live-standby system to run on a dissimilar platform from the primary system attracts decision makers and technical team members to build a sophisticated, one-of-a-kind disaster recovery site. Mostly designed to run on a mid-range Intel-based system powered by Oracle Linux. It delivers high-quality service and low-cost per transaction with best of class stability and reliability.

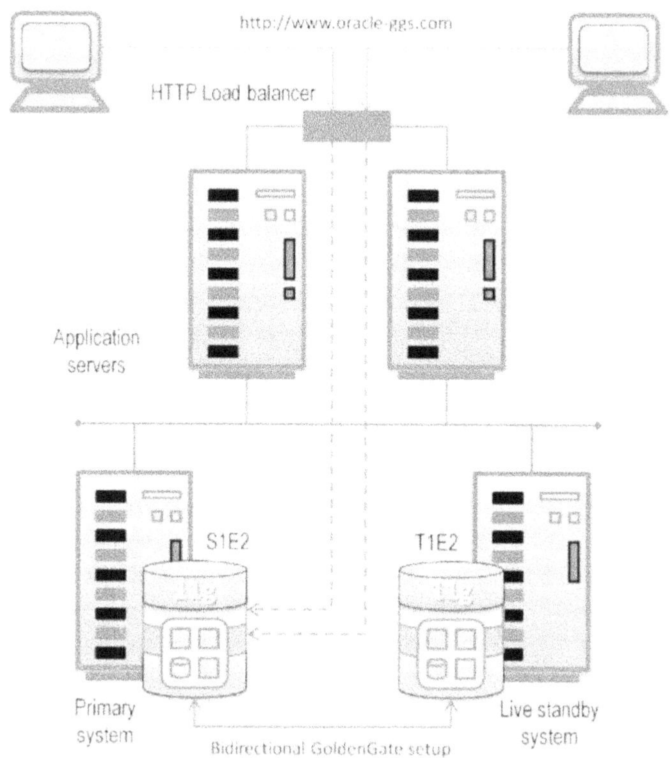

Figure 5-3: Disaster Recovery Connections

Oracle GoldenGate Value Proposition

A value proposition of Oracle GoldenGate is the certification with Oracle Database Standard Edition (SE). Small to mid-range server sites running Oracle Database SE can develop their disaster recovery solution using Oracle GoldenGate only. The demonstration of this chapter was developed using Oracle Database 11g SE running on Oracle Linux. This value proposition should not be underestimated!

```
SQL> SELECT * FROM v$version;

BANNER
-----------------------------------------------------------------
Oracle Database 11g Release 11.2.0.3.0 - 64bit Production
PL/SQL Release 11.2.0.3.0 - Production
CORE    11.2.0.3.0    Production
TNS for Linux: Version 11.2.0.3.0 - Production
```

```
NLSRTL Version 11.2.0.3.0 - Production
```

GoldenGate Disaster Recovery Considerations

The concept of disaster recovery (DR) requires a standby database to operate in read-only mode at all times. However, because Oracle GoldenGate requires that the database operates on read-write, it is only the synchronized tables that are restricted from DML operation outside of the Oracle GoldenGate apply session (Replicat). Also, even though the bi-directional setup is already in place, it is active from only one direction at any time. Other guidelines to consider when using Oracle GoldenGate for disaster recovery are listed below:

Live-Standby System

At all times, the data flow is active from only one direction. The live-standby database (target) remains on read-write mode but fundamentally inactive – used only by the Replicat sessions. Under normal situations, OLTP users are only connected to the primary system database (the "source" database). Utilizing the live-standby system for other applications should avoid interaction with mapped tables used by Oracle GoldenGate delivery processes (the "Replicats" database).

Operating Mode and Failover

The live-standby system database should be operated on ARCHIVELOG mode. This prepares the live-standby system for a planned switchover and unplanned failover. Oracle GoldenGate switchover and failover is an interactive operation and handled manually. Using tools such as Oracle GoldenGate Veridata and the Oracle GoldenGate Monitor are highly recommended to proactively avoid data divergence and minimizing latency.

Query Offloading

OLAP users are normally directed to the live-standby system database (the "target" database). It is the ideal platform for running long query reports, but the database should not be modified by creating additional objects such as indexes and materialized views. Otherwise, these created objects must be dropped as part of a failover/switchover operation.

Unsupported Data Types

The unsupported data types by Oracle GoldenGate is minimum. The most common applications data types not supported by Oracle GoldenGate is BFILE, which handled using the PL/SQL supplied API DBMS_LOB and DBMS_FILE_TRANSFER. Refer to Chapter 5 to learn more about using PL/SQL with Oracle GoldenGate. Evaluating the extent of unsupported data types is necessary to qualify using Oracle GoldenGate for disaster recovery solution. Refer to Chapter 1 to learn more about unsupported data types.

GoldenGate Disaster Recovery Implementation

A disaster recovery implementation using Oracle GoldenGate consists of the tasks listed in Table 5-1. Testing switchover and failover for moving users from the primary system to the live-standby system and then moving users back to the primary system is the last step and executed for planned & unplanned scenarios.

	Task
1.	Install software, configure manager process, and start Oracle GoldenGate instance.
2.	Enable database supplemental logging and archive log mode.
3.	Create Oracle GoldenGate database user and grant privileges.
4.	Login to the database from GGSCI and Add table-level logging.
5.	Prepare GLOBALS parameters and the checkpoint table.
6.	Perform initial load from primary (source) to live standby (target) systems.
7.	Configure, create, and deploy Oracle GoldenGate groups for bi-directional topology.
8.	Enable data capture and delivery from primary to live standby system.
9.	Perform moving users for planned & unplanned switchover and failover.

Table 5-1: Bi-Directional Configuration for High Availability and Disaster Recovery Solutions

The destination for each of the above tasks is shown in Figure 5-4. Since this is a bi-directional topology architecture, the tasks are performed on the primary system/source database and on the live-standby system/target database.

The live-standby system should have adequate resources to support the post-failover/ switchover operation timeframe. Having matched resources is recommended. Even though Oracle GoldenGate supports a heterogeneous database environment, it is absolutely not recommended when implementing high availability and disaster recovery solutions using Oracle GoldenGate. The primary and live-standby platform should have identical architecture. The planned switchover and the unplanned failover is a manual process. Automation is developed using Linux shell script and Oracle GoldenGate obey files. The use of Oracle GoldenGate Veridata for data consistency and the Oracle GoldenGate Monitor are highly recommended for such an environment.

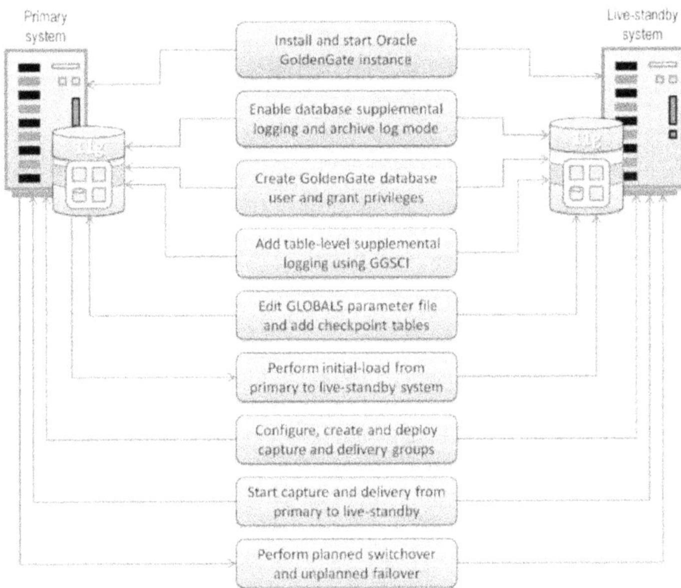

Figure 5-4: Bi-Directional Topology Architecture Tasks vs. Destinations

Software Installation

Successful installation of Oracle GoldenGate on the primary and live-standby systems must be successfully completed to proceed further. Consider the platform architecture. The chapter uses Oracle GoldenGate for Oracle Database 11g 64-bit.

The same bundle of Oracle GoldenGate 12c provides support for Oracle database enterprise and standard editions. Refer to Chapter 2 to learn about installing Oracle GoldenGate.

GoldenGate Supplemental Logging

Enable supplemental logging on the primary and live-standby databases. Also, ensure the databases are operating on ARCHIVELOG mode.

```
SQL> CONN / AS SYSDBA
Connected.

SQL> SELECT log_mode FROM v$database;

LOG_MODE
------------
ARCHIVELOG

SQL> ALTER DATABASE ADD SUPPLEMENTAL LOG DATA;

Database altered.
```

Refer to Chapter 2 to learn more about database supplemental logging settings. Even though the data flow is in one direction at any time, ensuring the database supplemental logging and ARCHIVELOG mode are enabled on the primary and Live-standby systems minimizes the meantime to migrate users and reverse the processing direction.

GoldenGate Database Users

Create Oracle GoldenGate database user on the primary and live-standby databases. The use of dedicated Oracle GoldenGate is required for active-active bi-directional topology. It is used for an endless loop detection purpose as explained in this chapter.

```
SQL> CREATE USER ggs_admin identified by oracle;

User created.

SQL> GRANT DBA TO ggs_admin;

Grant succeeded.

SQL> CONN ggs_admin/oracle

Connected.
```

Refer to Chapter 2 to learn more about the precise database privileges granted to Oracle GoldenGate users on the primary (source) and live-standby (target) database. The above command grants DBA which is considered an over grant and not recommended or even possible for some sites.

Start Oracle GoldenGate Instances

The primary system and live-standby system are running on Oracle Database 11g Standard Edition 64-bit. The primary system Oracle GoldenGate instance manager process is listening on port 7805 and the live-standby Oracle GoldenGate manager process is listening on port 7806. Using the GoldenGate Software Command Interface (GGSCI), configure and start the manager process on the primary and live-standby systems.

```
GGSCI (apps-srv1) 6> START MGR
Manager started.

GGSCI (apps-srv1) 7> INFO MGR

Manager is running (IP port apps-srv1.7805, Process ID 13632).

GGSCI (apps-srv1) 8>
```

Repeat the above GGSCI commands for the live-standby system.

```
GGSCI (apps-srv2) 2> START MGR
Manager started.

GGSCI (apps-srv2) 3> INFO MGR

Manager is running (IP port apps-srv2.7806, Process ID 30133).
```

Refer to Chapter 2 to learn more about the manager process common parameters settings for managing trails and unattended restart.

GoldenGate Checkpoint Table

The database checkpoint table is the default for the Replicat process checkpoint. Prepare the GLOBALS parameter file, then use GGSCI to create the checkpoint table. The GLOBALS parameter file contains the following one line only. Where GGS-ADMIN is the Oracle GoldenGate database schema.

```
CHECKPOINTTABLE ggs-admin.chkpttab

GGSCI (apps-srv1) 1> DBLOGIN USERID ggs_admin, PASSWORD oracle
Successfully logged into database.

GGSCI (apps-srv1) 2> ADD CHECKPOINTTABLE

No checkpoint table specified. Using GLOBALS specification
(ggs_admin.chkpttab)...

Successfully created checkpoint table ggs_admin.chkpttab.
```

Create the checkpoint table on primary system and live-standby systems. Remember to exit and restart GGSCI to activate parameters added to GLOBALS parameter file.

GoldenGate: Performing the Initial-Data Load

This is a major task that must be delivered 100% successfully. The live-standby system database must be established prior to beginning the configuration tasks. Even though this demonstration is from Oracle-to-Oracle database (homogenous), file to Replicat Oracle GoldenGate initial-data load method is used to establish the live-standby (target) database. Since we consider the initial load from an inactive database, the initial load is performed using the following steps:

- Configure and start the initial load Extract (ELOAD03)
- Configure the initial load Replicat (RLOAD03)
- Start the initial load Replicat (RLOAD03)

GoldenGate Initial Load Extract

Before starting the initial load extract, some analysis must be conducted to determine any unsupported column data types. Since this configuration is for developing a disaster recovery (DR), all tables must be included in the capture groups. For a very large list of tables, use the following PL/SQL code or the Extract and Replicat wild-card syntax format with exclude option to prepare the ELOAD03.PRM file.

```
SQL> CREATE DIRECTORY ggs_dir as '/d01/oracle/ggs/dirprm';
```

```
Directory created.
```

```
SQL> GRANT ALL ON DIRECTORY ggs_dir to public;
```

```
Grant succeeded.
```

```
SQL> DECLARE
        filehandler UTL_FILE.FILE_TYPE;
        CURSOR c1 is SELECT table_name
                     FROM   dba_tables
                     WHERE  owner='OSM$REPAPI';
        vtable_name VARCHAR2(30);
     BEGIN
        fileHandler := UTL_FILE.FOPEN('GGS_DIR', 'eload03.prm', 'W');
        UTL_FILE.PUTF(fileHandler, 'SOURCEISTABLE\n');
        UTL_FILE.PUTF(fileHandler, 'USERID ggs_admin, PASSWORD oracle\n');
        UTL_FILE.PUTF(fileHandler, 'RMTHOST apps-srv2, MGRPORT 7806\n');
        UTL_FILE.PUTF(fileHandler, 'RMTFILE ./dirdat/initload01.dat,
PURGE\n');
        OPEN c1;
        LOOP
           FETCH c1 into vtable_name;
```

```
        EXIT WHEN c1%NOTFOUND;
        UTL_FILE.PUTF(fileHandler, 'TABLE
osm$repapi.'||vtable_name||';\n');
     END LOOP;
     CLOSE c1;
     UTL_FILE.FCLOSE(fileHandler);
 EXCEPTION
     WHEN utl_file.invalid_path THEN
       raise_application_error(-20000, 'ERROR: Invalid GoldenGate
path.');
 END;
 /
```

```
GGSCI (apps-srv1) 1> EDIT PARAMS eload03
```

```
SOURCEISTABLE
USERID ggs_admin, PASSWORD oracle
RMTHOST apps-srv2, MGRPORT 7806
RMTFILE ./dirdat/initload03.dat, PURGE
TABLE osm$repapi.POLICY_TYPES;
TABLE osm$repapi.DISCOUNT_TYPES;
TABLE osm$repapi.CUSTOMERS;
TABLE osm$repapi.POLICIES;
```

```
GGSCI (apps-srv1) 1> SHELL ./extract pf ./dirprm/eload03.prm rf
./dirrpt/eload03.rpt
```

The *ggsci shell* command allows you to invoke programs and operating system shell commands from within Oracle GoldenGate. The parameter *sourceistable* directly reads records from the database tables, and must be the first parameter in the configuration file.

GoldenGate Initial Load Replicat

The initial load data file has been created on the live-standby system. Verify the existence of *./dirdat/initload03.dat* on the live standby. Before starting the Replicat program, create a special run Replicat process (RLOAD03) as shown below.

```
GGSCI (apps-srv2) 1> ADD REPLICAT rload03, SPECIALRUN
REPLICAT added.
```

```
GGSCI (apps-srv2) 2> EDIT PARAMS rload03
```

```
REPLICAT rload03
SPECIALRUN
ASSUMETARGETDEFS
HANDLECOLLISIONS
USERID ggs_admin, PASSWORD oracle
EXTFILE ./dirdat/initload03.dat
```

```
DISCARDFILE ./dirrpt/rload03.dsc, PURGE
MAP osm$repapi.*, TARGET osm$repapi.*;
END RUNTIME
```

```
GGSCI (apps-srv2) 1> SHELL ./replicat pf ./dirprm/rload03.prm rf
./dirrpt/rload03.rpt
```

Now, the live-standby database is established and identical to the primary database. Before proceeding further, verify ascertain the data using Oracle GoldenGate Veridata. Also, because the initial-load is done from an inactive database, review Oracle GoldenGate report generated from the initial-load Replicat process.

```
GGSCI (apps-srv2) 4> VIEW REPORT ./dirrpt/rload03.rpt
```

```
Reading ./dirdat/initloa3.dat, current RBA 37987353, 200007 records

Report at 2014-01-04 17:27:04 (activity since 2014-01-04 17:26:08)

From Table OSM$REPAPI.POLICY_TYPES to OSM$REPAPI.POLICY_TYPES:
       #                   inserts:         4
       #                   updates:         0
       #                   deletes:         0
       #                  discards:         0
From Table OSM$REPAPI.DISCOUNT_TYPES to OSM$REPAPI.DISCOUNT_TYPES:
       #                   inserts:         3
       #                   updates:         0
       #                   deletes:         0
       #                  discards:         0
From Table OSM$REPAPI.CUSTOMERS to OSM$REPAPI.CUSTOMERS:
       #                   inserts:    100000
       #                   updates:         0
       #                   deletes:         0
       #                  discards:         0
From Table OSM$REPAPI.POLICIES to OSM$REPAPI.POLICIES:
       #                   inserts:    100000
       #                   updates:         0
       #                   deletes:         0
       #                  discards:         0

Last log location read:
     FILE:      ./dirdat/initload03.dat
     RBA:       37987353
     TIMESTAMP: 2014-01-04 14:24:58.801283
     EOF:       NO
     READERR:   400
```

As per the report details, the initial load has been completed successfully. Refer to Chapter 3 for more details regarding initial data load techniques and options.

GoldenGate Bi-Directional Topology Configuration

The basic task of configuring Oracle GoldenGate to support a disaster recovery site is to have a working bi-directional data flow, from the primary system to the live-standby system and vice versa. The purpose of the basic configuration is to test the capture, route, and delivery groups on a bi-directional environment using automated database transactions developed in PL/SQL and run from the command line. Figure 5-5 depicts Oracle GoldenGate groups that are configured next.

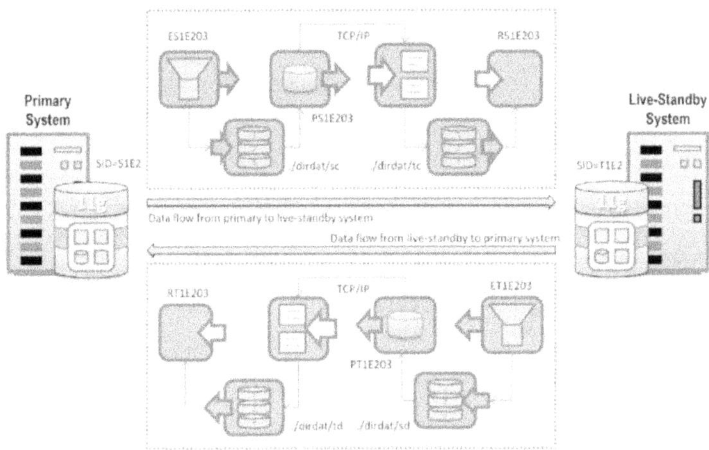

Figure 5-5: Bi-Directional Capture and Delivery Groups

After completing the bi-directional configuration, run and verify the transactional testing from both sides. The following procedure TRANS_LOAD is run as an anonymous PL/SQL block.

```
SQL> BEGIN
  2      FOR i IN 100901..101000 LOOP
  3          trans_load(1, i);
  4      END LOOP;
  5   END;
  6   /
```

Since the procedure *trans_load* does not handle primary key collision, ensure the lower and upper range of the loop statement is correctly bounded to avoid primary key violation error.

GoldenGate Intermediate Systems

The use of an intermediate system between the primary and live-standby systems is an option. This configuration is only recommended when the current active system needs to ship trail files to a third system, not really part of this high availability bi-directional topology. Other reasons for using an intermediate system is to offload the current active system (primary system) from routing trail records to the remote system, or network security prevents either system from sending trail records, and the need of a dedicated system for sending trail to the third system regardless of which system (primary or live-standby) is active. The disadvantage is increasing the latency, which increases the likelihood of data conflicts. Refer to Chapter 10 for details regarding intermediate systems.

GoldenGate Primary to Standby Data Flow

The configuration of the primary (source) to the live-standby (target) systems data flow is composed of deploying the primary & secondary extract groups and a delivery group. Figure 5-6 shows the components configured to move data from the primary to
the live-standby system.

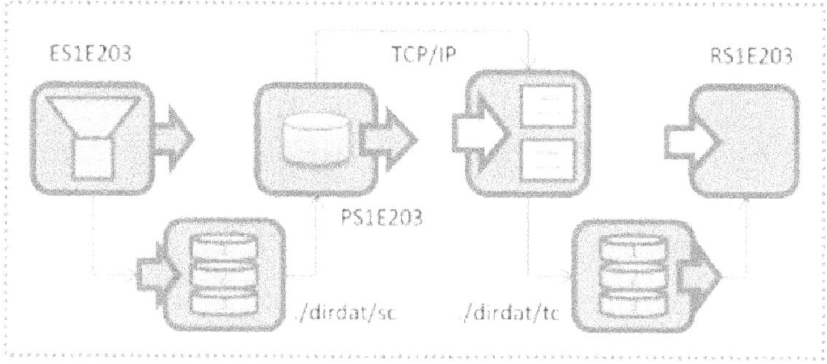

Figure 5-6: Primary to Standby Data Flow

GoldenGate Primary Extract Group

The primary group is composed of the parameter file ES1E203.PRM, the primary extract process ES1E203, the local trail ./dirdat/sc, and the checkpoint file ./dirchk/ES1E203.CPE. The primary extract ES1E203 is configured to capture from the transaction logs and writes to the local trail. The next two commands create the primary extract and its local trail. The local trail files is sized 128MB.

```
GGSCI (apps-srvl) 2> EDIT PARAMS es1e203
```

```
EXTRACT es1e203
SETENV   (ORACLE_SID=S1E2)
SETENV   (ORACLE_HOME="/d01/app/oracleSE")
SETENV   (NLS_LANG=AMERICAN_AMERICA.AR8ISO8859P6)
```

```
USERID  ggs_admin, password oracle
EXTTRAIL ./dirdat/sc
TABLE osm$repapi.CUSTOMERS;
TABLE osm$repapi.POLICIES;
```

```
GGSCI (apps-srv1) 3> ADD EXTRACT es1e203, TRANLOG, BEGIN now, THREADS 1
EXTRACT added.
```

```
GGSCI (apps-srv1) 5> ADD EXTTRAIL ./dirdat/sc, EXTRACT es1e203, MEGABYTES
128
EXTTRAIL added.
```

GoldenGate Secondary Extract Group

The secondary group is composed of the parameter file PS1E203.PRM, the data pump extract process PS1E203, the remote trail ./dirdat/tc, and the checkpoint file ./dirchk/PS1E203.CPE. The data pump extract PS1E203 sends data over TCP/IP to the live-standby system. The next commands create the secondary group (data pump) and its remote trail. The remote trail files is sized 128MB.

```
GGSCI (apps-srv1) 6> EDIT PARAMS ps1e203
```

```
GGSCI (apps-srv1) 6> EDIT PARAMS ps1e203 EXTRACT ps1e203
USERID ggs_admin, PASSWORD oracle
PASSTHRU
RMTHOST apps-srv2, MGRPORT 7806
RMTTRAIL ./dirdat/tc
TABLE osm$repapi.CUSTOMERS;
TABLE osm$repapi.POLICIES;
```

```
GGSCI (apps-srv1) 7> ADD EXTRACT ps1e203, EXTTRAILSOURCE ./dirdat/sc
EXTRACT added.
```

```
GGSCI (apps-srv1) 11> ADD RMTTRAIL ./dirdat/tc, EXTRACT ps1e203, MEGABYTES
128
RMTTRAIL added.
```

GoldenGate Delivery Group

The delivery group is composed of the parameter file RS1E203.PRM, the Replicat process PS1E203, the remote trail ./dirdat/tc, and the checkpoint file ./dirchk/ES1E203.CPR. The delivery process uses the live-standby database SQL Native Call to apply transactions to the database.

```
GGSCI (apps-srv2) 2> ADD REPLICAT rs1e203, EXTTRAIL ./dirdat/tc
REPLICAT added.
```

```
GGSCI (apps-srv2) 3>
```

GoldenGate Standby to Primary Data Flow

To support switchover and failover operations for planned and unplanned modes, the data flow from the standby to the primary systems must be in place. Figure 5-7 shows the data flow from the live-standby to the primary system.

The live-standby to primary data flow configuration remains inactive. It is activated only when users are moved from the primary system to the live-standby system. The application servers, where the applications are running, are configured to connect to one and only one specific system – either the primary system or the live-standby system, but not both.

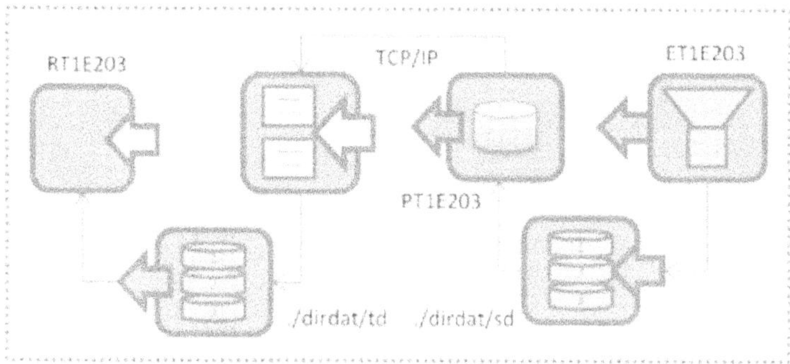

Figure 5-7: Standby to Primary Data Flow

GoldenGate Primary Extract Group

The primary group is composed of the parameter file ET1E203.PRM, the primary extract process ET1E203, the local trail ./dirdat/sd and the checkpoint file ./dirchk/ET1E203.CPE. The next commands create the primary extract and its local trail. The local trail files sized 128MB.

```
GGSCI (apps-srv2) 1> EDIT PARAMS et1e203
```

```
EXTRACT et1e203
SETENV (ORACLE_SID="T1E2")
SETENV (ORACLE_HOME="/d01/app/oracleSE/product/11.2.0/dbhome_1")
SETENV (NLS_LANG="AMERICAN_AMERICA.AL32UTF8")
USERID ggs_admin, PASSWORD oracle
EXTTRAIL ./dirdat/sd
TABLE osm$repapi.customers;
```

```
TABLE osm$repapi.policies;
```

```
GGSCI (apps-srv2) 5> ADD EXTRACT et1e203, TRANLOG, BEGIN now, THREADS 1
EXTRACT added.
```

```
GGSCI (apps-srv2) 6> ADD EXTTRAIL ./dirdat/sd, EXTRACT et1e203, MEGABYTES
128
EXTTRAIL added.
```

GoldenGate Secondary Extract Group

The secondary group is composed of the parameter file PT1E203.PRM, the data pump extract process PT1E203, the remote trail ./dirdat/td and the checkpoint file ./dirchk/PT1E203.CPE. The next commands create the secondary group (data pump) and its remote trail. The remote trail files sized 128MB.

```
GGSCI (apps-srv2) 7> EDIT PARAMS pt1e203
```

```
EXTRACT pt1e203
USERID ggs_admin, PASSWORD oracle
PASSTHRU
RMTHOST apps-srv1, MGRPORT 7805
RMTTRAIL ./dirdat/td
TABLE osm$repapi.customers;
TABLE osm$repapi.policies;
```

```
GGSCI (apps-srv2) 9> ADD EXTRACT pt1e203, EXTTRAILSOURCE ./dirdat/sd
EXTRACT added.
```

```
GGSCI (apps-srv2) 11> ADD RMTTRAIL ./dirdat/td, EXTRACT pt1e203, MEGABYTES
128
RMTTRAIL added.

GGSCI (apps-srv2) 12>
```

GoldenGate Delivery Group

The delivery group is composed of the parameter file RT1E203.PRM, the Replicat process PT1E203, the local trail ./dirdat/sd and the checkpoint file ./dirchk/ET1E203.CPR for reporting. The Replicat process ES1E203 uses a checkpoint table, which is the default location for checkpoint. The next command creates the delivery group (Replicat).

```
GGSCI (apps-srv1) 3> EDIT PARAMS rt1e203
```

```
REPLICAT rt1e203
SETENV (ORACLE_SID=S1E2)
```

```
SETENV (NSL_LANG=AMERICAN_AMERICA.AL32UTF8)
USERID ggs_admin, PASSWORD oracle
ASSUMETARGETDEFS
DISCARDFILE ./dirrpt/rt1e203.dsc, PURGE
MAP osm$repapi.customers, TARGET osm$repapi.customers;
MAP osm$repapi.policies, TARGET osm$repapi.policies;
```

```
GGSCI (apps-srv1) 4> ADD REPLICAT rt1e203, EXTTRAIL ./dirdat/td
REPLICAT added.

GGSCI (apps-srv1) 5>
```

This concludes Oracle GoldenGate bi-directional configuration. Under normal business operation, the data flow is always from the primary system (source) to the live-standby system (target). Users are temporary migrated to the live-standby system either due to switchover or failover operation.

GoldenGate Switchover and Failover

Moving users from the primary to the standby site is performed as a planned (switchover) or unplanned (failover) situation. A switchover is for well-planned specific system maintenance tasks such as primary site database upgrade, standby operating system upgrade, etc. The following sections describe the process workflow for a primary site protected by one live standby site, which may need to perform either a switchover or failover.

A switchover consists of the following tasks:

- Switchover for planned primary to standby site
- Moving users back to the primary site

A failover consists of the following tasks:

- Failover for unplanned primary to standby site
- Re-establish the primary site
- Moving users back to the primary site

During the switchover and failover operations, the primary system is referred to by (Primary) and the live standby system is referred to by (Live Standby). This distinction avoids executing commands on the wrong Oracle GoldenGate instance or database.

GoldenGate Planned Primary to Live-Standby Switchover Workflow

Database and system administrators plan and perform system maintenance tasks. For systems operating 24/7, temporarily moving users from the primary system to the live-standby system enables business continuity by sustaining the minimum downtime while ensuring data integrity. Figure 5-8 depicts the steps to move users from the primary to the live-standby system.

The two common maintenance task benefits from a planned switchover are:

- Database Upgrades
- Operating System Upgrades

Due to less resource availability on the live-standby system, the switchover is temporary. Users are moved back to the primary system after successfully performing the maintenance tasks.

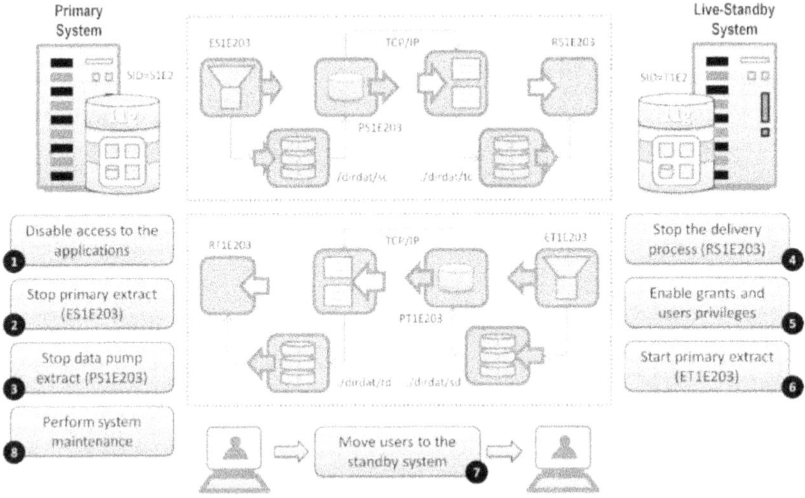

Figure 5-8: Planned Switchover from Primary to Standby System

Disable Access to the Applications (Primary)

For web-based applications accessing the database, shutdown of the application servers disables access to the database. To ascertain that no transactions were applied to the database during the switchover, after shutdown of the application servers, place the primary database on restricted sessions as shown below.

```
SQL> CONN / AS SYSDBA
Connected.
SQL> ALTER SYSTEM ENABLE RESTRICTED SESSION;

System altered.

SQL> GRANT RESTRICTED SESSION to ggs_admin;

Grant succeeded.

SQL> SELECT logins
  2  FROM   v$instance;

LOGINS
----------
RESTRICTED
```

The primary and secondary extracts are still running to complete capture and routing of the transaction after the shutdown of the application servers. After finishing Step 8 of Figure 5-8, revoke the restricted session privilege from the Oracle GoldenGate database user and disable the database restricted session.

```
SQL> REVOKE RESTRICTED SESSION FROM ggs_admin;

Revoke succeeded.

SQL> ALTER SYSTEM DISABLE RESTRICTED SESSION;

System altered.
```

Stop the Primary Extract (Primary)

Before stopping the primary extract (ES1E203), issue the LAG EXTRACT command until it returns the message "At EOF, no more records to process." This indicates the primary extract has processed the transactions logs and is ready to issue the STOP EXTRACT command.

```
GGSCI (apps-srv1) 2> LAG EXTRACT es1e203

Sending GETLAG request to EXTRACT ES1E203 ...
Last record lag 1 seconds.
At EOF, no more records to process.

GGSCI (apps-srv1) 3> STOP EXTRACT es1e203

Sending STOP request to EXTRACT ES1E203 ...
Request processed.
```

```
GGSCI (apps-srv1) 4>
```

Stop the Data Pump Extract (Primary)

Run the LAG EXTRACT command until it returns "At EOF, no more records to process." This indicates the data pump has sent all transactions to the live-standby system. Now, issue the STOP EXTRACT command.

```
GGSCI (apps-srv1) 5> LAG EXTRACT ps1e203

Sending GETLAG request to EXTRACT PS1E203 ...
Last record lag 4 seconds.
At EOF, no more records to process.

GGSCI (apps-srv1) 6> STOP EXTRACT ps1e203

Sending STOP request to EXTRACT PS1E203 ...
Request processed.

GGSCI (apps-srv1) 7>
```

Stop the Delivery Process (Live Standby)

Run the command LAG REPLICAT until it returns the message "At EOF, no more records to process." This indicates that the delivery process has applied all of the transaction to the live-standby database. Now, issue the STOP REPLICAT command.

```
GGSCI (apps-srv2) 2> LAG REPLICAT rs1e203

Sending GETLAG request to REPLICAT RS1E203 ...
Last record lag 7 seconds.
At EOF, no more records to process.

GGSCI (apps-srv2) 3> STOP REPLICAT rs1e203

Sending STOP request to REPLICAT RS1E203 ...
Request processed.

GGSCI (apps-srv2) 4>
```

Enable Grants and Constraints (Live Standby)

This step is site specific. To minimize the downtime, the database DDL commands to grant and enable constraints that should be developed prior to initiating the switchover.

Start the Primary Extract (Live Standby)

Prior to moving users to the standby system, run the ALTER EXTRACT command to change the BEGIN timestamp. Then, start the primary extract only. Do not start the data pump extract. Ensure the storage level for the local trail is preserved to handle the primary system maintenance timeframe.

```
GGSCI (apps-srv2) 6> ALTER EXTRACT et1e203, BEGIN now
EXTRACT altered.

GGSCI (apps-srv2) 7> START EXTRACT et1e203

Sending START request to MANAGER ...
EXTRACT ET1E203 starting

GGSCI (apps-srv2) 8>
```

Since the manager process is configured to handle local trail space management when the trail files are shipped, they are automatically purged and keep disk space level optimized.

Switch User to the Live-Standby System

Run the necessary commands (scripts) to switchover the application servers to connect to the standby system. This enables the user to connect and perform transactions on
the standby system.

Perform System Maintenance (Primary)

The time incurred to complete the system maintenance tasks impacts the storage level on the live-standby system. Performing the system maintenance on a separate test system minimizes the downtime of the primary system and reveals site specific issues.

The downtime for performing a planned switchover from the primary system to the live-standby system depends on Steps 5 & 7. These are the steps to run the database DDL commands to grant privileges, enable constraints, and start the application servers respectively. To successfully complete Steps 1 –7, it will take an estimated 10-30 minutes, when the commands are well-tested in the form script files.

GoldenGate Planned Standby to Primary Switchover Workflow

After completing the maintenance tasks on the primary system, a planned switchover from the live-standby to the primary system is performed. Figure 5-9 depicts the workflow steps to move users back to the primary system. Ascertain the current active database instance for a connected session using the following SQL statement:

```
SQL> CONN / AS SYSDBA
Connected.
SQL> COLUMN INSTANCE FORMAT A10
SQL> COLUMN DATABASE FORMAT A10
SQL> SELECT SYS_CONTEXT('USERENV', 'INSTANCE_NAME') INSTANCE,
  2         SYS_CONTEXT('USERENV', 'DB_NAME') DATABASE
  3  FROM   dual;

INSTANCE   DATABASE
---------- ----------
S1E2       S1E2
```

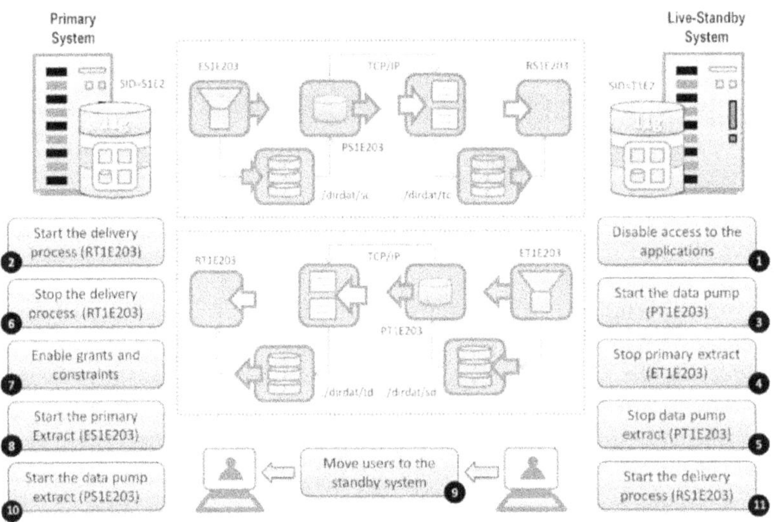

Figure 5-9: Planned Switchover from Live Standby to Primary System

Disable Application Access (Live Standby)

Start disabling users access to the applications by a shutdown of the application servers. The primary extract on the standby system remains running to capture the end of the transactions logs.

Start the Delivery Process (Primary)

To apply the transaction that occurred during the maintenance timeframe, start the delivery process (RT1E203).

```
GGSCI (apps-srv1) 9> START REPLICAT rt1e203

Sending START request to MANAGER ...
REPLICAT RT1E203 starting

GGSCI (apps-srv1) 10>
```

Start the Data Pump (Live Standby)

Since the data pump process stopped for the duration of the maintenance on the primary system, it needs to be started to send the transactions to the primary system.

```
GGSCI (apps-srv2) 9> START EXTRACT pt1e203

Sending START request to MANAGER ...
EXTRACT PT1E203 starting
```

Stop the Primary Extract (Live Standby)

While the applications are not running, keep issuing the command LAG EXTRACT until the message "At EOF, no more records to process" returns. This indicates all transaction logs are captured.

```
GGSCI (apps-srv2) 10> LAG EXTRACT et1e203

Sending GETLAG request to EXTRACT ET1E203 ...
No records yet processed.
At EOF, no more records to process.

GGSCI (apps-srv2) 11> STOP EXTRACT et1e203

Sending STOP request to EXTRACT ET1E203 ...
Request processed.

GGSCI (apps-srv2) 12>
```

Stop the Data Pump Extract (Live Standby)

Repeatedly issue the command LAG EXTRACT until it returns the message "At EOF, no more records to process." This indicates all transaction have been sent to the primary system. Then, issue the command STOP EXTRACT.

```
GGSCI (apps-srv2) 12> LAG EXTRACT pt1e203

Sending GETLAG request to EXTRACT PT1E203 ...
No records yet processed.
At EOF, no more records to process.


GGSCI (apps-srv2) 13> STOP EXTRACT pt1e203

Sending STOP request to EXTRACT PT1E203 ...
Request processed.

GGSCI (apps-srv2) 14>
```

Stop the Delivery Process (Primary)

The next step is to make sure the data processed during the maintenance is applied to the primary database. Keep issuing the command LAG REPLICAT until it returns "At EOF, no more records to process." This indicates all transactions have been applied to the primary database.

```
GGSCI (apps-srv1) 10> LAG REPLICAT rt1e203

Sending GETLAG request to REPLICAT RT1E203 ...
No records yet processed.
At EOF, no more records to process.

GGSCI (apps-srv1) 11> STOP REPLICAT rt1e203

Sending STOP request to REPLICAT RT1E203 ...
Request processed.

GGSCI (apps-srv1) 12>
```

Enable Grants and Constraints (Primary)

The primary system is now ready for switchover. Before doing so, run the database DDL command to grant privileges and enable constraints.

Start the Primary Extract (Primary)

Start the primary extract to capture from the transaction logs.

```
GGSCI (apps-srv1) 12> START EXTRACT es1e203

Sending START request to MANAGER ...
EXTRACT ES1E203 starting
```

Switch User Activity

Starting the application servers allows users to connect to the primary system. Now users are connected back to the primary system. Trails created need to be shipped to the live standby system.

Start the Data Pump (Primary)

Start the data pump to begin sending data to the live-standby system. In the case of data pump process failure due to connection rejection by the target system, verify the hostname or IP address is reachable by performing PING from within GGSCI command-line and the manager listening port on the live-standby system is correct.

```
GGSCI (apps-srv1) 13> START EXTRACT ps1e203

Sending START request to MANAGER ...
EXTRACT PS1E203 starting

GGSCI (apps-srv1) 14>
```

Start the Delivery Process (Live Standby)

The delivery process (RS1E203) is started to keep applying transactions to the live standby system.

```
GGSCI (apps-srv2) 14> START REPLICAT rs1e203

Sending START request to MANAGER ...
REPLICAT RS1E203 starting

GGSCI (apps-srv2) 15>
```

On the primary system, verify the status of the primary and secondary extracts. This is where users are currently executing transactions. On the live standby system, verify the status of the delivery process. Using tools such Oracle GoldenGate Veridata to compare the primary and live-standby databases allows database administrators to discover and fix missing rows, proactively. Another effective administration tool is the Oracle GoldenGate 11g Monitor, which is used for monitor health checks and diagnostics.

Unplanned Primary to Standby Failover Workflow

Situations such as a primary system disk failure are unplanned situations where users are moved to the live standby system until the primary system is recovered. Figure 5-10 depicts the steps to move users from the primary to the live-standby system. The unplanned failover from the primary to live-standby system presumes the live-standby Oracle GoldenGate configuration is in-place, and the database scripts to enable constraints are available.

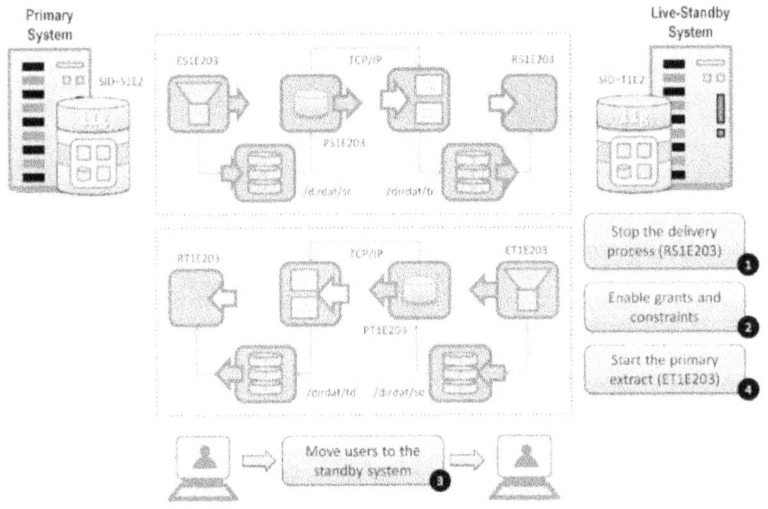

Figure 5-10: Primary to Standby Failover

Stop the Delivery Process (Live Standby)

Ensure transactions have been applied to the live standby system by continuing to issue the command LAG REPLICAT, until it returns "At EOF, no more records to process." This indicates all transactions have been applied to the live standby database.

```
GGSCI (apps-srv2) 1> LAG REPLICAT rs1e203

Sending GETLAG request to REPLICAT RS1E203 ...
Last record lag 8 seconds.
At EOF, no more records to process.

GGSCI (apps-srv2) 2> STOP REPLICAT rs1e203

Sending STOP request to REPLICAT RS1E203 ...
Request processed.

GGSCI (apps-srv2) 3>
```

Enable Grants and Constraints (Live Standby)

Since grants and constraints remain disabled during normal operation, before moving users, run the database DDL commands to grant database privileges and enable constraints.

Start the Primary Extract (Live Standby)

By starting the primary extract only, it continuously captures the transactions to the local trail, so that it is sent by the data pump when moving users back to the primary system.

```
GGSCI (apps-srv2) 4> START EXTRACT et1e203

Sending START request to MANAGER ...
EXTRACT ET1E203 starting

GGSCI (apps-srv2) 5>
```

Switch Users to Primary System

Redirect the application servers to the standby system. Since the primary system is not available until it is fixed, ensure the disk space is monitored to preserve the size of the local trail because the data pump is not available.

Unplanned Standby to Primary Failover Workflow

In the event of an unplanned failover, users are quickly moved to the standby system where business continues to operate. The downtime associated with an unplanned failover is minimal and mostly proportional to the unapplied amount of the remote trail files currently being applied to the live-standby system.

The next step is to determine the cause of the primary system failure and re-instantiate it from the live-standby system in preparation to move users back to the primary system. Figure 5-11 depicts the workflow for an unplanned live-standby to primary system failover.

The amount of downtime is greatly minimized by performing an initial load from the active live-standby system, then applying the transactions that occurred during the initial load timeframe to the primary system database. When Step 4 is completed, users are unable to execute transactions until Step 12 is completed (which enables the primary system database grants and constraints). Step 16 includes starting the application servers and moving users back to the primary system. The amount of downtime varies and depends on the size of the live-standby system local trail.

Task preformed on the primary system referred to by (Primary), whereas task performed on the live-standby system referred to by (Live Standby).

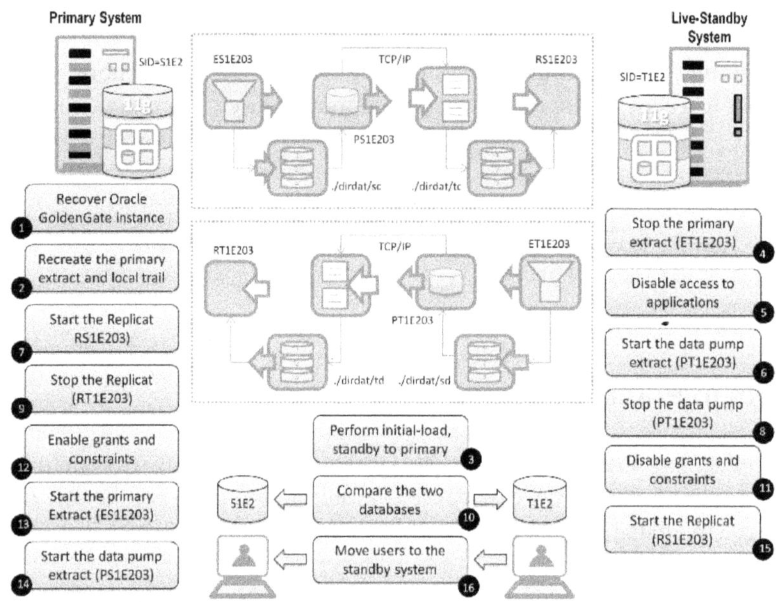

Figure 5-11: Unplanned Standby to Primary System Failover

Recover Oracle GoldenGate Instance (Primary)

Recovering Oracle GoldenGate instance may require installing the software, preferably to the same location to avoid modifying the instance parameter files. Then, restore the parameter files from the backup and start the manager process, using the same TCP/IP port to avoid modifying the manager and data pump parameter files. Verify the manager is running on the same port.

```
GGSCI (apps-srv1) 19> START mgr
Manager started.

GGSCI (apps-srv1) 20> INFO mgr

Manager is running (IP port apps-srv1.7805, Process ID 11252).

GGSCI (apps-srv1) 21>
```

Recreate the Primary Extract (Primary)

Regardless of the type of system failure, deleting and creating the primary extract is necessary. This avoids any type of reference to the old primary group.

```
GGSCI (apps-srvl) 13> DELETE EXTTRAIL ./dirdat/sc
Deleting extract trail ./dirdat/sc for extract ES1E203

GGSCI (apps-srvl) 14> DELETE EXTRACT esle203
Deleted EXTRACT ES1E203.
```

```
GGSCI (apps-srvl) 15> ADD EXTRACT esle203, TRANLOG, BEGIN now, THREADS 1
EXTRACT added.

GGSCI (apps-srvl) 16> ADD EXTTRAIL ./dirdat/sc, EXTRACT esle203, MEGABYTES
128
EXTTRAIL added.
```

Perform Initial Load

There are several techniques to establish the primary database from the live-standby database system. Refer to Chapter 3 for details regarding the available techniques. Oracle GoldenGate direct load technique is illustrated below.

Before performing initial load to establish the primary system database using the direct load method, the database table structure must be prepared. Several techniques are available including the Oracle Database Data Pump Utility.

For direct initial load method, start by preparing the initial load delivery process – as it will be referenced by the initial load extract. The objective is to perform initial load from an active live-standby system database to minimize the downtime.

Create the initial load Replicat using the SPECIALRUN option.

```
GGSCI (apps-srvl) 21> EDIT PARAMS rload03
```

```
REPLICAT rload03
SPECIALRUN
ASSUMETARGETDEFS
HANDLECOLLISIONS
USERID ggs_admin, PASSWORD oracle
EXTFILE ./dirdat/initload03.dat
DISCARDFILE ./dirrpt/rload03.dsc, PURGE
MAP osm$repapi.*, TARGET osm$repapi.*;
END RUNTIME
```

```
GGSCI (apps-srvl) 22> ADD REPLICAT rload03, SPECIALRUN
```

```
REPLICAT added.
```

Configure and create the initial load extract, ELOAD03. This extract reads from the active standby database and performs direct inserts using an initial load delivery process.

```
GGSCI (apps-srv2) 6> EDIT PARAMS eload03
```

```
EXTRACT eload03
USERID ggs_admin, PASSWORD oracle
RMTHOST apps-srv1, MGRPORT 7805
RMTTASK REPLICAT, GROUP rload03
TABLE osm$repapi.policy_types;
TABLE osm$repapi.discount_types;
TABLE osm$repapi.policies;
TABLE osm$repapi.customers;
```

```
GGSCI (apps-srv2) 7> ADD EXTRACT eload03, SOURCEISTABLE
EXTRACT added.
```

The primary system database is established by starting the initial load extract of the live standby system.

```
GGSCI (apps-srv2) 16> START EXTRACT eload03

Sending START request to MANAGER ...
EXTRACT ELOAD03 starting
```

The following shows part of the report to verify the successful completion of the initial load.

```
GGSCI (apps-srv1) 5> VIEW REPORT rload03
```

```
***********************************************************************
*                   ** Run Time Statistics **                         *
***********************************************************************
Report at 2014-01-24 17:28:40 (activity since 2014-01-24 17:27:48)

From Table OSM$REPAPI.POLICY_TYPES to OSM$REPAPI.POLICY_TYPES:
       #                   inserts:         4
       #                   updates:         0
       #                   deletes:         0
       #                  discards:         0
From Table OSM$REPAPI.DISCOUNT_TYPES to OSM$REPAPI.DISCOUNT_TYPES:
       #                   inserts:         3
       #                   updates:         0
       #                   deletes:         0
       #                  discards:         0
From Table OSM$REPAPI.POLICIES to OSM$REPAPI.POLICIES:
```

```
       #                   inserts:    102100
       #                   updates:         0
       #                   deletes:         0
       #                  discards:         0
From Table OSM$REPAPI.CUSTOMERS to OSM$REPAPI.CUSTOMERS:
       #                   inserts:    102100
       #                   updates:         0
       #                   deletes:         0
       #                  discards:         0
```

Disable Application Access (Live Standby)

Stop the applications. This is "application server dependent."

Stop the Primary Extract (Live Standby)

Stop the primary extract in preparation to applying the changes that occurred during the initial load timeframe. Issue the LAG EXTRACT before stopping the extract, this ensures all transactions have been processed by the extract.

```
GGSCI (apps-srv2) 19> LAG EXTRACT et1e203

Sending GETLAG request to EXTRACT ET1E203 ...
Last record lag 2 seconds.
At EOF, no more records to process.

GGSCI (apps-srv2) 20> STOP EXTRACT et1e203

Sending STOP request to EXTRACT ET1E203 ...
Request processed.
```

Start the Data Pump (Live Standby)

The data pump is started to send data to the primary system. These are the changes that occurred during the initial load.

```
GGSCI (apps-srv2) 21> START EXTRACT pt1e203

Sending START request to MANAGER ...
EXTRACT PT1E203 starting

GGSCI (apps-srv2) 22>
```

Start the Delivery Process (Primary)

Apply the changes to the primary database. Ensure handling collision to avoid a unique constraint error.

```
GGSCI (apps-srv1) 7> START REPLICAT rt1e203

Sending START request to MANAGER ...
REPLICAT RT1E203 starting

GGSCI (apps-srv1) 8>
```

Stop the Data Pump (Live Standby)

Stop the data pump on the standby system. Keep issuing the command LAG EXTRACT until it returns "At EOF, no more records to process." This indicates all transactions have been processed.

```
GGSCI (apps-srv2) 23> LAG EXTRACT pt1e203

Sending GETLAG request to EXTRACT PT1E203 ...
Last record lag 621,259 seconds.
At EOF, no more records to process.

GGSCI (apps-srv2) 24> STOP EXTRACT pt1e203

Sending STOP request to EXTRACT PT1E203 ...
Request processed.

GGSCI (apps-srv2) 25>
```

Stop the Delivery Process (Primary)

Stop the delivery process on the primary system. Keep issuing the command *lag replicat* until it returns "At EOF, no more records to process." This indicates all transactions have been applied to the primary database.

```
GGSCI (apps-srv1) 9> LAG REPLICAT rt1e203

Sending GETLAG request to REPLICAT RT1E203 ...
Last record lag 621,594 seconds.
At EOF, no more records to process.

GGSCI (apps-srv1) 10> STOP REPLICAT rt1e203

Sending STOP request to REPLICAT RT1E203 ...
Request processed.

GGSCI (apps-srv1) 11>
```

Compare Primary and Standby Databases

For data consistency, prior to proceeding, compare the primary and standby databases. Use tools such as Oracle GoldenGate Veridata to discover the missing rows or SQL*Plus to compare table rows count. For now, compare the two databases using rows count for tables CUSTOMERS and POLICIES using SQL*Plus for the tables.

```
SQL> conn osm$repapi/oracle
Connected.
SQL> select count(*) from customers;

  COUNT(*)
----------
    102100

SQL>
```

Execute the statement for the databases S1E2 and T1E2. Refer to Chapter 6 to learn more about Oracle GoldenGate Veridata.

Disable Grants and Constraints (Live Standby)

The receiving system must have grants and constraints disabled. This avoids referential integrity violations.

Enable Grants and Constraints (Primary)

Enable the database grants and constraints on the primary system.

Start the Primary Extract (Primary)

Start the primary extract. Since the primary was recreated, it will start transaction logs capture from the creation timestamp.

```
GGSCI (apps-srv1) 13> START EXTRACT es1e203

Sending START request to MANAGER ...
EXTRACT ES1E203 starting
```

Start the Data Pump (Primary)

Start the data pump. This starts sending data to the standby system.

```
GGSCI (apps-srv1) 15> START EXTRACT ps1e203
```

```
Sending START request to MANAGER ...
EXTRACT PS1E203 starting
```

Start the Delivery Process (Live Standby)

Start the delivery process to apply transactions sent to the standby system.

```
GGSCI (apps-srv2) 25> START REPLICAT rs1e203

Sending START request to MANAGER ...
REPLICAT RS1E203 starting
```

Move Users to the Primary System

Now, confirm the Replicat has applied all the transactions to the standby system database, start the application servers to move users back to the primary system. This step is application server/site specific. For example, if it's PL/SQL portal application such as Oracle APEX, it's changing the database connect string only from the live-standby system to the primary system database.

High Availability

Oracle High Availability has been always associated with Oracle Real Application Clusters (RAC), where within the same data center, multiple tightly coupled servers (nodes) access the same database. Another advanced architecture of RAC is Extended RAC, where nodes are loosely coupled and spread across two or more data centers. Figure 5-12 compares the high availability of Oracle GoldenGate and Extended RAC.

The upper part of Figure 5-12 is Oracle GoldenGate configured using an active-active bi-directional topology model. Over the TCP/IP network, data flows from the site A (node-1) to site B (node-2) and vice versa. The self-evident advantage of this solution is the unlimited distance between node-1 and node-2. The drawback is the chance of scalability and data conflict handling.

However, because the data is delivered in canonical format for a well-developed application, node-1 and node-2 may use different platforms. For example node-1 is Oracle Database 11g on Oracle Solaris while node-2 is Oracle Database 11g on Oracle Linux. Avoid heterogeneous database architecture for a high availability solution, unless the applications developed to support all database types transparently.

The lower part of Figure 5-12 shows Oracle Extended RAC. The databases are mirrored using dense wavelength division multiplexing (DWDM) over a dark fiber link. This enables always in-sync copies of the database. The self-evident advantage is out-of-box scalability and high availability. The drawback is the distance limitation between site A and site B for up to 100 kilometers and cost-factor.

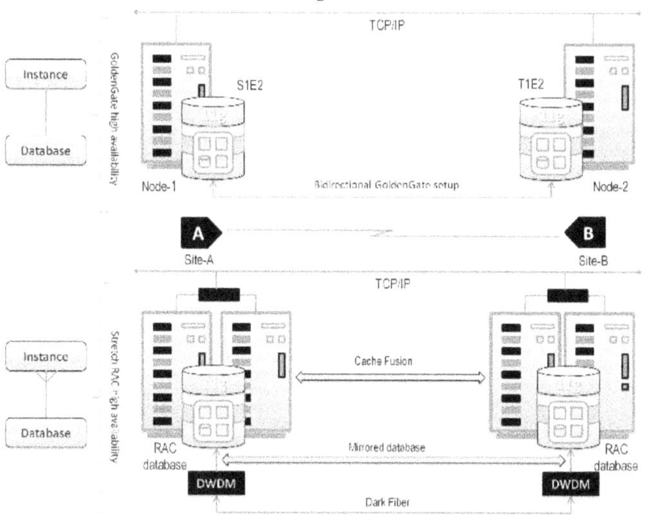

Figure 5-12: Comparison of 2-Node Oracle GoldenGate and Extended RAC

When using Oracle GoldenGate to implement a high availability platform, it is configured as an active-active bi-directional topology model. The source system (node-1) and target system (node-2) are available for user connections. Users may explicitly connect to either system based on predetermined attributes such as location, range of TCP/IP address, built-in application context, etc.

Implicit connections will be based on database and/or system workload. Users requests are routed to the system with minimal workload. This provides connection time workload evaluation to distribute database sessions across both systems. Figure 5-12 shows an implicit form of handling users connections. The database load balancer evaluates the preferred database, which is the database with lesser workload. Then, send the request to the application server which has its own HTTP load balancer. For more details regarding a high availability load balancer, refer to Figure 5-2.

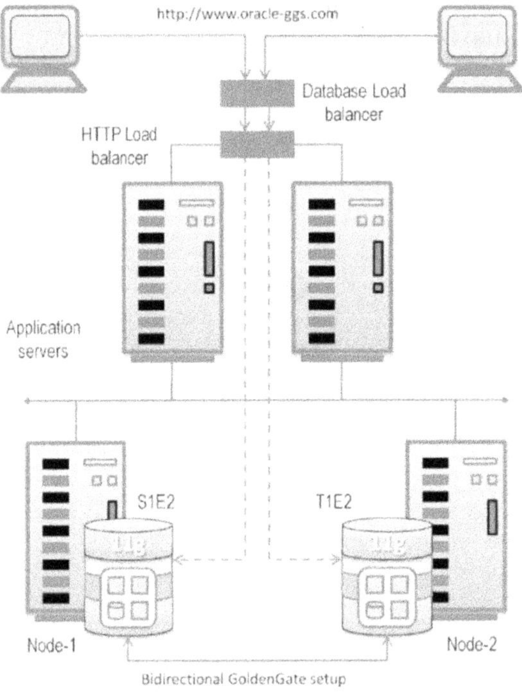

Figure 5-13: Load Balancing on Bi-Directional Topology

Applications running on Windows such as Oracle for .NET employ Oracle SQLNET to connect to the database. Whereas Java desktop applications employs JDBC drivers to connect to the database. For this type of applications, HTTP Servers are eliminated, the client applications establish stable types of database connections.

Bi-Directional Replication Considerations

Since data manipulation language (DML) statements may occurs at 'almost' the same time from either direction, the below must be considered and configured on a bi-directional active-active Oracle GoldenGate configuration.

Endless Loop Detection

In an active-active bi-directional topology, because the Extract and the Replicat are operating on the same table, the Replicat must be prevented from sending the same applied record back to the source to avoid an endless loop situation.

There are two techniques for loop detection to avoid re-extracting and re-replicating the same record:

- Replicat-Extract trace table
- Replicat-Extract parameter

Replicat-Extract Trace Table

When the Replicat applies transactions to the target database, it writes to a trace table which the Extract on the same system uses *for loop* detection by eliminating the Replicat transactions. When the Replicat starts, if the parameter *tracetable* is configured then it uses the specified trace table. If the parameter *tracetable* is not configured, it tries the default trace table name *ggs_table* owned by the Oracle GoldenGate user of the *dblogin* parameter. The following commands illustrate a non-default trace table *ggs_t1e2_trc* is created and configured as follows:

- Create the trace table *ggs_t1e2_trc*. This requires connecting to the database from within Oracle GoldenGate and issues the two GGSCI commands below:

```
GGSCI (apps-srv2) 1> DBLOGIN USERID ggs_admin, PASSWORD oracle
Successfully logged into database.

GGSCI (apps-srv2) 2> ADD TRACETABLE ggs_admin.ggs_t1e2_trc

Successfully created trace table GGS_ADMIN.GGS_T1E2_TRC.
```

- Add the parameter TRACETABLE to the Extract and the Replicat parameter file. The GGS_ADMIN is the Oracle GoldenGate database schema.

```
TRACETABLE ggs_admin.GGS_T1E2_TRC
```

Replicat Extract Parameter

The second method uses the Replicat *tranlogoptions* parameter only. This methods eliminates the processing overhead associated with using the database trace table explained above. The option *excludeuser* or *excludeuserid* of the parameter *tranlogoptions* explicitly avoid the re-capture of the transactions applied by specified user. This requires using a dedicated Oracle GoldenGate user so that transactions applied by this user are eliminated – avoiding re-sending the transaction back to the originated system. The *tranlogoptions* is shown next.

```
TRANLOGOPTIONS EXCLUDEUSER ggs_admin
```

Query DBA_USERS to replace the username with the user ID.

```
SQL> SELECT username, user_id
  2  FROM   dba_users
  3  WHERE  username='GGS_ADMIN';

USERNAME                          USER_ID
------------------------------ ----------
GGS_ADMIN                            1101
```

Data Conflicts in GoldenGate

This issue is related to data integrity that must be addressed comprehensively in an active-active bi-directional configuration. There are several types of conflict, avoidance, and detection techniques. Because applications are mostly not replication-ware, resolving data conflict is required and should be governed by the business rules. Oracle GoldenGate best practices recommend resolving data conflicts in the following order:

- Apply avoidance techniques of data segmentation and application partitioning
- Adapt Oracle GoldenGate automatic conflict detection and resolution (CDR)
- Develop custom conflict detection and resolution routines

Details regarding data conflicts and detection techniques are described in this chapter.

Truncate Table

Since the TRUNCATE TABLE command is not supported in an active-active bi-directional configuration, at any point in time, Extracts and Replicats must be configured for one-and-only-one dedicated system to issue the *truncate table* database command. This is achieved by adding the parameter *gettruncates* on the allowed system and the parameter *ignoretruncates* on the disallowed system. To ensure the *truncate table* command is issued from the allowed database only, revoke the *truncate table* privilege from the application roles.

Database Sequences in GoldenGate

When using database sequence numbers for a table primary and unique keys values on an active-active bi-directional configuration, we avoid primary and unique key uniqueness conflicts. There are several techniques for implementing database sequences on an active-active bi-directional configuration. Common techniques for using database sequences are:

- Node-1 database takes odd numbers, while node-2 database takes even numbers
- Node-1 database uses a different range of numbers than node-2 database
- Implement database sequence values based on built-in application contexts

Details regarding database sequence implementations are described in this chapter.

Real-Time Disconnected Transactions

When the applications retrieve and manipulate data synchronously from either of the two databases, database links are created which enable the application to fetch and to manipulate data from either databases. There is no data conflict. This is known as distributed database applications and adhere to database dependency, locks, and resource management as illustrated below.

Create two database links from S1E2 to T1E2 and from T1E2 to S1E2. Before creating the database link, ensure the database connect string is able to establish remote connection.

Create the database link from S1E2 to T1E2.

```
SQL> CREATE PUBLIC DATABASE LINK t1e2.precisetrace.com
  2  CONNECT TO osm$repapi IDENTIFIED BY oracle
  3  USING 'T1E2';

Database link created.
```

Create the database link from T1E2 to S1E2.

```
SQL> CREATE PUBLIC DATABASE LINK s1e2.precisetrace.com
  2  CONNECT TO osm$repapi IDENTIFIED BY oracle
  3  USING 'S1E2';

Database link created.
```

The following update statement executed remotely on S1E2 over the database link.

Do not issue COMMIT statement to continue locking resources.

```
SQL> host hostname
apps-srv2

SQL> CONN osm$repapi/oracle
Connected.
SQL> UPDATE customers@sle2 SET
  2     cust_email='falswaimil@gmai.com'
  3  WHERE cust_no=100100;

1 row updated.
```

The following update statement waits for the above remote transaction to release resources, issuing *commit* or *rollback*, then execute the update.

```
SQL> host hostname
apps-srv1

SQL> CONN osm$repapi/oracle
Connected.
SQL> UPDATE customers SET
  2     cust_email='falswaimil@yahoo.com'
  3  WHERE cust_no=100100;
```

This illustrates how synchronous transactions used by distributed applications do not trigger data conflict. They adhere to the target database resource management, locks, and queue handling.

However, for near real-time 'disconnected' transactions that are running asynchronously, the need to consider and handle data conflict caused by executing the applications is very obvious. Conflicts are either avoided using data and applications segmentation or they are handled using Oracle GoldenGate built-in and customs conflict detection and resolution. The section 'conflicts resolution' describes the built-in and advance custom techniques for handling data conflict.

Application and Database Design for High Availability

The key to avoid data conflict in an asynchronous environment is to partition data and application dynamically, which is referred to as "segmentation". This guarantees an application's group interacts and manipulates a logically partitioned subset of the database that is isolated from others application's groups. This is the fundamental concept of virtual private database (VPD). Figure 5-14 shows two application's groups in an active-active bi-directional topology model that are designed to be virtually isolated.

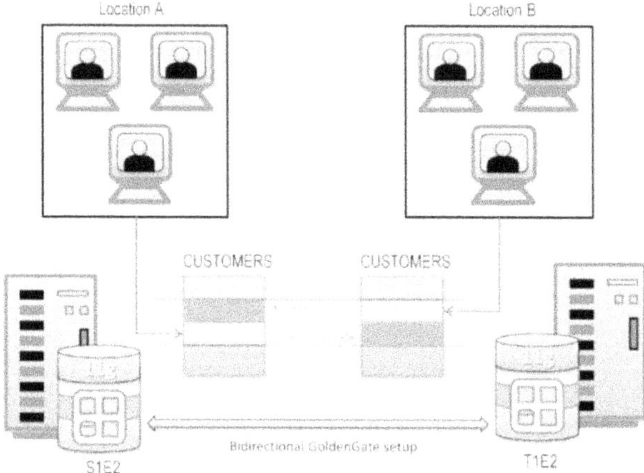

Figure 5-14: Conflict Avoidance Using Data & Applications Segmentation

The above data conflict avoidance technique is either implemented at the applications level or the database. Best practices recommend using the Oracle Database Enterprise Edition Virtual Private Database (VPD) feature. VPD uses policy functions for dynamically modifying SQL Statements to enforce data segmentation through data access control based on application contexts. Virtual Private Database implementation is explained in more detail in the section 'Virtual Private Database.'

An valuable feature for implementing segmentation by location is performance. Users are located in close proximity to access data. For example, a call center with two locations, where each location handles sales for specific products list avoids data conflict and has local data access which eliminates the overhead associated with network failure. Users continue to enter transactions locally. When the network becomes available, Oracle GoldenGate starts routing data to a remote system.

Bi-Directional Extract and Delivery Groups

The following Oracle GoldenGate configuration is built on the components used by the disaster recovery described above. Since Oracle GoldenGate high availability is deployed as an active-active bi-directional topology architecture, it is recommended to divide it into two phases:

- **Phase I: Working Bi-Directional Topology Architecture** – An end-to-end optimized and well-tested bi-directional replication capable of handling the transactions volume for near real-time data movement. Data conflict must be addressed as it's an unavoidable.

- **Phase II: Comprehensive Conflicts Handling** – Implementing avoidance and detection techniques for handling data conflicts. Since Oracle GoldenGate operates asynchronously, near real-time data movement minimizes conflict occurrences.

Figure 5-15 outlines the groups and trails. The upper part is for node-1 to node-2 data flow and the lower part is the opposite configuration, from node-2 to node-1.

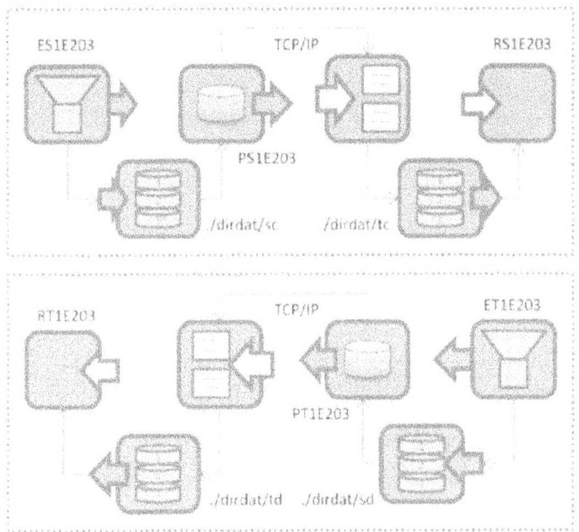

Figure 5-15: Bi-Directional High Availability Topology

Node-1 Parameter Files, Extracts, and Replicats Processes

Node-1 Oracle GoldenGate instance operates the processes listed in Table 5-2. Since an end-to-end data integrity among referenced tables must be enforced, designing multiple capture-and-delivery groups requires understanding the data model, our illustration is based on a single process architecture.

Component	Description
ES1E203	Primary capture process from the primary system transactions logs
./dirdat/sc	Local trail
PS1E203	Secondary extract data pump process send data to node-2 system
./dirdat/tc	Remote trail
RT1E203	Replicat process for node-2 database

Table 5-2: Node-1 Components

The parameter files must be modified to support bi-directional replication for conflict handling. Re-start the processes to activate the newly added parameters.

Node-1 primary extract process ES1E203 is shown below. Similarly modify Node-2 primary extract.

```
EXTRACT es1e203
SETENV  (ORACLE_SID=S1E2)
SETENV  (ORACLE_HOME="/d01/app/oracleSE")
SETENV  (NLS_LANG=AMERICAN_AMERICA.AR8ISO8859P6)
USERID  ggs_admin, password oracle
EXTTRAIL ./dirdat/sc
TABLE osm$repapi.CUSTOMERS;
TABLE osm$repapi.POLICIES
```

Node-2 delivery process RS1E203 is shown below. Similarly modify node-1 delivery process.

```
REPLICAT rt1e203
SETENV (ORACLE_SID=S1E2)
SETENV (NSL_LANG=AMERICAN_AMERICA.AL32UTF8)
USERID ggs_admin, PASSWORD oracle
ASSUMETARGETDEFS
DISCARDFILE ./dirrpt/rt1e203.dsc, PURGE
MAP osm$repapi.customers, TARGET osm$repapi.customers;
MAP osm$repapi.policies, TARGET osm$repapi.policies;
```

Verify the status of the processes on node-1 Oracle GoldenGate instance. The status of RUNNING indicates the Extract, the data pump, and the Replicat processes are configured correctly, at least.

The current status of the primary extract, ES1E203.

```
GGSCI (apps-srv1) 4> INFO EXTRACT es1e203
```

```
EXTRACT    ES1E203    Last Started 2014-01-28 22:23   Status RUNNING
Checkpoint Lag        03:42:54 (updated 00:00:05 ago)
Process ID            6378
Log Read Checkpoint   Oracle Redo Logs
                      2014-01-28 18:41:00  Thread 1, Seqno 30, RBA 39536
                      SCN 0.1997389 (1997389)
```

The local trail details, ./dirdat/sc.

```
GGSCI (apps-srv1) 5> INFO EXTTRAIL ./dirdat/sc
```

```
       Extract Trail: ./dirdat/sc
             Extract: ES1E203
               Seqno: 10
                 RBA: 1601
           File Size: 128M
```

The current status of the secondary (data pump) extract, PES1E203.

```
GGSCI (apps-srv1) 8> INFO EXTRACT ps1e203

EXTRACT    PS1E203   Last Started 2014-01-28 22:25   Status RUNNING
Checkpoint Lag       100:45:36 (updated 00:00:01 ago)
Process ID           6410
Log Read Checkpoint  File ./dirdat/sc000009
                     2014-01-24 17:40:22.000000  RBA 44546492
```

The current status delivery process from standby to primary system, RT1E203.

```
GGSCI (apps-srv1) 10> INFO REPLICAT rt1e203

REPLICAT   RT1E203   Last Started 2014-01-28 22:27   Status RUNNING
Checkpoint Lag       00:00:00 (updated 00:00:08 ago)
Process ID           6428
Log Read Checkpoint  File ./dirdat/td000008
                     First Record  RBA 45282
```

Node-2 Parameter Files, Extracts, and Replicats Processes

Node-2 Oracle GoldenGate instance operates the processes listed in Table 5-3. When Oracle GoldenGate is configured for high availability, node-1 and node-2 systems should have similar resources in terms of CPU speed and RAM size. This allows similar workload handling across the two nodes.

Component	Description
ET1E203	Primary Extract process from node-2 transactions logs
./dirdat/sd	Local trail
PT1E203	Secondary extract data pump process from node-2 to node-1
./dirdat/td	Remote trail
RS1E203	Replicat process on node-1

Table 5-3: Node-2 Components

Verify the status of the processes on node-2 Oracle GoldenGate instance.

```
GGSCI (apps-srv2) 4> INFO EXTRACT et1e203

EXTRACT    ET1E203   Last Started 2014-01-28 22:31   Status RUNNING
Checkpoint Lag       100:58:00 (updated 00:00:07 ago)
Process ID           17047
Log Read Checkpoint  Oracle Redo Logs
                     2014-01-24 17:33:26  Thread 1, Seqno 25, RBA 42078224
                     SCN 0.1889870 (1889870)
```

```
GGSCI (apps-srv2) 6> INFO EXTRACT pt1e203
```

```
EXTRACT    PT1E203   Last Started 2014-01-28 22:32   Status RUNNING
Checkpoint Lag       273:31:53 (updated 00:00:04 ago)
Process ID           17083
Log Read Checkpoint  File ./dirdat/sd000005
                     2014-01-17 13:00:31.000000  RBA 45235
```

```
GGSCI (apps-srv2) 8> INFO REPLICAT rs1e203
```

```
REPLICAT   RS1E203   Last Started 2014-01-28 22:32   Status RUNNING
Checkpoint Lag       00:00:29 (updated 00:00:00 ago)
Process ID           17097
Log Read Checkpoint  File ./dirdat/tc000016
                     2014-01-28 22:32:32.880946  RBA 1686454
```

Oracle Sequence for Artificial Primary Key Values

Oracle database sequence is a memory-based object. Hence, it is an efficient technique for generating primary key values. For a non-replicated database, sequences are suitable for generating primary key values without major issues. However, when it is used in a database synchronized by Oracle GoldenGate, it should be created to avoid primary key conflict for SQL insert statements. The following illustrates techniques for using Oracle sequences in databases synchronized in real-time by Oracle GoldenGate.

Odd-Even Numbers Distribution

The node-1 database fetches the odd number values only, while node-2 database fetches the even number values. Figure 5-16 depicts the sequence design created below:

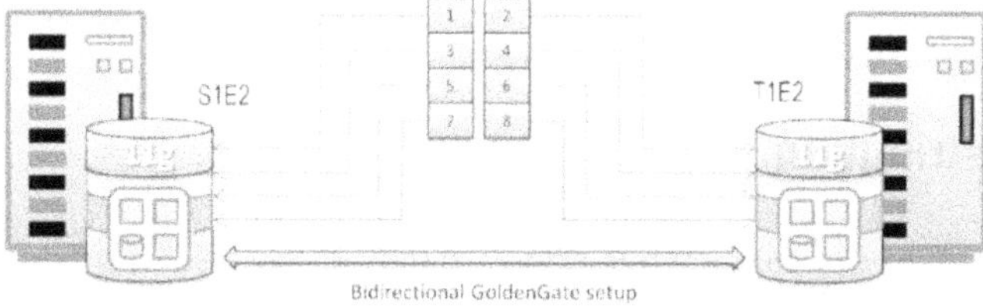

Figure 5-16: Odd-Even Numbers Sequencing

Node-1 database sequence is created to start with 1 and fetches odd numbers.

```
SQL> CREATE SEQUENCE cust_no_seq
  2  START WITH 1
  3  INCREMENT BY 2;

Sequence created.
```

```
SQL> SELECT cust_no_seq.nextval FROM dual;

   NEXTVAL
----------
         1

SQL> SELECT cust_no_seq.nextval FROM dual;

   NEXTVAL
----------
         3
```

Node-2 database sequence is created to start with 2 and fetches even numbers.

```
SQL> CREATE SEQUENCE cust_no_seq
  2  START WITH 2
  3  INCREMENT BY 2;

Sequence created.

SQL> SELECT cust_no_seq.nextval FROM dual;

   NEXTVAL
----------
         2

SQL> SELECT cust_no_seq.nextval FROM dual;

   NEXTVAL
----------
         4
```

Range Numbers Distribution

Node-1 database fetches from one range while node-2 database fetches from a second range. Figure 5-17 depicts the sequence design created below:

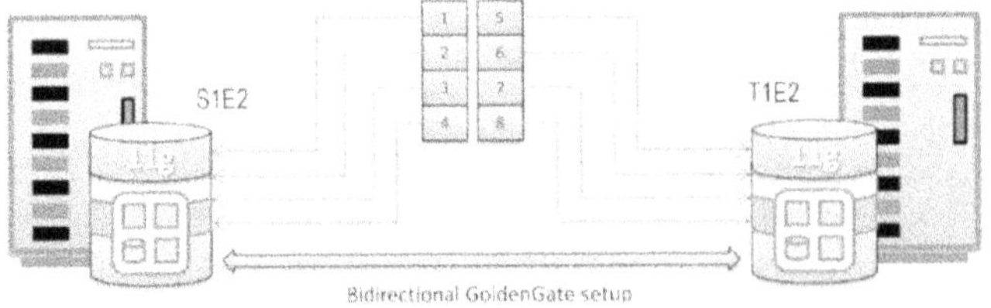

Figure 5-17: Range Numbers Sequencing

Node-1 database begins from 1 to n-1, where n is node-2 and begins sequence number.

```
SQL> CREATE SEQUENCE cust_no_seq
  2  START WITH 1;

Sequence created.

Node-2 begins at n, where n=5.

SQL> CREATE SEQUENCE cust_no_seq
  2  START WITH 5;

Sequence created.
```

Application Context of Numbers Distribution

The following illustrates the use of sequence to generate unique values based on the application context. Figure 5-18 depicts the application context value generator for a two-node architecture.

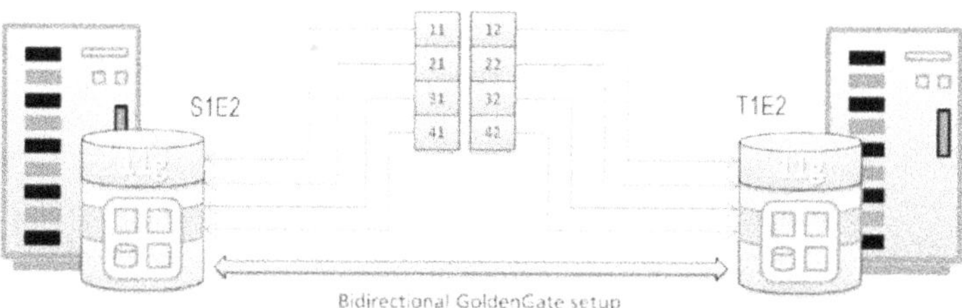

Figure 5-18: Numbers Sequencing based on Application Context

```
SQL> CREATE SEQUENCE cust_no_seq
  2  START WITH 1;

Sequence created.
```

Use the database function SYS_CONTEXT to concatenate the sequence number with the instance number (INSTANCE) for the session. This technique is similar to a sequence created with INCREMENT BY 10.

```
SQL> CREATE SEQUENCE cust_no_seq;
```

```
Sequence created.

SQL> SELECT TO_NUMBER(cust_no_seq.nextval||SYS_CONTEXT('USERENV',
'INSTANCE'))
  2  FROM   dual;

TO_NUMBER(CUST_NO_SEQ.NEXTVAL||SYS_CONTEXT('USERENV','INSTANCE'))
------------------------------------------------------------------
                                                                11
```

Instead of using the generated number by the sequence alone for the primary key values, when combined with SYS_CONTEXT('USERENV', 'DB_NAME), it generates a unique alphanumeric value of a character data type primary key.

Multi-Master Numbers Distribution

When Oracle GoldenGate is configured to support 3 systems for multi-master data replication, the first system sequence number begins at 1, the second system sequence begins at 2, and the third system sequence number begins at 3. All sequences increment by 3 as shown in Figure 5-19.

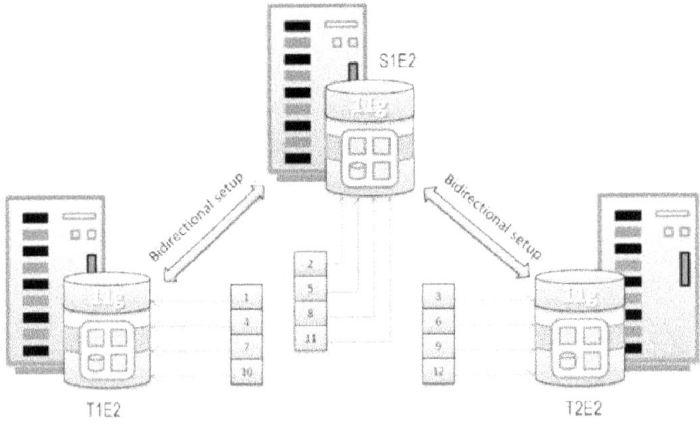

Figure 5-19: Multi-Master Numbers Sequencing

On node-1 (T1E2), create the sequence to begin at 1.

```
SQL> CREATE SEQUENCE cust_no_seq
  2  START WITH 1
  3  INCREMENT BY 3;

Sequence created.

SQL> SELECT cust_no_seq.nextval FROM dual;
```

```
   NEXTVAL
----------
         1

SQL> SELECT cust_no_seq.nextval FROM dual;

   NEXTVAL
----------
         4
```

On node-2 (S1E2), create the sequence to begin at 2.

```
SQL> CREATE SEQUENCE cust_no_seq
  2  START WITH 2
  3  INCREMENT BY 3;

Sequence created.

SQL> SELECT cust_no_seq.nextval FROM dual;

   NEXTVAL
----------
         2

SQL> SELECT cust_no_seq.nextval FROM dual;

   NEXTVAL
----------
         5
```

On node-3 (T2E2), create the sequence to begin at 3.

```
SQL> CREATE SEQUENCE cust_no_seq
  2  START WITH 3
  3  INCREMENT BY 3;

Sequence created.

SQL> SELECT cust_no_seq.nextval FROM dual;

   NEXTVAL
----------
         3

SQL> SELECT cust_no_seq.nextval FROM dual;

   NEXTVAL
----------
         6
```

Database sequences created to avoid SQL insert conflicts are not to be included on the TABLE and MAP statements. To avoid encountering gaps due to database restart, use the NOCACHE attribute when creating sequences. Since the sequence

START WITH and INCREMENT BY attributes are different on both systems, ascertain that the Oracle GoldenGate DDL replication is disabled when creating sequences and manually create them on both systems.

Data Conflicts in GoldenGate

Without explicit conflict detection, applications will continue processing transactions of inconsistent data. Logical data conflict and inconsistencies should be handled using either Oracle GoldenGate, a built-in, or custom developed conflict detection and resolution techniques. In addition, virtual private database implementation minimizes data conflict as explained in this chapter. The demonstrated conflict resolution techniques are developed for an online application system for a two-node configuration architecture, synchronized using Oracle GoldenGate. The primary database (node-1) is located at Boston, MA and the target database (node-2) is located at Albany, NY as shown in Figure 5-20.

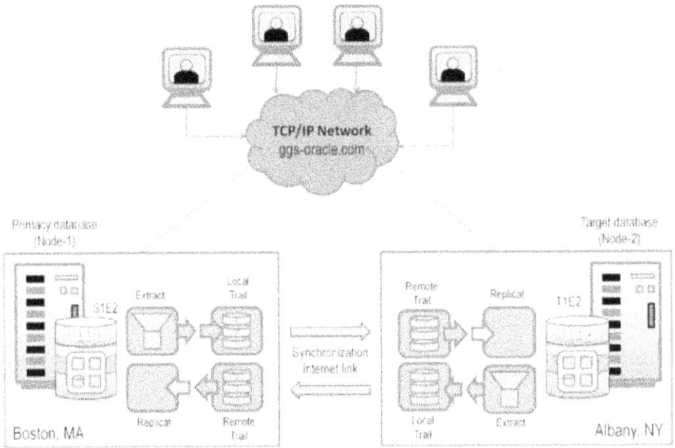

Figure 5-20: Bi-Directional Replication for Online Applications

Let us start by explaining the usages and applications of SQLEXEC parameter. This parameter is used in conjunction with custom data conflict handling technique developed in PL/SQL.

SQLEXEC Parameter

The use of the SQLEXC parameter extends Oracle GoldenGate capabilities, it enables invoking PL/SQL procedures and executes queries from within Oracle GoldenGate Extract or Replicat to support complex data conflict resolutions. The vast majority of data conflicts are handled using queries only, while procedures are mostly applied to more complex data conflicts and transformations.

Data manipulation and data conflict resolution are developed by utilizing Oracle GoldenGate built-in functions. The use of the functions @IF, @STREQ, @COMPUTE, @GETVAL and @GETENV is common. The following illustration of using SQLEXEC is developed to support a de-normalized POLICIES table which includes a PT_DESC column.

```
SQL> DESC policies
```

```
 Name                                      Null?    Type
 ----------------------------------------- -------- ---------------------
 POL_NO                                    NOT NULL NUMBER
 POL_FROM                                  NOT NULL DATE
 POL_TO                                    NOT NULL DATE
 POL_VALUE                                 NOT NULL NUMBER(8,2)
 POL_SUB_TOTAL                             NOT NULL NUMBER(8,2)
 PT_CODE                                   NOT NULL VARCHAR2(8)
 DT_CODE                                            VARCHAR2(8)
 POL_TOTAL                                 NOT NULL NUMBER(8,2)
 CUST_NO                                   NOT NULL NUMBER
 PT_DESC                                            VARCHAR2(128)
```

The PT_DESC (Policy Type Description) column exists on the target database only. Hence, a lookup operation within the Replicat is necessary to complete the transaction successfully.

SQLEXEC with Queries

The components of SQLEXEC with a query specifies the query ID, which is used by the built-in function @GETVAL to assign the value to the target column. The PARAMS clause lists the pair of parameter name and value used in the query. The last clause is the COLMAP to perform column mapping which references the query columns list using the query ID.

The Replicat MAP statement uses SQLEXEC to fetch the value for the column *pt_desc* using *pt_code* as a parameter.

```
MAP osm$repapi.policies, TARGET osm$repapi.policies, &
    SQLEXEC (ID lookup_pt, &
             QUERY " SELECT pt_desc
                     FROM   osm$repapi.policy_types
                     WHERE  pt_code = :pt_code_param ", &
             PARAMS (pt_code_param = pt_code)), &
             COLMAP (USEDEFAULTS, pt_desc = @GETVAL(lookup_pt.pt_desc));
```

The Replicat (RS1E203) parameter file using SQLEXEC with query clause.

```
REPLICAT rs1e203
SETENV (ORACLE_SID=T1E2)
SETENV (NSL_LANG=AMERICAN_AMERICA.AL32UTF8)
USERID ggs_admin, PASSWORD oracle
ASSUMETARGETDEFS
DISCARDFILE ./dirrpt/rs1e203.dsc, PURGE
MAP osm$repapi.customers, TARGET osm$repapi.customers;
MAP osm$repapi.policies, TARGET osm$repapi.policies, &
    SQLEXEC (ID lookup_pt, &
             QUERY " SELECT pt_desc
                     FROM   osm$repapi.policy_types
                     WHERE  pt_code = :pt_code_param ", &
             PARAMS (pt_code_param = pt_code)), &
             COLMAP (USEDEFAULTS, pt_desc = @GETVAL(lookup_pt.pt_desc));
```

SQLEXEC with Stored Procedures

SQLEXEC invokes stored procedure to perform advanced data transformations and conflicts resolutions. The simplest form of using SQLEXEC with stored procedure is performing a table look operation. The below PL/SQL database procedure performs a table look up operation instead of using query.

```
SQL> CREATE OR REPLACE PROCEDURE lookup_pt(pt_code_param IN VARCHAR2,
                                          pt_desc_param OUT VARCHAR2) IS
     BEGIN
        SELECT pt_desc into pt_desc_param
        FROM   osm$repapi.policy_types
        WHERE  pt_code = pt_code_param;
     END;
     /

Procedure created.

SQL> GRANT EXECUTE on lookup_pt to ggs_admin;

Grant succeeded.
```

The Replicat parameter file is modified to reference the stored procedure using the SQLEXEC parameter.

```
REPLICAT rs1e203
SETENV (ORACLE_SID=T1E2)
SETENV (NSL_LANG=AMERICAN_AMERICA.AL32UTF8)
USERID ggs_admin, PASSWORD oracle
ASSUMETARGETDEFS
DISCARDFILE ./dirrpt/rs1e203.dsc, PURGE
MAP osm$repapi.customers, TARGET osm$repapi.customers;
MAP osm$repapi.policies, TARGET osm$repapi.policies, &
    SQLEXEC (SPNAME osm$repapi.lookup_pt, &
```

```
            ID      lookup_pt, &
            PARAMS (pt_code_param = pt_code)), &
            COLMAP (USEDEFAULTS, &
                    pt_desc = @GETVAL(lookup_pt.pt_desc_param));
```

The above SQLEXEC invokes a stored procedure by specifying the following clauses:

SPNAME is the name of the stored procedure. Ascertain granting Oracle GoldenGate database user to EXECUTE privilege on the called procedure.

ID is the logical name for the procedure and is needed by the @GETVAL function to retrieve the look up value.

PARAMS is the list of input parameters and their initial values.

COLMAP performs column mapping which references the output parameters using the logical name.

SQLEXEC as Stand-Alone Parameter

The third form of SQLEXEC is a stand-alone. This is a one-time call-out to execute query, DDL command, or stored procedure. This type of SQLEXEC is valid for Extract and Replicat parameter files.

The next parameter files ES1E203.PRM use SQLEXEC parameters. The first parameter executes a query to avoid IDLE_TIME enforced by the user profile. The second parameter executes the DDL command TRUNCATE. The third parameter executes a stored procedure. Notice the procedure must not include input or output formal parameters.

```
EXTRACT es1e203
SETENV (ORACLE_SID=S1E2)
SETENV (ORACLE_HOME=/d01/app/oracleSE/product/11.2.0/dbhome_1)
SETENV (NLS_LANG=AMERICAN_AMERICA.AL32UTF8)
USERID ggs_admin, PASSWORD oracle
EXTTRAIL ./dirdat/sc
TRANLOGOPTIONS EXCLUDEUSER ggs_admin
SQLEXEC "SELECT * FROM DUAL" EVERY 55 MINUTES
SQLEXEC "TRUNCATE TABLE osm$repapi.logging" EVERY 1 DAYS
SQLEXEC "CALL send_notify()" EVERY 10 MINUTES
TABLE osm$repapi.customers;
TABLE osm$repapi.policies;
```

Custom Data Conflicts Handling

Consider an online application for managing a single inventory site. The inventory database is replicated across two cities – Boston, MA and Albany, NY as depicted in Figure 5-20. Customers' requests are directed to either database based on workload determined by the load balancer. Hence, data conflict is unavoidable. A classical data conflict may occur due to updates occurring at the time. When a conflict occurs, several resolutions are considered and should be governed by business rules.

- Use the net difference instead of using the after image value
- Perform comparison on other columns to accept, reject, or resolve transaction modifications
- Use the timestamp (date and time) then decide to accept or to reject the transaction modifications
- Manually handle the conflict by mapping data to an exception table

Conflicts Resolution Using SQLEXEC

When simultaneous bi-directional transactions update the same non-key row value on node-1 and on node-2, data divergence occurs slightly. This is a form of data conflict and must be detected and resolved.

Data Divergence Scenario

The customer has sent a change of email address request (non-key column). The request is received and routed to an agent at Boston. Shortly thereafter, the same customer sends another change of email address request with a different email from the previous request. The request is received and routed to an agent at Albany. Here is an illustration of processing this request without data conflict handling in place.

<table>
<tr><th>Node-1 Database: Boston</th><th>Node-2 Database: Albany</th></tr>
<tr><td><pre>SQL> SELECT cust_email
  2 FROM   customers
  3 WHERE cust_no=100200;

CUST_EMAIL
----
fawzi@yahoo.com

SQL></pre></td><td><pre>SQL> SELECT cust_email
  2 FROM   customers
  3 WHERE cust_no=100200;

CUST_EMAIL
----
fawzi@yahoo.com

SQL></pre></td></tr>
<tr><td>Data pump PS1E203 is down due to network failure</td><td>Data pump PT1E203 is down due to network failure</td></tr>
<tr><td><pre>SQL> UPDATE customers SET
  2 cust_email='fawzi@gmail.com'</pre></td><td><pre>SQL> UPDATE customers SET
  2 cust_email='fawzi@mail.com'</pre></td></tr>
</table>

`3 WHERE cust_no=100200;`
 	
`1 row updated.`
 	
`SQL> COMMIT;`
 	
`Commit complete.`
 	
`SQL>`
	`3 WHERE cust_no=100200;`
	
	`1 row updated.`
	
	`SQL> COMMIT;`
	
	`Commit complete.`
	
	`SQL>`

`SQL> SELECT cust_email`
`2 FROM customers`
`3 WHERE cust_no=100200;`
 	
`CUST_EMAIL`
`---------------`
`fawzi@gmail.com`
 	
`SQL>`
	`SQL> SELECT cust_email`
	`2 FROM customers`
	`3 WHERE cust_no=100200;`
	
	`CUST_EMAIL`
	`---------------`
	`fawzi@mail.com`
	
	`SQL>`

Network restored. The data pump PS1E203 started automatically.	Network restored. The data pump PT1E203 started automatically.

`SQL> SELECT cust_email`
`2 FROM customers`
`3 WHERE cust_no=100200;`
 	
`CUST_EMAIL`
`--------------`
`fawzi@mail.com`
	`SQL> SELECT cust_email`
	`2 FROM customers`
	`3 WHERE cust_no=100200;`
	
	`CUST_EMAIL`
	`---------------`
	`fawzi@gmail.com`

There is no error, but notice that the change of address resulted in mismatched CUST_EMAIL values between the two databases. This is a simple data conflict, yet critical to be addressed to avoid a data integrity problem.

Data Divergence Handling

Oracle GoldenGate captures before and after image of updates to support custom and built-in conflict resolutions by performing a compare operation before applying the transactions on the target database. Data divergence conflicts are prevented. Figure 5-21 shows the workflow of updating the email for CUST_NO=100200. Since there is no data segmentation at the application level, a custom data conflict is developed.

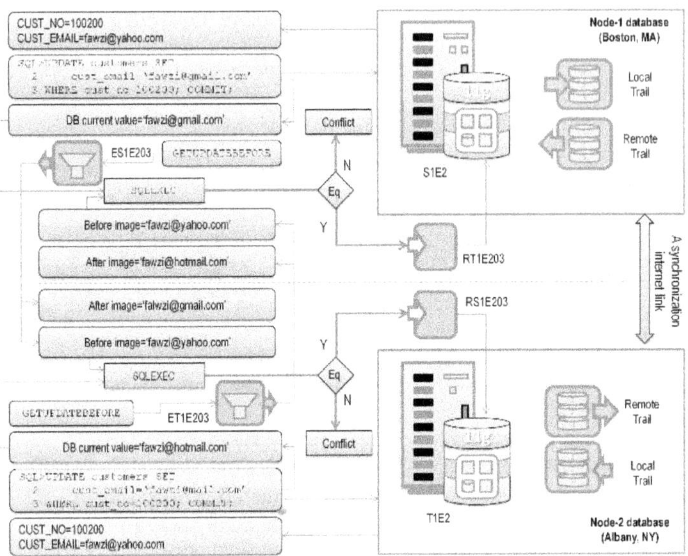

Figure 5-21: Resolving Conflict Using SQLEXEC

The Replicat applies the transaction to the database and the conflict occurs silently. The conflict is resolved either using the built-in conflict detection and resolution (CDR) or customer resolution using the SQLEXEC parameter. Using either technique, the database current value is compared with before image value from the trail record.

If the two values are equal, then the transaction is applied. Otherwise, a data conflict is detected and needs to be handled accordingly.

Using the parameter SQLEXEC to handle the above data conflict requires using a query or a procedure to fetch the current database value and compare with the before image from the trail record. If the two values are identical, then apply the transaction. Otherwise report or handle data conflict. The stored procedure GET_EMAIL for handling this type of update conflict follows.

```
SQL> CREATE OR REPLACE PROCEDURE get_email(pcust_no    IN NUMBER,
                                           pcust_email OUT VARCHAR2) IS
     BEGIN
        SELECT cust_email into pcust_email
        FROM   osm$repapi.customers
        WHERE  cust_no = pcust_no;
     END;
     /

Procedure created.
```

The Extract ES1E203 uses the parameter GETUPDATEBEFORES to force capture the transaction post values and before image values for use by the Replicat to detect conflict. Also, to support operation granularity, the parameter GETBEFORECOLS is used in conjunction with GETUPDATEBEFORES to associate the before image with the operation type of UPDATE, DELETE, or both. The argument ALL specifies
the before image value is for all columns. The example below illustrates using GETBEFORECOLS to capture the before image values for update and delete operations on the CUST_EMAIL column only. The argument KEYINCLUDING includes capture of the primary key before image value.

```
TABLE osm$repapi.customers &
      GETBEFORECOLS(ON UPDATE KEYINCLUDING (cust_email), &
                    ON DELETE KEYINCLUDING (cust_email));
```

The parameter GETUPDATEBEFORES remains in effect for all subsequent listed tables until the parameter IGNOREUPDATEBEFORES is encountered – enabling control of the before image capture for a specific list of tables.

```
EXTRACT es1e203
SETENV (ORACLE_SID=S1E2)
SETENV (ORACLE_HOME=/d01/app/oracleSE/product/11.2.0/dbhome_1)
SETENV (NLS_LANG=AMERICAN_AMERICA.AL32UTF8)
USERID ggs_admin, PASSWORD oracle
EXTTRAIL ./dirdat/sc
TRANLOGOPTIONS EXCLUDEUSER ggs_admin
GETUPDATEBEFORES
TABLE osm$repapi.customers GETBEFORECOLS(ON UPDATE ALL);
IGNOREUPDATEBEFORES
TABLE osm$repapi.policies;
```

The Replicat RS1E203 parameter file includes the SOURCEDEFS parameter for mapping non-identical tables structure. Using SQLEXEC to invoke the procedure GET_EMAIL returns the current database value for compression with the before image value. The COLMAP clause includes reference to the Oracle GoldenGate built-in function to detect conflict. If the built-in function @STREQ returns 1 (true) then
no conflict was detected. Otherwise, a conflict has been detected and the column CUST_EMAIL assigned the value 'conflict@pt.com' as a means of notification and intervention.

```
cust_email      = @IF(@STREQ(BEFORE.cust_email,
                      @GETVAL(get_email.pcust_email)),
                      cust_email, 'conflict@pt.com'),
```

```
REPLICAT rs1e203
SETENV (ORACLE_SID=T1E2)
SETENV (NSL_LANG=AMERICAN_AMERICA.AL32UTF8)
USERID ggs_admin, PASSWORD oracle
SOURCEDEFS /d01/oracle/ggs/dirdef/defgen.def
--ASSUMETARGETDEFS
DISCARDFILE ./dirrpt/rs1e203.dsc, PURGE
GETUPDATES
GETINSERTS
GETDELETES
MAP osm$repapi.customers, TARGET osm$repapi.customers, &
    SQLEXEC (ID get_email, &
        SPNAME osm$repapi.get_email, &
        PARAMS (pcust_no = cust_no)), &
        COLMAP (cust_no         = cust_no,
                cust_name       = cust_name,
                cust_email      = @IF(@STREQ(BEFORE.cust_email,
                                      @GETVAL(get_email.pcust_email)),
                                      cust_email, 'conflict@pt.com'),
                cust_mobile     = cust_mobile,
                cust_address    = cust_address,
                cust_commit_ts = @GETENV('GGHEADER', 'COMMITTIMESTAMP'));
--
MAP osm$repapi.policies, TARGET osm$repapi.policies, &
    SQLEXEC (SPNAME osm$repapi.lookup_pt, &
        ID      lookup_pt, &
        PARAMS (pt_code_param = pt_code)), &
        COLMAP (USEDEFAULTS, &
                pt_desc = @GETVAL(lookup_pt.pt_desc_param));
```

The following scenario illustrates conflict detection for an update operation. The Replicat applying the transaction detects the conflict and assigns the CUST_EMAIL column with temporary email 'conflict@pt.com' for further action.

Node-1 Database: Boston	**Node-2 Database: Albany**

`SQL> SELECT cust_email`
`  2  FROM   customers`
`  3  WHERE  cust_no=4846;`
 	
`CUST_EMAIL`
`--------------------`
`deema@yahoo.com`
 	
`SQL>`
	`SQL> SELECT cust_email`
	`  2  FROM   customers`
	`  3  WHERE  cust_no=4846;`
	
	`CUST_EMAIL`
	`--------------------`
	`deema@yahoo.com`
	
	`SQL>`

Data pump PS1E203 is down due to network failure	Data pump PT1E203 is down due to network failure

`SQL> UPDATE customers SET`
`  2  cust_email='deema@gmail.com'`
`  3  WHERE cust_no=4846;`
 	
`1 row updated.`
 	
`SQL> COMMIT;`
 	
`Commit complete.`
	`SQL> UPDATE customers SET`
	`  2      cust_email='deema@hotmail'`
	`  3  WHERE cust_no=4846;`
	
	`1 row updated.`
	
	`SQL> COMMIT;`
	
	`Commit complete.`

SQL>	SQL>

SQL> SELECT cust_email
  2 FROM   customers
  3 WHERE cust_no=4846;
 	
CUST_EMAIL
--------------- 	
deema@gmail.com
 	
SQL>
	SQL> SELECT cust_email
	  2 FROM customers
	  3 WHERE cust_no=4846;
	
	CUST_EMAIL
	-------------- 	
	deema@hotmail.com
	
	SQL>

Network restored. The data pump PS1E203 started automatically.	Network restored. The data pump PT1E203 started automatically.

SQL> SELECT cust_email
  2 FROM   customers
  3 WHERE cust_no=4846;
 	
CUST_EMAIL
------------- 	
deema@hotmail
 	
SQL>
	SQL> SELECT cust_email
	  2 FROM customers
	  3 WHERE cust_no=4846;
	
	CUST_EMAIL
	--------------- 	
	conflict@pt.com
	
	SQL>

Refer to Chapter 8 to learn more regarding generating the definition file and advanced transformation.

Applying Net Difference Resolution Using SQLEXEC

When the application manipulates a single entity such as inventory level, bank account, order entry, etc., in an active-active bi-directional Oracle GoldenGate topology, conflicts may occur and must be handled. Figure 5-22 illustrates an ATM workflow for simultaneous transactions executed at the same time.

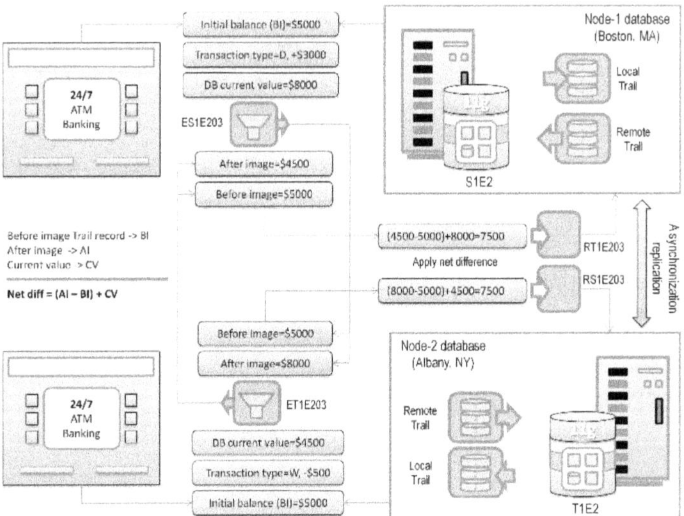

Figure 5-22: Applying Net Difference Resolution Using SQLEXEC

The initial account balance is $5,000. A deposit transaction (D) for the amount of $3,000 is entered using the primary ATM card. This transaction is located at Boston, MA increasing the account balance to $8,000.

Almost simultaneously, while the initial balance is still $5000, a withdrawal transaction (W) for the amount of $500 is entered using the secondary ATM card. This transaction is located at Albany, NY decreasing the account balance to $4,500.

When the Replicat applies the transaction on either database, conflict occurs. The database located at Boston, MA has a current value of $8,000 and the database located at Albany, NY has a current value of $4,500. By comparing the trail record and the current database values, the data conflict is detected and needs to be resolved — using either SQLEXEC for applying the net difference or Oracle GoldenGate built-in conflict detection and resolution (CDR) to calculate and apply the transaction correctly.

The resolution below is developed using SQLEXEC. The Replicat COLMAP clause determines and applies the net difference of: $5000+$3000-$500=$7500.

The net balance applied at Boston, MA is calculated as:

Net balance = ((Trail after image - Trail before image) + current value)
= ((4500 – 5000) + 8000) = $7,500

The net balance applied at Albany, NY is calculated as:

Net balance = ((Trail after image - Trail before image) + current value)
= ((8000 – 5000) + 4500) = $7,500

To demonstrate data conflict by applying the net difference value, the table CURRENT_ACCOUNTS exists on node-1 database (S1E2) and node-2 database (T1E2). It is configured on bi-directional configuration with transactions entered from both nodes.

```
SQL> DESC current_accounts

 Name                                  Null?    Type
 ------------------------------------- -------- ----------------
 ACCT_NO                               NOT NULL NUMBER
 ACCT_NAME                             NOT NULL VARCHAR2(64)
 ACCT_AMOUNT                                     NUMBER
 ACCT_TS                                         TIMESTAMP(6)

SQL> SELECT ACCT_AMOUNT
  2  FROM   current_accounts
  3  WHERE  acct_no=49664996;

ACCT_AMOUNT
-----------
       5000
```

The Extract parameter file lists the tables. The parameters GETUPDATEBEFORES and GETBEFORECOLS enable capture of the before image values.

```
EXTRACT es1e203
SETENV (ORACLE_SID=S1E2)
SETENV (ORACLE_HOME=/d01/app/oracleSE/product/11.2.0/dbhome_1)
SETENV (NLS_LANG=AMERICAN_AMERICA.AL32UTF8)
USERID ggs_admin, PASSWORD oracle
EXTTRAIL ./dirdat/sc
TRANLOGOPTIONS EXCLUDEUSER ggs_admin
GETUPDATEBEFORES
TABLE osm$repapi.customers &
      GETBEFORECOLS(ON UPDATE KEYINCLUDING (cust_email), &
                    ON DELETE KEYINCLUDING (cust_email));
IGNOREUPDATEBEFORES
TABLE osm$repapi.policies;
GETUPDATEBEFORES
TABLE osm$repapi.current_accounts &
      GETBEFORECOLS(ON UPDATE ALL);
IGNOREUPDATEBEFORES
```

The Replicat parameter file uses SQLEXEC to execute a query then compares the before image with the query return value. The COLMAP clause uses Oracle GoldenGate built-in @COMPUTE function to determine the net difference.

```
REPLICAT rs1e203
SETENV (ORACLE_SID=T1E2)
SETENV (NSL_LANG=AMERICAN_AMERICA.AL32UTF8)
USERID ggs_admin, PASSWORD oracle
SOURCEDEFS /d01/oracle/ggs/dirdef/defgen.def
DISCARDFILE ./dirrpt/rs1e203.dsc, PURGE
GETUPDATES
GETINSERTS
GETDELETES
MAP osm$repapi.customers, TARGET osm$repapi.customers, &
    SQLEXEC (ID       get_email, &
             SPNAME osm$repapi.get_email, &
             PARAMS (pcust_no = cust_no)), &
    COLMAP (cust_no          = cust_no,
            cust_name        = cust_name,
            cust_email       = @IF(@STREQ(BEFORE.cust_email,
                               @GETVAL(get_email.pcust_email)), cust_email,
                               'conflict@pt.com'),
            cust_mobile      = cust_mobile,
            cust_address     = cust_address,
            cust_commit_ts = @GETENV('GGHEADER', 'COMMITTIMESTAMP'));
--
MAP osm$repapi.policies, TARGET osm$repapi.policies, &
    SQLEXEC (SPNAME osm$repapi.lookup_pt, &
             ID     lookup_pt, &
             PARAMS (pt_code_param = pt_code)), &
             COLMAP (USEDEFAULTS, &
                     pt_desc = @GETVAL(lookup_pt.pt_desc_param));
--
MAP osm$repapi.current_accounts, TARGET osm$repapi.current_accounts,
    SQLEXEC (ID lookup_acct_amount, &
        QUERY " SELECT acct_amount FROM osm$repapi.current_accounts
                WHERE  acct_no = :vacct_no ", &
        PARAMS (vacct_no = acct_no)), &
        COLMAP (acct_no     = acct_no,
                acct_name   = acct_name,
                acct_amount = @COMPUTE(((acct_amount - BEFORE.acct_amount) +
                              @GETVAL(lookup_acct_amount.acct_amount))),
                acct_ts     = @GETENV('GGHEADER', 'COMMITTIMESTAMP'));
```

The below sequence of query and update statements demonstrates the same ACCT_NO is updated when the data pump is ABENDED due to network failure, which should lead to data conflict when the data pump is re-started. However, by applying the net difference value, the ACCT_AMOUNT value column is correctly calculated and converged.

Node-1 database, Boston	Node-2 database, Albany

`SQL> SELECT ACCT_AMOUNT`
`  2  FROM   current_accounts`
`  3  WHERE  acct_no=49664996;`
 	
`ACCT_AMOUNT`
`-----------`
`       5000`
 	
`SQL>`
	`SQL> SELECT ACCT_AMOUNT`
	`  2  FROM   current_accounts`
	`  3  WHERE  acct_no=49664996;`
	
	`ACCT_AMOUNT`
	`-----------`
	`       5000`
	
	`SQL>`

Data pump PS1E203 is down due to network failure	Data pump PT1E203 is down due to network failure

`SQL> UPDATE current_accounts SET`
`  2      acct_amount=acct_amount+3000`
`  3  WHERE  acct_no=49664996;`
 	
`1 row updated.`
 	
`SQL> COMMIT;`
	`SQL> UPDATE current_accounts SET`
	`  2      acct_amount=acct_amount-500`
	`  3  WHERE  acct_no=49664996;`
	
	`1 row updated.`
	
	`SQL> COMMIT;`

`SQL> SELECT acct_amount`
`  2  FROM   current_accounts`
`  3  WHERE  acct_no=49664996;`
 	
`ACCT_AMOUNT`
`-----------`
`       8000`
	`SQL> SELECT acct_amount`
	`  2  FROM   current_accounts`
	`  3  WHERE  acct_no=49664996;`
	
	`ACCT_AMOUNT`
	`-----------`
	`       4500`

Network restored. The data pump PS1E203 started automatically.	Network restored. The data pump PT1E203 started automatically.

`SQL> SELECT acct_amount`
`  2  FROM   current_accounts`
`  3  WHERE  acct_no=49664996;`
 	
`ACCT_AMOUNT`
`-----------`
`       7500`
 	
`SQL>`
	`SQL> SELECT acct_amount`
	`  2  FROM   current_accounts`
	`  3  WHERE  acct_no=49664996;`
	
	`ACCT_AMOUNT`
	`-----------`
	`       7500`
	
	`SQL>`

DML Conflict Types

Fundamentally, conflicts occur and must be handled. Why? It is because Oracle GoldenGate Replicat preserves data integrity when applying transactions. It does so by maintaining the transactions commit order and uses the target database native calls when applying transactions, which have database constraints enabled.

An active-active bi-directional configuration must implement, detect, and resolve data conflict techniques. These conflicts arising from DML transactions manipulate the same row stored on the source and target databases. The resolution is detected and resolved using either built-in or custom developed conflict detection and resolution techniques.

The resolution is developed as part of the transaction integrity or by applying basic resolution rules such as timestamps. There are (3) types of conflicts that occur when executing SQL statements on asynchronous mode:

Insert Conflicts

Due to enabled and valid primary key or unique key constraints on tables, insert conflicts occur when duplicate values violate the constraint. Without conflict handling the Replicat terminates with an error.

Update Conflicts

Modifying the same row at the same time results in update conflicts. However, because access to the updated row's before and after image is available, conflicts are resolved by applying suitable resolution methods.

Delete Conflicts

This type of conflict commonly occurs when the Replicat attempts to apply a delete transaction, but the row is not found on the target database. This is because the row is already deleted or updated by another transaction.

GoldenGate Data Conflict and Resolution Roadmap

The fundamental rule when developing conflict resolution is to consider the technique and consistency. This allows applying the same technique across the vast majority of the database tables. There are several approaches to data conflict avoidance, detection, and resolution. The combination of avoidance and resolution promotes data convergence and data consistency. Oracle GoldenGate provides its own built-in function and conflict detection and resolution (CDR). It is the distinctive feature of Oracle GoldenGate 11g Release 2, explained and demonstrated shortly.

The techniques and order for handling data conflicts in an active-active bi-directional topology is shown in Figure 5-23. Since Oracle GoldenGate is mostly deployed after the application, it is less likely the application is conflict-aware. To minimize the application changes and make Oracle GoldenGate data replication transparent on bi-directional topology, the roadmap begins by implementing data segmentation as an avoidance technique. When data segmentation may not totally avoid data conflict, partitioning the applications provides the second line of defense.

In addition to data segmentation and application partitioning, Oracle GoldenGate built-in conflict detection and resolution applies consistent methods to resolve conflicts using declarative parameter settings for all types of DML conflict types.

For complex data conflict detection and resolution, using the SQLEXEC parameter requires developing PL/SQL sub-programs and SQL queries that are invoked from within Oracle GoldenGate.

When SQLEXEC is not meeting the requirements, user exits is another option to consider for handling sophisticated conflicts beyond those provided by Oracle GoldenGate built-in functions and techniques. User exits are developed in C and C++ programming language and invoked from the Extract and Replicat, but mostly adapted for advanced integration and data transformation.

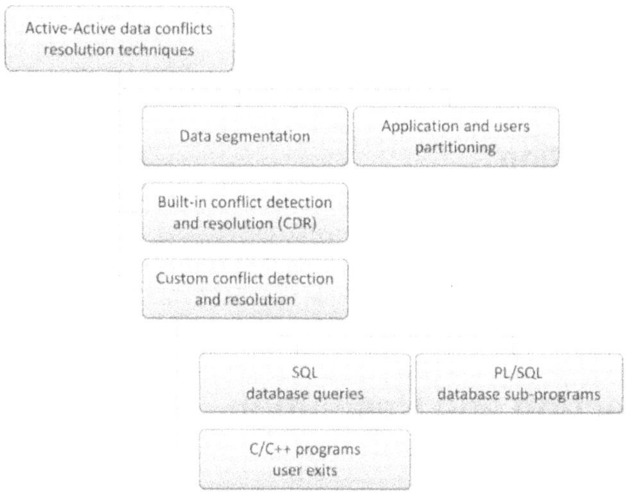

Figure 5-23: Conflicts Resolutions Roadmap

Data Segmentation

When the application is not replication-aware, then implementing data segmentation is the first approach of the data conflict avoidance technique. It is developed and deployed within the database only. An example is implementing Oracle Virtual Private Database (VPD) to dynamically apply a table-level security policy function to avoid the likelihood of having the same row concurrently accessed by multiple users.

Application Segmentation

Application segmentation is implemented from within the virtual private database – making the application replication-aware. Then by segregating applications so that groups of users are associated with an application, accessing a subset of tables reduces the possibility of data conflicts. Application segmentation is developed using application contexts such as locations, transaction type, etc. This is an avoidance technique to minimize and not to entirely eliminate data conflicts.

Built-In Conflict Detection and Resolution

Oracle GoldenGate 11g Release 2 is shipped with built-in conflict detection and resolution (CDR). This is a core feature of any data replication software. Using simple declarative conflicts and methods, Oracle GoldenGate handles the majority of conflicts for database applications accessing active-active bi-directional topology.

Custom Conflict Resolution

Using queries, PL/SQL sub-programs, and user exits enable developing conflict resolution beyond the capabilities of Oracle GoldenGate built-in conflict resolution methods. The technique extends the capabilities of Oracle GoldenGate to include using the database built-in features for events handling.

Built-In Conflict Detection and Resolution

While complex business logic custom data conflicts resolutions are developed using PL/SQL, SQL queries, and C/C++ user exits, the majority of data conflicts can be handled by adapting Oracle GoldenGate automatic conflicts detection and resolution (CDR) techniques.

The advantages of employing the built-in CDR are performance, consistency, and lower maintenance cost. Resolving conflicts using CDR delivers better performance when compared to custom resolution using SQLEXEC to invoke database PL/SQL procedures or SQL executing queries. The built-in resolution and detection avoid runtime context switching. Since the vast majority of tables are handled using similar conflict resolution methods, CDR delivers consistency using declarative conflict types and methods. Lower maintenance cost is also an advantage of using CDR. For example, when modifying CDR methods, deploying CDR new features, adding new table columns and database tables, maintenance is executed within GoldenGate only. Oracle GoldenGate built-in conflict detection and resolution uses the four parameters listed in Table 5-4, promoting ease of configuration and deployment.

Parameter	Description
GETUPDATEBEFORES	An Extract parameter. It forces capture of the transaction post values (after image) and before image values for use by the Replicat to detect conflicts.
GETBEFORECOLS	An Extract parameter. It associates the before image with the operation type of UPDATE, DELETE, or both and the column list.
COMPARECOLS	A Replicat parameter. It lists the columns to check for conflicts with the target database current value. A mismatch is a conflict and handled by the RESOLVECONFLICT settings.
RESOLVECONFLICT	A Replicat parameter. It specifies the operation type, the resolution type, and the method applied to resolve the conflict. The parameter is repeated for each resolution to handle the different operations.

Table 5-4: Built-In Conflict Detection and Resolution Parameters

For tables referenced by transactions on an active-active bi-directional topology, the parameter RESOLVECONFLICT is configured to handle conflicts. Within the same MAP statement, it resolves all types of data conflict transactions for UPDATE, DELETE, and INSERT SQL statements. The below illustrates resolving update conflicts. The named resolution DELTA_RESOLUTION_METHOD uses the method USEDELTA for the column ACCT_AMOUNT. The resolution MAX_RESOLUTION_METHOD uses the method USEMAX for the columns ACCT_NAME and ACCT_TS.

```
RESOLVECONFLICT (UPDATEROWEXISTS,
                    (DELTA_RESOLUTION_METHOD, USEDELTA, COLS (acct_amount)),
                    (MAX_RESOLUTION_METHOD, USEMAX(acct_ts),
                     COLS (acct_name, acct_ts))
```

Figure 5-24 depicts the hierarchy of using Oracle GoldenGate built-in conflict detection and resolution (CDR).

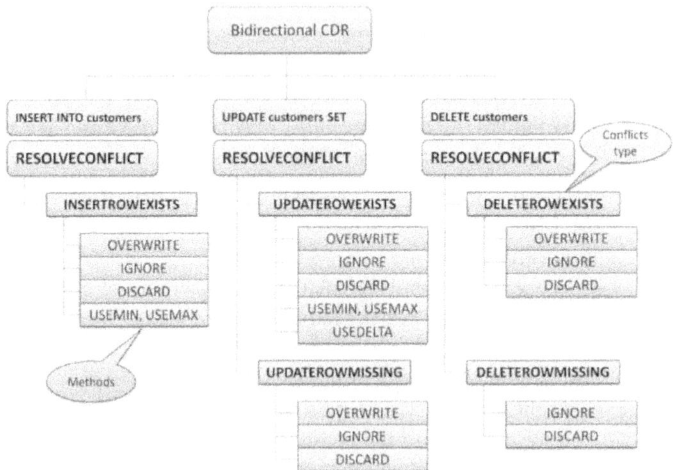

Figure 5-24: Built-In Conflicts Detection and Resolution

The parameter RESOLVECONFLICT takes any of the arguments listed in Table 5-5. Depending on the business rules for data conflict resolution handling, associate the argument with a resolution method.

Conflict type	Description
INSERTROWEXISTS	Handles unique constraint violation. The target database has primary key or unique key constraint enabled.
UPDATEROWEXISTS	Handles update data conflict when the before image value for one or more columns differ from the current database value.
UPDATEROWMISSING	Handles data conflict when the row does not exist on the target database.
DELETEROWEXISTS	Handles delete data conflict when before image value for one or more columns differ from the current database value.
DELETEROWMISSING	Handles data conflict when the row deleted on source does not exist on the target database.

Table 5-5: RESOVLECONFLICT Parameter Conflict Types

Each conflict type is associated with one resolution method. The following is the list of methods applied to a DEFAULT or named resolution:

- OVERWRITE
- IGNORE
- DISCARD
- USEMIN
- USEMAX
- USEDELTA

Figure 5-25 outlines the syntax of the Replicat built-in conflict detection and resolution. The combination of COMPARECOLS and RESOLVECONFLICT parameters handles the operation types and the conflict types. For each conflict type, a resolution method is selected and may be applied to one or more columns.

```
MAP  <source table>, TARGET <target table>,
COMPARECOLS (
  { ON UPDATE {ALL | KEY | KEYINCLUDING(col1, col2,..., coln) |
                          KEYEXCULDING(col1, col2,..., coln)}|
   ,ON DELETE {ALL | KEY | KEYINCLUDING(col1, col2,..., coln) |
                          KEYEXCULDING(col1, col2,..., coln)} )
RESOLVECONFLICT (
    { INSERTROWEXISTS   |
      UPDATEROWEXISTS   | UPDATEROWMISSING |
      DELETEROWEXISTS   | DELETEROWMISSING }
                 {
                   { DEFAULT | <resolution name>},
                   { USEMAX (column) |
                     USEMIN (column) |
                     DELTA           |
                     DISCARD         |
                     OVERWRITE }
                 },
                    COLS (col1, col2,..., coln)
             )
```

Figure 5-25: Built-In Conflict Detection and Resolution Syntax

Configuring Built-In Conflict Detection and Resolution

This section implements active-active configuration using Oracle GoldenGate built-in conflict detection and resolution (CDR). Consider the CURRENT_ACCOUNTS table, the Extract and Replicat are configured for CDR. The ACCT_AMOUNT column is handled using the DELTA method. The ACCT_NAME and ACCT_TS columns are handled using the USEMAX method.

```
SQL> DESC current_accounts
```

```
 Name                                      Null?    Type
 ----------------------------------------- -------- -------------------
 ACCT_NO                                   NOT NULL NUMBER
 ACCT_NAME                                 NOT NULL VARCHAR2(64)
 ACCT_AMOUNT                                        NUMBER
 ACCT_TS                                           TIMESTAMP(6)
```

As part of the change data capture (CDC), ensure to run the ADD TRANDATA command on node-1 and node-2 databases using the syntax below.

```
GGSCI (apps-srv1) 4> ADD TRANDATA osm$repapi.current_accounts ALLCOLS
```

Node-1 Extract and Replicat Parameter Files

The parameter files for node-1 configured to support the Extract ES1E203, the data pump PS1E203 and the Replicat RT1E203.

The use of the parameters GETUPDATEBEFORES, GETBEFORECOLS and IGNOREUPDATEBEFORES is for supporting capture of the before image on the trail records.

```
EXTRACT es1e203
SETENV (ORACLE_SID=S1E2)
SETENV (ORACLE_HOME=/d01/app/oracleSE/product/11.2.0/dbhome_1)
SETENV (NLS_LANG=AMERICAN_AMERICA.AL32UTF8)
USERID ggs_admin, PASSWORD oracle
EXTTRAIL ./dirdat/sc
TRANLOGOPTIONS EXCLUDEUSER ggs_admin
GETUPDATEBEFORES
TABLE osm$repapi.customers &
      GETBEFORECOLS(ON UPDATE KEYINCLUDING (cust_email), &
                    ON DELETE KEYINCLUDING (cust_email));
IGNOREUPDATEBEFORES
TABLE osm$repapi.policies;
GETUPDATEBEFORES
```

```
TABLE osm$repapi.current_accounts &
      GETBEFORECOLS(ON UPDATE ALL, ON DELETE ALL);
IGNOREUPDATEBEFORES
```

The data pump PS1E203 is configured on PASSTHRU mode, sending data to node-2 without transformation.

```
EXTRACT ps1e203
USERID ggs_admin, PASSWORD oracle
PASSTHRU
RMTHOST apps-srv2, MGRPORT 7806
RMTTRAIL ./dirdat/tc
TABLE osm$repapi.customers;
TABLE osm$repapi.policies;
TABLE osm$repapi.current_accounts;
```

The Replicat RT1E203 applies transactions to the node-1 database.

```
REPLICAT rt1e203
SETENV (ORACLE_SID=S1E2)
SETENV (NSL_LANG=AMERICAN_AMERICA.AL32UTF8)
USERID ggs_admin, PASSWORD oracle
ASSUMETARGETDEFS
DISCARDFILE ./dirrpt/rt1e203.dsc, PURGE
MAP osm$repapi.customers, TARGET osm$repapi.customers;
MAP osm$repapi.policies, TARGET osm$repapi.policies;
MAP osm$repapi.current_accounts, TARGET osm$repapi.current_accounts,
    COMPARECOLS (ON UPDATE ALL, ON DELETE ALL),
    RESOLVECONFLICT (UPDATEROWEXISTS,
                    (DELTA_RESOLUTION_METHOD, USEDELTA, COLS (acct_amount)),
                    (MAX_RESOLUTION_METHOD, USEMAX(acct_ts),
                     COLS (acct_name, acct_ts)),
                                        (DEFAULT, USEMAX(acct_ts))),
    RESOLVECONFLICT (UPDATEROWMISSING, (DEFAULT, OVERWRITE)),
    RESOLVECONFLICT (DELETEROWEXISTS,  (DEFAULT, OVERWRITE)),
    RESOLVECONFLICT (DELETEROWMISSING, (DEFAULT, DISCARD)),
    RESOLVECONFLICT (INSERTROWEXISTS,  (DEFAULT, USEMAX(acct_ts)));
```

Node-2 Extract and Replicat Parameter Files

The set of node-2 parameter files are similar to node-1. The parameter files support the Extract ET1E203, the data pump PT1E203 and the Replicat RS1E203.

The Extract ET1E203 parameter file.

```
EXTRACT et1e203
SETENV (ORACLE_SID="T1E2")
SETENV (ORACLE_HOME="/d01/app/oracleSE/product/11.2.0/dbhome_1")
SETENV (NLS_LANG="AMERICAN_AMERICA.AL32UTF8")
USERID ggs_admin, PASSWORD oracle
TRANLOGOPTIONS EXCLUDEUSER ggs_admin
EXTTRAIL ./dirdat/sd
```

```
TABLE osm$repapi.customers;
TABLE osm$repapi.policies;
GETUPDATEBEFORES
TABLE osm$repapi.current_accounts &
      GETBEFORECOLS(ON UPDATE ALL, ON DELETE ALL);
IGNOREUPDATEBEFORES
```

The data pump PT1E203 parameter file.

```
EXTRACT pt1e203
USERID ggs_admin, PASSWORD oracle
PASSTHRU
RMTHOST apps-srv1, MGRPORT 7805
RMTTRAIL ./dirdat/td
TABLE osm$repapi.customers;
TABLE osm$repapi.policies;
TABLE osm$repapi.current_accounts;
```

The Replicat RS1E203 parameter file.

```
REPLICAT rs1e203
SETENV (ORACLE_SID=T1E2)
SETENV (NSL_LANG=AMERICAN_AMERICA.AL32UTF8)
USERID ggs_admin, PASSWORD oracle
ASSUMETARGETDEFS
DISCARDFILE ./dirrpt/rs1e203.dsc, PURGE
GETUPDATES
GETINSERTS
GETDELETES
MAP osm$repapi.customers, TARGET osm$repapi.customers, &
    SQLEXEC (ID get_email, &
             SPNAME osm$repapi.get_email, &
             PARAMS (pcust_no = cust_no)), &
             COLMAP (cust_no        = cust_no,
                     cust_name      = cust_name,
                     cust_email     = @IF(@STREQ(BEFORE.cust_email,
                                      @GETVAL(get_email.pcust_email)),
                                      cust_email, 'conflict@pt.com'),
                     cust_mobile    = cust_mobile,
                     cust_address   = cust_address,
                     cust_commit_ts = @GETENV('GGHEADER',
                                              'COMMITTIMESTAMP'));
--
MAP osm$repapi.policies, TARGET osm$repapi.policies, &
    SQLEXEC (SPNAME osm$repapi.lookup_pt, &
             ID     lookup_pt, &
             PARAMS (pt_code_param = pt_code)), &
             COLMAP (USEDEFAULTS, &
                     pt_desc = @GETVAL(lookup_pt.pt_desc_param));
--
MAP osm$repapi.current_accounts, TARGET osm$repapi.current_accounts,
    COMPARECOLS (ON UPDATE ALL, ON DELETE ALL),
    RESOLVECONFLICT (UPDATEROWEXISTS,
                    (DELTA_RESOLUTION_METHOD, USEDELTA, COLS (acct_amount)),
                    (MAX_RESOLUTION_METHOD, USEMAX(acct_ts),
                                                COLS (acct_name, acct_ts)),
```

```
                                     (DEFAULT, USEMAX(acct_ts))),
    RESOLVECONFLICT (UPDATEROWMISSING, (DEFAULT, OVERWRITE)),
    RESOLVECONFLICT (DELETEROWEXISTS,  (DEFAULT, OVERWRITE)),
    RESOLVECONFLICT (DELETEROWMISSING, (DEFAULT, DISCARD)),
    RESOLVECONFLICT (INSERTROWEXISTS,  (DEFAULT, USEMAX(acct_ts)));
```

Highly Available Applications in GoldenGate

Most call center's applications are the front line for customer service companies that provide 24/7 services. Requests and inquiry calls coming from various input devices such as mobile phones, smart phone applications, and browser-based applications are system received and routed to the next available agent. Figure 5-26 shows the workflow for incoming customer calls. This is a high level description to demonstrate using Oracle Virtual Private Database (VPD) in supporting the data conflict avoidance technique for this kind of business environment.

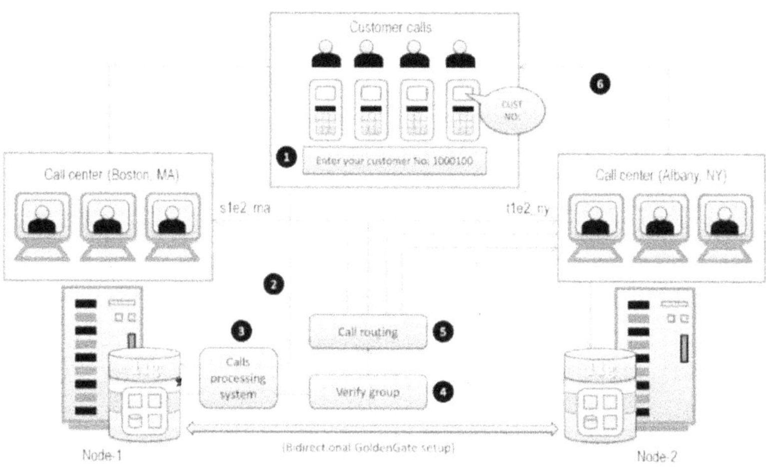

Figure 5-26: Call Center Applications Workflow

The customer calls in for inquires, such as requesting a policy renewal quotation. An automated system welcomes the customer. Then, the customer call is processed by assigning an agent to fulfill the request as follows:

1. The caller enters their customer number, which is the unique identifier.
2. The number is sent to the current database dedicated for receiving calls.
3. The call processing system validates the call and updates the calls log.
4. Based on the customer number, the owner group is determined.

5. Call routing is made based on the group name of the customer number.
6. An assigned agent receives the routed call and is locked with the customer.

The next section is developed on the basis of the above applications workflow. Data separation is achieved by routing requests and inquires to either Boston or Albany call centers. The objective is to maximize the return of investment (ROI) from licensing Oracle Database Enterprise Edition and Oracle GoldenGate software bundles for achieving a two-node architecture as an active-active topology applied for high availability and disaster recovery business requirements.

Transparent Avoidance Using Virtual Private Database

Virtual Private Database (VPD) is an advanced data conflict avoidance technique for transparent data segmentation. After creating database's table polices and implementing fine-grain access control and application contexts, SQL statements are dynamically modified to control rows (and columns) level access by database users. Figure 5-27 shows how users on node-1 and on node-2 access different subset of data, even when the session is connected to the same database. Fine-grain access control limits rows access by implementing a database function that returns a predicate clause (WHERE) to virtually limit row access by the database users.

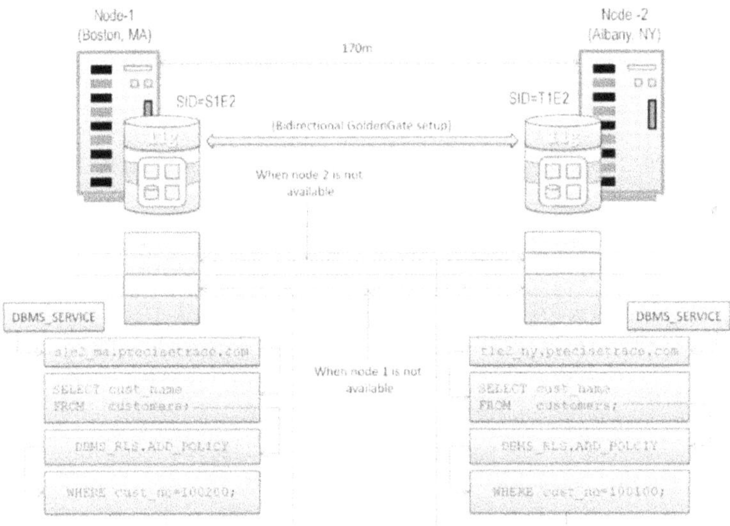

Figure 5-27: Data Segmentation Using Virtual Private Database

Our objective for using Virtual Private Database is to enforce data access based on ownership, so that a group of users within a database sees only their own accounts. The implementation is transparent – defined using policies that are independent of the applications. These active policies are cached in the SGA shared pool allowing in-memory access for faster evaluation and processing of fine-grain access control using SYS_CONTEXT function.

Begin by using DBMS_SERVICE PL/SQL supplied package to create non-default service names which will be used to associate a database user to one-and-only-one group at any time. However, in the event of a node failure, the user connects to the surviving node using the same service name but referencing the surviving node database service. Figure 5-27 shows the service name s1e2_ma for users connecting to node-1 database and t1e2_ny for users connecting to node-2 database.

The calls to DBMS_SERVICE.CREATE_SERVICE create the service names s1e2_ma and t1e2_ny, then start these service names for user connections. The procedure DBMS_SERVICE.CREATE_SERVICE requires the service name and service network name, use the service name to manage the service name.

```
SQL> BEGIN
     DBMS_SERVICE.CREATE_SERVICE(service_name=>'s1e2_ma',
                                 network_name=>'s1e2_am.precisetrace.com');
    END;
    /

PL/SQL procedure successfully completed.

SQL> EXEC DBMS_SERVICE.START_SERVICE('s1e2_ma');

PL/SQL procedure successfully completed.

SQL> BEGIN
     DBMS_SERVICE.CREATE_SERVICE(service_name=>'t1e2_ny',
                                 network_name=>'t1e2_ny.precisetrace.com');
    END;
    /

PL/SQL procedure successfully completed.

SQL> EXEC DBMS_SERVICE.START_SERVICE('t1e2_ny');

PL/SQL procedure successfully completed.
```

Use 'netca utility' to create the database connect string for the new service names and perform quick tests. By creating the two service names on node-1 and node-2 instances, they are readily available in the event of either node failure. The connect

string for s1e2_ma is configured (t1e2_ny is not shown), followed by a successful test using
the connect string s1e2_ma and t1e2_ny.

```
S1E2_MA =
  (DESCRIPTION =
    (ADDRESS_LIST =
      (ADDRESS = (PROTOCOL = TCP)(HOST = ggs_source)(PORT = 1521))
    )
    (CONNECT_DATA =
      (SERVICE_NAME = s1e2_ma.precisetrace.com)
    )
  )
```

```
SQL> CONN fawzi/oracle@s1e2_ma
Connected.

SQL> CONN deema/oracle@t1e2_ny
Connected.
```

How Does Virtual Private Database Work?

The major advantage for using Virtual Private Database is ease of deployment and flexibility. After the policy is created, developed, and enabled, it becomes part of the database and access control applies across all applications of the table or view. The workflow of executing an SQL application enforced by the Virtual Private Database security policy on the CUSTOMERS table is as follows:

1. The user accesses the CUSTOMERS table using SQL applications.
2. The application invokes the package for preparing and setting the context attribute values.
3. The policy function returns the predicate. It uses the session application context attributes stored in memory.
4. The database server dynamically modifies the statement by appending the returned predicate to SQL applications of step 1.
5. The session executes the dynamically generated SQL applications.

Implementing Virtual Private Database

The implementation of Virtual Private Database may require designing the database to provide the application context attribute values at runtime. Figure 5-28 shows a modified data model where customers are created by a group, meaning the customers and policies are owned and modified by a specific location (group). This model provides data conflict avoidance as the data is modified by transactions within the same database.

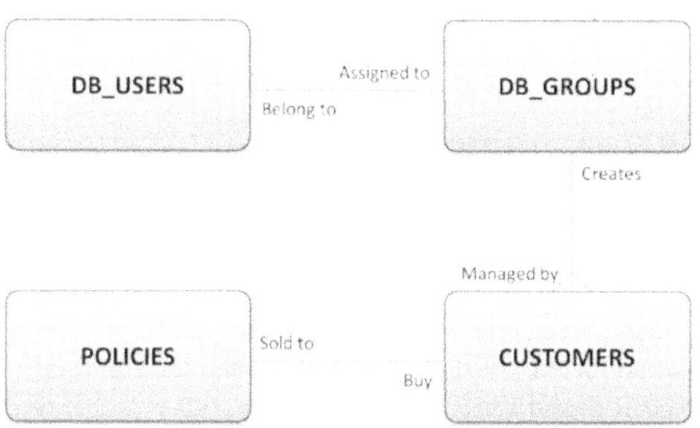

Figure 5-28: Data Modeling for VPD

The table structure of Figure 5-28 is listed below. The column GROUP_ID for each customer supports developing a conflict avoidance by group (location) and not by users. Transactions are processed as one unit of work and sent to the remote database after being processed by the local database.

```
SQL> DESC db_groups
```

```
Name                                      Null?    Type
----------------------------------------- -------- ----------------------
GROUP_ID                                  NOT NULL VARCHAR2(30)
GROUP_DESC                                NOT NULL VARCHAR2(128)
```

```
SQL> DESC db_users
```

```
Name                                      Null?    Type
----------------------------------------- -------- ----------------------
USER_ID                                   NOT NULL VARCHAR2(30)
USER_NAME                                 NOT NULL VARCHAR2(128)
GROUP_ID                                  NOT NULL VARCHAR2(30)
```

```
SQL> DESC customers
```

```
Name                                      Null? Type
---------------------------------------- -------- ---------------------
CUST_NO                                   NOT NULL NUMBER
CUST_NAME                                 NOT NULL VARCHAR2(128)
CUST_EMAIL                                NOT NULL VARCHAR2(128)
CUST_MOBILE                                        VARCHAR2(16)
CUST_ADDRESS                                       VARCHAR2(128)
GROUP_ID                                  NOT NULL VARCHAR2(30)
```

```
SQL> DESC policies
```

```
Name                                 Null?    Type
```

```
------------------------------------- -------- ---------------------
 POL_NO                                NOT NULL NUMBER
 POL_FROM                              NOT NULL DATE
 POL_TO                                NOT NULL DATE
 POL_VALUE                             NOT NULL NUMBER(8,2)
 POL_SUB_TOTAL                         NOT NULL NUMBER(8,2)
 PT_CODE                               NOT NULL VARCHAR2(8)
 DT_CODE                                        VARCHAR2(8)
 POL_TOTAL                             NOT NULL NUMBER(8,2)
 CUST_NO                               NOT NULL NUMBER
```

Next, using the PL/SQL supplied package DBMS_RLS to create the CUSTOMERS table, access control policy named CUST_POLICY_VPD adapted for transactions of type SELECT, UPDATE, INSERT, and DELETE.

Creating the Application Groups and Users

The groups are created to identify users' location. Each group is associated with a specific instance service name. The below INSERT statements creates two groups. Each correspond to a service name.

```
SQL> INSERT INTO db_groups VALUES('s1e2_ma', 's1e2_ma.precisetrace.com');

1 row created.

SQL> INSERT INTO db_groups VALUES('t1e2_ny', 't1e2_ny.precisetrace.com');

1 row created.

SQL> COMMIT;

Commit complete.
```

Then, the users are created using the format to associate them with the service network name for node 1 or node 2, but not both. For the database username 'fawzi', the application username is 'fawzi$s1e2_ma.precisetrace.com.'

```
SQL> INSERT INTO db_users VALUES
  2  ('fawzi$s1e2_ma.precisetrace.com', 'F. Alswaimil', 's1e2_ma');

1 row created.

SQL> INSERT INTO db_users VALUES
  2  ('deema$t1e2_ny.precisetrace.com', 'D. Alswaimil', 't1e2_ny');

1 row created.

SQL> COMMIT;

Commit complete.
```

Virtual Private Database Prerequisite

There are several related virtual private policy privileges that need to be granted to certain users for managing and troubleshooting objects encompassed by virtual private database policies. The following DDL statements grant capabilities to the application owner, Oracle GoldenGate database users, and SYSTEM administrative when working with tables and views enforced by Virtual Private Database.

```
SQL> CONN / as sysdba

Connected.

SQL> GRANT EXEMPT ACCESS POLICY TO SYSTEM;

Grant succeeded.

SQL> GRANT EXEMPT ACCESS POLICY TO ggs_admin;

Grant succeeded.

SQL> GRANT EXEMPT ACCESS POLICY TO osm$repapi;

Grant succeeded.

SQL> GRANT EXECUTE ON DBMS_RLS to osm$repapi;

Grant succeeded.
```

Create the Security Policy

Use the procedure DBMS_RLS.ADD_POLICY to create the policy CUST_POLICY_VPD. This implements fine grain row level access on the CUSTOMERS table. The STATEMENT_TYPES parameter lists the SQL application types enforced by this policy. The POLICY_FUNCTION parameter specifies the function name that returns the predicate.

```
SQL> BEGIN
       DBMS_RLS.ADD_POLICY(
          object_schema=>'system',
          object_name=>'customers',
          policy_name=>'cust_policy_vpd',
          function_schema=>'system',
          policy_function=>'ggs_security_p.cust_order',
          statement_types=>'select, insert, update, delete');
     END;
     /

PL/SQL procedure successfully completed.
```

Create the Context Management Package

Develop the package to prepare the application context using the function SYS_CONTEXT and set the context attributes values using the procedure DBMS_SESSION.SET_CONTEXT. For all transaction types, the package set the value for context attribute GROUP_ID according to the USER_ID.

```
SQL> CREATE OR REPLACE PACKAGE ggs_security is
        PROCEDURE set_user_group;
     END;
     /

Package created.

SQL> CREATE OR REPLACE PACKAGE BODY ggs_security is
       PROCEDURE set_user_group(puser_id varchar2)   IS
          vgroup_id VARCHAR2(30);
       BEGIN
          SELECT group_id into vgroup_id
          FROM   db_users
          WHERE  UPPER(user_id) =
                 UPPER(puser_id)||'$'||UPPER(SYS_CONTEXT('USERENV',
                 'SERVICE_NAME'));
          DBMS_SESSION.SET_CONTEXT('oeapp', 'group_id', vgroup_id);
       EXCEPTION
          WHEN OTHERS THEN
               DBMS_SESSION.SET_CONTEXT('oeapp', 'group_id', NULL);
       END;
     END;
     /

Package body created.
```

Create the Security Function

Develop the function to return the predicate clause (WHERE). The return predicate is appended to the existing where clause is using AND as logical operator.

```
SQL> CREATE OR REPLACE PACKAGE ggs_security_p is
        FUNCTION cust_order(object_schema VARCHAR2, object_name VARCHAR2)
        RETURN VARCHAR2;
     END;
     /

Package created.

SQL> CREATE OR REPLACE PACKAGE BODY ggs_security_p is
        FUNCTION cust_order(object_schema VARCHAR2, object_name VARCHAR2)
        RETURN VARCHAR2 IS
        BEGIN
           RETURN 'group_id=SYS_CONTEXT(''oeapp'', ''group_id'')';
        END;
```

```
END;
/

Package body created.
```

Create the Database Application Context

Connect as privileged user to create the context. The context references the package created above.

```
SQL> CREATE CONTEXT oeapp USING ggs_security;

Context created.
```

Execute the Application

Now, it is time to run the application accessing tables enforced by Virtual Private Database. Depending on the database username, the context attributes assign runtime values allowing dynamic modified SQL application to be executed.

Figure 5-29 shows the original SQL statement tunnel through the security policy CUST_POLICY_VPD, the ultimate modified SQL statement restricts access only to rows that are within the context of the username session.

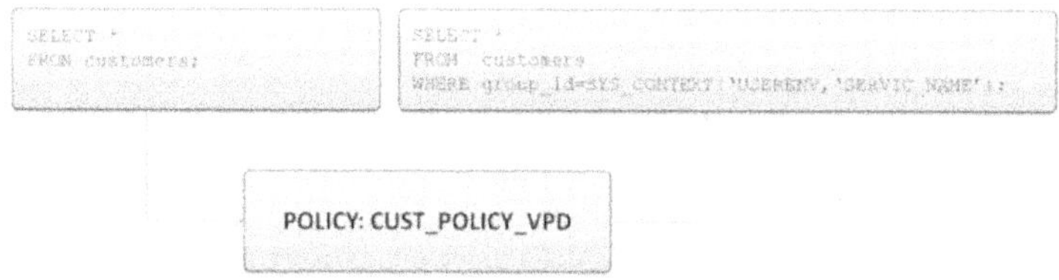

Figure 5-29: Dynamic SQL Modification for Data Access Control

The application starts by invoking the package that prepares and initializes the context attributes, which are used by the security function that return the predicate clause. The application heavily relies on the built-in database function SYS_CONTEXT which uses a pre-defined list of attributes such as DB_NAME and SERVICE_NAME
for application runtime.

The following shows how data segmentation is achieved. It considers the combination of the database username and the service name to produce an active row set specific to the user's session. The following demonstrates the row set when connected to the Albany, NY system.

```
SQL> CONN deema/oracle@t1e2_ny
Connected.
SQL> DECLARE
      CURSOR c1 IS SELECT * FROM system.customers;
      vcust system.customers%ROWTYPE;
   BEGIN
      SYSTEM.GGS_SECURITY.SET_USER_GROUP(USER);
      OPEN c1;
      LOOP
         FETCH c1 into vcust;
         EXIT WHEN c1%NOTFOUND;
         DBMS_OUTPUT.PUT_LINE(vcust.cust_name);
      END LOOP;
      CLOSE c1;
   END;
   /
```

```
CAROL P. THOMPSON
MARK B. MILLER
RONALD H. ALLEN
NANCY U. WILSON
JESSICA Z. WILSON
DAVID O. JOHNSON
SANDRA J. ALSWAIMIL
SARAH N. KING
KENNETH O. ROBINSON
LINDA K. WILSON

PL/SQL procedure successfully completed.
```

The following demonstrates when the user connects to the Boston, MA system. It is the same application driven by dynamic context attributes and values to retrieve different active row sets.

```
SQL> CONN fawzi/oracle@s1e2_ma
Connected.

SQL> DECLARE
      CURSOR c1 IS SELECT * FROM system.customers;
      vcust system.customers%ROWTYPE;
   BEGIN
      SYSTEM.GGS_SECURITY.SET_USER_GROUP(USER);
      OPEN c1;
      LOOP
         FETCH c1 into vcust;
         EXIT WHEN c1%NOTFOUND;
         DBMS_OUTPUT.PUT_LINE(vcust.cust_name);
      END LOOP;
      CLOSE c1;
   END;
   /
```

```
JOHN V. KING
NOUR Z. LEWIS
KAREN Y. WALKER
KIMBERLY O. THOMPSON
KAREN Q. ALIBRAHIM
SARAH P. WHITE
JOHN C. DAVIS
KEVIN H. ALIBRAHIM
MARK L. MILLER
CHARLES N. WALKER

PL/SQL procedure successfully completed.
```

Virtual Private Database Considerations

Be aware of Virtual Private Database (VPD) as an Oracle Database Enterprise feature. It is adapted mutually for data security by developing fine-grain access control at the row level and enhances application performance by reading metadata, context attribute values from Oracle shared pool memory of the System Global Area (SGA). The length of the returned predicate by the security function is limited to 4000 characters only, which may not be sufficient for some complex WHERE clauses. An alternative of DBMS_RLS is to use Oracle Enterprise Manager to create and manage policies from the graphical user interface (GUI).

Oracle GoldenGate High Availability Runtime

The following illustrates the runtime for high availability on an active-active bi-directional configuration. The building blocks for the demonstration are:

- Identical Tables Structure
- Oracle GoldenGate Active-Active Bi-Directional Topology Architecture
- Oracle GoldenGate Built-In Conflict Detection and Resolution
- Database Sequences, odd numbers for node-1 and even numbers for node-2
- Database Connections load-balancer for two-node Oracle GoldenGate high availability configuration

Figure 5-30 shows the load balancer used to handle high availability and workload balancing across the two databases, S1E2 and T1E2.

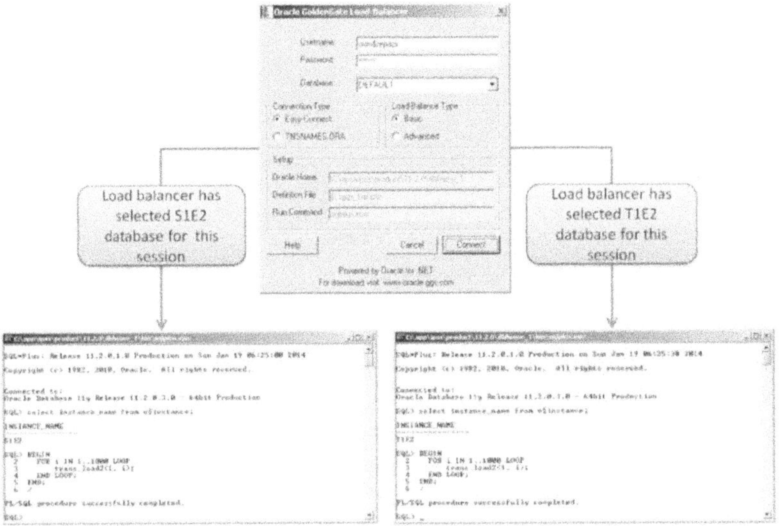

Figure 5-30: Runtime on High Availability Environment

Verify Transactions

The TRANS_LOAD2 is a workload program for generating database transactions. Oracle GoldenGate active-active bi-directional configuration synchronizes node-1 and node-2 databases, keeping the two databases identical using real-time data movement.

The test was completed successfully. The transaction size of 1000 performs concurrent 1000 inserts and replication. The logging table records conflict detection and error,
if any.

Database (S1E2)	Database (T1E2)

SQL> BEGIN
  2   FOR i IN 1..1000 LOOP
  3   trans_load2(1, i);
  4   END LOOP;
  5 END
  6 /
	SQL> BEGIN
	  2 FOR i IN 1..1000 LOOP
	  3 trans_load2(1, i);
	  4 END LOOP;
	  5 END
	  6 /

SQL> SELECT cust_no
  2 FROM   customers
  3 WHERE rownum < 11
  4 ORDER BY 1;
 	
   CUST_NO
---------- 	
	SQL> SELECT cust_no
	  2 FROM customers
	  3 WHERE rownum < 11
	  4 ORDER BY 1;
	
	   CUST_NO
	---------- 	

``` 1006007 1006009 1006010 1006011 1006012 1006013 1006014 1006015 1006016 1006017 ```	``` 1006007 1006009 1006010 1006011 1006012 1006013 1006014 1006015 1006016 1006017 ```

```
   1006007
   1006009
   1006010
   1006011
   1006012
   1006013
   1006014
   1006015
   1006016
   1006017

10 rows selected.

SQL>
```

```
   1006007
   1006009
   1006010
   1006011
   1006012
   1006013
   1006014
   1006015
   1006016
   1006017

10 rows selected.

SQL>
```

To effectively monitor data divergence and proactively detect data inconsistency, Oracle GoldenGate Veridata is a robust tool for detecting missing rows between source and target tables. Refer to Chapter 6 to learn about implementing and using Oracle GoldenGate Veridata.

Workload Simulator

Yes, Oracle GoldenGate is a non-destructive software. It is the software installable on a production environment without major negative performance impact. However, use of the workload simulator is not to be underestimated and can be used for:

- Data Replication Testing Environments
- Benchmarking the server performance for different levels of transaction volume
- Ejection of Data Conflict for detection and resolution

Summary

The use of Oracle GoldenGate 12c for business continuity has advantages and disadvantages in using the same bi-directional topology architecture to build the foundation for a disaster recovery site and high availability on supported platforms.

When using Oracle GoldenGate for disaster recovery (DR), the major point of discussion is unsupported data types. For applications not using any of the unsupported data types, Oracle GoldenGate is an option for disaster recovery solutions. Switchover and failover from the primary system to the live standby system and vice versa is an interactive process and requires manual execution of commands or scripts.

The downtime associated with switchover and failover is very low and varies from site-to-site. The chapter has illustrated the following:

- Planned moving of users from primary to live standby system for switchover
- Planned moving of users back from live standby to primary system for switchover
- Unplanned moving of users from primary to live standby system for failover
- Unplanned moving of users back from live standby to primary system for failover

When using Oracle GoldenGate for high availability (HA), detailed analysis is carried out to evaluate Oracle GoldenGate capability of achieving the level of scalability for low-high transactions volume. When Oracle GoldenGate is deployed from the ground up, the applications become replication-aware (transparent replication) which promote Oracle GoldenGate for a high availability platform. However, deploying Oracle GoldenGate at a later stage results in the challenge of handling data conflict. This chapter has discussed and illustrated techniques of handling data conflicts using:

- Data and Applications Segmentation
- Oracle GoldenGate Built-In Conflict Detection and Resolution (CDR)
- Develop PL/SQL Sub-Programs and implement callout using SQLEXEC
- Oracle Virtual Private Database (VPD) for total segmentation

Throughout the chapter, a two-node bi-directional topology architecture is demonstrated. A three-node topology architecture, multi-master brings challenges and should be carefully qualified for disaster recovery and high availability solutions. Oracle GoldenGate considerations, in respect of disaster recovery and high availability, are discussed to lead to a sound decision and minimize the impact of post-deployment changes.

The chapter also compared Oracle GoldenGate with Oracle Real Application Clusters (RAC) and Oracle Data Guard (DG). It was made clear, for an enterprise, Oracle GoldenGate complements RAC and DG rather than replaces them.

Comparison of High-Volume In-Flight Data Using Oracle GoldenGate Veridata

CHAPTER

Overview

This chapter covers the Oracle GoldenGate companion tool, *Oracle GoldenGate Veridata*. By all means, the continued deviation of data integrity and consistency severely impacts business reviews and escalates inaccurate results. Hence, the need for a tool to provide online detections and detailed analysis of data discrepancies is crucial and must be accomplished quickly. This is where Oracle GoldenGate Veridata plays the role — supporting data accuracy among heterogeneous data sets by performing advanced table comparisons without impacting online transactions.

To implement Oracle GoldenGate Veridata, it's necessary to perform the following activities:

1. Download and install Oracle GoldenGate Veridata agents.
2. Download and install Oracle GoldenGate Veridata server instance.
3. Explain and configure Oracle GoldenGate Veridata components.
4. Explain and configure Oracle GoldenGate Veridata configurable objects.
5. Perform compare jobs on compare pairs for compare groups.
6. Generate Out-Of-Sync (OOS) summary reports.
7. Develop data repair technique for data convergence.

Oracle GoldenGate Veridata becomes the primary tool when using Oracle GoldenGate for delivering these tasks:

- **Fast Upgrades:** Near zero-downtime database upgrade, Oracle GoldenGate Veridata is used to verify zero data-divergence before moving users to the target system.

- **High availability:** Oracle GoldenGate Veridata compares data set of the primary and the live standby database following failover/switchover operation.

- **Monitoring:** Unattended online monitor and notification of two data sources without impacting online transactions.

Let's begin by introducing Oracle GoldenGate architecture and building blocks, which are fundamentals for implementing Oracle GoldenGate Veridata.

GoldenGate Architecture for Veridata

Though there are several topologies to install and configure Oracle GoldenGate Veridata components, the overall architecture remains the same. Figure 6-1 depicts the common architecture, the all-in-one topology, for installing Oracle GoldenGate Veridata. This topology illustrates Oracle GoldenGate Veridata agents installed on the database servers. This avoids the network traffic when the agent is installed remotely.

The Oracle GoldenGate Veridata server and its database repository are installed on a dedicated server — configured to communicate with the two agents using JDBC drivers. Apache Tomcat web server is installed, integrated and configured to enable access to Oracle GoldenGate Veridata web interface applications. The Apache Tomcat web server administration tool supports managing groups and users for a secure environment. Oracle GoldenGate Veridata objects configuration deployed using Oracle GoldenGate Veridata server web interface, whereas the command-line utility VERICOM performs basic functions such as configuring and starting jobs.

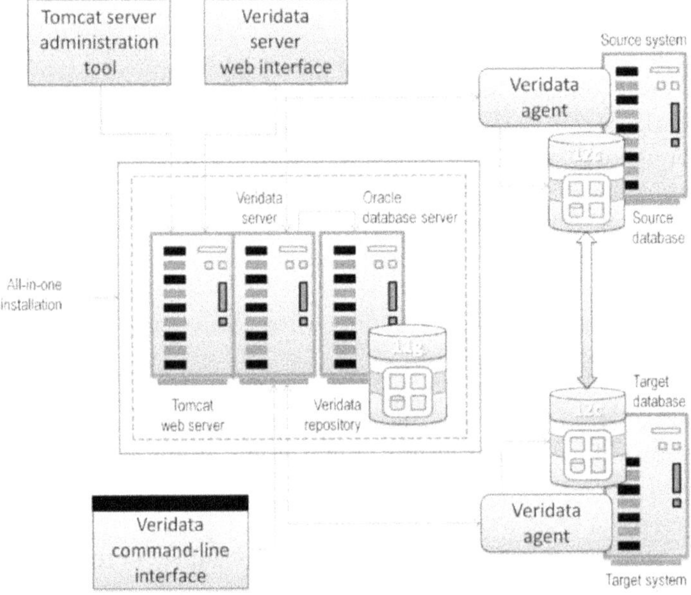

Figure 6-1: Oracle GoldenGate Veridata Architecture (All-In-0ne Topology)

Regardless of the options and topology adapted to install and configure Oracle GoldenGate Veridata, the components and data flow among them remains the same.

We will work with and manage the following Veridata components:

- Oracle GoldenGate Veridata Server
- Oracle GoldenGate Veridata Database Repository
- Oracle GoldenGate Veridata Agents
- Source and Target Database
- Apache Tomcat Web Server
- Oracle GoldenGate Veridata Web Interface
- Oracle GoldenGate Veridata Command-Line Interface

When designing Oracle GoldenGate Veridata topology, the aim is to reduce the processing overhead on the production servers and minimize the overhead of sending data across the network. An optimum topology is achieved by evaluating the alternatives by carefully distributing the components. For example, the agent's location is within the database server or remote. Oracle GoldenGate Veridata Database Repository is local or remote, single agent vs. multi-agent configurations, etc.

Before we proceed further, here are brief definitions of the Oracle GoldenGate Veridata components. Refer to Figure 6-1 for logical presentation and further understanding of the components.

Oracle GoldenGate Veridata Server

The Veridata server is the core of several integrated components. Ultimately, the function of the Oracle GoldenGate Veridata server is to identify out-of-sync pair of rows. This is achieved by performing the following steps:

- Establishing an agent connection for requesting data fetch from the source and target database.
- Receiving bulk data from the database agent in preparation of rows hash, sort (optional) and compare.
- Coordinating the activities and tasks by executing various Oracle GoldenGate Veridata programs.
- Building an in-memory, out-of-sync queue.
- Confirming out-of-sync data.
- Generating out-of-sync summary and runtime review reports.

When multiple Oracle GoldenGate Veridata server instances reference the same database repository, we prefer to use the shared data location on file system for all instances. The use of network file system (NFS) is necessary for all distributed instances.

Oracle GoldenGate Veridata Repository

There are several types of objects configured to enable Oracle GoldenGate Veridata to perform data comparisons and report about out-of-sync rows. The metadata about these objects is stored on a database schema called the repository. There are three supported database types:

1. Oracle Database
2. Oracle MySQL
3. Microsoft SQL Server

Preparation and configuration is database specific. This chapter uses the Oracle Database for the repository. Consider Oracle software license cost of the repository database, as it is not included with Oracle GoldenGate Veridata licensed software.

Oracle GoldenGate Veridata Agents

Upon request by the Oracle GoldenGate Veridata server, the agent connects to the target data source for performing sequence of data fetch. Oracle GoldenGate has two types of agents:

1. Java agent (J agent)

2. C agent

Java agent supports a wide range of platforms, since it uses JDBC drivers to connect to the target database. A certified Java Runtime Environment (JRE) is required to operate and manage Java agents. The agent is installable on the database server, on the Oracle GoldenGate Veridata server, or on a dedicated server. Moreover, Oracle provides a custom Java agent built for platforms certified by Oracle GoldenGate.

The C agent is only available for Enscribe/SQL/MP and Oracle database. Operating C agents demands Oracle GoldenGate instance and is installable on the database server only. C agent continues to support Oracle database, but there are no plans for further enhancements as of Version 11.2.1.0.0.

This chapter focuses and uses the Java agent, but also briefly explains the C agent.

Source and Target Database

The Oracle GoldenGate Veridata server performs data comparisons from two databases only – the source and target databases. Heterogamous database support is a key feature of the Oracle GoldenGate Veridata server. For example, the source database is an Oracle database while the target database might be a Microsoft SQL Server database.

Oracle GoldenGate Veridata server uses internal data types mapping for a heterogamous source and target database. Modifications of the default data type's settings are performed using Oracle GoldenGate Veridata web interface.

Apache Tomcat Web Server

GoldenGate uses an Apache HTTP server. It enables access to the Oracle GoldenGate Veridata server administration tools and applications from any web browser.

Oracle GoldenGate Veridata users' access is configured from within the Tomcat web server. Users, groups, roles, and privileges assignments are performed from within the Apache Tomcat web server administration tool. Further data related privileges are configured from Oracle GoldenGate Veridata.

Oracle GoldenGate Veridata Web Interface

A comprehensive set of web-based applications and reports is available for configuring and managing Oracle GoldenGate Veridata objects. The web interface creates connections, groups, jobs, profiles, and columns mapping. Figure 6-2 shows a Oracle GoldenGate Veridata homepage of a newly installed Oracle GoldenGate Veridata instance. The homepage is composed of the navigation panel, favorites, and display area. Access to the Oracle GoldenGate Veridata web interface requires a valid Tomcat web server username and password.

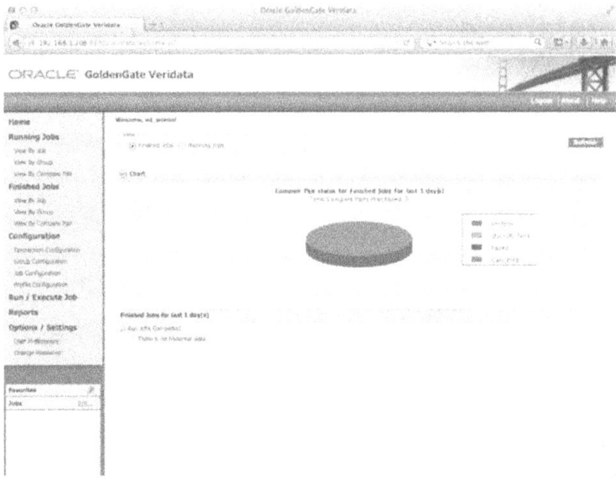

Figure 6-2: Oracle GoldenGate Veridata Web Interface

Oracle GoldenGate Veridata Command-Line Interface

The Oracle GoldenGate Veridata Command-Line Interface (CLI), VERICOM, is a client software installed with the Oracle GoldenGate Veridata server. It is intended for performing limited tasks such as running compare jobs, overriding runtime parameters and developing automated batch jobs for data comparison.

Veridata Supported Platforms

Oracle GoldenGate Veridata components (server, agents, and repository) are certified to run on any of the certified combination of database and operating systems listed on Table 6-1. The certification is version specific for the databases and operating systems.

Components	Database	Operating system
Oracle GoldenGate Veridata Java agent	▪ Oracle Database ▪ MS SQL Server ▪ Sybase ▪ Teradata	▪ Oracle Linux ▪ Red Hat EL ▪ Oracle Solaris ▪ Microsoft Windows ▪ IBM AIX ▪ HP-UX ▪ zOS
Oracle GoldenGate Veridata C agent	▪ Oracle Database	
	▪ Enscribe/SQL/MP	▪ HP NonStop
Oracle GoldenGate	▪ Oracle Database ▪ Oracle MySQL	▪ Oracle Linux ▪ Red Hat EL

Veridata server repository	▪ MS SQL Server	▪ Oracle Solaris ▪ MS Windows ▪ IBM AIX ▪ HP-UX

Table 6-1: Oracle Veridata Supported Platforms

Customers with a valid Oracle support agreement may request custom builds for Oracle GoldenGate and Java agent for currently unlisted certification.

Installing Oracle GoldenGate Veridata Agents

The GoldenGate veridata agent executes tasks on the database on behalf of the Oracle GoldenGate Veridata server. These tasks include:

- Fetch and return blocks of rows to compare.
- Return column level details for out-of-sync rows.

There are two types of agents, the C agent and Java agents. The C agent requires Oracle GoldenGate instance and configuring related manager parameters. Whereas, the Java agent is ready to use after configuring the agent parameters file, and Java agent is installable on the same system of the source and target database or on a remote server accessing the source and target server over the network. The recommended approach is to install the agent on the same source and target systems — saving the network overhead as a result of returning massive amounts of data to Oracle GoldenGate Veridata server.

C Agent Settings

The C agent is named "C" because it is written in the C language. It is the initial version of the Oracle GoldenGate Veridata agent and requires that the Oracle GoldenGate instance be shipped with the agent. The steps to install and configure C agent are:

1. Install the software by unpacking to the agent location
2. Start GGSCI from the agent root directory
3. Create sub-directory structure
4. Configure and start the agent manager

As of May 2014, the Oracle GoldenGate Veridata C agent is not available for download from the Oracle software delivery cloud. Hence, installation and configuration of the C agent is not covered in this book. Figure 6-3 shows the list of software available for Oracle GoldenGate Veridata Media Pack for Linux x86-64.

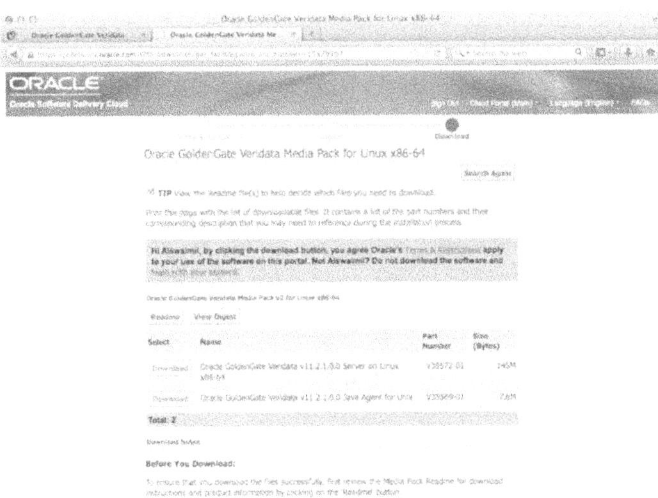

Figure 6-3: Oracle GoldenGate Veridata Media Packs

Java Agent Settings

This agent is written in Java language. It is the new version of the Oracle GoldenGate Veridata agent and does not require the Oracle GoldenGate instance. The Java agent uses JDBC to connect to the database. Hence, a Java environment JRE/JSDK is needed. The minimum version of JRE/JSDK is 1.5. Visit www.java.com for the Java download archive.

Software Installation

The installation steps apply to Linux and UNIX operating systems. For proper security settings, the agent must be installed using a non-root operating system user with the correct *umask* setting. These steps include:

1. Download agent software from the Oracle software delivery cloud.
2. Create the agent root directory. Move the download to this directory.
3. Extract the zipped file using: unzip Linux/UNIX utility.
4. Make a copy of *agent.properties.sample* and rename it as *agent.properties*.
5. Configure the parameters listed in Table 6-2.

The following executes step 3 by running unzip Linux/UNIX utility from the command-line.

```
$ unzip V35569-01.zip
Archive:  V35569-01.zip
   creating: agent/
   creating: agent/classes/
   creating: agent/drivers/
   creating: agent/lib/
   creating: agent/licenses/
  inflating: agent/JavaAgent.jar
  inflating: agent/agent.bat
  inflating: agent/agent.properties.sample
  inflating: agent/classes/log4j.properties
  inflating: agent/drivers/gvdb2.jar
  inflating: agent/drivers/gvsybase.jar
  inflating: agent/drivers/ojdbc6.jar
  inflating: agent/drivers/sqljdbc.jar
  inflating: agent/lib/commons-dbcp-1.2.2.jar
  inflating: agent/lib/commons-pool-1.3.jar
  inflating: agent/lib/log4j-1.2.12.jar
  inflating: agent/lib/ucp.jar
  inflating: agent/licenses/Apache-LICENSE-2.0.txt
  inflating: agent/licenses/notices.txt
  inflating: agent/agent.sh
  inflating: ogg-veridata-readme-11.2.1.0.0.doc
  inflating: ogg-veridata-readme-11.2.1.0.0.txt
  inflating: ogg_veridata_relnotes_11.2.1.0.0.doc
  inflating: ogg_veridata_relnotes_11.2.1.0.0.pdf $
```

For Step 4, the configuration file agent.properties.sample is copied to agent.properties and modified as follows:

```
server.port=4000
database.url=jdbc:oracle:thin:@S1E2
server.driversLocation = drivers
server.jdbcDriver=ojdbc6.jar
database.transaction.isolation=READ_COMMITTED
```

Table 6-2 describes the parameters for configuring Java agents. The *agent.properties* is a file located on the agent root directory. The sample file, *agent.properties.sample* provides database-specific values. Use the suggested values for the target database as per the table below.

Parameter	Description
server.port	The server.port property is the port where the Veridata agent listens for connection requests.
database.url	The database connect string that enables the agent to connect to the database using JDBC.

server.driversLocation	The location of the JDBC driver. Enter the location for non-default JDBC software installation.
server.jdbcDriver	The name of the JDBC driver. Agent release 11.2 is compatible with Java 6.
database.transaction.isolation	Specify the transaction level of isolation used during the initial comparison step. For Oracle, it only supports READ_COMMITTED value.

Table 6-2: Java Agent Parameters

Starting and Stopping the Java Agents

To start the Java agent, navigate to the agent root directory, export the location of Java runtime environment (JRE) using the JRE_HOME variable, then execute the program agent.sh as shown here:

```
$ export JRE_HOME=/usr/java/jre1.6.0_18
$ ./agent.sh start
```

To stop the Java agent, navigate to the agent root directory, export the location of Java runtime environment (JRE) using the JRE_HOME variable, then execute the program agent.sh as shown here:

```
$ export JRE_HOME=/usr/java/jre1.6.0_18
$ ./agent.sh stop
```

Java Agent Installation for Microsoft Windows

When the database server is running on Microsoft Windows and the agent to be installed on the same server, then the Oracle GoldenGate Veridata Java agent for Microsoft Windows is required. It is necessary to match the database server operating system architecture with the Oracle GoldenGate Veridata Java agent for Microsoft Windows. The software is available for 32-bit and 64-bit systems. The installation is self-explanatory as it adapts a Graphical User Interface (GUI) wizard-based installer.

Figure 6-4 shows step 5 of 10, which presents the database type and JDBC connection details.

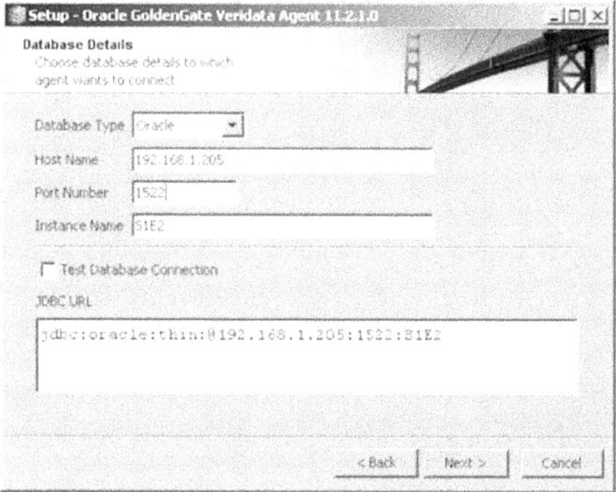

Figure 6-4: Veridata Java Agent Installation (Windows)

Oracle GoldenGate Veridata Setup

Since Oracle GoldenGate requires a database repository for storing configured objects metadata, the initial steps are to create the repository database, create the repository owner, grant database access privileges, and then start installing Oracle GoldenGate Veridata server software. First, it is recommended to install, configure, and start the Veridata agent. This enables performing a quick test after successfully installing the Oracle GoldenGate Veridata Server.

Database Repository

Oracle GoldenGate Repository stores details about the source and target database configured components.

Use any of the supported database management systems listed below:

- Oracle Database
- Oracle MySQL
- Microsoft SQL Server

The database repository configured using Oracle Database 11g has the following details on Figure 6-5 of the Oracle Database Configuration Assistant (DBCA).

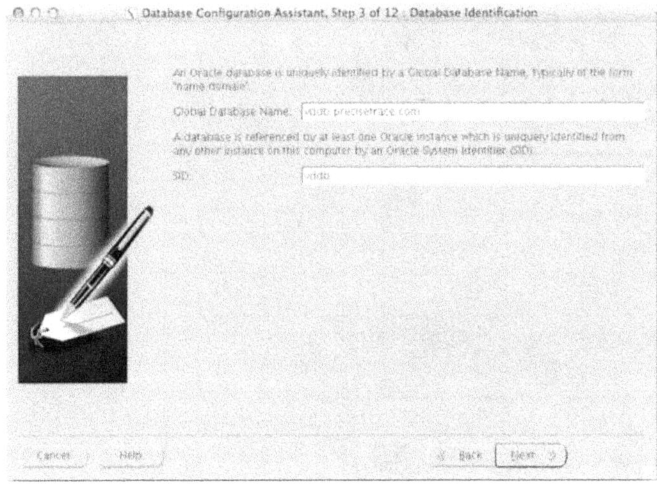

Figure 6-5: Create Database using DBCA

Database Name: vddb
Database Domain: precisetrace.com
Database Instance: vddb

Oracle Corporation recommends using the database automatic memory management (AMM), enabled by setting the *memory_target* parameter. This enables self-managed memory utilization when running compare jobs and reports. The overall database resource requirements are low and static. You should also operate the database in *archivelog* mode to enable online backup, restore, and recover operations.

Veridata Repository Database Sizing

Since the database repository is only dedicated for storing configured objects metadata created using Oracle GoldenGate Veridata server web applications, it is classified as a short transactions type where the default database sizing parameters are adequate for the majority of the installations.

However, when the Oracle GoldenGate Veridata Server performs sort operations using the database, the temporary tablespace should be configured to support the largest data set. Database best practices suggest to create the temporary tablespace using groups as illustrated next:

```
SQL> ALTER TABLESPACE temp TABLESPACE GROUP tmp_ts_group;

Tablespace altered.

SQL> CREATE TEMPORARY TABLESPACE temp2
  2  TEMPFILE '/d01/app/oracleSE/oradata/vddb/temp201.dbf' SIZE 1000M
  3  AUTOEXTEND ON;

Tablespace created.

SQL> ALTER USER vd_admin TEMPORARY TABLESPACE tmp_ts_group;

User altered.
```

We now create a dedicated tablespace for the Oracle GoldenGate Veridata repository owner. This promotes highly effective maintenance tasks such as upgrade, backup, etc.

```
SQL> CREATE TABLESPACE vddb_dat
  2  DATAFILE '/u01/app/oracle/oradata/vddb/vddb_dat01.dbf' SIZE 100M
  3  AUTOEXTEND on;
```

```
Tablespace created.
```

Now, we create Oracle GoldenGate Veridata database role, grant the database privileges, and create the repository owner and the role to the repository owner.

```
SQL> CREATE ROLE veridata_role;

Role created.

SQL> GRANT CREATE SESSION, CREATE TABLE, CREATE VIEW, CREATE PROCEDURE,
  2  CREATE SYNONYM TO veridata_role;

Grant succeeded.

SQL> CREATE USER vd_admin IDENTIFIED BY oracle
  2  DEFAULT TABLESPACE vddb_dat
  3  QUOTA UNLIMITED ON vddb_dat;

User created.

SQL> GRANT veridata_role TO vd_admin;

Grant succeeded.
```

Remote Repository Database

When the repository database for the Oracle GoldenGate Veridata Server is created on a remote system, then a database listener and a local database connect string must be configured. The local database connect string is specified during the installation.

Figure 6-6 represents the topology when the repository database is remotely located.

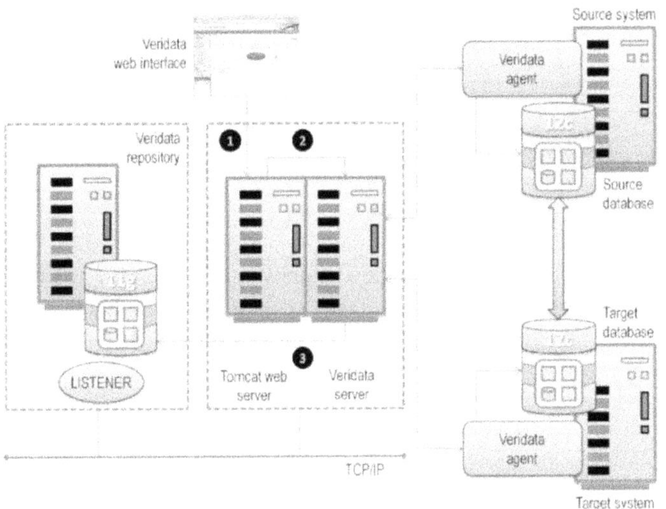

Figure 6-6: Veridata Remote Repository Database Topology

During Oracle GoldenGate Veridata Server installation, there are two options to connect to the repository database:

- Local Database Connect String
- EZCONNECT String

Before starting the installation of the Oracle GoldenGate Veridata Server, verify that the connection is successfully established using the database connect string which provides advanced listener settings.

```
SQL> conn vd_admin/oracle@vddb
Connected.
```

Oracle GoldenGate Veridata Server Sizing

Size the Oracle GoldenGate Veridata Server to sustain processing and memory requirements. The agent fetches data from the database, while the Veridata Server performs sorting and data comparisons. Consider the following when sizing the server:

- CPU Sizing for sort processing location: database or server.

- Memory Sizing for the sort maximum memory usage; default is 50MB.

- Storage Sizing for the temporary storage directory for source and target data.

The major resource consumers, on the Oracle GoldenGate Veridata server, are the row sorting operations of the initial comparison step when the profile sort parameter setting is on server vs. database. Depending on the available server resources, Oracle GoldenGate Veridata supports In-memory and In-disk sorts. The In-Memory sort requires approximately 2.5 the size of the data, whereas the In-disk sort depends on the number of passes (writes) to disk. A One Disk Pass sorts data and writes to the disk only once, a Two Disk Passes sorts data and writes to the disk twice, etc.

Software Installation

Now that the repository database is opened and the listener is started, it is time to begin the Oracle GoldenGate Veridata installation. The wizard-based Java installer interactively guides you through the process. Depending on the options selected, the installer steps vary accordingly. The installation employs an existing database user (VD_ADMIN) and the repository resides on an Oracle database 11g. There are two installation methods:

- Graphical User Interface (GUI) wizard-based installer
- Command-Line Interface (CLI) installer

This chapter adapts the Graphical User Interface (GUI) wizard-based installer. The command-line is only recommended in the absence of an X Window system on Linux/UNIX platforms for remote installations. The following installation of Oracle GoldenGate Veridata is remotely executed using an X Window system on Mac OS X.

```
$ unzip V35572-01.zip
Archive:  V35572-01.zip
  inflating: GoldenGate_Veridata_redhatAS40_x64.sh
  inflating: ogg_veridata_relnotes_11.2.1.0.0.pdf
  inflating: ogg_veridata_relnotes_11.2.1.0.0.doc
  inflating: ogg-veridata-readme-11.2.1.0.0.doc
  inflating: ogg-veridata-readme-11.2.1.0.0.txt
$ ./GoldenGate_Veridata_redhatAS40_x64.sh
Unpacking JRE ...
Starting Installer ...
```

Each step of the wizard-based installer is captured, given a title, and briefly described then followed by the launching of Oracle GoldenGate Veridata.

Step 1: Welcome

This step starts the Oracle GoldenGate Veridata programs installation. We click "Next" to proceed or Cancel to abort the installation. Before proceeding further, closing all currently running applications is recommended.

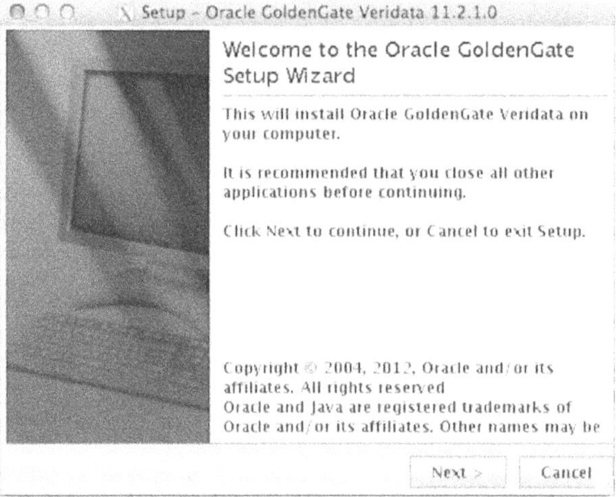

Figure 6-6a: Setup wizard

Step 2: Software Location

Specify the software location. For Linux/UNIX security fundamentals, proper directories and files permissions are enforced by setting the shell environment variable umask. Using umask 022 produces files permission setting of 644. Only the owner has read and write permissions; the group and others are read only.

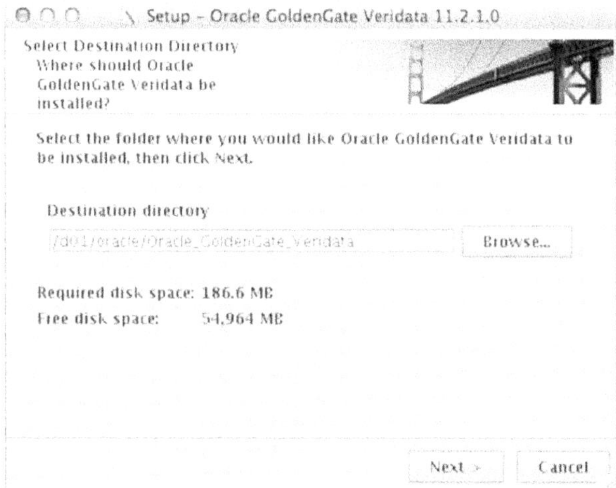

Figure 6-6b: Destination directory

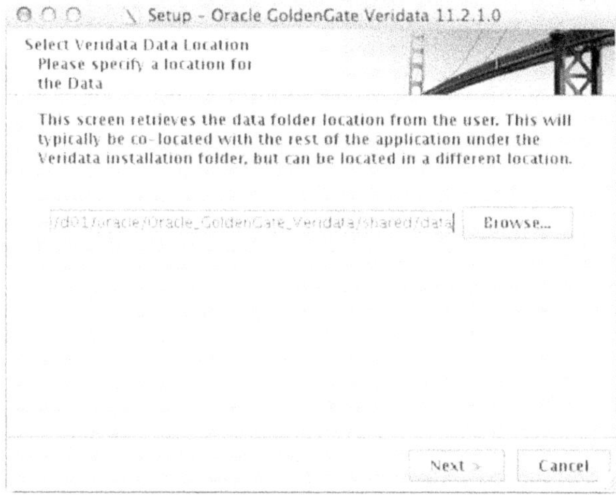

Figure 6-6c: Destination directory

Step 3: Runtime Data Location

Oracle GoldenGate Veridata stores comparison runtime results in files. Out-Of-Sync (OOS) data are stored in two formats, binary and XML. The XML structure describes the comparison pairs. OOS data is further classified by jobs and group names.

Step 4: Veridata Web Server

Oracle GoldenGate Veridata web server uses Apache Tomcat web server to run the applications for configuring Veridata objects such as connections, groups, comparison pairs, jobs and profiles. Use the URL http://<veridata data IP address>:8830 to access the Veridata web interface.

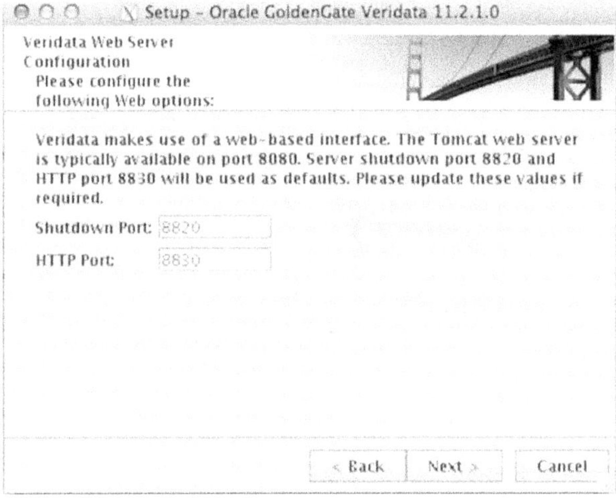

Figure 6-6c: Port entry

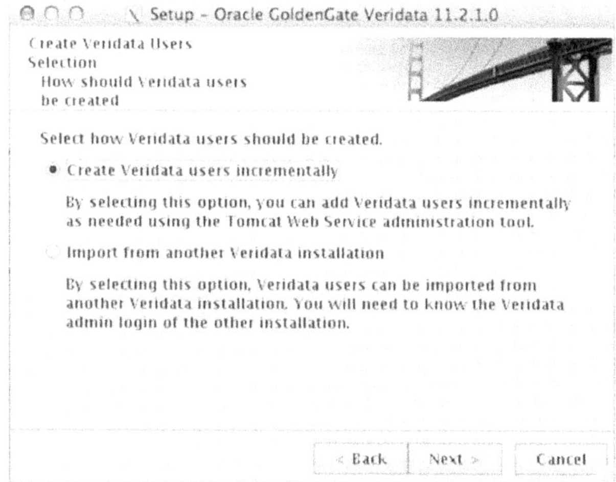

Figure 6-6d: Create users

Step 5: Veridata Server User Option

Oracle GoldenGate Veridata users must be authenticated to gain access to the Veridata web server. There are two options for creating users, either manually using Tomcat administration page or by importing Veridata users from another Veridata instance. The installation creates the first user with administration rights.

Step 6: Veridata Web Server User

Enter the Veridata web server administrator user name and password. The user *vd_admin* has administrative rights and is able to create additional users. Use the Tomcat web administration tool for creating groups, users, and assigning privileges.

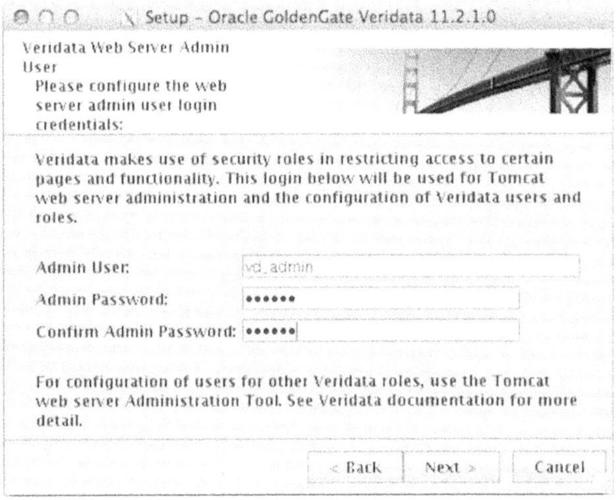

Setup - Oracle GoldenGate Veridata 11.2.1.0

Veridata Web Server Admin User

Please configure the web server admin user login credentials:

Veridata makes use of security roles in restricting access to certain pages and functionality. This login below will be used for Tomcat web server administration and the configuration of Veridata users and roles.

Admin User: vd_admin

Admin Password: ••••••

Confirm Admin Password: ••••••

For configuration of users for other Veridata roles, use the Tomcat web server Administration Tool. See Veridata documentation for more detail.

< Back | Next > | Cancel

Figure 6-6e: sign-on

Step 7: Veridata Repository

The repository stores Veridata metadata, runtime parameters (profiles), and Veridata configured objects. Specify the database type. This configuration uses Oracle Database 11g release 2 running on the Oracle Linux server.

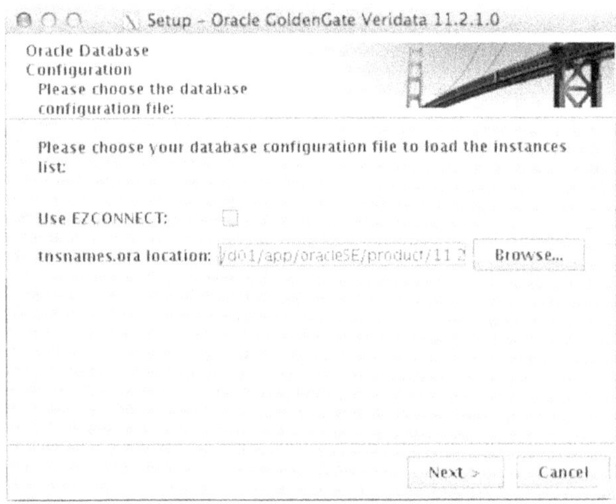

Figure 6-6f: tnsnames

Step 8: Network Files Location

Here, we specify the Oracle network files location. If you are uncertain, check the software location for VDDB instance by viewing the */etc/oratab* file. Also, verify if the shell environment variable TNS_ADMIN is already exported which overrides the default location. Oracle EZCONNECT is a flexible option for basic configuration.

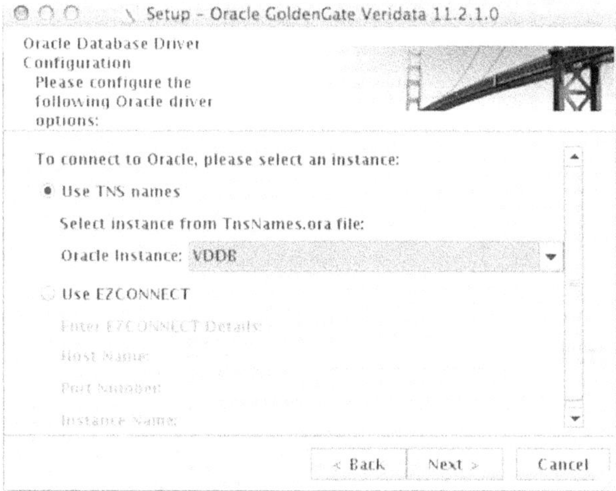

Figure 6-6g: Network Files Location

Step 9: Database Connection

The database connection to the repository database has two options: TNS names and EZCONNECT. It is preferred to use the TNS option which requires configuring the local database connect string on the TNSNAMES.ORA network file. Use the NETCA utility to create and test the connection.

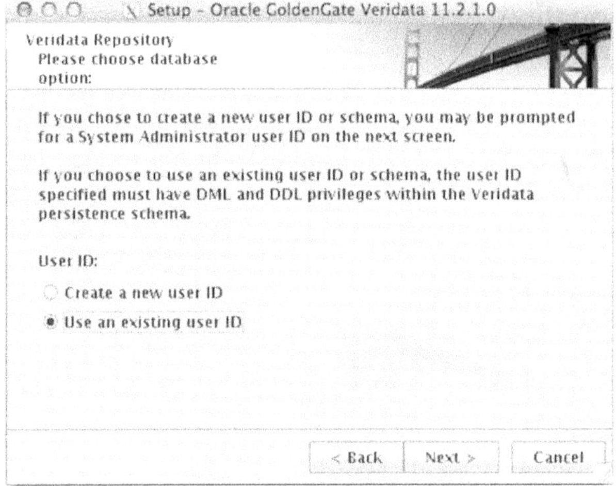

Figure 6-6h: Use existing User ID

Step 10: Veridata Repository

Veridata Repository schema is either an existing database user or newly created during the installation. In either option, this user should be dedicated to Oracle Veridata repository only. Repository maintenance tasks are easier when using a dedicated user.

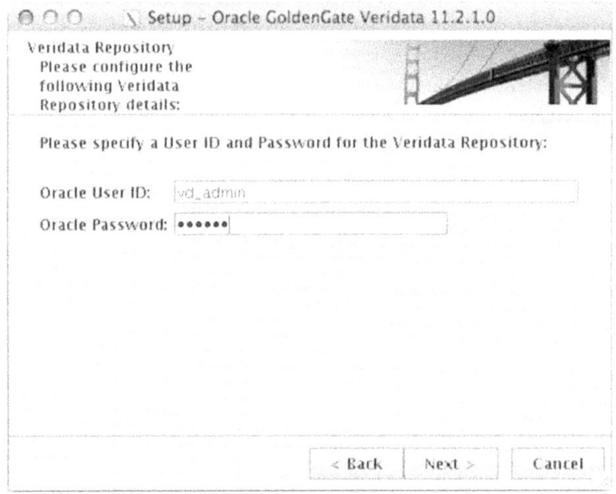

Figure 6-6i: Veridata Repository

Step 11: Repository Database Schema

Specify the repository database schema (owner) and password. This database schema must be authenticated to access the repository database. This schema assigns the default database profile for password restrictions and memory resource management.

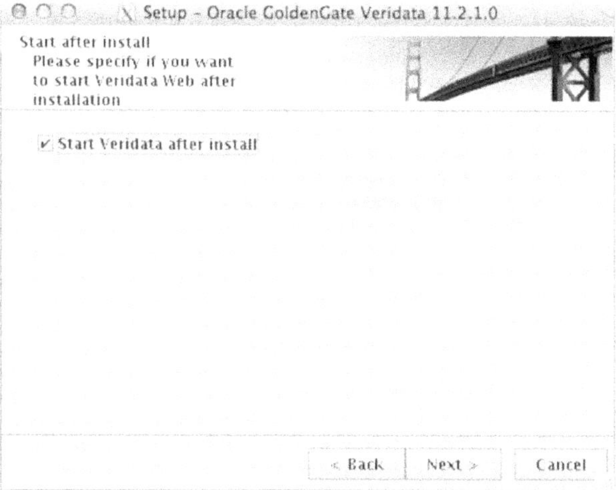

Figure 6-6j: Start Veridata

Step 12: Post Installation Tasks

By selecting 'Start Veridata after install', the Oracle GoldenGate Veridata web server is started after successful installation. If left unchecked, use the program *veridata_web.sh* to manually start and stop Veridata.

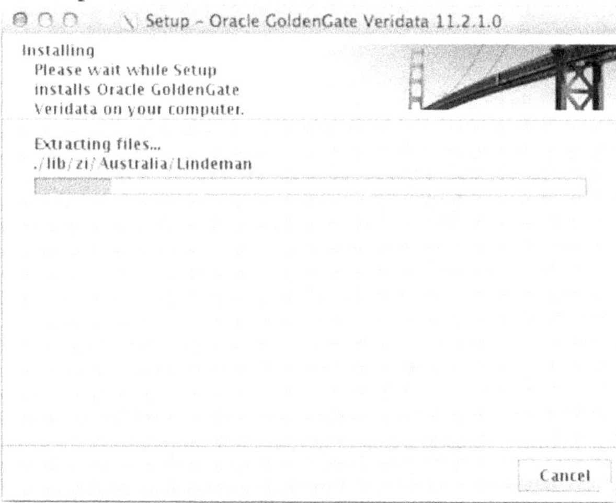

Figure 6-6k: Start Installation

Step 13: Information

Take notes of the information presented on this step. JDBC Driver URL is needed to configure the Java agent. Verify the software location is correct and start the installation by clicking Next. The database connect string is the alias from *tnsnames.ora* file.

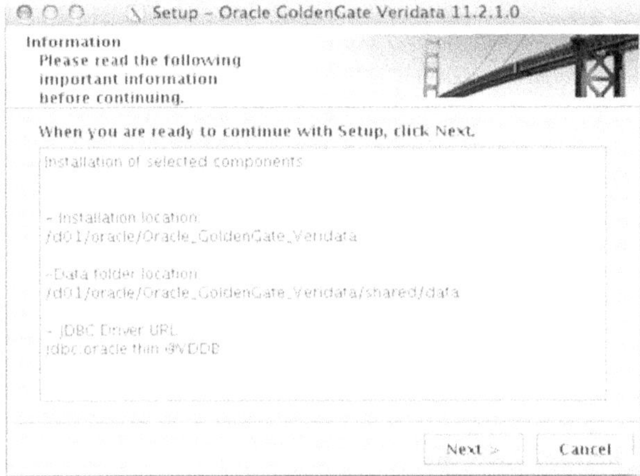

Figure 6-61: Installation of Selected Components

Step 14: Installation Progress

This is a quick installation that takes approximately 5-10 minutes to complete. It starts by extracting the software, creating the directory structure, and then proceeds with the installation on the specified software location.

Step 15: Successful installation

Click Finish to confirm successful installation. Verify the installation log files *installation.log*. Search for operating system related issues such as permissions, write access failed, etc. Now, Apache Tomcat web server and Oracle GoldenGate Veridata server are automatically started by the installation program.

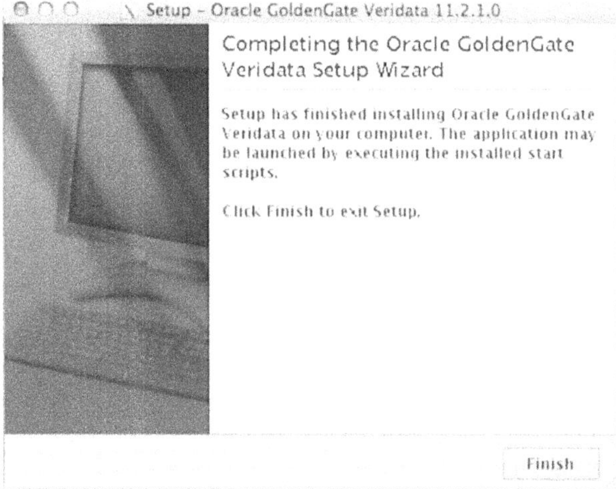

Figure 6-6m: Completing Veridata Setup

Verify Veridata Server Installation

We begin by accessing the Oracle GoldenGate Veridata server homepage at http://<veridata server IP address>:8830. For authentication, supply the username and password entered on Step 6. Port 8830 is the default HTTP for the first instance.

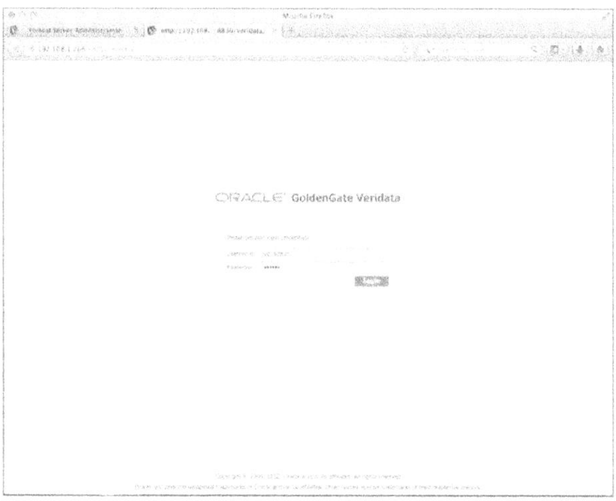

Figure 6-6n: Log In

Data Comparison Steps

To sustain online non-intrusive types of operations, data comparison is divided into two steps. This enables Oracle GoldenGate Veridata to account for data currently in the stream of change data capture and delivery — referred to as in-flight data. For non-key columns, data compare has two options, either the row hash (default) or the actual values of the columns.

The row hash value option uses a unique digital signature for calculating the row hash value to produce a compact source and target data. It is highly accurate (but not absolute) to be sent over the network to the Oracle GoldenGate Veridata server for comparison to determine if the two rows have the same or different column values. To make the data comparison absolute, configure the Oracle GoldenGate Veridata server to perform data compare using the actual column-to-column values. The drawback of the column-to-column approach is the increase overhead for processing data compare on tables with a large number of columns; it also increases the network overhead for sending data between the database and Oracle GoldenGate Veridata server.

Figure 6-7 illustrates the comparison steps and sub-steps workflow performed by the Oracle GoldenGate Veridata server to determine out-of-sync (OOS) rows between the source and target tables (compare pairs). The overall efficiency of the comparison is highly dependent on the integration among the different components executing various activities, independently.

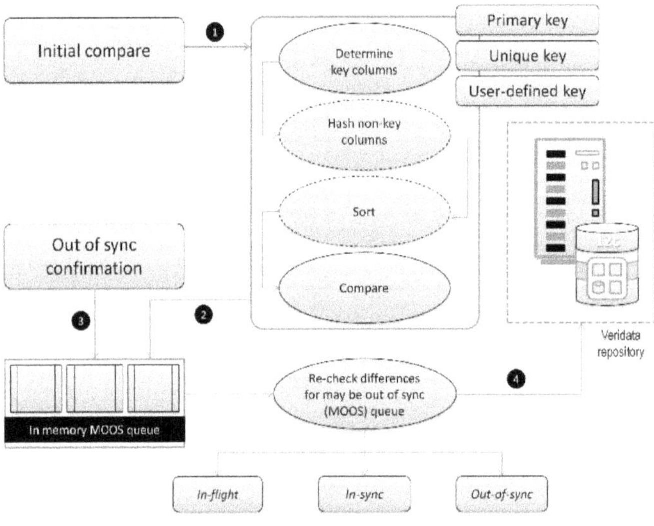

Figure 6-7: Oracle GoldenGate Veridata comparison steps

Unique Key

The Oracle GoldenGate Veridata Server must identify each row uniquely. There are three types of unique key identifiers (UID's):

1. Table Primary Key
2. Table Unique Key
3. User-Defined Unique Key

When the table has a primary key, the Oracle GoldenGate Veridata Server uses it for comparing two rows. However, in the absence of a primary key, it uses the table's smallest unique key. When the primary and unique keys are absent, a user-defined unique key is necessary. The user-defined key is created by the column mapping configuration which identifies the columns used as the key.

As shown in Figure 6-7, there are two major steps performed by the Oracle GoldenGate Veridata Server to determine out-of-sync rows. The following explains the two steps in further details.

Step 1: Initial Compare

This step relies on the key to determine the row uniqueness. The compare pair key columns are compared using value-to-value (literally) whereas non-key columns are compared using the hash value (default) evaluated using the row's unique digital signature. If the rows fetch returned by the agent is not sorted, then a sort operation is performed, and the row-to-row data compare operation is carried out. The outcome of the initial compare step is an in-memory, may be out-of-sync (MOOS) queue for accounting in-flight data, their status yet to be confirmed. The hash non-key column is the default. The option of using column-to-column literal value achieves absolute data compare results. The sort task is optional for the Oracle GoldenGate Veridata.

Step 2: Out-of-Sync Confirmation

This step uses the in-memory queue to reconfirm the status of compare pairs rows as in-flight, in-sync, or out-of-sync. The status is highly dependent on latency and transactions volume as data compare is performed while transactional replication is applied to the target database.

- **In-Flight Status**. Due to latency, the row was out-of-sync as determined by the initial step, but it has since been updated. If Oracle GoldenGate Veridata still cannot confirm the row as in-sync, the status is recorded as *in-flight.*

- **In-Sync Status**. The row was out-of-sync after completion of the initial step, but Oracle GoldenGate changed data capture and delivery streams have applied the row to the target database. Oracle GoldenGate Veridata confirmed current row match and the status is recorded as *in-sync.*

- **Out-Of-Sync Status**. The row was recorded out-of-sync by the initial step, but it has not been updated since the initial step took place. Therefore, the status is recorded as permanent *out-of-sync.*

The data compare results metadata is persistently recorded on the Oracle GoldenGate Veridata database repository; but out-of-sync data is recorded on the file system, ready for generating out-of-sync reports.

Tomcat Web Server Administration

Tomcat web server installed under Oracle GoldenGate root directory. Access Tomcat web server administration tool via http://<veridata server IP address>:8830/admin. Use the tool for performing fundamental administration tasks. Figure 6-8 shows the login page. Enter the user name and password submitted during the installation.

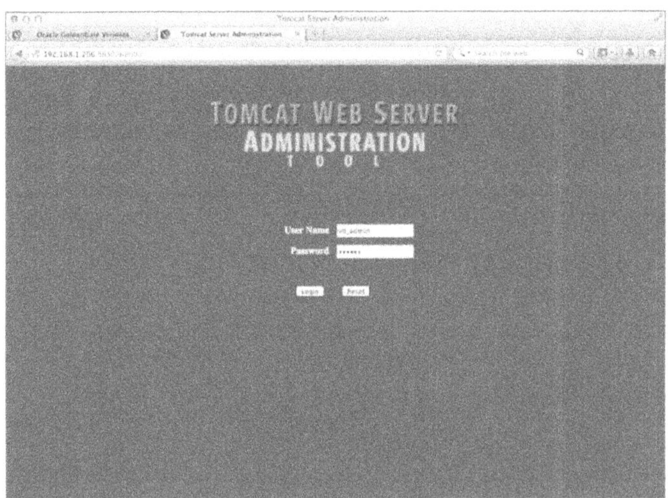

Figure 6-8: Tomcat Web Server

Tomcat Web Server Start-Up and Shutdown

Tomcat web server is an Apache HTTP server. Changes to configuration parameters and maintenance tasks demand to manually restart the Tomcat web server.
The following basic commands show how to perform start-up and shutdown.

Tomcat Start-Up

From Oracle GoldenGate Veridata root directory, change directory to /web/bin and execute the script catalina.sh as illustrated next:

```
$./catalina.sh start
```

Tomcat Shutdown

From Oracle GoldenGate Veridata root directory, change directory to /web/bin and execute the script catalina.sh as illustrated next:

```
$./catalina.sh stop
```

User and Group Administration

Oracle GoldenGate Veridata server installation creates the first administrative user, which is capable of creating additional groups and users. Figure 6-9 shows the Tomcat web server administration tool page. Management of groups, users and roles is performed from this web page.

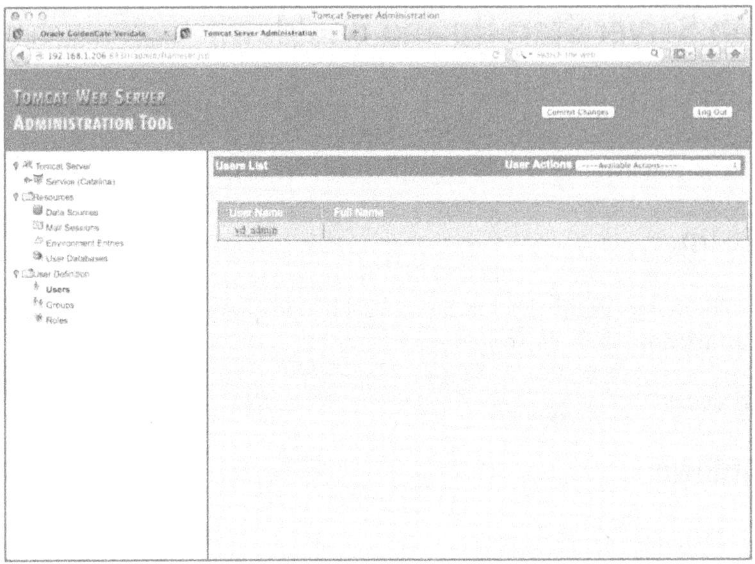

Figure 6-9: Groups, Users and Roles

For security and auditing standard practices, create multiple groups for classifying users then assign users to the relevant groups.

Using Oracle GoldenGate Veridata Web Interface

The Oracle GoldenGate Veridata web interface configures objects and rules for performing data comparison activities on compare pairs. Moreover, from the Oracle GoldenGate Veridata web interface, several activities are performed such as managing jobs, generating review and out-of-sync summary reports, and handling privileges for users. Figure 6-10 shows Oracle GoldenGate Veridata job, "Run Configuration." A job is linked to one-or-more compare groups and each is executed as a logical unit of work.

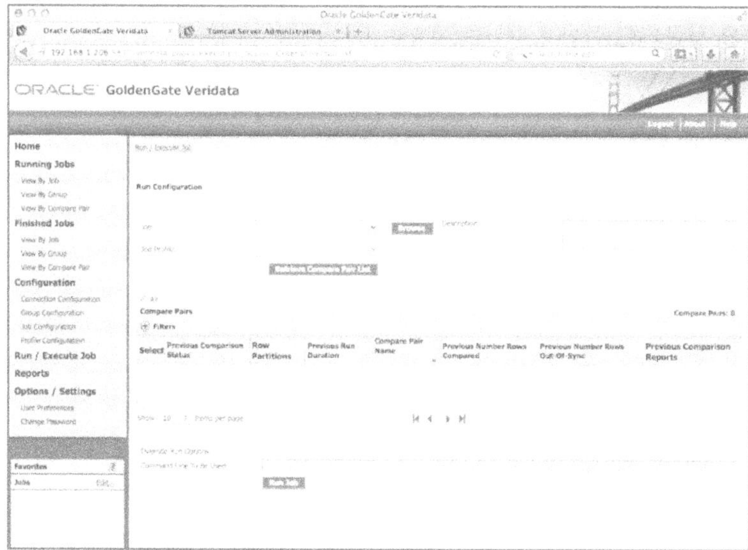

Figure 6-10: Oracle GoldenGate Veridata Web Interface

Stopping and Starting Oracle GoldenGate Veridata Server

For reasons such as altering Web server parameters, a restart of Oracle GoldenGate Veridata is required. From Oracle GoldenGate Veridata root directory, navigate to */web/bin* and execute the script *veridata_web.sh* as illustrated below:

Since Oracle GoldenGate Veridata server already started, execute the shell script veridata_web.sh using the argument "stop," this disables access to the Oracle GoldenGate Veridata web interface.

```
$ ./veridata_web.sh stop
CATALINA_HOME: /u01/app/Oracle_GoldenGate_Veridata/web
JRE_HOME: /u01/app/Oracle_GoldenGate_Veridata/jre
JAVA_OPTS: -Xms1024m -Xmx1024m -Djava.awt.headless=true -
Dveridata.home=/u01/app/Oracle_GoldenGate_Veridata -
Dveridata.log.dir=/u01/app/Oracle_GoldenGate_Veridata/shared/logs -
Dveridata.log.file=veridataweb.log
Using CATALINA_BASE:   /u01/app/Oracle_GoldenGate_Veridata/web
Using CATALINA_HOME:   /u01/app/Oracle_GoldenGate_Veridata/web
Using CATALINA_TMPDIR: /u01/app/Oracle_GoldenGate_Veridata/web/temp
Using JRE_HOME:        /u01/app/Oracle_GoldenGate_Veridata/jre
$
```

To enable access to the Oracle GoldenGate Veridata web interface, execute the shell script *veridata_web.sh* using the argument "start."

Configurable Veridata Objects

Regardless of how Oracle GoldenGate Veridata server components are installed and integrated, mandatory and optional objects are configured to enable the Oracle GoldenGate Veridata server to perform data comparison tasks and determine out-of-sync compare pairs. Figure 6-11 represents the associations (data model) among Oracle GoldenGate Veridata components and objects, then explained.

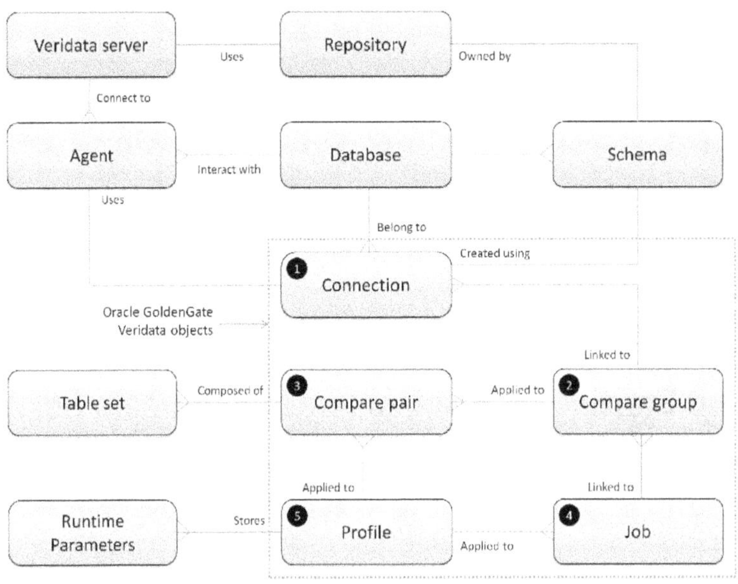

Figure 6-11: The Association among GoldenGate Veridata Objects

An Oracle GoldenGate Veridata Server connects to one or more agents; the agent listening port is required for creating the connections. Each connection is used by an agent to establish one or more database sessions. There can be several connections configured for a database, but this is not necessary. A compare pair belongs to one-and-only-one group (compare group), but a compare group contains one or more compare pairs — a 2-table set from the source and target database. A job is configured and linked to one or more compare groups to report out-of-sync compare pairs belonging to a compare group. Each compare pair consists of one or more database table sets. A profile is an optional object and in the absence of profiles, the internally defined default profile is applied implicitly. Non-default profiles are applied globally to one or more configured jobs, but also applied to one or more compare pairs to override certain runtime parameters. Non-default profiles inherit their parameters from the default profile. Modifications of profiles are applied dynamically to jobs and compare pairs.

Configure Connections

The Oracle GoldenGate Veridata agent utilizes successfully configured connections to establish database sessions. A single connection is sharable by multiple compare groups. Figure 6-12 shows the list of connections. Select the connection then Edit to modify, or Delete to remove. Click on New to configure a new connection. Testing connections requires the data source database to be available and the agent is started.

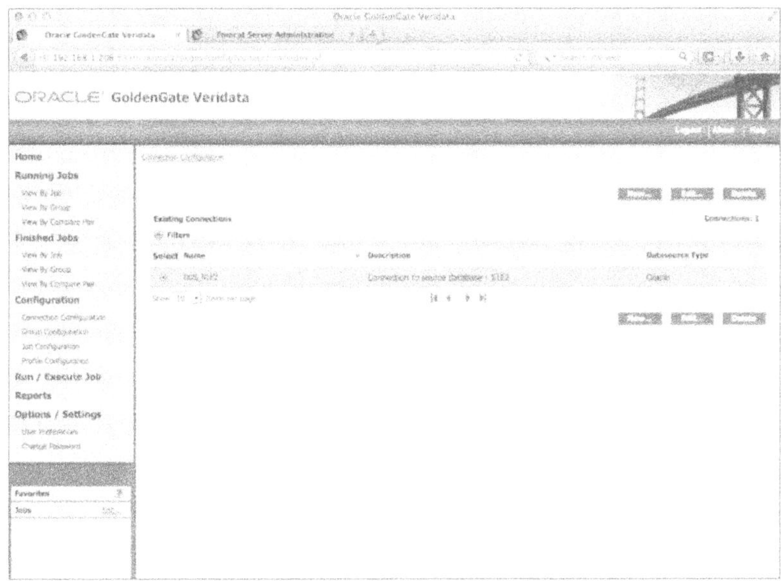

Fig 6-12: Configure Connections

Creating new connections require the following details:

- Agent Host Name or IP Address
- Agent Port
- Data Source Details

From the Oracle GoldenGate Veridata web interface navigation panel, under Configuration, click Connection Configuration. Follow the instructions for configuring the data sources connections.

Connection Name

Enter a unique connection name and a short description. For naming convention and consistency, make the database instance name (SID) as part of the connection name. Click Next to enter data source connection details.

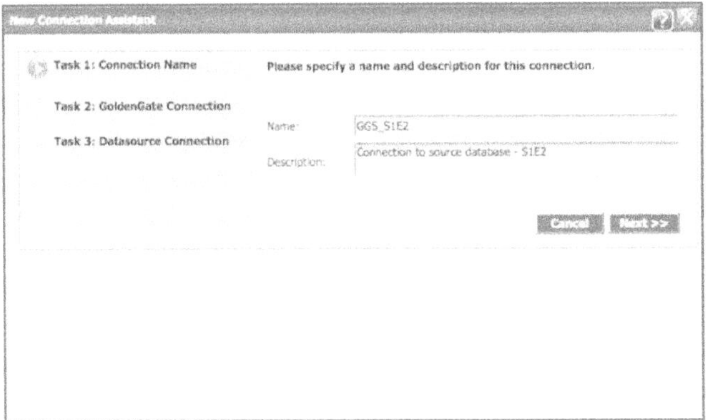

Fig 6-12a: Connection Name

GoldenGate Connections

Next, we enter the details for the GoldenGate Veridata agent; the host name or the IP address where the agent is installed, the agent connection port from the *agent.properties* file, and the database type. Click Verify and make sure the message "Datasource type verified. Please continue." is displayed.

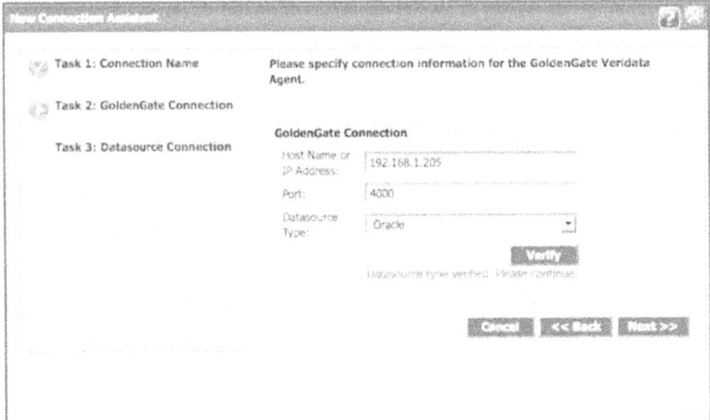

Fig 6-12b: GoldenGate Connections

The Oracle GoldenGate Veridata agent may be installed on the database server or elsewhere. The Oracle GoldenGate Veridata Server communicates with the agent using the connections configured. However, consider network traffic overhead when deciding where the agent should be installed.

Data Source Connection

Provide the data source connection details. Specify a database user with SELECT privilege on compare pairs tables. Click Test Connection. When the message "Datasource connection was successful" is displayed, click Finish.

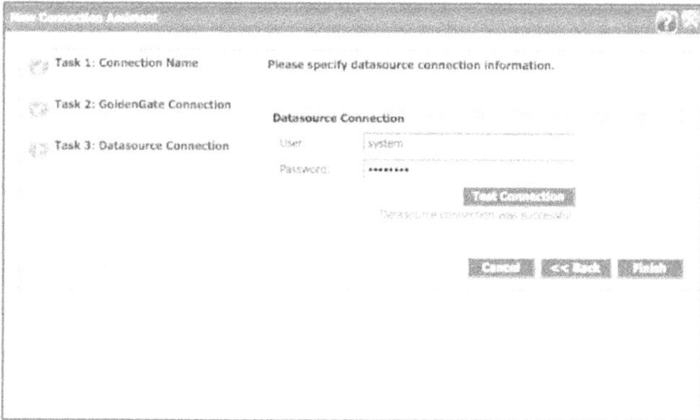

Fig 6-12c: Data Source Connections

To reconfigure an existing connection, click the connection name (link), Figure 6-13 shows the connection details, settings, and properties tabs. Make modifications, apply changes, but always verify the agent and test the database connection.

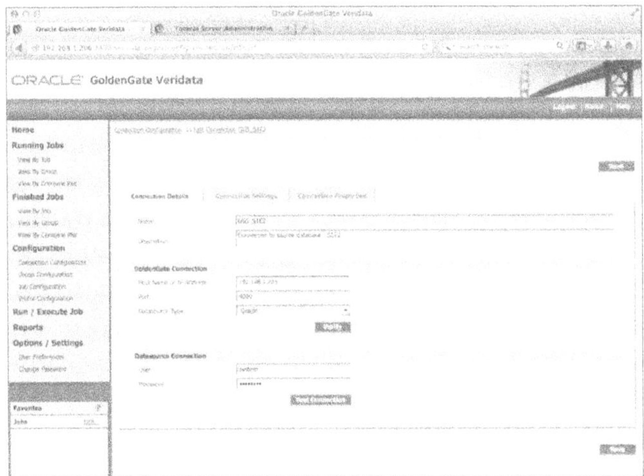

Figure 6-13: Connection Details, Settings, and Properties Tabs

Follow the above steps to configure the connection for the target database T1E2. Note that the target database agent must be running. The agent listening port and the host name/IP address are available to successfully create and test the connection.

Configure Groups

Groups or compare groups are logical containers to establish boundaries among compare pairs. Prior to creating compare groups, it is highly recommended to classify the database tables accessed and manipulated by the applications. The classification of database tables promotes data compares performance, compare pairs maintenance and data repairs. Start by creating the following compare groups:

- **Core Tables Compare Groups:** Contain set of compare pairs (2 tables) that are accessed and manipulated by transactions as one unit of work. Two rows mismatched on these compare pairs require immediate intervention by the application administrator. For example, the core tables compare groups may be further expanded to include lookup tables.
- **Lookup Tables Groups:** Contain static data referenced by other tables with minimal DML transactions. In general, it is appropriate to configure one compare group for all lookup tables compare pairs. For example, create multiple lookup table groups to further classify lookup tables groups by applications.
- **Non-Core Tables Compare Groups**: Contain set of compare pairs (2 tables) that are accessed and manipulated by isolated transactions. For example, create multiple lookup table groups to further classify lookup tables groups by applications or schemas.

For an application with partitioned database schema design, it is technically appropriate to map one compare group for each set of schema compare pairs. Figure 6-14 depicts examples for configuring groups.

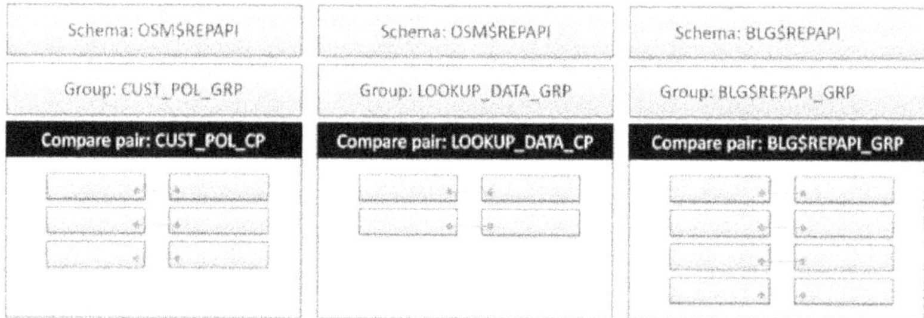

Figure 6-14: Examples of Configuring Compare Groups

Figure 6-15 shows the list of compare groups. Select the group name then Edit to modify or Delete to remove. Click on New to configure a new group (compare group). The next steps create the group CUST_POL_GRP, this compare group contains the compare pairs CUSTOMERS and POLICIES. The compare group needs the source and target connection names.

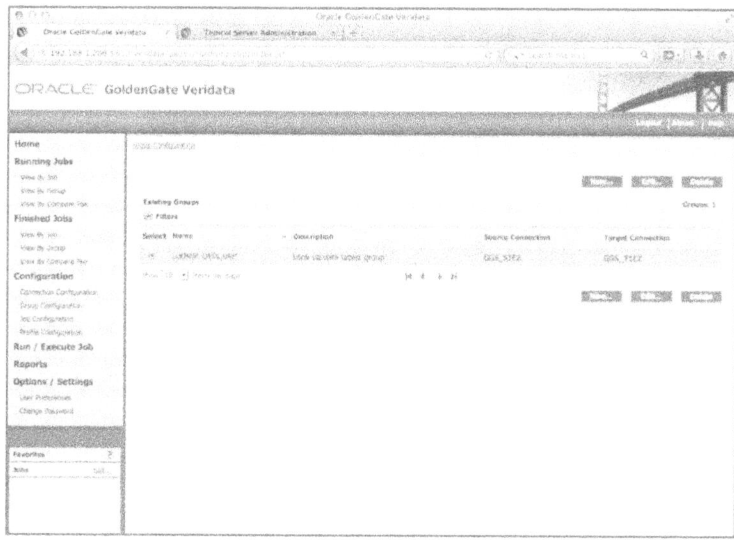

Figure 6-15: List of Compare Groups

Group Name

Enter a unique short name and a short description for the group. When using the option "Create new group using copy of existing group", select an existing group from the dropdown list of values.

When creating a group, consider the following:

- Since the space character is not permitted for multi-word group names, use characters such as "_" (underline) or "-" (hyphen) to define such group names. A group name such as CUST_POL_GRP is valid.

- Though group names are case insensitive, the use of upper, lower and mixed characters is valid. Follow a consistent naming convention.

- The maximum length for a group name is 200 characters, but the use of short descriptive group names is always preferable.

A unique constraint violation error is returned when entering an existing group name. View the list of groups as shown in Figure 6-15 above.

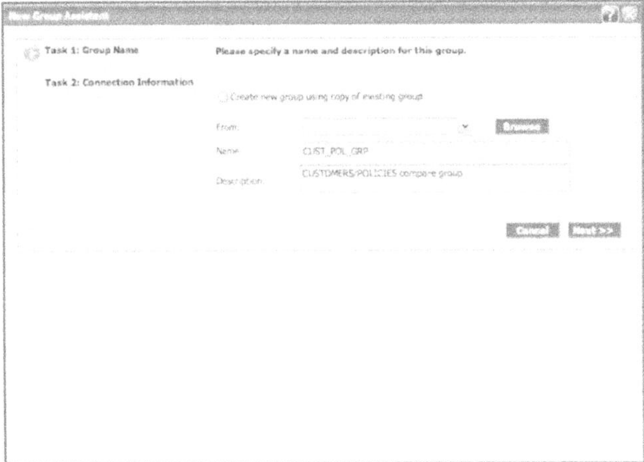

Fig 6-15a: Group Name

Data Source Connection

Enter the data source connections for this group. Carefully specify the source and target connection from the drop list. Click Finish to create the compare group.

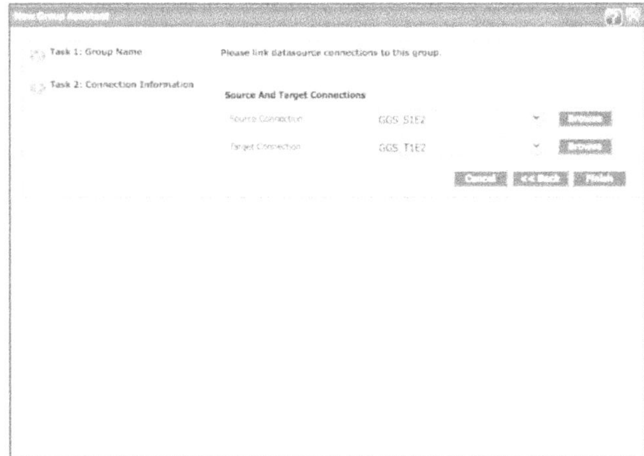

Fig 6-15b: Data Source Connections

Now we query the table VD_ADMIN.GROUPS, where VD_ADMIN is the repository schema for viewing compare group and the number of compare pairs. Do not update VD_ADMIN.GROUPS from outside of Oracle GoldenGate Veridata web interface.

```
T1E2>COLUMN name FORMAT A30
T1E2>SELECT name, status, num_compare_pairs
  2  FROM   groups;
```

```
NAME                               STATUS NUM_COMPARE_PAIRS
------------------------------ ---------- -----------------
POL_CUST_GRP                            0                 1
CUST_POL_GRP                            0                 2
LOOKUP_DATA                             0                 2
CUST_GRP                                0                 1
test                                    0                 0
CUSTOMERS_POLICIES_GRP                  0                 2
```

Configure Compare Pairs

The next object type configured is the compare pair. Compare pairs are contained within a compare group. Each compare pair is composed of a list of 2-table sets to be compared. Figure 6-16 shows each step and its associated methods/options, if any, for configuring compare pairs. If the compare group (group) is already created, it may have existing compare pairs. There are two mapping methods for adding compare pairs. Every time a compare pair is added, the compare pair must be generated and saved. Edit the column mapping, as necessary (e.g. specifying a user-defined unique key). The last step is to validate columns mapping. Only valid compare pairs are considered for data comparison. In case of an error, investigate, correct the error and re-validate the columns mapping in preparation of running compare pairs jobs for determining out-of-sync rows.

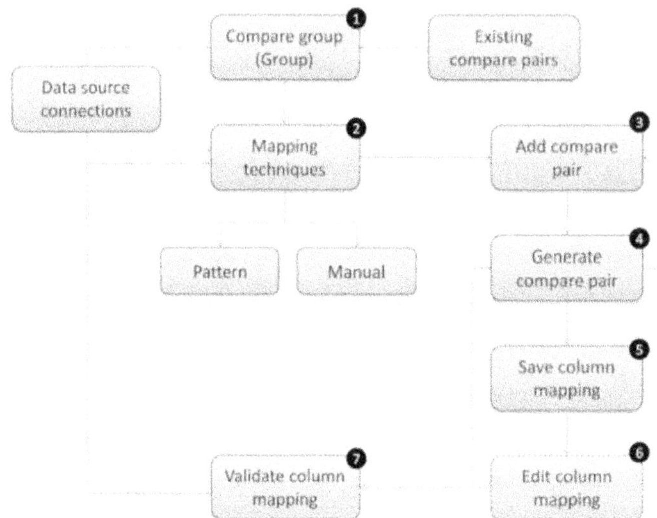

Figure 6-16: Configure Compare Pairs

Oracle GoldenGate Veridata has two techniques for configuring compare pairs.

1. Pattern Mapping
2. Manual Mapping

Veridata Pattern Mapping

The pattern mapping technique is suitable for a large set of source and target tables synchronized using Oracle GoldenGate. Without any kind of transformation where the Replicat MAP-TARGET clause has identical table names or wildcard for table names, then the pattern mapping technique is a sound option. Pattern mapping has three methods for creating the compare pairs list.

1. Map Source and Target Tables using exact names
2. Map Source and Target Tables using a SQL % wildcard pattern. Use only one % on each side.
3. Map Source and Target Tables using a GoldenGate * wildcard pattern. Use only one * on each side.

Veridata Manual Mapping

The manual mapping is sometimes preferred over the pattern mapping technique (e.g. where the table names are different or for creating a short-listed compare pair from a large list of tables).

The general steps to configure compare pairs are:

1. Identify the compare group name (group)
2. Choose the mapping technique
3. Add the compare pairs
4. Generate the compare pairs
5. Edit column mapping (optional)
6. Save column mapping
7. Validate column mapping

Compare Group Name

By clicking on the compare group, the compare group and connections details presented are followed by the compare pairs section. As shown in Figure 6-17, click on the link "Go to Compare Pair Configuration" to add new compare pairs or modify existing compare pairs for this compare group.

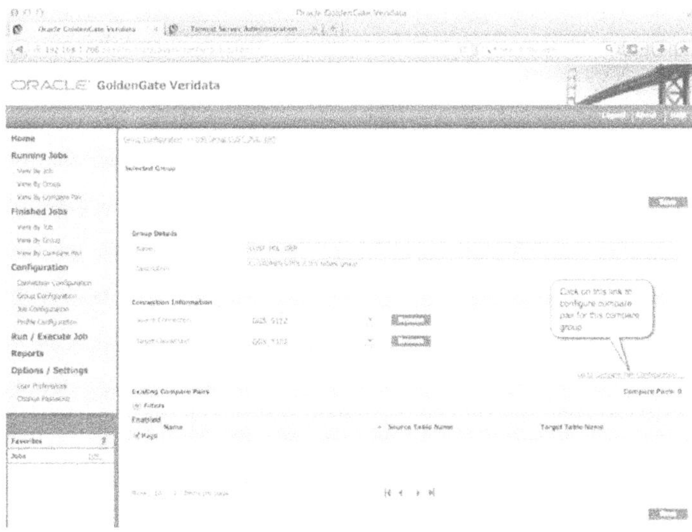

Figure 6-17: Configure A Group's Compare Pairs

Compare Pairs Mapping

For the group CUST_POL_GRP, the manual mapping technique is applied. Figure 6-18 displays the group name information and exiting compare pairs, if any. Click on Manual Mapping tab to select 2-table set from the list of source and target tables.

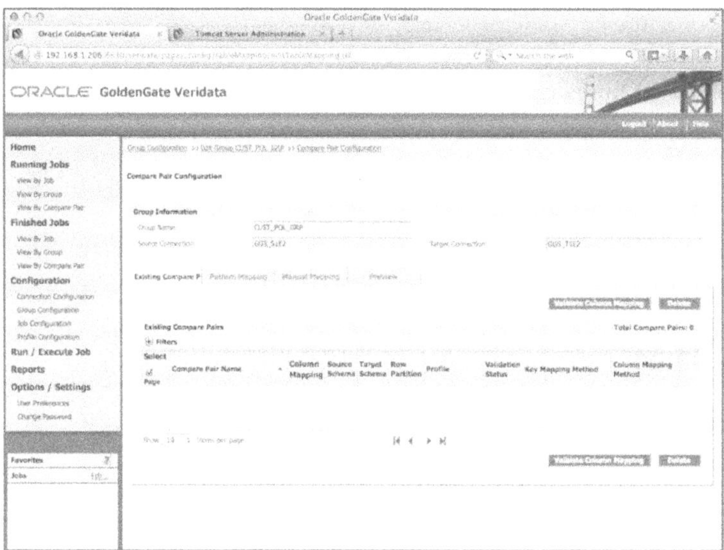

Figure 6-18: Configure Compare Pair Mapping

Adding Compare Pairs

Figure 6-19 shows the manual mapping technique from the data source information. Select the source and target schemes then iteratively build the compare pairs by selecting one table from the source database and mapped table from the target. When completed, click Save.

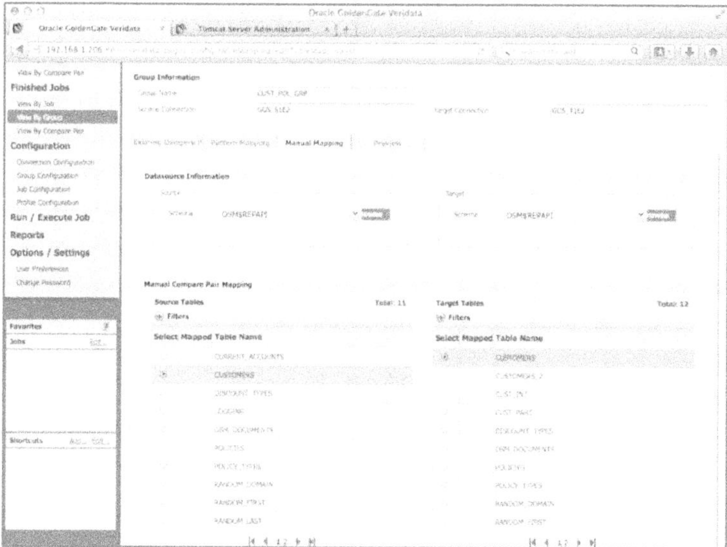

Figure 6-19: Compare Pair Mapping

Generate Compare Pairs

After adding each compare pair, click on Generate Compare Pair located at the bottom of the page. Figure 6-20 shows the added compare pairs for the compare group CUST_POL_GRP. The compare pairs table names are identical.

CUSTOMERS=CUSTOMERS
POLICIES=POLICIES

Applying user-configured profile to compare pair by selecting from the list of profiles, the profile is already created and modified to apply runtime parameters to override the group runtime parameters. Configure row partition to limit comparison to be performed against a subset of the table.

After modifying the compare pair, update the compare pair by clicking on Generate Compare Pair.

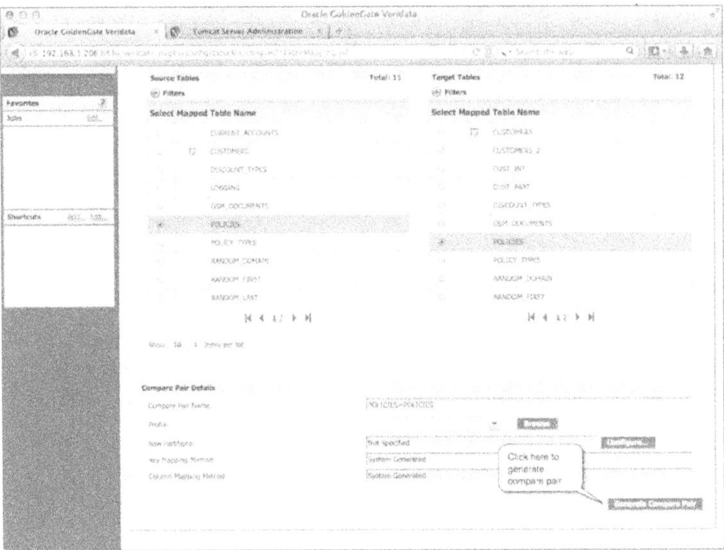

Figure 6-20: Generate Compare Pair

Save Column Mapping

After generating all compare pairs, select the Preview tab and click Save.

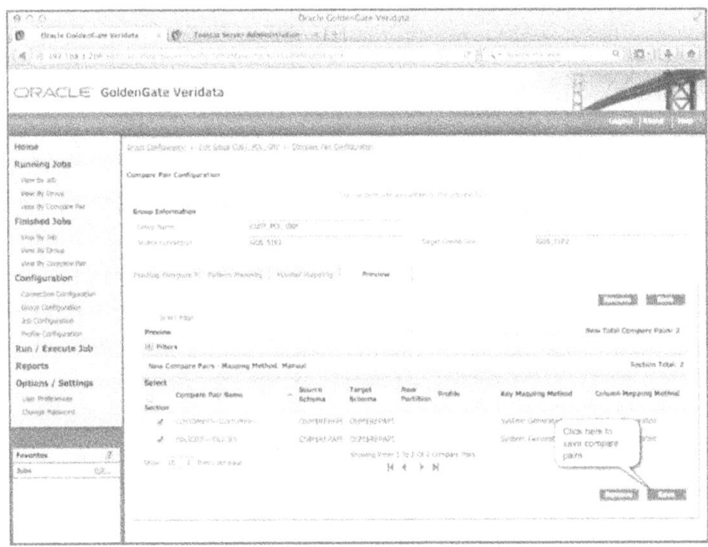

Figure 6-21: Save Compare Pairs

Edit Compare Pairs

The edit compare pair is used to alter key mapping method, comparison column mapping and the mapping type. Click the Edit link as shown in Figure 6-22.

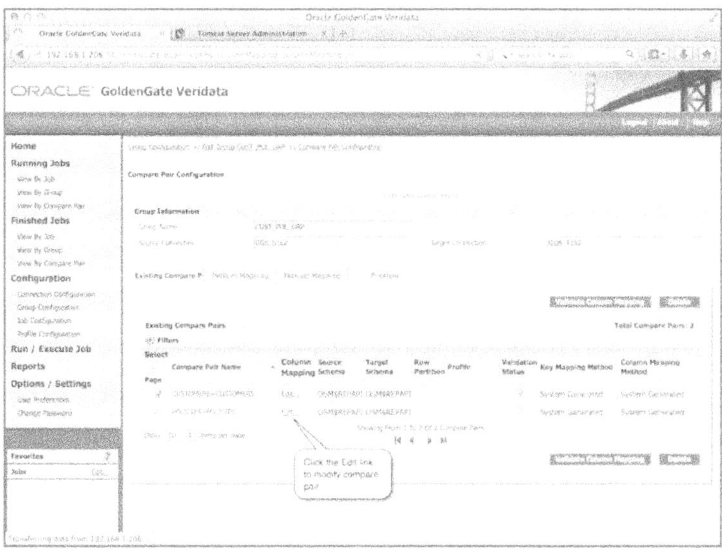

Figure 6-22: Edit Compare Pair Column Mapping

Figure 6-23 alters the mapping type from row hash to row literal. This allows an absolute data compare, but increases processing overhead proportional to the number of columns and their data types.

Figure 6-23: Edit Columns Mapping Type from Hash to Literal

Validate Compare Pairs

Whenever a compare pair is added or updated, it must be first saved then validated. Click on Review tab to generate the compare pair by clicking on Generate Compare Pair. Select the compare pairs then click on the Validate Compare Mapping. After the compare pair is successfully validated, the validation status is recorded. Figure 6-24 shows the compare validation step.

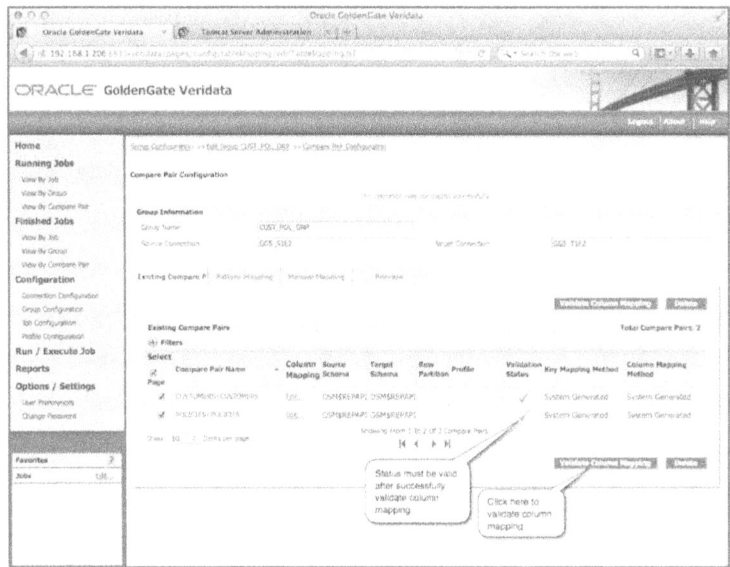

Figure 6-24: Validate Compare Pairs

Configure Jobs

A configured job is linked to one or more compare groups. The tasks to configure a job are:

- Provide the job name and description
- Link the job to one or more compare groups
- Override the compare group connections (optional)
- Specify non-default profile (optional)

From the navigation panel, under Configuration, click on Job Configuration. Figure 6-25 shows existing jobs. Click on New to create a new job. Edit to modify existing job, Delete to remove existing job, or Run to start the job. For more control, when running jobs, from the navigation panel, click on Run/Execute to select the job and modify the row partition by providing the SQL predicate statement.

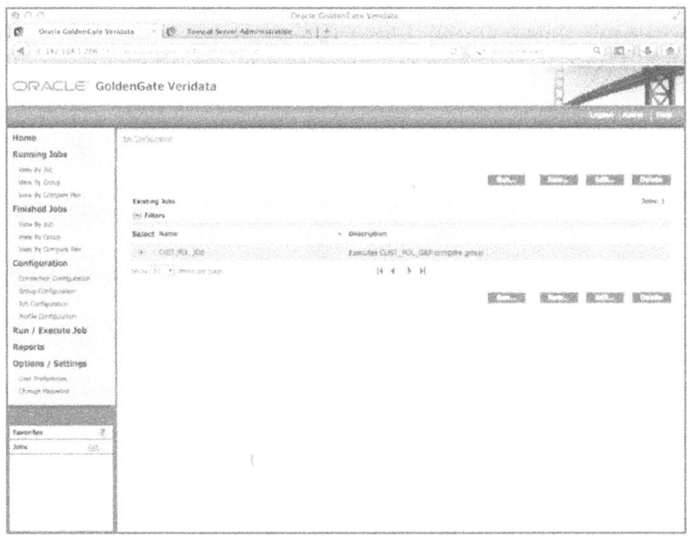

Figure 6-25: List of Jobs

Job Name

Enter the job name and short description. Click Next for connection information.

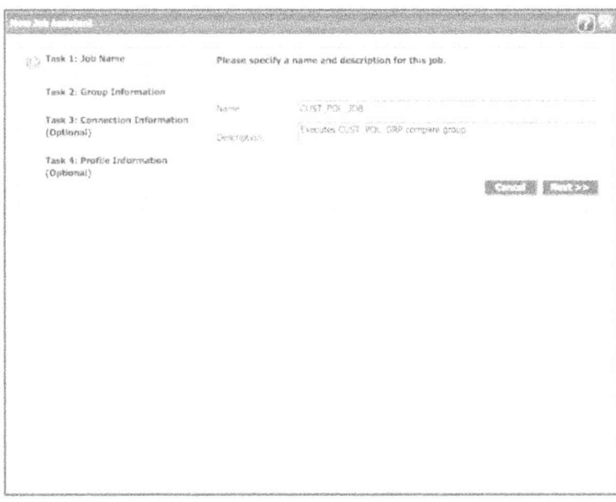

Figure 6-25a: Job Name

Group Information

A job is associated with one or more compare groups. We check the list of compare groups that are linked to a job, which executes the compare activities for each compare pair. Note that it is necessary to create multiple jobs for the different compare groups to promote effective resource management incurred during the comparison steps.

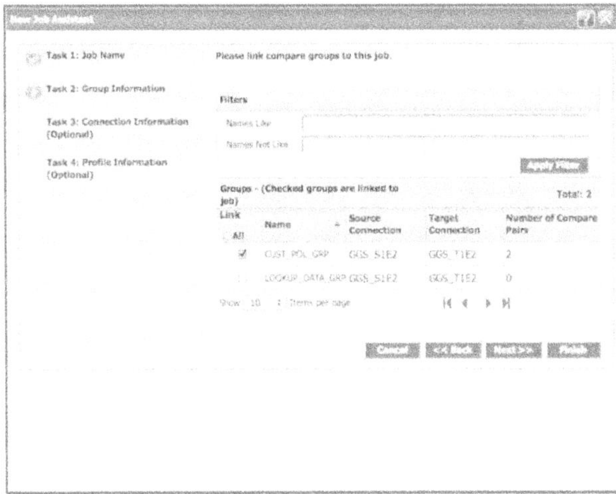

Figure 6-25b: Group Information

Connection Information

The connection information details are optional as they are already part of the compare group configuration. Specifying connection information overrides the compare group connections.

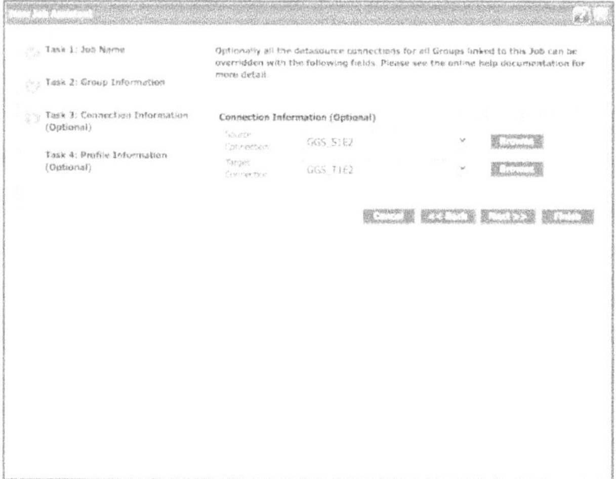

Figure 6-25c: List of Jobs

Profile Information

The profile information is optional. Oracle GoldenGate Veridata applies its default profile. When a user-defined profile is specified, it overrides the default profile.

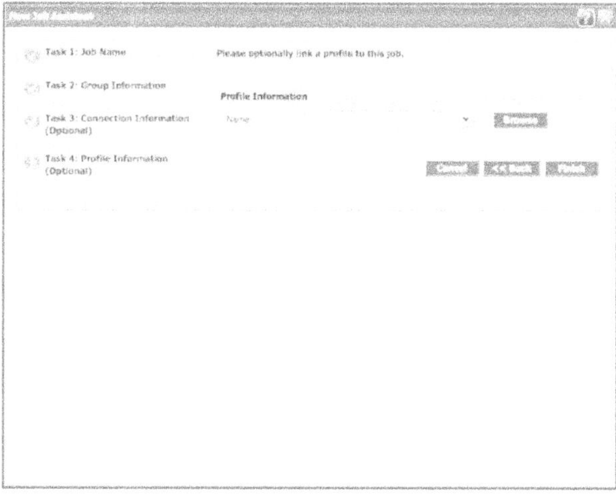

Figure 6-25d: Profile Information

Configure Profiles

Profiles stores runtime parameters. Oracle GoldenGate is shipped with a default profile, named Default. Explicit linking of profiles to jobs and compare pairs is optional, because jobs implicitly inherit runtime comparison parameters from the default profile.

For more control and more effective comparison activities, either modify the default profile parameters or create a new profile which inherits the default parameters setting. Then, assign the non-default profile to jobs and compare pairs.

From the navigation panel, click on Profile Configuration. Click on New to add new profile, Edit to modify existing profile and Delete to remove existing profile. Figure 6-26 shows the profile configuration page.

Profile Settings

The profile has four categories of parameters:

1. General
2. Sorting Method
3. Initial Compare
4. Confirm Out-Of-Sync

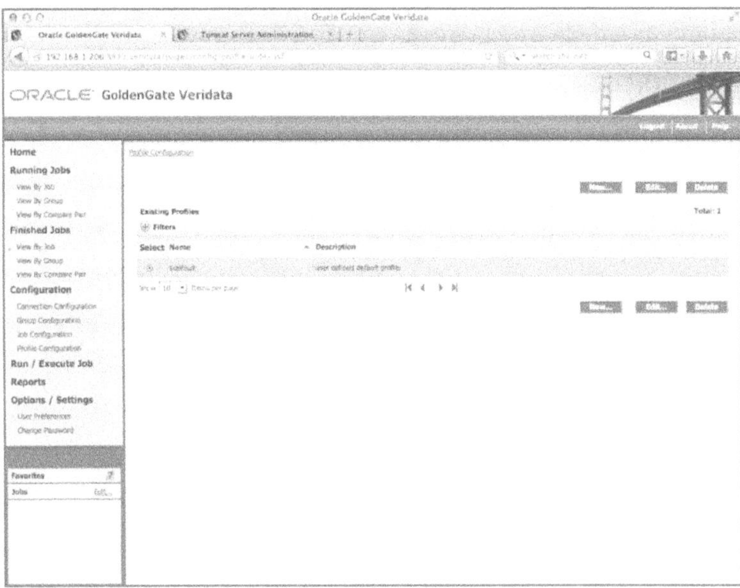

Figure 6-26: Configure Profiles Page

General Parameters

The general parameters default values should remain unchanged. For users interested to view out-of-sync rows in XML format, set the value for the parameter 'Out-Of-Sync Output Format' to XML by performing the following steps:

1. Uncheck Use Default
2. Select XML from the list of values
3. Click Save

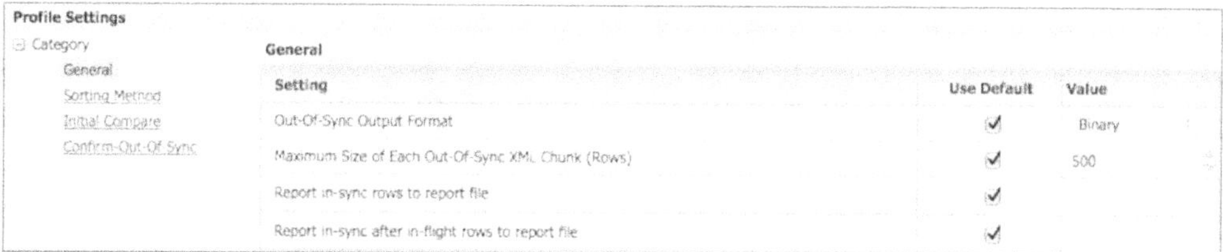

Figure 6-26a: Profile Settings

Out-of-sync files are stored under /shared/data of Oracle GoldenGate Veridata server root directory. Then, sub-directories are created using the name of the compare group.

Sorting Method Parameters

The transactions volume, number of columns and rows of the source and target database tables, has direct impact on setting these parameters. To increase the performance of compare pairs processing, increase the value for the parameter 'Maximum Memory Usage (MB)'. The default setting of 50MB is fairly low for large compare pairs.

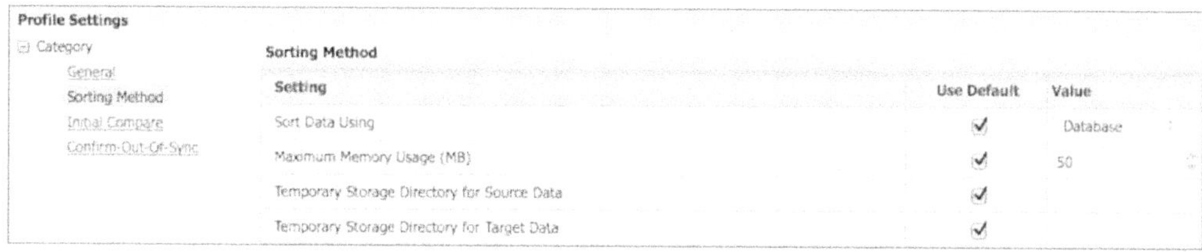

Figure 6-26b: Profile Settings

Since it is not possible to dynamically change memory usage for each table, use a value that will meet the majority of the compare pairs. Execute the following PL/SQL to report the average table size, which will be used as the value for the parameter.

```
SQL> DECLARE
    CURSOR c1 IS SELECT table_name, sum(bytes)/1024/1024 bytes
                 FROM (SELECT segment_name table_name, bytes
                       FROM user_segments
                  WHERE  segment_type = 'TABLE' and
                         segment_name IN ('POLICIES', 'CUSTOMERS'))
                 GROUP BY table_name;
    vAverageSize NUMBER:=0;
    vtable_name  VARCHAR2(30);
    vbytes       NUMBER;
    vcnt         NUMBER:=0;
  BEGIN
    OPEN c1;
    LOOP
       FETCH c1 into vtable_name, vbytes;
       EXIT WHEN c1%NOTFOUND;
       vcnt := vcnt+1;
       DBMS_OUTPUT.PUT_LINE(vtable_name||' size='||vbytes||' MB');
       vAverageSize :=  vAverageSize + vbytes;
    END LOOP;
    DBMS_OUTPUT.PUT_LINE('The average size='||vAverageSize/vcnt||' MB');
  END;
  /
```

```
POLICIES size=.0625 MB
CUSTOMERS size=.0625 MB
The average size=.0625 MB
```

Initial Compare Parameters

The initial compare parameters are categorized by initial compare, event reporting and agent. Setting the parameter 'Terminate when Maximum Records Out-Of-Sync' to lower values eliminates unnecessary overhead of continued comparison activities.

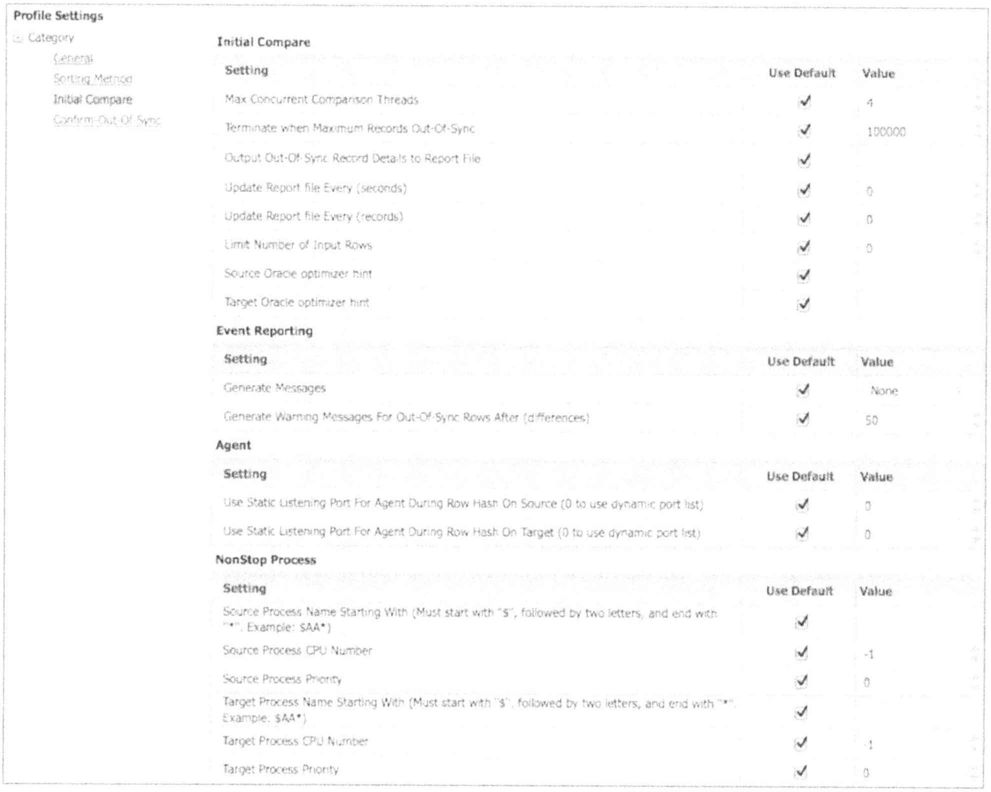

Profile Settings

- Category
  - General
  - Sorting Method
  - Initial Compare
  - Confirm-Out-Of-Sync

Initial Compare

Setting	Use Default	Value
Max Concurrent Comparison Threads	✓	4
Terminate when Maximum Records Out-Of-Sync	✓	100000
Output Out-Of-Sync Record Details to Report File	✓	
Update Report file Every (seconds)	✓	0
Update Report file Every (records)	✓	0
Limit Number of Input Rows	✓	0
Source Oracle optimizer hint	✓	
Target Oracle optimizer hint	✓	

Event Reporting

Setting	Use Default	Value
Generate Messages	✓	None
Generate Warning Messages For Out-Of-Sync Rows After (differences)	✓	50

Agent

Setting	Use Default	Value
Use Static Listening Port For Agent During Row Hash On Source (0 to use dynamic port list)	✓	0
Use Static Listening Port For Agent During Row Hash On Target (0 to use dynamic port list)	✓	0

NonStop Process

Setting	Use Default	Value
Source Process Name Starting With (Must start with "$", followed by two letters, and end with "*". Example: $AA*)	✓	
Source Process CPU Number	✓	-1
Source Process Priority	✓	0
Target Process Name Starting With (Must start with "$", followed by two letters, and end with "*". Example: $AA*)	✓	
Target Process CPU Number	✓	-1
Target Process Priority	✓	0

Figure 6-26c: Profile Settings

Confirm Out-Of-Sync Parameters

The out-of-sync profile parameters match the initial compare parameters, typically with lower values settings for parameters related to resources utilization. When changing the below parameters, perform adequate testing outside of Oracle GoldenGate. When the result is satisfactory, apply the values to profile parameters.

- Max Concurrent Comparison Threads
- Limit Number of Input Rows
- Source Oracle optimizer hint/Target Oracle optimizer hint

Execute Jobs

Jobs are executed to determine the compare pairs status within a compare group. From Oracle GoldenGate Veridata web interface navigation panel, click on Run / Execute Job option. The run configuration page has the list of configured jobs. To override the compare group runtime parameter, select the job profile from the available list of configured user-defined profiles. Figure 6-27 shows previous jobs completion status.

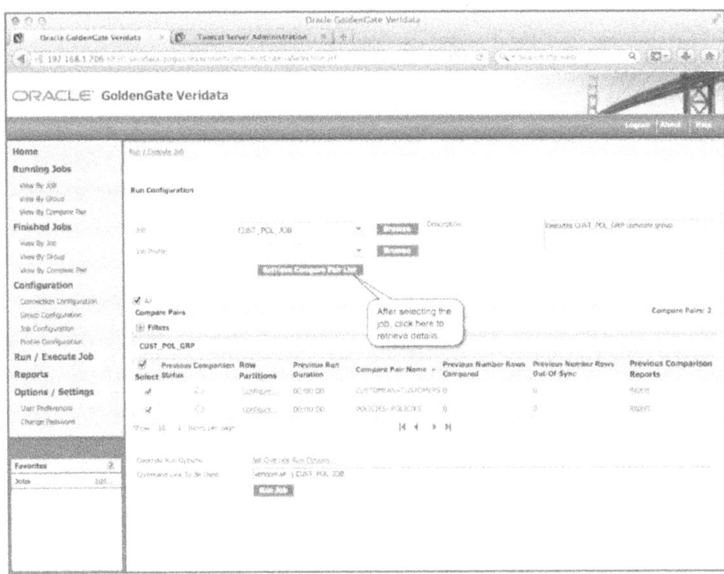

Figure 6-27: Run Job for a Compare Group

Row Partition

Row Partition technique filters the compare pair input data. It narrows down the initial compare by configuring row partition for each compare pair using a valid SQL predicate clause. By default, Oracle GoldenGate Veridata do not apply row partition.

Because the boundary of row partition is within a table only, apply the same row partition clause to all related tables for a consistent out-of-sync report. For example, if we need to limit rows compare to customer for CUST_NO > 100, apply the predicate to CUSTOMERS=CUSTOMERS compare pair and the referenced tables compare pair POLICIES=POLICIES. This yields consistent views of the out-of-sync report. Figure 6-28 shows adding SQL predicate to CUSTOMERS=CUSTOMERS compare pair. Click on New to add new SQL predicate statement. Click on Edit to modify existing SQL predicate statement. Click on Remove to delete existing SQL predicate statement.

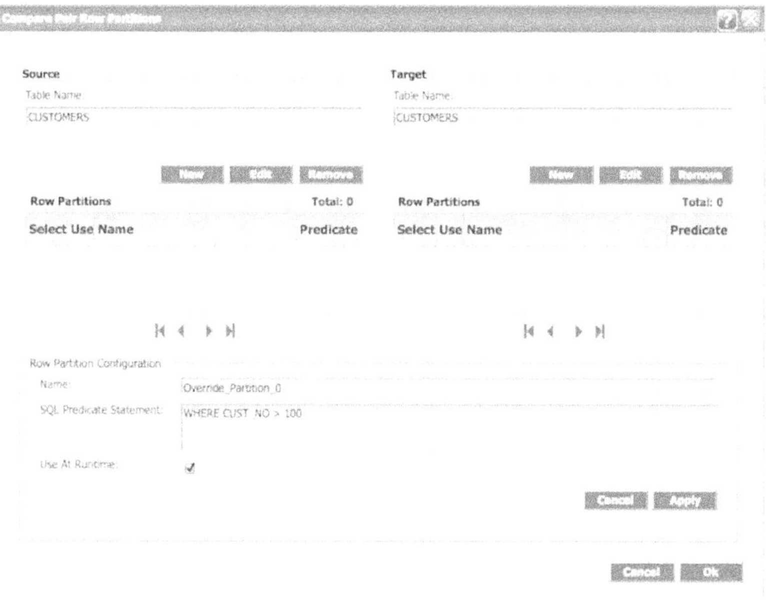

Figure 6-28: Configure Row Partition

Out-Of-Sync Reports

Oracle GoldenGate Veridata stores out-of-sync output data on the directory /shared/data/oos/<compare group name sub-directory> under the Oracle GoldenGate root directory.

The list of out-of-sync reported uses the compare group name.

```
$ ls -al
total 24
drwxr-x---   6 oracle oinstall 4096 Dec 11 23:01 .
drwx------   5 oracle oinstall 4096 Dec  8 18:32 ..
drwxr-x---   6 oracle oinstall 4096 Dec 16 00:31 CUST_JOB
drwxr-x---   4 oracle oinstall 4096 Dec 11 23:01 CUST_POL_GOB1
drwxr-x---  11 oracle oinstall 4096 Dec 10 23:05 CUST_POL_JOB
drwxr-x--- 175 oracle oinstall 4096 Dec 19 18:48 LOOKUP_DATA_JOB
$
```

To view the out-of-sync summary report from Oracle GoldenGate Veridata web interface navigation panel, under Finished Jobs, click View By Compare Pair option. Compare pairs that have out-of-sync has a link on OOS Rows column. Figure 6-29 shows the report output.

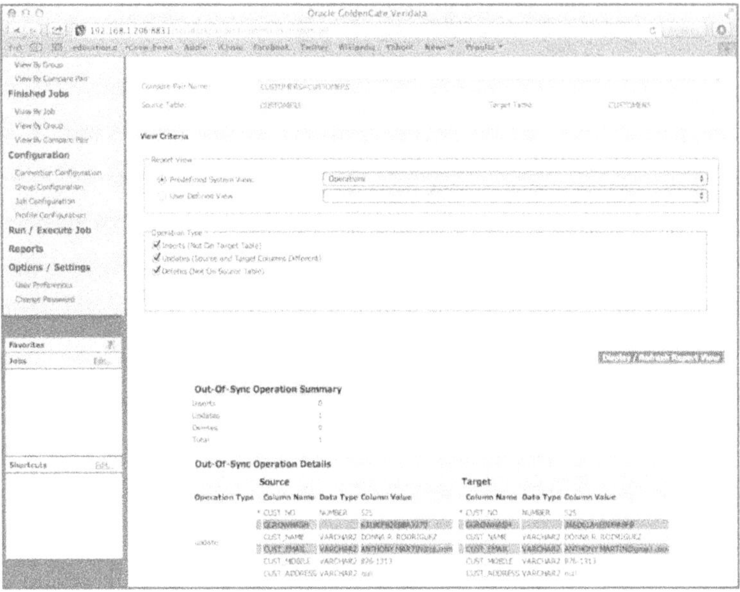

Figure 6-29: Out-Of-Sync Report Summary

The out-of-sync report summary view is customized by report type and operation types. For a tabular summary only, set the Preferred System View to Differences By Columns. The out-of-sync report view is customizable by operation of type:

- Inserts (Not On Target Table)
- Updates (Source and Target Column Different)
- Deletes (Not On Source Table)

The current release of Oracle GoldenGate Veridata functionality is limited to row-to-row compare only of the source and target tables. It does not provide a repair technique for rows differences. The data repair is implemented outside of Oracle GoldenGate Veridata. This chapter discusses Oracle database LogMiner as data repair techniques. Depending on two factors, the degree of out-of-sync compare pair and the causes of out-of-sync, it may be necessary to programmatically develop the repair utility. This requires configuring database links between the source and target system. Also, Oracle GoldenGate Extract and Replicat with intended settings and transformations enables handling out-of-sync from source to target and vice versa.

Oracle GoldenGate Reports

For executed jobs, Oracle GoldenGate Veridata generates various reports for analysis and troubleshooting. From the Oracle GoldenGate Veridata web interface navigation panel, click on Reports. Figure 6-30 shows the Oracle GoldenGate Veridata reports page.

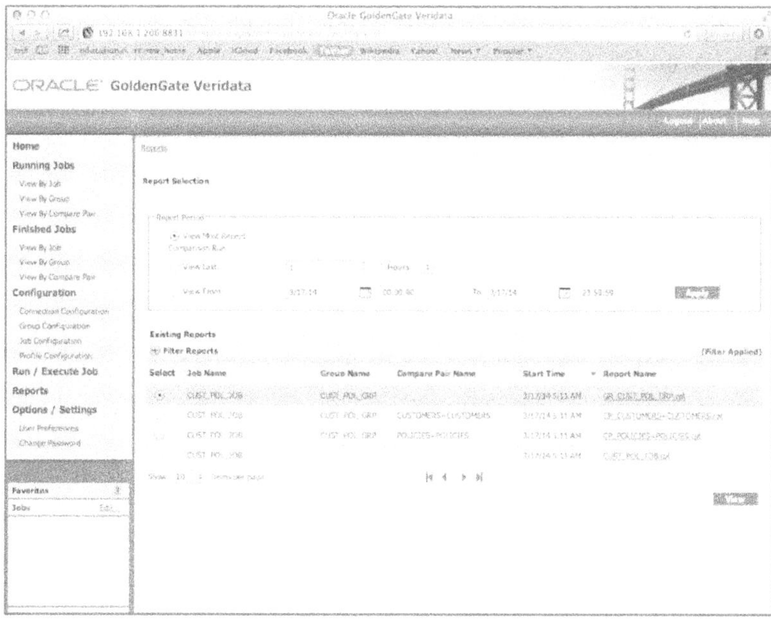

Figure 6-30: Compare Group Reports

Click on Report Name. The report outlines runtime parameters values and a summary for out-of-sync, if any. The report has the details for:

- Profile Applied
- Profile Applied General Parameters
- Sorting Method Parameters
- Initial Compare Parameters
- Confirm Out-Of-Sync Parameters
- Source and Target Agents
- Performance Statistics
- Summaries

Sections of the compare pair DISCOUNT_TYPES=DISCOUNT_TYPES report follows. The report name is constructed in the form <compare group name>.rpt.

```
**********************************************************************
                      Oracle GoldenGate Veridata
           11.2.1.0  OGGVDT_11.2.1.0.0_PLATFORMS_121108.1625

Copyright (C) 2004, 2012, Oracle and/or its affiliates. All rights reserved.

                    Starting at 2013-12-20 10:48:06

**********************************************************************

OS           : Linux
Version      : 2.6.18-164.el5xen
Node         : gss-target
Machine      : amd64
Process id   : 27538, Thread id : 38
Java version: 1.6.0_15
Java vendor : Sun Microsystems Inc.

Compare Pair: DISCOUNT_TYPES=DISCOUNT_TYPES
Run ID       : (1235,1,1)

Compare Parameters:

    Source connection: GG_S1E2
    Source host      : 192.168.1.205  (oracle)
    Target connection: GG_T1E2
    Target host      : 192.168.1.206  (oracle)
    Source table     : OSM$REPAPI.DISCOUNT_TYPES
    Target table     : OSM$REPAPI.DISCOUNT_TYPES

Profile: $default

General:
**********************************************************************
          Out-Of-Sync Output Format:* xml
   Maximum Size of Each Out-Of-Sync
                  XML Chunk (Rows): 500
 Report in-sync rows to report file: false
     Report in-sync after in-flight
               rows to report file: false

Sorting Method:
**********************************************************************
                   Sort Data Using: database
          Maximum Memory Usage (MB): 50
    Temporary Storage Directory for
                       Source Data:
    Temporary Storage Directory for
                       Target Data:

Initial Compare:
**********************************************************************
  Max Concurrent Comparison Threads: 4
     Terminate when Maximum Records
                       Out-Of-Sync: 100000
```

```
  Output Out-Of-Sync Record Details
                    to Report File: false
 Update Report file Every (seconds): 0
 Update Report file Every (records): 0
         Limit Number of Input Rows: 0
       Source Oracle optimizer hint:
       Target Oracle optimizer hint:

Initial Compare (Event Reporting):
**********************************************************************
                 Generate Messages: none
     Generate Warning Messages For
           Out-Of-Sync Rows After
                     (differences): 50

Initial Compare (Agent):
**********************************************************************
     Use Static Listening Port For
 Agent During Row Hash On Source (0
         to use dynamic port list): 0
     Use Static Listening Port For
 Agent During Row Hash On Target (0
         to use dynamic port list): 0

…
Confirm-Out-Of-Sync:
**********************************************************************
   Perform Confirm Out-Of-Sync Step: true
      Run Concurrently With Initial
                           Compare: true
      Delay Confirm-Out-Of-Sync By
                         (seconds): 0
     Terminate when Maximum Records
                       Out-Of-Sync: 100000
  Output Out-Of-Sync Record Details
                    to Report File: false
 Update Report file Every (seconds): 0
 Update Report file Every (records): 0
       Source Oracle optimizer hint:
       Target Oracle optimizer hint:

Confirm-Out-Of-Sync (Event Reporting):
**********************************************************************
                 Generate Messages: none
     Generate Warning Messages For
           Out-Of-Sync Rows After
                     (differences): 50

Confirm-Out-Of-Sync (Agent):
**********************************************************************
     Use Static Listening Port For
 Agent During Row Hash On Source (0
         to use dynamic port list): 0
     Use Static Listening Port For
 Agent During Row Hash On Target (0
         to use dynamic port list): 0

Starting  Veriagt session for source rowhash at  2013-12-20 10:48:06.
```

```
Initial Compare source Agent Information:
               JDBC URL: jdbc:oracle:thin:@192.168.1.205:1521:S1E2
             Session ID: 848
               SortNull: high
       NLS_CHARACTERSET: AL32UTF8

Starting  Veriagt session for target rowhash at  2013-12-20 10:48:06.

Initial Compare target Agent Information:
               JDBC URL: jdbc:oracle:thin:@192.168.1.206:1521:t1e2
             Session ID: 816
               SortNull: high
       NLS_CHARACTERSET: AL32UTF8

Performance Statistics for Source Rowhash at 2013-12-20 10:48:07.

    rows                : 3
    duration (secs)     : 00:00:00
    rows/sec            : 200
    row bytes           : 103
    row bytes/sec       : 6866
    bytes/row           : 34
    rows skipped        : 0
    blocks skipped      : 0
    time fetching       : 00:00:00
    time until first row: 00:00:00
    ipc msgs            : 8
    ipc bytes           : 2364
    bytes/msg           : 9

Comparing first row at 2013-12-20 10:48:07

*** Summarizing Initial Row Comparison Step ***

    Time                 : 2013-12-20 10:48:07
    Elapsed Time         : 00:00:00
    Comparisons performed: 3
    Rows per second      : 130
    Rows out-of-sync     : 0
    inserts              : 0
    updates              : 0
    deletes              : 0

Performance Statistics for Target Rowhash at 2013-12-20 10:48:07.

    rows                : 3
    duration (secs)     : 00:00:00
    rows/sec            : 28
    row bytes           : 103
    row bytes/sec       : 980
    bytes/row           : 34
    rows skipped        : 0
    blocks skipped      : 0
    time fetching       : 00:00:00
    time until first row: 00:00:00
    ipc msgs            : 8
    ipc bytes           : 2364
    bytes/msg           : 9
```

```
*** Summarizing Confirm Out-of-Sync Step ***

    Time                    : 2013-12-20 10:48:07
    Elapsed Time            : 00:00:00
    Rows confirmed          : 0
    Rows per second         : 0

*** Summarizing Persistently Out-of-Sync Rows ***

    Rows out-of-sync                  : 0
    inserts                           : 0
    updates                           : 0
    deletes                           : 0

*** Summarizing In-Sync-after-In-Flight Rows ***

    Rows in-sync-after-in-flight      : 0
    inserts                           : 0
    updates                           : 0
    deletes                           : 0

*** Summarizing Still-Changing Rows ***

    Rows in-flight                    : 0
    inserts                           : 0
    updates                           : 0
    deletes                           : 0

tables in sync: source OSM$REPAPI.DISCOUNT_TYPES, target
OSM$REPAPI.DISCOUNT_TYPES

Comparison terminated normally.
```

Veridata Command-Line Utility

While the majority of Oracle GoldenGate Veridata tasks and activities are performed using the web interface, the command-line interface is available for running non-configuration tasks.

Let us start by finding the version for your Veridata command-line. Login to Oracle GoldenGate Veridata server and enter the command below.

```
$ ./vericom.sh -v
```

```
VERIDATA_HOME /u01/app/Oracle_GoldenGate_Veridata
JRE_HOME: /u01/app/Oracle_GoldenGate_Veridata/jre
JAVA_OPTS: -Xmx1024m -Djava.awt.headless=true
Oracle GoldenGate Veridata Command Line Interface - Version 11.2.1.0
OGGVDT_11.2.1.0.0_PLATFORMS_121108.1625
```

Jobs created using Oracle GoldenGate Veridata web interface are executable from the command-line. Specify the –j flag followed by the job name.

```
$ ./vericom.sh -j LOOKUP_DATA_JOB
```

```
VERIDATA_HOME /u01/app/Oracle_GoldenGate_Veridata
JRE_HOME: /u01/app/Oracle_GoldenGate_Veridata/jre
JAVA_OPTS: -Xmx1024m -Djava.awt.headless=true
Oracle GoldenGate Veridata Command Line Interface - Version 11.2.1.0
OGGVDT_11.2.1.0.0_PLATFORMS_121108.1625
Job LOOKUP_DATA_JOB started
Run ID: (1037,0,0)
Number of Compare Pairs: 2
Number of Compare Pairs With Errors: 0
Number of Compare Pairs With OOS: 0
Number of Compare Pairs With No OOS: 2
Number of Compare Pairs Cancelled: 0
Job Report Filename:
/u01/app/Oracle_GoldenGate_Veridata/shared/data/rpt/LOOKUP_DATA_JOB/00001037
/LOOKUP_DATA_JOB.rpt
Run ID: (1037,0,0)
Job Completion Status: IN SYNC
```

Unattended Execution

One of the applications of VERICOM is to enable unattended execution of Oracle Veridata jobs. Data comparison is triggered using the operating system or the database scheduler. Since Oracle Veridata repository is stored on an Oracle database, use DBMS_SCHEDULER to execute Veridata jobs based on pre-determined intervals.

The following steps use DBMS_SCHEDULER to create a database job that executes Oracle GoldenGate Veridata job, LOOKUP_DATA_JOB.

Start by creating the program. This is an optional component, but promotes flexibility when working with DBMS_SCHEDULER. It separates the program from job definition.

```
T1E2>BEGIN
          DBMS_SCHEDULER.CREATE_PROGRAM (
            program_name=>'COMPARE_PAIRS',
            program_type=>'EXECUTABLE',
            program_action=>'/home/oracle/lookup_dat.sh',
            enabled=>TRUE,
            comments=>'Verify lookup tables');
  END;
  /
```

```
PL/SQL procedure successfully completed.
```

The PROGRAM_ACTION parameter specifies the shell script directory and name. The script invokes VERICOM using the flag –j followed by the job name. The shell script contains the two lines below with the correct operating system to execute permission settings.

```
#!/bin/bash
/u01/app/Oracle_GoldenGate_Veridata/vericom.sh -j LOOKUP_DATA_JOB
```

Next, create the schedule which is also optional and can be part of the job definition. Creating a schedule promotes flexibility when working with DBMS_SCHEDULER.

```
T1E2>BEGIN
    DBMS_SCHEDULER.CREATE_SCHEDULE (
       schedule_name=>'RUN_EVERY_1_HOUR',
       repeat_interval=>'FREQ=HOURLY; INTERVAL=1',
       comments=>'Run the jobs every hourly');
    END;
   /
```

```
PL/SQL procedure successfully completed.

T1E2>
```

The last step is to create the database job that will execute the Oracle GoldenGate Veridata job.

```
T1E2>BEGIN
     DBMS_SCHEDULER.CREATE_JOB (
        job_name=>'RUN_VD_COMPARE_LD',
        program_name=>'COMPARE_PAIRS',
        schedule_name=>'RUN_EVERY_1_HOUR',
        comments=>'Execute Veridata compare pair job every 1 hour',
        enabled=>TRUE);
   END;
   /
```

```
PL/SQL procedure successfully completed.

T1E2>
```

Manually run and verify that the job is executed without errors. Successful execution returns a status code of 0.

```
T1E2>BEGIN
      DBMS_SCHEDULER.RUN_JOB('RUN_VD_COMPARE_LD');
   END;
   /
```

```
PL/SQL procedure successfully completed.
```

```
T1E2>SELECT status, error#, SUBSTR(additional_info, 1, 10) INFO
  2  FROM   dba_scheduler_job_run_details
  3  WHERE  job_name='RUN_VD_COMPARE_LD';
```

```
STATUS                         ERROR#     INFO
------------------------------ ---------- ------------------------
SUCCEEDED                               0
```

Verify the job compare status from within the Oracle Veridata web interface. Figure 6-31 shows the result of the compare pairs is in-sync.

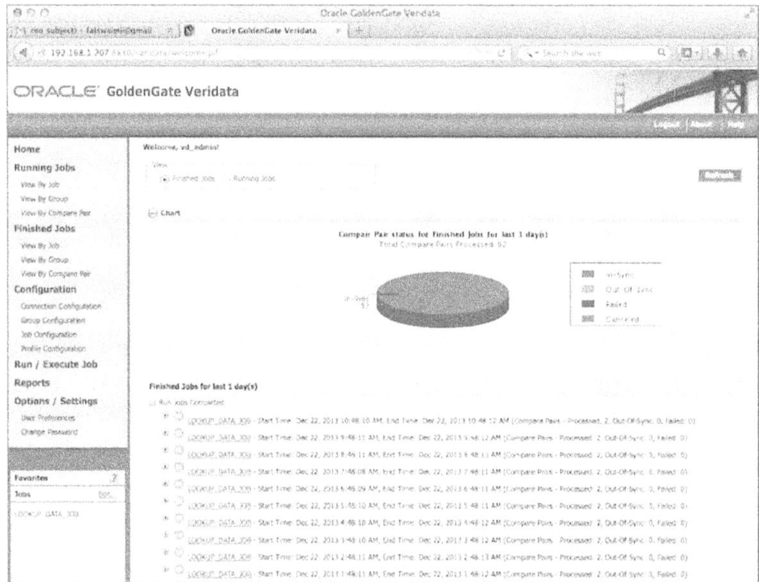

Figure 6-31: Data Compare Results for the Unattended Job

Veridata Server Parameters

Oracle GoldenGate Veridata server runtime uses server-side parameters. Some of the parameters define the instance properties, while others allocate resources for optimizing data compare activities. Oracle GoldenGate Veridata installation creates the parameter file veridata.cfg. The file defines and briefly describes each parameter. To find the location of the parameter file veridata.cfg, navigate to /shared/conf under the Oracle GoldenGate Veridata root directory.

```
# SERVER PARAMETERS
server.veridata_data                     /u01/app/Oracle_GoldenGate_Veridata/
                                         shared/data
```

```
server.persistence_db_type              ORACLE_OCI
server.persistence_db_instance          VDDB
server.persistence_db_name
server.persistence_db_port
server.persistence_db_username          vd_admin
server.persistence.oracle.tns_admin     /u01/app/oracle/product/11.2.0/
                                        dbhome_1/network/admin
server.meta_session_handle_timeout      900
server.max_concurrent_jobs                100
server.max_concurrent_comparison_threads  default
server.max_sort_memory                    default
server.max_comparison_sort_memory         default
server.sort_waiting_threshold             default
server.concurrent.writers                 default
server.concurrent.readers                 default
server.number_sort_threads                default

# WEB PARAMETERS
web.host                                localhost
web.OOS_User_Templates                  /u01/app/Oracle_GoldenGate_Veridata/
                                        shared/templates
web.persistence_db_url                  jdbc:oracle:thin:@VDDB
```

Data Repair Techniques

Oracle GoldenGate Veridata performs comparisons on data sets to identify data discrepancies. However, data discrepancies repairs are handled outside of Oracle GoldenGate Veridata. Depending on the extent of data discrepancies, identified in the out-of-sync (OOS) report, the repairs techniques are developed using any of the following options:

- Oracle GoldenGate
- Oracle Database Utilities
- In-House Developed Utilities
- Third-Party Utilities

The majority of the data discrepancies are resolved using either Oracle GoldenGate or Oracle Database utilities. However, it is case-specific for selecting and applying the most appropriate options. For example, for consistent pattern of data discrepancies, the use of in-house developed interactive utility is recommended. It is likely to use the out-of-sync (OOS) XML files as input.

When using Oracle GoldenGate to repair data discrepancies related to DELETE and INSERT DML operations, configure Oracle GoldenGate to capture and deliver from the source to target database and vice versa. The purpose of this configuration is for data repair only and not for an online synchronization. This kind of repair should adapt a one-time remote task configuration of the initial-load extract process in which the Extract communicates directly with the Replicat over TCP/IP to apply changes.

For data discrepancies related to UPDATE DML operations, configure Oracle GoldenGate to capture and deliver from source to target database and vice versa for an online replication. Consider the following when using Oracle GoldenGate to develop the data repair:

- Limit the Extract process capture using the option SQLPREDICATE of the TABLE clause for capturing the intended row(s) only.
- The Extract-Replicat direction depends on the operation type and target data source.
- Temporary disabling of foreign key constraints may be required for UPDATE DML statements.

Refer to chapter 3 and 4 for more details regarding initial-load techniques and configuring Oracle GoldenGate online synchronization. The Oracle GoldenGate Logdump utility supports data repair techniques. It searches trail files for detailed analysis, advanced filtering, and extracting columns values. Refer to chapter 9 for more details regarding performing filtering using the Director.

The following section will be dedicated to demonstrate the Oracle Database LogMiner utility for developing data repair to handle out-of-sync rows.

Oracle Database LogMiner Utility

LogMiner is a database utility for mining and analysis of the transactions logs stored as database archived log files. The utility independently extracts and rebuilds INSERT and DELETE DML transactions without the need to restore and perform point-in-time database recovery. Historically, LogMiner has been used as the primary tool for repairing logical data corruptions by applying SQL undo (SQL_UNDO) to the target database.

The following sections illustrate the use of Oracle database LogMiner utility as data repair technique by applying SQL_UNDO and SQL_REDO transactions to the target data source.

Create the LogMiner External Data Dictionary

The purpose of the file-based data dictionary is for mapping and translating obscure database objects codes to their corresponding data dictionary names. For example, the table object ID translates to table name and user ID translates to username. The next two steps create the file-based data dictionary.

Step 1: Configure the database parameter UTL_FILE_DEST. This enables PL/SQL write access to the directory specified by the parameter. The parameter is static and requires a database restart.

```
SQL> ALTER SYSTEM SET utl_file_dir='/home/oracle' SCOPE=spfile;
```

```
System altered.
```

```
SQL> conn sys/oracle_4U as sysdba
Connected.
SQL> STARTUP FORCE
ORACLE instance started.
```

```
Total System Global Area    843456512 bytes
Fixed Size                  2233040 bytes
Variable Size               637537584 bytes
Database Buffers            201326592 bytes
Redo Buffers                2359296 bytes
Database mounted.
Database opened.
```

Step 2: Use the DBMS_LOGMNR_D.BUILD procedure to create the file-based data dictionary. The input parameters are the name of the data dictionary file and directory location on the database server as specified by the parameter UTL_FILE_DEST. Ascertain the appropriate write/read operating system file permission settings on the directory specified.

```
SQL> CONN system/oracle_4U
Connected.
SQL>
SQL> BEGIN
  2     DBMS_LOGMNR_D.BUILD (
  3         dictionary_filename => 'T1E2lmdict.ora',
  4         dictionary_location => '/home/oracle');
  5  END;
  6  /
```

```
PL/SQL procedure successfully completed.
```

Build the LogMiner Archived Files Queue

Now, build the list of archived log files using DBMS_LOGMNR.ADD_LOGFILE procedure. Use the option DBMS_LOGMNR.NEW to create the list and add the first archived log file to the queue. Then, use the DBMS_LOGMNR.ADDFILE for the parameter option to add subsequent archived files (transactions logs).

```
SQL> BEGIN
  2      DBMS_LOGMNR.ADD_LOGFILE (
  3          options=>DBMS_LOGMNR.NEW,
  4          logfilename =>
'/d01/app/oracleSE/fast_recovery_area/T1E2/archivelog/2014_02_15/o1_mf_1_114
_9hxplrny_.arc');
  5  END;
  6  /

PL/SQL procedure successfully completed.

SQL> BEGIN
  2      DBMS_LOGMNR.ADD_LOGFILE (
  3          options=>DBMS_LOGMNR.ADDFILE,
  4          logfilename =>
'/d01/app/oracleSE/fast_recovery_area/T1E2/archivelog/2014_02_15/o1_mf_1_115
_9hzk9do8_.arc');
  5  END;
  6  /

PL/SQL procedure successfully completed.
```

Start the LogMiner Engine

Start the LogMiner session using DBMS_LOGMNR.START_LOGMNR procedure. The input of the procedure is the file-based data dictionary. This session reads from the file-based data dictionary and writes to v$logmnr_contents dynamic view.

```
SQL> BEGIN
  2      DBMS_LOGMNR.START_LOGMNR (
  3          dictfilename => '/home/oracle/T1E2lmdict.ora');
  4  END;
  5  /

PL/SQL procedure successfully completed.
```

Retrieve SQL_UNDO and SQL_REDO Transactions

From the same terminal session while the LogMiner session is active, query V$LOGMNR_CONTENT dynamic view to obtain SQL_UNDO and SQL_REDO DML transactions. Use Oracle GoldenGate Out-Of-Sync report details to narrow down the query output.

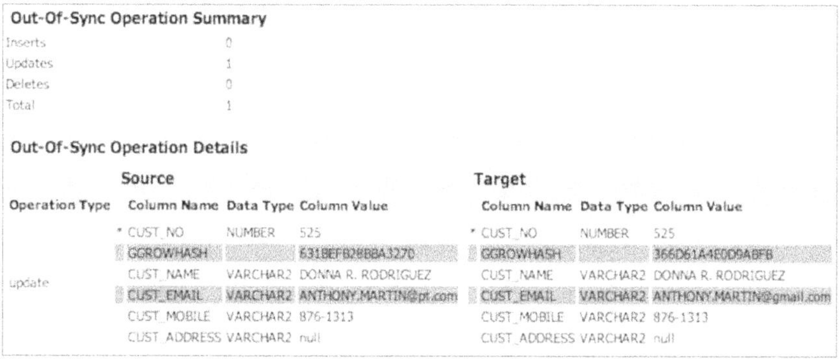

Out-Of-Sync Operation Summary

Inserts	0
Updates	1
Deletes	0
Total	1

Out-Of-Sync Operation Details

	Source			Target		
Operation Type	Column Name	Data Type	Column Value	Column Name	Data Type	Column Value
	* CUST_NO	NUMBER	525	* CUST_NO	NUMBER	525
	GGROWHASH		6318EFB28BBA3270	GGROWHASH		366D61A4E0D9ABFB
update	CUST_NAME	VARCHAR2	DONNA R. RODRIGUEZ	CUST_NAME	VARCHAR2	DONNA R. RODRIGUEZ
	CUST_EMAIL	VARCHAR2	ANTHONY.MARTIN@pt.com	CUST_EMAIL	VARCHAR2	ANTHONY.MARTIN@gmail.com
	CUST_MOBILE	VARCHAR2	876-1313	CUST_MOBILE	VARCHAR2	876-1313
	CUST_ADDRESS	VARCHAR2	null	CUST_ADDRESS	VARCHAR2	null

Figure 6-31a: Out of Sync Operation Summary

The query uses the CUST_EMAIL value in the WHERE clause to retrieve the SQL_UNDO (DELETE) and SQL_REDO (INSERT) statements.

```
SQL> SELECT sql_redo, sql_undo
  2  FROM   v$logmnr_contents
  3  WHERE  sql_undo like ' %DONNA R. RODRIGUEZ%';
```

```
SQL_REDO
----------------------------------------------------------------------------
SQL_UNDO
----------------------------------------------------------------------------
insert into
"OSM$REPAPI"."CUSTOMERS"("CUST_NO","CUST_NAME","CUST_EMAIL","CUST_MO
BILE","CUST_ADDRESS") values ('525','DONNA R.
RODRIGUEZ','ANTHONY.MARTIN@pt.com'
,'876-1313',NULL);
delete from "OSM$REPAPI"."CUSTOMERS" where "CUST_NO" = '525' and "CUST_NAME"
= '
DONNA R. RODRIGUEZ' and "CUST_EMAIL" = 'ANTHONY.MARTIN@pt.com' and
"CUST_MOBILE"
 = '876-1313' and "CUST_ADDRESS" IS NULL and ROWID = 'AAASepAAEAAAAFoABy';

SQL>
```

A possible solution for data repair is to re-apply the transaction by performing SQL_UNDO followed by SQL_REDO on S1E2 (source) database as illustrated next:

```
SQL> delete from "OSM$REPAPI"."CUSTOMERS" where "CUST_NO" = '525' and
"CUST_NAME" = 'DONNA R. RODRIGUEZ' and "CUST_EMAIL" =
'ANTHONY.MARTIN@gmail.com' and
"CUST_MOBILE" = '876-1313' and "CUST_ADDRESS" IS NULL and ROWID =
'AAASepAAEAAAAFoABy'
/

1 row deleted.

SQL> commit;
```

```
Commit complete.

SQL> insert into
"OSM$REPAPI"."CUSTOMERS"("CUST_NO","CUST_NAME","CUST_EMAIL","CUST_MOBILE","C
UST_ADDRESS") values
('525','DONNA R. RODRIGUEZ','ANTHONY.MARTIN@gmail.com','876-1313',NULL)
/
1 row created.

SQL> commit;
Commit complete.
```

End the LogMiner Session

Terminate LogMiner session by executing DBMS_LOGMNR.END_LOGMNR procedure. This stops the LogMiner internal engine.

```
SQL> BEGIN
  2      DBMS_LOGMNR.END_LOGMNR;
  3  END;
  4  /

PL/SQL procedure successfully completed.
```

Figure 6-32 shows the compare pair is in-sync after applying the DML (SQL_UNDO and SQL_REDO) from the LogMiner session.

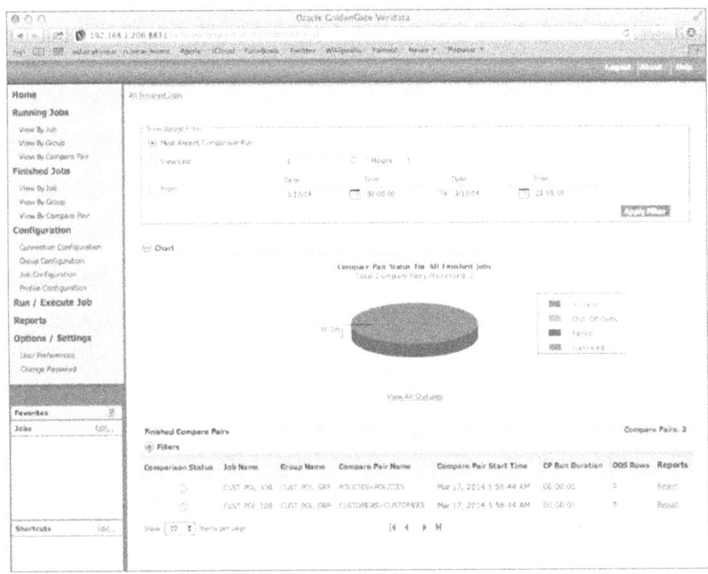

Figure 6-32: Compare Pair In-Sync

Summary

Business continuity relies on data accuracy. It is crucial to discover, as early as possible, any kind of data discrepancies when using Oracle GoldenGate for high availability, disaster recovery and near zero-downtime migration, and upgrade configurations. In general, a bi-directional topology needs an online comparison tool to detect out-of-sync data sets so that a repair solution is developed and adapted quickly.

This chapter has covered the details of implementing Oracle GoldenGate Veridata for data comparison and introduced one of the database data repair utilities, the Oracle LogMiner utility.

This implementation requires performing the following activities:

- Configure Veridata agents for data fetching from source and target database
- Configure Oracle GoldenGate Veridata Database Repository
- Install Oracle GoldenGate Veridata agents and server components
- Perform Tomcat web server fundamental tasks
- Configure Veridata components, connections, groups, jobs, and profiles
- Run compare jobs and view out-of-sync (OOS) tables
- Configure and execute Oracle LogMiner for data repair

The use of integrated systems requires using certified components only. Oracle GoldenGate Veridata server and agents must be certified on the host operating system and database.

Since Oracle GoldenGate Veridata does not carry out-of-sync data repair, the chapter covered Oracle database LogMiner as data repair techniques to complement Veridata. Given out-of-sync data is available and well organized in XML format, in-house developed utilities should be considered to handle consistent out-of-sync patterns.

The next chapter is a core function of Oracle GoldenGate. It is the near zero-downtime migration and upgrade technique. Oracle GoldenGate Veridata plays a crucial role in verifying no data discrepancies. It verifies the whole data sets of the two databases are identical before the database administrator disconnects users from the current system and moves them to the target system.

Near Zero-Downtime Database Migration and Upgrade

CHAPTER

Overview

The need to continue processing transactions while performing major tasks on the 24/7 production database server is becoming a necessity for Oracle installations running core business applications and mission critical systems. The objective of this chapter is to cover the techniques of using Oracle GoldenGate and Oracle Database technologies to perform an end-to-end database migration and upgrade with a flexible failback option — leaving no impact on business continuity to achieve near zero-downtime of database availability.

For mission critical systems, an Oracle Database upgrade is a strategic activity, and the upgrade project plan must be developed in accordance to Oracle's software policy life cycle. Database administrators must be aware of Oracle policy milestones and plan their upgrade project, accordingly. This keeps their database releases current with Oracle supported platforms for applying patches and avoiding the addition of premium support services fees. Nevertheless, the upgraded database should take advantage of Oracle software new release features and innovations which transparently enhances the database's functionality, performance, and security.

The near zero-downtime migration and upgrade activities are divided into a series of related phases. Each of the phases is composed of (7) tasks for completion.
The list of phases and their brief description are:

1. Deploy Oracle GoldenGate
2. Online Clone of the Production Database
3. Migrate to Automatic Storage Management
4. Upgrade to Oracle Database 12c
5. Applications Regressions Testing
6. Synchronize the Target Database
7. Data Verification

Though a merge of phases 2 and 3 is possible, this chapter illustrates them as two separate phases. The order of phase 3 and 4 is also exchangeable. This chapter adapts the order listed above — performing migration first then upgrade of the database.

However, Phase 5 is application specific and out of the scope of the book, but will be discussed briefly.

Deploy Oracle GoldenGate

Oracle GoldenGate is deployed as unidirectional topology — and the data flows from the source system (production) to the target system. The primary extracts create local trail files while the secondary extracts (data pumps) ship the transactions to the target system. Note that no transformations are performed on either extracts. The manager process on the source system is configured to optimize the storage level by purging local trail files upon being successfully shipped to the target system.

The remote trail files are maintained on the target system until the database upgrade is completed and ready to synchronize the target database — aiming for a sub-second latency in preparation of the application transition phase.

Online Clone of the Production Database

Cloning the database is the key for a near zero-downtime database upgrade project. It serves two purposes:

1. As an initial-load technique from an active database
2. Eliminates the various types of downtimes

The total database downtime is affected by two time factors: the timeframe of the database upgrade assistant (DBUA) to successfully upgrade the database and the timeframe of the applications' functional and technical testing.

By cloning the database, you avoid the DBUA shutting down the production database required during the database dictionary upgrade. At the same time, it develops a highly reliable and compatible platform for applications testing. The clone is performed using the Oracle Recovery Manager (RMAN) command-line with the Linux Network File System (NFS) and is configured to allow file sharing by RMAN between the source and target systems.

Migrate to Automatic Storage Management

It seems Oracle Automatic Storage Management (ASM) is a strategic direction for Oracle database storage. The migration from the file system to the ASM requires the provision of ASM disks by the storage administrator. For the purpose of the implementation, ASM disks are simulated by creating a raw files type using the Linux operating system "dd" command. This is an optional phase but highly recommended to be considered and can be executed using either Oracle Recovery Manager (RMAN) or Oracle Enterprise Manager Database control. We will use RMAN to complete the migration from a file system to an automatic storage management (ASM) environment.

Upgrade to Oracle Database 12c

The upgrade to Oracle Database 12c is executed on the cloned database. Oracle Database 12c binaries are installed on a separate software location (home). Prerequisites are verified in preparation of launching the Database Upgrade Assistant (DBUA). DBUA has two upgrade techniques — Graphical User Interface (GUI) and command-line. We will be using the recommended approach, GUI. The database is restarted to operate on archive log mode and the database flashback is enabled.

Applications Regressions Testing

There are two types of testing — technical and functional. For technical testing, adaption of the Oracle Real Applications Testing (RAT) Suite produces highly accurate and quick results. The functional testing is more time consuming. This is due to a complete transaction cycle testing followed by reports generation. It is preferred to conduct both tests on the cloned database to produce highly realistic results. The cloned database flashback feature is enabled for rewinding the database to remove data entered during the functional testing phase.

Synchronize the Target Database

It is necessary to flashback the target database after the functional testing is completed. The flashback rewinds the database to the system change number (SCN) as calculated by the RMAN *clone* command. The next step is to apply the remote trail files by starting the Replicat processes from the system change number calculated by RMAN. This avoids the overhead of data collision, if enabled, and Replicat terminates with errors due to duplicate records. Depending on the size of the remote trail, the number of Replicat configured and the current transaction volume, the timeframe to each the sub-second delay varies. This is necessary to achieve before the application transition phase begins.

Data Verification

Now that the Replicats have applied the transactions to the target database, it is time to verify data integrity and accuracy. Configure and deploy Oracle GoldenGate Veridata for data sets confirmation. The applications servers must be disconnected for a short period of time to allow the last streams of transactions to be applied to the target database, and this where the near zero-downtime occurs. Execute Oracle GoldenGate Veridata jobs to confirm all data sets are in "in-sync status", then route the application servers to the new database.

Migration Technical Architecture

Near zero-downtime migrations and upgrades from Oracle Database 11g to Oracle Database 12c is depicted in Figure 7-1. There are several major components to develop and execute for each phase. The Oracle technologies used to complete the migration and upgrade are:

- Oracle GoldenGate 12c
- Oracle GoldenGate 11g Veridata
- Oracle Database Automatic Storage Management (ASM)
- Oracle Database Recovery Manager (RMAN)
- Oracle Database Configuration Assistant (DBCA)
- Oracle Database Upgrade Assistant (DBUA)
- Oracle Database Flashback Technology
- Oracle Database Real Application Testing (RAT)

Keep in mind, depending on the scope of the project, some of the above components may become optional or adapted using alternative technologies. Since this chapter covers Oracle-to-Oracle Database upgrade, only the above list of Oracle components are adapted.

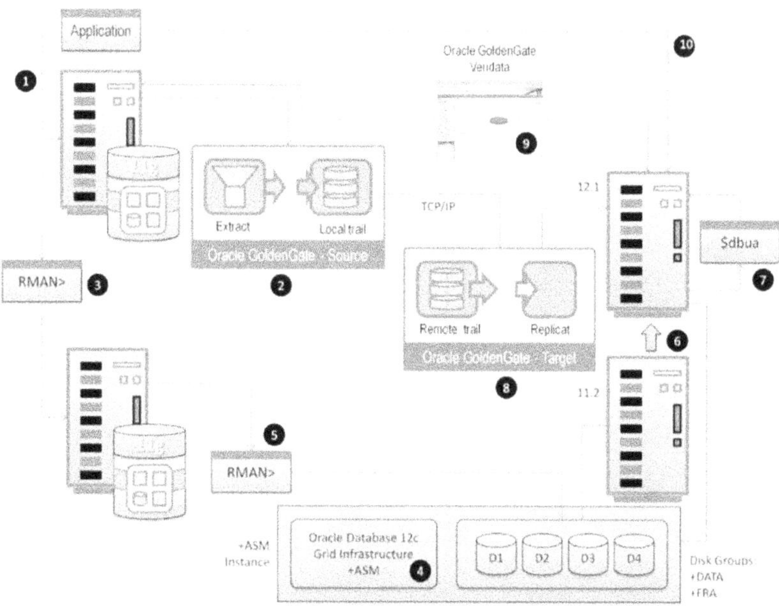

Figure 7-1: Near Zero-Downtime Migration and Upgrade Architecture

Figure 7-1 illustrates highly available applications running on the production system (Source – S1E2 database). Oracle GoldenGate unidirectional configuration is employed. The primary extracts work to capture the transaction logs and the data pumps send the data to the new remote system (Target). Oracle Database 12c Automatic Storage Management (ASM) instance manages database storage (Disk Groups). Online cloning of the production database leaves this database intact and avoids downtimes during the database data dictionary upgrade. Oracle Database 12c software is installed on the target system and the upgrade of the database is executed using DBUA.

The Replicat applies the remote trail files starting from the System Change Number (SCN) identified by the Oracle Recovery Manager (RMAN) "*duplicate*" command. Oracle GoldenGate Veridata ascertains the source and target database are identical before diverting the applications from the source to the target database.

Transactions Workload Simulator

The ultimate goal of this chapter is to implement near zero-downtime migration and upgrade using Oracle GoldenGate while users are concurrently processing business transactions. Hence, the transactions simulator, *trnas_load*, will remain running on the production system (S1E2 instance) until the upgrade is completed then interrupted and redirected to the target system (T1E2 instance). Oracle GoldenGate is deployed to capture and ship transactions to the target system in preparation of being applied after successfully upgrading Oracle Database 11g to Oracle Database 12c.

We start by opening a terminal window and execute the following anonymous PL/SQL block on the source system (production).

Note! *Do not close this terminal window. It must remain open for the duration of the migration and upgrade tasks.*

```
SQL> CONN osm$repapi/oracle

Connected.

SQL> DESC trans_load

PROCEDURE trans_load
 Argument Name                  Type                    In/Out Default?
 ------------------------------ ----------------------- ------ --------
 PLOAD_LEVEL                    NUMBER                  IN     DEFAULT
 PSTARTFROM                     NUMBER                  IN     DEFAULT

SQL> BEGIN
       FOR i IN 100001..1000000 LOOP
           TRANS_LOAD(1, i);
           DBMS_LOCK.SLEEP(2);
       END LOOP;
    END;
    /
```

Using the procedure DBMS_LOCK.SLEEP(2) allows an elapsed time of a two seconds delay for every transaction. The above transaction volume should last for the duration of the upgrade. Our objective is to ultimately interrupt the load simulator *trans_load* explicitly and move it to the migrated and upgraded environment.

Now let's look at deploying Oracle Goldengate.

Phase I: Deploy Oracle GoldenGate

Successfully deploying Oracle GoldenGate is a key requirement for a near zero-downtime migration and upgrade. While the applications continue to deliver business transactions, Oracle GoldenGate captures the transaction logs and sends data to the target system.

For applications with complex database design such as enterprise ERP where it is challenging to maintain the order of foreign keys referential integrity constraints, you are required that the target database foreign key constraints remain disabled during the synchronization process and successfully enabled before the applications are redirected to the new database. The disable/enable foreign key constraints step is developed using database scripts generated from the database dictionary.

Figure 7-2 shows Oracle GoldenGate deployed as a unidirectional classical capture configuration. Another alternative is to employ Oracle GoldenGate integrated capture where Oracle GoldenGate is installable on a downstream system. This avoids additional overhead to the production server as a result of the transaction logs capture processing and local trail storage. Refer to Chapter 10 for details regarding Oracle GoldenGate integrated capture implementation.

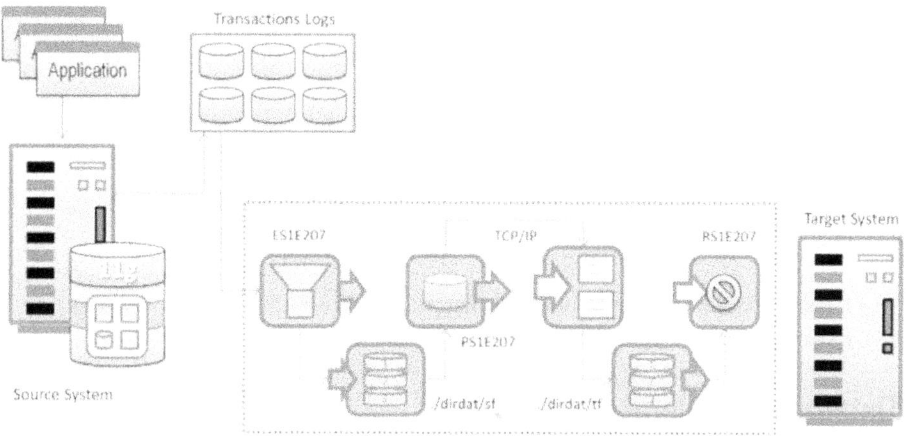

Figure 7-2: Oracle GoldenGate Unidirectional Setup

The configuration is composed of one or more primary extracts and one or more secondary extracts (data pumps). The primary extracts read the transaction logs for the configured list of database tables and create the corresponding local trails. The data pump extracts, over TCP/IP, ship the data to the remote system which creates corresponding remote trails. The Replicat processes remain stopped until the target database (cloned) is upgraded from Oracle Database 11g to Oracle Database 12c. Though the use of data pumps is optional, it is highly recommended for near zero-downtime implementation to eliminate production server overhead in the event of network unavailability to the target system. In a nutshell, phase I consists of the following tasks:

1. Oracle GoldenGate Software Installation
2. Preparation of the Source Database

3. Enable Table-Level Logging
4. Configure and Test Capture, Route, and Delivery
5. Start Primary Extract (ES1E207)
6. Start Data Pump Extract (PS1E207)

Oracle GoldenGate Software Installation

Successful installation of Oracle GoldenGate on the source (production) and target system must be completed to proceed further in your migration, and you must always consider the platform architecture.

This chapter uses Oracle GoldenGate 12c for Oracle Database 11g 64-bit. The same bundle of Oracle GoldenGate 12c is used for Oracle Database 12c 64-bit. Refer to Chapter 2 to learn about installing Oracle GoldenGate 12c.

Preparation of the Source Database

Prior to configuring Oracle GoldenGate Extracts and Replicats, the following database related tasks must be completed:

- Enable Database Supplemental Logging
- Create Oracle GoldenGate Database User

Database Supplemental Logging

Since the database supplemental logging is not enabled by default when the database is created, it is necessary to enable the minimum database supplemental logging – manually. The database supplemental logging records the primary key information for update and delete operations. Oracle GoldenGate locates the target row to update or delete on the target database using the primary key.

Query the data dictionary dynamic view *v$database* view to find out your level of supplemental logging.

```
S1E2> SELECT supplemental_log_data_min "Minimum",
   2         supplemental_log_data_pk  "Primary key",
   3         supplemental_log_data_ui  "Unique Key",
   4         supplemental_log_data_fk  "Foregin Key",
   5         supplemental_log_data_all "All"
   6  FROM   v$database;

Minimum  Pri Uni For All
-------- --- --- --- ---
NO       NO  NO  NO  NO

S1E2>
```

Refer to Chapter 1 for more details regarding supplemental logging.

The Oracle GoldenGate Database User

The use of a dedicated database user for Oracle GoldenGate is highly recommended, and you should avoid using an existing active database user. This user requires database privileges listed on Table 7-1.

Database Privilege	Source Database	Target Database
CREATE SESSION, ALTER SESSION	X	X
RESOURCE	X	X
CONNECT	X	X
SELECT ANY DICTIONARY	X	X
FLASHBACK ANY TABLE or FLASHBACK ON<owner.table>	X	
SELECT ANY TABLE or SELECT ON <owner.table>	X	X
INSERT, UPDATE, DELETE ON <target.table>		X
CREATE TABLE		X
EXECUTE on DBMS_FLASHBACK package	X	

Table 7-1: Database Privileges

Refer to Chapter 2 for more details regarding creating an Oracle GoldenGate database user.

Enabling Table-Level Logging

Table-Level is added from Oracle GoldenGate GGSCI command-line interface. The command *add trandata* adds table-level logging using different techniques:

- Specify the schema and table name
- Specify the schema followed by the Oracle GoldenGate wildcard character
- Execute *add trandata* using an obey file

The *add trandata* command requires login to the database from within GGSCI.

```
GGSCI (ggs-source) 1> DBLOGIN USERID ggs_admin, PASSWORD oracle
Successfully logged into database.

GGSCI (ggs-source) 2>
```

Refer to Chapter 2 for more details regarding adding table-level logging.

Configure and Test Capture, Route, and Delivery

At this point, the source database has been successfully prepared for Oracle GoldenGate capture. The configuration uses a data pump process to send data to the target system.

This enables the capture process to continue operating in the event that the target system becomes unreachable for a considerable timeframe. It also offloads the primary extract from TCP/IP communications with the target's server collector. The primary process becomes dedicated to capturing and creating the local trail only. The data pump process continues resending data up on the restoration of the network.

The next three sections implement the configuration. The delivery process remains stopped until the database upgrade is successfully completed and is ready to apply transactions to the target database.

- Configure the Primary Extract
- Configure the Secondary Extract
- Configure the Replicat

We begin by analyzing the database schemas and their tables. This enables the capture of schema by schema, mapping extract to schema and identifying unsupported data types. The following configuration uses the schema OSM$REPAPI.

```
SQL> SELECT table_name
  2  FROM   user_tables;

TABLE_NAME
------------------------------
RANDOM_DOMAIN
RANDOM_FIRST
RANDOM_MIDDLE
RANDOM_LAST
POLICY_TYPES
DISCOUNT_TYPES
CUSTOMERS
POLICIES
OSM_DOCUMENTS

9 rows selected.
```

Configure the Primary Extract

As we know, the primary extract reads the transaction logs (the "captures") and writes to the local trail. The extract begins capture from the time it is successfully created or altered to begin immediately before starting the database cloning task. Then, it continues to capture while the database upgrade is in progress.

We need to prepare the primary extract parameter file. It identifies the local trail and the list of target tables. For near zero-downtime implementation, the inclusion of all tables is likely required. However, to exclude specific tables, use the parameter *tableexeclude* followed by the list of tables to include. The *table* parameter uses the Oracle GoldenGate wildcard pattern represented by *osm$repapi.** to include the remaining tables.

```
EXTRACT es1e207
SETENV (ORACLE_SID="S1E2")
SETENV (ORACLE_HOME="/u01/app/oracle/product/11.2.0/dbhome_1")
SETENV (NLS_LANG="AMERICAN_AMERICA.AL32UTF8")
USERID ggs_admin, PASSWORD oracle
EXTTRAIL ./dirdat/sf
TABLEEXCLUDE osm$repapi.OSM_DOCUMENTS;
TABLE osm$repapi.*;
```

Next, we create the primary extract ES1E207. Since it is a single-instance database, the parameter THREADS 1 is specified. The extract starts transaction logs capture upon being successfully created, but it may be altered to begin capture just before the database cloning begins.

```
GGSCI (ggs-source) 4> ADD EXTRACT es1e207, TRANLOG, BEGIN now, THREADS 1
EXTRACT added.
```

Associate the primary extract ES1E207 to its local trail. Specify the maximum size of the local trail file. The default size is 100MB.

```
GGSCI (ggs-source) 6> ADD EXTTRAIL ./dirdat/sf, EXTRACT es1e207, MEGABYTES
16
EXTTRAIL added.
```

Configure the Secondary Extract

It is highly recommended that you configure the secondary extracts – the data pumps. We start by preparing the parameter file. Since no transformation is required, we specify the parameter *passthru* mode. The target system is specified by the parameter *rmthost*, followed by the Oracle GoldenGate manager listening port. Use the same *tableexeclude* and *table* parameters to identify the list of tables.

```
EXTRACT psle207
USERID ggs_admin, PASSWORD oracle
PASSTHRU
RMTHOST 192.168.1.209, MGRPORT 7812
RMTTRAIL ./dirdat/tf
TABLEEXCLUDE osm$repapi.OSM_DOCUMENTS;
TABLE osm$repapi.*;
```

Below we create the data pump extract. The data pump will read the local trail and send the replicated data to the remote system.

```
GGSCI (ggs-source) 5> ADD EXTRACT psle207, EXTTRAILSOURCE ./dirdat/sf
EXTRACT added.
```

Next, we associate the data pump extract with its remote trail. Note that we specify the maximum size of the local trail file, and that the default size is 100 MB. To re-attempt applying the transaction to the target database, we need to make sure that we do not configure the purge of the remote trail files until the database upgrade is completed.

```
GGSCI (ggs-source) 6> ADD RMTTRAIL ./dirdat/tf, EXTRACT psle207, MEGABYTES
16
RMTTRAIL added.
```

Configure the Replicat

Now, er prepare the Replicat parameter file. Since the Replicat requires a database table for a checkpoint, an initial database is created for testing the Replicat. Since database cloning is treated as the technique for initial data load, do not include the *handlecollisions* parameter. Rather, alter the Replicat to begin applying transactions using the System Change Number (SCN) of the database cloning. This saves unnecessary data collision overhead.

```
REPLICAT rsle207
SETENV (ORACLE_SID="T1C2")
SETENV (ORACLE_HOME="/u01/app/oracle/product/11.2.0/dbhome_1")
SETENV (NLS_LANG="AMERICAN_AMERICA.AL32UTF8")
USERID ggs_admin, PASSWORD oracle
ASSUMETARGETDEFS
DISCARDFILE ./dirrpt/rsle207.dsc, PURGE
MAPEXCLUDE osm$repapi.OSM_DOCUMENTS;
MAP osm$repapi., TARGET osm$repapi.*;
```

```
GGSCI (ggs-target) 3> ADD REPLICAT rsle207, EXTTRAIL ./dirdat/tf
REPLICAT added.
```

Next, we start the primary and secondary extracts. The Replicat remains stopped until the database upgrade is successfully completed.

Start the Primary Extract, ES1E207

Now, we start the primary extract. Make the status as RUNNING and it updates the checkpoint timestamp.

```
GGSCI (ggs-source) 31> START EXTRACT es1e207

Sending START request to MANAGER ...
EXTRACT ES1E207 starting

GGSCI (ggs-source) 32> INFO EXTRACT es1e207

EXTRACT    ES1E207   Last Started 2014-04-11 11:24   Status RUNNING
Checkpoint Lag       00:00:02 (updated 00:00:09 ago)
Process ID           32142
Log Read Checkpoint  Oracle Redo Logs
                     2014-04-11 11:25:11  Thread 1, Seqno 92, RBA 1688972
                     SCN 0.3623058 (3623058)
```

Start the Data Pump Extract, PS1E207

Next, we start the data pump extract. Make the status as RUNNING and it updates the checkpoint timestamp.

```
GGSCI (ggs-source) 33> START EXTRACT ps1e207

Sending START request to MANAGER ...
EXTRACT PS1E207 starting

GGSCI (ggs-source) 34> INFO EXTRACT ps1e207

EXTRACT    PS1E207   Last Started 2014-04-11 11:25   Status RUNNING
Checkpoint Lag       00:00:00 (updated 00:01:31 ago)
Process ID           32216
Log Read Checkpoint  File ./dirdat/sf000000
                     2014-04-11 11:24:22.000000  RBA 491227
```

Verify the Remote Trail

Next we use the Oracle GoldenGate Logdump utility to ascertain that the transactions have been captured and sent to the target system.

```
$ ls -al
total 476
drwxr-x---  2 oracle oinstall   4096 Apr 11 17:35 .
drwxr-xr-x 28 oracle oinstall   4096 Apr  1 23:42 ..
-rw-r-----  1 oracle oinstall 474974 Apr 11 17:37 tf000000
```

The following displays transaction details using the Oracle GoldenGate Logdump utility. We will perform this same verification on several remote trail files.

Open the Current Remote Trail File

Open the trail file and use the Logdump utility to open one trail file at a time.

```
Logdump 3 >OPEN ./dirdat/tf000000
Current LogTrail is /u01/app/ggs/12.1.0/gghome_1/dirdat/tf000000
```

Display Transactions Summary

Display summary details. Each trail file indicates the total number of records and each type of DML size.

```
Logdump 4 >COUNT
LogTrail /u01/app/ggs/12.1.0/gghome_1/dirdat/tf000000 has 2017 records
Total Data Bytes              244700
  Avg Bytes/Record               121
Insert                          2016
Others                             1
After Images                    2016

Average of 2017 Transactions
    Bytes/Trans .....          169
    Records/Trans ...            1
    Files/Trans .....            1

Logdump 5 >
```

Table-Level Transaction Details

This is an important Logdump utility command. Below we see how it shows specifics for each table, with all DML transaction details.

```
Logdump 6 >COUNT, DETAIL
LogTrail /u01/app/ggs/12.1.0/gghome_1/dirdat/tf000000 has 2017 records
Total Data Bytes              244700
  Avg Bytes/Record               121
Insert                          2016
Others                             1
After Images                    2016

Average of 2017 Transactions
    Bytes/Trans .....          169
    Records/Trans ...            1
    Files/Trans .....            1

*FileHeader*                                              Partition 0
```

```
Total Data Bytes              1456
  Avg Bytes/Record            1456
Others                           1

OSM$REPAPI.CUSTOMERS                                Partition 4
Total Data Bytes             97326
  Avg Bytes/Record              96
Insert                        1008
After Images                  1008

OSM$REPAPI.POLICIES                                 Partition 4
Total Data Bytes            145918
  Avg Bytes/Record             144
Insert                        1008
After Images                  1008
```

From within the Logdump command line, type help to display the list of options and operations that are available.

Phase II: Online Clone of the Source Database

Achieving near zero-downtime upgrade requires cloning the source database, which is an image copy of the database at a timestamp referred to as the System Change Number (SCN). The primary purpose of cloning the source database is to avoid a production database shutdown by the Database Upgrade Assistant (DBUA) during the database data dictionary upgrade.

There are several techniques for cloning the database. However, this chapter employs the Oracle Recovery Manager (RMAN) DUPLICATE command to clone the database S1E2 and create the target database T1C1. The database clone is an online operation. It does not incur the source database shutdown.

The adaption of RMAN to clone the source database allows the customization of the target database physical structure, such as:

- Exclusion of read-only tablespaces.
- Exclusion of named tablespaces; such as testing environment tablespaces, or inclusion of list of named tablespaces.
- Open the target database on RESTRICTED SESSION; the default, the target database is opened on READ/WRITE mode.
- Clone without applying archived redo log files.

Figure 7-3 represents a clone database from the source to target system.

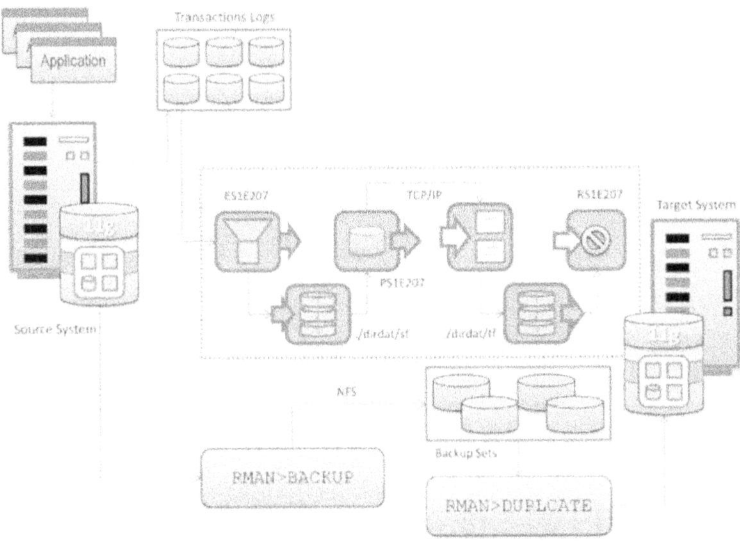

Figure 7-3: Database Cloning to Target System using RMAN

The cloned database uses a different unique Database Identifier (DBID) from the source database. Cloning the database is performed either from a backup or from an active database instance. It is created on the same system or remotely. The cloned database is one of the initial data load techniques. It includes the complete contents of the database. There are four techniques for cloning the database:

1. From an active database connected to the source and target instances
2. From a backup connected to the source and target instances
3. From a backup connected to the target instance and recovery catalog
4. From a backup connected to the target instance

This chapter uses technique 2 : from a backup connected to the source and target instances. The database and archive log files source database backup is completed using RMAN. Using Linux File System (NFS), the backup directory is shared on the remote system.

When database cloning is performed outside of this context, the source database/ instance is referred to as the 'Target' and the target database/instance is referred to as the 'Auxiliary'.

Another option of cloning the database is using Oracle Enterprise Manager Database Control (OEM). This is a Graphical User Interface (GUI) and commonly used by less experienced Database Administrators (DBA). Figure 7-4 represents cloning the database using OEM.

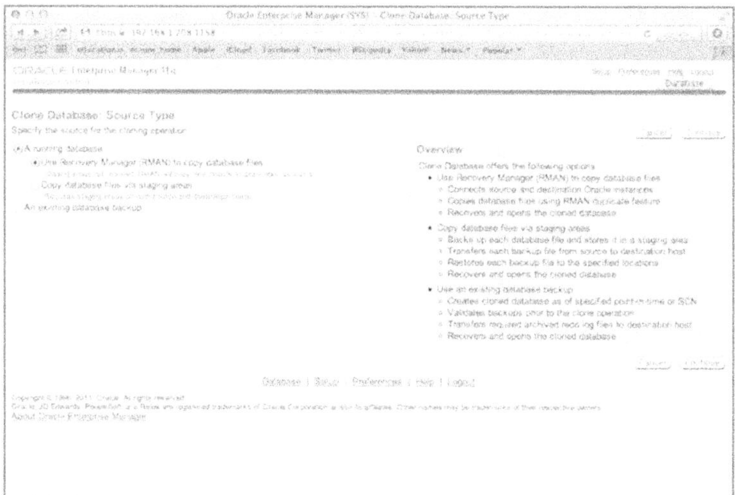

Figure 7-4: Database Cloning using Oracle Enterprise Manager (OEM)

Since the cloned database is created on a different system, configuring the Linux Network File System server and client is illustrated first.

Installing Oracle Database 11g

The database clone on a separate system requires the installation of Oracle Database 11g on the target system. The cloned database delivers three functions:

- Initial Data Load from an Active Source Database
- Migration and Upgrade Platform
- Application Testing Platform

Install Oracle Database 11g software only. Do not attempt to create the target database, as it will be created as a cloned database. Figure 7-5 shows Oracle Database 11g Universal Installer. In Step 3 of 10, select the 'install database software only'.

Remember, the installation of Oracle Database 11g requires adjusting the Operating System Kernel parameters as per the installation's guide. Another alternative is to simply copy the Kernel parameter file from the source system. Then activate the new parameters using the Operating System command – *sysctl*, as shown below.

```
# scp /etc/sysctl.conf root@192.168.1.209:/etc
# /sbin/sysctl -p
```

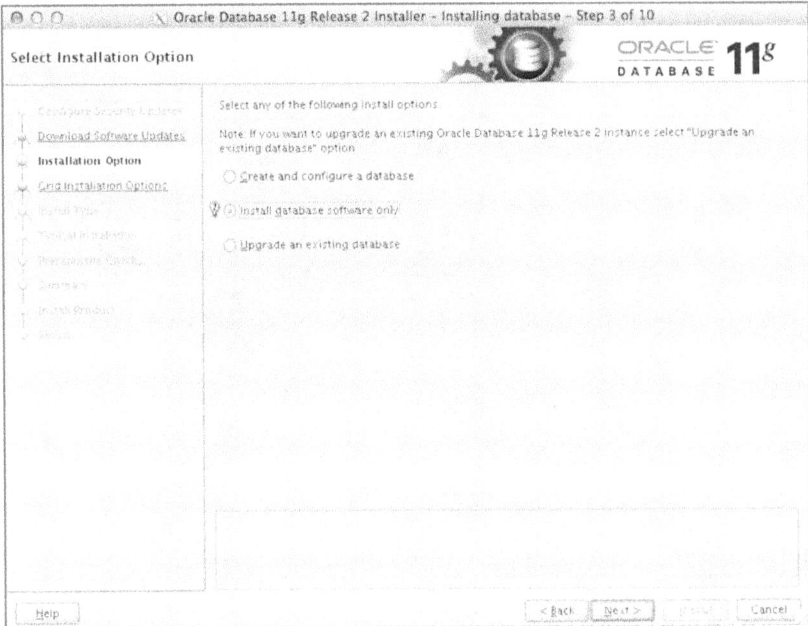

Figure 7-5: Oracle Database 11g Installation

Configure Linux Network File System

The purpose of configuring the Network File System (NFS) is to allow the target system to share directories (mount points) on the source system as if it is stored on the local system storage. This enables quick access to the backup files created by RMAN on the source system database when creating a backup-based clone database.

Considering the source system IP address is 192.168.1.213/192.168.1.208 and the target system is 192.168.1.214/192.168.1.209, execute the steps as follows:

Source System (Server)

Login as root user and execute the steps below.

- Create the shared directory used for RMAN backup files destination.

```
# mkdir -p /home/oracle/backup
# cd /home/oracle
# chown -R oracle:oinstall backup
```

- Allow the target system to mount the directory by modifying the file '/etc/exports.' Add the below line indicating the client IP address and allowed mount options.

```
/home/oracle/backup    192.168.1.214 (rw, sync)
```

- Restart NFS services to activate the configuration.

```
# /sbin/service nfs restart
Shutting down NFS mountd:                               [  OK  ]
Shutting down NFS daemon:                               [  OK  ]
Shutting down NFS quotas:                               [  OK  ]
Shutting down NFS services:                             [  OK  ]
Starting NFS services:                                  [  OK  ]
Starting NFS quotas:                                    [  OK  ]
Starting NFS daemon:                                    [  OK  ]
Starting NFS mountd:                                    [  OK  ]
# /sbin/service portmap restart
Stopping portmap:                                       [  OK  ]
Starting portmap:                                       [  OK  ]
#
```

- Verify NFS configuration settings.

```
# /usr/sbin/showmount -e 192.168.1.213
```

Target System (Client)

We login as the *root* user and execute the steps below.

- Create the directory used for RMAN backup files destination

```
# mkdir -p /home/oracle/backup
# cd /home/oracle
# chown -R oracle:oinstall backup
```

- Mount the directory '/home/oracle/backup' on the source system. Specify the IP address of the server followed by the source and target shared directory.

```
# mount -t nfs 192.168.1.213:/home/oracle/backup /home/oracle/backup
```

- Run the RMAN *backup* command to test NFS setup by specifying the backup location as the NFS mounted directory '/home/oracle/backup.'

```
$ rman

Recovery Manager: Release 11.2.0.3.0 - Production on Sat Apr 12 09:48:44
2014

Copyright (c) 1982, 2011, Oracle and/or its affiliates.  All rights
reserved.

RMAN> CONNECT TARGET

connected to target database: S1E2 (DBID=4279993164)

RMAN> BACKUP TABLESPACE users
2> FORMAT '/home/oracle/backup/user_%U.dbf';

Starting backup at 12-APR-14
using channel ORA_DISK_1
channel ORA_DISK_1: starting full datafile backup set
channel ORA_DISK_1: specifying datafile(s) in backup set
input datafile file number=00004
name=/u01/app/oracle/oradata/S1E2/users01.dbf
channel ORA_DISK_1: starting piece 1 at 12-APR-14
channel ORA_DISK_1: finished piece 1 at 12-APR-14
piece handle=/home/oracle/backup/user_03p5hkkf_1_1.dbf
tag=TAG20140412T095111 comment=NONE
channel ORA_DISK_1: backup set complete, elapsed time: 00:00:12
Finished backup at 12-APR-14
```

- Next, we verify RMAN backup is created on the target system, and we change the permission on the backup directory to avoid permission denied by the operating system during the restore operation.

```
$ cd /home/oracle/backup
$ ls -al
total 100404
drwxrwxrwx 2    500      501       4096 Apr 12 08:51 .
drwx------ 4 oracle oinstall       4096 Apr 12 00:56 ..
-rw-r----- 1    500      501 102694912 Apr 12 08:51 user_03p5hkkf_1_1.dbf
$ chown oracle:oinstall *
```

Creating a Backup-Based Clone Database

A backup-based clone database uses an online backup of the database files plus the archived redo log files. Since the target database (clone) is located on a separate system, we override the default backup destination, Fast Recovery Area (FRA). Use the FORMAT parameter to specify a shared directory configured using the Network File System (NFS). The NFS shared directory ensures the backup is immediately available for the RMAN *duplicate* command to clone the database.

The following RMAN script performs an online backup of the database and archived log files. It begins by allocating three channels to enable backup parallelism. The script begins backup of the database files, followed by the archived log files.

Both backups are written to the destination '/home/oracle/backup' accessible by the target system as an NFS mounted directory. Upon successful completion of the backup, the channels allocated are released.

Connect using the *target* option which designates the source database. Verify the database name and DBID returned.

```
RMAN> CONNECT TARGET

connected to target database: S1E2 (DBID=4279993164)

RMAN> RUN {
2> ALLOCATE CHANNEL c1 TYPE DISK;
3> ALLOCATE CHANNEL c2 TYPE DISK;
4> ALLOCATE CHANNEL c3 TYPE DISK;
5>    BACKUP DATABASE INCLUDE CURRENT CONTROLFILE
6>    FORMAT '/home/oracle/backup/db_bck_%U.dbf';
7>    SQL 'ALTER SYSTEM SWITCH LOGFILE';
8>    BACKUP ARCHIVELOG ALL
9>    FORMAT '/home/oracle/backup/db_bck_%U.arc';
10> RELEASE CHANNEL c1;
11> RELEASE CHANNEL c2;
12> RELEASE CHANNEL c3;
13> }
```

From the target system, we verify that the newly created backup and backup files owner, group, and global permission are set correctly. Otherwise, we manually execute the operating system shell commands 'chown' and 'chmod' for correcting the backup files permission and owner settings.

```
# cd /home/oracle/backup
# chown oracle:oinstall *; chmod 777 *
```

Backup File Name Format

The backup files created must be unique, an error is returned when the Recovery Manager (RMAN) tries to overwrite an existing file. The above script uses the substitution variable %U, this ascertains unique backup files names are generated. Other combination of substitution variables are available, but must be combined carefully to produce unique files names. The substitution variable %U combines the substitution variables %u, %p and %c.

As shown in Figure 7-6, the clone database is divided into 3 related phases:

1. Configure the Target Instance
2. Start the Target Instance in NOMOUNT Mode
3. Perform Clone Database using RMAN

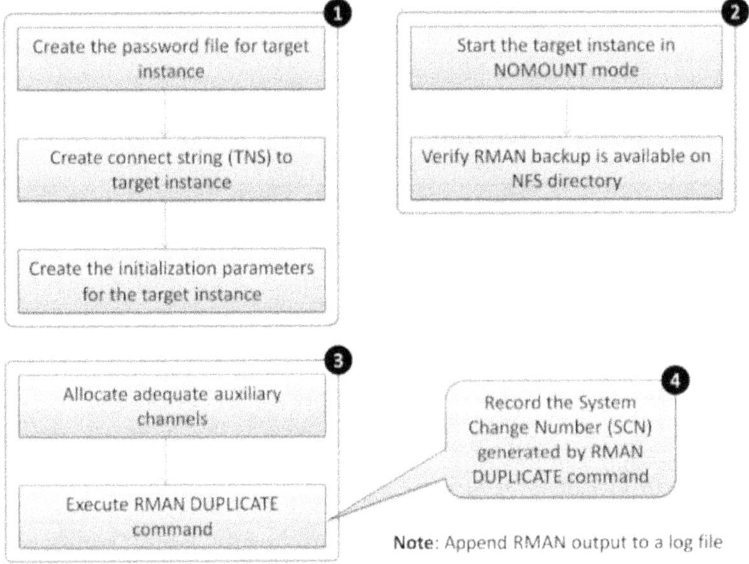

Figure 7-6: Clone Database from Backup

Configure the Target Instance

The configuration prepares the target instance for database cloning. Use the Oracle password utility *orapwd* command to create the password file, the Oracle NETMGR, or NETCA utility to create the TNS database connect string and create the parameter file, 'initS1E2.ora'.

- Create the password file on the default location $ORACLE_HOME/dbs

```
$ pwd
/u01/app/oracle/product/11.2.0/dbhome_1/dbs
$ orapwd file=orapwT1C1.ora password=oracle_4U force=y
$ ls
init.ora  orapwT1C1.ora
```

- Create the listener on the target system then create the database connect strings from source to target and vice versa. Test the database connect strings using Oracle *tnsping* utility command.

Source to Target Connect String Testing

```
$ tnsping T1C1

TNS Ping Utility for Linux: Version 11.2.0.3.0 - Production on 18-APR-2014
03:08:06

Copyright (c) 1997, 2011, Oracle.  All rights reserved.

Used parameter files:

Used TNSNAMES adapter to resolve the alias
Attempting to contact (DESCRIPTION = (ADDRESS_LIST = (ADDRESS = (PROTOCOL =
TCP)(HOST = 192.168.1.209)(PORT = 1521))) (CONNECT_DATA = (SERVICE_NAME =
T1C1.precisetrace.com)))
OK (40 msec)
[oracle@ggs-source ~]$

Target to Source Connect String Testing

$ tnsping S1E2

TNS Ping Utility for Linux: Version 11.2.0.3.0 - Production on 18-APR-2014
10:09:57

Copyright (c) 1997, 2011, Oracle.  All rights reserved.

Used parameter files:

Used TNSNAMES adapter to resolve the alias
Attempting to contact (DESCRIPTION = (ADDRESS_LIST = (ADDRESS = (PROTOCOL =
TCP)(HOST = 192.168.1.208)(PORT = 1521))) (CONNECT_DATA = (SERVICE_NAME =
S1E2.precisetrace.com)))
OK (10 msec)
```

- Create the target parameter file from the source database instance then modify it to the suite of the target database.

```
SQL> CONN / AS SYSDBA
Connected.

SQL> CREATE pfile FROM spfile;

File created.
```

```
*.audit_file_dest='/u01/app/oracle/admin/T1C1/adump'
*.audit_trail='db'
*.compatible='11.2.0.0.0'
*.control_files='/u01/app/oracle/oradata/T1C1/control01.ctl','/u01/app/oracl
e/fast_recovery_area/T1C1/control02.ctl'
*.db_block_size=8192
*.db_domain='precisetrace.com'
*.db_name='T1C1'
```

```
*.db_recovery_file_dest='/u01/app/oracle/fast_recovery_area'
*.db_recovery_file_dest_size=4322230272
*.diagnostic_dest='/u01/app/oracle'
*.dispatchers='(PROTOCOL=TCP) (SERVICE=T1C1XDB)'
*.log_archive_format='%t_%s_%r.dbf'
*.memory_target=2147483648
*.open_cursors=300
*.processes=150
*.remote_login_passwordfile='EXCLUSIVE'
*.undo_tablespace='UNDOTBS1'
*.db_file_name_convert='/u01/app/oracle/oradata/S1E2/',
                       '/u01/app/oracle/oradata/T1C1/'
*.log_file_name_convert='/u01/app/oracle/oradata/S1E2/',
                       '/u01/app/oracle/oradata/T1C1/'
```

Next, we modify then save the file as initT1C1.ora and copy it over to the target system.

```
$ scp initT1C1.ora

oracle@192.168.1.209:/u01/app/oracle/product/11.2.0/dbhome_1/dbs
```

And we create the directory structure as needed for the database instance T1C1.

```
$ cd $ORACLE_BASE/admin
$ mkdir -p T1C1/cdump T1C1/udump T1C1/adump
$ cd T1C1
$ ls
adump  cdump  udump
$ cd $ORACLE_BASE/oradata
$ mkdir T1C1
$ cd $ORACLE_BASE
$ cd fast_recovery_area/
$ mkdir T1C1
```

Startup the Target Instance

Start the target instance using the parameter file 'initT1C1.ora'. The instance is started in *nomount* mode. Then, create the server parameter file (spfileT1C1.ora). Shutdown and startup the instance in *mount* mode using the parameter file spfileT1C1.ora.

```
$ export ORACLE_HOME=/u01/app/oracle/product/11.2.0/dbhome_1
$ export ORACLE_SID=T1C1
$ sqlplus /nolog

SQL*Plus: Release 12.1.0.1.0 Production on Fri Apr 18 09:38:42 2014

Copyright (c) 1982, 2013, Oracle.  All rights reserved.

SQL> CONN / AS SYSDBA
Connected to an idle instance.
```

```
SQL> STARTUP NOMOUNT
pfile='/u01/app/oracle/product/11.2.0/dbhome_1/dbs/initT1C1.ora'
ORACLE instance started.

Total System Global Area  551165952 bytes
Fixed Size                  2230232 bytes
Variable Size             331352104 bytes
Database Buffers          213909504 bytes
Redo Buffers                3674112 bytes
SQL>

SQL> CREATE spfile FROM PFILE;
```

Perform Clone Database using RMAN

Now we are ready to perform the database clone. While logged in to the target system, connect to the target instance (T1C1) and remotely connect to the source instance (S1E2). The RMAN *duplicate* command runs in verbose mode.
To avoid 'permission denied error' returning from the operating system while RMAN restores backup files, prior to starting the command ascertain the correct permission settings on the target system NFS directory '/home/oracle/backup.'

```
$ export ORACLE_HOME=/u01/app/oracle/product/11.2.0/dbhome_1
$ cd $ORACLE_HOME/bin
$ ./rman

Recovery Manager: Release 11.2.0.3.0 - Production on Fri Apr 18 10:14:59
2014

Copyright (c) 1982, 2011, Oracle and/or its affiliates.  All rights
reserved.

RMAN> CONNECT AUXILIARY sys/oracle_4U

connected to auxiliary database: T1C1 (not mounted)

RMAN> CONNECT TARGET sys/oracle_4U@S1E2

connected to target database: S1E2 (DBID=4279993164)

RMAN>

RMAN> RUN {
2> DUPLICATE TARGET DATABASE TO T1C1
3> BACKUP LOCATION '/home/oracle/backup'
4> NOFILENAMECHECK;
5> }
```

The above RMAN *duplicate* script overrides the default backup location, the Fast Recovery Area (FRA) by specifying the non-default destination using the parameter *backup location.* The parameter *nofilenamecheck* prevents RMAN from checking whether source database data files with the same name as clone database data files are in use.

Specify this option when the source and clone database data files and redo log files have the same names. This option is specified because the clone database is on a different system with the same disk configuration, file system structure, and file names as the source database system. Without the parameter *nofilenamecheck*, the command will terminate with an error.

If you receive the error message ' RMAN-06025: no backup of archived log for thread 1 with sequence 255 and starting SCN of 8375157 found to restore', then we use the *noredo* option as illustrated below.

```
RMAN> RUN {
2> DUPLICATE TARGET DATABASE TO T1C1
3> NOREDO
4> BACKUP LOCATION '/home/oracle/backup'
5> NOFILENAMECHECK;
6> }
```

Target Replicat Starting SCN

The above RMAN *duplicate* command determined the System Change Number (SCN) for performing point in-time recovery and opened the target database in RESETLOGS mode.

The following section of the RMAN *duplicate* command log shows the SCN 14274705. This will be the application point of the Replicat for synchronizing the target database – T1C1.

```
contents of Memory Script:
{
   set until scn 14274705;
   set newname for datafile  1 to
 "/u01/app/oracle/oradata/T1C1/system01.dbf";
   set newname for datafile  2 to
 "/u01/app/oracle/oradata/T1C1/sysaux01.dbf";
   set newname for datafile  3 to
 "/u01/app/oracle/oradata/T1C1/undotbs01.dbf";
   set newname for datafile  4 to
 "/u01/app/oracle/oradata/T1C1/users01.dbf";
   restore
   clone database
   ;
}
```

Post Database Clone

Now, we modify the file '/etc/oratab' to include the clone database reference. To avoid a re-clone database in the event of failure, start a consistent database backup using RMAN. First, shutdown the database using the *immediate* option, then startup in MOUNT state.

```
RMAN> STARTUP MOUNT

connected to target database (not started)
Oracle instance started
database mounted

Total System Global Area     551165952 bytes

Fixed Size                     2230232 bytes
Variable Size                369100840 bytes
Database Buffers             176160768 bytes
Redo Buffers                   3674112 bytes

RMAN> BACKUP DATABASE;
```

Verify the Clone Database Structure

Since the RMAN *duplicate* command did not exclude any of the source database tablespaces after the clone database operation was successfully completed, the clone database (target) must have identical physical data file structures.

The following is the list of the clone database data files, control files, online redo log files, list of tables owned by OSM$REPAPI, and the current row counts of the table POLICIES.

```
$ . oraenv
ORACLE_SID = [oracle] ? T1C1
The Oracle base remains unchanged with value /u01/app/oracle
$ sqlplus /nolog

SQL*Plus: Release 11.2.0.3.0 Production on Fri Apr 18 18:51:14 2014

Copyright (c) 1982, 2011, Oracle.  All rights reserved.

SQL>CONN / AS SYSDBA
Connected.
SQL> SELECT file_name FROM dba_data_files UNION
  2  SELECT file_name FROM dba_temp_files UNION
  3  SELECT name      FROM v$controlfile  UNION
  4  SELECT member    FROM v$logfile;

FILE_NAME
--------------------------------------------------------------------
/u01/app/oracle/fast_recovery_area/T1C1/control02.ctl
/u01/app/oracle/oradata/T1C1/control01.ctl
/u01/app/oracle/oradata/T1C1/redo01.log
/u01/app/oracle/oradata/T1C1/redo02.log
/u01/app/oracle/oradata/T1C1/redo03.log
/u01/app/oracle/oradata/T1C1/sysaux01.dbf
/u01/app/oracle/oradata/T1C1/system01.dbf
```

```
/u01/app/oracle/oradata/T1C1/temp01.dbf
/u01/app/oracle/oradata/T1C1/undotbs01.dbf
/u01/app/oracle/oradata/T1C1/users01.dbf

10 rows selected.

SQL> SELECT table_name
  2  FROM   dba_tables
  3  WHERE  owner='OSM$REPAPI';

TABLE_NAME
------------------------------
RANDOM_DOMAIN
RANDOM_FIRST
RANDOM_MIDDLE
RANDOM_LAST
POLICY_TYPES
DISCOUNT_TYPES
CUSTOMERS
POLICIES
OSM_DOCUMENTS

9 rows selected.

SQL> SELECT count(*) FROM osm$repapi.policies;

  COUNT(*)
----------
    921740
```

Phase III: Migrate to Automatic Storage Management

The migration from the file system to Automatic Storage Management (ASM) allows the upgraded database to take advantage of high availability features delivered by ASM, which are necessary for supporting 24/7 systems.

After the migration is successfully completed, the database continues to function as it was before the migration. However, ASM enables the Database Administrator (DBA) to manage the database storage more effectively by performing online operations that may require database shutdown on a non-ASM environment. An example of an online operation delivered by ASM is adding and removing disk storage while the database is operational which avoids user interruption by keeping the database open during the operation execution.

Before migration from the file system to the ASM, perform the following configurations:

- Create, configure, and provision ASM disks
- Create and configure ASM disk groups

Figure 7-7 depicts ASM architecture and migrating database data file from file system to ASM using RMAN. The high-level component of ASM is the disk group, which logically groups ASM disks – the physical disk partitions provisioned for ASM. A single disk group may be referenced by one or more databases.

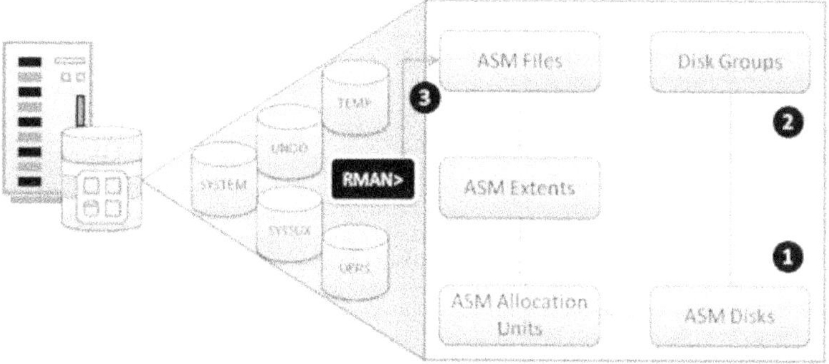

Figure 7-7: Automatic Storage Management Architecture

Oracle ASM disks are the storage devices associated with an Oracle ASM disk group. There are several forms of an ASM disk: an entire physical disk, combination of one or more disk partitions, a Logical Unit Number (LUN), a logical volume (LV), or network file system. Each ASM disk is composed of ASM allocation units, the smallest contiguous amount of disk space that ASM allocates. When you create an ASM disk group, the ASM allocation unit of 1, 2, 4, 8, 16, 32, or 64 MB is specified as a disk group attribute. The default is 1MB. ASM allocation units form an ASM extent associated with an ASM file. An Oracle ASM extent is the raw storage which holds the contents of an Oracle ASM file. An Oracle ASM file consists of one or more extents tracked using an extent map table.

Installation of Oracle 12c Grid Infrastructure

Before migration to the ASM, it is necessary to install Oracle 12c Grid Infrastructure and configure the disk groups. The installation requires using a dedicated operating system user that is different from Oracle Database 12c. Figure 7-8 shows the installation options.

The Oracle Universal Installer for Oracle 12c Grid Infrastructure has four installation options:

- Install and Configure Oracle Grid Infrastructure for a Cluster
- Install and Configure Oracle Grid Infrastructure for a Standalone Server

- Upgrade Oracle Grid Infrastructure or Oracle Automatic Storage Management
- Install Oracle Grid Infrastructure Software Only

Since the ASM disks are not provisioned yet, select the option 'Install Oracle Grid Infrastructure Software Only'. After the ASM disks are provisioned, then use Oracle Automatic Storage Management Configuration Assistant (ASMCA) to create, start the ASM instance +ASM and create and configure the disk groups +DATA and +FRA.

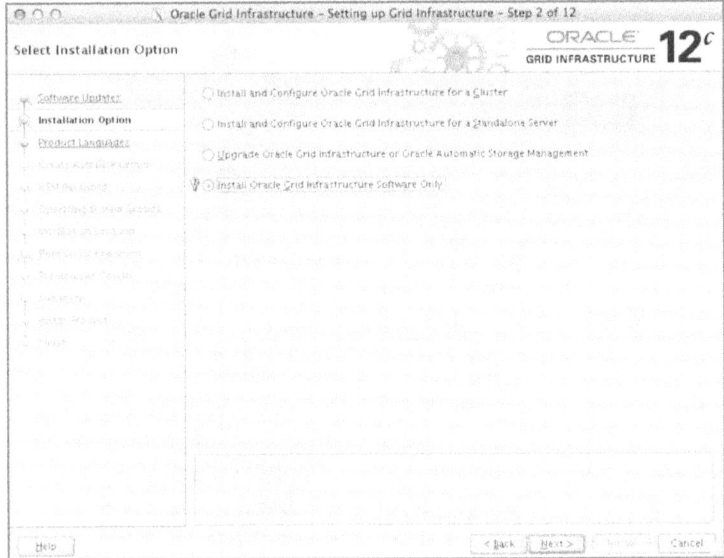

Figure 7-8: Oracle Grid Infrastructure 12c

For details regarding creating and providing ASM disks, refer to the section 'Building Virtual File System for ASM Disks.'

Working with ASM Instance

At this point, an ASM Instance is installed on Oracle Database 12c server. There must be one and only one ASM instance running on the system. The ASM instance must be started in order for the database instance to access data files. Connect as SYSASM to start the ASM instance, which mount the list of created and configured disk groups.

```
$ . oraenv
ORACLE_SID = [+ASM] ? +ASM
The Oracle base remains unchanged with value /u02/app/grid
$ sqlplus /nolog
```

```
SQL*Plus: Release 12.1.0.1.0 Production on Wed Apr 30 21:40:21 2014

Copyright (c) 1982, 2013, Oracle.  All rights reserved.

SQL> CONN / AS SYSASM
Connected to an idle instance.
SQL> STARTUP
ASM instance started

Total System Global Area   1135747072 bytes
Fixed Size                    2297344 bytes
Variable Size              1108283904 bytes
ASM Cache                    25165824 bytes
ASM diskgroups mounted
```

The ASM Instance uses fewer parameters than the database instance. The only mandatory parameter-value is *instance_type=asm.* View the ASM instance parameters related to list the auto-mounted disk groups and ASM disks storage devices.

```
SQL> SHOW PARAMETERS disk

NAME                                 TYPE        VALUE
------------------------------------ ----------- ----------------------
asm_diskgroups                       string      DATA, FRA
asm_diskstring                       string      /dev/x*
```

This instance works in conjunction with the database instance to handle database file management. When the database instance submits the following CREATE TABLESPACE statement:

```
SQL> CREATE TABLESPACE edge
  2  DATAFILE '+DATA' SIZE 50M AUTOEXTEND on;
Tablespace created.
SQL> SELECT file_name
  2  FROM   dba_data_files
  3  WHERE  tablespace_name='EDGE';
FILE_NAME
--------------------------------------------------------------
+DATA/t1c1/datafile/edge.267.846273245
```

The tablespace data file is created as an ASM file with the following characteristics:

1. The database requests creating the data file on the specified disk group, +DATA.
2. The ASM Instance allocates the storage based on the Allocation Unit (AU) of the disk group. ASM spreads the allocation units evenly across all ASM disks, within the disk group specified, to balance load and avoid hot spots. It also mirrors allocation units for the disk group with redundant normal or high attribute.
3. The database background process ASMB receives the extent map for the new file. The extent map is a table that maps data extents in a file to allocation units on disk. This allows the database instance access to the data.
4. The file is now open and the database process starts formatting the file.
5. The ASM Instance confirms the file creation and marks the file as created.
6. The file is closed and reopened by the database instance.

Database Disk Groups

There are two disk groups created; +DATA and +FRA. Remember, creating disk groups requires ASM disks. The +DATA disk group hosts all types of database data files and the +FRA disk group is dedicated for the Fast Recovery Area (FRA) files only.

Figure 7-9 is the Automatic Storage Management Configuration Assistant (ASMCA). It manages disk groups. Use ASMCA to create/alter/drop disk groups, add disks to a disk group, drop disks from a disk group, or mount /dismount disk groups.

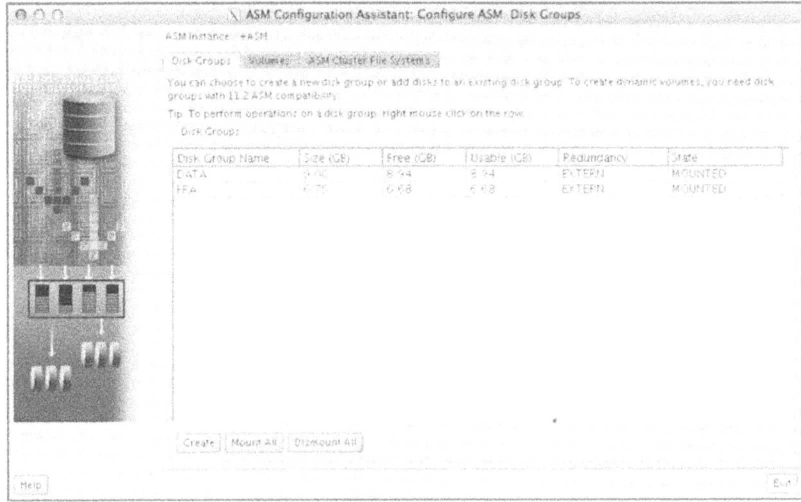

Figure 7-9: Automatic Storage Management Configuration Assistant (ASMCA)

ASM Instance has its own command-line – *asmcmd. asmcmd* adapts Linux-like file system management commands. The following illustrates the copy of the archived log file from ASM to file system using the copy command. The '+' character designates the ASM root directory. Use the change directory 'cd' command to navigate across the ASM directory structure.

```
$ . oraenv
ORACLE_SID = [grid] ? +ASM
The Oracle base has been set to /u02/app/grid
$ asmcmd
ASMCMD> ls
DATA/
FRA/
ASMCMD> cd +FRA/T1C1/ARCHIVELOG/2014_05_02
ASMCMD> ls
thread_1_seq_24.257.846500305
```

```
ASMCMD> cp * /home/grid/arc
copying +FRA/T1C1/ARCHIVELOG/2014_05_02/thread_1_seq_24.257.846500305 ->
/home/grid/arc/thread_1_seq_24.257.846500305
```

Testing the creation of tablespace in +DATA disk group. The next CREATE *tablespace* command creates the tablespace *edge*. The data file is auto extended with an initial size of 100MB.

```
$ . oraenv
ORACLE_SID = [+ASM] ? T1C2
The Oracle base has been changed from /u02/app/grid to /u01/app/oracle
$ sqlplus /nolog

SQL*Plus: Release 11.2.0.3.0 Production on Tue Apr 22 18:34:38 2014

Copyright (c) 1982, 2011, Oracle.  All rights reserved.

SQL> CONN / AS SYSDBA
Connected.
SQL> CREATE TABLESPACE edge
  2  DATAFILE '+DATA';

Tablespace created.

SQL> SELECT tablespace_name
  2  FROM   dba_tablespaces;

TABLESPACE_NAME
------------------------------
SYSTEM
SYSAUX
UNDOTBS1
TEMP
USERS
EDGE

6 rows selected.

SQL> DROP TABLESPACE edge;

Tablespace dropped.
```

The above commands were done on a test database – T1C2 and it is necessary to create a test database of type Automatic Storage Management (ASM). The test confirms Oracle Grid Infrastructure 12c is properly installed and disk groups are configured for the migration. View the +ASM instance alert file. Investigate and resolve errors found before proceeding from Migration to the Automatic Storage Management. Use DBCA to drop the test database. This will free disk groups space.

This next section outlines performing the migration to the Automatic Storage Management (ASM).

Migration to the Automatic Storage Management

Migration of the clone database storage from the file system to the Automatic Storage Management (ASM) is executed using either the Oracle Enterprise Manager (OEM) 'Migrate Database to ASM' wizard or the Oracle Recovery Manager (RMAN) *duplicate* command. Very Large Database (VLDB) environments benefit using RMAN for migrating the database gradually.

For example, processing the migration based on the disk storage availability and the ownership of tablespaces by applications allows faster and manageable restoration in case of failure. The RMAN *duplicate* command supports a database clone from an active database. This option minimizes the amount of trail files to synchronize the target database after successfully upgrading the database to Oracle Database 12c. Figure 7-10 represents the migration workflow using the RMAN *duplicate* command, which requires preparation of the disk groups +DATA and +FRA for the database file storage.

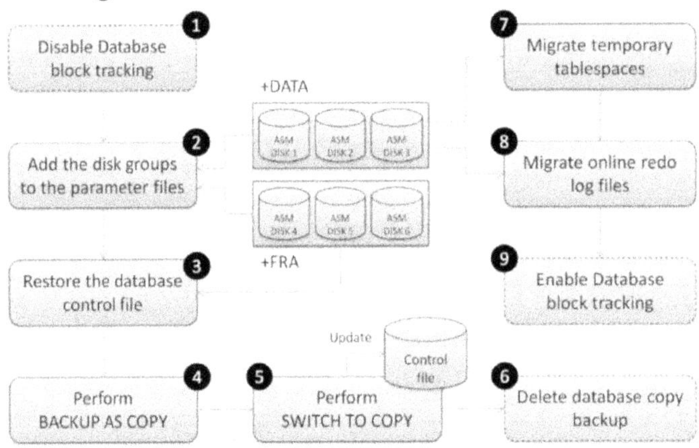

Figure 7-10: Migration Workflow using RMAN

The following steps are executed on the clone database using SQL*Plus and Oracle Recovery Manager (RMAN).

1. Disable the database block change tracking process
2. Modify the parameter file by adding the ASM disk groups
3. Migrate the control file
4. Migrate the data files
5. Migrate the temporary tablespaces
6. Migrate the online redo log files groups
7. Enable the database block change tracking process

Disable Block Change Tracking

When the block change tracking is enabled, for each database block that is changed, the background process CTWR writes the physical address to an external file – outside of the database. The purpose is to support RMAN incremental backups. During the migration to the ASM, if the database block change tracking process is enabled, then it must be disabled prior to starting the migration steps. To determine if the process is enabled or disabled, query the database dynamic view *v$block_change_tracking*. If the status column returns 'ENABLED', then we disable it, otherwise proceed to the next step.

```
SQL> SELECT status, filename FROM v$block_change_tracking;

STATUS     FILENAME
---------- ---------------------------------------------------------
ENABLED    /u01/app/oracle/…/T1C1/changetracking/o1_mf_9ozlbm2w_.chg

SQL> ALTER DATABASE DISABLE BLOCK CHANGE TRACKING;

Database altered.
```

Define Disk Groups

Migration to the Automatic Storage Management (ASM) requires the ASM disk groups to be created and mounted. This migration uses two disk groups, +DATA and +FRA. The disk group +DATA stores the database data files, redo log files, and control files. The disk group +FRA is the location of the database Fast Recovery Area (FRA), the default location for RMAN backup files, flashback log files, and the mirror copy of the control file and online redo log files.

- Determine the name and status of +DATA and +FRA disk groups by querying the ASM dynamic view V$ASM_DISKGROUP.

```
SQL> SELECT name, state
  2  FROM   v$asm_diskgroup;

NAME                           STATE
------------------------------ -----------
FRA                            MOUNTED
DATA                           MOUNTED
```

- Create the parameter file 'initT1C1.ora' from the server parameter file 'spfileT1C1.ora'. Use IMMEDIATE shutdown option to force checkpoint and closes the database files.

```
SQL> SHUTDOWN IMMEDIATE
Database closed.
Database dismounted.
ORACLE instance shut down.
SQL> CONN / AS SYSDBA
Connected to an idle instance.
SQL> CREATE pfile FROM spfile;

File created.
```

- Add and/or modify the parameters file by adding the disk groups +DATA and +FRA as the locations of the control files, data files, and online redo log files. Table 7-2 lists the modified parameters.

Parameter	Description
CONTROL_FILES	The location of Oracle managed control files.
DB_CREATE_ONLINE_LOG_DEST_1	The location of the first member of the online redo log files and control file.
DB_CREATE_FILE_DEST	The location of the data file
DB_RECOVERY_FILE_DEST	The location of the Fast Recovery Area (FRA).

Table 7-2: Automatic Storage Management File Locations

```
*.audit_file_dest='/u01/app/oracle/admin/T1C1/adump'
*.audit_trail='db'
*.compatible='11.2.0.0.0'
*.control_files=(+DATA, +FRA)
*.db_create_online_log_dest_1=+DATA
*.db_create_file_dest=+DATA
*.db_recovery_file_dest=+FRA
*.db_recovery_file_dest_size=4322230272
*.db_block_size=8192
*.db_domain='precisetrace.com'
*.db_name='T1C1'
*.db_recovery_file_dest_size=4322230272
*.diagnostic_dest='/u01/app/oracle'
*.dispatchers='(PROTOCOL=TCP) (SERVICE=T1C1XDB)'
*.log_archive_format='%t_%s_%r.dbf'
*.memory_target=2147483648
*.open_cursors=300
*.processes=150
*.remote_login_passwordfile='EXCLUSIVE'
*.undo_tablespace='UNDOTBS1'
```

- Next, we create the server parameter file 'spfileT1C1.ora' from the modified parameter file 'initT1C1.ora.' The two parameter files are currently stored on the default location - $ORACLE_HOME/dbs. After the migration to the ASM is completed, use the Oracle supplied PL/SQL package DBMS_FILE_TRANSFER to move the server parameter file to ASM storage.

```
SQL> CREATE spfile FROM pfile;

File created.
```

Control File Migration

The migration begins by restoring an image copy of the current control file to the location(s) specified by the parameter *control_files*. Start the Oracle Recovery Manager (RMAN), connect to the target database, start the instance in NOMOUNT mode and perform the RMAN *restore* command of the control file.

- Start Oracle Recovery Manager (RMAN) and start the instance in NOMOUNT mode:

```
$ rman

Recovery Manager: Release 11.2.0.3.0 - Production on Tue Apr 22 19:35:20
2014

Copyright (c) 1982, 2011, Oracle and/or its affiliates.  All rights
reserved.

RMAN> CONNECT TARGET

connected to target database (not started)

RMAN> STARTUP NOMOUNT

Oracle instance started

Total System Global Area     551165952 bytes

Fixed Size                     2230232 bytes
Variable Size                331352104 bytes
Database Buffers             213909504 bytes
Redo Buffers                   3674112 bytes
```

- Based on the current location of the control file identified from 'initT1C1.ora', use Oracle Recovery Manager (RMAN) RESTORE CONTROLFILE command to restore a copy of the control file to +DATA and +FRA.

```
RMAN> RESTORE CONTROLFILE FROM
2> '/u01/app/oracle/oradata/T1C1/control01.ctl';

Starting restore at 22-APR-14
using channel ORA_DISK_1
```

```
channel ORA_DISK_1: copied control file copy
output file name=+DATA/t1c1/controlfile/current.256.845581127
output file name=+FRA/t1c1/controlfile/current.257.845581127
Finished restore at 22-APR-14
```

Data File Migration

After the control is successfully restored, the next step is to migrate the database permanently and undo data files. One method to achieve this is by creating a backup copy of the database, which is a consistent backup of the database data files. The file location is explicitly identified by the FORMAT parameter as +DATA disk group. Using the RMAN COPY command creates an image copy of the data files to the location specified by the FORMAT parameter.

- Optionally, enable Recovery Manager (RMAN) parallelism. This enhances the data file copy operations by allocating multiple channels. A parallelism of 6 allocates six RMAN database channels to create the database image copy.

```
RMAN> STARTUP MOUNT

database is already started
database mounted
released channel: ORA_DISK_1

RMAN> CONFIGURE DEVICE TYPE DISK PARALLELISM 6;

new RMAN configuration parameters:
CONFIGURE DEVICE TYPE DISK PARALLELISM 6 BACKUP TYPE TO BACKUPSET;
new RMAN configuration parameters are successfully stored
```

- Create an image copy of the database data files to the +DATA disk group. The database is in MOUNT mode to create consistent image backup files. The COPY command excludes the files belonging to the database temporary tablespace, which will migrate separately.

```
RMAN> BACKUP AS COPY DATABASE FORMAT '+DATA';

Starting backup at 22-APR-14
allocated channel: ORA_DISK_1
channel ORA_DISK_1: SID=26 device type=DISK
allocated channel: ORA_DISK_2
channel ORA_DISK_2: SID=27 device type=DISK
allocated channel: ORA_DISK_3
channel ORA_DISK_3: SID=28 device type=DISK
allocated channel: ORA_DISK_4
channel ORA_DISK_4: SID=29 device type=DISK
allocated channel: ORA_DISK_5
channel ORA_DISK_5: SID=30 device type=DISK
```

```
allocated channel: ORA_DISK_6
channel ORA_DISK_6: SID=31 device type=DISK
channel ORA_DISK_1: starting datafile copy
input datafile file number=00002
name=/u01/app/oracle/oradata/T1C1/sysaux01.dbf
channel ORA_DISK_2: starting datafile copy
input datafile file number=00001
name=/u01/app/oracle/oradata/T1C1/system01.dbf
channel ORA_DISK_3: starting datafile copy
input datafile file number=00004
name=/u01/app/oracle/oradata/T1C1/users01.dbf
channel ORA_DISK_4: starting datafile copy
input datafile file number=00003
name=/u01/app/oracle/oradata/T1C1/undotbs01.dbf
output file name=+DATA/t1c1/datafile/users.259.845581373
tag=TAG20140422T194250 RECID=7 STAMP=845581412
channel ORA_DISK_3: datafile copy complete, elapsed time: 00:00:51
output file name=+DATA/t1c1/datafile/undotbs1.260.845581377
tag=TAG20140422T194250 RECID=8 STAMP=845581424
channel ORA_DISK_4: datafile copy complete, elapsed time: 00:00:57
output file name=+DATA/t1c1/datafile/system.258.845581371
tag=TAG20140422T194250 RECID=9 STAMP=845581560
channel ORA_DISK_2: datafile copy complete, elapsed time: 00:03:12
output file name=+DATA/t1c1/datafile/sysaux.257.845581371
tag=TAG20140422T194250 RECID=10 STAMP=845581564
channel ORA_DISK_1: datafile copy complete, elapsed time: 00:03:24
Finished backup at 22-APR-14

Starting Control File and SPFILE Autobackup at 22-APR-14
piece handle=+FRA/t1c1/autobackup/2014_04_22/s_845580320.258.845581577
comment=NONE
Finished Control File and SPFILE Autobackup at 22-APR-14
```

- Now, the control and data files are moved to Automatic Storage Management (ASM). The next step is to update the control files with the new locations of the database data files then open the database in normal mode. Note that the RMAN *switch* command updates the file names for a database, tablespace, and data files to the latest image copies available for the specified files or database.

```
RMAN> SWITCH DATABASE TO COPY;

using target database control file instead of recovery catalog
datafile 1 switched to datafile copy
"+DATA/t1c1/datafile/system.258.845581371"
datafile 2 switched to datafile copy
"+DATA/t1c1/datafile/sysaux.257.845581371"
datafile 3 switched to datafile copy
"+DATA/t1c1/datafile/undotbs1.260.845581377"
datafile 4 switched to datafile copy
"+DATA/t1c1/datafile/users.259.845581373"

RMAN> ALTER DATABASE OPEN;
```

```
database opened

RMAN> exit

Recovery Manager complete.
$
```

The database migration to the Automatic Storage Management (ASM) is partially completed and the database is open in read/write mode. The next steps manually migrate the remaining of the database – temporary and online redo log files. Migration of temporary and online redo log files is an in-place operation. The database remains open while executing migration commands.

Temporary Files Migration

The Recovery Manager (RMAN) command *backup as copy database* excludes the temporary tablespace files. It is performed by manually creating an interim temporary tablespace to allow the recreation of the existing temporary tablespace as Automatic Storage Management (ASM) type.

- Determine the name and size of the temporary files. Since the database is open, query the database data dictionary view DBA_TEMP_FILES.

```
SQL> CONN / AS SYSDBA
Connected.
SQL> SELECT file_name, bytes/1024/1204 MB
  2  FROM   dba_temp_files;

FILE_NAME                                                 MB
-------------------------------------------------- -----------
/u01/app/oracle/oradata/T1C1/temp01.dbf               549.42

SQL>
```

- Create an interim temporary tablespace then alter the default database-wide temporary tablespace. Query the data dictionary DATABASE_PROPERTIES view to ascertain the default database-wide temporary tablespace.

```
SQL> CREATE TEMPORARY TABLESPACE temp_1
  2  TEMPFILE '/u01/app/oracle/oradata/T1C1/temp02.dbf' SIZE 550M;

Tablespace created.

SQL> ALTER DATABASE DEFAULT TEMPORARY TABLESPACE temp_1;

Database altered.
```

- Now we drop and recreate the original temporary tablespace. Note that the new temporary tablespace is created as an Automatic Storage Management (ASM) file type. Make the temporary tablespace size match the original size.

```
SQL> DROP TABLESPACE temp INCLUDING CONTENTS;

Tablespace dropped.

SQL> CREATE TEMPORARY TABLESPACE temp
  2  TEMPFILE '+DATA' SIZE 550M;

Tablespace created.

SQL> ALTER DATABASE DEFAULT TEMPORARY TABLESPACE temp;

Database altered.
```

- Lastly, we drop the interim temporary tablespace and verify the temporary tablespace is created as an Automatic Storage Management (ASM) file type.

```
SQL> DROP TABLESPACE temp_1 INCLUDING CONTENTS;

Tablespace dropped.

SQL> SELECT file_name
  2  FROM   dba_temp_file;

FILE_NAME
--------------------------------------------------------------------------------
+DATA/t1c1/tempfile/temp.261.845582177

SQL>
```

Online Redo Log Files Migration

Since Oracle Recovery Manager (RMAN) does not backup online redo log files, the migration from a file system to Automatic Storage Management (ASM) type is performed manually. As illustrated below, it is an in-place operation and does not require shutdown of the database.

- List of the current online redo group members by a joint query of V$LOGFILE and V$LOG.

```
SQL> SELECT l.group#, lf.member, l.bytes/1024/1024
  2  FROM   v$logfile lf, v$log l
  3  WHERE  lf.group#=l.group#
  4  ORDER BY 1;

    GROUP# MEMBER                                  L.BYTES/1024/1024
---------- --------------------------------------- ----------------
```

```
         1 /u01/app/oracle/oradata/T1C1/redo01.log                    50
         2 /u01/app/oracle/oradata/T1C1/redo02.log                    50
         3 /u01/app/oracle/oradata/T1C1/redo03.log                    50

SQL>
```

- Create new online redo log groups, each group composed of two members. The first member is stored on the +DATA disk group and the second member on the +FRA disk group. According to the above query, the next three groups to be created are 4, 5 and 6. Use the same returned size.

```
SQL> ALTER DATABASE ADD LOGFILE GROUP 4 ('+DATA', '+FRA') SIZE 50M;

Database altered.

SQL> ALTER DATABASE ADD LOGFILE GROUP 5 ('+DATA', '+FRA') SIZE 50M;

Database altered.

SQL> ALTER DATABASE ADD LOGFILE GROUP 6 ('+DATA', '+FRA') SIZE 50M;

Database altered.
```

- Now we drop the non-ASM online redo log groups. We start by dropping INACTIVE and UNUSED groups only. The query below shows group 1 status is CURRENT and it cannot be dropped until several log switches are archived and it becomes INACTIVE.

```
SQL> SELECT group#, status FROM v$log;

    GROUP# STATUS
---------- ----------------
         1 CURRENT
         2 INACTIVE
         3 INACTIVE
         4 UNUSED
         5 UNUSED
         6 UNUSED

6 rows selected.

SQL> ALTER DATABASE DROP LOGFILE GROUP 2;

Database altered.

SQL> ALTER DATABASE DROP LOGFILE GROUP 3;

Database altered.
```

- To drop an active group, perform multiple log switches until the group status becomes INACTIVE.

```
SQL> SELECT group#, status FROM v$log;
```

```
    GROUP# STATUS
---------- ----------------
  1 CURRENT
  4 UNUSED
  5 UNUSED
  6 UNUSED

SQL> ALTER SYSTEM SWITCH LOGFILE;

System altered.

SQL> select GROUP#, STATUS from v$log;

    GROUP# STATUS
---------- ----------------
  1 INACTIVE
  4 CURRENT
  5 UNUSED
  6 UNUSED
SQL> ALTER DATABASE DROP LOGFILE GROUP 1;

Database altered.
```

- Lastly, we verify that the online redo log file migrated to the Automatic Storage Management (ASM). As per the query output below, there are two members for each group stored on the +DATA and +FRA disk groups. Multiplexing the online redo log groups avoids single point of failure.

```
SQL> SELECT member
  2  FROM   v$logfile;
MEMBER
----------------------------------------------------------------------
+DATA/t1c1/onlinelog/group_4.262.845583489
+FRA/t1c1/onlinelog/group_4.262.845583491
+DATA/t1c1/onlinelog/group_5.263.845583507
+FRA/t1c1/onlinelog/group_5.263.845583509
+DATA/t1c1/onlinelog/group_6.264.845583523
+FRA/t1c1/onlinelog/group_6.264.845583525
6 rows selected.

SQL>
```

This ends the migration of the database from the file system to the Automatic Storage Management (ASM). The ASM instance must remain operational to provide support for the database instance access of database files.

Verify New Database Storage

Verify that the database storage has been migrated to the Automatic Storage Management (ASM) files type. Use the SQL*Plus or ASMCMD command-line to confirm the database files are successfully migrated to the ASM.

```
SQL> SELECT file_name FROM dba_data_files UNION
  2  SELECT file_name FROM dba_temp_files UNION
  3  SELECT member    FROM v$logfile      UNION
  4  SELECT name      FROM v$controlfile;

FILE_NAME
----------------------------------------------------------------------
+DATA/t1c1/controlfile/current.256.845581127
+DATA/t1c1/datafile/sysaux.257.845581371
+DATA/t1c1/datafile/system.258.845581371
+DATA/t1c1/datafile/undotbs1.260.845581377
+DATA/t1c1/datafile/users.259.845581373
+DATA/t1c1/onlinelog/group_4.262.845583489
+DATA/t1c1/onlinelog/group_5.263.845583507
+DATA/t1c1/onlinelog/group_6.264.845583523
+DATA/t1c1/tempfile/temp.261.845582177
+FRA/t1c1/controlfile/current.257.845581127
+FRA/t1c1/onlinelog/group_4.262.845583491

FILE_NAME
----------------------------------------------------------------------
+FRA/t1c1/onlinelog/group_5.263.845583509
+FRA/t1c1/onlinelog/group_6.264.845583525

13 rows selected.

SQL>
```

The DBMS_FILE_TRANSFER Package

Another approach to migrate and copy files from the file system to the ASM is to use the Oracle supplied PL/SQL package DBMS_FILE_TRANSFER. The example below illustrates the use of the package to migrate a temporary tablespace from the file system to the Automatic Storage Management (ASM) using the following steps:

- Create and provide access to the source and target directories – SRCDIR and TGTDIR. The source data file is located on the directory '/home/oracle.' The target directory is the +DATA disk group.

```
SQL> CREATE DIRECTORY srcdir as '/home/oracle';

Directory created.

SQL> GRANT all ON DIRECTORY srcdir to system;

Grant succeeded.

SQL> CREATE DIRECTORY tgtdir as '+DATA';

Directory created.

SQL> GRANT all ON DIRECTORY tgtdir to system;
```

```
Grant succeeded.

SQL>
```

- Execute DBMS_FILE_TRANSFER.COPY_FILE procedure

```
SQL> BEGIN
  2     DBMS_FILE_TRANSFER.COPY_FILE(
  3          'SRCDIR', 'temp_1.dbf', 'TGTDIR', 'temp_1.f');
  4  END;
  5  /

PL/SQL procedure successfully completed.

SQL>
```

- Update the database data dictionary with the new file location. The tablespace must be either offline or the database is on MOUNT mode. Obtain the name of the copied file by querying V$ASM_FILES.

```
SQL> SHUTDOWN IMMEDIATE
Database closed.
Database dismounted.
ORACLE instance shut down.
SQL> STARTUP MOUNT
ORACLE instance started.

Total System Global Area        551165952 bytes
Fixed Size                        2230232 bytes
Variable Size                   352323624 bytes
Database Buffers                192937984 bytes
Redo Buffers                      3674112 bytes
Database mounted.
SQL> ALTER DATABASE RENAME FILE '/home/oracle/temp_1.dbf'
  2  TO '+DATA/temp_1.f';

Database altered.

SQL> ALTER DATABASE OPEN;

Database altered.

SQL>
```

- Verify the new location of the migrated temporary file.

```
SQL> SELECT tablespace_name, file_name
  2  FROM   dba_temp_files;

TABLESPACE_NAME      FILE_NAME
-------------------- --------------------------------------------------
TEMP_2               +DATA/t1c1/tempfile/copy_file.267.846281147
TEMP_1               +DATA/temp_1.f
TEMP                 +DATA/t1c1/tempfile/temp.263.846267555

SQL>
```

The next two steps are optional, but highly recommended to account for the disk space used by unneeded database files.

Delete Database Files

After migrating the database to the Automatic Storage Management (ASM), it is recommended that you remove all previous backups and data file copies. The process of removing files require RMAN and it should not be done manually. RMAN removes the files from the FRA. Below we update the control file and data dictionary.

```
$ rman

Recovery Manager: Release 11.2.0.3.0 - Production on Tue Apr 22 20:30:41
2014

Copyright (c) 1982, 2011, Oracle and/or its affiliates.  All rights
reserved.

RMAN> CONNECT TARGET

connected to target database: T1C1 (DBID=3821873595)

RMAN> RUN {
2> DELETE COPY OF DATABASE;
3> }

using target database control file instead of recovery catalog
allocated channel: ORA_DISK_1
channel ORA_DISK_1: SID=42 device type=DISK
allocated channel: ORA_DISK_2
channel ORA_DISK_2: SID=47 device type=DISK
allocated channel: ORA_DISK_3
channel ORA_DISK_3: SID=45 device type=DISK
allocated channel: ORA_DISK_4
channel ORA_DISK_4: SID=43 device type=DISK
allocated channel: ORA_DISK_5
channel ORA_DISK_5: SID=44 device type=DISK
allocated channel: ORA_DISK_6
channel ORA_DISK_6: SID=49 device type=DISK
List of Datafile Copies
=======================

Key     File S Completion Time Ckp SCN    Ckp Time
------- ---- - --------------- ---------- ---------------
11      1    A 22-APR-14       5993451    22-APR-14
        Name: /u01/app/oracle/oradata/T1C1/system01.dbf

12      2    A 22-APR-14       5993451    22-APR-14
        Name: /u01/app/oracle/oradata/T1C1/sysaux01.dbf

13      3    A 22-APR-14       5993451    22-APR-14
        Name: /u01/app/oracle/oradata/T1C1/undotbs01.dbf

14      4    A 22-APR-14       5993451    22-APR-14
```

```
        Name: /u01/app/oracle/oradata/T1C1/users01.dbf

Do you really want to delete the above objects (enter YES or NO)? YES
deleted datafile copy
datafile copy file name=/u01/app/oracle/oradata/T1C1/system01.dbf
RECID=11 STAMP=845581916
deleted datafile copy
datafile copy file name=/u01/app/oracle/oradata/T1C1/sysaux01.dbf
RECID=12 STAMP=845581916
deleted datafile copy
datafile copy file name=/u01/app/oracle/oradata/T1C1/undotbs01.dbf
RECID=13 STAMP=845581916
deleted datafile copy
datafile copy file name=/u01/app/oracle/oradata/T1C1/users01.dbf
RECID=14 STAMP=845581916
Deleted 4 objects

RMAN> exit

Recovery Manager complete.
```

Removal of Unneeded Files

After all database data files, online redo log files, and control files are migrated to the ASM, we remove the old files from the file system. Be careful when executing this step. Make sure your current directory is '/u01/app/oracle/oradata/T1C1.'

```
$ cd /u01/app/oracle/oradata/T1C1/
$ ls -al
total 167092
drwxr-xr-x 2 oracle oinstall      4096 Apr 22 20:31 .
drwxr-x--- 3 oracle oinstall      4096 Apr 18 10:04 ..
-rw-r----- 1 oracle oinstall  10076160 Apr 22 19:25 control01.ctl
-rw-r----- 1 oracle oinstall  52429312 Apr 22 20:20 redo01.log
-rw-r----- 1 oracle oinstall  52429312 Apr 22 20:12 redo02.log
-rw-r----- 1 oracle oinstall  52429312 Apr 22 20:12 redo03.log
-rw-r----- 1 oracle oinstall  49291264 Apr 22 19:21 temp01.dbf
-rw-r----- 1 oracle oinstall 209723392 Apr 22 19:55 temp02.dbf
$ rm *.log *.dbf *.ctl
$
```

Enable Block Change Tracking

This step is performed for testing purposes only. The block change tracking process should remain disabled during the next phase – the database upgrade.

```
$ sqlplus /nolog

SQL*Plus: Release 11.2.0.3.0 Production on Tue Apr 22 20:37:31 2014

Copyright (c) 1982, 2011, Oracle.  All rights reserved.
```

```
SQL> CONN / AS SYSDBA
Connected.

SQL> ALTER DATABASE ENABLE BLOCK CHANGE TRACKING;

Database altered.

SQL> ALTER DATABASE DISABLE BLOCK CHANGE TRACKING;

Database altered.

SQL>
```

Whole Database Backup

The database has been migrated from the file system to the Automatic Storage Management (ASM), before starting the Phase IV - Upgrade to Oracle Database 12c. Use Oracle Recovery Manager (RMAN) to perform a whole database backup. This backup is available in the event of failure during the database upgrade.

```
RMAN> CONFIGURE CONTROLFILE AUTOBACKUP on;

new RMAN configuration parameters:
CONFIGURE CONTROLFILE AUTOBACKUP ON;
new RMAN configuration parameters are successfully stored

RMAN> BACKUP DATABASE PLUS ARCHIVELOG TAG="Before_Upgrade";
```

Upon successful backup, the next step is to upgrade the clone database from Oracle Database 11g to Oracle Database 12c as illustrated in Phase IV.

Phase IV: Upgrade to Oracle Database 12c

There are several methods to upgrade the clone database to Oracle Database 12c. Our aim is to achieve a near zero-downtime database upgrade by keeping the source database up and running throughout the upgrade process. The database upgrade is performed using the Oracle Database Upgrade Assistant (DBUA) or manually using SQL upgrade commands. Oracle Corporation recommends using the DBUA Graphical User Interface (GUI) as illustrated in this section. Figure 7-11 shows the clone database upgrade.

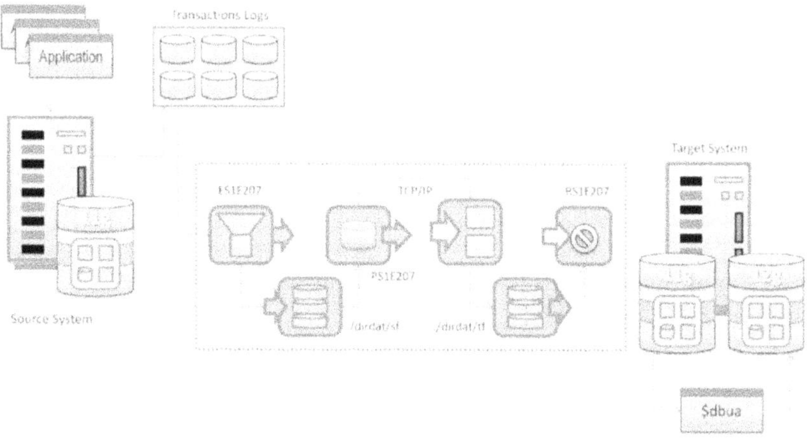

Figure 7-11: Clone Database Upgrade using the DBUA

Let's start by discussing the upgrade checklist. This ensures the database upgrade process is successfully executed.

Preparation Checklist

- Direct Upgrade Certification Path
- Delete the Database Recycle Bin
- Check for INVALID and Duplicate Objects in the SYS and SYSTEM Schemas
- Remove Outdated and Obsolete Parameters
- Check for INVALID Components
- Check for Mandatory Components
- Remove Obsolete Components
- Apply Patch Sets, Critical Patch Updates (CPUs), and Patches
- Minimum Disk Space Requirements
- Minimum Target Memory for SGA/PGA Settings

Direct Upgrade Certification Path

It is crucial to ascertain that the direct database upgrade is certified with Oracle Database 12c Release 1. For specific database releases, it may be required to perform an interim database upgrade to reach a certified source version for direct upgrade to Oracle Database 12c version 12.1.0.1.0. At the time of writing this book, the current direct upgrade path is shown in Table 7-1.

Source Database Release	Source Version	Direct Upgrade Support

Oracle Database 11g Release 2	11.2.0.2 and later	Yes
Oracle Database 11g Release 1	11.1.0.7	Yes
Oracle Database 10g Release 2	10.2.0.5	Yes

Table 7-1: Direct Upgrade Certification Path

Delete the Database Recycle Bin

The recycle bin must be purged before starting the database upgrade. Use the command below to empty the database recycle bin for all users on the source database.

```
SQL> PURGE DBA_RECYCLEBIN;

DBA Recyclebin purged.

SQL>
```

Invalid and Duplicate Objects

Here, we find out if there are invalid and duplicate objects owned by the SYS and SYSTEM users. We find and fix invalid and duplicate objects as illustrated below.

```
SQL> SELECT DISTINCT object_name, object_type, owner
  2  FROM   dba_objects
  3  WHERE  status='INVALID'
  4  ORDER BY owner, object_name, object_type;

no rows selected

SQL>
```

It's important to note that you do not start the database upgrade when there are invalid data dictionary objects. To recompile invalid objects, connect as SYSDBA and run the supplied script 'utlrp.sql' as shown below.

```
SQL> @?/rdbms/admin/utlrp.sql
```

Outdated Parameters

When Oracle develops a new database release, a parameter may become obsolete or depreciated. Obsolete parameters, underscore parameters and events must be removed prior to starting the database upgrade. Obsolete parameters on Oracle Database 12c Release 1 include:

- _app_ctx_vers
- _log_io_size

For a list of depreciated parameters, query the dynamic view *v$parameter* as show below.

```
SQL> SELECT name
  2  FROM   v$parameter
  3  WHERE  isdeprecated ='TRUE'
  4  ORDER BY name;

NAME
--------------------------------------------------------------------------
active_instance_count
background_dump_dest
buffer_pool_keep
buffer_pool_recycle
commit_write
cursor_space_for_time
fast_start_io_target
global_context_pool_size
instance_groups
lock_name_space
log_archive_local_first

NAME
--------------------------------------------------------------------------
log_archive_start
max_enabled_roles
parallel_automatic_tuning
parallel_io_cap_enabled
parallel_server
parallel_server_instances
plsql_debug
plsql_v2_compatibility
remote_os_authent
resource_manager_cpu_allocation
sec_case_sensitive_logon

NAME
--------------------------------------------------------------------------
serial_reuse
sql_trace
standby_archive_dest
user_dump_dest

26 rows selected.
```

Invalid Components

Query DBA_REGISTRY to list the components' status. The status for all components must be valid before attempting the upgrade. Also, the DBUA pre-upgrade script reports installed components' status.

```
SQL> SELECT comp_name component, version, status
  2  FROM   dba_registry;
```

```
COMPONENT                                VERSION        STATUS
---------------------------------------- ------------   ------
OWB                                      11.2.0.3.0     VALID
Oracle Application Express               3.2.1.00.12    VALID
Oracle Enterprise Manager                11.2.0.3.0     VALID
OLAP Catalog                             11.2.0.3.0     VALID
Spatial                                  11.2.0.3.0     VALID
Oracle Multimedia                        11.2.0.3.0     VALID
Oracle XML Database                      11.2.0.3.0     VALID
Oracle Text                              11.2.0.3.0     VALID
Oracle Expression Filter                 11.2.0.3.0     VALID
Oracle Rules Manager                     11.2.0.3.0     VALID
Oracle Workspace Manager                 11.2.0.3.0     VALID
Oracle Database Catalog Views            11.2.0.3.0     VALID
Oracle Database Packages and Types       11.2.0.3.0     VALID
JServer JAVA Virtual Machine             11.2.0.3.0     VALID
Oracle XDK                               11.2.0.3.0     VALID
Oracle Database Java Packages            11.2.0.3.0     VALID
OLAP Analytic Workspace                  11.2.0.3.0     VALID
Oracle OLAP API                          11.2.0.3.0     VALID

18 rows selected.
```

Mandatory Components

Oracle Database 12c Release 1 requires a few mandatory components. XDB (Oracle XML Database) is a mandatory component. It must be valid and upgraded successfully.

Obsolete Components

Oracle Database 12c Release 1 has made the following components obsolete:

- Enterprise Manager (EM) Database Control Repository
- UltraSearch

When performing upgrade using the DBUA, obsolete components are skipped. However, it is best to remove them from the clone database before starting the upgrade.

Database Patches

This is an imperative step and all required patches must be applied. The database patching is done to ensure having a certified source database version or to apply fixes necessary for a successful upgrade. Apply all patch sets, Patch Set Updates (PSUs) and patches to the clone database installation. By applying all patch types, it is likely that the database upgrade path will be confirmed as per the Oracle certification matrix.

Minimum Disk Space Requirements

The Database Upgrade Assistant (DBUA) reports the disk space usage and requirements. We ascertain how to meet the minimum recommended disk space for the ASM disk groups, flashback logs, and archived log files. The disk space requirements take into consideration the selected DBUA recovery option.
For a clone database created from backup, it is not necessary to preserve any kind of DBUA option as the clone database may be recreated in case of a database upgrade failure and reattempt.

System Global Area Requirements

Allocate enough memory to the shared and Java pools. This is done by using the Automatic Shared Memory Management (ASMM) or manually. Failure to allocate the required memory causes the database upgrade to terminate with errors. During the upgrade phase, the data dictionary PL/SQL packages and Java classes are recompiled. However; some of the Java classes need to allocate enough memory to compile successfully. To avoid the upgrade terminates with failure due to unable to allocate memory allocation, set a value of 2GB or higher for the database parameter *memory_target* (if you are not manually allocating your SGA pools).

Now, let's perform the actual upgrade phases: Pre-Upgrade, Upgrade, and Post-Upgrade. Figure 7-12 presents the upgrade as a top-down approach highlighting the tasks for a successful database upgrade project.

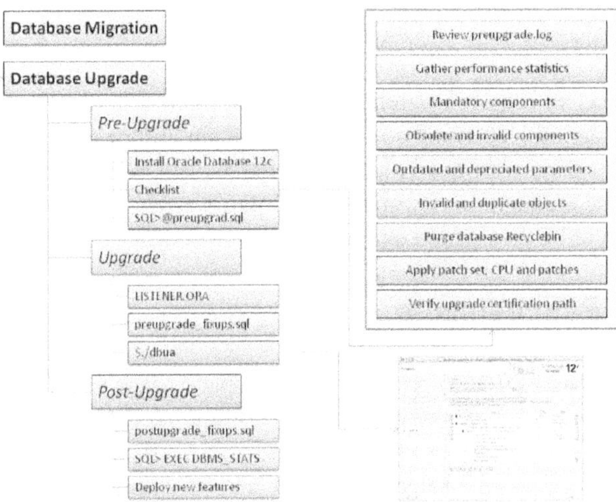

Figure 7-12: Database Upgrade Workflow

Database Pre-Upgrade

Before starting Oracle Database 12c Database Upgrade Assistant (DBUA), the pre-upgrade script (preupgrd.sql) must be executed. It quickly generates a pre-upgrade actions report. The pre-upgrade script is shipped with Oracle Database 12c and executed on the source database. It performs a sequence of checks against the database, but does not perform any action.

The pre-upgrade report includes the following sections:

- Renamed Parameters
- Obsolete and Depreciated Parameters
- Component List and Status
- Tablespace and their Space Usage
- Pre-Upgrade Checks and Required Actions
- Pre-Upgrade Recommendations

From the Oracle Database 12c software installation directory on the clone database server, follow the steps below to execute the pre-upgrade script.

```
$ cd /u01/app/oracle/product/12.1.0/db_1/rdbms/admin
$ sqlplus /nolog

SQL*Plus: Release 11.2.0.3.0 Production on Wed Apr 23 18:49:26 2014
```

```
Copyright (c) 1982, 2011, Oracle.  All rights reserved.

SQL> CONN / AS SYSDBA
Connected.
SQL> @preupgrd.sql
Loading Pre-Upgrade Package...
Executing Pre-Upgrade Checks...
Pre-Upgrade Checks Complete.
      ************************************************************

Results of the checks are located at:
 /u01/app/oracle/cfgtoollogs/T1C1/preupgrade/preupgrade.log

Pre-Upgrade Fixup Script (run in source database environment):
 /u01/app/oracle/cfgtoollogs/T1C1/preupgrade/preupgrade_fixups.sql

Post-Upgrade Fixup Script (run shortly after upgrade):
 /u01/app/oracle/cfgtoollogs/T1C1/preupgrade/postupgrade_fixups.sql

      ************************************************************

  Fixup scripts must be reviewed prior to being executed.

      ************************************************************

      ************************************************************
           ====>> USER ACTION REQUIRED       <<====
      ************************************************************

 The following are *** ERROR LEVEL CONDITIONS *** that must be addressed
           prior to attempting your upgrade.
    Failure to do so will result in a failed upgrade.

   You MUST resolve the above errors prior to upgrade.

      ************************************************************

SQL>
```

Since the clone database and Oracle Database 12c are on the same host, another listener (LISTENER2) is configured and started to support the upgraded database. Export the environment variables *tns_admin* and *ld_library_path* as shown below.

```
$export TNS_ADMIN=/u01/app/oracle/product/12.1.0/db_1/network/admin
$cd /u01/app/oracle/product/12.1.0/db_1/bin
$./lsnrctl start LISTENER2
$export LD_LIBRARY_PATH=/u01/app/oracle/product/12.1.0/db_1/lib
```

Database Upgrade

The Near Zero-Downtime Database Upgrade requires the use of Oracle GoldenGate as part of the database upgrade technique. There are two methods for upgrading an Oracle Database:

- Oracle Database Upgrade Assistant
- Manual Upgrade using SQL

Oracle Corporation recommends using the Oracle Database Assistant (DBUA). The completion of the Database Pre-Upgrade Checklist ascertains the successful completion of the database upgrade using the Oracle Database Assistant (DBUA). The database upgrade timeframe is approximately 90-180 minutes regardless of the database size and it does not add, modify, or delete data.

Database Upgrade Assistant

The Oracle Database Upgrade Assistant (DBUA) is the Oracle recommended method for upgrading the database. There are two interface options to execute the DBUA:

- Graphical User Interface (GUI)
- Silent Interface

The Database Upgrade Assistant (DBUA) guides you through the upgrade steps by finding and implementing recommendations to ensure the database is successfully completed. The DBUA interface shows the progress of the database component and the completion status and simultaneously writes to the log files. DBUA alters and/or creates auxiliary files to support the upgraded database and provision database recoverability in the event of failure and fully supports the database running on Real Application Clusters. For a highly integrated and automated upgrade, the DBUA is available on silent mode from the command-line.

However, when the Database Administrator requires full control of the database upgrade runtime, the upgrade is done manually using SQL upgrade commands only. This method is more error prone when compared with the DBUA.

Starting Oracle Database Upgrade Assistant

The Database Upgrade Assistant (DBUA) is started from Oracle Database 12c home by executing the following steps:

```
$ /u01/app/oracle/product/12.1.0/db_1/bin/dbua
```

Step 1 of 11: Select Operation

The Database Upgrade Assistant (DBUA) supports the following type of operations:

- Upgrade Oracle Database
- Merge Database from a Different Release 12.1 Oracle Home

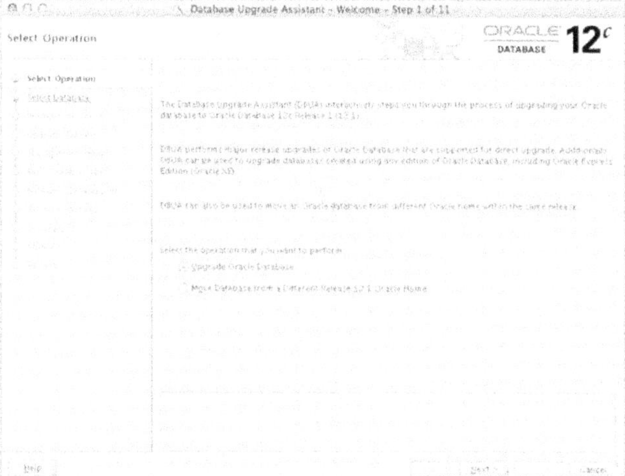

Figure 7-12a: Select Operation

Step 2 of 11: Select Database

Figure 7-12b: Select Database

DBUA detects the source and target database software releases from file '/etc/oratab'. From the list of databases, select the database name for upgrade. The status of the database must be up.

Step 3 of 11: Prerequisite Check

This step checks the prerequisite for the target database. Due to depreciated components and depreciated parameters, some alerts will be generated. Make sure to examine the alerts generated which may require taking actions before proceeding further.

Figure 7-12c: Prerequisite Check

Step 4 of 11: Upgrade Options

We select the database upgrade parallelism which is set to 4 by default. Parallelism enhances the database upgrade performance and reduces the downtime incurred during the database data dictionary upgrade. The degree of parallelism depends on the number of CPU's on the server and is generally set to *cpu_count – 1*. From the Upgrade Options, select 'Recompile Invalid Objects During Post Upgrade.' This eliminates the need of recompiling invalid objects manually by running the supplied script 'utlrp.sql'.

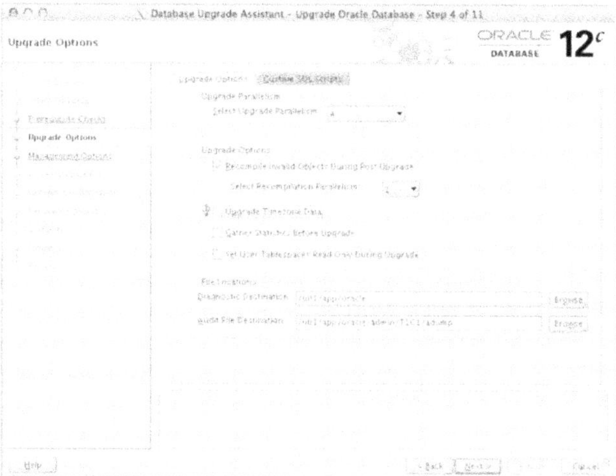

Figure 7-12d: Upgrade Options

Step 5 of 11: Management Options
Oracle Enterprise Manager 11g Database Control is depreciated by Oracle Database 12c. There are two available management options:

- Enterprise Manager (EM) Database Express
- Enterprise Manager (EM) Cloud Control

Figure 7-12e: Management Options

Step 6 of 11: Move Database Files
This enables you to move the database files and Fast Recovery Area (FRA) location. The storage types available are File System and Automatic Storage Management (ASM). For File System, you may select the Oracle Managed File (OMF) option.

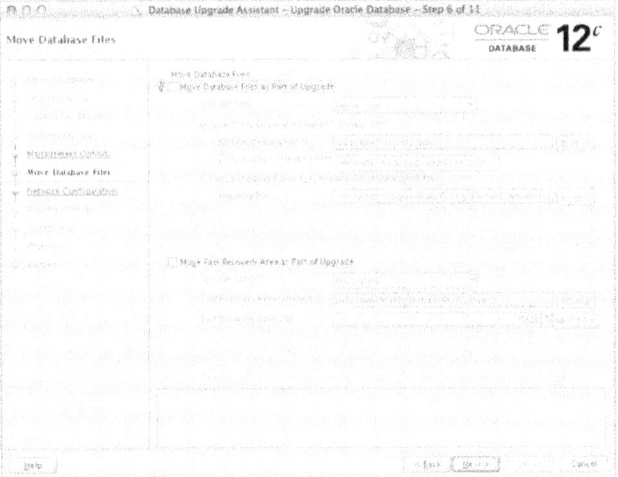

Figure 7-12f: Database Files

Step 7 of 11: Network Configuration

Select the listeners from the available list. The target database will be registered with the selected listeners. Or enter the listener name and the port number to be created by the DBUA.

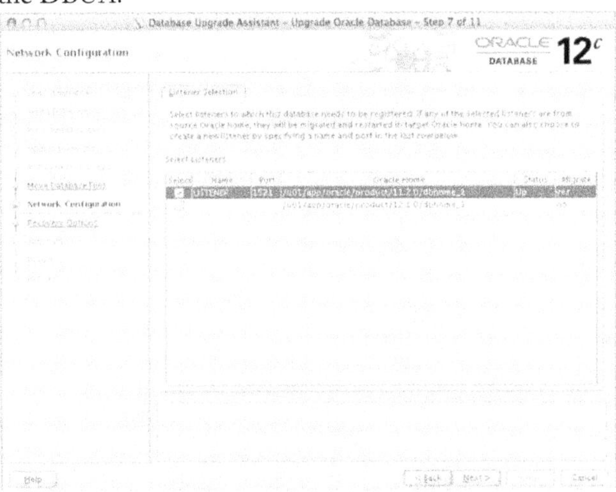

Figure 7-12g: Network Configuration

Step 8 of 11: Recovery Options

There are two recovery options: Use RMAN backup or Database Flashback. Since this is a clone database from an existing backup, select the option 'I have my own backup and restore strategy'. Consider the disk space requirements for +DATA, +FRA, flashback logs, and the archived log file. Disk space requirements must be met before proceeding further, if any.

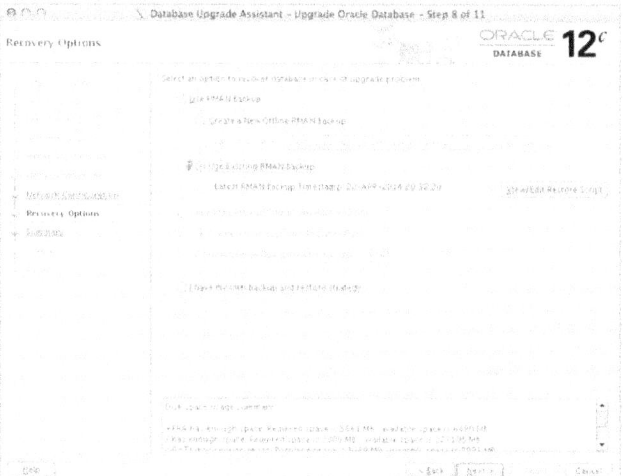

Figure 7-12h: Recovery Options

Step 9 of 11: Summary

Here we review the database upgrade summary sections. We begin by verifying the source and target database details – database name, release, and home. The Pre-Upgrade Checks section lists the issues found and the corresponding actions. The summary includes database parameters' old and changed values as recommended by the pre-upgrade script. Then we click 'Finish' to begin the database upgrade.

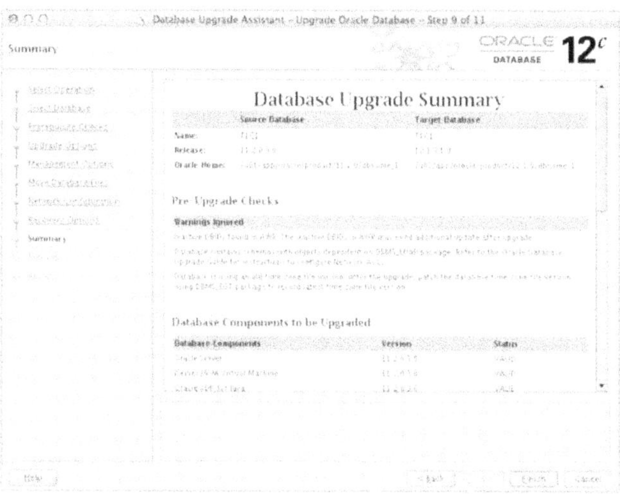

Figure 7-12i: Summary

Step 10 of 11: Progress

Depending on the number of components to upgrade, the timeframe varies. An average of 90-120 minutes is common to complete the upgrade for all components.

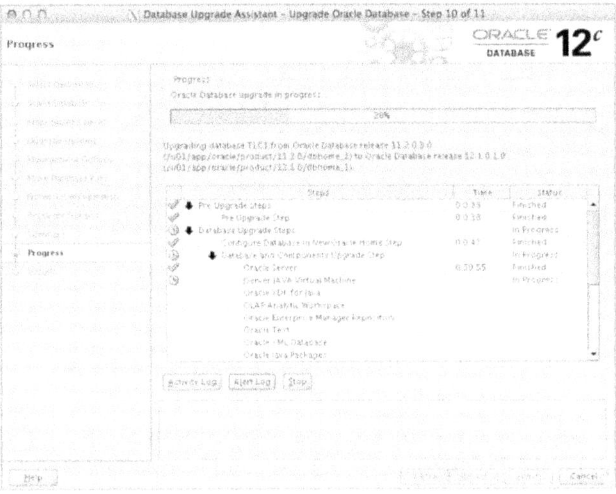

Figure 7-12j: Progress

Step 11 of 11: Upgrade Result

Review the upgrade results. For each step, DBUA generates a log file. Review the log files for recommendations as a post-upgrade step.

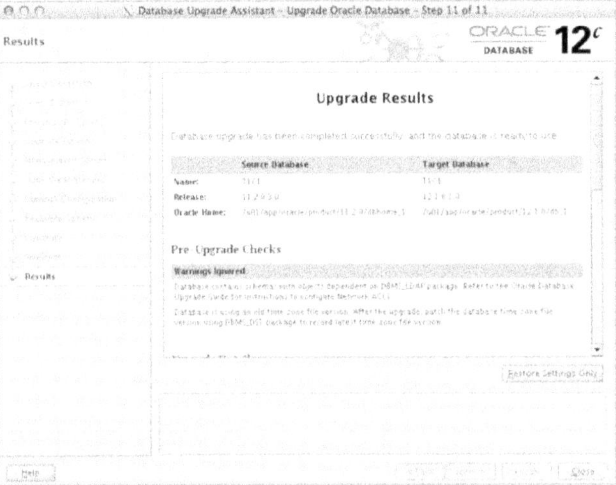

Figure 7-12k: Upgrade Result

Verify Database Upgrade

Congratulations! The database upgrade is successfully completed. The target database instance is started and the database is opened. Query the dynamic view V$VERSION to confirm the database core components versions.

```
$ . oraenv
ORACLE_SID = [T1C1] ? T1C1
The Oracle base remains unchanged with value /u01/app/oracle
$ sqlplus /nolog

SQL*Plus: Release 12.1.0.1.0 Production on Sun Apr 27 19:36:50 2014

SQL> CONN / AS SYSDBA
Connected.
SQL> SELECT banner
  2  FROM   v$version;

BANNER
--------------------------------------------------------------------------
----
Oracle Database 12c Enterprise Edition Release 12.1.0.1.0 - 64bit
Production
PL/SQL Release 12.1.0.1.0 - Production
CORE    12.1.0.1.0      Production
TNS for Linux: Version 12.1.0.1.0 - Production
NLSRTL Version 12.1.0.1.0 - Production
```

Silent Mode Upgrade

Another method of performing the database upgrade is running the DBUA on silent mode. The main reason for running the DBUA on silent mode is the absence of X Windows Manager. It also provides more control over the DBUA GUI runtime. The following script illustrates running the DBUA on silent mode:

```
$ /u01/app/oracle/product/12.1.0/db_1/bin/dbua -silent \
> -sid T1C1 \
> -oracleHome /u01/app/oracle/product/11.2.0.3/dbhome_1 \
> -diagnosticDest /u01/app/oracle \
> -autoextendFiles \
> -recompile_invalid_objects true \
> -degree_of_parallelism 2 \
> -upgradeTimezone \
> -emConfiguration NONE \
> -keepHiddenParams \
> -gatheringStatistics \
> -createGRP true \
> -upgrade_parallelism 2
```

The timeframe for the database upgrade using the DBUA silent mode is the same as the DBUA GUI mode. Performing the pre-upgrade checklist ensures database components are upgraded successfully.

Manual Upgrade

The manual upgrade provides you with more control when performing the database upgrade. The steps for performing a manual database upgrade using SQL command are highlighted below.

- On the source database, run the pre-upgrade script tool shipped with Oracle Database 12c. The script file is preupgrd.sql.
- Create a whole database backup using RMAN. This serves as the database recovery solution in the event of failure.
- The installation of Oracle Database 12c is already completed. Prepare the new Oracle Home database auxiliary files, parameters, password file and network files.
- Shutdown the source database.
- While still connected as SYSDBA, execute the SQL upgrade command startup *upgrade*.
- Restart the database instance.
- Run the post-upgrade script 'utlu121s.sql'
- Run the post-upgrade script 'catupst.sql,' which performs the remaining database upgrade operations.

Database Post-Upgrade

The post-upgrade configures files related to Oracle Database 12c. When using Oracle Database Configuration Assistant (DBCA), the database post-upgrade changes are minimal. The following is the list of post-upgrade changes:

- Update the Operating System environment variables
- Update '/etc/oratab' for Manual Upgrade
- Update Client Files
- Upgrade Recovery Manager Catalog, if used
- Enable Database Vault, if used.
- Deploy Oracle Database 12c new features, gradually.
- Enable Unified Auditing

Enable Flashback Database

Using the Flashback Database quickly brings the database to an earlier point in time by undoing changes that occurred since that time. The advantage of the database Flashback is its fast operation compared to the traditional RMAN restore-recover operations to perform point-time database recovery.

The Flashback Database step supports rewinding the database after Phase V – Application Regression Testing is completed. The purpose is to reestablish the target database without the need to re-clone the database. Follow the steps below to configure and enable Flashback Database.

Though there are several Flashback Database options which are: Timestamp, System Change Number (SCN), Restore Point and Flashback Sequence Number, use of the SCN or restore point is preferred. Begin by obtaining the current database System Change Number (SCN). This will be used on the subsequent step to flashback the database.

```
SQL> SELECT current_scn
  2  FROM   v$database;

CURRENT_SCN
-----------
    9294723
```

Enabling the Flashback Database starts a background process RVWR to write the Flashback logs to the Fast Recovery Area (FRA). The amount of Flashback is set to 129600 minutes (90 days) to target, but not to guarantee enough timeframe to complete the applications' functional testing. The Fast Recovery Area (FRA) size is proportional to the retention target.

```
SQL> ALTER SYSTEM SET DB_FLASHBACK_RETENTION_TARGET=129600
  2  SCOPE=both;

System altered.

SQL> ALTER DATABASE FLASHBACK on;

Database altered.

SQL> SELECT flashback_on
  2  FROM   v$database;

FLASHBACK_ON
------------------
YES

SQL>
```

Setting the parameter *db_flashback_retention_taret* is optional. It specifies an upper limit, in minutes, on how far back the database can be flashed back. The default value is 1440 minutes (1 day). When setting the value for the parameter *db_flashback_retention_taret*, consider two important elements – the timeframe to complete the testing and the size of the Fast Recovery Area (FRA) to sustain the accumulative database flashback logs.

We keep monitoring the storage requirement and usage while the Flashback Database is enabled. Use Oracle Enterprise Manager or perform queries against the database dynamic views:

v$flashback_database_log
v$flash_recovery_area_usage

Phase V: Applications Regression Testing

Before the transition to the new system, functional and technical testing must be thoroughly conducted. The purpose of various types of testing is to uncover issues that may arise due to changes and enhancements to the database management system internals. A very common area to address is the behavior of the application with the new database optimizer. Oracle Corporation has addressed this issue using the Oracle Real Application Testing suite, which consists of two solutions:

- Oracle Database Replay
- SQL Performance Analyzer

Oracle Database Replay

Oracle Database Replay is the database upgrade companion tool. The Database Replay enables users to perform real-time, real-world testing by capturing actual database workloads on the production system and replaying them on the clone database system. The test on the clone database can be performed with production characteristics including timing and transactions concurrency.

The main feature of Database Replay is it provides analysis and reporting to highlight potential problems such as slow completion of a report on the new environment. The Oracle Database Replay has two interfaces – Oracle Enterprise Manager and Oracle PL/SQL supplied packages. Figure 7-13 shows the Oracle Database Replay workflow, which is composed of three tasks:

- **Capture Workload.** Captures a workload from the production (source) environment. The capture is done during normal business hours to create a real-world baseline.
- **Pre-Process Workload.** This task prepares the capture files for replay on the target system. The workload capture files must be moved to the target system before the next task, when the pre-process is done on the source system.
- **Replay Workload.** This task replays the pre-processed workload on the clone database.

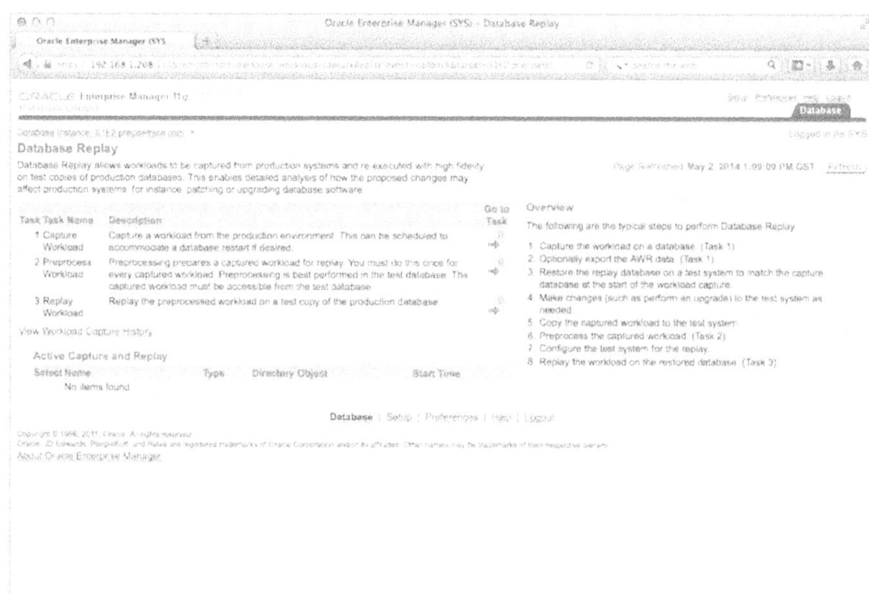

Figure 7-13: Oracle Database Replay

SQL Performance Analyzer

The SQL Performance Analyzer (SPA) can be used to quickly and accurately predict and prevent potential performance problems for any database changes that alter the original sequence of execution plan steps. The change can be any of the following:

- Database Upgrade
- Operating System Upgrade
- Database Migration
- Deploying New Application
- Database Schema Changes / Adding Indexes
- Statistics Gathering
- Database Parameter Changes

- Hardware and Operating System Changes

Figure 7-14 depicts the Oracle SQL Performance Analyzer (SPA). The workflow run is either a predetermined or guided workflow. Select the workflow that corresponds to the upgrade path or guided workflow.

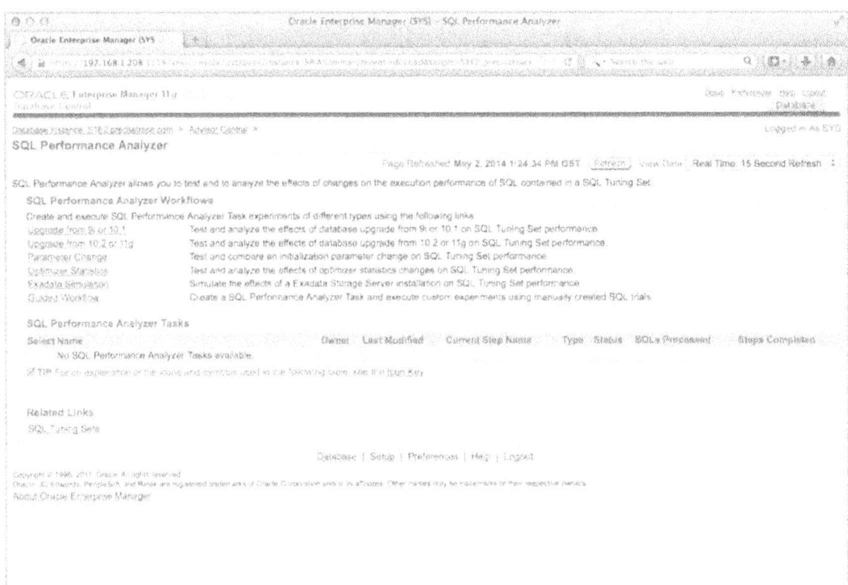

Fig 7-14: Oracle SQL Performance Analyzer (SPA)

This is an overview of Oracle Database Real Application Testing Suite solutions. Use either Oracle Database Replay or SQL Performance Analyzer. Phase V – Applications Regressions Testing is out of this book's scope, as our objective is limited to implementation of using Oracle GoldenGate 12c for Near Zero-Downtime Migration and Upgrade of the Oracle Database only.

Perform Flashback Database

After completing the functional and technical testing, the database must be restored to the state just after the upgrade is completed. The following procedure illustrates performing the Flashback Database.

```
SQL> SHUTDOWN IMMEDIATE
Database closed.
Database dismounted.
ORACLE instance shut down.
SQL> STARTUP MOUNT
ORACLE instance started.
```

```
Total System Global Area       551165952 bytes
Fixed Size                       2230232 bytes
Variable Size          373295144 bytes
Database Buffers               171966464 bytes
Redo Buffers             3674112 bytes
Database mounted.
SQL> FLASHBACK DATABASE TO SCN 9294723;
SQL> ALTER DATABASE OPEN RESETLOGS;

Database altered.

SQL>
```

Now, we query the dynamic view *v$session_longops* view to monitor the progress of the Flashback Database. Another method is to monitor the instance's alert log file.

```
$ cd /u01/app/oracle/diag/rdbms/t1c1/T1C1/trace
$ tail -f alert_T1C1.log
Flashback Restore Start
Flashback Restore Complete
Flashback Media Recovery Start
Serial Media Recovery started
Recovery of Online Redo Log: Thread 1 Group 6 Seq 3 Reading mem 0
  Mem# 0: +DATA/t1c1/onlinelog/group_6.266.846267799
  Mem# 1: +FRA/t1c1/onlinelog/group_6.260.846267803
Incomplete Recovery applied until change 9319751 time 05/03/2014
07:23:44
Flashback Media Recovery Complete
Completed: flashback database to scn 9319750
```

Disable Flashback Database

Now, we disable Flashback Database. The *disable* command terminates the Flashback background process RVWR and deletes existing Flashback logs stored at Fast Recovery Area (FRA).

```
SQL> ALTER DATABASE FLASHBACK off;

Database altered.

SQL> SELECT flashback_on FROM v$database;

FLASHBACK_ON
------------------
NO

SQL>
```

Phase VI: Apply Target Database Synchronization

Simultaneously, while the clone database is going through an upgrade to Oracle Database 12c, Oracle GoldenGate is running on the source system (S1E2). It is continuously capturing and sending transactions and trail files to the target system (T1C1). After successfully completing the database upgrade, the target database synchronization starts from the System Change Number (SCN) identified by the RMAN *duplicate* command.

This saves the Replicat processing time for reading, applying, and handling conflicts of unnecessary transactions. It is recommended that the target Oracle GoldenGate manager process is configured without the trail files purge option. Remote purge of trail files will be configured after the migration of users, when it is certain that the trail files are no longer needed. Figure 7-15 depicts the synchronization of the target database.

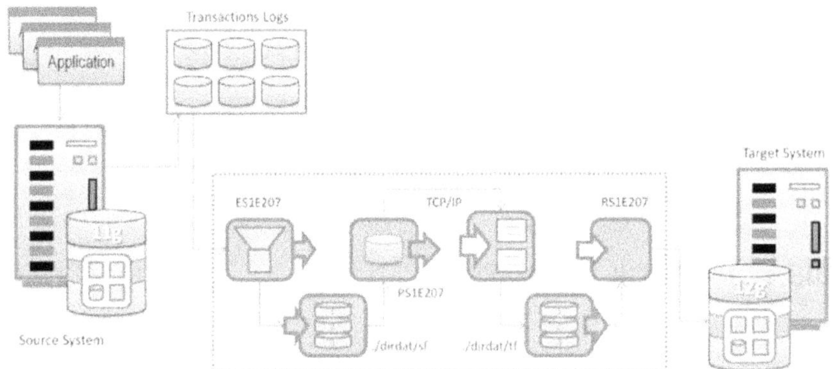

Figure 7-15: Synchronization of the Target Database

The Replicat process applies transactions to the target database in the order of the committed System Change Number (SCN), preserving data integrity of the target database while the applications continue to run on the source database. Implement parallel downstream Extract-Replicat processes carefully to avoid escalation of data integrity issues. The list of tables must be only related to tables handled by the Extract-Replicat group.

Remote Trail Files

Remote trail files are shipped from the source to target system using the data pump process. They are accumulated and ultimately applied to synchronize the target database. The size of the remote trail is proportional to the source transactions volume and the timeframe to complete the database migration and upgrade. Verify and compare the trail files on the source and its availability on the target system.

```
$ cd /u01/app/ggs/12.1.0/gghome_1/dirdat
$ ls -ltr
```

```
total 395056
-rw-r----- 1 oracle oinstall   492190 Apr 11 11:24 tf000000
-rw-r----- 1 oracle oinstall 15999967 Apr 11 21:00 tf000001
-rw-r----- 1 oracle oinstall 15999941 Apr 12 06:37 tf000002
-rw-r----- 1 oracle oinstall 15999756 Apr 12 16:15 tf000003
-rw-r----- 1 oracle oinstall 15999820 Apr 14 21:09 tf000004
-rw-r----- 1 oracle oinstall 15999990 Apr 15 06:50 tf000005
-rw-r----- 1 oracle oinstall 15999742 Apr 15 16:32 tf000006
-rw-r----- 1 oracle oinstall 15999867 Apr 16 02:15 tf000007
-rw-r----- 1 oracle oinstall 15999954 Apr 16 11:59 tf000008
-rw-r----- 1 oracle oinstall 15999940 Apr 16 21:44 tf000009
-rw-r----- 1 oracle oinstall 15999999 Apr 17 07:30 tf000010
-rw-r----- 1 oracle oinstall 15999852 Apr 17 17:17 tf000011
-rw-r----- 1 oracle oinstall 15999867 Apr 18 03:05 tf000012
-rw-r----- 1 oracle oinstall 15999872 Apr 18 12:59 tf000013
-rw-r----- 1 oracle oinstall 15999870 Apr 18 22:51 tf000014
-rw-r----- 1 oracle oinstall 15999906 Apr 19 08:44 tf000015
-rw-r----- 1 oracle oinstall 15999879 Apr 19 18:36 tf000016
-rw-r----- 1 oracle oinstall 15999783 Apr 20 04:29 tf000017
-rw-r----- 1 oracle oinstall 15999984 Apr 20 14:24 tf000018
-rw-r----- 1 oracle oinstall 15999955 Apr 21 00:19 tf000019
-rw-r----- 1 oracle oinstall 15999811 Apr 21 10:16 tf000020
-rw-r----- 1 oracle oinstall 15999790 Apr 21 20:14 tf000021
-rw-r----- 1 oracle oinstall 15999876 Apr 22 06:13 tf000022
-rw-r----- 1 oracle oinstall 15999796 Apr 22 16:12 tf000023
-rw-r----- 1 oracle oinstall 15999887 Apr 23 02:13 tf000024
-rw-r----- 1 oracle oinstall 15999797 Apr 23 12:16 tf000025
-rw-r----- 1 oracle oinstall  3440714 Apr 23 14:25 tf000026
```

Checkpoint Database Table

Create the checkpoint table used by the Replicat process. The default checkpoint location is a database table as defined by the GLOBALS parameter files.

```
GGSCI (ggs-target) 9> DBLOGIN USERID ggs_admin, PASSWORD oracle
Successfully logged into database.

GGSCI (ggs-target) 10> ADD CHECKPOINTTABLE

No checkpoint table specified. Using GLOBALS specification
(ggs_admin.chkpttab)...

Successfully created checkpoint table ggs_admin.chkpttab.

GGSCI (ggs-target) 11>
```

The Delivery Group

The delivery group is composed of the parameter file RS1E207.PRM, the Replicat process PS1E207, the remote trail ./dirdat/tf, and the checkpoint file ./dirchk/ES1E207.CPR. The delivery process uses the target database SQL native calls to apply transactions by reading the remote trail files.

Replicat Parameter File

Though the Replicat process starts from the System Change Number (SCN) identified by the RMAN *duplicate* command, to prevent a duplicate records error message, the *handlecolissions* parameter is enabled.

```
GGSCI (apps-srv1) 3> EDIT PARAMS rs1e207
```

```
REPLICAT rs1e207
SETENV (ORACLE_SID="T1C1")
SETENV (ORACLE_HOME="/u01/app/oracle/product/12.1.0/db_1")
SETENV (NLS_LANG="AMERICAN_AMERICA.AL32UTF8")
USERID ggs_admin, PASSWORD oracle
ASSUMETARGETDEFS
HANDLECOLISSIONS
DISCARDFILE ./dirrpt/rs1e207.dsc, PURGE
MAPEXCLUDE osm$repapi.OSM_DOCUMENTS;
MAP osm$repapi.*, TARGET osm$repapi.*;
```

Define Replicat Process

The Replicat process reads from the './dirdat/tf' remote trail and applies transactions to the target database – T1C1.

```
GGSCI (ggs-target) 12> ADD REPLICAT rs1e207, EXTTRAIL ./dirdat/tf
REPLICAT added.

GGSCI (ggs-target) 13>
```

Remote Trail Settings

Verify the details of the remote trail. The Replicat process applies the remote trail files to the target database.

```
$ ./ggsci
Oracle GoldenGate Command Interpreter for Oracle
Version 12.1.2.0.0 17185003 OGGCORE_12.1.2.0.0_PLATFORMS_130924.1316_FBO
Linux, x64, 64bit (optimized), Oracle 11g on Sep 25 2013 00:31:13
Operating system character set identified as UTF-8.
Copyright (C) 1995, 2013, Oracle and/or its affiliates. All rights
reserved.
```

```
GGSCI (ggs-source) 2> info rmttrail ./dirdat/tf

       Extract Trail: ./dirdat/tf
             Extract: PS1E207
               Seqno: 1
                 RBA: 9045389
           File Size: 16M

GGSCI (ggs-source) 3>
```

The GGSCI INFO command shows the location, the Replicat name, the current sequence, the current RBA (Relative Byte Address), and the trail file size.

Start and Monitor Replicat Process

The Replicat is started after a specified System Change Number (SCN) using the option AFTERCSN of the START REPLICAT GGSCI command.

```
GGSCI (ggs-target) 16> INFO replicat RS1E207

REPLICAT   RS1E207   Initialized   2014-05-04 05:16   Status STOPPED
Checkpoint Lag       00:00:00 (updated 95:49:26 ago)
Log Read Checkpoint  File ./dirdat/tf000000
                     First Record  RBA 0


GGSCI (ggs-target) 17> START REPLICAT rs1e207 AFTERCSN 14274705

Sending START request to MANAGER ...
REPLICAT RS1E207 starting


GGSCI (ggs-target) 18> INFO ALL

Program     Status      Group       Lag at Chkpt  Time Since Chkpt

MANAGER     RUNNING
REPLICAT    RUNNING     RS1E207     08:57:15      00:00:00

GGSCI (ggs-target) 19>
```

Perform quick basic test using SQL*Plus. This ascertains that the Replicat is applying transactions to the target database tables. Repeat to confirm rows count is changing.

```
SQL> CONN osm$repapi/oracle
Connected.
SQL> SELECT COUNT(*)
  2  FROM   customers;

  COUNT(*)
----------
   2553617
```

At this point, the source and target database are synchronizing with each other. The source transactions are applied in real-time to the target database achieving sub-seconds of latency. Now, the users migration to the new system occurs.

Phase VII: Data Verification

Prior to diverting applications from the source environment running Oracle Database 11g to the target environment running Oracle Database 12c, an important task must be performed and delivered with 100% accuracy - *Data Verification*. Data Verification compares data sets on the source and target databases and it is best performed using Oracle GoldenGate Veridata. Oracle GoldenGate Veridata assures data consistency without the need to rely on in-house developed SQL scripts or applications to compare table-to-table.

This becomes a complex task for a very large database (VLDB) environment with a large number of tables. In such an environment, Oracle GoldenGate Veridata plays the major rule by automating the creation of compare pair groups using different methods such as wildcard patterns. This eliminates creating compare pairs explicitly.

Oracle GoldenGate Veridata

Oracle GoldenGate Veridata performs advanced data comparisons between compare pair groups of the source and target databases. The use of Oracle GoldenGate Veridata requires software installation and configuration of:

- Oracle GoldenGate Server Database Repository
- Oracle GoldenGate Server
- Oracle GoldenGate Veridata Agent (Java Agent) on the source and target systems

To perform comparison on data sets, Oracle GoldenGate Veridata requires the configuration of related components. Use the Oracle GoldenGate Veridata web-based administration tool to execute the following:

- Configure connections to source (S1E2) and target (T1C1) databases
- Configure groups
- Configure compare pair groups
- Configure compare jobs

The process of performing comparisons of data sets between the source and target databases is illustrated by presenting the following major steps:

- Compare Pair Groups Job Runtime
- Initial Compare
- Out-of-Sync Confirmation

For details, refer to Chapter 6 regarding implementing Oracle GoldenGate Veridata.

Compare Pair Groups Job Runtime

After configuring connections, compare groups, compare pair groups and compare jobs, the job is executed for the compare groups as shown in Figure 7-16. There are two compare groups: OSM_APPS for transactional compare pairs and OSM_LOOKUP for lookup compare pairs.

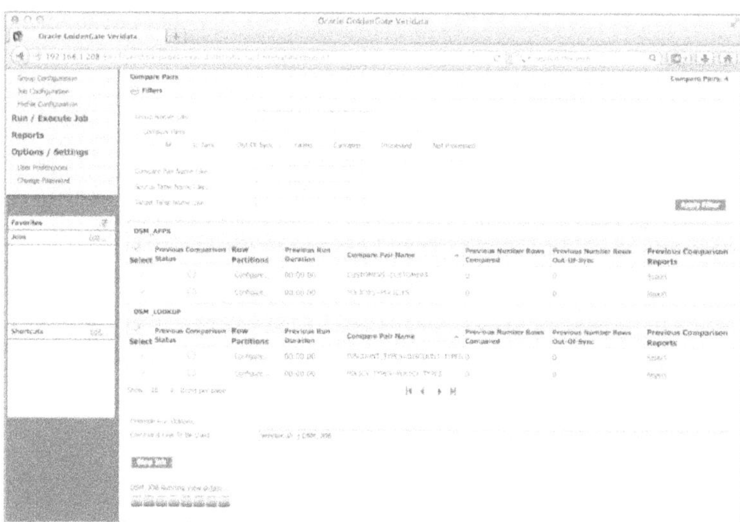

Figure 7-16: Compare Pair Group Job Runtime Progress

The compare groups and compare pairs configured are shown in Table 7-3.

Compare Group	Compare Pair
OSM_APPS	CUSTOMERS=CUSTOMERS POLICIES= POLICIES
OSM_LOOKUP	POLICY_TYPES= POLICY_TYPES DISCOUNT_TYPES= DISCOUNT_TYPES

Table 7-3: Compare Groups Configuration

Initial Compare

While Oracle GoldenGate is performing the Change Data Capture (CDC) on the source database — sending and applying the transactions to the target database — data deviation will continue to exist. To ascertain accurate compare results, the compare pair groups include all tables: transactional and lookup tables. Figure 7-17 shows the initial compare with out-of-sync results. This occurs because of the delay on applying the transactions to the target database.

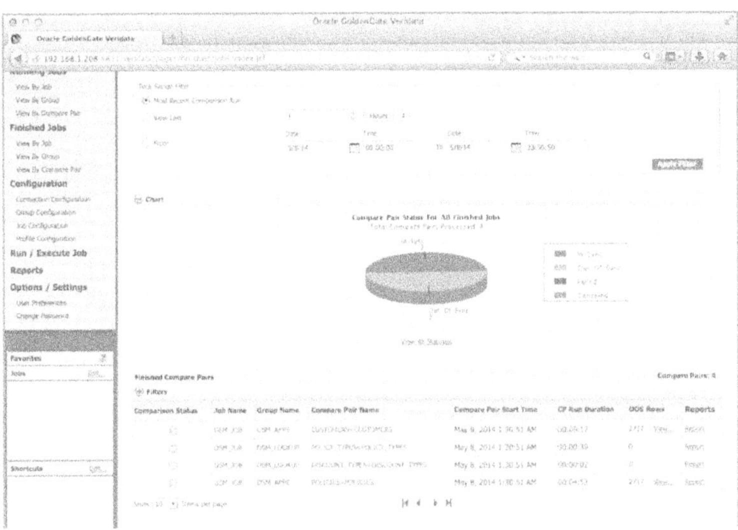

Figure 7-17: Initial Compare – Out of Sync

The OOS rows column indicates the extent of data mismatch, click on the View link to display the Out-of-Sync summary report. Out-of-Sync is expected to occur and the extent depends on the current transactions volume of the source database.

Out-of-Sync Confirmation

For an enterprise running multiple application servers, the next step is to disconnect the application servers gradually during the minimum database workload.
The purpose of using this approach is to achieve sub-seconds latency between the source and target databases. Use Oracle GoldenGate *ggsci lag* command to determine the current lag of the Replicat process. When it comes within the expected upgrade downtime timeframe, it is time to disconnect the remaining application servers to

allow data convergence. When the lag is zero, rerun the compare job to obtain the current Out-of-Sync result.

For our case, disconnecting the application server terminates the PL/SQL database application simulator by issuing the SQL *kill session* command.

```
SQL> SELECT s.sid, s.serial#
  2  FROM   v$session s, v$sqlarea a
  3  WHERE  s.username = 'OSM$REPAPI' AND
  4         s.sql_id = a.sql_id       AND
  5         UPPER(a.sql_text) like '%TRANS_LOAD%';

       SID    SERIAL#
---------- ----------
 19       1559

SQL> ALTER SYSTEM KILL SESSION '19, 1559' IMMEDIATE;

System altered.
```

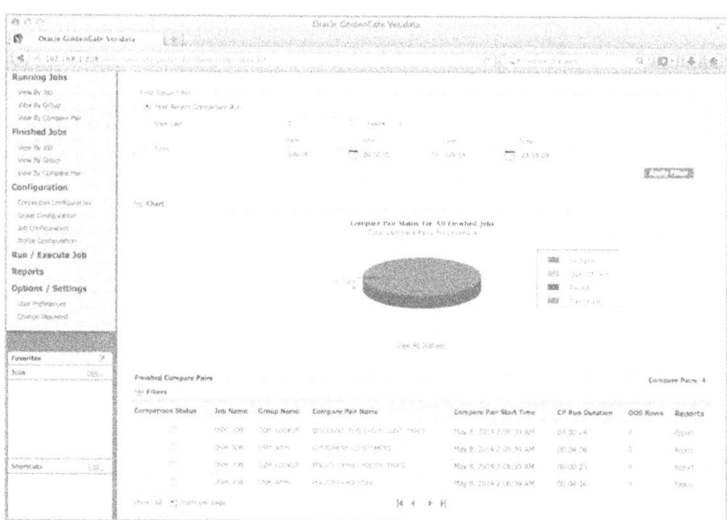

Fig 7-18: Synchronized Source and Target Databases

Figure 7-18 shows in-sync compare pair groups following termination of the PL/SQL transactions simulator. All transaction logs from the source database have been shipped and completely applied to the target database.

Achieving Near Zero-Downtime Optimization

The major factors impacting the database upgrade downtime are listed below. They are all related and listed in the order of higher-lower impact.

- Transactions volume on the source database during out-of-sync confirmation.

  High transactions volume affects the primary extracts capture from the transaction logs. Consider configuring parallelism of extracts, data pumps, and Replicat processes. Also, consider disabling applications access during low system activities to minimize the transaction logs.

- Extracts (primary and secondary) and Replicat lag.

  Within the downstream, there are three types of lags: The primary extract lag is the time difference of writing to the local trail and the transaction logs (online redo log file). The data pump extract lag is the time difference between writing to the remote trail and reading from the local trail. The Replicat lag is the time difference of applying transactions to the target database and reading from the remote trail. Fine tuning the lags reduces the downtime. Use the GGSCI LAG command to determine the current lag as shown below.

```
GGSCI (ggs-target) 5> LAG REPLICAT RS1E207

Sending GETLAG request to REPLICAT RS1E207 ...
No records yet processed.
At EOF, no more records to process.

GGSCI (ggs-target) 6>
```

- Application Servers Redirection Timeframe

  The redirection of Application Servers instances increases the downtime. An example is Oracle Application Express. The changes are made to DADS.CONF file to specify the new host name, listener port number, and SID. The preparation of redirection changes ahead of time and reduces the downtime as application servers are started immediately upon the confirmed synchronization of the source and target databases.

Removing Oracle GoldenGate Configurations

After the applications servers are diverted to the target system, perform the following tasks to remove Oracle GoldenGate instance configuration. However, do not de-install Oracle GoldenGate software and instance if there are more 24/7 databases to be upgraded. The following is the list of actions for removing the configurations:

- Stop, backup parameter files, and remove Extracts configurations on the source system.
- Stop the source instance manager.
- Delete the local trail files.
- Stop, backup parameter files, and remove Replicat configurations on the target system.
- Stop the target instance manager.
- Delete the remote trail files.
- Drop the checkpoint table.

Refer to Chapter 2 for details regarding Oracle GoldenGate 12c de-installation and removing configurations.

This concludes using Oracle GoldenGate for Near Zero-Downtime Migration and Upgrade. This chapter followed a phased approach which may vary by combining, adding, modifying, or eliminating specific tasks and/or phases. Ultimately, it is an outline for meeting the objective – Using Oracle GoldenGate for Near Zero-Downtime Migration and Upgrade.

Building Virtual File System for ASM Disks

Automatic Storage Management (ASM) employs provisioned disks for creating disk groups. The following steps instantiate the virtual disks used to create a virtual file system, without creating disks partitioning.

- Create zero-filled flat files

  Run the 'dd' command to create the zero-filled flat files. Optionally, in between each 'dd' command, the Operating System 'sync' command is executed to write buffered data to the disk, releasing memory for the next 'dd' command. The size of the file is specified using the 'count' attribute. The following example creates a zero-filled file of size 20GB.

```
#dd if=/dev/zero of=/u01/asmdsks/_asm_file_vdisk_01 bs=1k count=20971520
```

- Attach a loopback device for each file

  Use the Operating System utility 'losetup' to attach the first Linux loopback device with the flat file created. Ensure the loopback devices /dev/loop1 to /dev/loop7 are available. Test each loopback device availability; to test the first loopback device, type the following the command:

```
# /sbin/losetup /dev/loop1
```

- Link the virtual loopback device

  Use the command 'ln' to alias the loopback devices to be presented as virtual block devices.

- Create the ASM Disk

  The last step is to use Oracle ASM command 'oracleasm createdisk' to provision the files as virtual ASM disk.

Warning! This virtual disk setup is for training purposes. It should not be employed for a production environment. The script is designed to create up to 7 ASM disks only.

```
#-----------------------------------------------------------------
#-- DISCLAIMER:
#--
#-- This script is provided for educational purposes only.
#-- The script has been tested on an Oracle Database 11g instance
#-- and run as intended. However; prior to using the script on
#-- production systems, a dynamic test should be conducted prior
#-- to deployment.
#--
#------------------------------------------------------------------
#
#!/bin/bash
echo `date`
echo "Enter non-existing ASM directory or press ENTER to exit, "
echo "Example: /u01/ASMDSKS: "; read vdir
if [ -d $vdir ]; then
   echo "Directory exit"; exit -1
elif [[ $vdir != /* ]]; then
   echo "Invalid directory, example /u01/ASMDSKS"; exit -1
else
  echo "Enter number of virtual disks followed by size, "
  echo "Example: 4 4194304: "; read vdsk vsize
  if [[ "$vdsk" = *[!2-7]* ]]; then
      echo "Invalid argument value, Example: 2 4096"; exit -1
  else
     mkdir -p $vdir
     for i in $(eval echo "{1..$vdsk}")
     do
```

```
        sync; echo 3 > /proc/sys/vm/drop_caches
        echo "Creating $vdir/_asm_file_vdisk_0$i"
        dd if=/dev/zero of=$vdir/_asm_file_vdisk_0$i\
           bs=1024 obs=1024 count=$vsize status=noxfer
        echo "De-attaching /dev/loop$i"
        /sbin/losetup -d /dev/loop$i
        /sbin/losetup /dev/loop$i $vdir/_asm_file_vdisk_0$i
        case "$i" in
           2) echo "Creating ASM_DISK0$i";
              ln -s /dev/loop$i /dev/xvdd;
              /usr/sbin/oracleasm createdisk ASM_DISK0$i /dev/xvdd;;
           3) echo "Creating ASM_DISK0$i";
              ln -s /dev/loop$i /dev/xvde;
              /usr/sbin/oracleasm createdisk ASM_DISK0$i /dev/xvde;;
           4) echo "Creating ASM_DISK0$i";
              ln -s /dev/loop$i /dev/xvdf;
              /usr/sbin/oracleasm createdisk ASM_DISK0$i /dev/xvdf;;
           5) echo "Creating ASM_DISK0$i";
              ln -s /dev/loop$i /dev/xvdg;
              /usr/sbin/oracleasm createdisk ASM_DISK0$i /dev/xvdg;;
           6) echo "Creating ASM_DISK0$i";
              ln -s /dev/loop$i /dev/xvdh;
              /usr/sbin/oracleasm createdisk ASM_DISK0$i /dev/xvdh;;
           7) echo "Creating ASM_DISK0$i";
              ln -s /dev/loop$i /dev/xvdi;
              /usr/sbin/oracleasm createdisk ASM_DISK0$i /dev/xvdi;;
        esac
     done
     echo "Scanning ASM disk..."
     echo ""
     /usr/sbin/oracleasm listdisks
  fi
fi
```

Summary

Employing Oracle GoldenGate for near zero-downtime migration and upgrade demonstrates a key application area of the software. Since Oracle GoldenGate is a multitasking software for enterprises running 24/7 systems, the software may be used to achieve near zero-downtime migration and upgrade while it is already installed and running on the system performing query offloading. This is an Oracle GoldenGate Return on Investment (ROI) strategy when deployed using best practices.

This chapter has demonstrated the migration and upgrade from Oracle Database 11g to Oracle Database 12c, the multitenant database, providing an innovative approach for database consolidation. The topics covered were:

- Deploy Oracle GoldenGate on Source and Target Databases
- Online Clone of the Database
- Migration to the Automatic Storage Management
- Upgrade from Oracle Database 11g to Oracle Database 12c
- Target Database Synchronization and Data Verification

Though the chapter has demonstrated the upgrade from Oracle Database 11g to Oracle Database 12c, when using Oracle GoldenGate, it enables a jumping upgrade approach. For example, direct upgrade from Oracle Database 9i to Oracle Database 12c. The jumping upgrade uses an initial-load from an active database rather than a database clone. Such an approach provides higher flexibility when compared with the traditional upgrade methods such as using Oracle Database Export and Import.

The chapter specified upgrading Oracle Database 11g to Oracle Database 12c using the DBUA Graphical User Interface (GUI) as it is the recommended technique for database upgrade. Other database upgrade techniques are DBUA on Silent Mode and Manual Upgrade using SQL commands. The DBUA Silent Mode provides a similar level of control as the DBUA GUI. However, a manual upgrade is executed step-by-step which promotes more control throughout the upgrade process.

It is critical to verify the data before the application transition occurs. Using Oracle GoldenGate Veridata delivers the best result in terms of accuracy and performance.

The next chapter covers Oracle GoldenGate heterogeneity between Oracle Database 12c and Oracle MySQL. This combination positions Oracle GoldenGate distinctively for data replication.

Open-Source Heterogeneities Plugged-In: Oracle MySQL Database

CHAPTER

Overview

Oracle GoldenGate software is engineered to support the world's top database management systems, from the desktop to the mainframe platforms. This requires establishing a common and well-defined data structure to bridge the dissimilar platforms for achieving transparent *heterogeneity*. Yet, it also delivers high performance, dynamic data streaming for applications demanding real-time data acquisition. This enables a globally operating enterprise to operate side-by-side with global partners and affiliates without consideration of platforms' dissimilarities — sending and receiving data with sub-second delay as if it is coming from a unified environment.

The increase and advanced skills of open-source developers communities has highly reflected the open-source database management systems applications. Currently, *Oracle MySQL* is the leading database for online web applications. The open-source platforms have proven to be highly cost-effective and reliable to support the e-commerce applications; and do not underestimate MySQL when the top social media engines are powered by MySQL database. MySQL connectivity for Java, PHP, Python and Perl have become standard components to deliver business transactions for Small-Medium-Large (S-M-L) organizations.

However, enterprises need to have an insight of the business which requires moving data from the remote MySQL databases to a centralized Oracle Database running the business intelligence applications for real-time decision making. The need for sustainable real-time decision-making requires moving transactional data with sub-seconds delay, feeding the operational data warehouse for multiple concurrent high-bandwidth data streaming. This is where Oracle GoldenGate takes over to handle data consolidation, transformation and replication. It is beyond data replication.

Figures 8-1 and 8-2 depict the Oracle Database 12c multitenant heterogeneity, where each global MySQL database is mapped to a Pluggable Database (PDB). Oracle GoldenGate feeds the individual PDB, moving data on real-time. This architecture enables data protection solution and delivers unprecedented data consolidation and transformation for the corporate business intelligence (BI) applications.

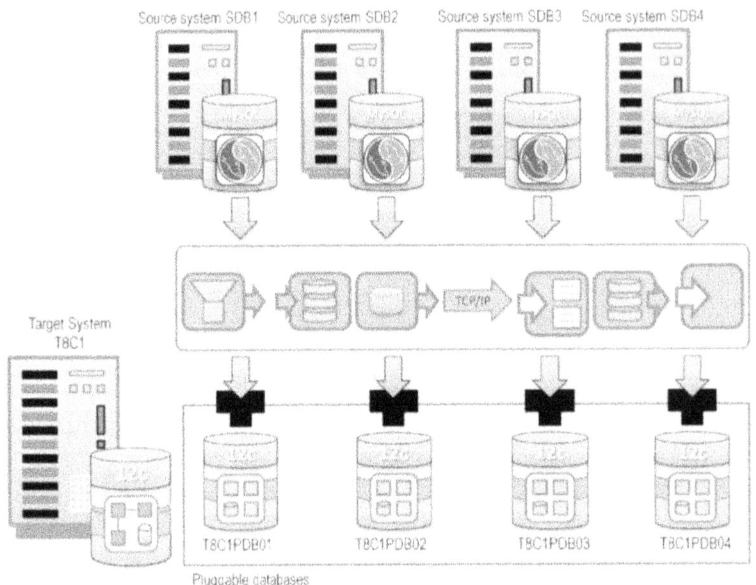

Figure 8-1: Heterogeneity, from Oracle MySQL to Oracle Multitenant Database

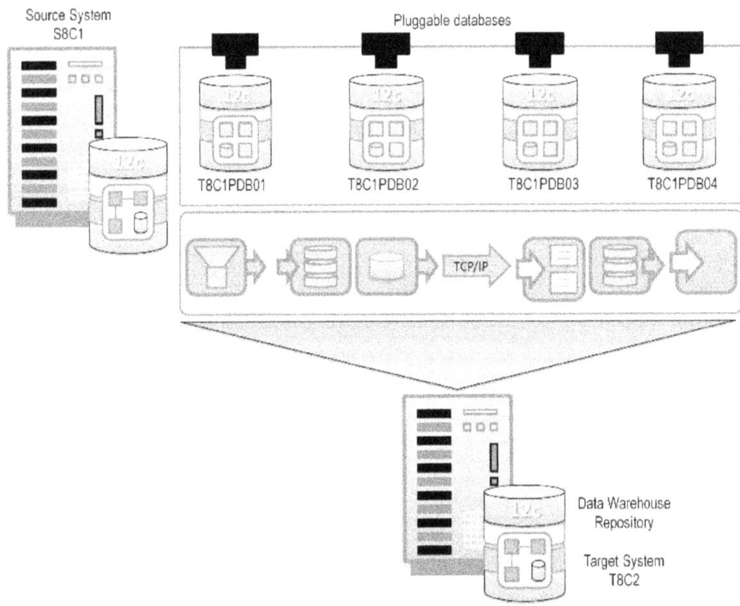

Figure 8-2: Data Consolidation, from Multitenant to the Data Warehouse Repository

What is the meaning of Heterogeneous?

It is referred to as dissimilar, a different kind, or unlike related entities. When the term heterogeneous is used within the context of Oracle GoldenGate, it refers to the extents of dissimilarity between the source and target database systems. With that said, Oracle GoldenGate bridges the two different kind of internal architectures without comprising database features and system resources and still remains.

> *GoldenGate provides low-impact capture, routing, transformation, and delivery of transactional data across heterogeneous environments in real-time, delivering advanced data replication and high-availability.*

This chapter is a deep dive of Oracle GoldenGate for moving data from four MySQL databases to a single Oracle database 12c — deploying the Oracle Linux Operating System for both the source and target which is the choice of open-source platforms.

Heterogeneous Database Support

Oracle GoldenGate supports the database management systems listed in Table 1-1. Do not attempt to install Oracle GoldenGate for an uncertified combination of database and operating systems. Since Oracle GoldenGate is unlikely to be application-specific, install the latest release and apply current patches. Oracle GoldenGate patches provide fixes to known issues discovered during the initial release. For details regarding Oracle GoldenGate certification, see http://support.oracle.com.

Database	Version	Operating System
MySQL	5.5 and 5.6	Linux Oracle Solaris Microsoft Windows
Oracle Database	11.1, 11.2 and 12.1	Linux Oracle Solaris Microsoft Windows HP-UX IBM AIX
Microsoft SQL Server	2008 and 2012	Microsoft Windows
IBM DB2	9.5, 9.7, 10.5 and 10.7	Linux Oracle Solaris Microsoft Windows IBM AIX
Sybase	15.0,15.5 and 15.7	Linux Oracle Solaris Microsoft Windows IBM AIX
HP Non-Stop SQL/MX	2.3 and 3.2	HP Non-Stop Itanium

Table 8-1: Oracle GoldenGate Certified Platforms

Oracle GoldenGate 12c Software Download

Figure 8-3 is the Oracle Software Delivery Cloud – http://edelivery.oracle.com. It lists Oracle GoldenGate for non-Oracle databases. Navigate to Oracle GoldenGate for Non-Oracle Databases v12.1.2 Media Pack for Linux x86-64 to list the current available builds. However, if the build is not listed, visit My Oracle Support Community (MOSC) http://support.oracle.com and submit a service request (SR) for Oracle Support Services to provide the download link for the specific build. A valid Customer Support Identification (CSI) is required for MOSC sign-on.

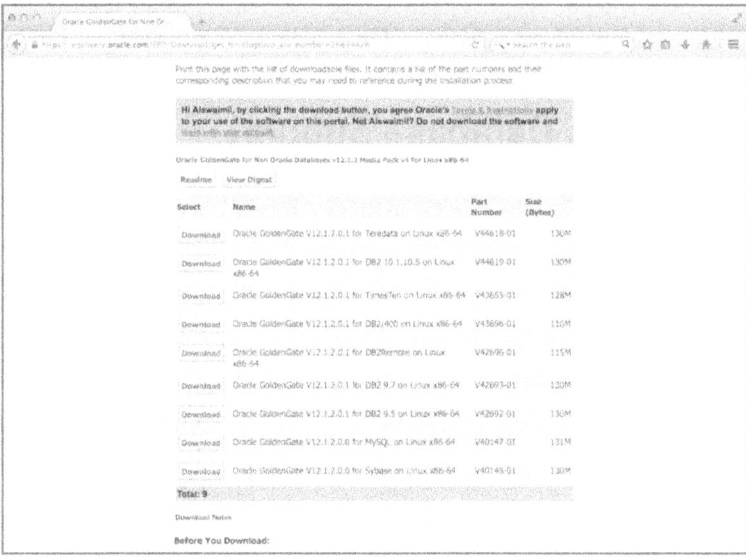

Figure 8-3: Oracle GoldenGate for MySQL on Linux x86-64 Download

Certification of Oracle GoldenGate and MySQL

Using certified software releases is essential. Certification ensures the combination of the installed Oracle software has been tested, issues are discovered, and fixes & workarounds are developed by Oracle Corporation. However, Oracle GoldenGate 12c for MySQL is certified with MySQL enterprise edition only. From MySQL command-line, execute the SHOW VARIABLES with the characters pattern '%version%' to display matching MySQL system variables related to software version details. Use of the wildcards characters ('%' and '_') and WHERE clause limits the returned system variables values.

```
mysql> SHOW VARIABLES LIKE '%version%';
+-------------------------+------------------------------------------------+
| Variable_Name           | Value                                          |
+-------------------------+------------------------------------------------+
| protocol_version        | 10                                             |
| version                 | 5.0.95-log                                     |
| version_bdb             | Sleepycat Software: Berkeley DB 4.1.24:        |
|                         | (December 16, 2011)                            |
| version_comment         | Source distribution                            |
| version_compile_machine | x86_64                                         |
| version_compile_os      | redhat-linux-gn                                |
+-------------------------+------------------------------------------------+
6 rows in set (0.01 sec)
```

At the time of writing the book, Oracle GoldenGate 12c (12.1.2.0) is certified with MySQL database version 5.5 and 5.6, and available for x86-64 platforms only. For the current certification matrix of Oracle GoldenGate and MySQL database, visit Oracle support services site – http://support.oracle.com.

Installation and Setup of MySQL

Since Oracle Linux Release 5 is bundled with MySQL, it is important to certify the pre-installed version of MySQL with Oracle GoldenGate for MySQL. Let us quickly start and verify the pre-installed Oracle MySQL version.

```
$ su -
Password:
# service mysqld start
Starting MySQL:                                            [  OK  ]
# mysql
Welcome to the MySQL monitor.  Commands end with ; or \g.
Your MySQL connection id is 2
Server version: 5.0.77 Source distribution

Type 'help;' or '\h' for help. Type '\c' to clear the buffer.

mysql> SELECT VERSION();
+-----------+
| VERSION() |
+-----------+
| 5.0.77    |
+-----------+
1 row in set (0.00 sec)
mysql>
```

For an unsupported release, an upgrade or de-install and install of MySQL is required. Typically, MySQL installation is performed using either the RedHat Linux Operating System package manager (rpm) or the Yum utility. The next section illustrates MySQL de-installation using 'rpm' and the installation using the Yum utility, which installs the certified Oracle MySQL release 5.6.19-2.

What is Yum?

Yum stands for Yellowdog Update Modified. It is a package manager for automating the installation of Linux Operating System packages (RPMs). The Yum utility uses a repository to resolve RPM conflicts and dependences. Before using the Yum utility to install MySQL, download the latest version of the MySQL Yum repository, which references the latest version of MySQL distribution packages. The repository is downloadable from the Oracle MySQL developers' site http://dev.mysql.com/downloads/repo.

The following are the basic options of the Yum utility:

- Installing distribution packages specifying the 'install' option followed by the repository definition. The flag [–y] enables a silent install session.

```
#yum install <distribution packages reference> [ -y ]
```

- Remove distribution packages by specifying the 'remove' option followed by the repository definition. The flag [–y] enables silent de-install session.

```
#yum remove <distribution packages reference > [ -y ]
```

- Query the existing installation for finding packages based on keywords or specific package name.

```
#yum search <package keyword>
```

Other Yum utility options include update, check update, provides, and local install. For software like MySQL running on Linux, it is highly recommended to employ the Yum utility to install software.

De-Installation of MySQL

Since the pre-shipped with Oracle Linux is not certified with Oracle GoldenGate 12 (12.1.2.0), perform the steps below to de-install the existing MySQL software using the 'rpm' command.

- Begin by querying the existing MySQL installed packages, then remove each software package individually as shown next. Do not remove the ODBC package as it is required by Oracle GoldenGate for MySQL.

```
[root@source-mysql1 ~]# rpm -qa | grep '^mysql-'
mysql-5.0.77-3.el5
mysql-connector-odbc-3.51.26r1127-1.el5
mysql-bench-5.0.77-3.el5
mysql-server-5.0.77-3.el5
mysql-devel-5.0.77-3.el5
mysql-5.0.77-3.el5
mysql-devel-5.0.77-3.el5
```

- Next, de-install MySQL software. Forced de-install is performed by supplying the two options '—allmatches' and '—nodeps'. The option '—allmatches' removes all versions of the packages with matching name — avoiding returning an error in case multiple matching packages exist. To avoid dependencies check, use the option '–nodeps'.

```
[root@source-mysql1 ~]# rpm -e --allmatches mysql-5.0.77-3.el5 --nodeps
[root@source-mysql1 ~]# rpm -e --allmatches mysql-bench-5.0.77-3.el5 --
nodeps
[root@source-mysql1 ~]# rpm -e --allmatches mysql-server-5.0.77-3.el5 --
nodeps
[root@source-mysql1 ~]# rpm -e --allmatches mysql-devel-5.0.77-3.el5 --
nodeps
[root@source-mysql1 ~]#
```

Repeat the de-installation steps on the four Oracle MySQL systems.

Installation of Oracle MySQL

The installation of MySQL is easily and quickly performed using the Yum utility by following the steps below:

- Begin by installing the latest MySQL repository package. The package is downloadable from http://dev.mysql.com/downloads/repo site.

```
[root@source-mysql1 rpm]# rpm -Uhv mysql-community-release-el5-
5.noarch.rpm
```

- Use the Yum utility to install Oracle MySQL server. The server must be able to connect to the repository to resolve packages dependencies and install the required software packages.

```
[root@source-mysql1 rpm]# yum install mysql mysql-server -y
```

- Query the installed MySQL packages details. This step can also be performed using the Yum utility.

```
[root@source-mysql1 rpm]# rpm -qa | grep '^mysql-'
mysql-5.6.19-2.el5
mysql-connector-odbc-3.51.26r1127-1.el5
mysql-community-client-5.6.19-2.el5
mysql-community-release-el5-5
mysql-community-server-5.6.19-2.el5
mysql-community-common-5.6.19-2.el5
mysql-community-libs-5.6.19-2.el5
mysql-5.6.19-2.el5
mysql-community-libs-compat-5.6.19-2.el5
[root@source-mysql2 rpm]#
```

- Start MySQL Linux services

```
[root@source-mysql1 rpm]# /sbin/service mysqld start
```

- Secure the installation by providing password for 'root' MySQL user.

```
root@source-mysql1 rpm]# /usr/bin/mysql_secure_installation
```

- Connect to MySQL server, create and query the list of databases.

```
[root@source-mysql1 rpm]# mysql -u root -p
Enter password:
Welcome to the MySQL monitor.  Commands end with ; or \g.
Your MySQL connection id is 13
Server version: 5.6.19 MySQL Community Server (GPL)

Copyright (c) 2000, 2014, Oracle and/or its affiliates. All rights
reserved.

Oracle is a registered trademark of Oracle Corporation and/or its
affiliates. Other names may be trademarks of their respective
owners.

Type 'help;' or '\h' for help. Type '\c' to clear the current input
statement.

mysql> create database SDB2;
Query OK, 1 row affected (0.00 sec)

mysql> show databases;
+--------------------+
| Database           |
+--------------------+
| information_schema |
| SDB2               |
| mysql              |
| performance_schema |
+--------------------+
4 rows in set (0.02 sec)

mysql>
```

Repeat the installation steps across the four Oracle MySQL systems.

MySQL Post-Installation

Perform the following steps to enable Oracle GoldenGate 12c to perform captures from MySQL transaction logs. Otherwise, Oracle GoldenGate trails are shipped excluding the database transactions.

- Change the Operating System group for the Operating System user 'mysql' to match the group for the Oracle GoldenGate user. Both users assigned the 'oinstall' group.

```
root@source-mysql1 rpm]# usermod -G oinstall mysql
```

- Modify the 'umask' environment variable to enable read permission for MySQL transaction log files. Add the environment variables MYSQL_HOME and LD_LIBRARY_PATH to .bash_profile shell startup file.

```
umask 077
MYSQL_HOME=/usr/bin; export MYSQL_HOME
LD_LIBRARY_PATH=$LD_LIBRARY_PATH:/u01/app/ggs/mysql; export
LD_LIBRARY_PATH
```

- Prepare MySQL parameter file /etc/my.cnf. This file overrides parameter files found elsewhere. Notice the format for the parameter 'log-bin', it is fully qualified as log-bin=/var/lib/mysql/<hostname>-bin.

```
[mysqld]
#
datadir=/var/lib/mysql
socket=/var/lib/mysql/mysql.sock
user=mysql
log-bin=/var/lib/mysql/localhost-bin
max_binlog_size=4096
binlog_format=row
#
# Disabling symbolic-links is recommended to prevent assorted security
# risks
symbolic-links=0
#
# Recommended in standard MySQL setup
sql_mode=NO_ENGINE_SUBSTITUTION,STRICT_TRANS_TABLES
#
[mysqld_safe]
log-error=/var/log/mysqld.log
pid-file=/var/run/mysqld/mysqld.pid
```

- Setup the 'socket' parameter to 'socket=/tmp/mysql.sock'. This is done creating the directory /tmp/mysql.sock or by creating a soft link to /tmp directory.

This step is required because Oracle GoldenGate requires the parameter 'socket' to be located on /tmp/mysql.sock.

```
[root@source-mysql1 rpm]# ln -s /var/lib/mysql/mysql.sock /tmp
```

- Create the ODBC initialization parameter file - /usr/local/etc/odbc.ini. Add the parameters required by Oracle MySQL ODBC connector.

```
[root@source-mysql1 etc]# pwd
/usr/local/etc

[ODBC 3.51 Data Source]
SDB2 = MyODBC 3.51 Driver DSN

[SDB1]
Driver = /usr/lib/libmyodbc3.so
Description = Connector/ODBC 3.51 Driver DSN
Server = localhost
Port = 3306
User = root
Password = oracle
Database = SDB1
Option = 3
Socket = /tmp/mysql.sock
```

Since most of the steps above are Oracle GoldenGate specific, do not proceed with the installation of Oracle GoldenGate 12c prior to successfully completing these steps. Stop and start the mysqld server and attempt to connect to MySQL. This will verify connections are affected by the new or modified parameters. After Oracle GoldenGate 12c for MySQL is installed, test the database connection from the GGSCI command-line by executing DBLOGIN. The SOURCEDB option refers to <db name>@<hostname>.

```
GGSCI (source-mysql1) 15> DBLOGIN SOURCEDB SDB1@source-mysql1, USERID root,
PASSWORD oracle
Successfully logged into database.

GGSCI (source-mysql1) 16>
```

Installation Oracle GoldenGate 12c for MySQL

With the introduction of the Oracle GoldenGate 11.2 integrated capture technique, Oracle GoldenGate for Oracle database is deployable in the same database server or in a downstream server receiving the Oracle database transaction logs. Refer to Chapter 8 for advanced data transformation and manipulation using Oracle GoldenGate. However, only the classic capture is available for non-Oracle database. For non-Oracle database such as MySQL, Oracle GoldenGate must be installed on the same database server. Hence, this chapter requires four Oracle GoldenGate

12c installations for MySQL to support the proposed topology. Unlike the Graphical User Interface (GUI) installer available for Oracle database, the installation of Oracle GoldenGate 12c for MySQL uses the command-line only; However, it is a relatively quick & simple setup task composed of (4) steps:

1. Unzip and extract the Media Pack using the Operating System commands
2. Start Oracle GoldenGate instance
3. Create Oracle GoldenGate subdirectory structure
4. Test database connection from GGSCI command-line

Create Software Location and Perform Media Extract

Now, we transfer the Media Pack zipped file to the Oracle GoldenGate 12c software location then unzip and extract the Media Pack on the same directory location. To avoid files' & directories' permission errors, verify 'oracle' is the owner and 'oinstall' is the group for the Media Pack (V40147-01.zip).

```
[root@source-mysql1 ~]# mkdir -p /u01/app/ggs/mysql
[root@source-mysql1 ~]# chown -R oracle:oinstall /u01
[oracle@source-mysql1 mysql]$ unzip V40147-01.zip
Archive:  V40147-01.zip
  inflating: ggs_Linux_x64_MySQL_64bit.tar
  inflating: OGG_WinUnix_Rel_Notes_12.1.2.0.0.pdf
  inflating: OGG_WinUnix_Rel_Notes_12.1.2.0.0.doc
  inflating: Oracle-GoldenGate-12.1.2.0-README.doc
  inflating: Oracle-GoldenGate-12.1.2.0-README.txt
[oracle@source-mysql1 mysql]$ tar -xvf ggs_Linux_x64_MySQL_64bit.tar
```

Starting Oracle GoldenGate Instance

While the current directory is Oracle GoldenGate 12c software location, start the GGSCI command-line. Failure to start the GGSCI is commonly due to incorrect setting of the environment variable LD_LIBRARY_PATH.

```
[oracle@source-mysql1 mysql]$ ./ggsci

Oracle GoldenGate Command Interpreter for MySQL
Version 12.1.2.0.0 17185003 OGGCORE_12.1.2.0.0_PLATFORMS_130924.1316
Linux, x64, 64bit (optimized), MySQL Enterprise on Sep 24 2013 15:32:47
Operating system character set identified as UTF-8.

Copyright (C) 1995, 2013, Oracle and/or its affiliates. All rights reserved.


GGSCI (source-mysql1) 1>
```

Create Sub-Directories and Start the Manager Process

The Oracle GoldenGate 12c directory structure is created manually. Create the instance manager process parameter file 'mgr.prm.' PORT is the only required parameter. Verify the manager process is successfully started before performing further configuration.

```
GGSCI (source-mysql1) 1> CREATE SUBDIRS

Creating subdirectories under current directory /u01/app/ggs/mysql

Parameter files                /u01/app/ggs/mysql/dirprm: already exists
Report files                   /u01/app/ggs/mysql/dirrpt: created
Checkpoint files               /u01/app/ggs/mysql/dirchk: created
Process status files           /u01/app/ggs/mysql/dirpcs: created
SQL script files               /u01/app/ggs/mysql/dirsql: created
Database definitions files     /u01/app/ggs/mysql/dirdef: created
Extract data files             /u01/app/ggs/mysql/dirdat: created
Temporary files                /u01/app/ggs/mysql/dirtmp: created
Credential store files         /u01/app/ggs/mysql/dircrd: created
Masterkey wallet files         /u01/app/ggs/mysql/dirwlt: created
Dump files                     /u01/app/ggs/mysql/dirdmp: created


GGSCI (source-mysql1) 5> EDIT PARAMS mgr

GGSCI (source-mysql1) 6> START mgr
Manager started.

GGSCI (source-mysql1) 7> INFO MGR

Manager is running (IP port source-mysql1.7823, Process ID 12476).

GGSCI (source-mysql1) 8>
```

Test Database Connection

Oracle GoldenGate runtime environments frequently requires connecting to the source and target database. The following DBLOGIN command successfully connect to the database by supplying the correct database name, hostname or IP address and privileged database credential.

```
GGSCI (source-mysql1) 10> DBLOGIN SOURCEDB SDB1@source-mysql1, USERID root,
PASSWORD oracle
Successfully logged into database.

GGSCI (source-mysql1) 11>
```

Changing MySQL User Host

The Oracle GoldenGate DBLOGIN command must explicitly specify the database name followed by the hostname (e.g.'SDB1@source-mysql1'). The following GRANT statement passes all the object's privileges for all databases to the user 'root' on the hostname 'source-mysql1'. The WITH GRANT OPTION enables the user to pass the privileges to other users. The FLUSH PRIVILEGES command immediately activates the previously executed GRANT ALL PRIVILEGES command.

```
mysql> GRANT ALL PRIVILEGES ON *.* TO 'root'@'source-mysql1'
    -> IDENTIFIED BY 'oracle' WITH GRANT OPTION;
Query OK, 0 rows affected (0.02 sec)

mysql> FLUSH PRIVILEGES;
Query OK, 0 rows affected (0.00 sec)

mysql> select host, user from user;
+---------------+------+
| host          | user |
+---------------+------+
| %             | root |
| 127.0.0.1     | root |
| ::1           | root |
| localhost     | root |
| source-mysql1 | root |
+---------------+------+
5 rows in set (0.00 sec)
```

Creating an Oracle Database 12c Container Database

The source MySQL databases are instantiated from an Oracle 12c Pluggable Database – S8C1PDB, using Oracle GoldenGate the initial-load technique for a heterogeneous environment – from Oracle Database to MySQL. The Oracle Database 12c Multitenant Container Database (CDB) 'S8C1' contains and manages (5) Pluggable Databases:

1. S8C1PDB, for establishing SDB1, SDB2, SDB3 and SDB4.
2. T8C1PDB1, mapped to MySQL database SDB1.
3. T8C1PDB2, mapped to MySQL database SDB2.
4. T8C1PDB3, mapped to MySQL database SDB3.
5. T8C1PDB4, mapped to MySQL database SDB4.

Figure 8-4 shows the Oracle Database Configuration Assistant (DBCA). Upon successfully completion, it creates the CDB database and the Pluggable Database S8C1PDB from which the MySQL databases are established. The Pluggable Database T8C1PDB1, T8C1PDB2, T8C1PDB3, and T8C1PDB3 are created from the SQL*Plus command-line as shown next:.

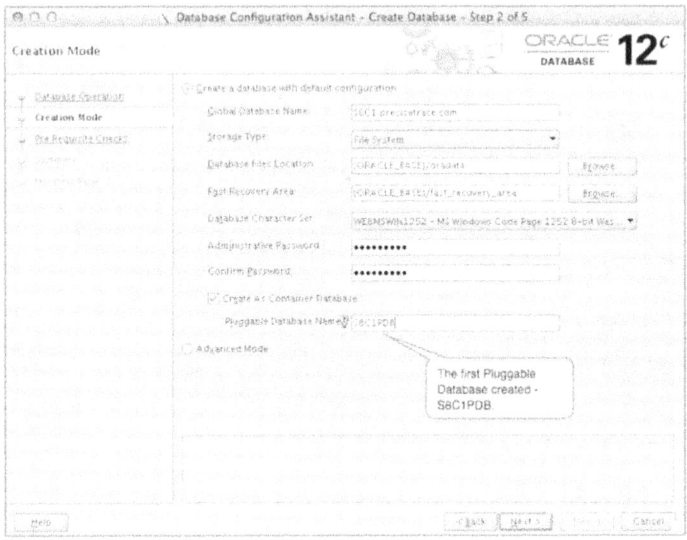

Figure 8-4: Create S8C1 as Multitenant Container Database (CDB)

Figure 8-5 shows the initial-load performed using the methods:

- Database utility (import) for establishing the Pluggable Database S8C1PDB, T8C1PDB1, T8C1PDB2, T8C1PDB3 and T8C1PDB4.
- File-to-Replicat for establishing MySQL SDB1, SDB2, SDB3 and SDB4.

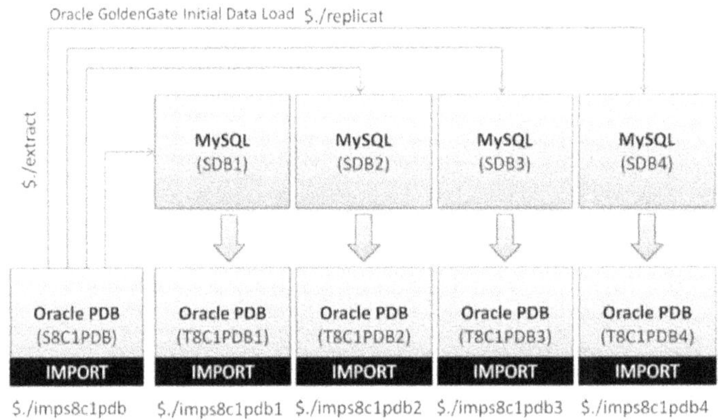

Figure 8-5: Data Import for Oracle Database and Initial-Load for MySQL

Create, Open, and Connect to Pluggable Databases

Oracle Database 12c is a multitenant RDBMS which is designed to support the deployment of large numbers of databases referred to as Pluggable Databases (PDBs). An example is deploying a series of departmental-level databases which are collectively formed in the enterprise database. These departmental-level databases are stored and managed using a single Oracle Database 12c system, where the data dictionary metadata is shared across all pluggable databases. This avoids having a dedicated data dictionary for each database. After the container database is created, the pluggable databases are created using a preferred method. The following pluggable databases are created from the seed pluggable database - PDB$SEED, which is like a template to quickly create pluggable databases (PDBs). Since Oracle Managed File (OMF) feature is enabled, the CREATE PLUGGABLE DATABASE command-line implicitly creates the pluggable database data files.

- The pluggable database 's8c1pdb' is created to perform the Oracle GoldenGate initial-load to each MySQL database. When using Oracle Database 12c DBUA to create the database as a Container Database, the first Pluggable Database must be specified. Other PDBs are created using the SQL*Plus command-line.

  Test connection to the Pluggable Database – S8C1PDB.

  ```
  $ sqlplus /nolog

  SQL*Plus: Release 12.1.0.1.0 Production on Mon Aug 4 05:10:30 2014

  Copyright (c) 1982, 2013, Oracle.  All rights reserved.

  SQL> CONN system/oracle_4U@S8C1
  Connected.
  SQL> CONN system/oracle_4U@S8C1PDB
  Connected.
  SQL>
  ```

- The pluggable database 't8c1pdb1'; mapped to MySQL database – 'SDB1'. Oracle GoldenGate Extract captures from SDB1 and applies the transaction to the 't8c1pdb1' pluggable database.

  ```
  SQL> CONN sys/oracle_4U@S8C1 AS SYSDBA
  Connected.
  SQL> CREATE PLUGGABLE DATABASE t8c1pdb1
    2  ADMIN USER pdb1_admin IDENTIFIED BY oracle_4U
    3  ROLES=(CONNECT);

  Pluggable database created.

  SQL> ALTER PLUGGABLE DATABASE t8c1pdb1 OPEN;

  Pluggable database altered.

  SQL> CONN system/oracle_4U@t8c1pdb1
  Connected.
  SQL>
  ```

- The pluggable database 't8c1pdb2'; mapped to MySQL database – 'SDB2'. Oracle GoldenGate Extract captures from SDB2 and applies the transaction to the't8c1pdb2' pluggable database.

```
SQL> CONN sys/oracle_4U@S8C1 AS SYSDBA
Connected.
SQL> CREATE PLUGGABLE DATABASE t8c1pdb2
  2  ADMIN USER pdb2_admin IDENTIFIED BY oracle_4U
  3  ROLES=(CONNECT);

Pluggable database created.

SQL> ALTER PLUGGABLE DATABASE t8c1pdb2 OPEN;

Pluggable database altered.

SQL> CONN system/oracle_4U@t8c1pdb2
Connected.
SQL>
```

- The pluggable database 't8c1pdb3'; mapped to MySQL database – 'SDB3'. Oracle GoldenGate Extract captures from SDB3 and applies the transaction to the't8c1pdb3' pluggable database.

```
SQL> CONN sys/oracle_4U@S8C1 AS SYSDBA
Connected.
SQL> CREATE PLUGGABLE DATABASE t8c1pdb3
  2  ADMIN USER pdb3_admin IDENTIFIED BY oracle_4U
  3  ROLES=(CONNECT);

Pluggable database created.

SQL> ALTER PLUGGABLE DATABASE t8c1pdb3 OPEN;

Pluggable database altered.

SQL> CONN system/oracle_4U@t8c1pdb3
Connected.
SQL>
```

- The pluggable database 't8c1pdb4'; mapped to MySQL database – 'SDB4'. Oracle GoldenGate Extract captures from SDB4 and applies the transaction to the 't8c1pdb4' pluggable database.

```
SQL> CONN sys/oracle_4U@S8C1 AS SYSDBA
Connected.
SQL> CREATE PLUGGABLE DATABASE t8c1pdb4
  2  ADMIN USER pdb4_admin IDENTIFIED BY oracle_4U
  3  ROLES=(CONNECT);

Pluggable database created.
```

```
SQL> ALTER PLUGGABLE DATABASE t8c1pdb4 OPEN;

Pluggable database altered.

SQL> CONN system/oracle_4U@t8c1pdb4
Connected.
SQL>
```

The data dictionary view CDB_PDBS lists the Pluggable Databases (PDBs) created and their status. The pluggable database PDB$SEED remains on read-only and cannot be dropped. The PDB PDB$SEED is an internal template to create other PDBs.

```
SQL> CONN / as SYSDBA
Connected.
SQL> SELECT SUBSTR(pdb_name, 1, 8) PDB_NAME, status
  2  FROM   cdb_pdbs;

PDB_NAME                            STATUS
--------------------------------    -------------
T8C1PDB1                            NORMAL
PDB$SEED                            NORMAL
T8C1PDB2                            NORMAL
T8C1PDB3                            NORMAL
T8C1PDB4                            NORMAL
S8C1PDB                             NORMAL

6 rows selected.

SQL>
```

CDB & PDB Network Files Configuration

The following listener configuration statically registers the CDB and PDBs with the default listener – LISTENER using the default TCP/IP port of 1521.

```
SID_LIST_LISTENER =
  (SID_LIST =
    (SID_DESC =
      (GLOBAL_DBNAME = S8C1.precisetrace.com)
      (ORACLE_HOME = /u01/app/oracle/product/12.1.0/dbhome_1)
      (SID_NAME = S8C1)
    )
    (SID_DESC =
      (GLOBAL_DBNAME = S8C1PDB.precisetrace.com)
      (ORACLE_HOME = /u01/app/oracle/product/12.1.0/dbhome_1)
      (SID_NAME = s8c1pdb)
    )
    (SID_DESC =
      (GLOBAL_DBNAME = t8c1pdb1.precisetrace.com)
      (ORACLE_HOME = /u01/app/oracle/product/12.1.0/dbhome_1)
      (SID_NAME = t8c1pdb1)
    )
    (SID_DESC =
```

```
      (GLOBAL_DBNAME = t8c1pdb2.precisetrace.com)
      (ORACLE_HOME = /u01/app/oracle/product/12.1.0/dbhome_1)
      (SID_NAME = t8c1pdb2)
    )
    (SID_DESC =
      (GLOBAL_DBNAME = t8c1pdb3.precisetrace.com)
      (ORACLE_HOME = /u01/app/oracle/product/12.1.0/dbhome_1)
      (SID_NAME = t8c1pdb3)
    )
    (SID_DESC =
      (GLOBAL_DBNAME = t8c1pdb4.precisetrace.com)
      (ORACLE_HOME = /u01/app/oracle/product/12.1.0/dbhome_1)
      (SID_NAME = t8c1pdb4)
    )
  )

LISTENER =
  (DESCRIPTION =
    (ADDRESS = (PROTOCOL = TCP)(HOST = target-cdb)(PORT = 1521))
  )

ADR_BASE_LISTENER = /u01/app/oracle
```

The database connect string for CDB and PDBs enables remote connections. Add the following TNS entries to TNSNAMES.ORA network file.

```
S8C1 =
  (DESCRIPTION =
    (ADDRESS_LIST =
      (ADDRESS = (PROTOCOL = TCP)(HOST = 192.168.1.42)(PORT = 1521))
    )
    (CONNECT_DATA =
      (SERVICE_NAME = s8c1.precisetrace.com)
    )
  )

S8C1PDB =
  (DESCRIPTION =
    (ADDRESS_LIST =
      (ADDRESS = (PROTOCOL = TCP)(HOST = 192.168.1.42)(PORT = 1521))
    )
    (CONNECT_DATA =
      (SERVICE_NAME = s8c1pdb.precisetrace.com)
    )
  )

T8C1PDB1 =
  (DESCRIPTION =
    (ADDRESS_LIST =
      (ADDRESS = (PROTOCOL = TCP)(HOST = 192.168.1.42)(PORT = 1521))
    )
    (CONNECT_DATA =
      (SERVICE_NAME = t8c1pdb1.precisetrace.com)
    )
  )

T8C1PDB2 =
```

```
  (DESCRIPTION =
    (ADDRESS_LIST =
      (ADDRESS = (PROTOCOL = TCP)(HOST = 192.168.1.42)(PORT = 1521))
    )
    (CONNECT_DATA =
      (SERVICE_NAME = t8c1pdb2.precisetrace.com)
    )
  )

T8C1PDB3 =
  (DESCRIPTION =
    (ADDRESS_LIST =
      (ADDRESS = (PROTOCOL = TCP)(HOST = 192.168.1.42)(PORT = 1521))
    )
    (CONNECT_DATA =
      (SERVICE_NAME = t8c1pdb3.precisetrace.com)
    )
  )

T8C1PDB4 =
  (DESCRIPTION =
    (ADDRESS_LIST =
      (ADDRESS = (PROTOCOL = TCP)(HOST = 192.168.1.42)(PORT = 1521))
    )
    (CONNECT_DATA =
      (SERVICE_NAME = t8c1pdb4.precisetrace.com)
    )
  )
```

Pluggable Database (PDB) Data Import

Prior to performing the heterogeneous, initial data load to establish the (4) MySQL databases – SDB1, SDB2, SDB3 and SDB4, let us designate and establish the Pluggable Database (S8C1PDB) as the source of the initial data load for MySQL. The Oracle Database 12c built-in data pump functionality is executed to import the data into the pluggable database, S8C1PDB, in preparation of the initial data load.

- Connect to the pluggable database T8C1PDB and create the default tablespace for the schema OSM$REPAPI.

```
SQL> CONN system/oracle_4U@T8C1PDB
SQL> CREATE TABLESPACE users;

Tablespace created.
```

- Run the shell following shell script (imps8c1pdb.sh). The script connect to the pluggable database – S8C1PDB creates the database schema OSM$REPAPI, creates the database directory - IMPDIR, grants database privileges and imports data into the pluggable database S8C1PDB.

```
export ORACLE_HOME=/u01/app/oracle/product/12.1.0/dbhome_1
export ORACLE_SID=S8C1
sqlplus system/oracle_4U@S8C1PDB <<EOF
create user osm\$repapi identified by oracle
default tablespace users
quota unlimited on users;
grant  dba, create session to osm\$repapi;
create directory impdir as '/stage/dmp';
grant all on directory impdir to public;
host impdp system/oracle_4U@S8C1PDB directory=impdir dumpfile=osm2.dmp
tables='osm\$repapi.RANDOM_DOMAIN', 'osm\$repapi.random_first',
'osm\$repapi.random_middle', 'osm\$repapi.random_last',
'osm\$repapi.policy_types', 'osm\$repapi.discount_types'
host impdp system/oracle_4U@S8C1PDB directory=impdir dumpfile=osm2.dmp
tables='osm\$repapi.customers', 'osm\$repapi.policies'
EOF
```

- Connect to the pluggable database 'S8C1PDB' to verify the data import operation was executed successfully.

```
SQL> CONN osm$repapi/oracle@s8c1pdb
Connected.
SQL> SELECT table_name
  2  FROM   user_tables;

TABLE_NAME
----------------------------------------------------------------------
RANDOM_DOMAIN
RANDOM_FIRST
RANDOM_MIDDLE
RANDOM_LAST
POLICY_TYPES
DISCOUNT_TYPES
CUSTOMERS
POLICIES

8 rows selected.

SQL>
```

Repeat the above data import for the pluggable databases T8C1PDB1, T8C1PDB2, T8C1PDB3 and T8C1PDB4. Supply the appropriate pluggable database connect string. After completing the Oracle GoldenGate 12c initial-load for MySQL database SDB1,SDB2, SDB3 and SDB4, four pairs of identical databases are established in preparation of the Oracle GoldenGate 12c Change Data Capture (CDC) and change delivery — from MySQL to the Oracle Database 12c Container Database.

GoldenGate Extract-Replicat Architecture

The components and data flow of Oracle GoldenGate processes is shown in Figure 8-6 and Figure 8-7. It is based on a unidirectional at two levels: (i) from the MySQL database to the pluggable Oracle Database 12c and (ii) from the Oracle Database 12c CDB to the Oracle Database 12c non-CDC. Table 8-2 lists Oracle GoldenGate Extracts, Data Pumps and Replicats processes from (4) MySQL databases mapped to (4) of the Oracle Database 12 pluggable databases.

Process	Type	Description
MGR	Manager	PORT 7823
E01SDB01	Extract process	Capture process writes to local trail
./dirdat/sa	Local trail	Local trail associated with E01SDB01
P01SDB01	Data pump process	Data pump process to the remote pluggable database
./dirdat/ta	Remote Trail	Remote trail created by P01SDB01
R01SDB01	Replicat process	Replicat at the Pluggable database T8C1PDB1
MGR	Manager	PORT 7824
E01SDB02	Extract process	Capture process writes to local trail
./dirdat/sb	Local trail	Local trail associated with E01SDB02
P01SDB02	Data pump process	Data pump process to the remote pluggable database
./dirdat/tb	Remote Trail	Remote trail created by P018SDB02
R01SDB02	Replicat process	Replicat at the Pluggable database T8C1PDB2
MGR	Manager	PORT 7833
E01SDB03	Extract process	Capture process writes to local trail
./dirdat/sc	Local trail	Local trail associated with E01SDB03
P01SDB03	Data pump process	Data pump process to the remote pluggable database
./dirdat/tc	Remote Trail	Remote trail created by P01SDB03
R01SDB03	Replicat process	Replicat at the Pluggable database T8C1PDB3
MGR	Manager	PORT 7834
E01SDB04	Extract process	Capture process writes to local trail
./dirdat/sd	Local trail	Local trail associated with E01SDB04
P01SDB04	Data pump process	Data pump process to the remote pluggable database
./dirdat/td	Remote Trail	Remote trail created by P01SDB04
R01SDB04	Replicat process	Replicat at the Pluggable database T8C1PDB4

Table 8-2: Oracle GoldenGate Process for Oracle MySQL Databases

Figure 8-6 depicts the processes and data flow. Oracle GoldenGate deploys on the MySQL systems. The Extract process writes to its local trail. The data pump process sends data to the corresponding Oracle 12c Pluggable Database. Through TCP/IP, the Pluggable database's Server Collector reassembles the data and writes to its remote trail. The Replicat process uses the target database SQL native calls to apply the transactions to the database. Data flow parallelism may be developed for each database, based on transactions' data replication volumes.

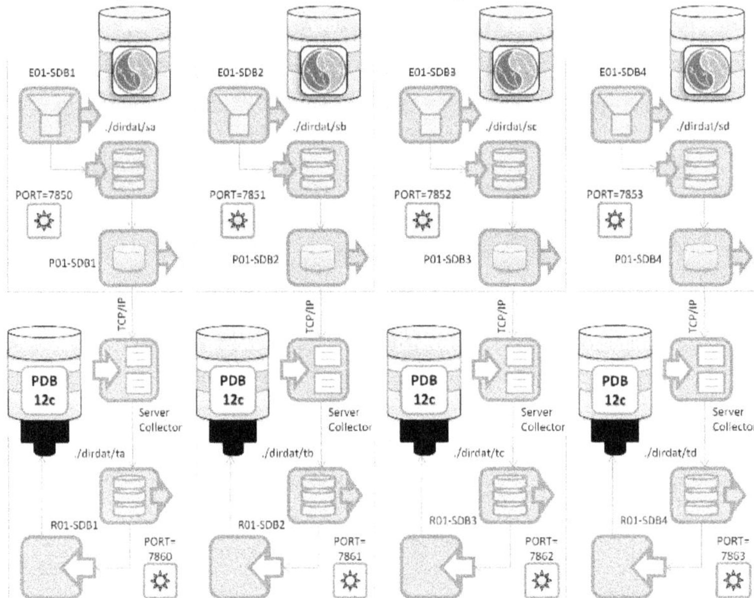

Figure 8-6: MySQL to Oracle Pluggable Database Components and Workflow

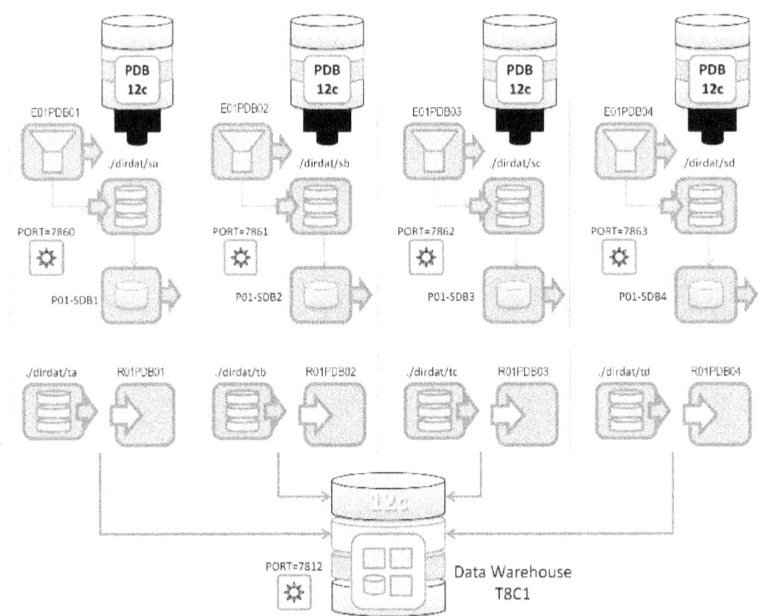

Figure 8-7: Oracle Pluggable Databases to Data Warehouse Repository

Figure 8-7 depicts the consolidation of the Pluggable databases into the data warehouse repository database. Oracle GoldenGate Extract processes are configured for each of the pluggable databases, moving data to Oracle Database 12c. For high performance business analytics, the adaption of the Oracle EXADATA database machine delivers the performance and scalability for queries' intensive applications.

GoldenGate Heterogeneous Configuration Considerations

On a heterogeneous Oracle GoldenGate environment, the majority of the tasks remain the same as on a homogenous environment. However, database-specific components are created accordingly. The following are the list of issues discussed and developed.

- MySQL Database Tables
- Oracle Multitenant Database Users
- Tables' Primary Keys
- Data Types Mapping
- Source Definition Files
- Data Transformations
- Login to MySQL Database

MySQL Database Tables

The Oracle GoldenGate initial-load capture and delivery for establishing MySQL database requires that the database tables structure is created with equivalent data types. Oracle GoldenGate handles data types mapping using source definition files, target definition files, or both. Begin by creating the MySQL database SDB1, SDB2, SDB3 and SDB4 using the CREATE DATABASE command, these are the databases mapped to Oracle 12c Pluggable Databases.

The following CREATE TABLE DDL statements are executed on database SDB1, SDB2, SDB3 and SDB4.

```
mysql> USE SDB1
Database changed
```

```
mysql> CREATE TABLE RANDOM_MIDDLE (
RM_NAME VARCHAR(32) NOT NULL,
PRIMARY KEY(RM_NAME));
```

```
Query OK, 0 rows affected (0.72 sec)

mysql> CREATE TABLE RANDOM_LAST (
RL_NAME VARCHAR(32) NOT NULL,
PRIMARY KEY(RL_NAME));
Query OK, 0 rows affected (0.34 sec)

mysql> CREATE TABLE RANDOM_FIRST (
RF_NAME VARCHAR(32) NOT NULL,
PRIMARY KEY(RF_NAME));Query OK, 0 rows affected (0.13 sec)

mysql> CREATE TABLE RANDOM_DOMAIN (
RD_NAME VARCHAR(32) NOT NULL,
PRIMARY KEY(RD_NAME));Query OK, 0 rows affected (0.19 sec)

mysql> CREATE TABLE POLICY_TYPES (
PT_CODE VARCHAR(8) NOT NULL,
PT_DESC VARCHAR(128) NOT NULL,
PRIMARY KEY(PT_CODE));
Query OK, 0 rows affected (0.30 sec)

mysql> CREATE TABLE DISCOUNT_TYPES (
DT_CODE VARCHAR(8) NOT NULL,
DT_DESC VARCHAR(128) NOT NULL,
DT_PERC INT,
PRIMARY KEY(DT_CODE));
Query OK, 0 rows affected (0.18 sec)

mysql> CREATE TABLE CUSTOMERS (
CUST_NO INT NOT NULL,
CUST_NAME VARCHAR(128) NOT NULL,
CUST_EMAIL VARCHAR(128) NOT NULL,
CUST_MOBILE VARCHAR(16),
CUST_ADDRESS VARCHAR(128),
PRIMARY KEY(CUST_NO));
Query OK, 0 rows affected (0.11 sec)

mysql> CREATE TABLE POLICIES (
POL_NO INT NOT NULL,
POL_FROM DATE NOT NULL,
POL_TO DATE NOT NULL,
POL_VALUE FLOAT(8,2) NOT NULL,
POL_SUB_TOTAL FLOAT(8,2) NOT NULL,
PT_CODE VARCHAR(8) NOT NULL,
DT_CODE VARCHAR(8),
POL_TOTAL FLOAT(8,2) NOT NULL,
CUST_NO INT NOT NULL,
PRIMARY KEY(POL_NO));
Query OK, 0 rows affected (0.13 sec)

mysql>
```

Oracle Database 12c Container Database Users

When running Oracle GoldenGate for Oracle Database 12c Container Database (CDB), the Oracle GoldenGate Extracts and Replicats processes are authenticated differently from the non-CDB. Since the Extract processes perform change data capture (CDC) from the database transaction logs, it connects to the CDB$ROOT container using a common database user. The Replicat processes apply transactions to the target database using the local database user. To find out users' details in the Oracle Database 12c Container Database, query the data dictionary views CDB_USERS. The next query displays the username, the type of user (common or local), and the container identification - pluggable database.

```
SQL> SELECT username, common, con_id
  2  FROM   cdb_users
  3  WHERE  username like '%GGS%';
```

Figure 8-8 shows how the local and common users are related. A common user is available across all pluggable databases, enforced by fine-grain database privileges.

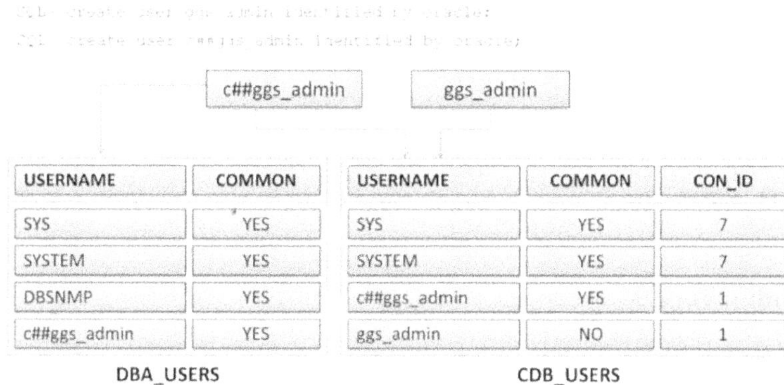

Figure 8-8: Oracle Database 12c Multitenant Users Data Dictionary

CDB$ROOT Users

The database administrators SYS, SYSTEM, and database pre-defined users belong to the CDB$ROOT container. These database users connect to CDB$ROOT and pluggable databases, as shown below. Use the SHOW CON_NAME to display the current pluggable database name.

- Connect to the root Container Database (CDB$ROOT)

```
SQL> CONN system/oracle_4U
Connected.
SQL> SHOW con_name

CON_NAME
------------------------------
CDB$ROOT
```

- Connect to the pluggable database (T8C1PDB1) using the database connect string

```
SQL> CONN system/oracle_4U@t8c1pdb1
Connected.
SQL> SHOW con_name

CON_NAME
------------------------------
T8C1PDB1
```

- Connect to the current pluggable database (T8C1PDB1) by the setting the session's default container.

```
SQL> CONN system/oracle_4U
Connected.
SQL> ALTER SESSION SET CONTAINER = T8C1PDB1;

Session altered.

SQL> SHOW con_name

CON_NAME
------------------------------
T8C1PDB1
SQL>
```

Local Users

Local database users are known to its own pluggable database only. Database privileges and roles are granted and exercised within the user's pluggable database only. CDB local users are managed in the same manner as users in the non-CDB database. The following commands create a local user in the current pluggable database (container).

```
SQL> create user ggs_admin identified by oracle;

User created.

SQL> grant dba to ggs_admin;

Grant succeeded.

SQL>
```

Common Users

Common Database Users are created in the CDB$ROOT container and are common to all pluggable databases (containers), subject to fine-grain privileges. Notice the common database users start with the characters 'c##'.

```
SQL> create user c##ggs_admin identified by oracle;

User created.

SQL> grant dba to c##ggs_admin;

Grant succeeded.

SQL>
```

The following illustrates using the common user 'c##ggs_admin' to connect to the database from GGSCI command-line.

```
GGSCI (target-cdb) 1> DBLOGIN userid c##ggs_admin, PASSWORD oracle;
Successfully logged into database CDB$ROOT.
~
GGSCI (target-cdb) 2>
```

Primary Key in GoldenGate Data Warehouse Repository

The tables' primary key uniquely identifies rows. The primary key is used by the Replicat to locate the target rows for DML transactions of type UPDATE and DELETE. In the absence of a primary key, Oracle GoldenGate has the KEYCOLS option of the TABLE or MAP statement to define the primary key's column(s).

In a data warehouse, the table's primary key may require additional attributes to uniquely identify rows as a result of consolidations and/or data transformations. Figure 8-9 depicts the consolidation of (4) MySQL POLICIES tables into a single Oracle Database POLICIES table. By adding the attribute policy's source to the primary key and using Oracle GoldenGate functions to identify the policy source, rows are uniquely & globally identified.

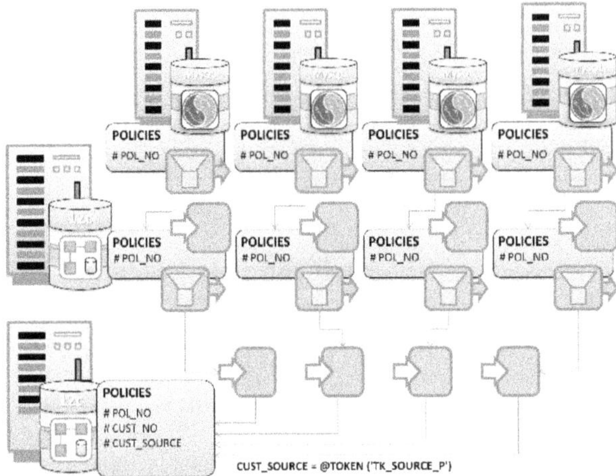

Figure 8-9: Globally Defined Primary Key Value

The technique implemented using Oracle GoldenGate TOKEN, to capture the data source, corresponds to the Extract process group name.

The POLICIES table structure for MySQL database matches the POLICIES table structure for the Oracle Pluggable database.

```
mysql> desc POLICIES;
+---------------+------------+------+-----+---------+-------+
| Field         | Type       | Null | Key | Default | Extra |
+---------------+------------+------+-----+---------+-------+
| POL_NO        | int(11)    | NO   | PRI | NULL    |       |
| POL_FROM      | date       | NO   |     | NULL    |       |
| POL_TO        | date       | NO   |     | NULL    |       |
| POL_VALUE     | float(8,2) | NO   |     | NULL    |       |
| POL_SUB_TOTAL | float(8,2) | NO   |     | NULL    |       |
| PT_CODE       | varchar(8) | NO   |     | NULL    |       |
| DT_CODE       | varchar(8) | YES  |     | NULL    |       |
| POL_TOTAL     | float(8,2) | NO   |     | NULL    |       |
| CUST_NO       | int(11)    | NO   |     | NULL    |       |
+---------------+------------+------+-----+---------+-------+
9 rows in set (0.04 sec)

mysql>
```

However, the POLICIES table structure for the data warehouse repository has the additional column CUST_SOURCE, which is part of the primary key columns.

```
SQL> DESC osm$repapi.policies
 Name                                      Null?    Type
 ----------------------------------------- -------- ----------------------------
 POL_NO                                    NOT NULL NUMBER
 POL_FROM                                  NOT NULL DATE
 POL_TO                                    NOT NULL DATE
```

```
 POL_VALUE                          NOT NULL NUMBER(8,2)
 POL_SUB_TOTAL                      NOT NULL NUMBER(8,2)
 PT_CODE                            NOT NULL VARCHAR2(8)
 DT_CODE                                     VARCHAR2(8)
 POL_TOTAL                          NOT NULL NUMBER(8,2)
 CUST_NO                            NOT NULL NUMBER
 CUST_SOURCE                        NOT NULL VARCHAR2(32)

SQL>
```

The Extract name for each pluggable database (source database) is identified as the policy source. The TABLE statement uses the TOKENS option to store the Extract name (source) in a user's defined Oracle GoldenGate environment variable of type token, TK_SOURCE_P.

```
EXTRACT E01PDB1
SETENV (ORACLE_SID=S8C1)
SETENV (NLS_LANG=AMERICAN_AMERICA.AL32UTF8)
SETENV (ORACLE_HOME="/u01/app/oracle/product/12.1.0/dbhome_1")
USERID c##ggs_admin@s8c1, PASSWORD oracle
EXTTRAIL ./dirdat/sa
TABLE T8C1PDB1.osm$repapi.customers, TOKENS (TK_SOURCE_C = @GETENV
('GGENVIRONMENT', 'GROUPNAME'));
TABLE T8C1PDB1.osm$repapi.policies, TOKENS (TK_SOURCE_P = @GETENV
('GGENVIRONMENT', 'GROUPNAME'));
```

The Replicat of the target database performs columns' mapping. The Replicat employs the Oracle GoldenGate function @TOKEN to retrieve the row source stored in the variable 'TK_SOURCE_P'.

```
REPLICAT R01PDB1
SETENV (ORACLE_SID=bwdb)
SETENV (NLS_LANG=AMERICAN_AMERICA.AL32UTF8)
USERID ggs_admin@bwdb, PASSWORD oracle
SOURCEDEFS ./dirdef/oracle1.def
DISCARDFILE ./dirrpt/r01pdb1.dsc
MAP T8C1PDB1.osm$repapi.CUSTOMERS, TARGET osm$repapi.CUSTOMERS, &
COLMAP (USEDEFAULTS, CUST_SOURCE = @TOKEN ('TK_SOURCE_C'));
MAP T8C1PDB1.osm$repapi.POLICIES, TARGET osm$repapi.POLICIES, &
COLMAP (USEDEFAULTS, CUST_SOURCE = @TOKEN ('TK_SOURCE_P'));
```

Data Types Compatibility and Column Mapping

The internal implementation of data types differ among databases. Column mapping of the source and target table is defined and referenced using Oracle GoldenGate definition files. In some cases, the default column size can cause issues and must be explicitly defined. Table 8-3 compares Oracle Database and MySQL data types.

Oracle	MySQL
VARCHAR2(size [BYTE | CHAR])	VARCHAR(n)

NVARCHAR2(size)	NVARCHAR(n)
NUMBER [(p [, s])]	DECIMAL(p,s)
FLOAT [(p)]	DOUBLE
LONG	LONGTEXT
DATE	DATETIME
BINARY_FLOAT	FLOAT
BINARY_DOUBLE	DOUBLE
TIMESTAMP [(fractional_seconds_precision)]	DATETIME(p)
TIMESTAMP [(fractional_seconds_precision)] WITH TIME ZONE	DATETIME(p)
TIMESTAMP [(fractional_seconds_precision)] WITH LOCAL TIME ZONE	DATETIME(p)
INTERVAL YEAR [(year_precision)] TO MONTH	VARCHAR(30)
INTERVAL DAY [(day_precision)] TO SECOND [(fractional_seconds_precision)]	VARCHAR(30)
RAW(size)	BINARY(n)
LONG RAW	LONGBLOB
ROWID	CHAR(10)
UROWID [(size)]	VARCHAR(n)
CHAR [(size [BYTE | CHAR])]	CHAR(n)
NCHAR[(size)]	NCHAR(n)
CLOB	LONGTEXT
NCLOB	NVARCHAR(n)
BLOB	LONGBLOB
BFILE	VARCHAR(255)

Table 8-3: Comparing Oracle and MySQL Data Types

Definition Files

The Oracle GoldenGate definition files are required for a heterogeneous environment, column mapping, and data transformations. When developing a data warehouse repository, it is very common that the dimensions of the fact table are the results of data transformations. Figure 8-10 illustrates a high-level presentation of a typical data warehouse design.

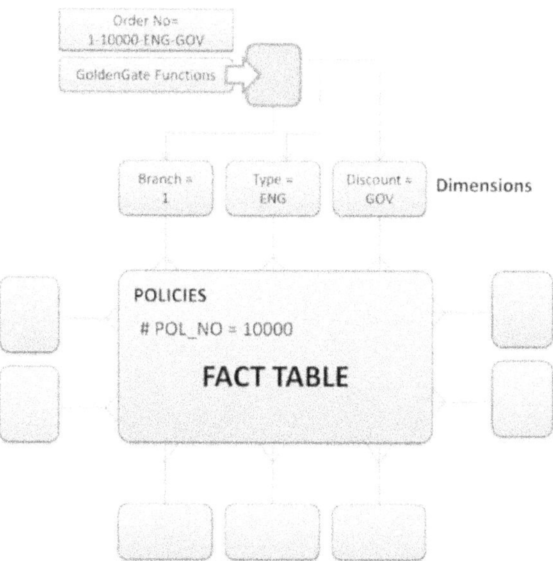

Figure 8-10: Replicat Feeding the Fact-Table

The chapter heterogeneous architecture requires several definition files. Figure 8-11 depicts the definition files created to support:

- Initial-load from the Oracle Pluggable Database (S8T1PDB) to MySQL databases SDB1, SDB2, SDB3 and SDB4.
- Data movement from MySQL to the Oracle Database pluggable databases.
- Data movement from the Oracle Database pluggable databases to the data warehouse repository.

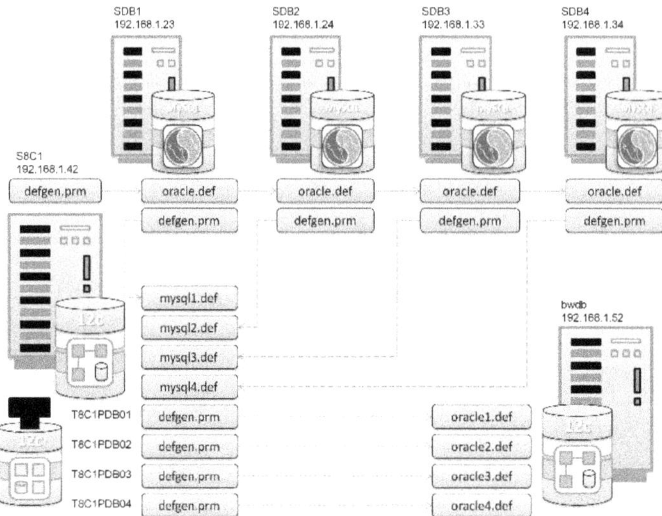

Figure 8-11: Definition File Names and Locations

Initial-Load Definition File

Since the initial-load extract is generated from one specific pluggable database, only one definition file is required – 'oracle.def'. The same definition file is copied across all of the MySQL systems. The following steps create the initial-load definition file.

- On system 'S8C1PDB', create the parameter file – 'defgen.prm'. The file defines the definition file and lists the candidate tables. The table name is constructed using the container name, schema, and table name.

```
DEFSFILE ./dirdef/oracle.def, PURGE
USERID system@s8c1pdb, PASSWORD oracle_4U
TABLE s8c1pdb.osm$repapi.RANDOM_DOMAIN;
TABLE s8c1pdb.osm$repapi.RANDOM_FIRST;
TABLE s8c1pdb.osm$repapi.RANDOM_MIDDLE;
TABLE s8c1pdb.osm$repapi.RANDOM_LAST;
TABLE s8c1pdb.osm$repapi.POLICY_TYPES;
TABLE s8c1pdb.osm$repapi.DISCOUNT_TYPES;
TABLE s8c1pdb.osm$repapi.CUSTOMERS;
TABLE s8c1pdb.osm$repapi.POLICIES;
```

- Use the DEFGEN utility to create the source definition file. Verify the report file ./dirrpt/defgen.rpt is generated for the list of tables.

```
$ ./defgen PARAMFILE ./dirprm/defgen.prm REPORTFILE ./dirrpt/defgen.rpt
```

- Transport the source definition file – 'oracle.def' to the target systems. Figure 8-11 depicts this step.

Pluggable Databases Definition Files

The architecture shows the presence of (4) MySQL databases corresponding to (4) Oracle Pluggable databases. Hence, (4) definition files are created and transferred to the Multitenant system as listed on Table 8-4.

Replicat	Parameter File	Source Definition File	Target System
R01SDB01	./dirprm/defgen.prm	./dirdef/mysql1.def	192.168.1.42
R01SDB02	./dirprm/defgen.prm	./dirdef/mysql2.def	192.168.1.42
R01SDB03	./dirprm/defgen.prm	./dirdef/mysql3.def	192.168.1.42
R01SDB04	./dirprm/defgen.prm	./dirdef/mysql4.def	192.168.1.42

Table 8-4: Pluggable Databases Definition Files

Definition File for Replicat – R01SDB01

- On the source mysql1 (SDB1) system, prepare the parameter file – 'defgen.prm'.

```
DEFSFILE ./dirdef/mysql1.def, PURGE
SOURCEDB SDB1@source-mysql1, USERID root, PASSWORD oracle
TABLE SDB1.CUSTOMERS;
TABLE SDB1.POLICIES;
```

- Run the DEFGEN utility to create the source definition file. Verify the result on the file ./dirrpt/defgen.rpt.

```
$ ./defgen PARAMFILE ./dirprm/defgen.prm REPORTFILE ./dirrpt/defgen.rpt
```

- Transport the source definition file – mysql1.def to ./dirdef/ of the target system.

Definition File for Replicat – R01SDB02

- On the source mysql2 (SDB2) system, prepare the parameter file – 'defgen.prm'.

```
DEFSFILE ./dirdef/mysql2.def, PURGE
SOURCEDB SDB2@source-mysql2, USERID root, PASSWORD oracle
TABLE SDB2.CUSTOMERS;
TABLE SDB2.POLICIES;
```

- Run the DEFGEN utility to create the source definition file.

```
$ ./defgen PARAMFILE ./dirprm/defgen.prm REPORTFILE ./dirrpt/defgen.rpt
```

- Transport the source definition file – mysql2.def to ./dirdef/ of the target system.

Definition File for Replicat – R01SDB03

- On the source mysql3 (SDB3) system, prepare the parameter file – 'defgen.prm'.

```
DEFSFILE ./dirdef/mysql3.def, PURGE
SOURCEDB SDB3@source-mysql3, USERID root, PASSWORD oracle
TABLE SDB3.CUSTOMERS;
TABLE SDB3.POLICIES;
```

- Run the DEFGEN utility to create the source definition file.

```
$ ./defgen PARAMFILE ./dirprm/defgen.prm REPORTFILE ./dirrpt/defgen.rpt
```

- Transport the source definition file – mysql3.def to ./dirdef/ of the target system.

Definition File for Replicat – R01SDB04

- On the source mysql4 (SDB4) system, prepare the parameter file – 'defgen.prm'.

```
DEFSFILE ./dirdef/mysql4.def, PURGE
SOURCEDB SDB4@source-mysql4, USERID root, PASSWORD oracle
TABLE SDB4.CUSTOMERS;
TABLE SDB4.POLICIES;
```

- Run the DEFGEN utility to create the source definition file.

```
$ ./defgen PARAMFILE ./dirprm/defgen.prm REPORTFILE ./dirrpt/defgen.rpt
```

- Transport the source definition file – mysql4.def to ./dirdef/ of the target system.

Now, the Oracle Database 12c CDB target system (192.168.1.42) has (4) MySQL source definition files. Each is referenced by the associated pluggable database, Replicat. Verify the definition files from the Operating System:

```
[oracle@target-cdb dirdef]$ pwd
/u01/app/ggs/product/12.1.2/gghome_1/dirdef
[oracle@target-cdb dirdef]$ ls -al mysql*.def
-rw-r----- 1 oracle oinstall 2422 Jul  2 18:06 mysql1.def
-rw-r----- 1 oracle oinstall 2422 Jul  5 00:01 mysql2.def
-rw-r----- 1 oracle oinstall 2422 Jul  2 18:04 mysql3.def
-rw-r----- 1 oracle oinstall 2422 Jul  2 18:02 mysql4.def
[oracle@target-cdb dirdef]$
```

Data Warehouse Repository Definition Files

The data warehouse repository is synchronized using four Replicats – R01PDB1, R01PDB2, R01PDB3 and R01PDB4. Each of the Replicat requires its own definition file. Hence, (4) definition files are created as listed on Table 8-5.

Replicat	Parameter File	Source Definition File	Target System
R01PDB1	./dirprm/defgen1.prm	./dirdef/oracle1.def	192.168.1.52
R01PDB2	./dirprm/defgen2.prm	./dirdef/oracle2.def	192.168.1.52
R01PDB3	./dirprm/defgen3.prm	./dirdef/oracle3.def	192.168.1.52
R01PDB4	./dirprm/defgen4.prm	./dirdef/oracle4.def	192.168.1.52

Table 8-5: Data Warehouse Repository Definition Files

Definition File for Replicat – R01PDB1

- On the Oracle Database 12c source system, prepare the parameter files – 'defgen1.prm'

```
DEFSFILE ./dirdef/oracle1.def, PURGE
USERID c##ggs_admin@s8c1, PASSWORD oracle
TABLE T8C1PDB1.osm$repapi.customers;
TABLE T8C1PDB1.osm$repapi.policies;
```

- Run the DEFGEN utility to create the source definition file.

```
$ ./defgen PARAMFILE ./dirprm/defgen1.prm REPORTFILE
./dirrpt/defgen1.rpt
```

- Transport the source definition file – oracle1.def to ./dirdef/ of the target system.

Definition File for Replicat – R01PDB2

- On the Oracle Database 12c source system, prepare the parameter files – 'defgen1.prm'

```
DEFSFILE ./dirdef/oracle2.def, PURGE
USERID c##ggs_admin@s8c1, PASSWORD oracle
TABLE T8C1PDB2.osm$repapi.customers;
TABLE T8C1PDB2.osm$repapi.policies;
```

- Run the DEFGEN utility to create the source definition file.

```
$ ./defgen PARAMFILE ./dirprm/defgen2.prm REPORTFILE
./dirrpt/defgen2.rpt
```

- Transport the source definition file – oracle2.def to ./dirdef/ of the target system.

Definition File for Replicat – R01PDB3

- On the Oracle Database 12c source system, prepare the parameter files – 'defgen1.prm'

```
DEFSFILE ./dirdef/oracle3.def, PURGE
USERID c##ggs_admin@s8c1, PASSWORD oracle
TABLE T8C1PDB3.osm$repapi.customers;
TABLE T8C1PDB3.osm$repapi.policies;
```

- Run the DEFGEN utility to create the source definition file.

```
$ ./defgen PARAMFILE ./dirprm/defgen3.prm REPORTFILE
./dirrpt/defgen3.rpt
```

- Transport the source definition file – oracle3.def to ./dirdef/ of the target system.

Definition File for Replicat – R01PDB4

- On the Oracle Database 12c source system, prepare the parameter files – 'defgen1.prm'

```
DEFSFILE ./dirdef/oracle4.def, PURGE
USERID c##ggs_admin@s8c1, PASSWORD oracle
TABLE T8C1PDB4.osm$repapi.customers;
TABLE T8C1PDB4.osm$repapi.policies;
```

- Run the DEFGEN utility to create the source definition file.

```
$ ./defgen PARAMFILE ./dirprm/defgen4.prm REPORTFILE
./dirrpt/defgen4.rpt
```

- Tranport the source definition file – oracle1.def to ./dirdef/ of the target system.

Now on Oracle Database 12c Data Warehouse Repository target system (192.168. 1.52), there are (4) source definition files. Each is referenced by a Replicat. Verify the definition files using the operating system:

```
[oracle@target-bw dirdef]$ pwd
/u01/app/ggs/product/12.1.2/gghome_1/dirdef
[oracle@target-bw dirdef]$ ls -al
total 24
drwxr-x---  2 oracle oinstall 4096 Jun 28 23:07 .
drwxr-xr-x 30 oracle oinstall 4096 Jun 28 22:09 ..
-rw-r-----  1 oracle oinstall 2443 Jun 27 09:34 oracle1.def
-rw-r-----  1 oracle oinstall 2443 Jun 28 23:06 oracle2.def
-rw-r-----  1 oracle oinstall 2443 Jun 28 23:07 oracle3.def
-rw-r-----  1 oracle oinstall 2443 Jun 28 23:07 oracle4.def
[oracle@target-bw dirdef]$
```

Using GoldenGate Functions for Data Transformation

Data Transformation is a core feature of Oracle GoldenGate. Data structure in terms of data type and value transformation may occur at different places, at the source, target, and an intermediate system.

The consolidation of several Oracle 12c Pluggable Databases into the data warehouse repository requires dynamic data transformation, and it is best done using Oracle GoldenGate built-in functions. For example, the attribute CUSTOMERS .CUST_NO from the pluggable database is transformed to CUSTOMERS .CUST_NOn, where n refers to the pluggable database ID (the source). POLICIES.POL_NO is transformed to POLICIES.POL_NOn. There are two advantages of this transformation technique:

- Identifying the Unique Key Value
- Identifying the Data Source

The following Replicat MAP parameter illustrates data transformation technique performed at the data warehouse repository Oracle GoldenGate instance. Using Oracle GoldenGate functions delivers a higher performance than using the database functions.

- The Extract TABLE statement uses the function @GETENV to retrieve the Extract group name and assigns it to the Oracle GoldenGate variable TK_SOURCE_C.

```
TABLE T8C1PDB1.osm$repapi.customers, TOKENS (TK_SOURCE_C = @GETENV
('GGENVIRONMENT', 'GROUPNAME'));
```

- The Replicat MAP statement performs functions' nesting using @NUMSTR, @STRCAT, @STREXT and @TOKEN to transform the CUST_NO column as depicted in Figure 8-12.

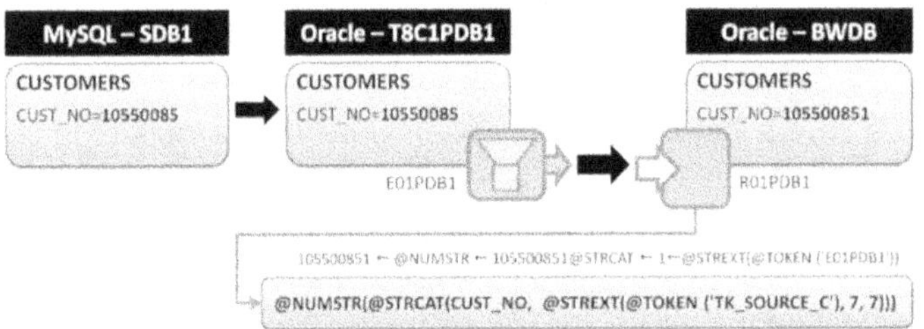

Figure 8-12: Oracle GoldenGate Functions Nesting for Data Transformation

The following shows the Replicat MAP statement for performing data transformation for CUST_NO and POL_NO.

```
MAP T8C1PDB1.osm$repapi.CUSTOMERS, TARGET osm$repapi.CUSTOMERS, &
COLMAP (USEDEFAULTS, CUST_NO = @NUMSTR(@STRCAT(CUST_NO,
                             @STREXT(@TOKEN ('TK_SOURCE_C'), 7, 7))),
                     CUST_SOURCE = @TOKEN ('TK_SOURCE_C'));
MAP T8C1PDB1.osm$repapi.POLICIES, TARGET osm$repapi.POLICIES, &
COLMAP (USEDEFAULTS, CUST_NO = @NUMSTR(@STRCAT(CUST_NO,
                             @STREXT(@TOKEN ('TK_SOURCE_C'), 7, 7))),
                     POL_NO = @NUMSTR(@STRCAT(POL_NO,
                             @STREXT(@TOKEN ('TK_SOURCE_C'), 7, 7))),
                     CUST_SOURCE = @TOKEN ('TK_SOURCE_P'));
```

Login to MySQL Using GGSCI

Access to Oracle MySQL from within Oracle GoldenGate is performed using the following syntax. The SOURCEDB refers to the database and hostname.

```
GGSCI (source-mysql1) 5> DBLOGIN SOURCEDB SDB1@source-mysql1, USERID root,
password oracle
Successfully logged into database.

GGSCI (source-mysql1) 6>
```

The next three sections implement the stages depicted on Figure 8-13 using a 3-stage approach. The stages must be developed and executed sequentially.

Stage I: Heterogeneous Initial Data Loading establishes the (4) Oracle MySQL databases from an existing pluggable database.

Stage II: Heterogeneous Online Synchronization performs an online unidirectional data movement from the Oracle MySQL to the Oracle 12c Pluggable Database.

Stage III: Feeding the Operational Data Warehouse Repository performs real-time data movement and transformation (consolidation).

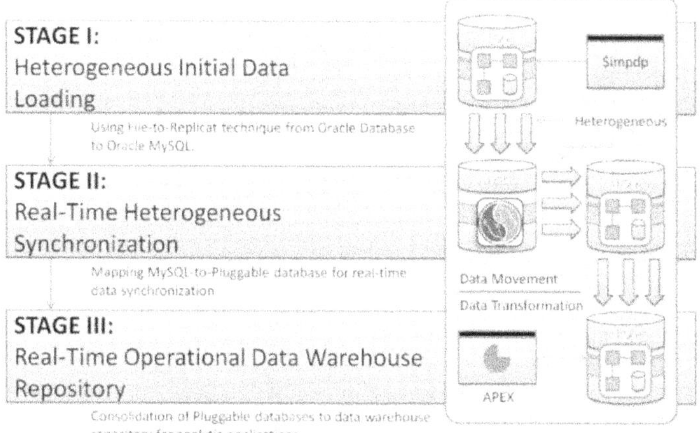
STAGE I:
Heterogeneous Initial Data Loading
Using File-to-Replicat technique from Oracle Database to Oracle MySQL.
STAGE II:
Real-Time Heterogeneous Synchronization
Mapping MySQL-to-Pluggable database for real-time data synchronization
STAGE III:
Real-Time Operational Data Warehouse Repository
Consolidation of Pluggable databases to data warehouse repository for analytic applications
$impdp
Heterogeneous
Data Movement
Data Transformation
APEX

Figure 8-13: A 3-Stage Approach for Operational Data Warehouse Repository

Stage I: Heterogeneous Initial Data Loading

In a heterogeneous database environment, a best practice approach is to configure and apply a suitable Oracle GoldenGate initial load method for establishing the MySQL database. The commonly used initial load methods for such environment are:

- Loading Data from File to Replicat
- Loading Data with an Oracle GoldenGate direct load

The next sequence of initial loads is performed using 'Loading Data from File to Replicat' method. Figure 8-14 shows the method's workflow. The Oracle Pluggable Database T8C1PDB is treated as the source database to instantiate the MySQL databases: SDB1, SDB2, SDB3 and SDB4. Since the above initial load methods tend to be slow in processing rows, consider designing parallelism for the initial load capture and delivery.

The 'Loading Data from File to Replicat' initial load method is composed of these (4) steps:

1. Capture/Run the initial load Extract (RLPDB01) to create the extract file './dirdat/initload08.ora'.
2. Generate the source definition file 'oracle.def'.
3. Transfer/Copy the extract file and definition file across all MySQL systems.
4. Apply/Run the initial load Replicat (RLSDB0n), where n=1, 2, 3 and 4.

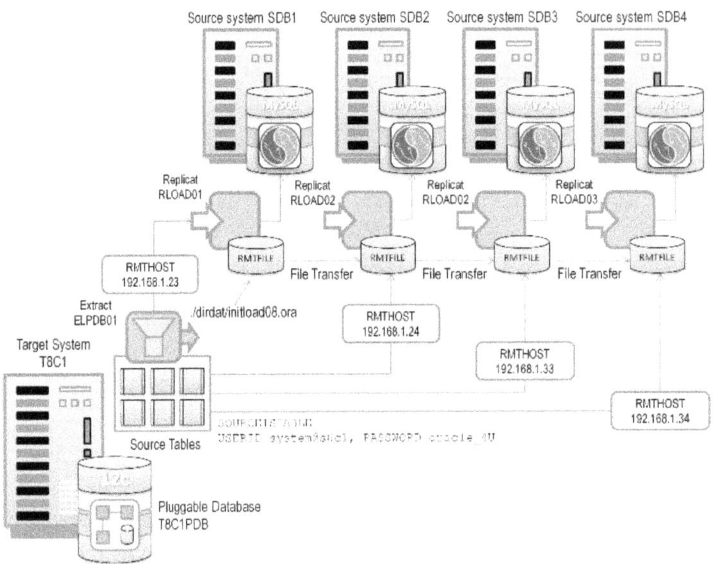

Figure 8-14: Initial Load File to Replicat Method

The initial load Extract 'ET8C1PDB' reads the source database tables from the pluggable database 'T8C1PDB'. Using the parameters RMTHOST and RMTFILE, the Extract 'ET8C1PDB' creates the initial load extract file 'initload08.ora' in canonical format on the target MySQL database, SDB01. Instead of running a separate initial load Extract for each MySQL database, the extract file is manually copied across all MySQL servers running the databases: SDB2, SDB3 and SDB4. Then, the Replicat processes RLOAD01 on SDB1, RLOAD02 on SDB2, RLOAD03 on SDB3 and RLOAD04 on SDB4 are defined and executed. The Replicat process uses the MySQL database native SQL interface to establish the target database.

Refer to Chapter 3 for more details regarding Oracle GoldenGate Initial Load techniques.

Creating MySQL Database Tables

Prior to executing the initial load Extract-Replicat to establish the MySQL databases, the table's structure must have been created using compatible columns data types. For packaged applications, the reverse engineering of the source Oracle database fully automates the generation of the MySQL DDL scripts necessary to create the database tables. A second approach is to migrate the Oracle Database to MySQL using the MySQL Workbench Migration Wizard.

MySQL Workbench Migration Wizard migrates an ODBC compliant database to MySQL. It is considered an offline initial load method. The runtime options enable fine-grain control of:

- Source and Target Schemas Selection
- Manual Editing
- Target Creation Options
- Data Migration

Figure 8-15 shows the MySQL Workbench Migration Wizard. The tools are available for Linux, Windows, and Mac OS X platforms.

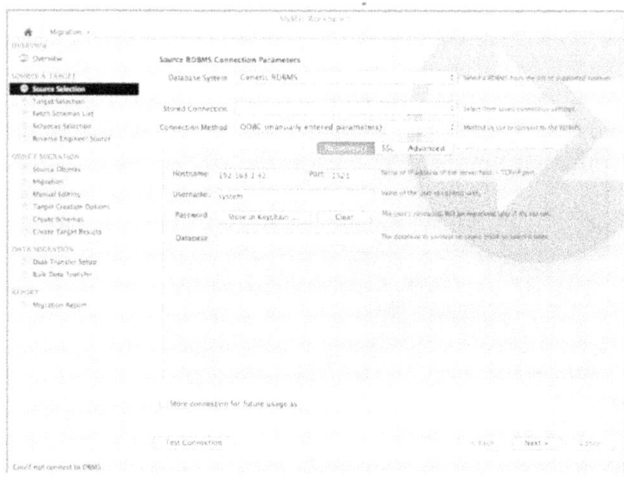

Figure 8-15: MySQL Workbench Migration Wizard

Initial Load for the MySQL SDB1 Database

MySQL SDB1 database is established using the Oracle GoldenGate initial load, File to Replicat method. The selection of this method is more appropriate because the same initial load extract file is copied across the other MySQL systems for use by the initial load Replicat. Oracle GoldenGate macros simplifies the creation of similar configuration files by grouping identical parameters in a macro file and referencing these parameters, where necessary.

Initial Load Capture

The initial load Extract reads the source database tables instructed by the parameter SOURCEISTABLE. In a multitenant database, the Extract must login to the root container database (CDB$ROOT). The Oracle GoldenGate error 'OGG-06206. The database connection must be to the root level database' and returned when using a pluggable level database user.

The initial load extract file 'initload08.dat' is created on the target system as instructed by the parameters RMTHOST and MGRPORT. The list of tables is fully qualified using the format: <pluggable database name.schema.table name>. An alternative is to add the parameter SOURCECATALOG, which specifies the default container in the Oracle Database 12c Multitenant Database.

The following shows the initial load Extract parameters followed by the Extract execution from the command-line. The Extract program uses the required argument 'pf' (parameter file) and the optional argument 'rf' (report file).

```
SOURCEISTABLE
USERID system@s8c1, PASSWORD oracle_4U
RMTHOST 192.168.1.23, MGRPORT 7823
RMTFILE ./dirdat/initload08.dat, PURGE
TABLE S8C1PDB.osm$repapi.RANDOM_DOMAIN;
TABLE S8C1PDB.osm$repapi.RANDOM_FIRST;
TABLE s8c1pdb.osm$repapi.RANDOM_MIDDLE;
TABLE s8c1pdb.osm$repapi.RANDOM_LAST;
TABLE s8c1pdb.osm$repapi.POLICY_TYPES;
TABLE s8c1pdb.osm$repapi.DISCOUNT_TYPES;
TABLE s8c1pdb.osm$repapi.CUSTOMERS;
TABLE s8c1pdb.osm$repapi.POLICIES;
```

```
$ ./extract pf dirprm/eload08.prm rf dirrpt/eload08.rpt
```

Ascertain that the initial load extract file '/dirdat/initload08.dat' has been created on the target system.

Using the Parameter SOURCECATALOG

To keep the format of the TABLE parameter similar to non-CDB, specify the parameter SOURCECATALOG. It dynamically amends the TABLE parameter to include the pluggable database name. The parameter SOURCECATALOG must proceed the TABLE parameter as shown below.

```
SOURCEISTABLE
USERID system@s8c1, PASSWORD oracle_4U
RMTHOST 192.168.1.23, MGRPORT 7823
RMTFILE ./dirdat/initload08.dat, PURGE
SOURCECATALOG S8C1PDB
TABLE osm$repapi.RANDOM_DOMAIN;
TABLE osm$repapi.RANDOM_FIRST;
TABLE osm$repapi.RANDOM_MIDDLE;
TABLE osm$repapi.RANDOM_LAST;
TABLE osm$repapi.POLICY_TYPES;
TABLE osm$repapi.DISCOUNT_TYPES;
TABLE osm$repapi.CUSTOMERS;
TABLE osm$repapi.POLICIES;
```

View Initial Load Capture Report

Ascertain that the initial load capture is successfully completed by viewing the Oracle GoldenGate logging file 'ggserr.log', which shows the operation's status. Also, view the initial load Extract report. The report run-time statistics indicate the status of the initial load capture for the list of tables.

The following is the section related to Run Time Statistics. It displays the number of inserts executed for each listed database table.

```
GGSCI (target-cdb) 5> VIEW REPORT dirrpt/eload08.rpt
```

```
***********************************************************************
*                   ** Run Time Statistics **                         *
***********************************************************************


Report at 2014-06-26 19:23:10 (activity since 2014-06-26 19:22:30)

Output to ./dirdat/initload08.dat:

From Table S8C1PDB.OSM$REPAPI.RANDOM_DOMAIN:
       #                   inserts:         5
       #                   updates:         0
       #                   deletes:         0
       #                  discards:         0
From Table S8C1PDB.OSM$REPAPI.RANDOM_FIRST:
       #                   inserts:        11
       #                   updates:         0
       #                   deletes:         0
       #                  discards:         0
From Table S8C1PDB.OSM$REPAPI.RANDOM_MIDDLE:
       #                   inserts:         6
       #                   updates:         0
       #                   deletes:         0
       #                  discards:         0
From Table S8C1PDB.OSM$REPAPI.RANDOM_LAST:
       #                   inserts:        11
       #                   updates:         0
```

```
       #                   deletes:         0
       #                  discards:         0
From Table S8C1PDB.OSM$REPAPI.POLICY_TYPES:
       #                   inserts:         4
       #                   updates:         0
       #                   deletes:         0
       #                  discards:         0
From Table S8C1PDB.OSM$REPAPI.DISCOUNT_TYPES:
       #                   inserts:         3
       #                   updates:         0
       #                   deletes:         0
       #                  discards:         0
From Table S8C1PDB.OSM$REPAPI.CUSTOMERS:
       #                   inserts:    100000
       #                   updates:         0
       #                   deletes:         0
       #                  discards:         0
From Table S8C1PDB.OSM$REPAPI.POLICIES:
       #                   inserts:    100000
       #                   updates:         0
       #                   deletes:         0
       #                  discards:         0


*** Session Pool Statistics ***
     #    Newly Created Sessions:        1
     #           Reused Sessions:       200040
     #        Timed-out Sessions:        0
     #           Active Sessions:        1
     #         Released Sessions:        0

REDO Log Statistics
  Bytes parsed                     0
  Bytes output              39589217

GGSCI (target-cdb) 6>
```

The above GGSCI report shows a successful initial load Extract. The initial load Extract is performed on the Oracle Database 12c Container Database, S8C1PDB, for the database tables listed on Table 8-6.

Database Schema	Table Name	Rows Extracted
OSM$REPAPI	RANDOM_DOMAIN	5
OSM$REPAPI	RANDOM_FIRST	11
OSM$REPAPI	RANDOM_MIDDLE	6
OSM$REPAPI	RANDOM_LAST	11
OSM$REPAPI	POLICY_TYPES	4
OSM$REPAPI	DISCOUNT_TYPES	3
OSM$REPAPI	CUSTOMERS	100000
OSM$REPAPI	POLICIES	100000

Table 8-5: Initial-Load Extract Tables

Creating the Checkpoint Table

The Replicat's default, and recommended, checkpoint system is a database table. Add the parameter CHECKPOINTTABLE to the Oracle GoldenGate instance GLOBALS parameter file. Changes to the global parameter file requires a restart of the GGSCI, then execute the command ADD CHECKPOINTTABLE as follows:

- Edit the GLOBALS parameter file:

```
checkpointtable SDB1.chkpttab
```

- Exit GGSCI. Restart the GGSCI and login to the database:

```
GGSCI (source-mysql1) 10> DBLOGIN SOURCEDB SDB1@source-mysql1, USERID
root, PASSWORD oracle
Successfully logged into database.
```

- Add the checkpoint database table:

```
GGSCI (source-mysql1) 11> ADD checkpointtable

No checkpoint table specified. Using GLOBALS specification
(SDB1.chkpttab)...

Successfully created checkpoint table SDB1.chkpttab.
GGSCI (source-mysql1) 12>
```

Initial Load Delivery

Having successfully completed the initial load capture, it is now time to execute the initial load delivery. The essential configuration parameters are TARGETDB and SOURCEDEFS. The parameter TARGETDB enables the login to the MySQL database by specifying the database name and the hostname – SDB1@source-mysql1. The parameter SOURCEDEFS specifies the source definition file generated at the source and transfers it to the target system - source-mysql1.

```
REPLICAT rload08
SPECIALRUN
TARGETDB SDB1@source-mysql1, USERID root, PASSWORD oracle
SOURCEDEFS ./dirdef/oracle.def, PURGE
HANDLECOLLISIONS
EXTFILE ./dirdat/initload08.dat
DISCARDFILE ./dirrpt/rload08.dsc, PURGE
SOURCECATALOG S8C1PDB
MAP osm$repapi.RANDOM_DOMAIN, TARGET SDB1.RANDOM_DOMAIN;
MAP osm$repapi.RANDOM_FIRST, TARGET SDB1.RANDOM_FIRST;
MAP osm$repapi.RANDOM_MIDDLE, TARGET SDB1.RANDOM_MIDDLE;
MAP osm$repapi.RANDOM_LAST, TARGET SDB1.RANDOM_LAST;
MAP osm$repapi.POLICY_TYPES, TARGET SDB1.POLICY_TYPES;
MAP osm$repapi.DISCOUNT_TYPES, TARGET SDB1.DISCOUNT_TYPES;
MAP osm$repapi.CUSTOMERS, TARGET SDB1.CUSTOMERS;
MAP osm$repapi.POLICIES, TARGET SDB1.POLICIES;
END RUNTIME
```

Prior to executing the Replicat program, define the SPECIALRUN Replicat, which uses the parameter EXTFILE as an input to apply the transactions to the target tables.

```
GGSCI (source-mysql1) 5> ADD REPLICAT RLOAD08, EXTFILE
./dirdat/initload08.dat
REPLICAT added.

GGSCI (source-mysql1) 6>
```

```
$ ./replicat pf dirprm/rload08.prm rf dirrpt/rload08.rpt
```

Initial Load Delivery Report

Execute the VIEW GGSCI command to view the initial load Replicat runtime statistics.

```
GGSCI (source-mysql1) 1> VIEW REPORT dirrpt/rload08.rpt
```

```
***********************************************************************
*                   ** Run Time Statistics **                         *
***********************************************************************

Last record for the last committed transaction is the following:
___________________________________________________________________
Trail name :  ./dirdat/initload08.dat
Hdr-Ind    :     E  (x45)     Partition  :     .  (x04)
UndoFlag   :     .  (x00)     BeforeAfter:     A  (x41)
RecLength  :   144 (x0090)    IO Time    : 2014-06-26 11:24:30.996706
IOType     :     5  (x05)     OrigNode   :   255  (xff)
TransInd   :     .  (x03)     FormatType :     R  (x52)
SyskeyLen  :     0  (x00)     Incomplete :     .  (x00)
AuditRBA   :          0       AuditPos   : 0
Continued  :     N  (x00)     RecCount   :     1  (x01)

2014-06-26 11:24:30.996706 Insert             Len   144 RBA 39590363
Name: S8C1PDB.OSM$REPAPI.POLICIES
___________________________________________________________________

Reading ./dirdat/initload08.dat, current RBA 39590585, 200040 records

Report at 2014-06-26 11:51:59 (activity since 2014-06-26 11:50:53)

From Table S8C1PDB.OSM$REPAPI.RANDOM_DOMAIN to SDB1.RANDOM_DOMAIN:
       #                   inserts:         5
       #                   updates:         0
       #                   deletes:         0
       #                  discards:         0
From Table S8C1PDB.OSM$REPAPI.RANDOM_FIRST to SDB1.RANDOM_FIRST:
       #                   inserts:        11
       #                   updates:         0
       #                   deletes:         0
```

```
       #                  discards:         0
From Table S8C1PDB.OSM$REPAPI.RANDOM_MIDDLE to SDB1.RANDOM_MIDDLE:
       #                   inserts:         6
       #                   updates:         0
       #                   deletes:         0
       #                  discards:         0
From Table S8C1PDB.OSM$REPAPI.RANDOM_LAST to SDB1.RANDOM_LAST:
       #                   inserts:        11
       #                   updates:         0
       #                   deletes:         0
       #                  discards:         0
From Table S8C1PDB.OSM$REPAPI.POLICY_TYPES to SDB1.POLICY_TYPES:
       #                   inserts:         4
       #                   updates:         0
       #                   deletes:         0
       #                  discards:         0
From Table S8C1PDB.OSM$REPAPI.CUSTOMERS to SDB1.CUSTOMERS:
       #                   inserts:    100000
       #                   updates:         0
       #                   deletes:         0
       #                  discards:         0
From Table S8C1PDB.OSM$REPAPI.POLICIES to SDB1.POLICIES:
       #                   inserts:    100000
       #                   updates:         0
       #                   deletes:         0
       #                  discards:         0

Last log location read:
     FILE:      ./dirdat/initload08.dat
     RBA:       39590585
     TIMESTAMP: 2014-06-26 11:24:30.996706
     EOF:       NO
     READERR:   400
```

An alternative, to verify the initial load delivery, is using the MySQL SQL command-line. Issue the following COUNT(*) queries to ascertain the rows count for the CUSTOMERS and POLICICES tables.

```
mysql> USE SDB1;
Database changed
mysql> SELECT COUNT(*)
    -> FROM   CUSTOMERS;
+----------+
| COUNT(*) |
+----------+
|   100000 |
+----------+
1 row in set (0.10 sec)

mysql> SELECT COUNT(*)
    -> FROM   POLICIES;
+----------+
| COUNT(*) |
+----------+
|   100000 |
+----------+
1 row in set (0.06 sec)

mysql>
```

The same initial load extract file – 'initload08.dat' is used for establishing the remaining MySQL databases – SDB2, SDB3 and SDB4. This eliminates the need to perform initial load capture for each of MySQL database.

Initial Load for MySQL SDB2 Database

Since the MySQL SDB2 database has the same table structure as SDB1, the initial load delivery uses the same initial load extract file created for SDB1. We transfer the initial load extract file 'initload08.dat' to the MySQL SDB2 server, then start the Replicat program. The definition file 'oracle2.def' is generated for referencing SDB2 database.

Initial-load Definition File

The definition file is generated on the source system (S8C1) and moved to the MySQL server. The following steps create the definition file using the Oracle GoldenGate DEFGEN utility:

- Prepare the parameter file – defgen.prm. The parameter DEFSFILE specifies the name of the definition file – oracle.def.

```
DEFSFILE ./dirdef/oracle.def, PURGE
USERID system@s8c1pdb, PASSWORD oracle_4U
TABLE s8c1pdb.osm$repapi.RANDOM_DOMAIN;
TABLE s8c1pdb.osm$repapi.RANDOM_FIRST;
TABLE s8c1pdb.osm$repapi.RANDOM_MIDDLE;
TABLE s8c1pdb.osm$repapi.RANDOM_LAST;
TABLE s8c1pdb.osm$repapi.POLICY_TYPES;
TABLE s8c1pdb.osm$repapi.DISCOUNT_TYPES;
TABLE s8c1pdb.osm$repapi.CUSTOMERS;
TABLE s8c1pdb.osm$repapi.POLICIES;
```

- Run the DEFGEN utility. It creates the definition files for the list of tables.

```
$ ./defgen PARAMFILE ./dirprm/defgen.prm REPORTFILE ./dirrpt/defgen.rpt
```

- Transfer the file 'oracle.def' to MySQL system. The definition files default location is ./dirdef directory. It references using the Replicat parameter, SOURCEDEFS.

Initial Load Delivery

The main components required by the initial load delivery are the initial load definition file – 'oracle.def' and the initial load extract file – 'initload08.dat'. We prepare the initial load delivery parameter file – 'rload08.prm.'and then define the special run Replicat group 'rload08' and execute the Replicat program as shown below.

```
REPLICAT rload08
SPECIALRUN
TARGETDB SDB2@source-mysql2, USERID root, PASSWORD oracle
SOURCEDEFS ./dirdef/oracle.def, PURGE
HANDLECOLLISIONS
EXTFILE ./dirdat/initload08.dat
DISCARDFILE ./dirrpt/rload08.dsc, PURGE
MAP S8C1PDB.osm$repapi.RANDOM_DOMAIN, TARGET SDB2.RANDOM_DOMAIN;
MAP S8C1PDB.osm$repapi.RANDOM_FIRST, TARGET SDB2.RANDOM_FIRST;
MAP s8c1pdb.osm$repapi.RANDOM_MIDDLE, TARGET SDB2.RANDOM_MIDDLE;
MAP s8c1pdb.osm$repapi.RANDOM_LAST, TARGET SDB2.RANDOM_LAST;
MAP s8c1pdb.osm$repapi.POLICY_TYPES, TARGET SDB2.POLICY_TYPES;
MAP s8c1pdb.osm$repapi.DISCOUNT_TYPES, TARGET SDB2.DISCOUNT_TYPES;
MAP s8c1pdb.osm$repapi.CUSTOMERS, TARGET SDB2.CUSTOMERS;
MAP s8c1pdb.osm$repapi.POLICIES, TARGET SDB2.POLICIES;
END RUNTIME
```

```
$ ./replicat pf dirprm/rload08.prm rf dirrpt/rload08.rpt
```

Verify Initial Load Delivery Report

Ensure the initial load delivery is successfully completed. The database SDB2 must be identical to SDB1.

```
GGSCI (localhost.localdomain) 3> VIEW REPORT dirrpt/rload08.rpt
```

```
***********************************************************************
*                   ** Run Time Statistics **                         *
***********************************************************************

Last record for the last committed transaction is the following:
___________________________________________________________________
Trail name :  ./dirdat/initload08.dat
Hdr-Ind    :     E  (x45)     Partition  :     .  (x04)
UndoFlag   :     .  (x00)     BeforeAfter:     A  (x41)
RecLength  :   144  (x0090)   IO Time    : 2014-06-26 11:24:30.996706
IOType     :     5  (x05)     OrigNode   :   255  (xff)
TransInd   :     .  (x03)     FormatType :     R  (x52)
SyskeyLen  :     0  (x00)     Incomplete :     .  (x00)
AuditRBA   :          0       AuditPos   : 0
Continued  :     N  (x00)     RecCount   :     1  (x01)
```

```
2014-06-26 11:24:30.996706 Insert           Len   144 RBA 39590363
Name: S8C1PDB.OSM$REPAPI.POLICIES
___________________________________________________________________

Reading ./dirdat/initload08.dat, current RBA 39590585, 200040 records

Report at 2014-07-18 14:11:29 (activity since 2014-07-18 14:10:17)

From Table S8C1PDB.OSM$REPAPI.RANDOM_DOMAIN to SDB2.RANDOM_DOMAIN:
       #                   inserts:         5
       #                   updates:         0
       #                   deletes:         0
       #                  discards:         0
       #         insert collisions:         5
From Table S8C1PDB.OSM$REPAPI.RANDOM_FIRST to SDB2.RANDOM_FIRST:
       #                   inserts:        11
       #                   updates:         0
       #                   deletes:         0
       #                  discards:         0
       #         insert collisions:        11
From Table S8C1PDB.OSM$REPAPI.RANDOM_MIDDLE to SDB2.RANDOM_MIDDLE:
       #                   inserts:         6
       #                   updates:         0
       #                   deletes:         0
       #                  discards:         0
       #         insert collisions:         6
From Table S8C1PDB.OSM$REPAPI.RANDOM_LAST to SDB2.RANDOM_LAST:
       #                   inserts:        11
       #                   updates:         0
       #                   deletes:         0
       #                  discards:         0
       #         insert collisions:        11
From Table S8C1PDB.OSM$REPAPI.POLICY_TYPES to SDB2.POLICY_TYPES:
       #                   inserts:         4
       #                   updates:         0
       #                   deletes:         0
       #                  discards:         0
       #         insert collisions:         4
From Table S8C1PDB.OSM$REPAPI.DISCOUNT_TYPES to SDB2.DISCOUNT_TYPES:
       #                   inserts:         3
       #                   updates:         0
       #                   deletes:         0
       #                  discards:         0
       #         insert collisions:         3
From Table S8C1PDB.OSM$REPAPI.CUSTOMERS to SDB2.CUSTOMERS:
       #                   inserts:    100000
       #                   updates:         0
       #                   deletes:         0
       #                  discards:         0
       #         insert collisions:    100000
From Table S8C1PDB.OSM$REPAPI.POLICIES to SDB2.POLICIES:
       #                   inserts:    100000
       #                   updates:         0
       #                   deletes:         0
       #                  discards:         0
       #         insert collisions:    100000
```

```
Last log location read:
     FILE:      ./dirdat/initload08.dat
     RBA:       39590585
     TIMESTAMP: 2014-06-26 11:24:30.996706
     EOF:       NO
     READERR:   400
```

So far, the initial load for SDB1 and SDB2 has been successfully completed. Repeat the steps performed for SDB2 to perform the initial load delivery for the MySQL databases SDB3 and SDB4.

Stage II: Real-Time Heterogeneous Synchronization

Real-Time Data Movement from the MySQL to the Oracle 12c Pluggable Database is a major step for data consolidation and building an online operational data warehouse repository that will receive data originated from up to 252 MySQL databases. This value refers to the maximum number of pluggable databases supported by a single Oracle Database 12c Container Database (CDB). This configuration enables data transformation to occur at the Replicat side running at the data warehouse, Oracle GoldenGate instance, rather than at each Oracle 12c Pluggable Database instance.

For a linearly growing large-scale environment, a more suitable and scalable option is to configure an Oracle GoldenGate intermediate system dedicated for handling data transformations functions, which forwards the data to the data warehouse Replicats for immediate application to the change delivery without transformations. Figure 8-16 depicts the architecture when deploying an intermediate system to perform data routing and transformation. Refer to Chapter 10 for more details regarding configuring Oracle GoldenGate intermediate systems.

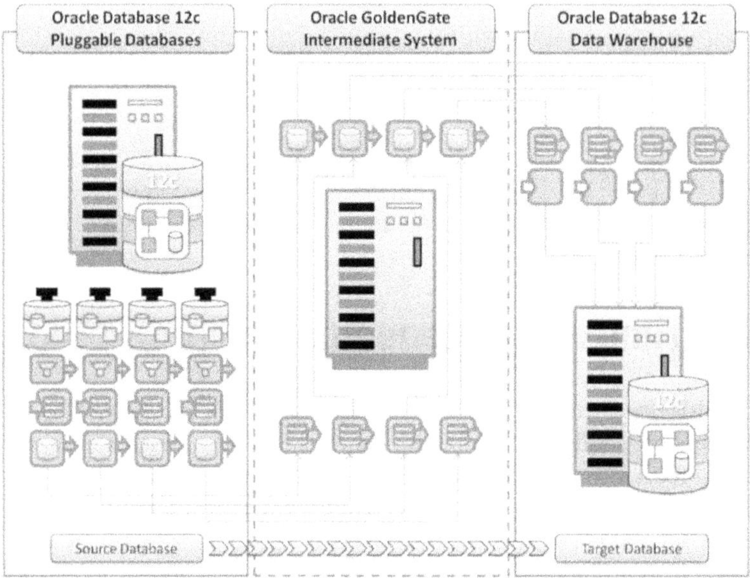

Figure 8-16: Intermediate System for Data Transformation

There are (4) separate configurations to enable data movement from the MySQL to the Oracle Database 12c Container Database (CDB).

- Configure Data Capture and Apply from the MySQL SDB1 to the Oracle 12c Pluggable Database T8C1PDB1.
- Configure Data Capture and Apply from the MySQL SDB2 to the Oracle 12c Pluggable Database T8C1PDB2.
- Configure Data Capture and Apply from the MySQL SDB3 to the Oracle 12c Pluggable Database T8C1PDB3.
- Configure Data Capture and Apply from the MySQL SDB4 to the Oracle 12c Pluggable Database T8C1PDB4.

Configure Data Capture and Apply From SDB1 to T8C1PDB1

The individual MySQL database is mapped to an Oracle 12c Pluggable Database (PDB). The unidirectional heterogeneous online capture and route enables a sub-second delay for near real-time data movement. The configuration follows a best practice approach using a data pump. It is configured for routing data to the target system, where the primary Extract of MySQL performs the capture and writes it to the local trail only. The Replicat of Oracle Database 12c CDB applies transactions to the target database. Figure 8-17 shows the Extracts and Replicat processes workflow.

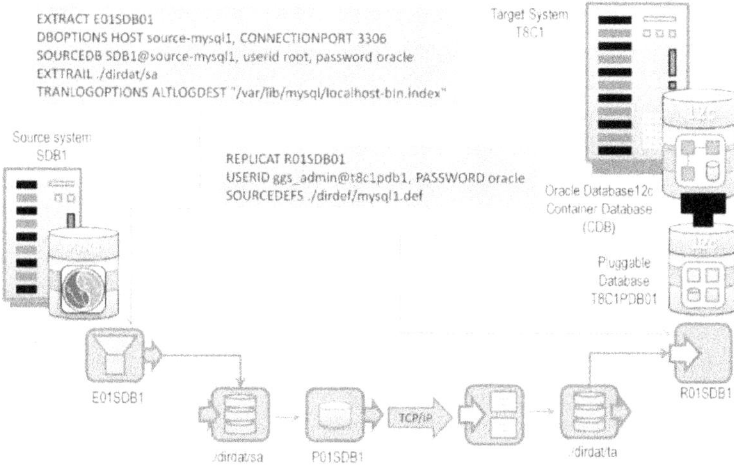
EXTRACT E01SDB01
DBOPTIONS HOST source-mysql1, CONNECTIONPORT 3306
SOURCEDB SDB1@source-mysql1, userid root, password oracle
EXTTRAIL ./dirdat/sa
TRANLOGOPTIONS ALTLOGDEST "/var/lib/mysql/localhost-bin.index"
Target System
T8C1
Source system
SDB1
REPLICAT R01SDB01
USERID ggs_admin@t8c1pdb1, PASSWORD oracle
SOURCEDEFS ./dirdef/mysql1.def
Oracle Database12c
Container Database
(CDB)
Pluggable
Database
T8C1PDB01
E01SDB1
TCP/IP
R01SDB1
./dirdat/sa
P01SDB1
./dirdat/ta

Figure 8-17: Data Movement from SDB1 to T8C1PDB1

Configure the Change Data Capture

The change data capture consists of two related components. The main function of the primary Extract is to continuously perform data capture from the database transactions logs. While the main function of the secondary Extract is to continuously send data to the dynamic collector for creating the remote trail. See Chapter 1 for more details regarding the Oracle GoldenGate components. The next section creates the following groups:

- Primary Extract Group
- Secondary Extract Group

Creating the Primary Extract Group

The MySQL Primary Extract Group, 'E01SDB01' is composed of the following components:

- Parameter File - e01sdb01.prm
- Primary Extract – E01SDB01
- Local Trail - ./dirdat/sa
- Checkpoint File - E01SDB01.cpe

For MySQL, the Primary Extract configuration uses the parameter DBOPTIONS to specify the hostname or IP address and the connection port. The MySQL default port is 3306. The parameter SOURCEDB for logging to MySQL database uses the database name, hostname, and privileged credentials of username and password. The TRANSLOGOPTIONS specify the MySQL transactions log locations and the index file name, which manages the transactions log files. The change data capture is for the tables CUSTOMERS and POLICIES only.

The following steps prepare the parameter file. Add the Primary Extract (E01SDB01) and define the local trail of the Primary Extract.

```
GGSCI (source-mysql1) 3> edit params E01SDB01
```

```
EXTRACT E01SDB01
DBOPTIONS HOST localhost, CONNECTIONPORT 3306
SOURCEDB SDB1@localhost, userid root, password oracle
EXTTRAIL ./dirdat/sa
TRANLOGOPTIONS ALTLOGDEST "/var/lib/mysql/localhost-bin.index"
TABLE SDB1.CUSTOMERS;
TABLE SDB1.POLICIES;
```

```
GGSCI (source-mysql1) 5> ADD EXTRACT E01SDB01, TRANLOG, BEGIN now
EXTRACT added.

GGSCI (source-mysql1) 6>
```

```
GGSCI (source-mysql1) 10> ADD EXTTRAIL ./dirdata/sa, EXTRACT E01SDB01,
MEGABYTES 30
EXTTRAIL added.

GGSCI (source-mysql1) 11>
```

After successfully defining the Primary Extract and local trail, start the Extract process and confirm the status. The Replicat RLOAD08 should remain stopped or dropped to avoid unintentional start.

```
GGSCI (source-mysql1) 20> START EXTRACT E01SDB01

Sending START request to MANAGER ...
EXTRACT E01SDB01 starting

GGSCI (source-mysql1) 21> INFO ALL

Program     Status      Group       Lag at Chkpt  Time Since Chkpt

MANAGER     RUNNING
EXTRACT     RUNNING     E01SDB01    01:10:52      00:00:05
REPLICAT    STOPPED     RLOAD08     00:00:00      01:36:28

GGSCI (source-mysql1) 22>
```

Creating the Secondary Extract Group

Next, configure the Secondary Extract Group. It is composed of the following:

- Parameter File - p01sdb01.prm
- Data Pump Extract – P01SDB01
- Remote Trail - ./dirdat/ta
- Checkpoint File - P01SDB01.cpe

The parameter PASSTHRU indicates the source MySQL SDB1 database has an identical structure as the target Oracle 12c Pluggable Database T8C1PDB1.

The following steps prepare the parameter file. Add the Secondary Extract (P01SDB01) and define the remote trail.

```
GGSCI (source-mysql1) 25> EDIT PARAMS P01SDB01
```

```
EXTRACT P01SDB01
PASSTHRU
RMTHOST 192.168.1.42, MGRPORT 7842
RMTTRAIL ./dirdat/ta
TABLE osm$repapi.CUSTOMERS;
TABLE osm$repapi.POLICIES;
```

```
GGSCI (source-mysql1) 26> ADD EXTRACT P01SDB01, EXTTRAILSOURCE ./dirdat/sa
EXTRACT added.
GGSCI (source-mysql1) 27>
```

```
GGSCI (source-mysql1) 27> ADD RMTTRAIL ./dirdat/ta, EXTRACT P01SDB01,
MEGABYTES 30
RMTTRAIL added.
GGSCI (source-mysql1) 28>
```

After successfully defining the Secondary Extract and remote trail, start the Extract process and confirm the status.

```
GGSCI (source-mysql1) 33> START EXTRACT P01SDB01
Sending START request to MANAGER ...
EXTRACT P01SDB01 starting

GGSCI (source-mysql1) 34> INFO ALL
Program     Status      Group       Lag at Chkpt  Time Since Chkpt
MANAGER     RUNNING
EXTRACT     RUNNING     E01SDB01    00:00:00      00:00:06
EXTRACT     RUNNING     P01SDB01    00:00:00      00:00:12
REPLICAT    STOPPED     RLOAD08     00:00:00      01:51:03
GGSCI (source-mysql1) 35>
```

Configure Change Delivery Group

Having completed the change data capture and route groups, now configure the change delivery group. The change delivery group consists of the following related components:

- Checkpoint Database Table – ggs_admin.chkpttab
- Source Definition File – mysql1.def
- Replicat Group

Creating the Replicat Checkpoint Database Table

The default checkpoint for the Replicat is a database table. The GoldenGate schema 'ggs_admin' of the pluggable database T8C1PDB1 owns the checkpoint table. Use the global GoldenGate instance configuration parameter CHECKPOINTTABLE to create and activate the checkpoint table for the Replicats.

```
CHECKPOINTTABLE ggs_admin.chkpttab
```

Login to the database and execute the command ADD CHECKPOINTTABLE as shown next.

```
GGSCI (target-cdb) 3> DBLOGIN USERID ggs_admin@t8c1pdb1, PASSWORD oracle
Successfully logged into database T8C1PDB1.

GGSCI (target-cdb) 4> ADD CHECKPOINTTABLE

No checkpoint table specified. Using GLOBALS specification
(ggs_admin.chkpttab)...
Logon catalog name T8C1PDB1 will be used for table specification
T8C1PDB1.ggs_admin.chkpttab.

Successfully created checkpoint table T8C1PDB1.ggs_admin.chkpttab.

GGSCI (target-cdb) 5>
```

Creating the Source Definition File

The definition file created uses the DEFGEN Oracle GoldenGate utility.
The definition file mysql1.def is created on the source system, then transferred to the target system. The file is placed on './dirdef/' directory and referenced by the Replicat process for mapping and converting column data types.

```
$ ./defgen PARAMFILE ./dirprm/defgen.prm REPORTFILE ./dirrpt/defgen.rpt
```

The following is the portion of the report file 'defgen.rpt.' It lists the table's definition and the created definition file.

```
***********************************************************************
**            Run with the Following Parameters                   **
***********************************************************************
DEFSFILE ./dirdef/mysql1.def, PURGE
sourcedb osm$repapi@localhost.localdomain, userid root, password ******
TABLE osm$repapi.CUSTOMERS;
Retrieving definition for osm$repapi.CUSTOMERS.
TABLE osm$repapi.POLICIES;
Retrieving definition for osm$repapi.POLICIES.

Definitions generated for 2 tables in ./dirdef/mysql.def.
```

Creating the Replicat Group

The Replicat reads the transaction logs from the remote trails './dirdat/ta.' It uses the remote database, native SQL calls to apply the transactions to the database. The Replicat group is composed of the following:

- Parameter File - r01sdb01.prm
- Replicat Process – R01SDB1
- Remote Trail (Extract Trail) - ./dirdat/ta
- Replicat Checkpoint File - R01SDB01.cpr

The Replicat parameter SOURCEDEFS specifies the location of the source definition file, followed by the MAP statement which associates the source and target tables. Use the ADD REPLICAT to create the change delivery group.

```
GGSCI (target-cdb) 2> EDIT PARAMS R01SDB01
```

```
REPLICAT R01SDB01
USERID ggs_admin@s8c1pdb1, PASSWORD oracle
SOURCEDEFS ./dirdef/mysql1.def
DISCARDFILE ./dirrpt/r01sdb01.dsc
MAP osm$repapi.CUSTOMERS, TARGET osm$repapi.CUSTOMERS;
MAP osm$repapi.POLICIES, TARGET osm$repapi.POLICIES;
```

```
GGSCI (target-cdb) 3> ADD REPLICAT R01SDB01, EXTTRAIL ./dirdat/ta
REPLICAT added.

GGSCI (target-cdb) 4>
```

After successfully defining the Replicat group, start the Replicat process and confirm the status.

```
GGSCI (target-cdb) 13> START REPLICAT R01SDB01

Sending START request to MANAGER ...
REPLICAT R01SDB01 starting

GGSCI (target-cdb) 14> INFO ALL

Program     Status      Group       Lag at Chkpt  Time Since Chkpt

MANAGER     RUNNING
REPLICAT    RUNNING     R01SDB01    00:00:00      00:00:02

GGSCI (target-cdb) 15>
```

Generate GoldenGate Report

Use the GGSCI VIEW command to view the Replicat runtime environment. The sequence of logging is of type informational (INFO) followed by the current remote opened trail file.

```
GGSCI (target-cdb) 18> VIEW REPORT R01SDB01
```

```
***********************************************************************
                 Oracle GoldenGate Delivery for Oracle
 Version 12.1.2.0.0 17185003 OGGCORE_12.1.2.0.0_PLATFORMS_130924.1316_FBO
   Linux, x64, 64bit (optimized), Oracle 12c on Sep 25 2013 02:54:11

Copyright (C) 1995, 2013, Oracle and/or its affiliates. All Rights Reserved.


                    Starting at 2014-07-30 15:04:23
***********************************************************************

Operating System Version:
Linux
Version #1 SMP Tue Sep 10 20:33:17 PDT 2013, Release 2.6.39-400.209.1.el5uek
Node: target-cdb
Machine: x86_64
                         soft limit   hard limit
Address Space Size   :    unlimited    unlimited
Heap Size            :    unlimited    unlimited
File Size            :    unlimited    unlimited
CPU Time             :    unlimited    unlimited

Process id: 64683

Description:

***********************************************************************
**           Running with the following parameters                   **
***********************************************************************

2014-07-30 15:04:23  INFO    OGG-03059  Operating system character set
identified as UTF-8.
```

```
2014-07-30 15:04:23  INFO    OGG-02695  ANSI SQL parameter syntax is used
for parameter parsing.
REPLICAT R01SDB01
USERID ggs_admin@t8c1pdb1, PASSWORD ******

2014-07-30 15:04:31  INFO    OGG-02679  The Replicat process logged on to
database T8C1PDB1 and can only apply to that database.
SOURCEDEFS ./dirdef/mysql1.def

2014-07-30 15:04:31  INFO    OGG-03528  The source database character set,
as determined from the table definition file, is ISO-8859-1.
DISCARDFILE ./dirrpt/r01sdb01.dsc
MAP SDB1.CUSTOMERS, TARGET osm$repapi.CUSTOMERS;

2014-07-30 15:04:31  INFO    OGG-02669  Default catalog name T8C1PDB1 will
be used for target table name osm$repapi.CUSTOMERS mapping.
MAP SDB1.POLICIES, TARGET osm$repapi.POLICIES;

2014-07-30 15:04:31  INFO    OGG-02669  Default catalog name T8C1PDB1 will
be used for target table name osm$repapi.POLICIES mapping.

2014-07-30 15:04:31  INFO    OGG-06451  Triggers will be suppressed by
default.

2014-07-30 15:04:31  INFO    OGG-01815  Virtual Memory Facilities for: COM
    anon alloc: mmap(MAP_ANON)  anon free: munmap
    file alloc: mmap(MAP_SHARED)  file free: munmap
    target directories:
    /u01/app/ggs/product/12.1.2/gghome_1/dirtmp.

CACHEMGR virtual memory values (may have been adjusted)
CACHESIZE:                              2G
CACHEPAGEOUTSIZE (default):             8M
PROCESS VM AVAIL FROM OS (min):         4G
CACHESIZEMAX (strict force to disk):   3.41G

Database Version:
Oracle Database 12c Enterprise Edition Release 12.1.0.1.0 - 64bit Production
PL/SQL Release 12.1.0.1.0 - Production
CORE 12.1.0.1.0     Production
TNS for Linux: Version 12.1.0.1.0 - Production
NLSRTL Version 12.1.0.1.0 - Production

Database Language and Character Set:
NLS_LANGUAGE     = "AMERICAN"
NLS_TERRITORY    = "AMERICA"
NLS_CHARACTERSET = "AL32UTF8"

***********************************************************************
**                      Run Time Messages                            **
***********************************************************************

Opened trail file ./dirdat/ta000059 at 2014-07-30 15:04:33

2014-07-30 15:04:33  INFO    OGG-03522  Setting session time zone to source
database time zone 'Asia/Riyadh'.

GGSCI (target-cdb) 11>
```

Dynamic Report Viewer

Practitioners prefer to monitor the logging on real-time on a separate Linux Terminal. Use the Linux command 'tail –f –n.' The tail command keeps streaming the logs as they generated.

```
$ tail -f -n 5 ggserr.log
2014-08-12 17:58:30  INFO    OGG-00987  Oracle GoldenGate Command
Interpreter for Oracle:  GGSCI command (oracle): INFO REPLICAT R01SDB01.
2014-08-12 17:59:02  INFO    OGG-00987  Oracle GoldenGate Command
Interpreter for Oracle:  GGSCI command (oracle): INFO REPLICAT R01SDB01
showch.
2014-08-12 18:00:15  INFO    OGG-00987  Oracle GoldenGate Command
Interpreter for Oracle:  GGSCI command (oracle): info all.
2014-08-12 18:00:23  INFO    OGG-01021  Oracle GoldenGate Delivery for
Oracle, r01sdb01.prm:  Command received from GGSCI: GETLAG.
```

We repeat the above configurations and GGSCI commands for data capture and apply from the MySQL SDB2 to the Oracle 12c Pluggable Database T8C1PDB2, MySQL SDB2 to Oracle 12c Pluggable Database T8C1PDB3, and MySQL SDB4 to Oracle 12c Pluggable Database T8C1PDB4.

Configure Data Capture and Apply from SDB2 to T8C1PDB2

The source, MySQL database SDB2 is associated with the remote Oracle 12c Pluggable Database T8C1PDB2. Figure 8-18 shows the data capture and apply from SDB2 to T8C1PDB2.

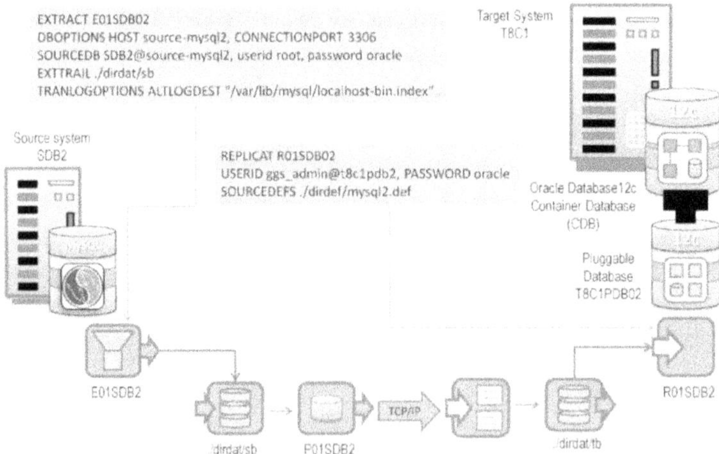

EXTRACT E01SDB02
DBOPTIONS HOST source-mysql2, CONNECTIONPORT 3306
SOURCEDB SDB2@source-mysql2, userid root, password oracle
EXTTRAIL ./dirdat/sb
TRANLOGOPTIONS ALTLOGDEST "/var/lib/mysql/localhost-bin.index"
Target System
T8C1
Source system
SDB2
REPLICAT R01SDB02
USERID ggs_admin@t8c1pdb2, PASSWORD oracle
SOURCEDEFS ./dirdef/mysql2.def
Oracle Database12c
Container Database
(CDB)
Pluggable
Database
T8C1PDB02
E01SDB2
R01SDB2
TCP/IP
./dirdat/sb
P01SDB2
./dirdat/tb

Figure 8-18: Data Capture and Application from SDB2 to T8C1PDB2

Configure the Change Data Capture

The change data capture consists of the following related configurations:

- Primary Extract Group
- Secondary Extract Group

Creating the Primary Extract Group

The Primary Extract Group is composed of the following components:

- Parameter File - e01sdb02.prm
- Primary Extract – E01SDB02
- Local Trail - ./dirdat/sb
- Checkpoint File - E01SDB02.cpe

```
GGSCI (source-mysql2) 6> edit params E01SDB02
```

```
EXTRACT E01SDB02
DBOPTIONS HOST source-mysql2, CONNECTIONPORT 3306
SOURCEDB SDB2@source-mysql2, userid root, password oracle
EXTTRAIL ./dirdat/sb
TRANLOGOPTIONS ALTLOGDEST "/var/lib/mysql/localhost-bin.index"
TABLE SDB2.CUSTOMERS;
TABLE SDB2.POLICIES;
```

```
GGSCI (source-mysql2) 5> ADD EXTRACT E01SDB02, TRANLOG, BEGIN now
EXTRACT added.

GGSCI (source-mysql2) 7>
```

```
GGSCI (source-mysql2) 8> ADD EXTTRAIL ./dirdata/sa, EXTRACT E01SDB02,
MEGABYTES 30
EXTTRAIL added.

GGSCI (source-mysql2) 9>
```

After successfully defining the Primary Extract and local trail, start the Extract process and confirm the status.

```
GGSCI (source-mysql2) 31> START E01SDB02

Sending START request to MANAGER ...
EXTRACT E01SDB02 starting

GGSCI (source-mysql2) 32> INFO ALL

Program     Status      Group       Lag at Chkpt  Time Since Chkpt
```

```
MANAGER      RUNNING
EXTRACT      RUNNING      E01SDB02     00:00:00      00:00:09
REPLICAT     STOPPED      RLOAD08      00:00:00      608:39:09

GGSCI (source-mysql2) 33> Creating the Secondary Extract Group
```

The Secondary Extract Group is composed of the following components:

- Parameter File - p01sdb02.prm
- Secondary Extract – P01SDB02
- Remote Trail - ./dirdat/tb
- Checkpoint File - P01SDB02.cpe

```
GGSCI (source-mysql2) 30> EDIT PARAMS P01SDB02
```

```
EXTRACT P01SDB02
PASSTHRU
RMTHOST 192.168.1.42, MGRPORT 7842
RMTTRAIL ./dirdat/tb
TABLE SDB2.CUSTOMERS;
TABLE SDB2.POLICIES;
```

```
GGSCI (source-mysql2) 31> ADD EXTRACT P01SDB02, EXTTRAILSOURCE ./dirdat/sb
EXTRACT added.

GGSCI (source-mysql2) 32>
```

```
GGSCI (source-mysql2) 32> ADD RMTTRAIL ./dirdat/tb, EXTRACT P01SDB02,
MEGABYTES 30
RMTTRAIL added.

GGSCI (source-mysql2) 33>
```

After successfully defining the Secondary Extract and remote trail, start the Extract process and confirm the status.

```
GGSCI (source-mysql2) 33> START P01SDB02

Sending START request to MANAGER ...
EXTRACT P01SDB02 starting

GGSCI (source-mysql2) 34> INFO ALL

Program      Status       Group        Lag at Chkpt  Time Since Chkpt

MANAGER      RUNNING
EXTRACT      RUNNING      E01SDB02     00:00:00      00:00:06
EXTRACT      RUNNING      P01SDB02     00:00:00      689:15:44
REPLICAT     STOPPED      RLOAD08      00:00:00      608:41:38

GGSCI (source-mysql2) 35>
```

Configure Change Delivery Group

The Change Delivery Group consists of the following components:

- Checkpoint Database Table (optional, but highly recommended)
- Source Definition File
- Change Delivery Group

Creating the Replicat Checkpoint Database Table

Prepare the Oracle GoldenGate instance global parameter file – GLOBALS. Add the checkpoint table by executing the command ADD CHECPOINTTABLE. The checkpoint table created is T8C1PDB2.ggs_admin.chktabtab.

```
GGSCI (target-cdb) 4> DBLOGIN USERID ggs_admin@t8c1pdb1, PASSWORD oracle
Successfully logged into database T8C1PDB1.

GGSCI (target-cdb) 5> ADD CHECKPOINTTABLE

No checkpoint table specified. Using GLOBALS specification
(ggs_admin.chkpttab)...
Logon catalog name T8C1PDB1 will be used for table specification
T8C1PDB1.ggs_admin.chkpttab.

Successfully created checkpoint table T8C1PDB1.ggs_admin.chkpttab.

GGSCI (target-cdb) 6>
```

Creating the Source Definition File

Create the Source Definition File. The file is specifically for mapping the table from the MySQL SDB2 to the Oracle 12c Pluggable Database T8C1PDB2. Prepare the source definition parameter file 'degen.prm.' Use the Oracle GoldenGate DEFGEN to generate the source definition file 'mysql2.def.'

```
DEFSFILE ./dirdef/mysql2.def, PURGE
sourcedb SDB2@source-mysql2, userid root, password oracle
TABLE SDB2.CUSTOMERS;
TABLE SDB2.POLICIES;
```

```
$ ./defgen PARAMFILE ./dirprm/defgen.prm REPORTFILE ./dirrpt/defgen.rpt
```

Creating the Change Delivery Group

The last step is to create the change delivery group. Prepare the parameter file – r01sdb02.prm, then define the Replicat R01SDB2.

```
GGSCI (target-cdb) 8> EDIT PARAMS R01SDB02
```

```
REPLICAT R01SDB02
USERID ggs_admin@s8c1pdb2, PASSWORD oracle
SOURCEDEFS ./dirdef/mysql2.def
DISCARDFILE ./dirrpt/r01sdb02.dsc
MAP osm$repapi.CUSTOMERS, TARGET osm$repapi.CUSTOMERS;
MAP osm$repapi.POLICIES, TARGET osm$repapi.POLICIES;
```

```
GGSCI (target-cdb) 9> ADD REPLICAT R01SDB02, EXTTRAIL ./dirdat/tb
REPLICAT added.

GGSCI (target-cdb) 10>
```

After successfully defining the Replicat group, start the Replicat process and confirm the status.

```
G GGSCI (target-cdb) 8> START REPLICAT R01SDB02

Sending START request to MANAGER ...
REPLICAT R01SDB02 starting

GGSCI (target-cdb) 9> INFO ALL

Program     Status      Group       Lag at Chkpt  Time Since Chkpt

MANAGER     RUNNING
EXTRACT     RUNNING     E01PDB1     00:00:06      00:00:05
REPLICAT    RUNNING     R01SDB01    00:00:00      00:00:09
REPLICAT    RUNNING     R01SDB02    00:00:00      00:00:07

GGSCI (target-cdb) 10>
```

Configure Data Capture and Apply from SDB3 to T8C1PDB3

The source, MySQL database SDB3 is associated with the remote Oracle 12c Pluggable Database T8C1PDB3. Figure 8-19 shows the data capture and apply from SDB3 to T8C1PDB3.

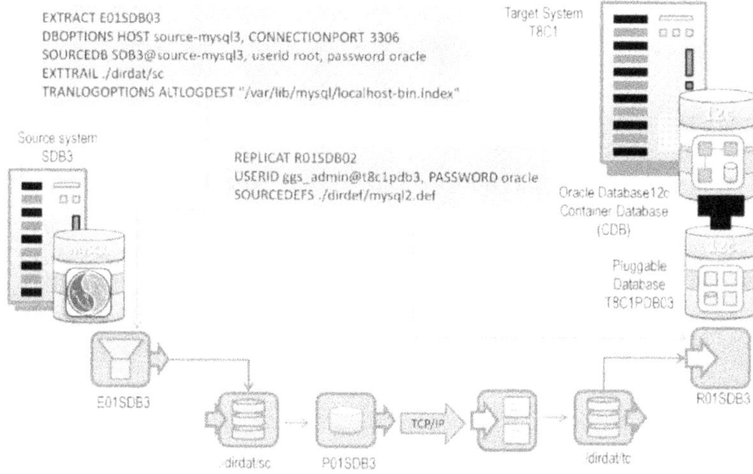
EXTRACT E01SDB03
DBOPTIONS HOST source-mysql3, CONNECTIONPORT 3306
SOURCEDB SDB3@source-mysql3, userid root, password oracle
EXTTRAIL ./dirdat/sc
TRANLOGOPTIONS ALTLOGDEST "/var/lib/mysql/localhost-bin.index"
Target System
T8C1
Source system
SDB3
REPLICAT R01SDB02
USERID ggs_admin@t8c1pdb3, PASSWORD oracle
SOURCEDEFS ./dirdef/mysql2.def
Oracle Database12c
Container Database
(CDB)
Pluggable
Database
T8C1PDB03
E01SDB3
R01SDB3
TCP/IP
dirdat/sc
P01SDB3
/dirdat/tc

Figure 8-19: Data Movement from SDB3 to T8C1PDB3

Configure the Change Data Capture

The change data capture consists of the following related configurations:

- Primary Extract Group
- Secondary Extract Group

Creating the Primary Extract Group

The Primary Extract group is composed of the following components:

- Parameter File - e01sdb03.prm
- Primary Extract – E01SDB03
- Local Trail - ./dirdat/sc
- Checkpoint File - E01SDB03.cpe

```
GGSCI (source-mysql3) 3> edit params E01SDB03
```

```
EXTRACT E01SDB03
DBOPTIONS HOST source-mysql3, CONNECTIONPORT 3306
SOURCEDB SDB3@source-mysql3, userid root, password oracle
EXTTRAIL ./dirdat/sc
TRANLOGOPTIONS ALTLOGDEST "/var/lib/mysql/localhost-bin.index"
TABLE SDB3.CUSTOMERS;
TABLE SDB3.POLICIES;
```

```
GGSCI (source-mysql3) 5> ADD EXTRACT E01SDB03, TRANLOG, BEGIN now
EXTRACT added.

GGSCI (source-mysql3) 6>
```

```
GGSCI (source-mysql3) 10> ADD EXTTRAIL ./dirdat/sc, EXTRACT E01SDB03,
MEGABYTES 30
EXTTRAIL added.

GGSCI (source-mysql3) 11>
```

After successfully defining the Primary Extract and local trail, start the Extract process and confirm the status.

```
GGSCI (source-mysql3) 7> START EXTRACT E01SDB03

Sending START request to MANAGER ...
EXTRACT E01SDB03 starting


GGSCI (source-mysql3) 8> INFO ALL

Program     Status      Group       Lag at Chkpt  Time Since Chkpt

MANAGER     RUNNING
EXTRACT     STOPPED     E01SDB03    00:00:00      00:00:29
REPLICAT    STOPPED     RLOAD08     00:00:00      759:08:49

GGSCI (source-mysql3) 9>
```

Creating the Secondary Extract Group

The Secondary Extract Group is composed of the following components:

- Parameter File - p01sdb03.prm
- Secondary Extract – P01SDB03
- Remote Trail - ./dirdat/tc
- Checkpoint File - P01SDB03.cpe

```
GGSCI (source-mysql3) 10> EDIT PARAMS P01SDB03
```

```
EXTRACT P01SDB03
PASSTHRU
RMTHOST 192.168.1.42, MGRPORT 7842
RMTTRAIL ./dirdat/tc
TABLE SDB3.CUSTOMERS;
TABLE SDB3.POLICIES;
```

```
GGSCI (source-mysql3) 11> ADD EXTRACT P01SDB03, EXTTRAILSOURCE ./dirdat/sc
EXTRACT added.

GGSCI (source-mysql3) 12>
```

```
GGSCI (source-mysql3) 12> ADD RMTTRAIL ./dirdat/tc, EXTRACT P01SDB03,
MEGABYTES 30
RMTTRAIL added.

GGSCI (source-mysql3) 13>
```

After successfully defining the secondary Extract and remote trail, start the Extract process and confirm the status.

```
GGSCI (source-mysql3) 13> START EXTRACT P01SDB03

Sending START request to MANAGER ...
EXTRACT P01SDB03 starting


GGGSCI (source-mysql3) 14> INFO ALL

Program     Status      Group       Lag at Chkpt  Time Since Chkpt

MANAGER     RUNNING
EXTRACT     RUNNING     E01SDB03    562:59:57     00:00:05
EXTRACT     RUNNING     P01SDB03    00:00:00      00:00:19
REPLICAT    STOPPED     RLOAD08     00:00:00      759:13:59


GGSCI (source-mysql3) 17>
```

Configure Change Delivery Group

The change Delivery Group consists of the following components:

- Checkpoint Database Table – optional, but highly recommended.
- Source Definition File
- Change Delivery Group

Creating the Replicat Checkpoint Database Table

Prepare the Oracle GoldenGate instance global parameter file – GLOBALS.
Add the checkpoint table by executing the command ADD CHECPOINTTABLE.
The checkpoint table created is T8C1PDB3.ggs_admin.chktabtab.

```
GGSCI (target-cdb) 3> DBLOGIN USERID ggs_admin@t8c1pdb3, PASSWORD oracle
Successfully logged into database T8C1PDB3.

GGSCI (target-cdb) 4> ADD CHECKPOINTTABLE

No checkpoint table specified. Using GLOBALS specification
(ggs_admin.chkpttab)...
Logon catalog name T8C1PDB3 will be used for table specification
T8C1PDB1.ggs_admin.chkpttab.

Successfully created checkpoint table T8C1PDB3.ggs_admin.chkpttab.

GGSCI (target-cdb) 5>
```

Creating the Source Definition File

Create the source definition file. The file is specifically for mapping the table from the MySQL SDB2 to the Oracle 12c Pluggable Database T8C1PDB3. Prepare the source definition parameter file 'degen.prm' and use the Oracle GoldenGate DEFGEN to generate the source definition file 'mysql3.def.'

```
DEFSFILE ./dirdef/mysql3.def, PURGE
sourcedb SDB3@source-mysql3, userid root, password oracle
TABLE SDB3.CUSTOMERS;
TABLE SDB3.POLICIES;
```

```
$ ./defgen PARAMFILE ./dirprm/defgen.prm REPORTFILE ./dirrpt/defgen.rpt
```

Creating the Change Delivery Group

The last step is to create the change delivery group. Prepare the parameter file – r01sdb03.prm, then define the Replicat R01SDB3.

```
GGSCI (target-cdb) 2> EDIT PARAMS R01SDB03
```

```
REPLICAT R01SDB03
USERID ggs_admin@s8c1pdb3, PASSWORD oracle
SOURCEDEFS ./dirdef/mysql3.def
DISCARDFILE ./dirrpt/r01sdb03.dsc
MAP osm$repapi.CUSTOMERS, TARGET osm$repapi.CUSTOMERS;
MAP osm$repapi.POLICIES, TARGET osm$repapi.POLICIES;
```

```
GGSCI (target-cdb) 3> ADD REPLICAT R01SDB03, EXTTRAIL ./dirdat/tc
REPLICAT added.

GGSCI (target-cdb) 4>
```

After successfully defining the Replicat group, start the Replicat process and confirm the status.

```
GGSCI (target-cdb) 13> START REPLICAT R01SDB03

Sending START request to MANAGER ...
REPLICAT R01SDB03 starting

GGSCI (target-cdb) 14> INFO ALL

Program     Status      Group       Lag at Chkpt  Time Since Chkpt

MANAGER     RUNNING
EXTRACT     RUNNING     E01PDB1     00:00:06      00:00:05
REPLICAT    RUNNING     R01SDB01    00:00:00      00:00:09
REPLICAT    RUNNING     R01SDB02    00:00:00      00:00:07
REPLICAT    RUNNING     R01SDB03    00:00:00      00:00:11

GGSCI (target-cdb) 15>
```

Configure Data Capture and Apply from SDB4 to T8C1PDB4

The source, MySQL database SDB4 is associated with the remote Oracle 12c Pluggable Database T8C1PDB4. Figure 8-20 shows the data capture and apply from the SDB4 to T8C1PDB4 process flow.

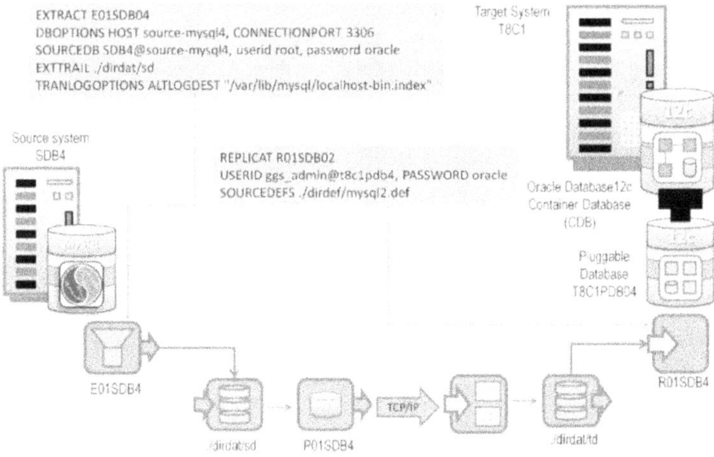
EXTRACT E01SDB04
DBOPTIONS HOST source-mysql4, CONNECTIONPORT 3306
SOURCEDB SDB4@source-mysql4, userid root, password oracle
EXTTRAIL ./dirdat/sd
TRANLOGOPTIONS ALTLOGDEST "/var/lib/mysql/localhost-bin.index"
Target System
T8C1
Source system
SDB4
REPLICAT R01SDB02
USERID ggs_admin@t8c1pdb4, PASSWORD oracle
SOURCEDEFS ./dirdef/mysql2.def
Oracle Database12c
Container Database
(CDB)
Pluggable
Database
T8C1PDB04
E01SDB4
TCP/IP
R01SDB4
./dirdat/sd
P01SDB4
./dirdat/td

Figure 8-20: Data Movement from the SDB4 to T8C1PDB4

Configure the Change Data Capture

The change data capture consists of the following related configurations:

- Primary Extract Group
- Secondary Extract Group

Creating the Primary Extract Group

The Primary Extract Group is composed of the following components:

- Parameter File - e01sdb04.prm
- Primary Extract – E01SDB04
- Local Trail - ./dirdat/sd
- Checkpoint File - E01SDB04.cpe

```
GGSCI (source-mysql4) 14> edit params E01SDB04
```

```
EXTRACT E01SDB04
DBOPTIONS HOST source_mysql4, CONNECTIONPORT 3306
SOURCEDB SDB4@source-mysql4, userid root, password oracle
EXTTRAIL ./dirdat/sd
TRANLOGOPTIONS ALTLOGDEST "/var/lib/mysql/localhost-bin.index"
TABLE SDB4.CUSTOMERS;
TABLE SDB4.POLICIES;
```

```
GGSCI (source-mysql4) 15> ADD EXTRACT E01SDB04, TRANLOG, BEGIN now
EXTRACT added.

GGSCI (source-mysql4) 16>
```

```
GGSCI (source-mysql4) 16> ADD EXTTRAIL ./dirdata/sd, EXTRACT E01SDB04,
MEGABYTES 30
EXTTRAIL added.

GGSCI (source-mysql4) 17>
```

After successfully defining the primary Extract and local trail, start the primary Extract process and confirm the status.

```
GGSCI (source-mysql4) 17> START EXTRACT E01SDB04

Sending START request to MANAGER ...
EXTRACT E01SDB04 starting
```

```
GGSCI (source-mysql4) 18> INFO ALL

Program     Status      Group       Lag at Chkpt  Time Since Chkpt

MANAGER     RUNNING
EXTRACT     RUNNING     E01SDB04    00:00:00      00:01:53
REPLICAT    STOPPED     RLOAD08     00:00:00      759:19:51

GGSCI (source-mysql4) 19>
```

Creating the Secondary Extract Group

The Secondary Extract group composed of the following components:

- Parameter File - p01sdb04.prm
- Secondary Extract – P01SDB04
- Remote Trail - ./dirdat/td
- Checkpoint File - P01SDB04.cpe

```
GGSCI (source-mysql4) 25> EDIT PARAMS P01SDB04
```

```
EXTRACT P01SDB04
PASSTHRU
RMTHOST 192.168.1.42, MGRPORT 7842
RMTTRAIL ./dirdat/td
TABLE osm$repapi.CUSTOMERS;
TABLE osm$repapi.POLICIES;
```

```
GGSCI (source-mysql1) 26> ADD EXTRACT P01SDB04, EXTTRAILSOURCE ./dirdat/sd
EXTRACT added.

GGSCI (source-mysql4) 27>
```

```
GGSCI (source-mysql4) 27> ADD RMTTRAIL ./dirdat/td, EXTRACT P01SDB04,
MEGABYTES 30
RMTTRAIL added.

GGSCI (source-mysql4) 28>
```

After successfully defining the secondary Extract and remote trail, we can start the secondary Extract process and confirm the status.

```
GGSCI (source-mysql4) 28> START EXTRACT P01SDB04

Sending START request to MANAGER ...
EXTRACT P01SDB04 starting

GGSCI (source-mysql4) 29> INFO ALL
```

```
Program     Status      Group       Lag at Chkpt  Time Since Chkpt

MANAGER     RUNNING
EXTRACT     RUNNING     E01SDB04    00:00:00      00:00:06
EXTRACT     RUNNING     P01SDB04    00:00:00      00:00:12
REPLICAT    STOPPED     RLOAD08     00:00:00      01:51:03

GGSCI (source-mysql4) 30>
```

Configure Change Delivery Group

The Change Delivery Group consists of the following components:

- Checkpoint Database Table (optional, but highly recommended)
- Source Definition File
- Change Delivery Group

Creating the Replicat Checkpoint Database Table

Prepare the Oracle GoldenGate instance global parameter file – GLOBALS.
Add the checkpoint table by executing the command ADD CHECPOINTTABLE.
The checkpoint table created is T8C1PDB4.ggs_admin.chktabtab.

```
GGSCI (target-cdb) 3> DBLOGIN USERID ggs_admin@t8c1pdb4, PASSWORD oracle
Successfully logged into database T8C1PDB4.

GGSCI (target-cdb) 4> ADD CHECKPOINTTABLE

No checkpoint table specified. Using GLOBALS specification
(ggs_admin.chkpttab)...
Logon catalog name T8C1PDB4 will be used for table specification
T8C1PDB4.ggs_admin.chkpttab.

Successfully created checkpoint table T8C1PDB4.ggs_admin.chkpttab.

GGSCI (target-cdb) 5>
```

Creating the Source Definition File

Create the source definition file. The file is specifically for mapping table from the MySQL SDB4 to the Oracle 12c Pluggable Database T8C1PDB4. Prepare the source definition parameter file 'degen.prm' and use the Oracle GoldenGate DEFGEN to generate the source definition file 'mysql4.def.'

```
DEFSFILE ./dirdef/mysql4.def, PURGE
sourcedb SDB4@source-mysql4, userid root, password oracle
TABLE SDB4.CUSTOMERS;
TABLE SDB4.POLICIES;
```

```
$ ./defgen PARAMFILE ./dirprm/defgen.prm REPORTFILE ./dirrpt/defgen.rpt
```

Creating the Change Delivery Group

The last step is to create the change delivery group. Prepare the parameter file – r01sdb04.prm, then define the Replicat R01SDB4.

```
GGSCI (target-cdb) 2> EDIT PARAMS R01SDB04
```

```
REPLICAT R01SDB04
USERID ggs_admin@s8c1pdb4, PASSWORD oracle
SOURCEDEFS ./dirdef/mysql4.def
DISCARDFILE ./dirrpt/r01sdb04.dsc
MAP osm$repapi.CUSTOMERS, TARGET osm$repapi.CUSTOMERS;
MAP osm$repapi.POLICIES, TARGET osm$repapi.POLICIES;
```

```
GGSCI (target-cdb) 3> ADD REPLICAT R01SDB04, EXTTRAIL ./dirdat/td
REPLICAT added.

GGSCI (target-cdb) 4>
```

After successfully defining the Replicat group, start the Replicat process and confirm the status.

```
GGSCI (target-cdb) 13> START REPLICAT R01SDB04

Sending START request to MANAGER ...
REPLICAT R01SDB04 starting

GGSCI (target-cdb) 14> INFO ALL

Program     Status      Group       Lag at Chkpt  Time Since Chkpt

MANAGER     RUNNING
EXTRACT     RUNNING     E01PDB1     00:00:06      00:00:05
REPLICAT    RUNNING     R01SDB01    00:00:00      00:00:09
REPLICAT    RUNNING     R01SDB02    00:00:00      00:00:07
REPLICAT    RUNNING     R01SDB03    00:00:00      00:00:11
REPLICAT    RUNNING     R01SDB04    00:00:00      00:00:11


GGSCI (target-cdb) 15>
```

Stage III: Real-Time Operational Data Warehouse Repository

Now, Oracle Database 12c Container Database (CDB) is globally synchronized on real-time, with data feed from the MySQL databases SDB1, SDB2, SDB3 and SDB4. The next step is to perform a real-time data consolidation from the Oracle Database 12c CDB to the Oracle Database 12c data warehouse repository. The data warehouse transformations may occur at the source, the target, or both the source & target systems. For complex resource intensive transformations, an Oracle GoldenGate intermediate system is the ideal platform for performing data transformations. The real-time operational data warehouse system is dedicated to run business intelligence (BI) and SQL analytic applications, delivering real-time data presentations for real-time decision making without impacting the transactional systems.

Oracle Database 12c Container Database Users

The change data capture (CDC) from the Oracle Database 12c Container Database (CDB) requires using a common database user. The common user has access to all Oracle 12c Pluggable Databases, subject to database privileges.

Creating Common Database User

The next steps create and grant privileges to the common user 'c##ggs_admin' for enabling database access. This user is used by the Extract processes to perform change database capture (CDC) from Oracle Database 12c Container Database transaction logs. Ensure the common database user is able to connect to all pluggable databases.

- Create the common database user :

```
SQL> CONN / AS SYSDBA
Connected.
SQL> CREATE USER c##ggs_admin
  2  IDENTIFIED BY oracle;

User created.
```

- Grant database privileges CREATE SESSION and DBA, for testing purpose only.

```
SQL> CONN sys/oracle_4U@T8C1PDB1 AS SYSDBA
Connected.
SQL> GRANT CREATE SESSION, DBA TO c##ggs_admin;

Grant succeeded.

SQL> CONN sys/oracle_4U@T8C1PDB2 AS SYSDBA
Connected.
SQL> GRANT CREATE SESSION, DBA TO c##ggs_admin;

Grant succeeded.

SQL> CONN sys/oracle_4U@T8C1PDB3 AS SYSDBA
Connected.
SQL> GRANT CREATE SESSION, DBA TO c##ggs_admin;
```

```
Grant succeeded.

SQL> CONN sys/oracle_4U@T8C1PDB4 AS SYSDBA
Connected.
SQL> GRANT CREATE SESSION, DBA TO c##ggs_admin;

Grant succeeded.
```

- Verify connection to pluggable databases

```
SQL> CONN c##ggs_admin/oracle@T8C1PDB1
Connected.
SQL> CONN c##ggs_admin/oracle@T8C1PDB2
Connected.
SQL> CONN c##ggs_admin/oracle@T8C1PDB3
Connected.
SQL> CONN c##ggs_admin/oracle@T8C1PDB4
Connected.
SQL>
```

Refer to Chapter 2 for more details regarding database privileges required by the Oracle GoldenGate database user on the source & target databases.

Creating Local Database User

Local database users own the checkpoint table and it is created for each of the Oracle 12c Pluggable Databases. The following SQL commands create the local database user 'ggs_admin' for the pluggable database 'T8C1PDB1'. This user is used by the Replicat to apply transactions to the target pluggable database.

- Issue an explicit DBA connection to the pluggable database. Create the local database user and grant privileges. The database privileges CREATE SESSION and DBA are for testing purposes only.

```
SQL> CONN system/oracle_4U@T8C1PDB1
Connected.
SQL> CREATE USER ggs_admin
  2  IDENTIFIED BY oracle;

User created.

SQL> GRANT CREATE SESSION, DBA TO ggs_admin;

Grant succeeded.

SQL> CONN system/oracle_4U@T8C1PDB2
Connected.
SQL> CREATE USER ggs_admin
  2  IDENTIFIED BY oracle;

User created.
```

```
SQL> GRANT CREATE SESSION, DBA TO ggs_admin;

Grant succeeded.

SQL> CONN system/oracle_4U@T8C1PDB3
Connected.
SQL> CREATE USER ggs_admin
  2  IDENTIFIED BY oracle;

User created.

SQL> GRANT CREATE SESSION, DBA TO ggs_admin;

Grant succeeded.

SQL> CONN system/oracle_4U@T8C1PDB4
Connected.
SQL> CREATE USER ggs_admin
  2  IDENTIFIED BY oracle;

User created.

SQL> GRANT CREATE SESSION, DBA TO ggs_admin;

Grant succeeded.
```

- Verify the connection to the pluggable database :

```
SQL> CONN ggs_admin/oracle@T8C1PDB1
Connected.
SQL> CONN ggs_admin/oracle@T8C1PDB2
Connected.
SQL> CONN ggs_admin/oracle@T8C1PDB3
Connected.
SQL> CONN ggs_admin/oracle@T8C1PDB4
Connected.
SQL>
```

Refer to Chapter 2 for more details regarding databases' privileges.

The real-time operational data warehouse repository requires configuration of data transformation, capture and apply from pluggable database T8C1PDB1, T8C1PDB2, T8C1PDB3 and T8C1PDB4 to BWDB.

Configure Data Capture, Transformation and Apply from T8C1PDB1 to BWDB

The change data capture (CDC) for Oracle 12c Pluggable Database 'T8C1PDB1' is configured using a secondary Extract option. The Primary Extract performs change data capture and writes to its associated local trail. The Secondary Extract (data pump) sends data to the remote system for writing to its associated remote trail via the data server collector.

For the Oracle Database 12c Container Database, the Extract process must be first registered with its associated Pluggable Database, then be defined as an integrated Extract. Figure 8-21 depicts the change data capture (CDC) by the Extract E01PDB1, routing by P01PDB1 and change delivery by R01PDB1.

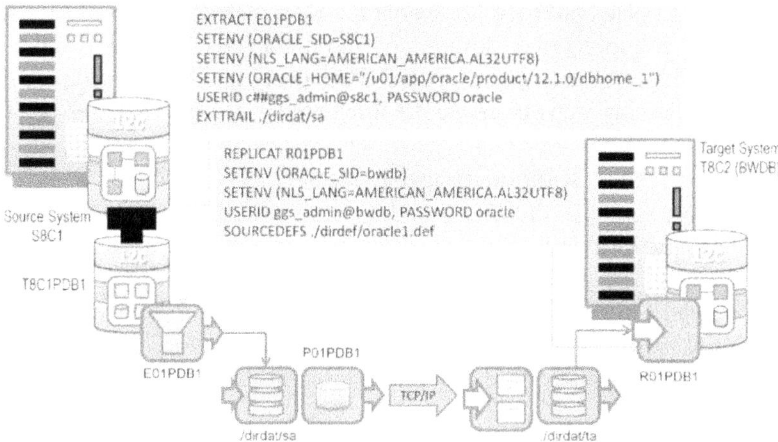

Figure 8-21: Data Capture, Transformation and Apply from T8C1PDB1 to BWDB

Creating Table Level Logging

The change data capture (CDC) is based on the database transaction logs, supplemented by the table's logging. There are (2) methods for creating table logging: (i) The ADD TRANDATA command enables table-level logging (ii) The ADD SCHEMATRANDATA command is required for integrated capture. It enables schema-level supplemental logging for current & future tables, which is similar when using the wildcard character '*' with the ADD TRANDATA.

The following ADD SCHEMATRANDATA uses the option ALLCOLS to enable logging for all columns.

```
GGSCI (target-cdb) 1> DBLOGIN USERID c##ggs_admin@t8c1pdb1, PASSWORD oracle
Successfully logged into database T8C1PDB1.

GGSCI (target-cdb) 2> ADD SCHEMATRANDATA osm$repapi ALLCOLS

2014-07-03 19:44:25  INFO    OGG-01788  SCHEMATRANDATA has been added on
schema osm$repapi.
```

```
2014-07-03 19:44:25  INFO    OGG-01976  SCHEMATRANDATA for scheduling
columns has been added on schema osm$repapi.

2014-07-03 19:44:25  INFO    OGG-01977  SCHEMATRANDATA for all columns has
been added on schema osm$repapi.
```

Creating the Integrated Capture Group

When working with the Oracle Database 12c Container Database (CDB), the Extract process must be created as a integrated capture type and not a classic capture. Login to the Oracle Database 12c root container, CDB$ROOT using the database common user and perform the following steps to create the integrated capture group:

- Register the Primary Extract with the pluggable database
- Add the Primary Extract – E01PDB1, using the integrated option
- Link the Extract to the local trail ./dirdat/sa

Notice that the integrated capture Extract TABLE statement uses the TOKEN option to capture the group name. The source of the transaction is used for identifying the primary key value after the data transformation.

- Prepare the Primary Extract Parameter File

```
GGSCI (target-cdb) 2> EDIT PARAMS E01PDB1
```

```
EXTRACT E01PDB1
SETENV (ORACLE_SID=S8C1)
SETENV (NLS_LANG=AMERICAN_AMERICA.AL32UTF8)
SETENV (ORACLE_HOME="/u01/app/oracle/product/12.1.0/dbhome_1")
USERID c##ggs_admin@s8c1, PASSWORD oracle
EXTTRAIL ./dirdat/sa
TABLE T8C1PDB1.osm$repapi.customers, TOKENS (TK_SOURCE_C = @GETENV
('GGENVIRONMENT', 'GROUPNAME'));
TABLE T8C1PDB1.osm$repapi.policies, TOKENS (TK_SOURCE_P = @GETENV
('GGENVIRONMENT', 'GROUPNAME'));
```

- Register the extract with the pluggable database

```
GGSCI (target-cdb) 4> DBLOGIN USERID c##ggs_admin@s8c1, PASSWORD oracle
Successfully logged into database CDB$ROOT.

GGSCI (target-cdb) 5>

GGSCI (target-cdb) 8> REGISTER EXTRACT E01PDB1 DATABASE CONTAINER (T8C1PDB1)
Extract E01PDB1 successfully registered with database at SCN 4338453.

GGSCI (target-cdb) 9>
```

- Add the Primary Extract and the associated local trail

```
GGSCI (target-cdb) 13> ADD EXTRACT E01PDB1, INTEGRATED TRANLOG, BEGIN now
EXTRACT added.

GGSCI (target-cdb) 14> ADD EXTTRAIL ./dirdat/sa, EXTRACT E01PDB1
EXTTRAIL added.
```

Creating the Secondary Group

Add the Secondary Extract (data pump) – P01PDB1. The data pump reads the local trail './dirdat/sa' of its pluggable database and routes data to the remote system for writing to the remote trail. The Extract P01PDB1 is linked to the remote trail './dirdat/ta.'

- Prepare the Parameter File.

```
GGSCI (target-cdb) 3> EDIT PARAMS P01PDB1
```

```
EXTRACT P01PDB1
PASSTHRU
RMTHOST 192.168.1.52, mgrport 7852
RMTTRAIL ./dirdat/ta
TABLE T8C1PDB1.osm$repapi.customers;
TABLE T8C1PDB1.osm$repapi.policies;
```

- Add the Primary Extract and its local trail.

```
GGSCI (target-cdb) 15> ADD EXTRACT P01PDB1, EXTTRAILSOURCE ./dirdat/sa,
BEGIN now
EXTRACT added.

GGSCI (target-cdb) 16> ADD RMTTRAIL ./dirdat/ta, EXTRACT P01PDB1
RMTTRAIL added.

GGSCI (target-cdb) 17>
```

Creating the Change Delivery Group

The change delivery group is created on the target system. The ADD REPLICAT command defines and links the Replicat R01PDB1 with the remote trail './dirdat/ta.' Postpone starting the Replicat until all Replicats are created.

Notice that the Replicat uses the GoldenGate function @TOKEN to read the token value when performing column mapping. The token value is assigned to the table column CUST_SOURCE to identify the source and implement a composite primary key.

```
GGSCI (target-bw) 2> EDIT PARAMS R01PDB1
```

```
REPLICAT R01PDB1
SETENV (ORACLE_SID=bwdb)
SETENV (NLS_LANG=AMERICAN_AMERICA.AL32UTF8)
USERID ggs_admin@bwdb, PASSWORD oracle
SOURCEDEFS ./dirdef/oracle1.def
DISCARDFILE ./dirrpt/r01pdb1.dsc
MAP T8C1PDB1.osm$repapi.CUSTOMERS, TARGET osm$repapi.CUSTOMERS, &
COLMAP (USEDEFAULTS, CUST_SOURCE = @TOKEN ('TK_SOURCE_C'));
MAP T8C1PDB1.osm$repapi.POLICIES, TARGET osm$repapi.POLICIES, &
COLMAP (USEDEFAULTS, CUST_SOURCE = @TOKEN ('TK_SOURCE_P'));
```

```
GGSCI (target-bw) 5> ADD REPLICAT R01PDB2, EXTTRAIL ./dirdat/ta
REPLICAT added.
```

Repeat the above configuration for data-transformation capture-apply from T8C1PDB2 to BWDB, T8C1PDB3 to BWDB and T8C1PDB4 to BWDB.

Starting Extracts and Replicats

On the source database, the Replicat R01SDB01, R01SDB02, R01SDB03 and R01SDB04 have been already started. Start and verify the primary and secondary Extracts E01PDB1, P01PDB1, E01PDB2, P01PDB2, E01PDB3, P01PDB3, E01PDB4 and P01PDB4.

```
GGSCI (target-cdb) 76> INFO ALL

Program     Status      Group       Lag at Chkpt  Time Since Chkpt

MANAGER     RUNNING
EXTRACT     RUNNING     E01PDB1     00:00:51      00:00:04
EXTRACT     RUNNING     E01PDB2     00:00:51      00:00:04
EXTRACT     RUNNING     E01PDB3     00:10:53      00:00:02
EXTRACT     RUNNING     E01PDB4     00:05:16      00:00:02
EXTRACT     RUNNING     P01PDB1     00:00:00      00:00:07
EXTRACT     RUNNING     P01PDB2     00:00:00      00:00:07
EXTRACT     RUNNING     P01PDB3     00:00:00      00:00:07
EXTRACT     RUNNING     P01PDB4     00:00:00      00:00:07
REPLICAT    RUNNING     R01SDB01    00:00:00      00:00:07
REPLICAT    RUNNING     R01SDB02    00:00:00      00:00:07
REPLICAT    RUNNING     R01SDB03    00:00:00      00:00:07
REPLICAT    RUNNING     R01SDB04    00:00:00      00:00:07
```

On the target database, start the Replicat R01PDB1, R01PDB2, R01PDB3 and R01PDB4.

```
GGSCI (target-bw) 18> INFO ALL
Program     Status      Group       Lag at Chkpt  Time Since Chkpt
MANAGER     RUNNING
REPLICAT    RUNNING     R01PDB1     00:00:00      00:00:00
REPLICAT    RUNNING     R01PDB2     00:00:00      00:00:08
REPLICAT    RUNNING     R01PDB3     00:00:00      00:00:08
REPLICAT    RUNNING     R01PDB4     00:00:00      00:00:08
```

Deleting an Integrated Extract

For reasons such as rebuilding the environment, deleting an integrated extract is a two-step command: DELETE and UNREGISTER. Deleting an integrated extract requires logging into the database using the database common user account.

```
GGSCI (target-cdb) 112> DBLOGIN USERID c##ggs_admin@s8c1, PASSWORD oracle
Successfully logged into database CDB$ROOT.
GGSCI (target-cdb) 113> DELETE E01PDB1
Deleted EXTRACT E01PDB1.
GGSCI (target-cdb) 114> UNREGISTER EXTRACT E01PDB1 DATABASE
Successfully unregistered EXTRACT E01PDB1 from database.
```

Data Transformations for Very Large Database

Oracle Database 12c Enterprise Edition supports the deployment of an extremely Very Large Database (VLDB) environment. A data warehouse repository database is handled differently in terms of the database design and storage. There are (2) key Oracle Database Enterprise Edition features for super-charging read-mostly, database applications performance without impacting the applications design:

- Database Table and Index Partitioning
- Database Materialized Views

Database Table and Index Partitioning

Database Table Indexes are partitioned without impacting the applications – *application transparent*. Instead of managing the database table and index as one segment, it is created as partitioned and managed as multiple segments of its type. There are several partitioning methods, for data warehouse applications. The *list* partition method is suitable when the partitioning key is mapped to a dimension attribute. For partitioned tables of type LIST, a list of discrete values for each partition is specified. INSERT statements are mapped to a partition (segment) by comparing the value of the partitioning key column value against the partition's list of values.

The following CREATE TABLE DDL Oracle SQL command creates a list-partitioned CUSTOMERS table using the column CUST_SOURCE. The discrete list of values is composed of the group names of the Replicat processes of the associated Oracle 12c Pluggable Database.

```
SQL> CREATE TABLE osm$repapi.customers (
CUST_NO         NUMBER NOT NULL,
CUST_NAME       VARCHAR2(128) NOT NULL,
CUST_EMAIL      VARCHAR2(128) NOT NULL,
CUST_MOBILE     VARCHAR2(16) NOT NULL,
CUST_ADDRESS    VARCHAR2(128),
CUST_SOURCE     VARCHAR2(32) NOT NULL)
PARTITION BY LIST (CUST_SOURCE)
  (PARTITION RPDB1 VALUES ('R01PDB1', 'R02PDB1', 'R03PDB1'),
   PARTITION RPDB2 VALUES ('R01PDB2', 'R02PDB2', 'R03PDB2'),
   PARTITION RPDB3 VALUES ('R01PDB3', 'R02PDB3', 'R03PDB3'),
   PARTITION RPDB4 VALUES ('R01PDB4', 'R02PDB4', 'R03PDB4'));

Table created.
```

Next, create the partitioned index as a LOCAL partitioned index. A local index partition is implicitly partitioned using the partitioned table's partitioning key – CUST_SOURCE column.

```
SQL> CREATE UNIQUE INDEX osm$repapi.cust_pk_1
ON osm$repapi.customers (cust_no, cust_source)
LOCAL;

Index created.

SQL> ALTER TABLE osm$repapi.customers ADD CONSTRAINT cust_pk_1
PRIMARY KEY (cust_no, cust_source);

Table altered.
SQL>
```

Query the data dictionary views DBA_PART_TABLES, DBA_PART_KEY_COLUMNS and DBA_TAB_PARTITIONS for details about the table's partitions and partitioning key columns.

```
SQL> SELECT PARTITION_NAME
FROM   DBA_TAB_PARTITIONS
WHERE  TABLE_NAME='CUSTOMERS2' and TABLE_OWNER='OSM$REPAPI';

PARTITION_NAME
--------------------------------------------------------------------------------
RPDB1
RPDB2
RPDB3
RPDB4

SQL>
```

For online conversion to a partitioned table, use a DBMS_REDEFINITION PL/SQL package to convert a non-partitioned to partitioned table. See Chapter 4 for more details regarding using DBMS_REDEFINITION.

Database Materialized Views

The second application's transparent Oracle Database 12c Enterprise Edition feature is designed for data warehouse applications and is the database materialized view. It is a database segment that stores the result of an SQL query which enable the dynamic re-write of the SQL applications after internally evaluating the execution plan.

The following SQL is the basis of creating the materialized view and the materialized view log. When any application executes, instead of performing the query against the original query database tables, it is dynamically re-written to execute against the materialized view.

```
SQL> SELECT cust_source, COUNT(*)
     FROM   osm$repapi.customers
     GROUP BY cust_source
     ORDER BY 1;
```

```
CUST_SOURCE                        COUNT(*)
-------------------------------  ---------
E01PDB1                            85083
E01PDB2                            83856
E01PDB3                            249054
E01PDB4                            202202
```

```
SQL> CONN osm$repapi/oracle

SQL> CREATE MATERIALIZED VIEW LOG ON customers
     WITH PRIMARY KEY;
```

```
Materialized view log created.
```

```
SQL> CREATE MATERIALIZED VIEW customers_mv
     BUILD IMMEDIATE
     REFRESH FAST AS
     SELECT cust_source, COUNT(*)
     FROM   osm$repapi.customers
     GROUP BY cust_source
     ORDER BY 1;
```

```
Materialized view created.

SQL>
```

Now when the applications execute, the Oracle Database 12c performs a query re-write when the database queries the optimizer. It determines the materialized view and performs more efficiently than the base table.
Refer to Chapter 3 for more details regarding enabling a query re-write.

Example: Real-Time Operational Data Warehouse Repository

The objective is to enable a real-time business monitor without impacting the Online Transaction Processing (OLTP) systems. Figure 8-22 depicts the processes workflow from the MySQL to the Oracle Database 12c Data Warehouse Repository.

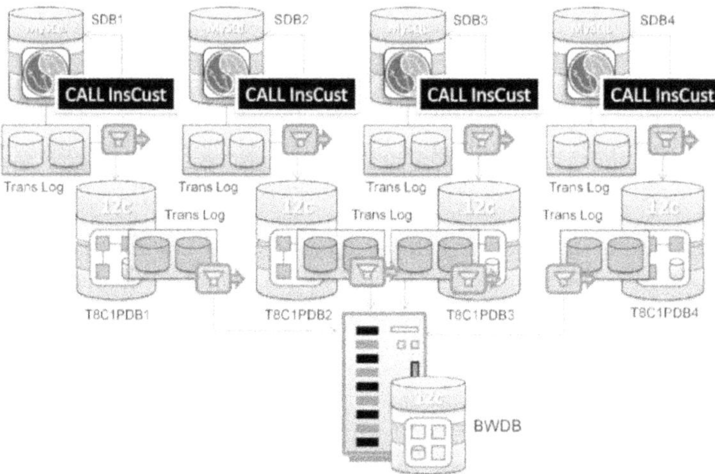

Figure 8-22: Transactions and Processes Workflow from MySQL to BWDB

Create MySQL Application

Create the following MySQL procedure for SDB1, SDB2, SDB3 and SDB4. The procedure has (2) input parameters, X and Y. Parameter X is the starting CUST_NO. Parameter Y is the terminating CUST_NO. Hence, the true condition of X < Y is required for the program to execute.

```
USE SDB1
DELIMITER ##
-- ==================================
-- x is the starting CUST_NO
-- y is the ending CUST_NO
-- The procedure terminates when x=y
-- ==================================
DROP PROCEDURE IF EXISTS InsCust##
CREATE PROCEDURE InsCust(x INT, y INT)
BEGIN
IF x < y THEN
    DECLARE fn VARCHAR(30);
    DECLARE ln VARCHAR(30);
    DECLARE mn VARCHAR(30);
    DECLARE dn VARCHAR(128);
    DECLARE vCUST_NO       INT;
    DECLARE vCUST_NAME     VARCHAR(128);
    DECLARE vCUST_EMAIL    VARCHAR(128);
```

```
    DECLARE vCUST_MOBILE  VARCHAR(32);
    DECLARE vCUST_ADDRESS VARCHAR(32);
    DECLARE vPOL_VALUE    FLOAT(8, 2);
    DECLARE pt VARCHAR(8);
    DECLARE dt VARCHAR(8);
    EOL: LOOP
       IF x = y THEN
           LEAVE  EOL;
       END IF;
       SET x = x + 1;
       SET vCUST_NO = x;
       SELECT UPPER(rf_name) into @fn
       FROM RANDOM_FIRST ORDER BY rand() LIMIT 1;
       SELECT UPPER(rm_name) into @mn
       FROM RANDOM_MIDDLE ORDER BY rand() LIMIT 1;
       SELECT UPPER(rl_name) into @ln
       FROM RANDOM_LAST ORDER BY rand() LIMIT 1;
       SELECT UPPER(rd_name) into @dn
       FROM RANDOM_DOMAIN ORDER BY rand() LIMIT 1;
       SET vCUST_MOBILE =  CONCAT('704-', FLOOR(RAND() * 999), '-',
                              FLOOR(RAND() * 9999));
       SET vCUST_NAME = CONCAT(@fn, ' ', @mn, ' ', @ln);
       SET vCUST_EMAIL =  CONCAT(@fn, '.', @ln, '@', @dn, '.COM');
       SET vCUST_ADDRESS =  CONCAT('PO BOX ', FLOOR(RAND() * 99999), ',
                                NC 27306, USA');
       INSERT INTO CUSTOMERS VALUES(vCUST_NO, vCUST_NAME, vCUST_EMAIL,
                                vCUST_MOBILE, vCUST_ADDRESS);
       COMMIT;
       SELECT pt_code INTO @pt FROM POLICY_TYPES ORDER BY rand() LIMIT 1;
       SELECT dt_code INTO @dt FROM DISCOUNT_TYPES ORDER BY rand() LIMIT 1;
       SET vPOL_VALUE = ROUND(RAND() * 9999.99, 2);
       INSERT INTO POLICIES VALUES(1000+vCUST_NO, CURDATE(),
                               DATE_ADD(CURDATE(), INTERVAL 1 YEAR),
                               vPOL_VALUE, vPOL_VALUE, @pt, @dt,
                               vPOL_VALUE, vCUST_NO);
       COMMIT;
    END LOOP;
END IF;
END;
##

DELIMITER ;
```

Execute the Applications

Run the applications for SDB1, SDB2, SDB3 and SDB4. Query the maximum value to avoid a primary key constraint violation.

```
mysql> USE SDB1
Database changed
mysql> SELECT MAX(cust_no) FROM CUSTOMERS;
+--------------+
| MAX(cust_no) |
+--------------+
|     10550084 |
+--------------+
1 row in set (0.21 sec)
```

```
mysql> CALL InsCust(10550085, 10550100);
Query OK, 0 rows affected (2.02 sec)

mysql>

mysql> USE SDB2
Database changed
mysql> SELECT max(cust_no) FROM CUSTOMERS;
+--------------+
| max(cust_no) |
+--------------+
|     10548858 |
+--------------+
1 row in set (0.16 sec)

mysql> CALL InsCust(10548859, 10548900);
Query OK, 0 rows affected (3.56 sec)

mysql>

mysql> USE SDB3
Database changed
mysql> SELECT max(cust_no) FROM CUSTOMERS;
+--------------+
| max(cust_no) |
+--------------+
|     10548765 |
+--------------+
1 row in set (0.16 sec)

mysql> CALL InsCust(10548766, 10548800);
Query OK, 0 rows affected (3.56 sec)
mysql>
mysql> USE SDB4
Database changed
mysql> SELECT max(cust_no) FROM CUSTOMERS;
+--------------+
| max(cust_no) |
+--------------+
|     10548234 |
+--------------+
1 row in set (0.16 sec)
mysql> CALL InsCust(10548235, 10548300);
Query OK, 0 rows affected (3.56 sec)

mysql>
```

Building Data Warehouse Reports Using Oracle APEX

Oracle Application Express (APEX) allows a user to quickly build sophisticated reports using different views. It's treated as a feature of the database, hence it down not require additional license fees. APEX requires minimal configuration since it is already installed when the database successfully created. Oracle APEX uses an advanced security model built on top of the Oracle Database security; The created components are stored inside the database, shared among users per Oracle APEX privileges and take unlimited advantage of the hosting database features, options, performance and scalability.

Login to Oracle APEX

When the database created using the Database Configuration Assistant (DBCA), Oracle APEX is automatically deployed. The default HTTP port for Oracle APEX is 8082. Login to the APEX homepage by entering the URL: http://hostname: 8082/apex. Figure 8-23 shows the login to Oracle APEX; Enter the Workspace, Username and Password.

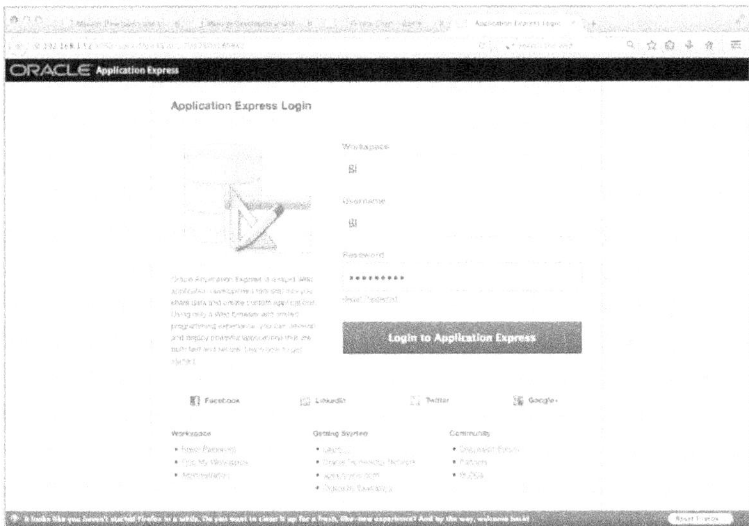

Figure 8-23: Oracle APEX Login

In case of login attempt failures, APEX users' profile is configured to lock the account. The UNLOCK_ACCOUNT procedure unlock the accounts. To change the password, run the supplied SQL script 'apxchpwd.sql' while connected as DBA.

```
SQL> alter session set current_schema = APEX_040200;

Session altered.

SQL> begin
  2      wwv_flow_security.g_security_group_id := 10;
  3      wwv_flow_fnd_user_api.UNLOCK_ACCOUNT('ADMIN');
  4      commit;
  5  end; /

PL/SQL procedure successfully completed.
```

Develop Applications using Oracle APEX

Applications are developed using browser-based wizard environment. Forms and reports applications are developed and deployed instantly. Figure 8-24 and 8-25 show two of the steps of the Create Page wizard – Chart Type and Query Worksheet.

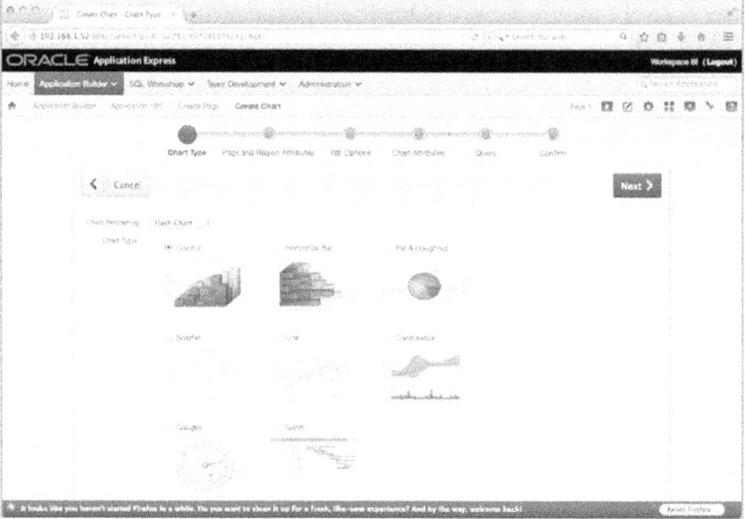

Figure 8-24: Select the Chart Type

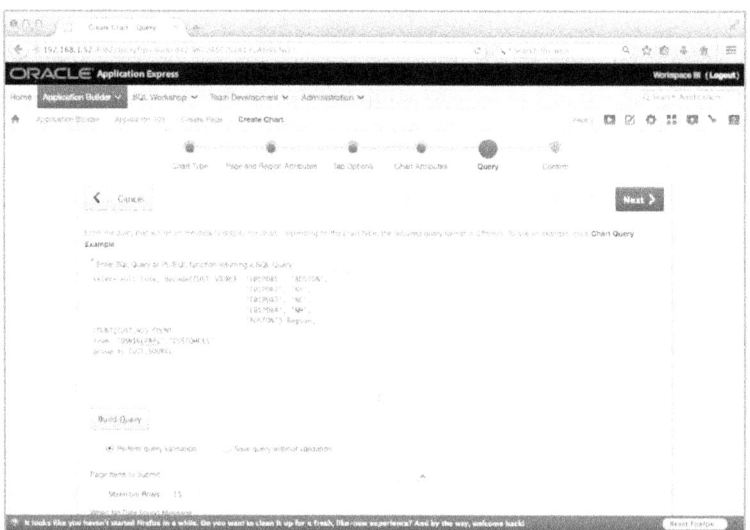

Figure 8-25: The Query Builder

APEX Application Runtime

The last step of the Create Page wizard runs the application. The application may be modified and re-run at any time.

Figure 8-26 shows the APEX runtime on the BWDB. It displays a highly optimized execution plan for the query below.

```
SQL> select decode(CUST_SOURCE, 'E01PDB1', 'BOSTON',
                                'E01PDB2', 'NY',
                                'E01PDB3', 'NC',
                                'E01PDB4', 'NM',
                                'BOSTON') Region, COUNT(CUST_NO) COUNT
     from  "OSM$REPAPI"."CUSTOMERS"
     group by CUST_SOURCE;

REGION      COUNT
------      ----------
NY          83856
NC          249054
NM          202202
BOSTON      85083

SQL>
```

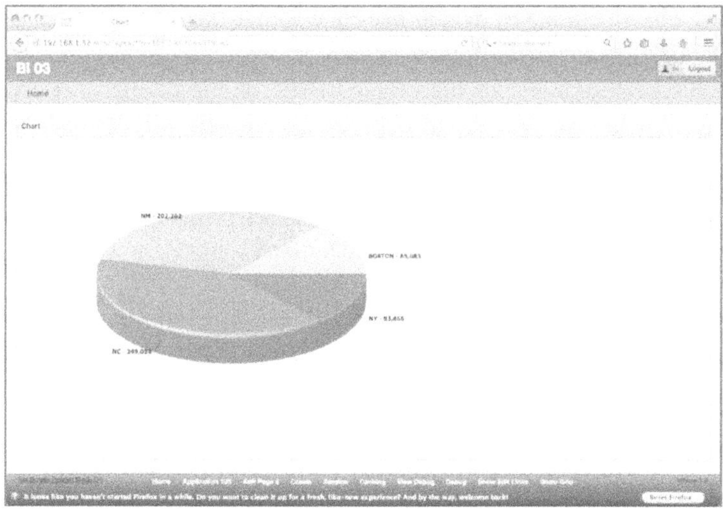

Figure 8-26: APEX Runtime

Summary

The combination of the Oracle Database 12c Multitenant for the Pluggable Database (PDB) and Oracle GoldenGate is a state-of-the-art platform for unifying a globally-operated business model. It is all about data consolidation, where databases are plugged into the corporate data warehouse repository. This chapter has covered the ultimate feature of Oracle GoldenGate, *heterogeneity*; between the Oracle Database 12c and MySQL.

The first task is to establish the remote MySQL databases. It is performed using the Oracle GoldenGate initial load method. There are (2) methods that are suitable for this task: File to Replicat and Direct Load. The File to Replicat was implemented.

Then, perform a heterogeneous online data synchronization. The data movement is developed by mapping each of the MySQL databases to an Oracle 12c Pluggable Database. The Extract performs online capture, data pump routes the trails, and the Replicat applies the transactions to the target Oracle 12c Pluggable Database.

The last step is to consolidate the data from all of the Oracle 12c Pluggable Databases into a single database, the data warehouse repository. To enable building online business analytic applications, data transformation is developed and delivered by Oracle GoldenGate. The streaming of data in real-time allows the decision making process without the need for manual offline data feeding.

The use of Oracle GoldenGate functions is key for performing data transformation and manipulation. The use of the database Pl/SQL sub-programs extend data transformation capabilities. These PL/SQL sub-programs are invoked from within Oracle GoldenGate Extracts and Replicats. Refer to Chapter 10 for advanced data transformation and manipulation using Oracle GoldenGate.

The chapter also demonstrated using Oracle APEX for real-time reporting. The Oracle APEX report was powered by the Oracle Database partitioning and materialized view for enabling a high-performance report engine. Oracle APEX is an embedded database and requires minimal configurations and skills for generating powerful report capabilities.

The next chapter covers Oracle GoldenGate management options, namely Oracle GoldenGate Director, Oracle GoldenGate Monitor, and Oracle Cloud Control Plug-In. These programs require separate licenses, configurations and deployments.

GoldenGate Management Pack for Managing Complex Topologies

CHAPTER

Overview

The development of front-end, user friendly Graphical User Interface (GUI) has become an essential component of the enterprise software. The goal of the front-end system is to provide a consistent interface to the Application Programmatic Interface (API), eliminating the complexity when using the command-line interface and the avoidance and ease of recovery from destructive commands. In certain cases, the software functionalities are best achieved only when the function is developed using GUI, a common example is when the function is workflow-oriented, the GUI wizard executes the steps in pre-defined sequence ensuring all mandatory API input parameters are valid — in proper order and evaluated before proceeding to the next step.

For highly sophisticated applications, the server software requires persistent metadata. Hence, a flat-file or a database repository is integrated. The repository is the component for building a front-end reporting system and analytical applications. Users drill down on the web-based report for further details and actions. Due to the repository being persistent with a manageable purge interval, it's used as a baseline for future analysis. Without a GUI, it's time-consuming to generate reports to evaluate accurately and effectively.

The most recent media form of a front-end interface is a smartphone. A standard feature of most of the monitoring applications send notification e-mails for events occurring on the system. The smartphone is one of the options. An example is a background process that is abnormally terminated (ABENDED). Given metadata being available in persistent form, e-mail notifications may present the triggering events and the causes, findings, impacts, and resolutions.

Nonetheless, GUI software is adapted more rapidly. It minimizes the learning curve for novice users and tasks are completed in proportion of the time for advanced users. Additionally, the back-end (server) software enhancements and fixed bugs rarely affect the front-end applications which maintain the same presentation for end-users. Certainly, the HTTP protocol has moved the front-end GUI from the desktop to the web browser. The HTTP protocol enabled the development of the front-end, web-based applications that extended the software capabilities using plug-ins from third parties to provide more sophisticated features and capabilities.

Oracle GoldenGate is not an exception. Oracle Corporation has developed not one but three products for deploying and managing complex Oracle GoldenGate topologies. These are tightly integrated with running Oracle GoldenGate Instances:

- Oracle GoldenGate Director
- Oracle GoldenGate Monitor
- Oracle GoldenGate Enterprise Manager Plug-In

Figure 9-1 presents the GoldenGate Management Pack, starting from inner to outer. The core of the Oracle GoldenGate comprises the instances. The GoldenGate Software Command-Line Interface (GGSCI) is the console that interacts with the instance manager and processes. The Director is an intuitive Graphical User Interface (GUI) for creating advanced configurations quickly and easily through Java Desktop applications and the Web Client. Basic monitoring is performed by the Oracle Enterprise Manager Plug-In while advanced monitoring is delivered by the Monitor. Oracle GoldenGate VeriData is an advanced data comparison tool. It employs a complex algorithm, in-disk and in-memory data verification, to monitor data divergence of the source and the target database.

This is a complete enterprise management system for heterogeneous platforms targeting organizations running complex Oracle GoldenGate topologies. Refer to Chapter 6 for details regarding Oracle GoldenGate Veridata.

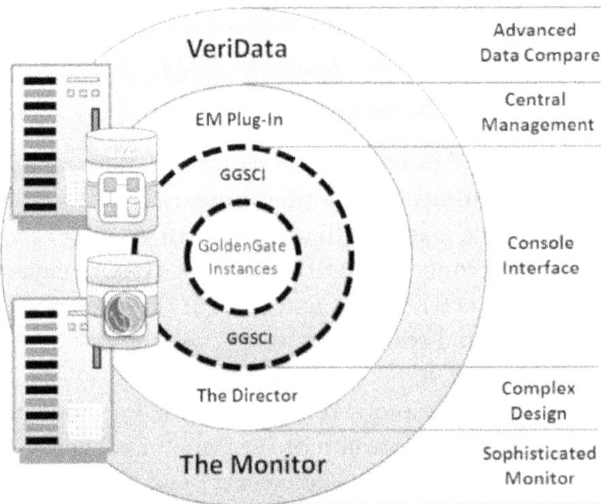

Figure 9-1: Oracle GoldenGate Management Pack

Overview of the Oracle GoldenGate Director

The Oracle GoldenGate Director is the face of Oracle GoldenGate. It provides the Graphical User Interface (GUI) for creating, deploying, and managing the complex Oracle GoldenGate topologies using several Java desktop and web-based applications. An Oracle GoldenGate architect has (3) options for configuring and managing Oracle GoldenGate Instances:

1. The Command-Line, using GGSCI
2. The Graphical User Interface, using the Director
3. The GGSCI and the Director

For sites purchased, the Oracle GoldenGate Director, Option 3 is very intuitive. The Director provides the visual presentation and diagramming capabilities of the capture, delivery processes, and trails. In a complex topology with a large number of source, target and parallel Extract and Replicat processes, the Director network diagramming helps understanding of the data and process flow. With a mouse click, the Director drills down the process group details and supported components.

Here is a summarized list of features of Oracle GoldenGate Director 12.1.2:

- Java Desktop Client and Web-based Applications Interface
- (3) Options of Database Repository
- Visual Presentation of new & existing Oracle GoldenGate instance processes
- Real-Time Alerts Status Reporting for Oracle GoldenGate instance processes
- Verifies Database Pre-requisites for supplemental logging
- Fine-Grain Management for users accounts, data sources, definition files, checkpoint tables and agents.
- Reporting capabilities for Extract and Replicat processes.
- View & Manage log files and run history
- E-mail Notification and Watch Lists

GoldenGate Director Architecture

The Director Architecture is a multi-tier Java client-server application which enables the Director to configure & manage multiple, heterogeneous Oracle GoldenGate Instances. Figure 9-2 shows the core layer of the Director architecture which is the *Director Server*, it's composed of the following components:

- The Director Application Server
- The Director Monitor Agent
- The Director Database Repository
- The Director Web Server

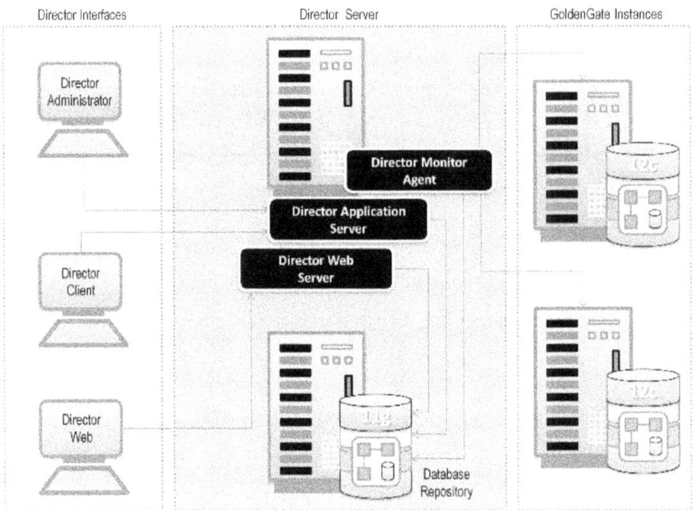

Figure 9-2: Oracle GoldenGate Architecture

The distribution of the server components delivers a more scalable, secure environment. The physical separation of the HTTP server and Database repository is recommended, but best when virtualized.

The Director Application Server

A set of Java EE applications is used by the Director Administrator and Director Client interface. The Director Application Server communicates with the Monitor Agent to establish the GGSCI session. Configuration develops though the Director Application services being consistently stored on the Director Repository.
The Director Server must be started and remain running as the background or foreground process enables access to the client applications. The Director Application Server provides the Application Programmatic Interface (API) for the Director Java desktop clients, Java Desktop Administrator clients, and the browser based for centralized remote management.

The Director Monitor Agent

Connect to Oracle GoldenGate GGSCI (GoldenGate Software Command Interface) to establish sessions and execute commands. The Director Server communicates with the Director Monitor Agent using the GoldenGate instance manager port to obtain status of processes and various levels of event information.

The Director Database Repository

The repository provides persistent metadata for configuration and properties of Oracle GoldenGate Instances. The Director uses a security model for which elements may be shared among accounts. The Database Repository is best hosted on a dedicated database, or on dedicated tablespace of an existing database. Since the repository can employ an Oracle Database Enterprise Edition, advanced Oracle Database features such as high-availability and advanced security are deployed easily.

The Director Web Server

The Oracle GoldenGate Director Server is powered by Oracle WebLogic HTTP Server. The Director Web Client connects to the Director Web Server to run the Director applications and manage the GoldenGate Instances, without the need to install additional components. Oracle GoldenGate Director supports the following browsers:

- Microsoft Internet Explorer Version 6.0 or higher
- Mozilla Firefox Version 2.0 or higher

GoldenGate Director Interface Components

There are (3) methods to access the Oracle GoldenGate Director Server. These are Java client-server and web-based tools for configuring & managing Oracle GoldenGate Instances using the Director.

The Director Administrator

The set of administrator tools for configuring the Director Server are: User Accounts, Data Sources, Monitor Agents, and Domain Suffix.

The Director Client

The Director Client is a Java client-server tool run by the Director users. The Director Client delivers the following features:

- Network Diagrams of GoldenGate Instances
- Configuration of Oracle GoldenGate Extract and Replicat components
- Management of Oracle GoldenGate Extract and Replicat components
- Review Status of Oracle GoldenGate Extract and Replicat components
- Establishes GGSCI sessions and creates & manages notification alerts

The Director Web Client

The Director Web Client uses a supported browser to remotely access the Director Server. No software installation is required to run the Director Web Client. The Director Web Client performs a similar function as the Java Director Client with the exception of creating Oracle GoldenGate visual presentations - diagrams.

Oracle GoldenGate Director Installation Phases

The installation of Oracle GoldenGate Director requires multiple software installations. Figure 9-3 presents the installation phases required by the Director. The order of the installation phases is highly recommended to be performed as outlined in Figure 9-3. However, the order of Phase 1 and 2 is flexible. Phase 2 must precede Phase 3 and the order of Phase 3 and 4 is also flexible. For best performance, the isolation of these systems is advised. Since the Director Database repository is relatively small, it can use an existing database with proper tablespace configuration. Since the Oracle WebLogic Server installation is dedicated for the Director, it's sufficient to create the new install location on an existing Oracle WebLogic Server. Installing the Director Server on the same WebLogic Server minimizes network traffic. Use a dedicated workstation for the Director Client, and it can run on Windows or Linux platforms.

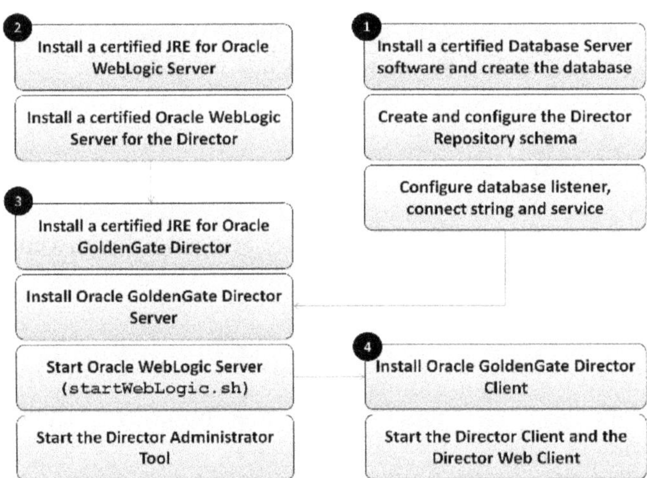

Figure 9-3: The Director Installation and Configuration Phases

Step 1 uses an Oracle Database 12c Enterprise Edition. The use of other database types is supported. The option of using an Oracle MySQL or MS SQL Server is not covered in this chapter. Refer to the product documentation for details.

Phase 1: Installation of the Database Server

The Director uses a database repository for storing and manipulating metadata and configuration details. Hence, a certified database type is required and an existing or new database hosts the Repository. A dedicated schema is created and granted only when the required database privileges are met to minimize the principle of least privileges. The chapter uses Oracle Database 12c to host the Director's repository.

Phase 2: Installation of the Oracle WebLogic Server

The Director uses Oracle WebLogic Server to run the Java EE applications. Hence, the installation of a certified Oracle WebLogic Server is installed. Prior to installing the Oracle WebLogic Server, install a certified version of Java Runtime Environment (JRE). *Do not create a Oracle WebLogic Server domain. It will be created when the Director Server is installed.* Alter and note the default values of the Oracle WebLogic installation needed by subsequence phases.

Phase 3: Installation of the Oracle Director Server

After Phase 1 and Phase 2 are successfully completed, install the Director Server. The Director Server installation requires the database repository schema and Oracle WebLogic install location. Prior to installing the Director Server, install a certified version of Java Runtime Environment (JRE).

Phase 4: Installation of the Oracle Director Client

The Director Client is a desktop "stand alone" installation. When installing the Director Client on a separate system from the Director Server, install a certified version of Java Runtime Environment (JRE). The Director Client is available for all platform supporting Java. Figure 9-4 shows the Director Java Client.

The Director Client provides access to the Director major functionalities. Use the Director Java Client to create and manage new diagrams via drag-and-drop technique, access to Oracle GoldenGate parameter files, interface to Oracle GoldenGate command-line interface (GGSCI), log files and alerts. The Director Client is secure interface and requires successful authentication to gain access to defined source and target Oracle GoldenGate instances.

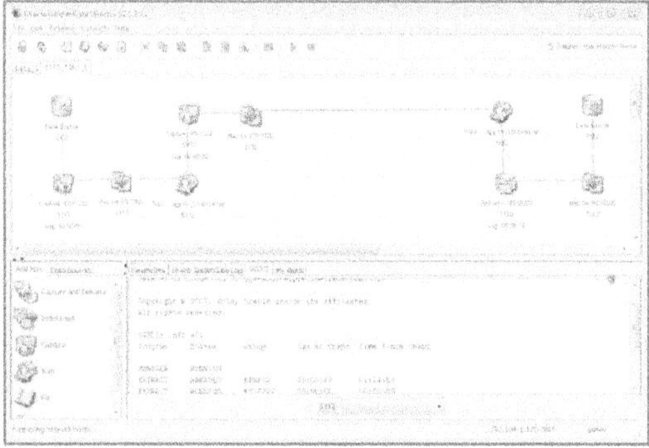

Figure 9-4: The Director Java Client Interface

Domain Name Server Configuration

It's necessary to register the Oracle GoldenGate Instances and the Director systems (the Director Server, the Director Client and the Director Repository) with the Domain Name Server (DNS). The Director Server must communicate with the Oracle GoldenGate Instances using the fully qualified host name. Also, it's recommended to define the suffix of the Director Server host as shown in Figure 9-5.

Figure 9-5: Defining the Director Sever Suffix

For the Linux/UNIX environment, we incorporate all systems in the local DNS /etc/hosts file for all hosts. The configuration includes the following systems:

- Oracle GoldenGate Source & Target Systems
- Oracle GoldenGate Intermediate Systems (if used)
- Oracle GoldenGate Director Servers
- Oracle GoldenGate Director Clients (if not installed on the Director Server)
- Oracle GoldenGate Director Repository (if not installed on the Director Server)

The Java Runtime Environment

Oracle GoldenGate Director is developed using Java. Hence, the Java Runtime Environment (JRE) is required to be installed and verified. It's important to install a certified JRE based on the version of the Oracle WebLogic Server. For consolidated installation, the use of a unified supported version of JRE is recommended. It promotes flexibility when defining the environment variables required by the Director utilities and runtime. For WebLogic Server 11g, the JRE must be at least version 6 (1.6.x). For WebLogic Server 12c, the JRE must be at least version 1.6.0_20 or 1.7. For all platforms, the JRE must be a 64-bit architecture.

Download and Install Java Runtime Environment

Visit http://www.java.com for downloading the JRE for Linux. Then, use the Linux Operating System utility RPM to install the JRE.

Installing Java Runtime Environment

Stage the JRE on a directory, login as the 'root' user, then run the RPM utility as shown below:

```
# rpm -ihv jre-7u67-linux-x64.rpm
Preparing...              ########################################### [100%]
   1:jre                  ########################################### [100%]
Unpacking JAR files...
     rt.jar...
     jsse.jar...
     charsets.jar...
     localedata.jar...
     jfxrt.jar...
#
```

Verify Java Runtime Environment Installation

When multiple versions of JRE installed on the system, verify a supported JRE is installed. Use the RPM utility to query all the installed JRE on the system. Login as the 'root' user and run the command:

```
[root@gg-director ~]# rpm -q jre
jre-1.7.0_67-fcs
[root@gg-director ~]#
```

Oracle WebLogic Server Installation

The Director Server is powered by the Oracle WebLogic Server. It's the application server for running the Director Web Server. The Director 12c (12.1.2) is certified with the Oracle WebLogic Standard Edition Version 10.3.1, 10.3.2, 10.3.3, 10.3.4, 12.1.1 or 12.1.2.

From the Oracle Software Delivery Cloud (http://edelivery.oracle.com), download Oracle Fusion Middleware 11g Media Pack for Linux x86-64. Figure 9-6 shows the list of downloads for Oracle WebLogic Server Version 11.3.4.

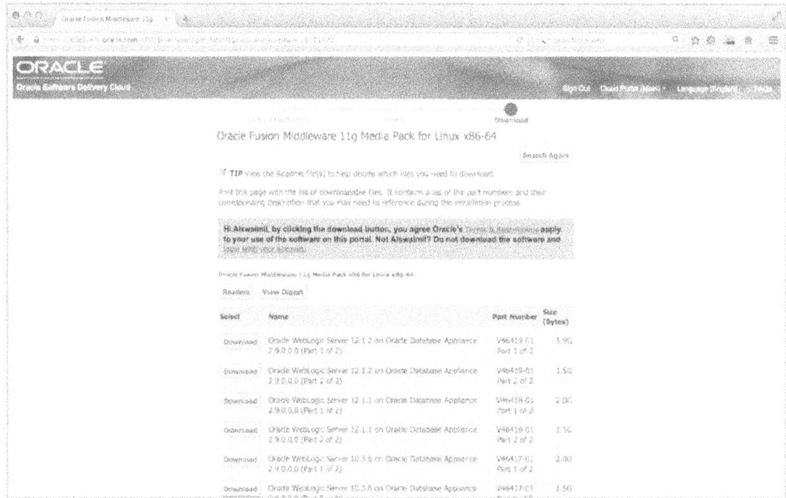

Figure 9-6: Download of Oracle WebLogic Server 11gR1 (10.3.4)

This section illustrates the basic installation of Oracle WebLogic 11g Standard Edition Version 10.3.4. *Do not create a domain for the Oracle GoldenGate Director Server. A domain under the Director Server directory is created by the installation of the GoldenGate Director.*

Starting the Oracle WebLogic 11g Installer

This chapter uses the default Operating System user 'oracle' for installing the WebLogic 11g Server. When using a non-oracle user, ascertain that the environment variable 'umask' is correctly assigned and that the user is a member of a secured group. Verify the settings as follows:

```
$ umask
0022
$ id
uid=54321(oracle) gid=54321(oinstall) groups=54321(oinstall),54322(dba)
[oracle@ggs-target ~]$
```

Ascertain that the 'umask' Linux Shell variable is set to 022 and that the Operating System's primary & secondary groups are correct. Stage and unpack the Oracle WebLogic 11g media into the Director Server system. Performing a remote Graphical User Interface installation (GUI) requires starting the X Windows System on the client workstation. The installation below uses the X Windows System from XQuartz for Mac OS X Version 10.8.3.

Start the installer as shown next.

```
$ export DISPLAY=192.168.1.9:0.0
$ java -jar wls1034_generic.jar
Extracting 0%....
```

Welcome

When ready, click "Next" to start the installation of Oracle WebLogic Version 10.3.4.0. It's important to install a certified version of Oracle WebLogic. The installer wizard guides you through the installation steps.

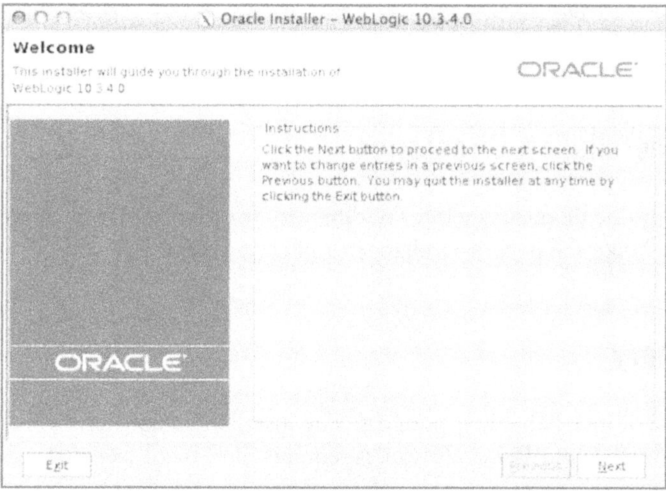

Figure 9-6a: Oracle Installer Welcome

Choose Middleware Home Directory

Specify the location for the Oracle Middleware software. Use the default directory as shown. When changing to a non-default directory, ensure the file system permission is correctly assigned. Verify that the 'umask' environment variable setting is 022.

Register for Security Updates

This is an optional step for delivering automated updates to security patches. Enter the e–mail address/username and password linked to the valid Oracle Support CSI. Uncheck 'security updates', click "Next" to proceed.

Choose Installation Type

For the Oracle GoldenGate Director Server, select "Typical" as the installation type. This installs the Oracle WebLogic Server and Oracle Coherence. Oracle Coherence enables faster data access and optimized resource utilization by the applications. Select "Typical" then click "Next" to proceed.

JDK Selection

Check the Local Java Development Kit (JDK). Ensure the select JDK is certified by the Oracle WebLogic Server. Visit http://www.java.com for a download of a supported Java release.

Choose Product Installation Directories

Under the Middleware home directory, select the directory for the WebLogic Server and Oracle Coherence. Make the necessary changes and click "Next."

Installation Summary

Here, below, are the list of installable components. The installation size depends on the installation type. For a "Typical" installation, it requires 664MB of free disk space.

Installation Complete

The installation is quick and should finish in less than 15 minutes. Uncheck the "Run Quickstart" option and click "Done." Do not make any customizations to the Oracle WebLogic installation.

GoldenGate Director Database Repository

The Oracle GoldenGate Director uses a database repository to store the metadata about Oracle GoldenGate instance configurations. The Director supports the following databases:

- Oracle Database 9i or higher
- MySQL 5.x Enterprise Edition
- SQL Server 2005 & 2008

This chapter uses Oracle Database 12c as the database repository. It's installed on the same host of the Oracle GoldenGate Director. The database name is GGDR, dedicated for the repository only.

```
SQL> select banner
  2  from   v$version;

BANNER
--------------------------------------------------------------------------------
Oracle Database 12c Enterprise Edition Release 12.1.0.1.0 - 64bit Production
PL/SQL Release 12.1.0.1.0 - Production
CORE 12.1.0.1.0     Production
TNS for Linux: Version 12.1.0.1.0 - Production
NLSRTL Version 12.1.0.1.0 - Production
SQL>
```

Creating Repository Tablespace

Depending on the number and size of the Oracle GoldenGate Instances to manage using the Director, the size of the tablespace varies. Dedicating a tablespace for the Director repository enables flexible administration and troubleshooting. The following SQL command creates the tablespace GGDR_DAT with an AUTOEXTEND data file:

```
SQL> create tablespace GGDR_DAT
  2  datafile '/u01/app/oracle/oradata/GGDR/datafile/ggdr_dat01.dbf'
  3  size 200M autoextend on;
Tablespace created.

SQL>
```

Creating and Granting Privileges to the Repository Owner

The following SQL command creates the repository owner DIR_ADMIN and grants the database privileges CONNECT and RESOURCE.

```
SQL> create user dir_admin identified by oracle
  2  default tablespace GGDR_DAT
  3  quota unlimited on GGDR_DAT;

User created.

SQL> grant connect, resource to dir_admin;

Grant succeeded.

SQL> connect dir_admin/oracle
Connected.
SQL>
```

The Director Database Tables and Indexes

Successful installation of the Director creates the repository. Table 9-1 lists the database repository tables and its associated indexes.

Table Name	Index Name
ACCOUNTB	PK_ACCOUNTB
ACLB	ACLBEAN_OWNER_IDX PK_ACLB
ACLENTRYB	ACLENTRYBEAN_OWNER_IDX PK_ACLENTRYB
ACNTGROUPREL	PK_ACNTGROUPREL
ACNTPROPB	ACCOUNTPROP_ACCOUNT_IDX PK_ACNTPROPB SYS_IL0000092015C00003$$
ACONPROCSB	ACONPROCSBEAN_COMMONNAME_IDX ACONPROCSBEAN_PROCNAME_IDX ACONPROCSBEAN_PROCTYPE_IDX PK_ACONPROCSB
ACONWATCHB	PK_ACONWATCHB SYS_IL0000092021C00005$$ ACONWATCHBEAN_USERID_IDX
ALERTB	GGALERTBEAN_ACTIVE_IDX GGALERTBEAN_TYPE_IDX GGALERTBEAN_ACCOUNT_IDX SYS_IL0000092025C00009$$ PK_ALERTB

AUTOINCB	PK_AUTOINCB
CONTCACHEB	PK_CONTCACHEB SYS_IL0000092102C00006$$
GDSCVERS	
GROUPB	PK_GROUPB
HOSTINFOB	HOSTINFO_COMMONNAME_IDX PK_HOSTINFOB
LOGENTRYB	PK_LOGENTRYB GGLOGENTRYBEAN_SEQUENCE_IDX
MANAGERREFB	PK_MANAGERREFB MANAGERREFBEAN_STAGE_IDX MANAGERREFBEAN_URI_IDX
MONAGENTB	PK_MONAGENTB
NODESTATEB	NODESTATEBEAN_URISTRING_IDX NODESTATEBEAN_STAGE_IDX NODESTATEBEAN_VISIBILITY_IDX PK_NODESTATEB
OBJECTSTATEB	PK_OBJECTSTATEB
STAGEB	STAGEBEAN_ACCOUNT_IDX STAGEBEAN_NAME_IDX STAGEBEAN_VISIBLE_IDX PK_STAGEB
STATSENTRYB	PK_STATSENTRYB GGSTATSENTRYBEAN_IDX
SUFFIXB	PK_SUFFIXB
UISPROPB	UISUPPORTPROP_PROPKEY_IDX PK_UISPROPB SYS_IL0000092056C00003$$

Table 9-1: The Director Database Objects

Database Listener

During the installation, the details about the database listener are required. Obtain the listener details for the database repository.

```
LSNRCTL> services
Connecting to (DESCRIPTION=(ADDRESS=(PROTOCOL=TCP)(HOST=gg-
director.precisetrace.com)(PORT=1521)))
Services Summary...
Service "GGDR.precisetrace.com" has 1 instance(s).
  Instance "GGDR", status UNKNOWN, has 1 handler(s) for this service...
    Handler(s):
      "DEDICATED" established:0 refused:0
         LOCAL SERVER
The command completed successfully
LSNRCTL>
```

The above output shows the database listener is on port 1521. Use the Oracle Network utility "NETCA" to create the default listener, then register the database with the listener using the Oracle utility "NETMGR."

GoldenGate Director Installation

After performing the Oracle WebLogic installation, configure the Director database repository. The next step is to install the Oracle GoldenGate Director components.

There are (2) required GoldenGate Director software installations. The recommended order of installation to be performed is:

- Oracle GoldenGate Director Server
- Oracle GoldenGate Director Client

When installing on a Linux/UNIX environment, the Director Installer requires an X Windows System. The next two sections illustrate installing the Oracle GoldenGate Director for Oracle Linux using the X Windows System shipped with Apple Mac OS X. Oracle GoldenGate Director is available on MS Windows. The configurations developed in the next sections use the Oracle Director for MS Windows.

Verify the database connection, using the database repository schema and connection string, is successful. Always ensure the database listener is running and accepting connections by performing a quick connection test using the database connect string. Query the database service name as it's needed by the repository wizard step.

```
SQL> SELECT sys_context('USERENV', 'SERVICE_NAME')
  2  FROM   dual;

SYS_CONTEXT('USERENV','SERVICE_NAME')
------------------------------------------------------------------
GGDR.precisetrace.com

SQL>
```

Installation of the GoldenGate Director Server

Navigate to the directory where the Director is staged. Unpack the Media Pack and run the installer as shown here:

```
$ cd /stage/dir-server/
$ $ ./gg-director-serversetup_unix_v12_1_2_0_1.sh
Starting Installer ...
```

Welcome

The Director Server is installed on the server. Using the agent, the Director Server connects to the Oracle GoldenGate Instance; and using JDBC, the Director Server connects to the database repository. Click "Next" to proceed.

Choose the Installation Location

Specify the Director Server software location. Ensure the file system has the proper Operating System permissions. The Oracle WebLogic Server domain for the Director is created under this location. Enter the Director Server location and click "Next" to proceed.

Select your WebLogic Install Location

Provide the software location for the Oracle WebLogic Server installation. This Oracle WebLogic Server is dedicated for the GoldenGate Director Server. Do not attempt to change to an alternative Oracle WebLogic installation once the Director Server is successfully installed.

WebLogic Install Location Details

This step confirms the version and location of Oracle WebLogic Server details. Click "Next" to proceed. When changing the install location, ascertain to set up the directory permission recursively.

Choose the HTTP Port

Specify the HTTP Port. The default port is 7001. This port is used when connecting using the Director Clients. Verify the port is not currently used by running the Operating System command: `#nmap -sT -O localhost`.

Select a Database

The Oracle GoldenGate Director Server Repository has (3) options: Oracle Database, MySQL Enterprise Edition Database, and MS SQL Server Database. This chapter uses Oracle Database 11g Enterprise Edition for the Director Repository. Ascertain that the Repository Schema is already created as explained above.

Database Driver Configuration

Depending on the database type for the repository, the Database Driver Configuration varies. For Oracle Database, it requires the Server Host Name, SID or Service Name, and the Database Port.

Database User

The Repository Schema hosts the Director Server Application Programmatic Interface (API). Enter the database User ID and Password. The password is subject to a strong security function. It must contain upper & lower case characters, special characters, and be at least 8 characters in length. The Password used is 'Oracle_4U'.

Pre-Installation Summary

This step summarizes important information. Given that multiple Oracle GoldenGate Director installations may exist, review and take notes of the details pertaining to this installation.

Installing

The Director Server installation takes less than 15 minutes to complete. Folders and files are placed under the software location directory.

Completing the Oracle GoldenGate Director Server Setup Wizard

The Director Server setup has finished. The next setup is to install the Director Client to test the installation of the Director Server. Click "Finish" to exit and confirm completion.

Starting the Oracle WebLogic Server

At this time, the Director's repository database is open and the listener is running. Perform a quick test for the Director Server installation by starting the Oracle Web Logic Server. Under the Director home location, navigate to the directory 'domain' and execute the shell script – "startWebLogic.sh." Oracle WebLogic Server is then started as a foreground process.

```
$ cd /u01/app/oracle/gg_director/domain
$ ./startWebLogic.sh
```

Review the end of the online messages log. It indicates the Director host name/ IP address, the HTTP listening port, and the running mode.

```
<Sep 26, 2014 10:44:02 AM AST> <Notice> <Server> <BEA-002613> <Channel
"Default" is now listening on 192.168.1.170:7001 for protocols iiop, t3,
ldap, snmp, http.>
<Sep 26, 2014 10:44:02 AM AST> <Notice> <WebLogicServer> <BEA-000331>
<Started WebLogic Admin Server "gg-director.precisetrace.com" for domain
"domain" running in Development Mode>
<Sep 26, 2014 10:44:03 AM AST> <Notice> <WebLogicServer> <BEA-000365>
<Server state changed to RUNNING>
<Sep 26, 2014 10:44:03 AM AST> <Notice> <WebLogicServer> <BEA-000360>
<Server started in RUNNING mode>
```

Installation of the GoldenGate Director Client

The next step is to install the Director Client on a dedicated install location. The client software provides the interface for the Director Server and (2) client interfaces are installed:

- Oracle GoldenGate Director Administrator Tool
- Oracle GoldenGate Director

The Director Administrator Tool creates and manages the mandatory components to enable using the Director diagramming tool. Accounts, Data Sources, and Monitor Agents are defined to allow using the Director Client and the Director Web Client.

Navigate to the directory where the Oracle GoldenGate Director Client Media Pack is staged. Export the DISPLAY environment variable then execute the installer script. The following illustrates installing the Oracle GoldenGate Director Client on Linux:

```
$ cd /stage/dir-cleint/
$ export DISPLAY=192.168.1.9:0.0
$ ./gg-director-clientsetup_unix_v12_1_2_0_1.sh
Starting Installer ...
```

Introduction

Using visual representation and a drag & drop technique, the Director Client is capable of managing existing and newly defined Oracle GoldenGate Instances. It manages and administers the components from a centralized Java Desktop console. Click "Next" to proceed.

Choose Install Folder

Specify the location for The Director Client software. Ascertain that the file system permission is correctly assigned. When the environment variable 'umask' is set to 022, files are created with permission 644, it sets the "read/write" permission for the owner, and a "read only" permission for groups and others. The installer displays the required and available disk space. Click "Next" to proceed.

Select the Directory for Symlinks

For Linux/UNIX platforms, ignore this step. It is specific to MS Windows platforms and creates a shortcut for the Director Client programs on the destination directory specified. Click "Next" to proceed.

Pre-Installation Summary

This step summarizes important information. Given that multiple Oracle GoldenGate Director installations may exist, review and take notes of the details pertaining to this installation. Click 'Next' to proceed.

Completing the Oracle GoldenGate Director Client Setup Wizard

The Director Client setup has finished. Click "Finish" to exit and confirm completion. The next step is to configure the Director components to enable using the Director Client and the Director Web Client.

Installing Oracle GoldenGate Director for MS Windows

Oracle GoldenGate Director, for MS Windows platforms, is available for a 64-bit architecture only. The setup wizard installs these Director tools:

- Oracle GoldenGate Director Administrator Tool
- Oracle GoldenGate Director

Prior to starting the installation, the Java Runtime Environment (JRE) must available on the workstation. Unpack the Oracle GoldenGate Director Media then run the setup program. The wizard steps are similar to the steps described above for Linux.

Figure 9-7 shows the Oracle GoldenGate Director Client interface installation wizard for MS Windows.

The following screen captures are obtained from Oracle GoldenGate Director and Administrator Tool for MS Windows.

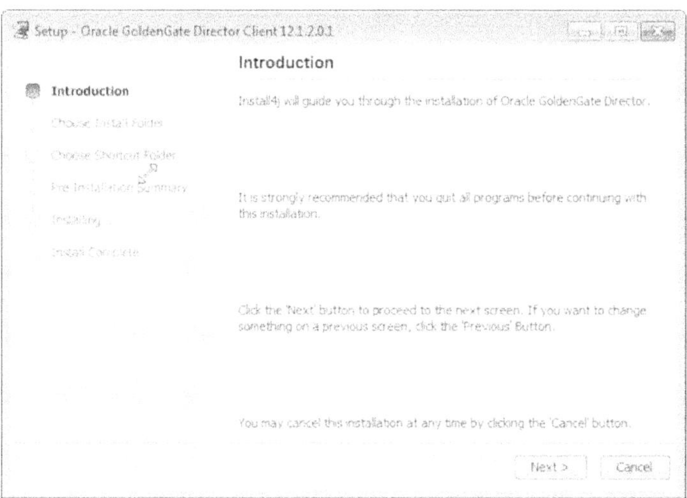

Figure 9-7: Oracle GoldenGate Director for MS Windows

Starting the Oracle GoldenGate Director Administrator Tool

The Director Administrator Tool is available for Linux/UNIX and MS Windows platforms. Prior to launching the Director Client, start the Director Server.

Start the Director Administrator Tool on Linux/UNIX by exporting the DISPLAY environment variable, Navigate to '/bin/' under the Director Client install location and execute the shell script 'run-admin.sh'. The shell script 'run-director.sh' launches the Director Diagramming Tool.

```
$ export DISPLAY=192.168.1.5:0.0
$ cd gg_director_client/bin
$ ./run-admin.sh
INITIALDIR: /u01/app/oracle/gg_director_client/bin
```

Figure 9-8 shows the administrator tool. It requires providing the User Name, Password, the Server Host Name and the HTTP port. The initial credential is provided during the Director Server installation.

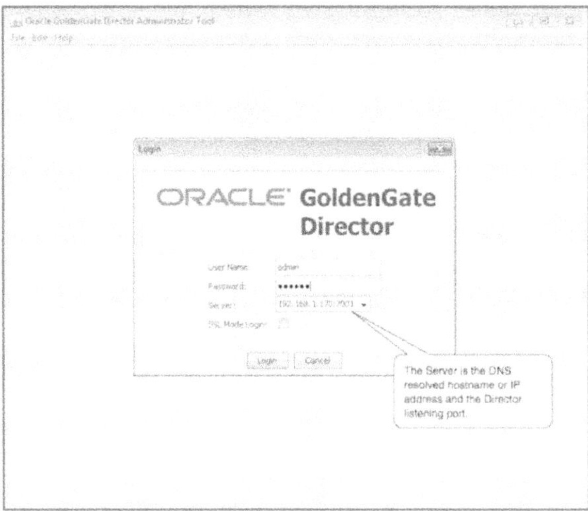

Figure 9-8: Starting Director Administrator Tool

Managing the Oracle GoldenGate Director Server

Under the Director Server install location, the directory '/domain/bin' is created, this is the location of the shell scripts for managing the Director Server. Startup and shutdown of the Director Server are performed by executing related scripts. It's recommended to add startup and shutdown shell scripts to the Operating System init daemon to automate the startup and shutdown of the Director Server. The primary startup and shutdown shell script is '***directorControl.sh***', which is explained in the next sections.

```
$ pwd
/u01/app/oracle/gg_director/domain/bin
$ ls -al
total 60
drwxr-xr-x 5 oracle oinstall  4096 Aug 30 08:37 .
drwxr-xr-x 9 oracle oinstall  4096 Aug 30 17:53 ..
-rwxr-x--- 1 oracle oinstall  2698 Aug 30 08:37 directorControl.sh
drwxr-xr-x 2 oracle oinstall  4096 Aug 30 08:37 nodemanager
drwxr-xr-x 2 oracle oinstall  4096 Aug 30 08:37 server_migration
drwxr-xr-x 2 oracle oinstall  4096 Aug 30 08:37 service_migration
-rwxr-x--- 1 oracle oinstall 10654 Aug 30 08:37 setDomainEnv.sh
-rwxr-x--- 1 oracle oinstall  3065 Aug 30 08:37 startManagedWebLogic.sh
-rwxr-x--- 1 oracle oinstall   380 Aug 30 08:37 startPointBaseConsole.sh
-rwxr-x--- 1 oracle oinstall  5986 Aug 30 08:37 startWebLogic.sh
-rwxr-x--- 1 oracle oinstall  2316 Aug 30 08:37 stopManagedWebLogic.sh
-rwxr-x--- 1 oracle oinstall  1119 Aug 30 08:37 stopWebLogic.sh
$
```

Starting the Director Server

To gain access to the Oracle GoldenGate Director Administrator client, the Director Server must be started and remain running. There are (2) modes to start the Director Server — as a foreground or as a background process. However, before starting the Director Server, ascertain that the pre-requisites are met:

- Repository Database is open.
- Database Listener is running.
- Repository Owner is not locked.

There are (2) methods to start the Director Server. For quick startup and shutdown, use the shell script 'startWebLogic.sh' found under the 'domain' directory. For startup with an option, use the shell script 'directorControl.sh' found under the 'domain/bin' directory.

Typing the shell script 'directorControl.sh' on the shell prompt displays the supported options.

```
$ pwd
/u01/app/oracle/gg_director/domain/bin
$ ./directorControl.sh
-------------------------------------------------------------------
USAGE:
   ./directorControl.sh start               : to start in foreground
   ./directorControl.sh stop                : to stop
   ./directorControl.sh -b start            : to start in background.
   ./directorControl.sh -b start <out_file> : to start in background,
                                              redirect to a file.
-------------------------------------------------------------------
$
```

The following starts the Oracle GoldenGate Director as a foreground process. Use either of the shell scripts for the Director Server startup.

```
$ pwd
/u01/app/oracle/gg_director/domain
$ ./startWebLogic.sh
```

Or navigate to the 'domain/bin' directory and execute 'directorControl.sh' with the start option.

```
$ pwd
/u01/app/oracle/gg_director/domain/bin
$ ./directorControl.sh start
```

Do not attempt to close the terminal when the Director Server is running as a foreground process. Closing the terminal will cause the Director Server to terminate.

Start the Oracle GoldenGate Director as a background process by supplying the argument '-b' when executing the 'directorControl.sh' script.

```
$ pwd
/u01/app/oracle/gg_director/domain/bin
$ ./directorControl.sh -b start
Starting in background
There is no redirection of logs to a file...
Please check domain server logs to find out any details ...
$
```

Start the Oracle GoldenGate Director as a background process and redirect messages log to a file by supplying the argument '-b' followed by the log file name when executing the 'directorControl.sh' script.

```
$ ./directorControl.sh -b start /tmp/WLS.log
Starting in background
Logging the output in to file /tmp/WLS.log
Be careful about the size of the file, it grows regularly ..
$ cd /tmp
$ ls -al WLS.log
-rw-r--r-- 1 oracle oinstall 17578 Sep 27 07:06 WLS.log
$
```

Do not alter the WebLogic installation or upgrade JRE to an uncertified version by the Oracle WebLogic Server.

Stopping the Director Server

When the Director Server is running as a foreground process on the console, pressing CTRL+C terminates the Director Server. If running from another terminal, use the shell script 'directorControl.sh'. When the Director Server is running as a background process, navigate to the directory '/domain/bin' under the Director Server install location and execute the shell script 'directorControl.sh' with the 'stop' argument.

```
$ pwd
/u01/app/oracle/gg_director/domain/bin
$ ./directorControl.sh stop
stoping weblogic...
Stopping Weblogic Server. Please wait...
```

Creating the GoldenGate Director Server Components

In order to utilize the Director diagramming tool for creating and managing Capture and Delivery processes, use the Director Administrator Tool to define the following components:

- User Accounts
- Data Sources
- Monitor Agents
- Default Suffix

Data Sources and Monitor Agents are mandatory components, while User Accounts and Default Suffix are optional components.

Configuring User Accounts

The default account 'admin' is a super user. While logged in as an admin, create additional users. Adapt a non-shared account environment as a standard security procedure and access control. Figure 9-9 shows the "Accounts" tab. To add a new account, click on "New/Clear" to remove an existing account. Select the account and click "Delete." To modify an existing account, select the account, modify, and save changes. When adding a new account, the only mandatory inputs are the User ID and Password. Passwords are not subject to security roles.

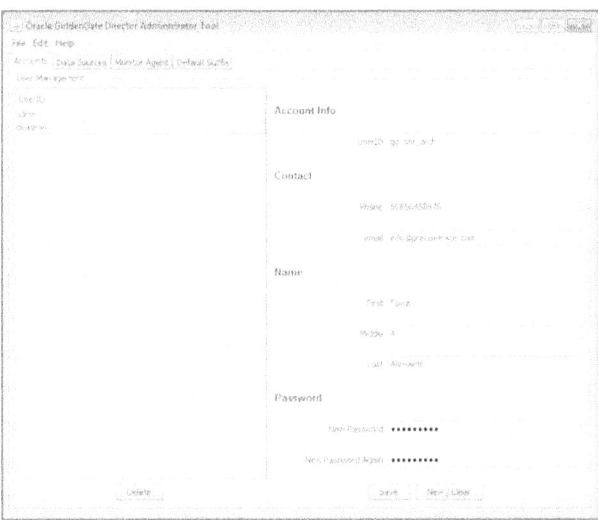

Figure 9-9: Adding, Removing, and Modifying Accounts

Configuring Data Source

An Oracle GoldenGate instance is comprised of the Oracle GoldenGate install location and the manager process. Defining the data sources is a mandatory Director Server component. Each Data Source is mapped to the source or target system. Figure 9-10 shows the "Data Source" tab. All sections of the "Data Source" tab inputs are mandatory.

The *Host Identity* defines the Data Source Name (S1T2) that is associated with an Oracle GoldenGate instance. Enter the fully qualified domain name as it's defined by the local DNS (/etc/hosts for Linux). Verify the connection is valid by clicking on "Check Connection."

The *GoldenGate Info* is essential for adapting the Operating System platform. The Host Operating System WU stands for Windows and Linux/UNIX. The database ORA stands for the Oracle Database and GoldenGate Version by the Director to identify the trail format and features.

The *Default DB Credential* is database specific. DNS is for a non-Oracle database. No input is required. Enter the User Name for the Oracle GoldenGate Database user who is designated with sufficient privileges to perform the Capture and Delivery. Supply and confirm the user's password.

The *Access Control* assigns an owner for the Data Source. The owner is an existing Director account. If the "Host is Observable" attribute is checked, then non-owners of that data source are able to observe, monitor, and view configuration information on that host, but will not be able to alter anything on that host.

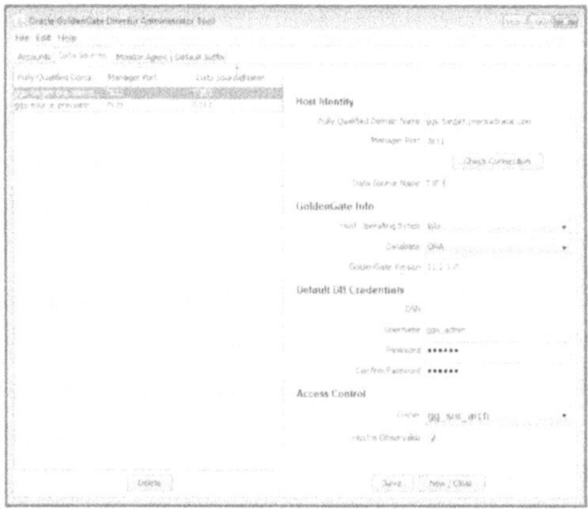

Figure 9-10: Configure Data Sources

Configuring the Monitor Agent

After registering an Oracle GoldenGate instance with the Director by creating the associated data source, a thread is created to monitor the status of the manager process. These threads are referred to as Monitor Agents. Figure 9-11 shows the "Monitor Agent" tab. The Monitor Agent Settings control the runtime environment and resources. Make the necessary changes and click "Save and Restart" to activate modifications.

- **Go Back Hours**. Represents the number of hours of recent history captured.
- **Host Wait Seconds**. This is the amount of time that a GoldenGate instance waits for an event before sending a status report to appear on the Director Client user diagrams. A lower value indicates that more report files are created.
- **Log Purge Hours**. Represents the number of hours to keep information in
- the GoldenGate Log before purging the data to optimize disk space.

  Ignore Alert Events Older Than (Minutes). This setting is relevant only when using e–mail alerts. Specify the age, in minutes, of the oldest alert to keep.

The Monitor and Manager Status display the status of the GoldenGate instance manager and the Monitor Agent with which it's registered. Select the Monitor for a Data Source, click "Start Selected Monitor" to start the monitor or click "Stop Selected Monitor" to stop the monitor.

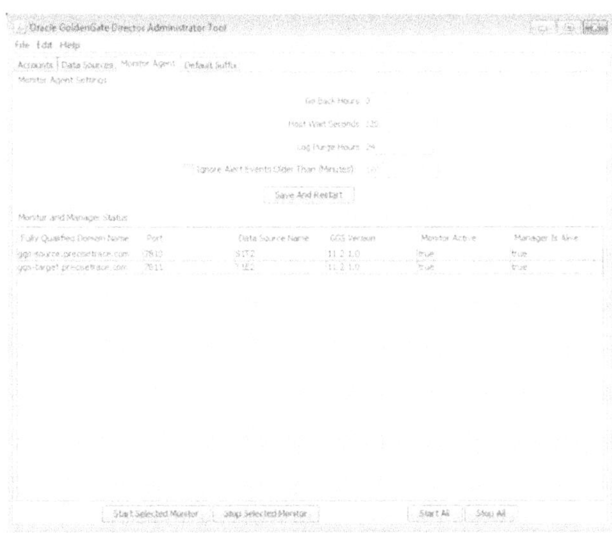

Figure 9-11: Configuring Monitor Agents

Configuring Default Suffix

The Director Server always attempts to resolve host names or IP addresses into fully qualified domain names. Prior to creating the Director components, ascertain that the local DNS defines all host names participating in the configuration.

```
192.168.1.170    gg-director.precisetrace.com    ggs-director
192.168.1.111    ggs-source.precisetrace.com     ggs-source
192.168.1.110    ggs-target.precisetrace.com     ggs-target
```

Figure 9-12 shows the "Default Suffix" tab. Add or delete domain suffixes for the GoldenGate Director Server to use when attempting to qualify a non–qualified host name that appears in a GoldenGate parameter file. For example, if the domain is 'precisetrace.com' and the fully qualified domain name of a server is 'ggs-target.precisetace.com,' put 'precisetace.com' into the suffix table.

Click "Add" to add new default suffixes. To delete a default suffix, select that suffix from the list and click "Delete."

Figure 9-12: Configuring Default Suffix

Working with the Oracle GoldenGate Director Client

The Director Client creates visual network topologies for existing and new Oracle GoldenGate Instances. The Director Client needs correctly configured accounts, data sources, monitor agents, and (optionally) suffixes by the Director Administrator as illustrated above. Then using the Director Client wizard, basic configurations are developed and deployed instantly. By means of drag-and-drop capabilities, the basic configurations are extended by adding Extracts and Replicats for more optimized configurations. Bi–directional configurations are achieved by running the Director Client wizard in reverse order — configuring Capture at the target and Delivery at the source database.

A major function of the Director Client is table mapping. Suggested tables are added to the selected Extract and these tables are automatically mapped to the selected Replicat. Data transformation is a key feature of Oracle GoldenGate. Hence, the Oracle GoldenGate Director Client supports data transformation by implementing Oracle GoldenGate functions for the selected Extract or Replicat.

Comprehensive management is achieved using the Director Client. Starting, stopping, and viewing details of selected Extracts and Replicat are performed using the Director Client. Changing configurations by adding, modifying, and deleting parameters are also performed using the Director Client. Log Management, GGSCI sessions, and alerts are available using the Director Client.

The next illustrations and examples presented are developed using the Oracle GoldenGate Director Client running on an MS Windows 7 workstation — connecting remotely to the Director Server running on an Oracle Linux server.

Login to the Director Server

Authentication of the Director Client is mandatory for gaining access to the Director Server. The login uses existing Director Server account credentials. After successfully launching the Director Client from the main menu, click on "File" then select the "Login" option or from the toolbar click on the icon "Login to Server."

Figure 9-13 shows the Login details. Enter the User Name, Password, and the Server. The Server is the Director Server host name or TCP/IP address followed by the listening port. In case of logging errors, run the Director Server as a foreground process. Ascertain that the last log message says <Server started in RUNNING mode> and the combination of host name and listening port (hostname:port) matches the details entered during the installation of the Director Server.

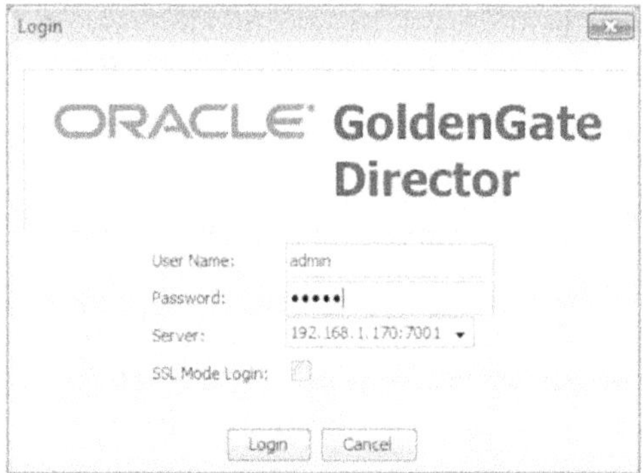

Figure 9-13: Director Server Login

The Director Client Functions

The Director Client performs the functions highlighted in Figure 9-14. The interface creates diagrams using a drag-and-drop technique. This ensures processes are correctly placed on the diagram according to the receiving component.

The technique to create a diagram is as follows:

- Drag and drop the data sources on the diagram area
- Drag and drop an item on a data source or receiving item
- Modify an existing item for table mapping
- Modify existing item parameters

To perform any of the functions, use the toolbar icons or the menu items. Function keys replace certain toolbar and menu items.

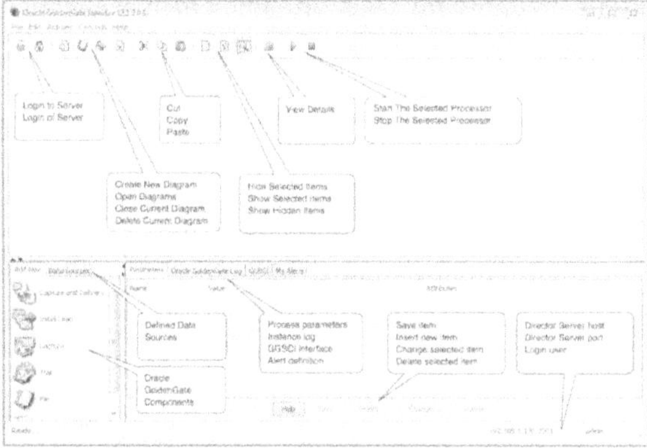

Figure 9-14: Director Client View

Next, use the Director Client diagramming tool only. The following configurations are implemented, deployed, and managed. This illustrates a complete cycle for creating an Oracle GoldenGate configuration using the Director Client:

- Initial-load using the direct method
- Uni-directional, wizard-based configuration
- Uni-directional configuration for a new Oracle GoldenGate instance
- Bi-directional configuration for an existing Oracle GoldenGate instance

Configure Initial-Load Using the Director Client

The delivered initial-load method by the Director Client is the direct initial-load technique. The direct initial-load method uses an initial-load extract for reading the source database tables across the TCP/IP — sending data directly to the target system initial-load replicate. The special run replicate process applies the data to the target database using the native database interface. This method is suitable for target systems that are in place and ready for performing the initial-load. It also eliminates the need of staging remote files on the target systems, which avoids issues related to creating and managing remote files. Since this method is relatively slow, a considerable timeframe should be allocated for the initial-load phase.
Data transformation capabilities is available using Oracle GoldenGate built-in functions. The next series of screen captures illustrates using the Director for configuring the initial-load.

Creating a New Diagram

On the toolbar, Click on "Create New Diagram." Enter the name of the new diagram and Click "OK." The name of the diagram is tabbed to the header of the diagramming area. Click on the diagram tab name to display the diagram.

Add Data Sources

From the lower panel, click on the "Data Sources" tab. Drag and drop the source and target database to the diagramming area. Select the data source to display the manager's parameter details. Click on "Insert" to add a parameter, "Change" to modify a parameter, and "Delete" to delete a parameter.

Add Initial-Load Extract

Drag and drop the initial-load extract to the source database.

Define a New Initial-Load Task

Configure the Source database initial-load capture. Enter the Capture Name, Description (optional) and the Database Access, User Name and Password. Optionally, check the password encryption feature.

Configure the Target database initial-load Replicat. Enter the Delivery Name, Description (optional) and select "Assume" for identical structure or "Use Source" to specify the source definition file generated using the DEFGEN utility. Enter the database access details by providing the database user name and password. Click "OK" to create the initial-load Capture and Delivery configuration.

Direct Initial-Load Configuration

The configuration created displays the Data Source (S1T2), the Capture Task (E09LOAD), Mapped Tables, Delivery Task, Mapped Tables(E09LOAD), and the target Data Source.

Select the component to review the basic parameters settings. Edit the initial parameters generated for the connected components as necessary. Remember, the direct-load method employs the target Replicat running as remote task.

Edit Parameters

Creates components configured using basic parameters. Select the component, right-click mouse at the bottom for the option, "Advanced and Edit Parameter File." Click "Edit" and insert additional applicable parameters then click "Save."

This initial configuration generates the basic parameters only. Table mapping is created manually as shown next.

```
extract ELOAD09
userid ggs_admin, password oracle
discardfile /u01/app/ogg/10.2.0/dirrpt/ELOAD09.dsc, purge

rmthost ggs-target.precisetrace.com, mgrport 7811
rmttask replicat, group RLOAD09
```

Capture Task Tables Mapping

Select the Map for the Capture Task to start the table mapping process. Click "Add Blank Mapping" by clicking on the plus sign (+), enter the Source table names, check the entries and click "Save."

Verify Table Mapping

Select the Capture Task, right-click mouse for "Advanced and Edit Parameter File." A warning message is displayed. Click "Continue" to view the parameters.

Modify Delivery Task

The Delivery Task has the basic configuration only. The next step is to perform table mapping and enable "handle collisions" feature.

Target Table Mapping

Select the Map for the Delivery Task to start table mapping process. Enter the Target table names, check the entries, and click "Save." Click "Add Blank Mapping" by clicking on the plus sign (+) for manually adding the Source and Target tables.
View the mapped tables by selecting the Delivery Task then right-click mouse for "Advanced and Edit Parameters File."

After performing table mapping operations, verify the source and target mapped table using the Edit parameter option. Modify as necessary before proceeding further.

Configuration Parameters

Click on the components for the relevant parameters to be displayed. For the Delivery Task, the HANDLECOLLISION parameter is to be added.

Insert Parameters

Select the Delivery Task, the current parameters are displayed. Click "Insert" then scroll down and select "handle collisions" parameter. Click "Insert" to add the parameter, click "Done" when finished.

Start the Capture Task

This a direct-load method. It uses a remote Replicat task started by the initial-load Extract. Select the Capture Task, right-click mouse and click on "Start." The Delivery Task starts shortly thereafter and is highlighted in green.

Note: This data load method is relatively slow. For homogenous systems, the use database method such as RMAN is recommended and it's mostly suitable for heterogeneous environments.

Initial-Load Statistics

Depending on the data volume of the initial-load from the source tables, the Delivery task applies the rows to the target tables. Once completed, the Delivery Task is terminated automatically.

Configure Basic Capture and Delivery

The purpose of the wizard is to quickly configure the Capture and Delivery processes. The wizard delivers the foundation for building complex configurations.
The following illustrates using the wizard to configure Capture from a S1T2 and Delivery to T1E2 data source.

Create a New Diagram

The first task is to create a new diagram by clicking "Create New Diagram" on the toolbar or select "File→New Diagram." Enter the "Name of the New Diagram" – (S1T2-T1E2-01). The diagram is automatically saved and a new tab is created for the new diagram.

Select Data Sources

The Source and Target database are already defined. Drag and drop the data sources on the diagramming area. Upon dragging the source data S1T2 into the diagramming area, the existing defined components are displayed. Click on "Show Hidden Items" to clear out the diagramming area. Click on the data source to display the manager's parameters.

Step 1: Configure Data Capture

Drag and drop the "Capture and Delivery" icon to the data source S1T2, the Configure data capture from S1T2 has the following input:

Input	Description
Capture Name	The name of the capture (Extract).
Description	Enter a short description (optional).
Source is Table	Used for initial-load Capture only.
Begin	Specify the Capture timestamp.
Database Access	Database user name and password (with encryption option).

Step 2: Configure Destination

Select the destination database (T1E2) and enter the following details.

Input	Description
In Directory	Location of trail files.
With Prefix	(2) Character prefix (name) & the maximum size of the trail file.
Trail Access	Local on the same host or remote using TCP/IP.
Format Release	Enter the (4) digits of the Oracle GoldenGate instance version.

Step 3: Configure Data Delivery

The delivery process runs on the Target database. It uses the following details:

Input	Description
Delivery Name	The name of the Delivery (Replicat).
Description	Short Description (optional).
Replicat Type	o Special Run: A one-time Capture and Delivery. o Extract File: Reads from an initial-load extract file. o Extract Trail: Apply Change Data Capture (CDC) to target.
Target Definition	o Use "Assume" of identical table structure.

	o Specify a source definition file for a dissimilar environment.
Checkpointing Info	o File-based, refer to using file system as <group name.cpr>. o Global Checkpoint Table, refer to GLOBAL parameter file. o Specify the schema and table name.
Database Access	Database user name and password (with encryption option).

First-Cut Configuration

Click "Finish" to generate the first-cut configuration. This configuration uses capture of a primary type extract only — sending the data directly to the target collector server.

The above configuration uses a secondary capture process (data pump). Hence, the primary capture is dedicated for delivering real-time data capture using the database transaction logs, while the secondary process is dedicated for sending data to the remote collector server for writing to the remote trail.

Creating Source Mapping

Select the Capture Map icon. Begin by clicking "Show Tables" which lists the tables owned by the schema specified by the parameter, 'USERID.' The next step is to manually create the table mapping as follows:

1. Click on "Add Blank Mapping" — the plus sign (+).
2. Enter the Source table. Use the format <Schema.Tablename>.
3. Repeat steps 1 and 2 to map more tables.
4. Check the candidate tables and click "Save."

Create Target Mapping

Select the Map icon for the Delivery. The list of candidate tables from the Capture mapping is displayed. The next step is to manually create the table mapping using:

1. Enter the Target table. Use the format <Schema.Tablename>.
2. Click on "Add Blank Mapping", the plus sign (+), when the extract uses a wildcard for table names.
3. Check candidate tables.
4. Click "Save."

Start Capture and Delivery

Select the Capture icon. Right-click mouse to display the menu options relevant to Captures. Click on the "Start" option to begin the Extract process. Successful startup is indicated by the green line.

There are (2) options to start the Delivery: Quick Start or Start. The Quick Start does not prompt for the start-up option. The Replicat attempts to start-up in "Normal" mode using the checkpoint information. However, the Start option provides (4) choices to start the selected Replicat.

The Replicat Start options are:

- Normal, which uses the checkpoint to start-up from the last Relative Byte Address (RBA).
- Skip Transaction, which uses the checkpoint to skip the last Relative Byte Address (RBA) and attempts to start-up.
- ATCSN, which starts at a specific Commit System Number (CSN) corresponding to the database System Change Number (SCN).
- AFTERCSN, which starts after a specific Commit System Number (CSN) corresponding to the database System Change Number (SCN).

View Capture and Delivery Details

Oracle GoldenGate stores manager, capture, and delivery logs under the directory './dirrpt.' In addition to the report file, the Director Client reports major process details. Select the process, right-click mouse and select "View Details."

- "Report" reads the process log file from the './dirrpt directory.'
- "Info" displays information about the process.
- "Checkpoint Log" reads the checkpoint file for the Capture and checkpoint file and/or checkpoint table for Delivery.
- "Statistics" - Lag detail.
- "Discards" - discards record details.

The next two sections are jointly developed. They're composed of (2) parts:

Part I configures uni-directional synchronization, capture from the source S1T2 to target T1E2 database.

Part II configures bidirectional synchronization, it's the reverse of Part I for performing bi-directional synchronization from the target T1E2 to the source S1T2 database. Refer to Chapter 5 for details regarding database design considerations and conflict detections & resolutions on an online bi-directional setup.

Part I: Configure Uni-Directional Change Data Capture and Delivery

In preparation for bi-directional configuration, Part I is the setup of a Uni-Directional Change Data Capture (CDC) and Delivery. The configuration is developed manually and customized to perform data capture and synchronization from the source (S1T2) to the target (T1E2) database.

Oracle GoldenGate best practice for configuring an online synchronization is to define primary & secondary Extracts. Figure 9-15 shows the architecture and processes flow. The Director Client is adapted to build and manage the configuration.

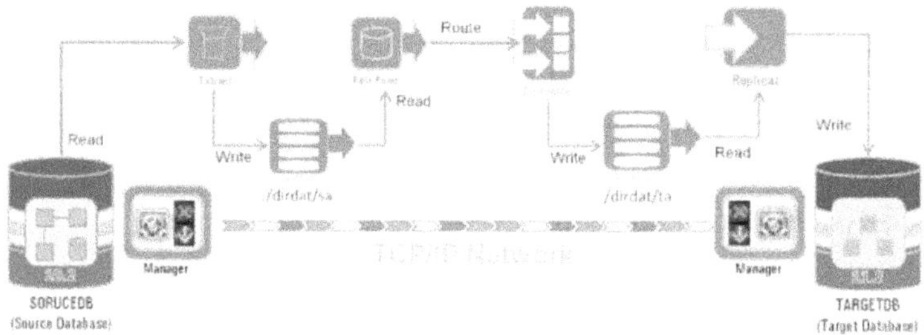

Figure 9-15: Uni-Directional Change Data Capture and Delivery Processes

Creating New Diagrams

The first task is to create a new diagram by clicking "Create New Diagram" on the toolbar or select "File→New Diagram." Enter the "Name of New Diagram" (S1T2-T1E2-01). The diagram is automatically saved and a new tab is created for the new diagram. Connect as the Director Client repository owner to query the diagrams created by using the following statement:

```
SQL> select STAGENAME from STAGEB;
```

Add Data Sources

The Source and Target database are already defined. Drag and drop the data sources on the diagramming area. Upon dragging the source data S1T2 into the diagramming area, the existing defined components are displayed. Click on "Show Hidden Items" to clear out the diagramming area. Click on the data source to display the manager's parameters. Click on the data source to display the manager's parameters' name, value, and attributes. There are two options to change the manager parameters by: (i) Insert, Change, or Delete or (ii) navigate to "Advanced → Edit Parameter File."

Define Capture

Drag and drop the Capture icon into the data source (S1T2). A New Capture for the Data Source will be displayed. Enter the Capture Name (up to 8 characters) and description (optional). The Source is "Table (Create a Task)" for the initial-load Extract. Select "Now to Begin" and the Database Access as defined with encryption support. Select the Capture for a basic parameters review. There are two options to change the Capture parameters by using (i) Insert, Change and Delete or (ii) navigate to "Advanced → Edit Parameter File."

Define the Local Trail

Drag and drop the Trail icon on the Primary Capture. This defines and associates a local trail with the Capture – E03S1T2. Enter the two letter prefix and size. The format is specified when the target Oracle GoldenGate instance version mismatches the source instance. The usage of a local trail is highly recommended to prevent network failure and offload the Primary Capture from sending transactions to the target Collector Server. The suggested maximum trail file size is 5MB, which is a very low size. Enter an appropriate size considering the size of the database redo log files.

Define the Secondary Capture

Drag and drop the Capture on the local trail. This defines the secondary Capture (Data Pump). Enter the Capture Name and Description (optional). Review the parameter to ascertain the capture source.

The PASSTHRU parameter instructs the data pump to operate on a pass-through mode. The Extract process does not uses table definition. The source and target tables must be identical without any forms of data transformations.

Define Remote Trail

Now, the secondary Capture is defined. It must be associated with a remote trail. Choose the host as S1T2. Drag and drop the Trail icon on the secondary Capture – P03S1T2. Enter the remote trail two letter prefix then modify the size, preferably to be consistent with the size of the local trail.

The Trail Access is of type use TCP/IP. This enables the secondary Capture to send data to the target host defined by the RMTHOST and MGRPORT parameters. Select the secondary Capture to review the parameters.

Define the Delivery

The Delivery applies transactions to the target using the database native SQL interface. Drag and drop the Delivery icon into the remote trail. This brings up the New Capture window. Enter the Delivery name – R03S1T2 and description (optional). Since the Delivery is for online synchronization, select the following: Replicat Type is Extract Trail, Target Definition is Assume, and Checkpointing Info. is the Global Checkpoint Table. Leave the Database Access as defined using GGS_ADMIN without any password encryption, yet.

Map the Primary Capture

Select the Map Capture E03S1T2 icon. Click "Add Blank Mapping"- (+).
Enter the Schema.TableName, check mapping, then click on "Save." Repeat the steps for additional mapping. Using the wildcard character OSM$REPAPI.*. is permutable.

When using the wildcard syntax and need to exclude tables, select the Primary Capture, right-click mouse → "Advanced → Edit Param File." Click "Edit."
Add the "Exclude Parameter" then click "Save."

Map the Secondary Capture

Select the Map Capture P03S1T2 icon. Tables mapping is fetched to match the Primary Capture. Check and click "Save." When using the wildcard syntax on the Primary Capture, click "Add Blank Mapping" - (+). Enter the schema.table name, check, then click on "Save." Repeat the steps as necessary. Using the wildcard character is permutable using OSM$REPAPI.*.

When using the wildcard syntax and need to exclude tables, select the Primary Capture, right-click mouse → "Advanced → Edit Param File." Click Edit.
Add the "Exclude Parameter" and click "Save."

Map Delivery

Select the Map Capture R03S1T2 icon. Tables mapping is fetched to match the Capture. Enter the target table, check then click "Save." When using wildcard syntax on the Capture, click the "Add Blank Mapping" icon - (+). Enter the schema.table name, check and click on "Save." Repeat the steps as necessary. Using the wildcard character is permutable using OSM$REPAPI.*.

When using the wildcard syntax and need to exclude tables, select the Primary Capture, right-click mouse → "Advanced → Edit Param File.". Click Edit. Add the "Exclude Parameter" and click "Save."

Start the Primary Capture

Select the Primary Capture, right-click mouse and select "Start"...
After the Primary Capture is successfully started, the Capture flow turns green.

Start the Secondary Capture

Select the Secondary Capture, right-click mouse and select "Start"...
After the Secondary Capture is successfully started, the Capture flow turns green.

Start the Delivery

Select the Delivery, right-click mouse and select "Quick Start" ...

After the Delivery is successfully started, the Capture flow turns green. The Delivery Start options are:

- Normal, which uses the checkpoint to start from the last Relative Byte Address (RBA).
- Skip Transaction, which uses the checkpoint to skip the last Relative Byte Address.
- ATCSN, which starts at a specific Commit System Number (CSN) corresponding to the database System Change Number (SCN).
- AFTERCSN, which starts after a specific Commit System Number (CSN) corresponding to the database System Change Number (SCN).

Primary Capture Status

The process status is one of the following: STARTING, STOPPED, ABENDED or RUNNING.

Select the Primary Capture, right-click mouse and select "View Details."
"View Details" has (5) tabs: Report, Info, Checkpoint Lag, Statistics, and Discards.

Secondary Capture Status

Select the Secondary Capture, right-click mouse and select "View Details."
"View Details" has (5) tabs: Report, Info, Checkpoint Lag, Statistics, and Discards.
The Secondary Capture uses the RMTHOST and MGRPORT to send transactions to the remote target. In the event of network failure, the target system becomes unavailable and the process is ABENDED. Configure the manager process to restart failed captures to support an automated and unattended restart.

Click on "Previous" to review older report files.

Delivery Status

Select Delivery, right-click mouse and select "View Details." "View Details" has (5) tabs: Report, Info, Checkpoint Lag, Statistics, and Discards.

Configuration Files - Summary

Since the status of the Primary Capture, Secondary Capture and Delivery is RUNNING as indicated by the connected green line, the setup is ready for data synchronization from Source (S1T2) to Target (T1E2) database.

The configuration files generated by the Client Director are outlined below.
These parameter files are Primary Extract, Secondary Extract, and Delivery groups.
Select the process name → right-click mouse → Advanced → Edit Param File.

Here is the configuration file for the Primary Capture E03S1T2. Using the capture group name, the Extract E03S1T2 is defined and the checkpoint E03S1T2.cpe is created and associated with a local trail.

```
extract E03S1T2
userid ggs_admin, password oracle
```

```
discardfile /u01/app/ogg/10.2.0/dirrpt/E03S1T2.dsc, purge
tranlogoptions excludeuser ggs_admin

exttrail /u01/app/ogg/10.2.0/dirdat/sk
table osm$repapi.customers;
```

Here is the configuration file for the Secondary Capture (Data Pump) P03S1T2.. Using the capture group name, the Extract P03S1T2 is defined and the checkpoint P03S1T2.cpe is created and associated with a remote trail.

```
extract P03S1T2
userid ggs_admin, password oracle
rmthost ggs-target.precisetrace.com, mgrport 7811
rmttrail /u01/app/ogg/11.2.0/dirdat/tk
table osm$repapi.customers;
```

Here is the configuration file for the Delivery R03S1T2. Using the delivery group name, the Replicat R03S1T2 is defined and the checkpoint R03S1T2.cpe is created and associated with the Oracle GoldenGate instance global database checkpoint table.

```
replicat R03S1T2
discardfile /u01/app/ogg/11.2.0/dirrpt/R03S1T2.dsc, purge
assumetargetdefs

userid ggs_admin, password oracle
map osm$repapi.customers, target osm$repapi.customers;
```

Part II: Configure Bi-Directional Change Data Capture and Delivery

The best practice approach when building an Oracle GoldenGate bi-directional setup is to completely deploy an *optimized* uni-directional configuration that is highly *stable* & *scalable* and delivers a sustainable *performance* for near real-time data movement. For strict data replication, the bi-directional configuration is the reverse of uni-directional configuration — sharing Capture and Delivery parameter files segments using Oracle GoldenGate macros. Figure 9-16 shows the architecture designed by the Director Client. The Director Client graphically depicts the network design, promotes consistencies, and minimizes the manual interaction to manage the environment.

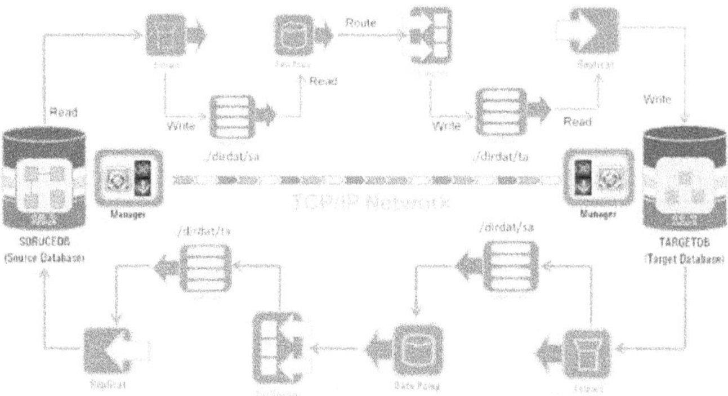

Figure 9-16: Bi-Directional Change Data Capture and Delivery

In a bi-directional setup, additional considerations are addressed and implemented to avoid different types of failures which lead to data-related errors and ABENDED processes. The database design, the applications coding, and the network stability are equally important components on an Oracle GoldenGate configuration. In an ideal environment, Data/System/Security Analysts, Database Administrators, and Network & Oracle GoldenGate Architects aim to produce database and application infrastructure to operate in complex Oracle GoldenGate topologies. In doing so, seamless data acquisition occurs without comprising data integrity & security.

Database Design

The database design should address proper implementations of primary key and database sequences. The database design helps to produce sophisticated data and application segmentations for minimizing data conflicts. Oracle Database Virtual Private Database (VPD) is an advanced data and application segmentation technique.

Infinite Loop Detection

Infinite Loop Detection is an essential step to be implemented in a bi-directional setup to avoid endless circular transactions or Delivery processes that are ABENDED due to data conflicts. Oracle GoldenGate supports two methods for infinite loop detection: (i) using the database trace table or (ii) using the exclude user name or User ID parameters.

Table-Level Supplemental Logging

In a bi-directional setup with built-in Conflict Detection and Resolution (CDR), the primary & column values must be logged, which are part of Conflict Detection and Resolution. Consider the growing size of the database transaction logs when the Table-Level is enabled for all columns.

The following GGSCI TRANDATA command enables Table-Level logging for all columns.

```
GGSCI (ggs-source) 4> ADD TRANDATA osm$repapi.current_accounts ALLCOLS
```

Here is an alternative of the Table-Level Logging for specific columns:

```
GGSCI (ggs-source) 9> ADD TRANDATA osm$repapi.customers, COLS(cust_name,
cust_email, cust_mobile, cust_address)
```

Conflict Detection and Resolution

The asynchronous data flow from the source to target system and vice versa escalates to different types of data conflicts causing data divergence, database errors, and ABENDED processes. Oracle GoldenGate built-in Conflict Detection and Resolution (CDR) are implemented at the table to address data conflict for Data Manipulation Language (DML) - Update, Insert, and Delete statements.
The following is an example for configuring built-in CDR:

```
MAP osm$repapi.customers, TARGET osm$repapi.customers, &
    COMPARECOLS (ON UPDATE KEYINCLUDING (cust_name, cust_email, cust_mobile,
                                         cust_address),
                 ON DELETE KEYINCLUDING (cust_name, cust_email, cust_mobile,
                                         cust_address)),
    RESOLVECONFLICT (UPDATEROWEXISTS,   (DEFAULT, OVERWRITE)),
    RESOLVECONFLICT (UPDATEROWMISSING,  (DEFAULT, OVERWRITE)),
    RESOLVECONFLICT (DELETEROWEXISTS,   (DEFAULT, OVERWRITE)),
    RESOLVECONFLICT (DELETEROWMISSING,  (DEFAULT, IGNORE)),
    RESOLVECONFLICT (INSERTROWEXISTS,   (DEFAULT, IGNORE));
```

Refer to Chapter 5 for more details regarding considerations on a bi-directional setup. The following bi-directional configuration is built on top of a successfully deployed uni-directional setup.

Define the Primary Capture

Drag and drop Capture icon into the data source (T1E2). A New Capture for the Data Source will be displayed. Enter the Capture Name (up to 8 characters) and description (optional). The Source is Table (Create a Task) for the initial-load Extract. Select Now to begin and the Database Access as defined with encryption support.

Select the Capture for a basic parameters review. There are (2) options to change the Capture parameters: (i) using Insert, Change, and Delete or (ii) navigate to Advanced → Edit Param File.

Define the Local Trail

Drag and drop the Trail icon on the Primary Capture. This defines and associates a local trail with the Capture – E03T1E2. Enter the two letter prefix and size. The format is specified when the target Oracle GoldenGate instance version mismatches the source instance. The usage of the local trail is highly recommended to prevent network failure and offload the Primary Capture from sending transactions to the target Collector Server. The suggested maximum trail file size is 5MB, which is a very low size. Enter an appropriate size considering the database redo log files size.

Define the Secondary Capture

Drag and drop the Capture on the local trail. This defines a Secondary Capture (Data Pump). Enter the Capture Name and Description (optional). Review the parameter to ascertain the capture source.

The PASSTHRU parameter instructs the data pump to operate on pass-through mode. The Extract process does not use table definition. The source and target tables must be identical without any forms of data transformations.

Define the Remote Trail

Now, the Secondary Capture is defined. It must be associated with a remote trail. Choose the host as S1T2. Drag and drop the Trail icon on the Secondary Capture – P03T1E2. Enter the remote trail two letter prefix and modify the size, preferably to be consistent with the size of the local trail.

The Trail Access is of type use TCP/IP. This enables the Secondary Capture to send data to the target host defined by the RMTHOST and MGRPORT parameters. Select the Secondary Capture to review the parameters.

Define the Delivery

The Delivery applies transactions to the target using the database native SQL interface. Drag and drop the Delivery icon into the remote trail. This brings up the New Capture window. Enter the Delivery Name – R03S1T2 and description (optional). Since the Delivery is for online synchronization, select the following: Replicat Type is Extract Trail, Target Definition is Assume, and Checkpointing Info is the Global Checkpoint Table. Leave the Database Access as defined using GGS_ADMIN without any password encryption, yet.

Map for the Primary Capture

Select the Map Capture E03S1T2 icon. Click the "Add Blank Mapping" icon - (+). Enter the Schema.TableName, check mapping and click on Save. Repeat the steps for additional mapping. Using the wildcard character, OSM$REPAPI.*., is permutable.

When using the wildcard syntax and need to exclude tables, select the Primary Capture, right-click mouse → "Advanced → Edit Param File." Click Edit. Add the "Exclude Parameter" and click "Save."

Map for the Secondary Capture

Select the Map Capture P03S1T2 icon. Tables mapping is fetched to match the Primary Capture. Check and click "Save." When using the wildcard on the Primary Capture, click the "Add Blank Mapping" icon - (+). Enter the schema.table name, check and click on "Save." Repeat the steps as necessary. Using the wildcard character, OSM$REPAPI.*., is permutable.

When using the wildcard syntax and need to exclude tables, select the Primary Capture, right-click mouse → "Advanced → Edit Param File." Click Edit. Add the "Exclude Parameter" and click "Save."

Map for the Delivery

Select the Map Capture R03S1T2 icon. Tables mapping is fetched to match the Capture. Enter the target table. Check and click "Save." When using the wildcard on the Capture, click the "Add Blank Mapping" icon - (+).

Enter the schema.table name, check and click on "Save." Repeat the steps as needed. Using the wildcard character, OSM$REPAPI.*., is permutable.

When using the wildcard syntax and need to exclude tables, select the Primary Capture, right-click mouse → Advanced → Edit Param File. Click Edit. Add the "Exclude Parameter" and click "Save."

Loop Detection

When configuring a bi-directional topology, loop detection is required to avoid an endless capture and delivery.

Start the Primary Capture

Select the Primary Capture, right-click mouse and select "Start" …

After the Primary Capture is successfully started, the Capture flow turns green.

Start the Secondary Capture

Select the Secondary Capture, right-click mouse and select "Start" …

After the Secondary Capture is successfully started, the Capture flow turns green.

Start the Delivery

Select the Delivery, right-click mouse and select "Quick Start" …

After the Delivery is successfully started, the Capture flow turns green. The Delivery Start options are:

- Normal, which uses the checkpoint to start from the last Relative Byte Address (RBA).
- Skip Transaction, which uses the checkpoint to skip the last Relative Byte Address.

- ATCSN, which starts at a specific Commit System Number (CSN) corresponding to the database System Change Number (SCN).
- AFTERCSN, which starts after a specific Commit System Number (CSN) corresponding to the database System Change Number (SCN).

Primary Capture Status

The process status is one of the following: STARTING, STOPPED, ABENDED or RUNNING.

Select the Primary Capture, right-click mouse, and select "View Details." "View Details" has (5) tabs: Report, Info, Checkpoint Lag, Statistics, and Discards.

Secondary Capture Status

Select the Secondary Capture, right-click mouse, and select "View Details." "View Details" has (5) tabs: Report, Info, Checkpoint Lag, Statistics, and Discards. The secondary uses the RMTHOST and MGRPORT to send transactions to the remote target. In the event of network failure, the target system becomes unavailable and the process is ABENDED. Configure the manager process to restart failed captures to support an automated and unattended restart.

Click on "Previous" to review older report files.

Delivery Status

Select Delivery, right-click mouse, and select "View Details." "View Details" has (5) tabs: Report, Info, Checkpoint Lag, Statistics, and Discards.

Configuration Files - Summary

Since the status of the Primary Capture, Secondary Capture, and Delivery is RUNNING as indicated by the connected green line, the setup is ready for data synchronization from Target (T1E2) to Source (S1T2) database.

The configuration files generated by the Client Director are outlined below. These parameter files are Primary Extract, Secondary Extract, and Delivery groups. Select the process name → click right-mouse → Advanced → Edit Param File.

Here is the configuration file for the Primary Capture E03T1E2. Using the capture group name, the Extract E03T1E2 is defined and the checkpoint E03T1E2.cpe is created and associated with a local trail.

```
extract E03T1E2
userid ggs_admin, password oracle
discardfile /u01/app/ogg/11.2.0/dirrpt/E03T1E2.dsc, purge
tranlogoptions excludeuser ggs_admin

exttrail /u01/app/ogg/11.2.0/dirdat/sk
table osm$repapi.customers;
```

Here is the configuration file for the Secondary Capture (Data Pump) P03T1E2. Using the capture group name, the Extract P03T1E2 is defined and the checkpoint P03T1E2.cpe is created and associated with a remote trail.

```
extract P03T1E2
userid ggs_admin, password oracle
rmthost ggs-source.precisetrace.com, mgrport 7810
rmttrail /u01/app/ogg/10.2.0/dirdat/tk
table osm$repapi.customers;
```

Here is the configuration file for the Delivery R03T1E2. Using the delivery group name, the Replicat R03T1E2 is defined and the checkpoint R03T1E2.cpe is created and associated with the Oracle GoldenGate instance global database checkpoint table.

```
replicat R03T1E2
discardfile /u01/app/ogg/10.2.0/dirrpt/R03T1E2.dsc, purge
assumetargetdefs

userid ggs_admin, password oracle
map osm$repapi.customers, target osm$repapi.customers;
```

Viewing Runtime Details

Oracle GoldenGate Director Client has a "View Details" option. Select the Capture or Delivery icon, right-click mouse → View Details. There are (5) navigation tabs:

- Report
- Info
- Checkpoint Lag
- Statistics
- Discards

Figure 9-17 shows the Checkpoint Lag details for the capture E03S1T2. The capture Checkpoint Lag equates to the difference of generating the trail and transaction commit timestamps. A fraction of the second Checkpoint Lag indicates that the Oracle GoldenGate configuration is optimized and currently delivering a near real-time data movement between the source and target systems.

Figure 9-17: View Details – Checkpoint Lag

Statistics provides the details on the current transactions volume. Statistics are grouped as Total, Daily, Hourly, and Latest. DML transaction statistics are viewed as Total or as Rate Per Hour, Minute, or Second. Figure 9-18 shows the Statistics details for the capture E03S1T2. The statistic report is grouped as Total and DML statistics calculated per second.

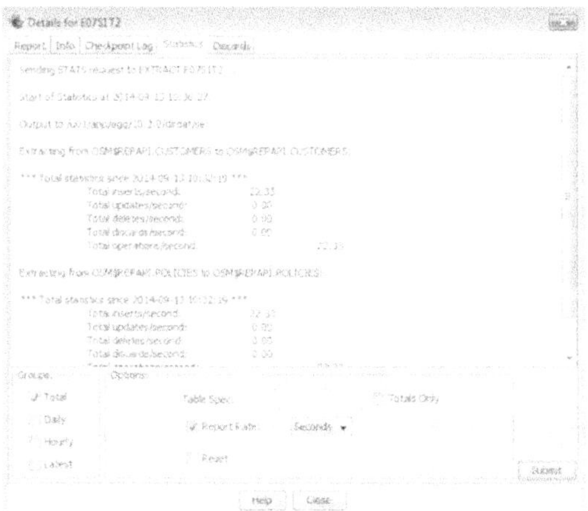

Figure 9-18: View Details - Statistics

Implementing Oracle GoldenGate Functions Using the Director Client

Data transformation is performed using Oracle GoldenGate built-in functions. For an online data capture and delivery, the location of data transformations may occur at different levels:

- The Source System
- The Target System
- The Source and Target Systems
- The Intermediate System

Figure 9-19 shows an example of performing data transformation at the source & target systems. At the source system, Oracle GoldenGate concatenates the first character of the first name with the last name. At the target system, Oracle GoldenGate performs upper case conversion and concatenation to form an alternative e-mail address.

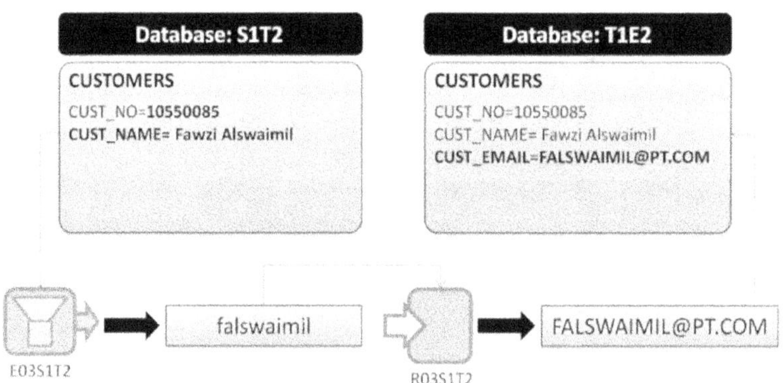

Figure 9-19: Data Transformation at the Source and Target Systems

The Oracle Director Client develops the above data transformation using a simple Graphical User Interface (GUI).

Source System Data Transformation

From an opened diagram, select "Map" for the capture. The list of mapped tables will be displayed. Select the mapped table and proceed as follows:

1. Click on "Add Blank Mapping"- (+)
2. Create the column mapping for the selected table by entering the source & target column names
3. Save the changes
4. Click "Edit column conversion"
5. From the list of conversion functions, select the function name, click "Insert" to add the function to the editor window
6. Click "Save"

Figure 9-20 shows implementation of the source data conversion using functions STRCAT and STREXT.

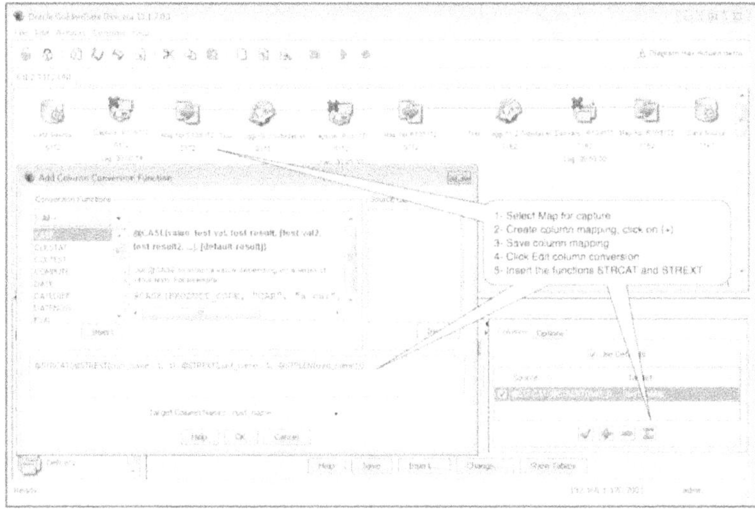

Figure 9-20: Source Conversion Functions for Data Transformations

Verify the configuration syntax by performing parameters validation from within the Director Client. Select the Capture → Advanced → Edit Param File → Edit → Check Syntax. Here is the parameter file for the capture process after adding the conversion functions:

```
extract E10S1T2
userid ggs_admin, password oracle
discardfile /u01/app/ogg/10.2.0/dirrpt/E10S1T2.dsc, purge

exttrail /u01/app/ogg/10.2.0/dirdat/sn
table osm$repapi.customers, colmap ((cust_name=@STRCAT(@STREXT(cust_name ,
1,  1), @STREXT(cust_name , 1,  @STRLEN(cust_name))), cols
```

```
(@STRCAT(@STREXT(cust_name , 1,  1), @STREXT(cust_name , 1,
@STRLEN(cust_name))))) exttrail /u01/app/ogg/10.2.0/dirdat/st);

exttrail /u01/app/ogg/10.2.0/dirdat/sm
```

Target System Data Transformation

At the target system, the GoldenGate functions are used to construct the e-mail format, convert to upper case, and perform the column mapping.

From an opened diagram, select "Map" for the capture. The list of mapped tables is displayed. Select the mapped table and proceed as follows:

1. Click on "Add Blank Mapping" - (+)
2. Create the column mapping for the selected table by entering the source & target column names
3. Save the changes
4. Click "Edit column conversion"
5. From the list of conversion function, select the function name, click "Insert" to add the function to the editor window
6. Click "Save"

Figure 9-21 shows implementation of the target system data conversion using functions STRCAT and STREXT.

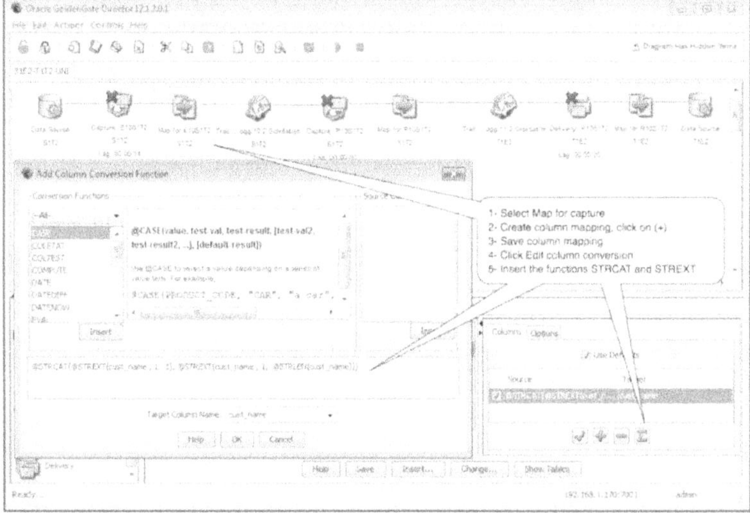

Figure 9-21: Target Conversion Functions for Data Transformations

Verify the configuration syntax by performing parameters validation from within the Director Client. Select the Capture → Advanced → Edit Param File → Edit → Check Syntax. Here is the parameter file for the capture process after adding the conversion functions:

```
extract E10S1T2
userid ggs_admin, password oracle
discardfile /u01/app/ogg/10.2.0/dirrpt/E10S1T2.dsc, purge

exttrail /u01/app/ogg/10.2.0/dirdat/sn
table osm$repapi.customers, colmap ((cust_name=@STRCAT(@STREXT(cust_name ,
1,  1), @STREXT(cust_name , 1,  @STRLEN(cust_name))), cols
(@STRCAT(@STREXT(cust_name , 1,  1), @STREXT(cust_name , 1,
@STRLEN(cust_name))))) exttrail /u01/app/ogg/10.2.0/dirdat/st);

exttrail /u01/app/ogg/10.2.0/dirdat/sm
```

Working with the GoldenGate Director Web Client

Oracle GoldenGate Director is a web-based, real-time management tool for Oracle GoldenGate Instances. It's an alternative tool for monitoring Oracle GoldenGate Extract and Replicat processes. The Director Web Client is integrated with the Director Server and does not require additional software components. Ascertain that the browser is certified by the Director to avoid unexpected problems.

The following outlines the major features & functionalities of the GoldenGate Director Web Client:

- No Installation is required. It's part of the Director Java application server and runs using only a browser.
- Configures, starts, stops, kills, and manages Oracle GoldenGate processes and tasks
- Manages process parameter files
- Provides preview reports, statistics, and discard files
- Manages alerts and watch lists

Login to the Oracle GoldenGate Director Web Client

The Director Server remains running to enable access to Oracle Director Clients. The Director Web Client is the web-based Director Server console and accessible via the URL "http://Server_Name:Port/acon," which starts the Login Page. The Director Web Client interface is accessible by entering valid credentials. Use the same credential for accessing the Director Client.

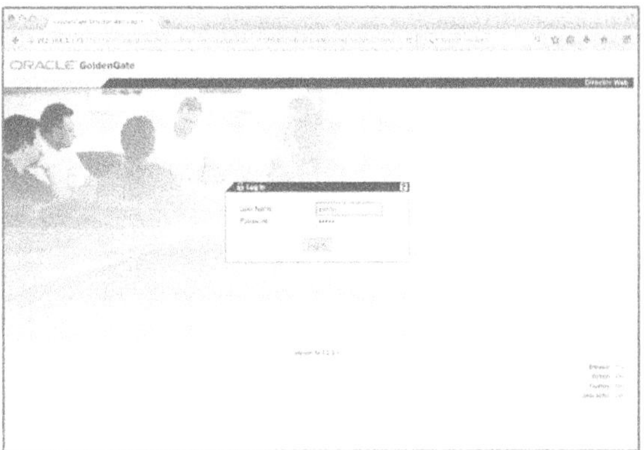

Figure 9-22: Login to the Director Web Client

The login page verifies the browser certification and version. Cookies and Java Scripts are enabled. Do not proceed until the green 'OK' is visible. Figure 9-22 represents the Director Web Client username and password window for login.

Oracle GoldenGate Director Web Client Interface

The Director Web Client Interface allows quick navigation to the different components managing Oracle GoldenGate Instances. The console's navigation displays the Data Sources, Processes and Tasks, Watch Lists, and Alerts. Expand the Data Source to display the associated processes and tasks. Password Change and Live Monitoring features are available from the Director Web Client. Figure 9-23 represents the Director Console, the Navigation Panel, Processes and Tasks Tabs and the Event Log.

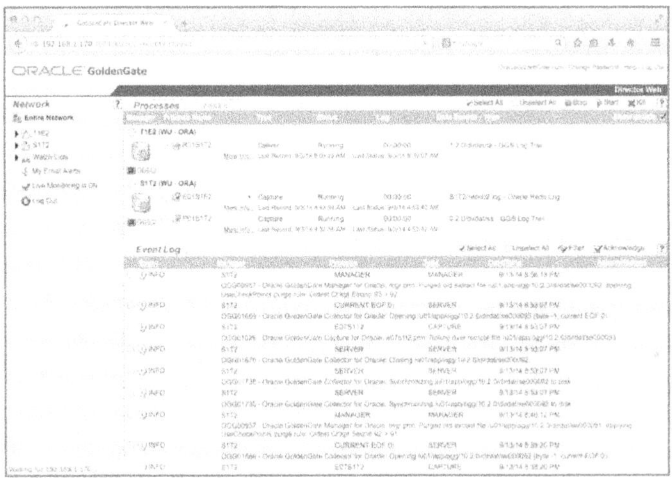

Figure 9-23: The Director Web Client Interface

Managing with Processes and Tasks using the Director Web Client

The tabs at the top of the Director Web Client console list Processes and Tasks. Click on "Processes" to display the list of defined processes and click on "Task" to display the list of defined tasks. The processes and tasks are defined using the GGSCI command-line or the Director Client.

The GGSCI commands STOP, START, and KILL are performed on selected processes and tasks.

- The Stop operation terminates one or more selected Capture or Delivery. Click on the "Info More" link to verify the current status.
- The Start operation for one or more selected Capture or Delivery. Click on the "Info More" link to verify the current status.
- The Kill operation forces a process to stop. Click on the "Info More" link to verify the current status.

The consoles have a real-time refresh. Figure 9-24 presents the list of defined processes and their status.

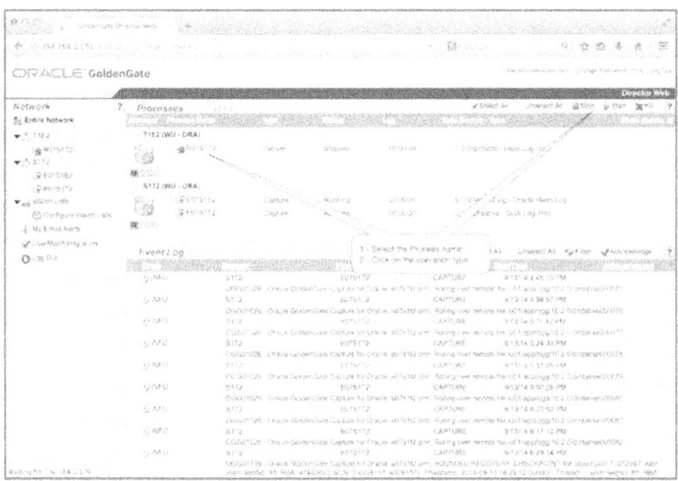

Figure 9-24: Managing Processes using the Director Web Client

Figure 9-25 represents the list of defined tasks. After the task is completed, the status remains stopped until it's restarted. Select the task name. Click "Stop" to terminate a running task, click "Start" to begin the task or "Kill" to force terminate the task. For each task there is a "More Info" link, click on the link to navigate the (4) Windows tabs. The "Report File" tab displays the last report with navigation to the previous report link, the "Info Details" tab displays the task status, type, and checkpoint lag, the "Lag History" tab displays lagging details (if any), and the "Discard File" tab displays record-specific runtime errors and bind variable values.

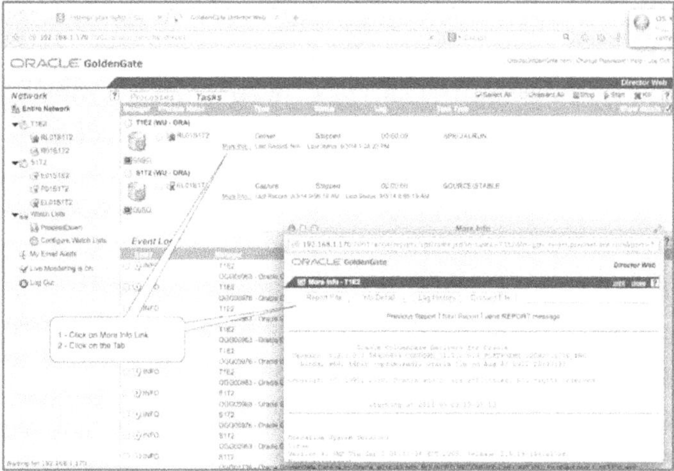

Figure 9-25: Managing Tasks using the Director Web Client

View Runtime Details using the Director Web Client

Enable Processes/Tasks details by checking the "Show" details. Then click on the "More Info" link to display the process's runtime details. The details displayed are in real-time and are the result of internally executing GGSCI commands.

Figure 9-26 shows the default display. Click on "Show details" to display more details on the default page.

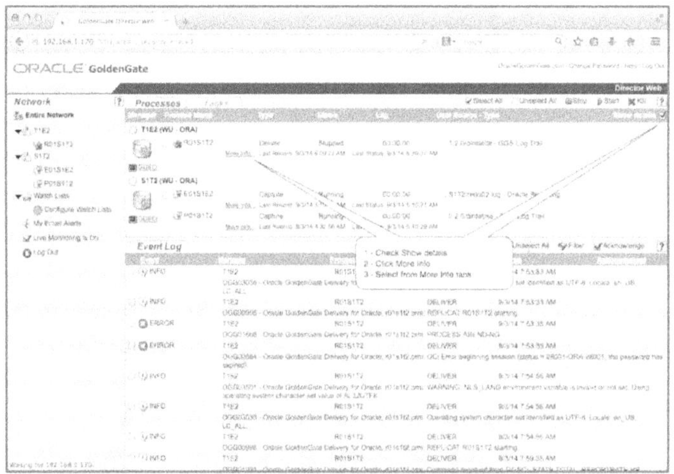

Figure 9-26: View Processes and Tasks Details

The "More Info" window has (4) tabs: Report File, Info Detail, Lag History, and Discard File. Click on "Report File" to display the current report file, click on "Info Details" to display current status, click on "Lag History" to display the process's lag details and click on "Discard File" to display the last runtime error details as shown in Figure 9-27.

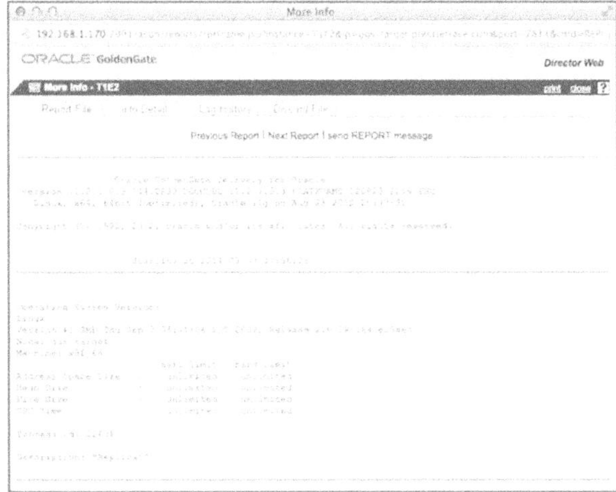

Figure 9-27: More Info Tabs

Edit Director Web Client Parameter Files

A click on the process name displays the parameter file on "Edit" mode. Edit the file by adding and/or removing parameters. Click "Save" to save changes. Stop and restart the process to activate the modified parameters.

Figure 9-28 shows the "Edit Parameter" window.

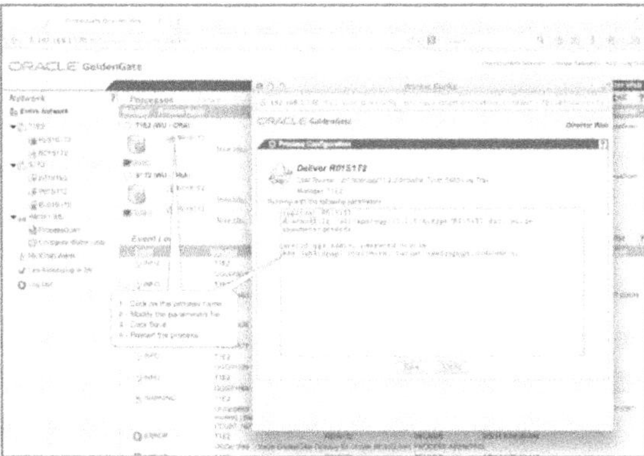

Figure 9-28: Edit Parameter Window

Invoking GGSCI from the Director Web Client

Simply click on the GGSCI link to invoke the GGSCI window. The GGSCI window is "process specific." Enter the GGSCI command and click the "Run" link to execute the command. Click on "Edit Script" to invoice the Script Editor for creating obey files. Figure 9-29 shows the GGSCI window.

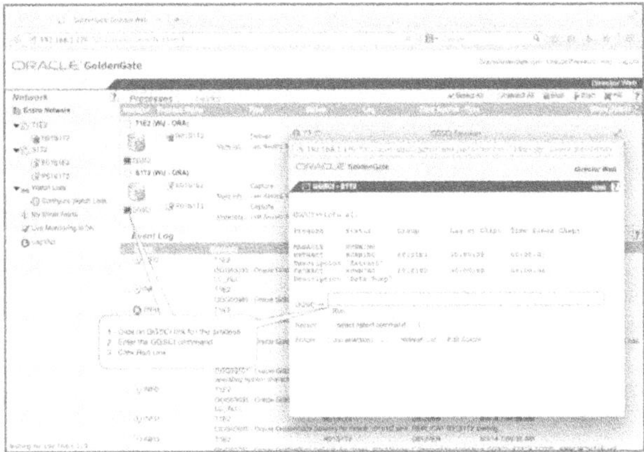

Figure 9-29: Invoking GGSCI from the the Director Web Client

Creating Alerts

Click on the "My Email Alert" link to query existing alert and create new alert. Select "New Alert" to enter new alert details or query an existing alert. Figure 9-30 shows the "Create Alert" window.

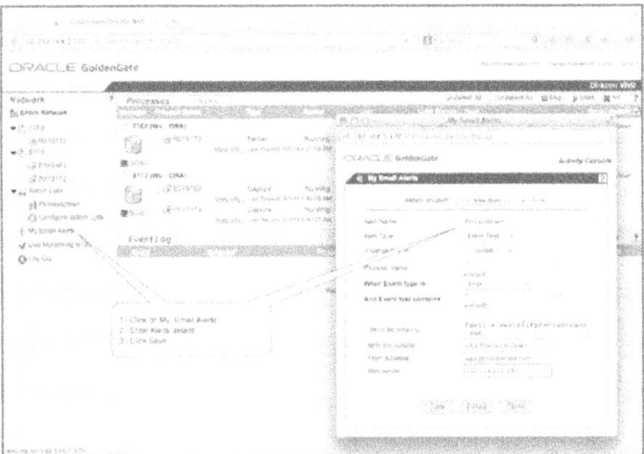

Figure 9-30: Creating Alerts

Creating Watch Lists

Watch Lists are created to monitor grouped entities. These entities should be related but not necessarily. Click on the "Configure Watch Lists" link to query existing and create new watch lists. Enter watch list details and "Save" to create the watch list.

A watch list can be created and shared with the Director users. The Event Log Filter controls the error type and the page size. The default is 100 events.

Watch List Name: Enter the Watch List Name
Author: Logged in User
Shared with other users: Checked
Include in list: Check the instance's manager. Select one or more process names
Event Log Filter: Check the level of details

Figure 9-31 shows the "Create Watch List" window.

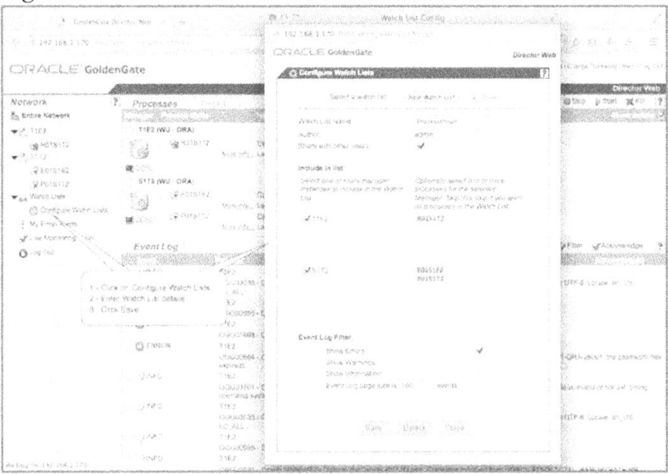

Figure 9-31: Creating Watch Lists

Oracle GoldenGate Monitor - An Overview

Oracle GoldenGate Monitor, aka the Monitor, delivers an advanced real-time monitoring capability for Oracle GoldenGate Instances. The Monitor is a web-based application. It provides integrated management systems to effectively monitor Oracle GoldenGate instances using graphical views. Similar to the Director, the Monitor employs a smart drag-and-drop technique to view an Oracle GoldenGate instance.

The Monitor focuses on the following functionalities:

- Real-Time Capture and Delivery Processes Status Management
- Advanced Alerts and Events Handling
- Runtime Statistics Reporting

The Monitor discovers targets using the Agent running on the Oracle GoldenGate instance systems. However, it does not alter Oracle GoldenGate configuration. The alteration is a function provided by the Director.

Architecture

The Monitor is composed of the Monitor Server, the GoldenGate instances, the Database Repository, the Monitor Agent, and the interfaces. Figure 9-32 shows the Monitor building blocks. The Monitor Agent is installed on the Oracle GoldenGate instance system. The Monitor Server communicates with the Monitor Agent for executing tasks and requesting processes' status information. Setup of the Monitor Server for each GoldenGate instance is performed from the client interface and command-line. The Monitor uses a database repository for persistently storing configuration and runtime statistics. The historical data displays details regarding previously occurred events. Though the illustrations on this chapter use the Oracle Database, the Monitor also supports a MS SQL Server, MySQL database, and IBM DB2.

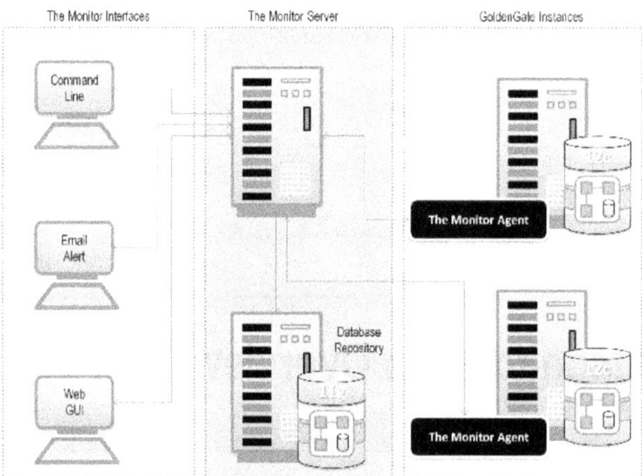

Figure 9-32: Oracle GoldenGate Monitor Building Blocks

Oracle GoldenGate Instances

An operational Oracle GoldenGate instance is composed of the source database, the manager process, the capture processes, the trails, the delivery processes and the target database. For real-time monitoring, each Oracle GoldenGate instance must have an installed and configured Oracle GoldenGate Monitor Agent.

Oracle GoldenGate Monitor Agent

The Monitor communicates with the Oracle GoldenGate instance via its agent. The Agent installed on each system sends information and status details to the Monitor Server. The agent uses JMX or SSL for communication with the Monitor Server.

Oracle GoldenGate Monitor Server

The Monitor Server oversees the monitoring of all discovered targets – Oracle GoldenGate instance host, database, manager process, and the associated objects. The Server controls user access, manages runtime history, events, and notifications. Monitoring the health of an Oracle GoldenGate instance and process information is received from the Agent. The Monitor Server uses a database repository for consistent configuration.

Oracle GoldenGate Monitor Repository

The repository stores metadata for operating the Monitor. Alerts, notifications, events, and history are consistently stored on the database repository. The repository handles users, groups, and access roles for secure connections. The repository supports the following database types:

- Oracle Database
- Oracle Database (enabled for edition-based redefinition)
- Microsoft SQL Server
- IBM DB2
- MySQL Database

Using various protocol, the Monitor Server communicates and handles requests for the various Monitor interfaces.

Oracle GoldenGate Monitor Interfaces

The Monitor interfaces display information and defines the Monitor components. Each interface uses its protocol as listed here:

- E-Mail – SMTP
- Web Browser – HTTP/HTTPS
- External Monitoring Systems – SNMP
- Command-Line

Download Oracle GoldenGate Management Pack Software

The Monitor software is downloadable from Oracle Technology Network (OTN); However, the Oracle Software Delivery Cloud – "http://edelivery.oracle.com" has bundled the Oracle GoldenGate Management Pack into one Media Pack, V44427-01. It's found under the Oracle Fusion Middleware 12c Media Pack page as shown in Figure 9-33. The current downloadable versions of the Monitor are: 11.1.1 and 12.1.3. Since there have been major new features added to release 12.1.3, it's highly recommended to use this release. This chapter illustrates deploying Oracle GoldenGate Monitor 12c, release 12.1.3. The Media Pack includes the following components:

- Oracle GoldenGate Veridata Server and Veridata Agent
- Oracle GoldenGate Monitor Server and Monitor Agent

The wizard based installer has the option "Complete Install" which completely installs the Oracle GoldenGate Management Pack.

Software Installations

The installation of the Monitor consists of prerequisites and the Monitor components. Before starting the Monitor Server installation, the following prerequisite installations must be completed successfully:

- Java Development Kit (Version 1.7 or higher)
- Oracle WebLogic 12c (Version 12.1.3)
- Oracle WebLogic 12c Infrastructure (Version 12.1.3)
- The Repository Database (Oracle Database Version 11g R1, 11 R2 or 12c R1)

There are (2) installations for the Monitor:

- The Monitor Server Installation
- The Monitor Agent

Install JDK1.7

Ensure installing the Java Development Kit (JDK) version 1.7 or higher. Installation and verification of the JDK using RPM is illustrated below:

```
[root@ggs-source tmp]# rpm -ihv jdk-7u67-linux-x64.rpm
Preparing...                ########################################### [100%]
   1:jdk                    ########################################### [100%]
Unpacking JAR files...
     rt.jar...
     jsse.jar...
     charsets.jar...
     tools.jar...
     localedata.jar...
     jfxrt.jar...
[root@ggs-source tmp]#
```

In case a JDK is already installed and it's necessary to verify the existence of JDK version 1.7, the RPM option –qa is as follows:

```
[root@ggs-source tmp]# rpm -qa | grep jdk-1.7.0
java-1.7.0-openjdk-1.7.0.25-2.3.10.5.0.1.el5_9
jdk-1.7.0_67-fcs
[root@ggs-source tmp]#
```

Install Oracle Fusion Middleware 12c Infrastructure

The Oracle Fusion Middleware 12c Infrastructure provides Oracle WebLogic Server, Oracle Coherence, and the Java Required Files (JRF). The Monitor Server is certified with Oracle WebLogic Server, Version 12.1.3. This installation uses Oracle Linux 6, Update 1.
Follow the WebLogic Server install wizard steps for installing the software.
Launch the installer by executing Java using –jar option.

```
[oracle@gg-monitor wls]$ export DISPLAY=192.168.1.3:0.0
[oracle@gg-monitor wls]$ java -jar fmw_12.1.3.0.0_infrastructure.jar
Launcher log file is /tmp/OraInstall2014-11-30_03-05-49AM/launcher2014-11-
30_03-05-49AM.log.
Extracting files..............
```

For a system with java-1.6.0-openjdk installed, an error "The OpenJDK JVM" is not supported on this platform. In this case, run the Java from the JDK software location.

```
/usr/java/jdk1.7.0_67/bin
```

```
[oracle@gg-monitor bin]$ ./java -jar
/stage/wls/fmw_12.1.3.0.0_infrastructure.jar
Launcher log file is /tmp/OraInstall2014-11-30_03-28-34AM/launcher2014-11-
30_03-28-34AM.log.
Extracting files......
```

Confirm the inventory directory location and Operating System Group. Click 'OK' to use the default values. Otherwise, enter new values for the Inventory Directory and Operating System Group. The following screen shots depict the installation of Oracle Fusion Middleware 12c Infrastructure:

Welcome

The Monitor set of applications are powered by Oracle WebLogic Server Version 12.1.3. Before proceeding further, while logged in as 'oracle', create the installation location base folder or use the default location '/home/oracle.' Click "Next" to continue.

Installation Location

The Installation Location is the Oracle Home for Oracle Fusion Middleware 12c WebLogic Server and Coherence. Use the Browse button or type the name of the directory. Verify the directory specified by clicking "View." It lists the feature sets of the specified directory.

Installation Types

Select the option, "Complete with Example." This option installs the Oracle WebLogic Server and Coherence: Core Server, Administrative Tools, Database Support, Open Source Components, and Oracle Installation Infrastructure.

Prerequisite Checks

This is an essential step and must be completed successfully. It assesses platform compatibility by checking the operating system and Java certification. In the event of an unsuccessful one or more prerequisite checks, apply the required fix, then re-attempt Step 4.

Security Updates

It's a must to keep Oracle Fusion Middleware software up to date by applying any security-related patches and workarounds delivered by Oracle Support. To do so, type your e-mail address and Oracle Support password.

Installation Summary

Verify that the Oracle Home Location is correct. The summary lists the "Feature Sets to install." For future silent mode installations, create the "Response File" by clicking on the "Save Response File" button. The silent install option applies standards and conventions for future Oracle Fusion Middleware 12c software.

Installation Progress

The installation goes through several phases. It starts by imaging the software on the install location — generating the libraries which are platform/architecture specific. The installation timeframe is relatively short, less than 20 minutes to complete.

Installation Complete

Step 8 of 8 confirms the status of the installation completion by listing the feature sets installed and location. Do not check the "Automatically Launch the Configuration Wizard" option. It will be run after installing the Monitor Server.

The Repository Database

Since the Monitor Repository database is relatively small and passive, the use of an existing database should meet the Monitor's requirements. Figure 9-34 shows the DBCA for creating the database to host the Monitor's Repository. During the creation of the Monitor Repository, it requires the following details.

Host Name: gg-director.precisetrace.com (IP Address)
Administrative User: SYS or SYSTEM
Service Name: GGDB.precisetrace.com
Listener Port: 1521

Since the Monitor's Repository utility makes an EZCONNECT to the database, verify the database connection is successful using an EZCONNECT method.

```
SQL> conn system/oracle_4U@192.168.1.170:1521/GGDB.precisetrace.com
Connected.
SQL> select sys_context('USERENV', 'SERVICE_NAME')
  2  from dual;

SYS_CONTEXT('USERENV','SERVICE_NAME')
--------------------------------------------------------------------
GGDB.precisetrace.com

SQL>
```

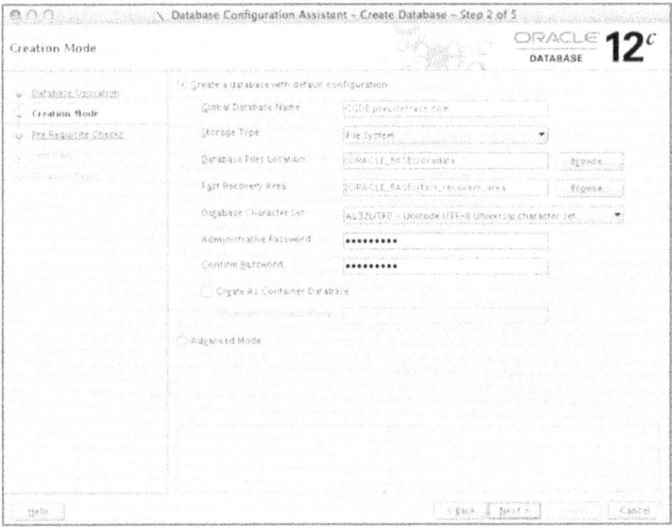

Figure 9-34: The Monitor Database Repository Details

Install Oracle GoldenGate Monitor Server

Now it's time to install the Oracle GoldenGate Monitor Server software on its dedicated host. The Monitor installation is composed of (2) parts:

Part I: Installation of the Monitor Software

Using the Oracle GoldenGate Monitor and Veridata installer, select the Oracle GoldenGate Monitor Server. The Monitor agent is separately installed on each Oracle GoldenGate Instance.

Part II: Creation of the Repository

The repository components of tablespaces and schemas and metadata are created. A successful JDBC connection to the repository database is mandatory during the creation of the repository.

Starting the Monitor Server Installation

While logged in as user 'oracle', execute the installer as shown below:

```
[oracle@gg-monitor bin]$ ./java -jar /stage/wls/fmw_12.1.3.0.0_ogg.jar
```

```
Launcher log file is /tmp/OraInstall2014-12-02_02-32-08AM/launcher2014-12-
02_02-32-08AM.log.
Extracting files........................
Starting Oracle Universal Installer
```

The installer tries to create the inventory directory, if it does not already exist. As shown, the installer suggests default values for the Inventory Directory and Operating System Group. Make the necessary changes and click "OK" to continue.

Welcome

The unified installer, The Oracle Fusion Middleware 12c (12.1.3.0.0) GoldenGate Monitor and Veridata installer performs installation for the Oracle GoldenGate Monitor and Veridata. It requires the installation of Oracle Fusion Middleware Infrastructure 12c.

Installation Location

The Installation Location directory is an existing Oracle Fusion Middleware 12c home. Select an existing home and click on "View" to display the installed feature sets.

Installation Types

Since the GoldenGate Source and Target Instances are installed on separate systems from the Monitor Server system, select the option "Oracle GoldenGate Monitor Server." The agent installation is performed on the source and target systems.

Prerequisite Checks

The prerequisite checks verify the operating system and Java version. In case of a failed verification, cancel the installation and re-attempt. For certification details, visit http://support.oracle.com."

Installation Summary

Verify the installation location. Review the disk space and feature sets to be installed. The Log File location is located on the "/tmp directory" for post-installation review. When ready, click "Install."

Installation Progress

The Monitor installation is relatively fast, between 10-15 minutes. Wait until all (8) steps are completed successfully, then click "Next" to review or "Finish" to exit the Installer.

Installation Complete

The last step displays the installation summary: installation location, installation log file, and the feature sets. Move the log file and the parameter file, 'oraparam.ini', to a permanent location for future reference.

Create the Oracle GoldenGate Monitor Repository

The Monitor Repository stores the Monitor metadata. The consistent configuration environment allows effective management for and monitoring of multiple and complex Oracle GoldenGate Instances.

Starting the Repository Utility

Start the shell repository management utility to create the Monitor database repository. Though there are several database type supports, this Repository uses an Oracle Database 12c, Release 1. From the Monitor software location, navigate to the 'oracle_common/bin' directory, start the repository utility as illustrated below:

```
[oracle@gg-monitor bin]$ pwd
/home/oracle/Oracle/Middleware/Oracle_Home1/oracle_common/bin
[oracle@gg-monitor bin]$ export DISPLAY=192.168.1.3:0.0
[oracle@gg-monitor bin]$ ./rcu
```

Welcome

The Repository Creation Utility (RCU) creates and configures the database repository for the Oracle GoldenGate Monitor. The utility verifies connection to the repository database using a JDBC connect string.

Create the Repository

The Repository Creation Utility (RCU) has (2) options: "Create Repository" and "Drop Repository." Select the "Create Repository" option with System Load and

Product Load. This option requires DBA privileges for creating tablespaces, schemas, and database objects such as tables and indexes.

Database Connection Details

The Database Connection Details require the database type of the repository: Host Name, Database Listener Port, Service Name, and Username with DBA or SYSDBA privilege.

Select Components

Provide the prefix for the repository components. Select all "AS Common Schemas" and the GoldenGate Monitor Server. The Schema Owner is automatically prefixed using the new prefix. Click "Next" to continue. For a re-run of the utility, drop the existing repository before re-creating.

Schema Passwords

Use the default password option – Use the same password for all schemas. Enter and confirm the password. For users with database advanced password policies, using the option – "Specify different passwords for all schemas" may be required. Click "Next" to continue.

Map Tablespaces

The Repository Creation Utility (RCU) creates a list of permanent tablespaces and one temporary tablespace. The utility uses the prefix to create the tablespaces and the schemas. Query the data dictionary views DBA_TABLESPACES and DBA_USERS to display the list of tablespaces and schemas. You may modify the tablespaces properties by clicking on "Manage Tablespaces." Click "Next" to continue.

Summary

For each component, the RCU shows the schema default (permanent) and temporary tablespace. Click "Create" to start the process of creating the Repository components. A failure may require a drop and re-create of the repository.

Completion Summary

The Completion Summary page is a preview of successfully creating the repository. The page provides access to log files – "rcu.log" and the individual component log file. Click "Close" to terminate the RCU and begin starting the WebLogic Server and the Oracle GoldenGate Monitor Server.

Managing the Oracle WebLogic Managed Server

Prior to accessing the Monitor, it requires successfully starting the WebLogic Server and the Monitor Managed Server. Use the HTTP ports identified during the installation of the Oracle WebLogic and the Monitor Server.

Starting the Oracle GoldenGate Monitor

The first step is to start the Oracle WebLogic Server using the start shell script created on the domain directory.

```
[oracle@ggs-mp ggm_domain1]$ pwd
/home/oracle/domains/ggm_domain1
[oracle@ggs-mp ggm_domain1]$ ./startWebLogic.sh
```

The end of the messages log indicates the running status as shown here.

```
<Oct 7, 2014 3:12:03 PM AST> <Notice> <WebLogicServer> <BEA-000360> <The
server started in RUNNING mode.>
<Oct 7, 2014 3:12:03 PM AST> <Notice> <WebLogicServer> <BEA-000365> <Server
state changed to RUNNING.>
```

Ascertain that the server status is RUNNING. The next step is to start the Monitor Server by starting the WebLogic Managed Server. The default managed server name is 'MONITORSERVER_server1', followed by the WebLogic console URL.

```
[oracle@ggs-mp bin]$ pwd
/home/oracle/domains/ggm_domain1/bin
[oracle@ggs-mp bin]$ ./startManagedWebLogic.sh MONITORSERVER_server1
http://ggs-mp.precisetrace.com:7001
```

The end of the messages log indicates the running status as shown here.

```
<Oct 7, 2014 3:22:45 PM AST> <Notice> <WebLogicServer> <BEA-000330> <Started
the WebLogic Server Managed Server "MONITORSERVER_server1" for domain
"ggm_domain1" running in production mode.>
<Oct 7, 2014 3:22:46 PM AST> <Notice> <WebLogicServer> <BEA-000360> <The
server started in RUNNING mode.>
<Oct 7, 2014 3:22:46 PM AST> <Notice> <WebLogicServer> <BEA-000365> <Server
state changed to RUNNING.>
```

Stopping Oracle GoldenGate Monitor

Since the Oracle WebLogic Server and the Monitor Managed Server are running as foreground processes, terminate the Monitor Managed Server then the WebLogic Server by pressing Control-C command.

Login to Oracle WebLogic Server

The Oracle WebLogic Server console, services, and applications are accessed using a certified web browser. The Login details of Host Name, HTTP Port, Username, and Password are identified during the Oracle WebLogic installation.

To access the console, use the URL http://WebLogicServerName:port/console. The login page, below, is accessed via "http://192.168.1.102:7001/console." Figure 9-35 shows the Login to Oracle WebLogic Server Administration Console 12c.

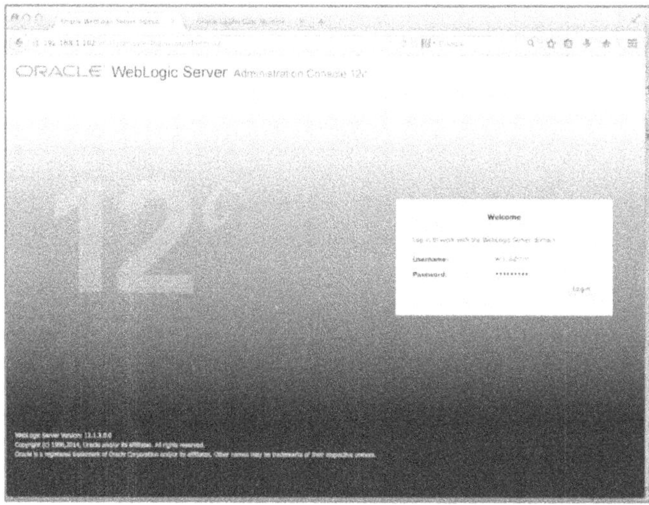

Figure 9-35: Login to Oracle WebLogic Server

Creating GoldenGate Monitor Users

While logged in as a privileged user, create additional users while considering the principle of least privilege promotes a well-managed and secure environment. Users are assigned to one or more groups which identify availability of resources.

The steps for creating additional WebLogic users are:

- Access to the Security Realms

- Create New User
- Assignment of Groups

Security Realms

Security Realms creates a logical representation of resources. From the navigation panel, click "Security Realms." The list of Oracle WebLogic instance Security Realms will be displayed.

Click on the Security Realm 'myrealm' to navigate to the realm settings. The user setting tabs are: Configuration, Users and Groups, Roles and Policies, Credential Mapping, Providers, and Migration.

Users and Groups

Click on 'New' to create a new user. The mandatory details for creating a new user are username and password only. The next step is to assign the user to be a member of one or more groups.

The 'Group' tab displays the available groups. Add one or more groups. Select the group 'Monitor' to enable the user's use of the Oracle GoldenGate Monitor. Table 9-2 lists the parent groups and a brief description.

Group Name	Description
Monitor	Views and modifies all resource attributes and performs operations not restricted by roles.
OGGAdministrator	OGG MonitorServer Administrators Group
OGGOperator	OGG MonitorServer Operators Group
OGGPowerOperator	OGG MonitorServer Power Operators Group
OGGSuperAdmin	OGG MonitorServer Super Administrator Group

Table 9-2: The Monitor User's Groups

Login to the Monitor Server

The Login to the Monitor Server requires supplying the valid credentials of Username and Password. Access to the Monitor Server consoles is composed of the Host Name and HTTP Port followed by '/monitor/faces/loginPage.jspx.'

Enter the URL "http://192.168.1.92:7003/monitor/faces/loginPage.jspx" to access the Monitor console. The HTTP port is identified during the Monitor Server installation.

Figure 9-36 shows the Login page to the Monitor.

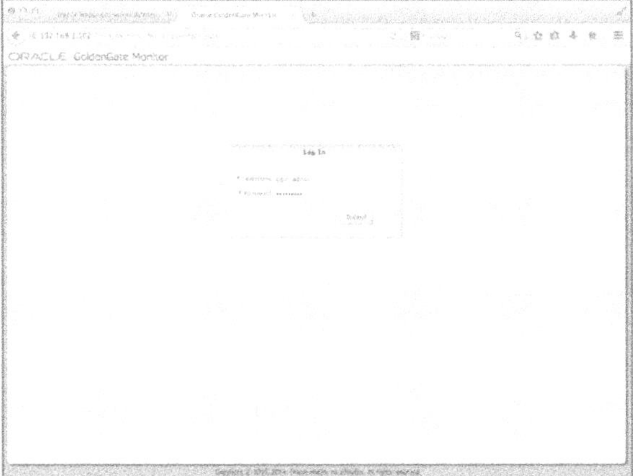

Figure 9-36: Login Page to the Monitor

Without installing and configuring the Oracle GoldenGate Monitor Agent, the Monitor console does not reflect any of the runtime details for Oracle GoldenGate Instances. Only the Monitor system status is displayed. Since the Agent is not installed yet, Figure 9-37 shows the host objects only without Oracle GoldenGate Instances.

The Monitor console consists of the following sections:

- Navigation pane, for displaying discovered objects from the source and target, where the agent installed.
- Diagram work area, for creating new and existing diagrams and solutions.
- Overview, provides a drill-down function on existing diagram.
- Attributes, display details status and error messages.

The Monitor Console includes the following tabs to navigate the environment and make features accessible.

- Data and Alerts View
- Logs
- Configuration
- Problem Summary
- Historical Data
- Alert History
- Alert Definition
- User Management

Install the Oracle GoldenGate Monitor Server Agent

To enable the Monitor to provide real-time monitoring and analysis, perform the Monitor Agent software installation and configuration on all Oracle GoldenGate Instance systems. The data captured by the Agent from the Oracle GoldenGate Instance is forwarded to the Monitor Server for analysis and interpretation. Start the installation by navigating to the Agent Media Pack directory and run the Oracle Fusion Middleware 12c Monitor and Veridata Installation.

```
$ export DISPLAY=192.168.1.3:0.0
$ ./java -jar /stage/fmw_12.1.3.0.0_ogg.jar
Launcher log file is /tmp/OraInstall2014-12-17_10-11-26AM/launcher2014-12-17_10-11-26AM.log.
Extracting files...........
```

Welcome

In addition to certifying the Operating System and Java versions, the installation of Oracle Fusion Middleware Infrastructure 12c is a prerequisite. For further details, refer to the "Install Oracle Fusion Middleware 12c Infrastructure" section.

Installation Location

Enter the directory for installation of the Oracle GoldenGate Agent. Press "View" to display the existing installed 'Feature Sets.' The permission settings of '755' means the owner has read, write, and execute permissions. The group and others have only read and execute permissions.

Installation Type

There are several installation options related to the Oracle GoldenGate 12c Monitor and Veridata. Since the installation is on the source and target systems, select 'Oracle GoldenGate Monitor Agent'. Click "Next'" to continue.

Prerequisite Checks

An additional interview phase is done by the installer to verify the prerequisites. The installer verifies the Operating System and Java versions. Click "Next" to continue.

Installation Summary

The Installation Summary presents the software location, the log location, disk space details, and the feature set to install. When ready, click "Install" to start the installation of the Agent.

Installation Progress

The installation passes through several phases. All the phases must be completed successfully. Click on "View Log" to display the log file. Click on "Finish" to terminate the installer or "Next" to display the 'Installation Complete' confirmation page.

Installation Complete

The 'Installation Complete' page confirms that Oracle GoldenGate is successfully installed. It outlines the locations of the Agent's home and the log file. Click "Finish" to terminate the installer.

Configure the Monitor Server

In order to start using the Monitor console, configuration of the Monitor Server and the Agent is required. Since the Oracle GoldenGate Agent communicates with the Monitor Server, configure the local DNS to avoid unexpected errors by including all hostnames to /etc/hosts. Edit the Monitor Server configuration file, "monitor.properties" which is located under the following directory:

/home/oracle/domains/GGM1_domain/config/monitorserver/cfg

The configuration zones of the Monitor Server are performed for setting properties parameters.

- JMX Server Properties
- SMTP Alert Properties
- CLI Alert Properties

The majority of the configuration parameters are assigned default values and require no changes. Configure the necessary components only. For example, ignoring SMTP Server Properties settings avoids sending e-mail notifications by the Monitor Server.

JMX Server Configuration

The JMX Server is enabled by default and it's required for registering the Agent. The following lists the JMX Server parameters and their settings:

```
monitor.jmx.server.enabled=true
monitor.jmx.server.host=gg-monitor
monitor.jmx.server.port=5502
monitor.jmx.server.user=jmxsvrusr
```

Target Database Configuration

Depending on the database type of the repository, uncomment the relevant line for the target database. The configuration file defines database platforms for an Oracle Database and MS SQL Server.

```
eclipselink.target-
database=org.eclipse.persistence.platform.database.OraclePlatform
```

SMTP Configuration

To enable the Monitor Server for sending notification e-mails, set the following properties:

```
monitor.smtp.host=smtp.awalnet.net.sa
monitor.smtp.port=25
monitor.smtp.secure=false
monitor.smtp.user=Fawzi.alswaimil@precisetrace.com
monitor.smtp.alerts.enabled=false
```

SNMP Configuration

To enable SNMP alerts, set the parameter 'monitor.snmp.alerts.enabled' to true, otherwise false.

```
monitor.snmp.alerts.enabled=true
```

CLI Configuration

To enable CLI alerts, set the parameter 'monitor.cli.alerts.enabled' to true, otherwise false.

```
monitor.cli.alerts.enabled=true
```

Security Configuration

The following list of properties is for enhanced security.

```
monitor.ssl=false
monitor.keystore.file=monitorKeyStore
monitor.truststore.file=jagentKeyStore
monitor.cm.event.max.size=1000
monitor.ssoLogOutUrl=/oamsso/logout.html?end_url=/monitor
```

General Parameters Configuration

The following list of properties is for general usage. Be cautious when changing the default values.

```
monitor.default_agent_connection.interval=30
monitor.supported.agent.metadata.version=1.0
monitor.events.dispatcher.threads_size=30
eclipselink.weaving=static
monitor.cm.event.timeout=2000
```

Configure the Agent

Prepare the Agent configuration file '<Agent_Home>/cfg/Config.properties' for all Oracle GoldenGate Instances. Assign values for non-default parameters. The following is the list of parameters. Non-Default Parameter values are highlighted.

```
####################################################################
## jagent.host: Host name of the machine where jAgent is running ###
## Note: This host name has to be reachable from Monitor Server  ###
####################################################################
jagent.host=ggs-source.precisetrace.com

####################################################################
## jagent.jmx.port: jAgent's JMX port number                     ###
####################################################################
jagent.jmx.port=5555

####################################################################
## interval.regular, interval.quick:                              ###
## jAgent's regular and quick polling interval for new            ###
## Monitoring Point values.                                       ###
## Default values are 60 and 30 seconds                           ###
####################################################################
interval.regular=60
interval.quick=30

####################################################################
## monitor.host: Monitor Server Host Name.                        ###
## Note: This property has to be the same with the property:      ###
## monitor.jmx.server.host in monitor.properties file             ###
## on Monitor Server side                                         ###
####################################################################
monitor.host=gg-monitor

####################################################################
## monitor.jmx.port: Monitor Server JMX port number               ###
####################################################################
monitor.jmx.port=5502

####################################################################
## monitor.jmx.username: Monitor Server JMX username               ###
## This is the JMX username defined during Monitor Installation  ###
####################################################################
```

```
monitor.jmx.username=jmxsvrusr

####################################################################
## jagent.username: jAgent username                              ###
## It can be any name. This jAgent username will be passed to    ###
## Monitor Server during jAgent registration.                    ###
####################################################################
jagent.username=oggmajmxusr

####################################################################
## reg.retry.interval: jAgent incremental registration           ###
## retry interval in seconds; when connection exception          ###
## occurs while jAgent is connecting to Monitor Server for the   ###
## first time                                                    ###
## Default value is 60 seconds                                   ###
####################################################################
reg.retry.interval=10

####################################################################
## instance.query.initial.interval:                              ###
## If only manager process is running, jAgent will wait for      ###
## 15 seconds by default before starting to register             ###
## to Monitor Server. After this waiting period of time,         ###
## if there are still no other running processes such as         ###
## extract and replicat beside the manager process, JAgent will  ###
## go ahead and register to Monitor Server.                      ###
####################################################################
instance.query.initial.interval=5

####################################################################
## incremental.registration.quiet.interval:                      ###
## jAgent will incrementally register to Monitor Server after    ###
## a new process is configured. However, jAgent will wait for    ###
## a period of 5 seconds by default before each                  ###
## incremental registration started.                             ###
####################################################################
incremental.registration.quiet.interval=5

####################################################################
## maximum.message.retrieval:                                    ###
## Maximum number of message to retrieve from cagent/core when   ###
## jagent starts                                                 ###
####################################################################
maximum.message.retrieval=500


####################################################################
## mgr.host: Host name of the machine where Manager is running   ###
## Note: This host name has to be reachable from JAgent          ###
## There is no need to define this property if JAgent is         ###
## running on the same machine with OGG Deployment               ###
####################################################################
mgr.host=ggs-source.precisetrace.com

####################################################################
## mgr.port: Manager port number                                 ###
## There is no need to define this property if JAgent is         ###
## running on the same machine with OGG Deployment               ###
####################################################################
```

```
mgr.port=7812

####################################################################
## jagent.rmi.port                                               ###
## RMI Port which EM Agent will use to connect to JAgent         ###
## RMI Port will only be used if agent.type.enabled=OEM          ###
####################################################################
jagent.rmi.port=5559

####################################################################
## agent.type.enabled : Choose either OEM or OGGMON              ###
## Choosing OGGMON will allow JAgent to register to              ###
## Monitor Server and JMX RMI connector will not be enabled.     ###
## Choosing OEM will enable JMX RMI connector which will be used ###
## by EM Agent to connect to JAgent and JAgent will not register ###
## to Monitor Server.                                            ###
####################################################################
agent.type.enabled=OGGMON

####################################################################
## status.polling.interval: polling interval for status changes  ###
## in second. Newly added process will be detected based on this ###
## polling interval.Default is 5 seconds.                        ###
####################################################################
status.polling.interval=5

####################################################################
## message.polling.interval: polling interval for message        ###
## changes in second. Default is 5 seconds.                      ###
####################################################################
message.polling.interval=5

## This property is not being used at the moment
reg.retry.times=-1

####################################################################
## jagent backward compatibility                                 ###
####################################################################
jagent.backward.compatibility=false

################### Start SSL Properties ###########################

####################################################################
## jagent SSL Enabled property                                   ###
####################################################################
jagent.ssl=false

####################################################################
## keystore file - value for SSL property javax.net.ssl.keyStore ###
####################################################################
jagent.keystore.file=jagentKeyStore

####################################################################
## truststore file-value for SSL property javax.net.ssl.trustStore #
####################################################################
jagent.truststore.file=jagentKeyStore

#################### End SSL Properties ############################
```

Edit the GLOBALS parameter file. Add the parameter ENABLEMONITORING. This parameter is mandatory for the Monitor. Execute the START JAGENT command as shown here.

- Stop and restart the Manager process.

```
GGSCI (ggs-source.precisetrace.com) 1> stop mgr!

Sending STOP request to MANAGER ...
Request processed.
Manager stopped.

GGSCI (ggs-source.precisetrace.com) 2> start mgr
Manager started.
```

- Start the Monitor agent.

```
GGSCI (ggs-source.precisetrace.com) 3> start jagent

Sending START request to MANAGER ...
GGCMD JAGENT starting

GGSCI (ggs-source.precisetrace.com) 4>
```

- Verify the status for the manager and agent.

```
GGSCI (ggs-source.precisetrace.com) 4> INFO ALL

Program     Status      Group       Lag at Chkpt  Time Since Chkpt

MANAGER     RUNNING
JAGENT      RUNNING

GGSCI (ggs-source.precisetrace.com) 5>
```

Perform the agent configuration on Source and Target systems.

```
[oracle@ggs-source ogg_agent]$ ./create_ogg_agent_instance.sh
Please enter absolute path of Oracle GoldenGate home directory :
/u01/app/ggs/12.1.0/gghome_1
Please enter absolute path of OGG Agent instance :
/u01/app/ggs/12.1.0/agent_1
OGG Agent instance directory already exists, do you want to overwrite the
contents (yes | no) : yes
Sucessfully created OGG Agent instance.
[oracle@ggs-source ogg_agent]$

[oracle@ggs-source bin]$ ./pw_agent_util.sh -create
JAVA_HOME not found
Enter JAVA_HOME : /usr/java/jdk1.7.0_67
/usr/java/jdk1.7.0_67
Please create a password for Java Agent:
```

```
Please confirm password for Java Agent:
Please enter Monitor Server JMX password:
Please confirm Monitor Server JMX password:
Oct 08, 2014 7:01:13 PM oracle.security.jps.JpsStartup start
INFO: Jps initializing.
Oct 08, 2014 7:01:18 PM oracle.security.jps.JpsStartup start
INFO: Jps started.
Wallet is created successfully.
[oracle@ggs-source bin]$
```

Using the Oracle GoldenGate Monitor

The monitor is composed of several tab pages, either for viewing the real-time Oracle GoldenGate Instance or to provide an input for the Monitor settings. Figure 9-38 shows the Monitor default page after successful authentication. The Monitor default page includes the following tab pages:

- Data and Alert View
- Logs
- Configuration
- Problem Summary
- Historical Data
- Alert History
- Alert Definition
- User Management
- View Management

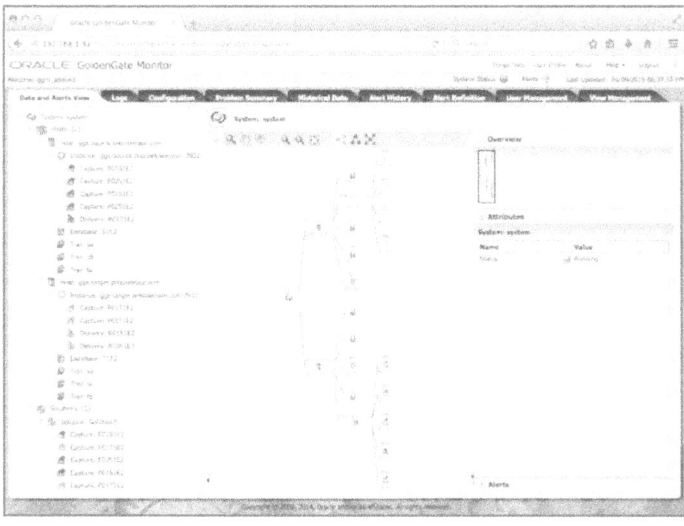

Figure 9-38: The Monitor Default Page

Navigation Tree and Diagram View

The Navigation Tree and Diagram View page is rendered based on the tab selected. When the 'Data and Alert View' tab is selected, it displays all discovered components. Click on a particular component to drill-down and focus for a more detailed view. Figure 9-39 shows the source of the Oracle GoldenGate Instance.

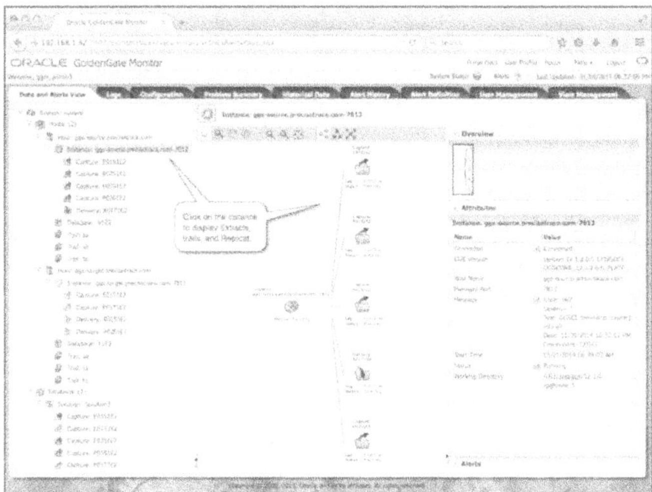

Figure 9-39: Navigation Tree and Diagram View

Creating the Monitor Alerts

A core function of the Monitor is alerts. Alerts help GoldenGate administrators to take corrective action before problems further escalate. Use the following steps to configure Alerts.

Click on the 'Alert Definition' tab. It displays the list of configured Alerts. Click on 'New Alert Definition' at the bottom, as shown in Figure 9-40.

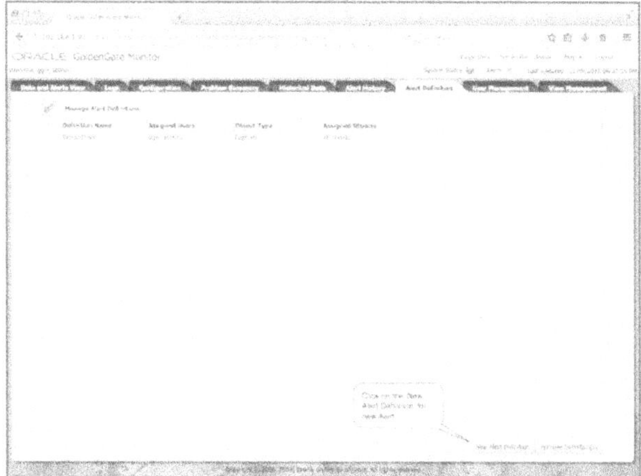

Figure 9-40: Alert Definition List

Let's define an Alert for notification when a specific Extract is not functioning.

```
GGSCI (ggs-source.precisetrace.com) 1> info all
Program      Status       Group        Lag at Chkpt  Time Since Chkpt
MANAGER      RUNNING
JAGENT       RUNNING
EXTRACT      RUNNING      E01S1E2      00:00:00      00:00:04
EXTRACT      RUNNING      E02S1E2      00:00:00      00:00:07
EXTRACT      RUNNING      P01S1E2      00:00:00      00:00:06
EXTRACT      RUNNING      P02S1E2      00:00:00      00:00:06
REPLICAT     RUNNING      R01T1E2      00:00:00      00:00:06

GGSCI (ggs-source.precisetrace.com) 2>
```

'Enter the Definition Name,' 'Assign the Alert Severity.' 'Select Group Name or Expression Attribute', 'Enter the value, Name of Extract,' 'Select Assigned Users,' and 'Select Assigned Objects.'

Submit the Alert Definition. Click on the 'Data and Alert View' tab.

Kill the monitored Extract E01S1E2 to trigger the Alert.

```
GGSCI (ggs-source.precisetrace.com) 8> KILL EXTRACT E01S1E2
Sending KILL request to MANAGER ...
Killed process (4504) for EXTRACT E01S1E2
GGSCI (ggs-source.precisetrace.com)
```

Restarting the Extract E01S1E2 clears the System Status.

It may take several minutes for the System Status to change to 'Running'.

```
GGSCI (ggs-source.precisetrace.com) 9> Start E01S1E2

Sending START request to MANAGER ...
EXTRACT E01S1E2 starting

GGSCI (ggs-source.precisetrace.com) 10> info all
```

```
Program     Status      Group       Lag at Chkpt  Time Since Chkpt

MANAGER     RUNNING
JAGENT      RUNNING
EXTRACT     STARTING    E01S1E2     00:00:00      00:10:23
EXTRACT     RUNNING     E02S1E2     00:00:00      00:00:00
EXTRACT     RUNNING     P01S1E2     00:00:00      00:00:06
EXTRACT     RUNNING     P02S1E2     00:00:00      00:00:04
REPLICAT    RUNNING     R01T1E2     00:00:00      00:00:04

GGSCI (ggs-source.precisetrace.com) 11>
```

Creating the Monitor Customized Views

Customized Views enable GoldenGate administrators to monitor specific areas of more complex solutions.
The following demonstrate creating a view of the Extract and its local trail only. It associates an alert to monitor the activities of the capture and writing to the local trail. The following steps illustrate creation of the solution.

- Click on the 'View Management' tab. It displays existing solutions, if any.

- Click on 'New View.' Enter the 'View Name' and 'Description' (optional). Create the view by performing a drag-and-drop on the view area. The view component is linked automatically. Click 'Submit' to save the diagram.

- Continue performing drag-and-drop until all related objects are linked. The following solution illustrates a bi-directional topology.

Dropping the Monitor Repository

In case of a failure creating the Monitor WebLogic Server domain, it may be a good idea to drop and re-create the repository. By dropping and recreating the repository, database schema issues and unused metadata are avoided. The following steps show the process of dropping the repository using the Repository Utility.

Starting the Repository Creation Utility

The Repository Creation Utility enables the creating and dropping of the Monitor Server Database Repository. We start the Repository Creation Utility by navigating to '/home/oracle/Oracle/Middleware/Oracle_Home1/oracle_common/bin' and execute the script 'rcu' as illustrated here:

```
[oracle@gg-monitor bin]$ pwd
```

```
/home/oracle/Oracle/Middleware/Oracle_Home1/oracle_common/bin
[oracle@gg-monitor bin]$ ./rcu
```

Prior to starting the Repository Creation Utility to drop the repository, ascertain that none of the active sessions are related to the Monitor Server. Otherwise, the Repository Creation Utility is prevented from being successfully completed.

Use the following Domain prefix to query the Monitor's database active sessions and terminate them using the 'KILL SESSION' command as illustrated here:

```
SQL> SELECT username, sid, serial#
  2  FROM   v$session
  3  WHERE  username LIKE 'GGM1%';

USERNAME                              SID    SERIAL#
------------------------------ ---------- ----------
GGM1_OPSS                              47      64709

SQL> ALTER SYSTEM KILL SESSION '47, 64709' IMMEDIATE;

System altered.

SQL>
```

If the database is dedicated to the Monitor Server Database Repository, a shutdown and start of the database instance is also an option. Use this method to avoid issuing multiple 'KILL SESSION' commands.

Welcome

Dropping the Monitor's Repository is a very destructive operation. It removes all database-related components and is unrecoverable. The drop operation removes the database tablespaces and schemas. Click 'Cancel' to terminate the utility or click 'Next' to proceed dropping the Repository.

Drop Repository

Select the 'Drop Repository' option. To avoid a privilege-related error, use database users with 'DBA' or 'SYSDBA' as shown in Step 2. Click 'Next' to proceed.

Database Connection Details

Depending on the 'Database Type' selected, the inputs change accordingly. Selecting 'Oracle Database' requires providing the following values:

- Host Name or IP address.
- Database Listener Port (default 1521) and Service Name.
- Database Username, Password and Role, SYSDBA for SYS Username.

Select Components

Select the prefix. Check the 'AS Common Schemas' and 'Oracle GoldenGate' options. Click 'Next' to proceed.

Summary

Review the Summary page. It outlines the Database details and the operation type. It also includes the list of database components, database schemas, and tablespaces. To proceed, click 'Drop'.

Completion Summary

The 'Drop' operation is relatively short. It takes less than 10 minutes to complete. Review the status and the log file.
Click 'Close' to terminate the Repository Creation Utility.

Summary

This chapter covered the Oracle GoldenGate Management Pack, which delivers an end-to-end Oracle GoldenGate Graphical User Interface (GUI) platform. This platform promotes much needed ease-of-use, productivity, and set standards & conventions throughout the development process. This chapter covered the following products:

- Oracle GoldenGate Director
- Oracle GoldenGate Monitor

The Oracle GoldenGate Director (The Director) and a Graphical User Interface (GUI) is used for configuring Oracle GoldenGate Capture and Delivery processes. It provides an intuitive diagramming tool using a drag-and-drop technique quickly, which creates an end-to-end data movement environment. It has a Java Desktop Client and Web Client. The Administration Client defines the building blocks for the Director – Data Sources, Accounts, Monitor Agents, and Suffix. The Director Client is the diagramming tool for defining the different types of Capture and Delivery processes. The web client is a browser-based set of applications for basic replication monitoring.

The Oracle GoldenGate Monitor (The Monitor), a browser-based set of applications interfaces for advanced monitoring of the Oracle GoldenGate environment. Using a drag-and-drop technique, the Monitor creates network views for Oracle GoldenGate existing topologies. Various advanced alert systems are available which cover a comprehensive set of conditions for Capture and Delivery processes. When the condition is satisfied, the notification is sent to the various receiving clients. Since metadata and configuration are consistent, alert history is available for trend analysis and performance impacts and prediction.

Oracle GoldenGate Management Pack also includes the Oracle Enterprise Manager (EM) Plug-In, an integrated console for basic monitoring and management of Oracle GoldenGate. Capture and Delivery processes of real-time status are tracked and graphing of lags and statistics are available from a single console. EM GoldenGate Plug-In uses an existing infrastructure and repository. Hence, it is deployed instantly — making it an attractive Oracle GoldenGate Management solution.

An extended version of Chapter 9 including all screenshots is available:

www.rampant.cc/GoldenGate-Chap9.pdf

An extended version of Chapter 9 including all screenshots is available:

www.rampant.cc/GoldenGate-Chap9.pdf

Oracle GoldenGate Advanced Integrations & Replications

CHAPTER

Overview

Enterprise Database Applications employ the database features for different purposes. Mission Critical Applications run on a deployed, clustered database environment using Oracle Real Application Clusters (RAC). For regulation and compliance, database applications connect to a primary database protected by one or more physical standby databases deployed using Oracle Data Guard (DG). Oracle GoldenGate highly supports these types of advanced environments.

The Oracle GoldenGate strategic direction has depreciated Oracle Streams. Customers are advised to migrate their data replication from Oracle Streams to Oracle GoldenGate. Oracle GoldenGate 11g release 2 for Oracle database supports of integrated capture for enabling downstream systems support and removing major limitations found in classic capture. For best scalability of large scale systems with massive transformation, intermediate systems promote data management scalability and eliminate overhead on the source and target systems.

The need to replicate Data Definition Language (DDL) is essential for dynamic in-house, developed database applications. Changes to the source database objects are replicated transparently — eliminating the need for the Database Administrators (DBAs) to manage actively changing database schemas.

This chapter covers advanced Oracle Database features requiring a high level of Oracle database administration skills. This chapter illustrates and explains the following:

- Oracle Data Guard (DG) Integration
- Migration from Oracle Streams to GoldenGate
- Integrated Capture for Oracle Database
- Intermediate Systems Support for Extreme Scalability
- Data Definition Language (DDL) Statements Replication

Although this chapter was developed using Oracle GoldenGate 12c for Oracle Database 12c, the same concepts and configuration parameters apply to Oracle Database 11g, with the exception of Oracle Database 12c Multi-Tenant.

Oracle Data Guard (DG) Integration

Oracle Data Guard is designed for deploying disaster recovery (DR) solutions. For some organizations, the availability of Data is very crucial for daily operations. Mirroring of Data using hardware is by far more costly and requires a greater level of experience to manage the different components. The Data Guard is an integrated component of the Oracle database and uses the Online Redo Log architecture to implement the "industry most reliable yet cost effective" disaster recovery solution for businesses. Depending on business requirements, Data Guard can be configured using different modes. Oracle Data Guard can be implemented with maximum protection, maximum availability, and maximum performance. A decision is made by evaluating Data availability and Data protection to decide on the Data Guard protection mode.

For systems requiring continuous availability, planned and unplanned downtimes are not an acceptable option. These systems need to be designed so that they are protected to be operational during either type of downtime situations to ensure the continuity of the business. Planned downtime occurs for a specific purpose during a specific time interval. Upgrading the system is a very common planned downtime. To minimize the downtime and the loss of data, production databases are protected by the complete infrastructure known as Oracle Data Guard. Unplanned downtime may occur as a result of instance failure, disk failure, data corruption, complete disaster, or human error. Based on the business requirement for high availability, it may be necessary to switch to a standby database to avoid such downtime intervals. Since failover to a standby database is a one-way operation and requires a rebuild afterwards, a decision has to be made whether to repair the production database or to failover to the standby database. Depending on the type of failure, the proper recovery technique is used. For example, a user error can be fixed using "Flashback" without the need of a standby failover.

GoldenGate and Data Guard Architecture

One of the objectives for integrating an Oracle GoldenGate in a Data Guard environment is to spin off a read-write database instance used by other application systems. Figure 10-1 illustrates the installed components and the install locations of Oracle GoldenGate. The Oracle Database S1C1 is the primary database (source) which is protected by a physical standby database. The Data Guard broker performs an asynchronous redo transport to a maintained synchronized read-only remote database. Oracle GoldenGate captures from the standby archived file and delivers to the remote database T1C1. This database is open on a read-write mode operating with the Flashback database enabled suitable for testing, reporting and other applications.

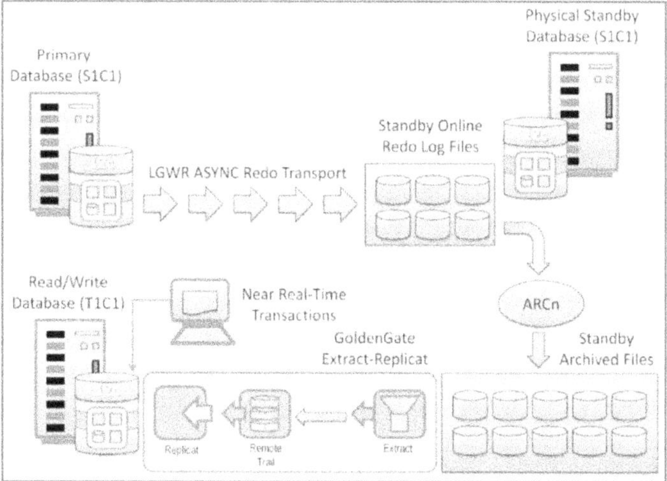

Figure 10-1: Oracle GoldenGate in a Data Guard Environment

Since the Extract ES1C101 is configured to operate on the "Archived Log Only" (ALO) mode, the target database remains behind the source database. When T1C1 is supporting non-critical application types, the capture is implemented to write directly to a remote trail – './dirdat/ta' rather than using a secondary capture (Data Pump). The Replicat RT1C101 applies the transactions to the target database using the native database interface. The use of a parallel Replicat is recommended to support heavy volume of archived redo log files. Refer to Chapter 1 for more details regarding implementing capture and delivery parallelism.

Creating Physical Standby Using RMAN

There are several methods for creating a physical standby database. The following sections illustrates the creation of a standby database using the Recovery Manager (RMAN). Use the following steps to create the physical standby database for the primary database S1C1.

- Enable and verify a database force logging option (Primary)
- Configure the standby redo log files (Primary)
- Configure archive log location parameters (Primary)

- Configure Data Guard Broker parameters (Primary)
- Enable database archive option (Primary)
- Perform an online backup using RMAN (Primary)
- Configure the Oracle SQLNET Network (Standby)
- Transfer the Oracle password file to the standby system
- Create the basic parameter file (Standby)
- Create the directories structure (Standby)
- Start the instance on the NOMOUNT state (Standby)
- Prepare and run the RMAN DUPLICATE command (Primary)
- Verify transactions' log shipping (Primary, Standby)
- Start the Data Guard Broker (Primary, Standby)
- Verify Data Guard Broker configuration (Primary, Standby)
- Verify database's Data Guard transport and application (Primary, Standby)

Enable and Verify Database Force Logging Option (Primary)

By default, the Oracle database force logging option is disabled at the database level while enabled at the tablespace and object level. However, to guarantee that the transaction logging of the primary database logging is overridden at the tablespace or object levels, it's required by the Data Guard to enable the database logging at the database level. This overrides no forced logging when specified at tablespace or object levels.

```
SQL> CONN / AS SYSDBA
Connected.
SQL> SELECT force_logging
  2  FROM   v$database;

FORCE_LOGGING
---------------------------------------
NO

SQL> ALTER DATABASE FORCE LOGGING;

Database altered.

SQL> SELECT force_logging
  2  FROM   v$database;

FORCE_LOGGING
---------------------------------------
YES

SQL>
```

Configure the Standby Redo Log Files (Primary)

When the database is operating on standby role, the received transaction logs are written to the standby redo log files and not to the online redo log files. Primarily, to avoids creating the standby redo log files manually on the standby database in the event of database role change. Because best practices suggest identical transactions log configuration, the online standby redo log files are created on the primary database and copied over to the standby database using RMAN. To avoid contention on the standby redo log files, the number of standby redo log groups should be one more than the online redo log groups.

```
SQL> SELECT group#, bytes/1024/1024 "M"
  2  FROM   v$log;

    GROUP#          M
---------- ----------
         1         50
         2         50
         3         50

SQL> ALTER DATABASE ADD STANDBY LOGFILE
  2  '/u01/app/oracle/fast_recovery_area/S1C1/onlinelog/stdby01.log'
  3  SIZE 50M;

Database altered.

SQL> ALTER DATABASE ADD STANDBY LOGFILE
  2  '/u01/app/oracle/fast_recovery_area/S1C1/onlinelog/stdby02.log'
  3  SIZE 50M;

Database altered.

SQL> ALTER DATABASE ADD STANDBY LOGFILE
  2  '/u01/app/oracle/fast_recovery_area/S1C1/onlinelog/stdby03.log'
  3  SIZE 50M;

Database altered.

SQL> ALTER DATABASE ADD STANDBY LOGFILE
  2  '/u01/app/oracle/fast_recovery_area/S1C1/onlinelog/stdby04.log'
  3  SIZE 50M;

Database altered.

SQL>
```

Configure Archive Log Location Parameters (Primary)

Add the following parameters needed to operate a standby database. Best practices uses the Fast Recovery Area (FRA) as the local archived files location. The redo transport will be operating on Maximum Performance mode as it's configured using the parameter LOG_ARCHIVE_DEST_2.

Parameter	Description
LOG_ARCHIVE_DEST_1	The Archive Log File Destination
LOG_ARCHIVE_CONFIG	The List of Database Unique Names
LOG_ARCHIVE_DEST_2	The Mode, Valid Role, and Unique Names' Specification
DG_BROKER_START	The Enable Data Guard Command-Line

```
SQL> ALTER SYSTEM SET log_archive_dest_1 =
  2  'LOCATION=USE_DB_RECOVERY_FILE_DEST';

System altered.

SQL>
```

Configure Data Guard Broker Parameters (Primary)

The Data Guard uses the list of unique database names (S1C1 and T2C1) for managing the broker's configuration. The parameter LOG_ARCHIVE_CONFIG lists the unique names for the primary and standby databases. The parameter LOG_ARCHIVE_DEST_2 configures the redo transport, the protection mode, and the optional optimization parameters.

```
SQL> ALTER SYSTEM SET log_archive_config =
  2  'dg_config=(S1C1, T1C1)';

System altered.

SQL> ALTER SYSTEM SET
  2  log_archive_dest_2 = 'service=T1C1 ASYNC
  3  valid_for=(online_logfile,primary_role)
  4  db_unique_name=T1C1';

System altered.

SQL>
```

Enable Database Archive Option (Primary)

Enabling the database archive mode, the archived destination is the Fast Recovery Area (FRA) as it's configured using LOG_ARCHIVE_DEST_1.

```
SQL> SHUTDOWN IMMEDIATE
Database closed.
Database dismounted.
ORACLE instance shut down.
SQL> STARTUP MOUNT
```

```
ORACLE instance started.

Total System Global Area   413372416 bytes
Fixed Size                   2289016 bytes
Variable Size              331350664 bytes
Database Buffers            75497472 bytes
Redo Buffers                 4235264 bytes
Database mounted.
SQL> ALTER DATABASE ARCHIVELOG;

Database altered.

SQL> ALTER DATABASE OPEN;

Database altered.

SQL>
```

Perform an Online Backup Using RMAN (Primary)

Perform an online database backup which will be used by the RMAN DUPLICATE command to instantiate the standby database. Set the size of the FRA to support the backup of the database and archived log files while considering the retention policy of database & archived log files.

```
SQL> ALTER SYSTEM SET
  2  db_recovery_file_dest_size=10G;

System altered.

SQL> exit
Disconnected from Oracle Database 12c Enterprise Edition Release 12.1.0.1.0
- 64bit Production
With the Partitioning, OLAP, Advanced Analytics and Real Application Testing
options
[oracle@source1 ~]$ rman

Recovery Manager: Release 12.1.0.1.0 - Production on Tue Feb 24 15:18:17
2015

Copyright (c) 1982, 2013, Oracle and/or its affiliates.  All rights
reserved.

RMAN> CONNECT TARGET

connected to target database: S1C1 (DBID=130281323)

RMAN> BACKUP DATABASE PLUS ARCHIVELOG;


Starting backup at 24-FEB-15
current log archived
using target database control file instead of recovery catalog
allocated channel: ORA_DISK_1
channel ORA_DISK_1: SID=40 device type=DISK
```

```
channel ORA_DISK_1: starting archived log backup set
channel ORA_DISK_1: specifying archived log(s) in backup set
input archived log thread=1 sequence=5 RECID=1 STAMP=872522132
input archived log thread=1 sequence=6 RECID=2 STAMP=872522350
channel ORA_DISK_1: starting piece 1 at 24-FEB-15
channel ORA_DISK_1: finished piece 1 at 24-FEB-15
piece
handle=/u01/app/oracle/fast_recovery_area/S1C1/backupset/2015_02_24/o1_mf_an
nnn_TAG20150224T151912_bgrv20ro_.bkp tag=TAG20150224T151912 comment=NONE
channel ORA_DISK_1: backup set complete, elapsed time: 00:00:01
Finished backup at 24-FEB-15

Starting backup at 24-FEB-15
using channel ORA_DISK_1
channel ORA_DISK_1: starting full datafile backup set
channel ORA_DISK_1: specifying datafile(s) in backup set
input datafile file number=00001
name=/u01/app/oracle/oradata/S1C1/datafile/o1_mf_system_bgqw43fp_.dbf
input datafile file number=00003
name=/u01/app/oracle/oradata/S1C1/datafile/o1_mf_sysaux_bgqw1d5w_.dbf
input datafile file number=00004
name=/u01/app/oracle/oradata/S1C1/datafile/o1_mf_undotbs1_bgqw74ps_.dbf
input datafile file number=00006
name=/u01/app/oracle/oradata/S1C1/datafile/o1_mf_users_bgqw73dz_.dbf
channel ORA_DISK_1: starting piece 1 at 24-FEB-15
channel ORA_DISK_1: finished piece 1 at 24-FEB-15
piece
handle=/u01/app/oracle/fast_recovery_area/S1C1/backupset/2015_02_24/o1_mf_nn
ndf_TAG20150224T151914_bgrv22dc_.bkp tag=TAG20150224T151914 comment=NONE
channel ORA_DISK_1: backup set complete, elapsed time: 00:01:37
channel ORA_DISK_1: starting full datafile backup set
channel ORA_DISK_1: specifying datafile(s) in backup set
including current control file in backup set
including current SPFILE in backup set
channel ORA_DISK_1: starting piece 1 at 24-FEB-15
channel ORA_DISK_1: finished piece 1 at 24-FEB-15
piece
handle=/u01/app/oracle/fast_recovery_area/S1C1/backupset/2015_02_24/o1_mf_nc
snf_TAG20150224T151914_bgrv54wb_.bkp tag=TAG20150224T151914 comment=NONE
channel ORA_DISK_1: backup set complete, elapsed time: 00:00:01
Finished backup at 24-FEB-15

Starting backup at 24-FEB-15
current log archived
using channel ORA_DISK_1
channel ORA_DISK_1: starting archived log backup set
channel ORA_DISK_1: specifying archived log(s) in backup set
input archived log thread=1 sequence=7 RECID=3 STAMP=872522454
channel ORA_DISK_1: starting piece 1 at 24-FEB-15
channel ORA_DISK_1: finished piece 1 at 24-FEB-15
piece
handle=/u01/app/oracle/fast_recovery_area/S1C1/backupset/2015_02_24/o1_mf_an
nnn_TAG20150224T152054_bgrv56s9_.bkp tag=TAG20150224T152054 comment=NONE
channel ORA_DISK_1: backup set complete, elapsed time: 00:00:01
Finished backup at 24-FEB-15
RMAN>
```

Configure Oracle SQLNET Network (Standby)

Configure the standby database listener and bi-directional connection for SQL NET. Test connections using the TNSPING utility before proceeding further. Perform configuration and test it, bi-directionally.

```
[oracle@target1 ~]$ cat /etc/hosts
# Do not remove the following line, or various programs
# that require network functionality will fail.
127.0.0.1           localhost.localdomain localhost
::1         localhost6.localdomain6 localhost6
192.168.1.152       target1.precisetrace.com
192.168.1.140       source1.precisetrace.com
[oracle@target1 ~]$ tnsping S1C1

TNS Ping Utility for Linux: Version 12.1.0.1.0 - Production on 23-FEB-2015
16:47:09

Copyright (c) 1997, 2013, Oracle.  All rights reserved.

Used parameter files:


Used TNSNAMES adapter to resolve the alias
Attempting to contact (DESCRIPTION = (ADDRESS_LIST = (ADDRESS = (PROTOCOL =
TCP)(HOST = source1.precisetrace.com)(PORT = 1521))) (CONNECT_DATA =
(SERVICE_NAME = S1C1.precisetrace.com)))
OK (0 msec)
[oracle@target1 ~]$ tnsping T1C1

TNS Ping Utility for Linux: Version 12.1.0.1.0 - Production on 23-FEB-2015
16:47:19

Copyright (c) 1997, 2013, Oracle.  All rights reserved.

Used parameter files:


Used TNSNAMES adapter to resolve the alias
Attempting to contact (DESCRIPTION = (ADDRESS_LIST = (ADDRESS = (PROTOCOL =
TCP)(HOST = target1.precisetrace.com)(PORT = 1521))) (CONNECT_DATA =
(SERVICE_NAME = T1C1.precisetrace.com)))
OK (0 msec)
[oracle@target1 ~]$
```

Transfer the Oracle Password File to the Standby System

The transport services use the password to authenticate the SYS user remote using the password file. Transfer the password file of the primary database to the standby database. The change of permission setting may be necessary.

```
[root@source1 dbs]# scp orapwS1C1
root@target1.precisetrace.com:/u01/app/oracle/product/12.1.0/dbhome_1/dbs
```

```
root@target1.precisetrace.com's password:
orapwS1C1                                    100% 7680     7.5KB/s   00:00
[root@target1 dbs]# chown oracle:oinstall orapwS1C1
[root@target1 dbs]#
```

Create the Basic Parameter File (Standby)

Prepare the standby database parameter file. It will contain the database name parameter only - DB_NAME=T1C1. Other parameters are applied by the RMAN DUPLICATE command. The list of related standby parameters are:

- db_unique_name
- db_create_file_dest
- db_recovery_file_dest
- db_recovery_file_dest_size
- control_files
- log_archive_max_processes
- fal_client
- fal_server
- standby_file_management

Create the Directories Structure (Standby)

Create the directory structure with proper permissions to avoid read/write errors when running the RMAN DUPLICATE command. Login as oracle and verify that the umask environment is set to 022.

```
[oracle@target1 ~]$ cd /u01/app/oracle/admin/
[oracle@target1 admin]$ mkdir T1C1
[oracle@target1 admin]$ cd T1C1
[oracle@target1 T1C1]$ mkdir adump dpdump pfile
[oracle@target1 T1C1]$
```

Start the Instance on NOMOUNT State (Standby)

Use the parameter file to start the standby instance on NOMOUNT state. This allows the DUPLICATE command to create the standby control file as specified by the parameter CONTROL_FILES.

```
SQL> STARTUP NOMOUNT PFILE='$ORACLE_HOME/dbs/initT1C1.ora'
ORACLE instance started.
Total System Global Area   217157632 bytes
Fixed Size                   2286656 bytes
Variable Size              159386560 bytes
Database Buffers            50331648 bytes
Redo Buffers                 5152768 bytes
SQL>
```

Prepare and Run the RMAN DUPLICATE Command (Primary)

Prepare and run the RMAN DUPLCIATE command. Before attempting to run the command, check the syntax using the RMAN command 'checksyntax' as illustrated below. There are several methods to run the RMAN DUPLICATE command. The command below is executed using an active database, which absolutely eliminates database downtime.

```
[oracle@source1 dbs]$ rman

Recovery Manager: Release 12.1.0.1.0 - Production on Tue Mar 3 05:25:19 2015

Copyright (c) 1982, 2013, Oracle and/or its affiliates.  All rights
reserved.

RMAN> connect target sys/oracle_4U@S1C1

connected to target database: S1C1 (DBID=130281323)

RMAN> connect auxiliary sys/oracle_4U@T1C1

connected to auxiliary database: T1C1 (not mounted)

RMAN> @rmandup.txt

run {
allocate channel s1c11 type disk;
allocate channel s1c12 type disk;
allocate channel s1c13 type disk;
allocate channel s1c14 type disk;
allocate auxiliary channel t1c11 type disk;
duplicate target database for standby from active database NOFILENAMECHECK
spfile
parameter_value_convert 'S1C1','T1C1'
set db_unique_name='T1C1'
set db_create_file_dest='/u01/app/oracle/oradata/T1C1/datafile'
set db_file_name_convert='/u01/app/oracle/oradata/S1C1/datafile',
'/u01/app/oracle/oradata/T1C1/datafile'
setlog_file_name_convert='/u01/app/oracle/fast_recovery_area/S1C1/onlinelog'
, '/u01/app/oracle/fast_recovery_area/T1C1/onlinelog'
set db_recovery_file_dest='/u01/app/oracle/fast_recovery_area'
set db_recovery_file_dest_size='8G'
set control_files='/u01/app/oracle/oradata/T1C1/datafile/controlfile'
set log_archive_max_processes='5'
set fal_server='S1C1'
set fal_client='T1C1'
set standby_file_management='AUTO'
set log_archive_config='dg_config=(S1C1,T1C1)'
set log_archive_dest_1='LOCATION=/u01/app/oracle/archivelog
valid_for=(all_logfiles, all_roles) db_unique_name=S1C1'
set log_archive_dest_2='service=T1C1 LGWR ASYNC
valid_for=(ONLINE_LOGFILES,PRIMARY_ROLES) db_unique_name=T1C1'
set log_archive_dest_state_1='enable'
set log_archive_dest_state_2='enable';
}
```

```
using target database control file instead of recovery catalog
allocated channel: s1c11
channel s1c11: SID=79 device type=DISK

allocated channel: s1c12
channel s1c12: SID=77 device type=DISK

allocated channel: s1c13
channel s1c13: SID=67 device type=DISK

allocated channel: s1c14
channel s1c14: SID=73 device type=DISK

allocated channel: t1c11
channel t1c11: SID=21 device type=DISK

Starting Duplicate Db at 03-MAR-15

contents of Memory Script:
{
   backup as copy reuse
   targetfile  '/u01/app/oracle/product/12.1.0/dbhome_1/dbs/orapwS1C1'
auxiliary format
 '/u01/app/oracle/product/12.1.0/dbhome_1/dbs/orapwT1C1'   targetfile
 '/u01/app/oracle/product/12.1.0/dbhome_1/dbs/spfileS1C1.ora' auxiliary
format
 '/u01/app/oracle/product/12.1.0/dbhome_1/dbs/spfileT1C1.ora'   ;
   sql clone "alter system set spfile=
''/u01/app/oracle/product/12.1.0/dbhome_1/dbs/spfileT1C1.ora''";
}
executing Memory Script

Starting backup at 03-MAR-15
Finished backup at 03-MAR-15
…
…
executing Memory Script

datafile 1 switched to datafile copy
input datafile copy RECID=1 STAMP=873264744 file
name=/u01/app/oracle/oradata/T1C1/datafile/o1_mf_system_bgqw43fp_.dbf
datafile 3 switched to datafile copy
input datafile copy RECID=2 STAMP=873264744 file
name=/u01/app/oracle/oradata/T1C1/datafile/o1_mf_sysaux_bgqw1d5w_.dbf
datafile 4 switched to datafile copy
input datafile copy RECID=3 STAMP=873264744 file
name=/u01/app/oracle/oradata/T1C1/datafile/o1_mf_undotbs1_bgqw74ps_.dbf
datafile 6 switched to datafile copy
input datafile copy RECID=4 STAMP=873264744 file
name=/u01/app/oracle/oradata/T1C1/datafile/o1_mf_users_bgqw73dz_.dbf
Finished Duplicate Db at 03-MAR-15
released channel: s1c11
released channel: s1c12
released channel: s1c13
released channel: s1c14
released channel: t1c11
RMAN> **end-of-file**

RMAN>
```

Login to the Standby database and verify the database state and role.

```
SQL> CONN sys/oracle_4U AS SYSDBA
Connected.
SQL> SELECT open_mode, database_role
  2  FROM   v$database;

OPEN_MODE            DATABASE_ROLE
-------------------- ----------------
MOUNTED              PHYSICAL STANDBY

SQL>
```

Verify Transactions Log Shipping (Primary, Standby)

Perform a manual online redo log file switch command. This verifies that the database is shipping the archived redo log files to the standby database system. Also, verify the archived file shipping and application are consistent.

```
SQL> CONN sys/oracle_4U@S1C1 AS SYSDBA
Connected.
SQL> SELECT MAX(sequence#)
  2  FROM   v$archived_log;

MAX(SEQUENCE#)
--------------
            66

SQL> CONN sys/oracle_4U@T1C1 AS SYSDBA
Connected.
SQL> SELECT MAX(sequence#)
  2  FROM   v$archived_log;

MAX(SEQUENCE#)
--------------
            66

SQL>
```

Start and Configure the Data Guard Broker (Primary or Standby)

Enable the Data Guard Broker for the primary & standby databases by setting the parameter DG_BROKER_START=TRUE.

```
SQL> ALTER SYSTEM SET dg_broker_start=TRUE SCOPE=BOTH;

System altered.

SQL>

DGMGRL> CREATE CONFIGURATION 'DGENV' AS
```

```
> PRIMARY DATABASE IS 'S1C1'
> CONNECT IDENTIFIER IS 'S1C1';
Configuration "DGENV" created with primary database "S1C1"
DGMGRL> ADD DATABASE 'T1C1' AS
> CONNECT IDENTIFIER IS 'T1C1';
Database "T1C1" added
DGMGRL> ENABLE CONFIGURATION;
Enabled.
```

Verify Data Guard Broker Configuration (Primary, Standby)

Perform this step from the primary & standby Data Guard instance. It will list the current primary & physical standby database. Ensure the status is 'SUCCESS' before proceeding to the next step. In case of warning due to inconsistent parameter settings, use the 'EDIT Data Guard' command to synchronize the settings. Review the Data Guard parameters settings as shown below.

```
DGMGRL> SHOW CONFIGURATION;

Configuration - DGENV

  Protection Mode: MaxPerformance
  Databases:
  S1C1 - Primary database
    T1C1 - Physical standby database

Fast-Start Failover: DISABLED

Configuration Status:
SUCCESS

DGMGRL> SHOW DATABASE VERBOSE 'S1C1';

Database - S1C1

  Role:              PRIMARY
  Intended State:    TRANSPORT-ON
  Instance(s):
    S1C1

  Properties:
    DGConnectIdentifier              = 'S1C1'
    ObserverConnectIdentifier        = ''
    LogXptMode                       = 'ASYNC'
    RedoRoutes                       = ''
    DelayMins                        = '0'
    Binding                          = 'optional'
    MaxFailure                       = '0'
    MaxConnections                   = '1'
    ReopenSecs                       = '300'
    NetTimeout                       = '30'
    RedoCompression                  = 'DISABLE'
    LogShipping                      = 'ON'
    PreferredApplyInstance           = ''
    ApplyInstanceTimeout             = '0'
```

```
    ApplyLagThreshold                = '0'
    TransportLagThreshold            = '0'
    TransportDisconnectedThreshold   = '30'
    ApplyParallel                    = 'AUTO'
    StandbyFileManagement            = 'MANUAL'
    ArchiveLagTarget                 = '0'
    LogArchiveMaxProcesses           = '4'
    LogArchiveMinSucceedDest         = '1'
    DbFileNameConvert                = ''
    LogFileNameConvert               = ''
    FastStartFailoverTarget          = ''
    InconsistentProperties           = '(monitor)'
    InconsistentLogXptProps          = '(monitor)'
    SendQEntries                     = '(monitor)'
    LogXptStatus                     = '(monitor)'
    RecvQEntries                     = '(monitor)'
    StaticConnectIdentifier          =
'(DESCRIPTION=(ADDRESS=(PROTOCOL=tcp)(HOST=source1.precisetrace.com)(PORT=15
21))(CONNECT_DATA=(SERVICE_NAME=S1C1_DGMGRL.oracle-
ggs.com)(INSTANCE_NAME=S1C1)(SERVER=DEDICATED)))'
    StandbyArchiveLocation           = '/u01/app/oracle/archivelog'
    AlternateLocation                = ''
    LogArchiveTrace                  = '0'
    LogArchiveFormat                 = '%t_%s_%r.dbf'
    TopWaitEvents                    = '(monitor)'

Database Status:
SUCCESS

DGMGRL>
```

Test the Switchover Using the Data Guard (Primary, Standby)

Now, test the Switchover command. Perform the command from the primary database to perform a database role change, followed by a switch from the original standby (current primary) to reverse the database role.

```
DGMGRL> SWITCHOVER TO 'T1C1';
Performing switchover NOW, please wait...
Operation requires a connection to instance "T1C1" on database "T1C1"
Connecting to instance "T1C1"...
Connected as SYSDBA.
New primary database "T1C1" is opening...
Operation requires startup of instance "S1C1" on database "S1C1"
Starting instance "S1C1"...
ORACLE instance started.
Database mounted.
Switchover succeeded, new primary is "T1C1"
DGMGRL> CONNECT sys/oracle_4U
Connected as SYSDG.
DGMGRL> SHOW CONFIGURATION;

Configuration - DGConfig

  Protection Mode: MaxPerformance
  Databases:
```

```
  T1C1 - Primary database
    S1C1 - Physical standby database

Fast-Start Failover: DISABLED

Configuration Status:
SUCCESS

DGMGRL> SWITCHOVER TO 'S1C1';
Performing switchover NOW, please wait...
Operation requires a connection to instance "S1C1" on database "S1C1"
Connecting to instance "S1C1"...
Connected as SYSDBA.
New primary database "S1C1" is opening...
Operation requires startup of instance "T1C1" on database "T1C1"
Starting instance "T1C1"...
ORACLE instance started.
Database mounted.
Switchover succeeded, new primary is "S1C1"
DGMGRL> SHOW CONFIGURATION;

Configuration - DGConfig

  Protection Mode: MaxPerformance
  Databases:
  S1C1 - Primary database
    T1C1 - Physical standby database

Fast-Start Failover: DISABLED

Configuration Status:
SUCCESS

DGMGRL>
```

Configure Oracle GoldenGate for the Standby Database

The next step is to configure the Oracle GoldenGate capture using the "Archived Log Only" (ALO) mode. The capture process reads from the Standby database archived log files and the delivery process writes to the target database, opened on read/write mode. To minimize the lag, create a series of primary database online redo log groups with a log switch to sustain the lag maximum target.

Enabling Archived Log Only Mode

The purpose of operating Oracle GoldenGate on the Archived Log Only (ALO) mode is for the non-real-time data capture to be acceptable. It's configured using the parameter 'TRANLOGOPTIONS'. The options of this parameter are database-specific for controlling non-standard log-based extract options. The following summarizes the common options when used for capture from Oracle archived log files.

```
TRANLOGOPTIONS ARCHIVEDLOGONLY
TRANLOGOPTIONS ALTARCHIVELOGDEST PRIMARY /u01/app/oracle/archivelog/
TRANLOGOPTIONS ALTARCHIVEDLOGFORMAT %t_%s_%r.dbf
```

If the error 'OGG-00730' (no minimum supplemental logging is enabled), this may cause the extract process to handle key update incorrectly if the key column is not in the first row piece. If this happens, then take the action below.

1. Disable supplemental logging temporarily by adding the parameter 'TRANLOGOPTIONS DISABLESUPPLOGCHECK.'
2. Advance the extract position using the 'GGSCI ALTER' command:

   ```
   GGSCI (target1.precisetrace.com) 6> ALTER EXTRACT E01S1C1, BEGIN now
   EXTRACT altered.
   ```

3. Start the extract and wait until it processes beyond the RBA position
4. Stop the extract and disable the parameter 'TRANLOGOPTIONS DISABLESUPPLOGCHECK' and start it again.

Configure the Primary Extract Process

The primary extract capture transaction using the archived log file is a technique that's exclusive when using the option 'ARCHIVELOGONLY.' The Extract 'ES1C101' capture behavior is controlled by the parameter 'TRANLOGOPTIONS.'

```
GGSCI (target1.precisetrace.com) 4> EDIT PARAMS E01S1C1
```

```
EXTRACT E01S1C1
SETENV (ORACLE_SID=T1C1)
SETENV (ORACLE_HOME="/u01/app/oracle/product/12.1.0/dbhome_1")
SETENV (NLS_LANG=AMERICAN_AMERICA.AL32UTF8)
USERID ggs_admin, PASSWORD oracle SYSDBA
RMTHOST 192.168.1.70, MGRPORT 7810
RMTTRAIL ./dirdat/sa
DISCARDFILE ./dirrpt/E01S1C1.dsc, APPEND
REPORTCOUNT EVERY 30 MINUTES, RATE
-- TRANLOGOPTIONS DISABLESUPPLOGCHECK
TRANLOGOPTIONS ARCHIVEDLOGONLY
TRANLOGOPTIONS ALTARCHIVELOGDEST PRIMARY /u01/app/oracle/archivelog/
TRANLOGOPTIONS ALTARCHIVEDLOGFORMAT %t_%s_%r.dbf
FETCHOPTIONS, NOUSESNAPSHOT, NOUSELATESTVERSION, MISSINGROW REPORT
TABLE ggs_admin.customers, keycol(col1);
```

```
GGSCI (target1.precisetrace.com) 11> ADD EXTRACT E01S1C1, TRANLOG, BEGIN NOW
EXTRACT added.

GGSCI (target1.precisetrace.com) 12> ADD RMTTRAIL ./dirdat/sa, EXTRACT
E01S1C1
```

```
RMTTRAIL added.

GGSCI (target1.precisetrace.com) 13>
```

Configure the Delivery Process

The delivery process applies the transactions to the target database that is opened for read-write operations. Since the Extract captures the transactions from the standby database archived log files only and Extract & Replicat lags, the target database always is relatively out-of-sync with the primary database. Configuring a small size of the online redo groups and increasing the number of database archive processes reduces the gap between the primary & target databases.

```
GGSCI (t2c1.precisetrace.com) 3> EDIT PARAMS R01S1C1
```

```
REPLICAT R01S1C1
SETENV (ORACLE_SID=T1C1)
SETENV (NLS_LANG=AMERICAN_AMERICA.AL32UTF8)
USERID ggs_admin, PASSWORD oracle
ASSUMETARGETDEFS
DISCARDFILE ./dirrpt/r01S1C1.dsc, PURGE
MAP ggs_admin.customers, TARGET ggs_admin.customers;
```

```
GGSCI (t2c1.precisetrace.com) 8> ADD REPLICAT R01S1C1, EXTTRAIL ./dirdat/sa
REPLICAT added.

GGSCI (t2c1.precisetrace.com) 9>
```

Starting Replicat and Extract Processes

Begin by starting the Replicat 'R01S1C1.' The Replicat applies the remote trails to the target database – T1C1.

```
GGSCI (t2c1.precisetrace.com) 10> START REPLICAT R01S1C1

Sending START request to MANAGER ...
REPLICAT R01S1C1 starting


GGSCI (t2c1.precisetrace.com) 11> INFO ALL

Program     Status      Group       Lag at Chkpt  Time Since Chkpt

MANAGER     RUNNING
REPLICAT    RUNNING     R01S1C1     00:00:00      00:00:01


GGSCI (t2c1.precisetrace.com) 12>
```

Next, start the primary Extract 'E01S1C1.' Since there is no secondary extract (data pump) configured, the primary Extract performs the capture & route functions. It captures from the standby database archive log files and routes to the target database.

```
GGSCI (target1.precisetrace.com) 14> START EXTRACT E01S1C1

Sending START request to MANAGER ...
EXTRACT E01S1C1 starting


GGSCI (target1.precisetrace.com) 15> INFO ALL

Program     Status      Group       Lag at Chkpt  Time Since Chkpt

MANAGER     RUNNING
EXTRACT     RUNNING     E01S1C1     00:00:00      00:06:50


GGSCI (target1.precisetrace.com) 16>
```

Verify Extract, Replicat, and Lagging

During a normal database operation, there will be a gap. The database remains relatively unsynchronized and the target database is behind the primary database. Oracle GoldenGate lag is measured between the standby database and the target database only. For precise measurement, the use of Oracle GoldenGate Veridata between the primary (the target) is an excellent option.

```
GGSCI (t2c1.precisetrace.com) 12> LAG REPLICAT R01S1C1

Sending GETLAG request to REPLICAT R01S1C1 ...
No records yet processed.
At EOF, no more records to process.

GGSCI (t2c1.precisetrace.com) 13>
```

Migration from Oracle Streams to GoldenGate

Oracle Streams is an internal component of the Oracle database. Oracle Streams delivers a high-performance Oracle database replication only. Enterprises running multiple database types need a single software to support multiple database vendors with a flexible configuration environment.

According to Oracle strategic direction for data replication, Oracle GoldenGate has deprecated Oracle Streams. Oracle Streams will continue to be part of the database, but without taking advantage of the new release of Oracle Database.

Customers are encouraged to migrate from Oracle Streams to GoldenGate. The following illustrates the migration phases from Oracle Streams to Oracle GoldenGate. The migration is online and delivers near-zero downtime.

Migration Architecture

Enterprises running critical mission system demands on an online migration from Oracle Streams to Oracle GoldenGate. Users continue to access the existing database until the new target database is completely synchronized with the source database. For highly secured environments, the option of deploying Oracle GoldenGate integrated capture eliminates the requirement of installing Oracle GoldenGate on the production system. Instead, it's installed on a downstream system receiving a continuous streams of the database transaction logs for capture, routing, and delivery to the target database.

As shown in Figure 10-2, the migration consists of the following components:

- The Source Oracle Database (S1C1)
- Oracle Database Streams
- The Target Oracle Database (T1C1) for Oracle Streams
- Oracle GoldenGate Installation on the Source and Target Databases
- The Target Oracle Database (T2C1) for Oracle GoldenGate
- Oracle GoldenGate Veridata

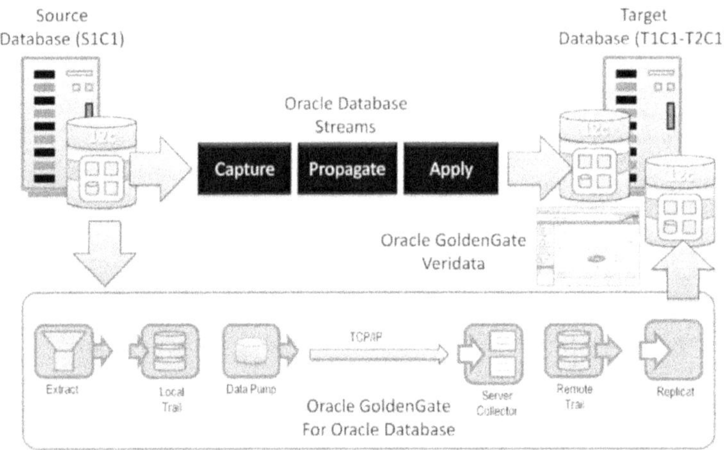

Figure 10-2: Migration from Streams to Oracle GoldenGate Components

GoldenGate Veridata helps make the decision to disable Oracle Streams after verifying the source and new target are synchronized. The downtime incurred is proportional to the database transactions volume at the time of momentarily disabling the source (production) database. Hence, the such decision should be carefully chosen during the lowest database transactions volume.

Oracle Streams Database Parameters

Oracle Streams set–up requires database parameters setting. These parameters have initial values. However, changing them enhances Oracle Streams performance and reliability.

```
SQL> ALTER DATABASE RENAME GLOBAL_NAME TO S2C1.ggs.com;

Database altered.

SQL> ALTER SYSTEM SET  aq_tm_processes = 1 SCOPE=BOTH;

System altered.

SQL> ALTER SYSTEM SET  job_queue_processes = 1000 SCOPE=BOTH;

System altered.

SQL>
```

Streams Database Administrator User

Oracle Streams needs a dedicated database user who is granted the privileges for performing the functions of Oracle Streams. The following statements create the tablespace and the user then grant the database privileges required by Oracle Streams.

Execute the below commands on the source and destination databases.

```
SQL> CREATE TABLESPACE STREAMSDB
  2  DATAFILE '/u01/app/oracle/oradata/S2C1/datafile/streamsdb01.dbf'
  3  SIZE 100M
  4  AUTOEXTEND ON;

Tablespace created.

SQL> CREATE USER streamadmin IDENTIFIED BY oracle
  2  DEFAULT TABLESPACE STREAMSDB
  3  QUOTA UNLIMITED ON STREAMSDB;

User created.

SQL> GRANT CONNECT, RESOURCE, AQ_ADMINISTRATOR_ROLE,DBA TO streamadmin;

Grant succeeded.

SQL> EXECUTE DBMS_STREAMS_AUTH.GRANT_ADMIN_PRIVILEGE('STREAMADMIN');
```

```
PL/SQL procedure successfully completed.

SQL> GRANT EXECUTE ON DBMS_AQADM TO streamadmin;

Grant succeeded.

SQL> GRANT EXECUTE ON DBMS_APPLY_ADM TO streamadmin;

Grant succeeded.

SQL> GRANT EXECUTE ON DBMS_CAPTURE_ADM TO streamadmin;

Grant succeeded.

SQL> GRANT EXECUTE ON DBMS_PROPAGATION_ADM TO streamadmin;

Grant succeeded.

SQL> GRANT EXECUTE ON DBMS_STREAMS TO streamadmin;

Grant succeeded.

SQL> GRANT EXECUTE ON DBMS_STREAMS_ADM TO streamadmin;

Grant succeeded.

SQL> BEGIN
  2  DBMS_RULE_ADM.GRANT_SYSTEM_PRIVILEGE(
  3  privilege =>DBMS_RULE_ADM.CREATE_RULE_SET_OBJ,
  4  grantee =>'streamadmin',
  5  grant_option =>FALSE);
  6  END;
  7  /

PL/SQL procedure successfully completed.

SQL>
```

Database Links

Oracle Streams uses Database Links to propagate database to the destination database. The database links connect to the Oracle Streams Schema created above. The following SQL commands create the database link and perform a basic test. Query the data dictionary view DBA_DB_LINKS to find database link details.

```
SQL> CREATE PUBLIC DATABASE LINK D1C1.ggs.com
  2  CONNECT TO streamadmin IDENTIFIED BY oracle
  3  USING 'D1C1.ggs.com';

Database link created.

SQL> SELECT * FROM dual@D1C1.ggs.com;

D
-
```

```
X

SQL> CREATE PUBLIC DATABASE LINK S2C1.ggs.com
  2  CONNECT TO streamadmin IDENTIFIED BY oracle
  3  USING 'S2C1.ggs.com';

Database link created.

SQL> SELECT * FROM dual@S2C1.ggs.com;

D
-
X

SQL>
```

Configure Streams Capture and Apply Queues

The capture and apply queues are created using multiple steps. The following PL/SQL steps create Oracle Streams ANYDATA queue, proration rules, and instantiation of the destination schema.

- Before creating any of Oracle Streams components, use the 'PL/SQL DBMS_STREAMS_ADM.SET_UP_QUEUE' to create any 'ANYDATA' queue. This queue is used by the capture, propagation, and application processes.

```
SQL> CONN streamadmin/oracle@S2C1.ggs.com
Connected.
SQL> BEGIN
  2  DBMS_STREAMS_ADM.SET_UP_QUEUE(
  3  queue_name =>'STREAMS_Q1',
  4  queue_table =>'STREAMS_Q1_TAB',
  5  queue_user =>'STREAMADMIN');
  6  END;
  7  /

PL/SQL procedure successfully completed.

SQL> CONN streamadmin/oracle@D1C1.ggs.com
Connected.
SQL> BEGIN
  2  DBMS_STREAMS_ADM.SET_UP_QUEUE(
  3  queue_name =>'STREAMS_Q1',
  4  queue_table =>'STREAMS_Q1_TAB',
  5  queue_user =>'STREAMADMIN');
  6  END;
  7  /

PL/SQL procedure successfully completed.
```

- Determine included and excluded messages. Use the package 'DBMS_STREAMS_ADM.ADD_TABLE_PROPAGATION_RULES.'

Specify the same Streams name, source queue, and destination queue as defined for the existing propagation.

```
SQL> CONN streamadmin/oracle@S2C1.ggs.com
Connected.
SQL> BEGIN
DBMS_STREAMS_ADM.ADD_GLOBAL_PROPAGATION_RULES(
streams_name =>'STREAMS_PROP_R1',
source_queue_name =>'STREAMADMIN.STREAMS_Q1',
destination_queue_name =>'STREAMADMIN.STREAMS_Q1@D1C1.ggs.com',
include_dml =>TRUE,
include_ddl =>TRUE,
source_database =>'S2C1.ggs.com');
END;
/

PL/SQL procedure successfully completed.

SQL> BEGIN
DBMS_STREAMS_ADM.ADD_GLOBAL_RULES(
streams_type =>'CAPTURE',
streams_name =>'STREAMADMIN_CAPTURE',
queue_name =>'STREAMADMIN.STREAMS_Q1',
include_dml =>TRUE,
include_ddl =>TRUE,
source_database =>'S2C1.ggs.com');
END;
/

PL/SQL procedure successfully completed.

SQL> CONN streamadmin/oracle@D1C1.ggs.com
Connected.
SQL> BEGIN
DBMS_STREAMS_ADM.ADD_GLOBAL_RULES(
streams_type =>'APPLY',
streams_name =>'STREAMADMIN_APPLY',
queue_name =>'STREAMADMIN.STREAMS_Q1',
include_dml =>TRUE,
include_ddl =>TRUE,
source_database =>'S2C1.ggs.com');
END;
/

PL/SQL procedure successfully completed.

SQL> BEGIN
DBMS_APPLY_ADM.SET_PARAMETER(
apply_name =>'STREAMADMIN_APPLY',
parameter =>'disable_on_error',
value =>'n');
END;
/

PL/SQL procedure successfully completed.
```

- From the source database, manually instantiate the destination schema as shown below. The instantiation uses the System Change Number (SCN) to ensure source and target objects are consistent from the determined SCN.

```
SQL> CONN streamadmin/oracle@S2C1.ggs.com
Connected.
SQL> DECLARE
       vscn NUMBER;
     BEGIN
        vscn:=DBMS_FLASHBACK.GET_SYSTEM_CHANGE_NUMBER();
        DBMS_APPLY_ADM.SET_SCHEMA_INSTANTIATION_SCN@S2C1.ggs.com(
        SOURCE_SCHEMA_NAME => 'SCOTT',
        SOURCE_DATABASE_NAME => 'D1C1.ggs.com',
        INSTANTIATION_SCN => vscn,
        RECURSIVE => TRUE);
     END;
     /

PL/SQL procedure successfully completed.

SQL> conn streamadmin/oracle@D1C1.ggs.com
Connected.
SQL> DECLARE
       vscn NUMBER;
     BEGIN
        vscn:=DBMS_FLASHBACK.GET_SYSTEM_CHANGE_NUMBER();
        DBMS_APPLY_ADM.SET_SCHEMA_INSTANTIATION_SCN@D1C1.ggs.com(
        SOURCE_SCHEMA_NAME => 'SCOTT',
        SOURCE_DATABASE_NAME => 'S2C1.ggs.com',
        INSTANTIATION_SCN => vscn,
        RECURSIVE => TRUE);
     END;
     /

PL/SQL procedure successfully completed.

SQL>
```

Starting the Application and Capture Processes

The final step is to start the application on the destination and capture on the source database.

```
SQL> CONN streamadmin/oracle@D1C1.ggs.com
Connected.
SQL> BEGIN
     DBMS_APPLY_ADM.START_APPLY(
     apply_name =>'STREAMADMIN_APPLY');
     END;
     /

PL/SQL procedure successfully completed.

SQL> CONN streamadmin/oracle@S2C1.ggs.com
```

```
Connected.
SQL> BEGIN
  2  DBMS_CAPTURE_ADM.START_CAPTURE(
  3  capture_name =>'STREAMADMIN_CAPTURE');
  4  END;
  5  /

PL/SQL procedure successfully completed.

SQL>
```

Initial Data Load

The new database (D2C1) must be instantiated and there are several initial data load techniques. For homogenous, Oracle-to-Oracle environments, the Recovery Manager (RMAN) is an option. For heterogeneous environments, Oracle GoldenGate initial-load methods and the Oracle database utilities are alternative options.

Next, the Oracle GoldenGate Direct Load method is illustrated to establish the new target database (D2C1). The Direct Load method implements an initial-load Extract, the Extract reads and sends data directly to a remote task (Replicat). The Replicat uses the native database SQL calls to perform sequential database insert statements.

Refer to Chapter 3 for more details regarding the initial load techniques.

Configure Initial-Load Extract

The Initial Load Extract (ILE1S2C1) fetches data from the source tables through the TCP/IP and sends the data to a target Replicat remote task.

```
GGSCI (source1.precisetrace.com) 3> EDIT PARAMS ILE1S2C1
```

```
EXTRACT ILE1S2C1
USERID ggs_admin@S2C1, PASSWORD oracle
RMTHOST t2c1.precisetrace.com, MGRPORT 7813
RMTTASK REPLICAT, GROUP ILR1S2C1
TABLE scott.salgrade;
TABLE scott.bonus;
TABLE scott.dept;
TABLE scott.emp;
```

```
GGSCI (source1.precisetrace.com) 6> ADD EXTRACT ILE1S2C1, SOURCEISTABLE
EXTRACT added.

GGSCI (source1.precisetrace.com) 7>
```

Configure Initial-Load Replicat

The Initial-Load Replicat (ILR1S2C1) is configured to be used as a special task. It's started by the Initial-Load Extract.

```
GGSCI (t2c1.precisetrace.com) 5> EDIT PARAMS ILR1S2C1
```

```
REPLICAT ILR1S2C1
USERID ggs_admin@D2c1, password oracle
ASSUMETARGETDEFS
HANDLECOLLISIONS
DISCARDFILE ./dirrpt/initILR1S2C101.dsc, PURGE
MAP scott.*, TARGET scott.*;
```

```
GGSCI (t2c1.precisetrace.com) 4> ADD REPLICAT ILR1S2C1, SPECIALRUN
REPLICAT added.

GGSCI (t2c1.precisetrace.com) 5>
```

Starting the Initial Data Load Processes

The Initial Data Load capture and delivery is performed by starting the Initial Data Load capture only. The Extract automatically starts the Initial Load Replicat as a special task process. After the Initial Data Load capture is completed, the Initial Data Load Replicat applies the last transactions then gracefully terminates.

```
GGSCI (source1.precisetrace.com) 5> START EXTRACT ILE1S2C1

Sending START request to MANAGER ...
EXTRACT ILE1S2C1 starting

GGSCI (source1.precisetrace.com) 6
```

Verify the Initial Data Load

Run the 'GGSCI REPORT' command from the source and/or the target database. The "Run Time Statistics" section of the report displays the occurred inserts for each table configured for the Initial Data Load.

```
GGSCI (source1.precisetrace.com) 1> VIEW REPORT ILE1S2C1
```

```
***********************************************************************
*                   ** Run Time Statistics **                         *
***********************************************************************


Report at 2015-03-27 14:39:00 (activity since 2015-03-27 14:38:34)

Output to ILR1S2C1:
```

```
From Table SCOTT.SALGRADE:
        #                  inserts:          8
        #                  updates:          0
        #                  deletes:          0
        #                 discards:          0
From Table SCOTT.DEPT:
        #                  inserts:          4
        #                  updates:          0
        #                  deletes:          0
        #                 discards:          0
From Table SCOTT.EMP:
        #                  inserts:         14
        #                  updates:          0
        #                  deletes:          0
        #                 discards:          0

REDO Log Statistics
--More--(98%)
```

Deploying Changed Data Synchronization

After the new destination (target) is successfully instantiated, the following sequence of steps configure the Changed Data Synchronization from the source to the target database. The synchronization is performed in parallel with the Capture-Propagate-Apply of Oracle Streams. As per best practices, the configuration deploys a secondary capture (data pump) for sending data to the remote Data Collector Server. The data pump enables data capture continuity in the event of a network failure. The Primary Extract continues to capture and write to the local trails. After the network is restored and the data pump process is restarted, the target database synchronization resumes.

For an environment with a multiple independent database schema design, create a separate Extract-Data pump and Replicat. For tables with high-volume transactions, consider the use of a parallel capture and delivery design. Refer to Chapter 1 for details regarding creating a parallel Extract and Replicat configuration.

Configure the Primary Extract Process

Prepare the parameter file for the extract 'E01S2C1.' This extract process writes to the local trail './dirdat/sa.' It captures data for the objects listed by the 'TABLE' parameters.

```
GGSCI (source1.precisetrace.com) 5> EDIT PARAMS E01S2C1
```

```
EXTRACT E01S2C1
SETENV (ORACLE_SID=S2C1)
SETENV (ORACLE_HOME="/u01/app/oracle/product/12.1.0/dbhome_1")
SETENV (NLS_LANG=AMERICAN_AMERICA.AL16UTF16)
USERID ggs_admin@S2C1, PASSWORD oracle
EXTTRAIL ./dirdat/sa
TABLE scott.dept;
TABLE scott.emp;
TABLE scott.bonus;
TABLE scott.salgrade;
```

The 'ADD EXTRACT' command creates the primary extract – 'E01S2C1.' The 'ADD EXTTRAIL' creates the local trail - ./dirdata/sa, and links it with the primary extract – 'E01S2C1.'

```
GGSCI (source1.precisetrace.com) 9> ADD EXTRACT E01S2C1, TRANLOG, BEGIN now,
THREADS 1
EXTRACT added.

GGSCI (source1.precisetrace.com) 10> ADD EXTTRAIL ./dirdat/sa, EXTRACT
E01S2C1
EXTTRAIL added.

GGSCI (source1.precisetrace.com) 11>
```

Configure the Secondary Extract Process

As per Oracle GoldenGate best practices, a secondary extract process (data pump) configuration is deployed. Prepare the parameter file for the data pump – 'P01S2C1.' The data pump reads the local trail and sends it to the destination (target database).

```
GGSCI (source1.precisetrace.com) 12> EDIT PARAMS P01S2C1
```

```
EXTRACT P01S2C1
USERID ggs_admin@S2C1, PASSWORD oracle
PASSTHRU
RMTHOST t2c1.precisetrace.com, MGRPORT 7813
RMTTRAIL ./dirdat/ta
TABLE scott.dept;
TABLE scott.emp;
TABLE scott.bonus;
TABLE scott.salgrade;
```

The command 'ADD EXTRACT' creates the data pump extract, the option 'EXTTRAILSOURCE' instructs the extract to read from the local trail.

```
GGSCI (source1.precisetrace.com) 18> ADD EXTRACT P01S2C1, EXTTRAILSOURCE
./dirdat/sa
EXTRACT added.

GGSCI (source1.precisetrace.com) 19> ADD RMTTRAIL ./dirdat/ta, EXTRACT
P01S2C1
RMTTRAIL added.

GGSCI (source1.precisetrace.com) 20>
```

Configure the Replicat Process

On the destination system, prepare the parameter file for the Replicat – 'R01S2C1.' The Replicat uses the target database native SQL interface to apply the transactions. The MAP command uses the wildcard character '*'. It designates all objects associated with the data pump 'TABLE' parameters.

```
GGSCI (t2c1.precisetrace.com) 3> EDIT PARAMS R01S2C1
```

```
REPLICAT R01S2C1
SETENV (ORACLE_SID=D2C1)
SETENV (NLS_LANG=AMERICAN_AMERICA.AL16UTF16)
USERID ggs_admin@D2C1, PASSWORD oracle
ASSUMETARGETDEFS
DISCARDFILE ./dirrpt/r01s2c1.dsc, PURGE
MAP scott.*, TARGET scott.*;
```

As per best practices and default settings, the Replicat requires a checkpoint table. Ensure the table created is already created or use the 'ADD CHECKPOINTTABLE' command to create a new database table.

Refer to Chapter 1 for more details regarding creating the checkpoint table.

```
GGSCI (t2c1.precisetrace.com) 5> INFO CHECKPOINTTABLE

No checkpoint table specified. Using GLOBALS specification
(ggs_admin.chkpttab)...

Checkpoint table ggs_admin.chkpttab created 2015-03-27 15:22:16.
```

The command 'ADD REPLICAT' creates the Replicat process. Specify the remote trail name.

```
GGSCI (t2c1.precisetrace.com) 6> ADD REPLICAT R01S2C1, EXTTRAIL ./dirdat/ta
REPLICAT added.

GGSCI (t2c1.precisetrace.com) 7>
```

Start and Verify Oracle GoldenGate Extracts and Replicat Processes

Now, it's time to start the Extracts and Replicat processes. From the source system, the command 'START *' starts the primary and secondary extracts. Use the 'INFO ALL' to verify the status.

```
GGSCI (source1.precisetrace.com) 22> START *

Sending START request to MANAGER ...
EXTRACT E01S2C1 starting

Sending START request to MANAGER ...
EXTRACT P01S2C1 starting

GGSCI (source1.precisetrace.com) 23> INFO ALL

Program     Status      Group       Lag at Chkpt  Time Since Chkpt

MANAGER     RUNNING
EXTRACT     RUNNING     E01S2C1     00:23:41      00:00:03
EXTRACT     RUNNING     P01S2C1     00:00:00      00:00:00

GGSCI (source1.precisetrace.com) 24>
```

From the destination system (target), the command 'START *' starts the Replicat process. Use the 'INFO ALL' to verify the status.

```
GGSCI (t2c1.precisetrace.com) 8> START *

Sending START request to MANAGER ...
REPLICAT R01S2C1 starting


GGSCI (t2c1.precisetrace.com) 9> INFO ALL

Program     Status      Group       Lag at Chkpt  Time Since Chkpt

MANAGER     RUNNING
REPLICAT    RUNNING     R01S2C1     00:00:00      00:00:02


GGSCI (t2c1.precisetrace.com) 10>
```

Data Verification and Failback Option

The purpose of using Oracle GoldenGate Veridata is to ensure the target database is fully synchronized with the source database prior to making the final decision for the switchover. Figure 10-3 shows Oracle GoldenGate Veridata.

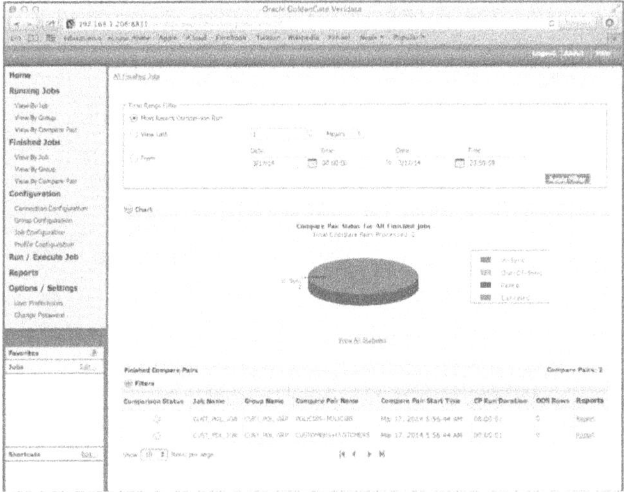

Figure 10-3: Oracle GoldenGate Veridata

The failback option is already in place by concurrently running Oracle Streams and Oracle GoldenGate. A worst case failback scenario is to rebuild the GoldenGate instance with impacting the source and destination system. Refer to Chapter 6 for more details regarding Oracle GoldenGate Veridata implementation.

Without using Oracle GoldenGate Veridata, the admin user can verify the concurrent data manipulation and movement by Oracle Streams and Oracle GoldenGate.

- Insert data into the source system (S2C1)

```
SQL> CONN system/oracle_4U@S2C1
Connected.
SQL> INSERT INTO scott.emp VALUES (
  2  8001, 'FAWZI', 'ANALYST', 7698, SYSDATE, 10000, NULL, 10);

1 row created.

SQL> COMMIT;

Commit complete.

SQL>
```

- Verify transaction movement maintained by Oracle Streams

```
SQL> CONN system/oracle_4U@D1C1.GGS.COM
Connected.
```

```
SQL> SELECT count(*) FROM scott.emp
  2  WHERE  EMPNO=8001;

  COUNT(*)
----------
         1

SQL>
```

- Verify the same transaction movement maintained by Oracle GoldenGate

```
SQL> CONN system/oracle_4U@D2C1
Connected.
SQL> SELECT count(*) FROM scott.emp
  2  WHERE  EMPNO=8001;

  COUNT(*)
----------
         1

SQL>
```

The above deployment is performed using Oracle GoldenGate classic capture. For highly restricted and secured environments, the Oracle GoldenGate Integrated Capture is deployed on a downstream system. The downstream system does not require the installation of Oracle GoldenGate on the production system. The next section addresses the details of configuration the Oracle GoldenGate integrated capture, a new Oracle GoldenGate 11.2 and above for Oracle Database only.

Integrated Capture for Oracle Database

For Oracle Database only, Oracle GoldenGate 11.2 supports two types of capture — classic and integrated. The primary purpose of the integrated capture is to overcome the major limitations of the classic capture. As the name suggests, it's the integration of the Oracle GoldenGate capture technique with the Oracle Database RDBMS. Hence the name derived – Integrated Capture. The integrated capture understands the internal format of the database's Logical Change Record (LCR) produced by the Logmining server. In regard to the database backup and recovery, the Recovery Manager (RMAN) manages the database archives by retaining archived log files needed by the integrated capture, which is not the case with the classic capture.

Unlike the classic capture, the integrated capture has support for the following database features:

- Basic and OLTP Compression
- Exadata Hybrid Columnar Compression
- IOTs Support

- XML Files (stored as binary)
- Parallel DML on a Real Application Cluster (RAC)

The integrated capture and classic capture can work together, where a set of objects are captured by the classic capture and another set of objects are captured by the integrated capture. However, existing Oracle GoldenGate installations are highly recommended to migrate to the integrated capture.

Architecture

The Integrated Capture core component is the Logmining Database. The Logmining Database creates the Logical Change Record (LCR) from the database transactions log, online redo log files for real-time capture, or archived files for deferred capture. The integrated capture has two deployment modes— local and downstream deployments. Figure 10-4 shows the components of the two deployment options. Regardless of the deployment type, the Logmining Database must be release 11.2.0.3 or higher. Because the data is not written to the database files, the Logmining Database has a small footprint database without overhead of the source database data files, it has only the metadata and infrastructure required for processing the online redo log or archive files. The Integrated Capture is highly integrated with the Recovery Manager (RMAN); hence, it's capable of switching among mirrors of the archive log files when operating on a deferred configuration. For Oracle Database release 10.2.0.0, the integrated capture must be operated as a downstream system, this has the advantage of offloading the source database from the capture processing and avoiding installing Oracle GoldenGate on a highly secured OLTP environment.

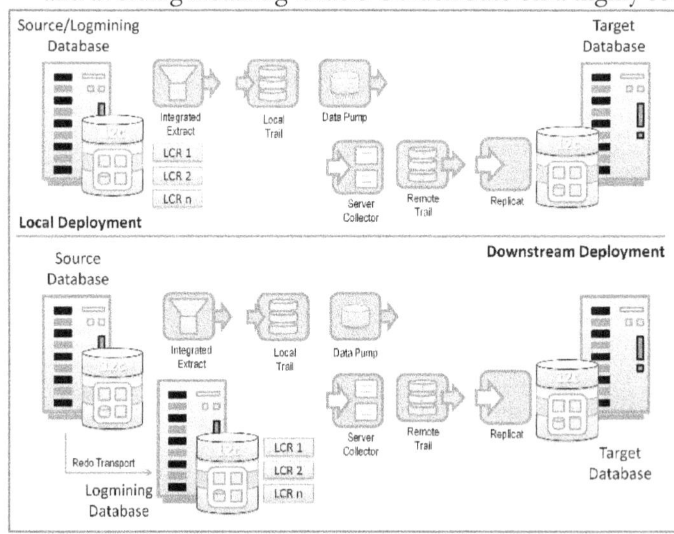

Figure 10-4 Integrated Capture Deployment Modes

Downstream Deployment Mode

The Logmining Database operates on a separate system (downstream system). The source system sends the transaction logs using the TCP/IP to the Logmining Database designated destination. The configuration of the source database parameters are similar to the parameters settings for the Data Guard configuration. Sending the data from the source database to the Logmining Database performed using either Asynchronous or Synchronous transport mode. The major advantage required by enterprises, the database configuration parameters are dynamic, which enables an online deployment of Oracle GoldenGate on a downstream deployment mode. Presumably, the source database is operating on Archive Log mode. The bottom section of Figure 10-4 shows the downstream deployment mode. This mode requires additional configuration to send the database transaction logs to the downstream system for creating the LCR and performing the preferred capture.

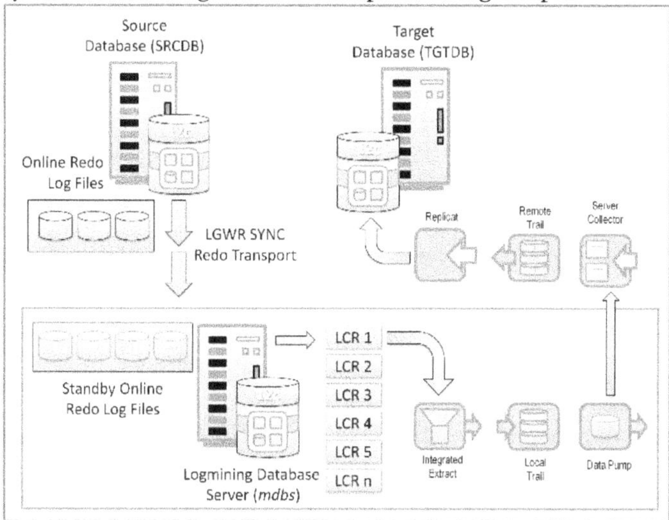

Figure 10-5: Downstream Mode Integrated Capture

Local Deployment Mode

The Logmining Database operates using the same source database instance and infrastructure. The Logmining Database creates the Logical Change Record (LCR) on the same instance designated destination, then the Integrated Capture acts on the Logical Change Record (LCR) for writing to the local or the remote trail. The top section of Figure 10-4 shows the local deployment option. Because redo transport is not required, this mode requires no additional database configuration parameters. Figure 10-6 depicts the components for a local integrated capture.

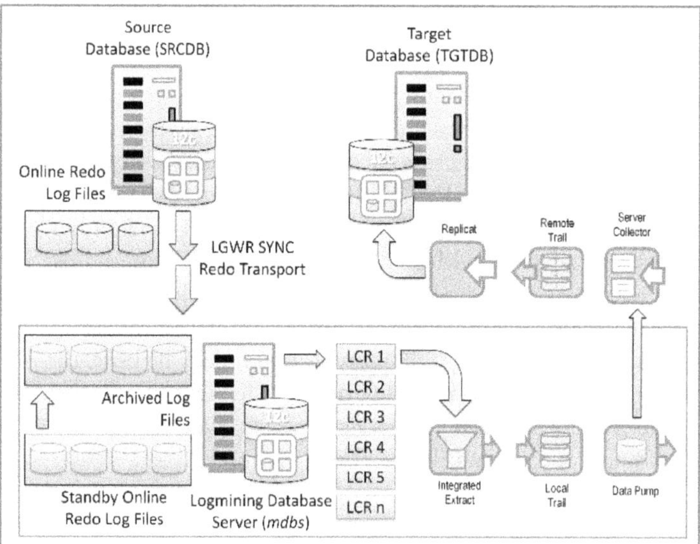

Figure 10-6: Local Mode Integrated Capture

Whether the integrated capture deployed locally or using a downstream system, the capture is configurable as a real-time or deferred capture.

Real-Time Integrated Capture Configuration

The real-time integrated capture is enabled using the standby online redo log file by the Logmining Database. The redo transport should be delivered on Synchronous mode to deliver an absolute real-time capture.

Deferred Integrated Capture Configuration

The deferred integrated capture is enabled using the archive files by the Logmining Database. The redo transport delivered on Synchronous or Asynchronous mode. The Integrated Capture (Extract) lag is proportional to the log switch occurs on the standby online redo log files, which is inherited from the source database online redo log groups, in term of group size and number.

The Downstream Logmining Database Server

This is where the integrated capture is defined. The Downstream Logmining Database Server must operate on Archive Log Mode. It must be configured to archive the redo or archived log files received from the source database.

Integrated Capture Prerequisites and Options

The following database settings must be performed on the source database, which are specific to an integrated capture.

- Memory Requirement Settings
- Enable an Integrated Capture Specific Database Supplemental Logging
- Create and Grant Oracle GoldenGate Database User

Database Memory Requirements for Integrated Capture

The integrated capture uses the database System Global Area (SGA) for creating the Logical Change Records (LCR). It utilizes the Streams Pool memory structure; The recommended size is approximately 700MB. When the SGA is dynamically allocated, manually allocate enough Streams Pool for an Oracle GoldenGate integrated capture. Query the data dictionary V$SGAINFO to display the current allocated memory size for the different System Global Area (SGA) components, if the Stream Pool Size reported is less than 700MB, then change the setting using the ALTER SYSTEM command.

```
SQL> SELECT NAME, BYTES
  2  FROM   v$sgainfo;

NAME                                  BYTES
-------------------------------- ----------
Fixed SGA Size                      2289016
Redo Buffers                        4235264
Buffer Cache Size                 159383552
Shared Pool Size                  138412032
Large Pool Size                     8388608
Java Pool Size                      4194304
Streams Pool Size                   4194304
Shared IO Pool Size                 4194304
Data Transfer Cache Size                  0
Granule Size                        4194304
Maximum SGA Size                  413372416

NAME                                  BYTES
-------------------------------- ----------
Startup overhead in Shared Pool   113301824
Free SGA Memory Available          92274688
```

```
13 rows selected.

SQL> ALTER SYSTEM SET streams_pool_size=700M SCOPE=BOTH;

System altered.

SQL>
```

INTEGRATEDPARAMS Options

For fine-grain memory sizing, Logmining Database server degree of parallelism and real-time mode employed by the integrated capture, use the Oracle GoldenGate parameter 'TRANLOGOPTIONS INTEGRATEDPARAMS' as outlined below.

```
TRANLOGOPTIONS INTEGRATEDPARAMS (max_sga_size 128)
TRANLOGOPTIONS INTEGRATEDPARAMS (parallelism 2)
TRANLOGOPTIONS INTEGRATEDPARAMS (downstream_real_time_mine Y)
```

The parameter 'max_sga_size' specifies the amount (in Gegabytes) of the System Global Area (SGA) used by the Logmining Database server. If the database parameter streams_pool_size is greater than 1GB, it defaults to 1GB. Otherwise, it's calculated as 75% of the streams_pool_size value.

The parameter 'parallelism' specifies the maximum number of processes spawned by the Logmining Database server. Be careful when setting the degree of parallelism, setting the degree to a large number may consume unnecessary system resources without taking advantage of optimized parallel processing. The default value is 0 (parallelism is disabled).

The parameter 'downstream_real_time_mine' is for downstream deployment mode only. When setting the parameter to 'Y', the integrated capture performs a real-time capture from the standby online redo log files. When setting the parameter to 'N' (Default), the integrated capture performs a delayed capture from the archive log file.

Enable GoldenGate Replication

For an integrated capture, Oracle Database 12.1 requires setting the database parameter 'ENABLE_GOLDENGATE_REPLICATION' to 'TRUE.' It enables supplemental logging for new data types. The parameter is dynamic as shown below.

```
SQL> ALTER SYSTEM SET ENABLE_GOLDENGATE_REPLICATION=TRUE SCOPE=BOTH;

System altered.

SQL>
```

Set the parameter for the source and target database.

GoldenGate Database User

For the integrated capture, the Oracle GoldenGate database user needs to be granted 'SELECT' privilege on the 'V_$DATABASE' dynamic view. In addition, execute the PL/SQL database package 'DBMS_GOLDENGATE_AUTH' to grant the administrative role to the GoldenGate database user.

```
SQL> GRANT DBA TO ggs_admin IDENTIFIED BY oracle;

Grant succeeded.

SQL> BEGIN
       DBMS_GOLDENGATE_AUTH.GRANT_ADMIN_PRIVILEGE
            (grantee=>'GGS_ADMIN',
             privilege_type=>'capture',
             grant_select_privileges=>true,
             do_grants=>TRUE);
     END;
     /

PL/SQL procedure successfully completed.

SQL> GRANT SELECT ON V_$DATABASE to ggs_admin;

Grant succeeded.

SQL>
```

Deploying an Integrated Capture on the Local System

The deployment of an integrated capture on the local system eliminates the major limitations of the classic capture. The Logmining Database server is the same source database instance. Hence, using the source online redo log files to generate the Logical Charge Record (LCR) passed to the integrated capture for processing. The only step required for deploying an integrated capture on the local system is registering the Extract with the source database.

The steps to deploy an integrated capture on the local system are:

- Login to the source database using 'DBLOGIN' to register the Extract
- Specify the 'TRANLOGOPTIONS INTEGRATEDPARAMS' parameter options
- Add the Extract group specify 'INTEGRATED TRANLOG' mode

Register the Integrated Capture with the Database

Registering the capture process with the database enables the capture to understand that the format of the Logical Change Record (LCR) is passed by the Logmining Database server.

For locally deployed integrated captures, the Logmining database is the same as the source database. Login to the source database using 'DBLOGIN' and issue a 'REGISTER EXTRACT' command. It's not required to login using 'MININGDBLOGIN' to register the integrated capture extract.

```
GGSCI (oltp01.oracle-ggs.com) 1> DBLOGIN USERID ggs_admin, PASSWORD oracle
Successfully logged into database.

GGSCI (oltp01.oracle-ggs.com) 2> REGISTER EXTRACT E01SRCDB WITH DATABASE
Extract E01SRCDB successfully registered with database at SCN 1828148.

GGSCI (oltp01.oracle-ggs.com) 3>
```

After successfully registering the integrated capture Extract, query the database dictionary view 'DBA_CAPTURE' to list the currently registered captures. Unregistering the Extract with the database removes the Oracle GoldenGate integrated capture from the capture list. The query below verifies the above Extract registration with the database.

```
SQL> desc dba_capture
 Name                                      Null?    Type
 ----------------------------------------- -------- -------------

 CAPTURE_NAME                              NOT NULL VARCHAR2(30)
 QUEUE_NAME                                NOT NULL VARCHAR2(30)
 QUEUE_OWNER                               NOT NULL VARCHAR2(30)
 RULE_SET_NAME                                      VARCHAR2(30)
 RULE_SET_OWNER                                     VARCHAR2(30)
 CAPTURE_USER                                       VARCHAR2(30)
 START_SCN                                          NUMBER
 STATUS                                             VARCHAR2(8)
 CAPTURED_SCN                                       NUMBER
 APPLIED_SCN                                        NUMBER
 USE_DATABASE_LINK                                  VARCHAR2(3)
 FIRST_SCN                                          NUMBER
 SOURCE_DATABASE                                    VARCHAR2(128)
 SOURCE_DBID                                        NUMBER
 SOURCE_RESETLOGS_SCN                               NUMBER
 SOURCE_RESETLOGS_TIME                              NUMBER
 LOGMINER_ID                                        NUMBER
 NEGATIVE_RULE_SET_NAME                             VARCHAR2(30)
 NEGATIVE_RULE_SET_OWNER                            VARCHAR2(30)
 MAX_CHECKPOINT_SCN                                 NUMBER
 REQUIRED_CHECKPOINT_SCN                            NUMBER
 LOGFILE_ASSIGNMENT                                 VARCHAR2(8)
```

```
 STATUS_CHANGE_TIME                                         DATE
 ERROR_NUMBER                                               NUMBER
 ERROR_MESSAGE                                              VARCHAR2(4000)
 VERSION                                                    VARCHAR2(64)
 CAPTURE_TYPE                                               VARCHAR2(10)
 LAST_ENQUEUED_SCN                                          NUMBER
 CHECKPOINT_RETENTION_TIME                                  NUMBER

SQL> SELECT capture_name, client_name, purpose
  2  FROM   dba_capture;

CAPTURE_NAME                   CLIENT_NAME PURPOSE
------------------------------ ----------  ------------------------------
OGG$CAP_E01SRCDB                E01SRCDB   GoldenGate Capture

SQL>
```

Enable Table Level Supplemental Logging

This can be performed for each table or using the Oracle GoldenGate wildcard character to add supplemental logging for the schema's table.

```
GGSCI (oltp01.oracle-ggs.com) 8> DBLOGIN USERID ggs_admin, PASSWORD oracle
Successfully logged into database.

GGSCI (oltp01.oracle-ggs.com) 9> ADD TRANDATA scott.*
```

The table without a primary key received a warning message— suggesting to use the 'KEYCOL' option of the TABLE statement.

Prepare and Define the Primary Integrated Extract

The integrated capture (E01SRCDB) is already registered with the database. This database has supplemental log data and forced logging is enabled. Use the 'EDIT' command to prepare the parameter file. Notice the parameter 'TRANLOGOPTIONS' has been extended to include the 'INTEGRATEDPARAMS' option. Then execute the 'ADD EXTRACT' command to define the Extract in the 'INTEGRATED TRANLOG' mode. The last step, when defining the primary extract, is to execute the 'ADD EXTTRAIL' command to link the Extract (E01SRCDB) with the local trail './dirdat/sa.'

```
GGSCI (oltp01.oracle-ggs.com) 3> EDIT PARAMS E01SRCDB
```

```
EXTRACT E01SRCDB
USERID ggs_admin@SRCDB, PASSWORD oracle
TRANLOGOPTIONS INTEGRATEDPARAMS (max_sga_size 128)
TRANLOGOPTIONS INTEGRATEDPARAMS (parallelism 2)
EXTTRAIL ./dirdat/sa
TABLE scott.*;
```

```
GGSCI (oltp01.oracle-ggs.com) 6> ADD EXTRACT E01SRCDB, INTEGRATED TRANLOG,
BEGIN now
EXTRACT added.
```

```
GGSCI (oltp01.oracle-ggs.com) 7> ADD EXTTRAIL ./dirdat/sa, EXTRACT E01SRCDB,
MEGABYTES 15
EXTTRAIL added.

GGSCI (oltp01.oracle-ggs.com) 8>
```

In order to allow the primary integrated extract to receive current redo logs from the source database, execute the SQL statement to perform a log switch.

```
SQL> ALTER SYSTEM SWITCH LOGFILE;

System altered.

SQL>
```

Prepare and Define the Secondary Extract

The Secondary Extract is optional, but a highly recommend Oracle GoldenGate practice. The purpose is to offload the primary extract from forwarding data to the target system and to provide system resilience in case of a network disconnect. The following 'GGSCI' command prepares the parameter file, defines the Secondary Extract, and links the remote trail with the Secondary Extract (data pump).

```
GGSCI (oltp01.oracle-ggs.com) 8> EDIT PARAMS P01SRCDB
```

```
EXTRACT P01SRCDB
USERID ggs_admin@SRCDB, PASSWORD oracle
RMTHOST 192.168.1.78, MGRPORT 7809
RMTTRAIL ./dirdat/sb
PASSTHRU
TABLE scott.*;
```

```
GGSCI (oltp01.oracle-ggs.com) 10> ADD EXTRACT P01SRCDB, EXTTRAILSOURCE
./dirdat/sa
EXTRACT added.

GGSCI (oltp01.oracle-ggs.com) 11> ADD RMTTRAIL ./dirdat/sb, EXTRACT
P01SRCDB, MEGABYTES 15
RMTTRAIL added.

GGSCI (oltp01.oracle-ggs.com) 12>
```

Start Primary and Secondary Extract

Start and verify the Extracts' status. The 'INFO ALL' command shows the status is RUNNING. If not, use the 'VIEW REPORT' command to display the report file which indicates the cause of failure.

```
GGSCI (oltp01.oracle-ggs.com) 39> START EXTRACT *

Sending START request to MANAGER ...
EXTRACT E01SRCDB starting

Sending START request to MANAGER ...
EXTRACT P01SRCDB starting

GGSCI (oltp01.oracle-ggs.com) 40> INFO ALL

Program     Status      Group       Lag at Chkpt  Time Since Chkpt

MANAGER     RUNNING
EXTRACT     RUNNING     E01SRCDB    00:00:41      00:00:05
EXTRACT     RUNNING     P01SRCDB    00:00:00      00:00:04

GGSCI (oltp01.oracle-ggs.com) 41>
```

Prepare and Define the Replicat

Regardless of the capture mode, the Replicat is configured to read the remote trail and apply the transactions using the database native SQL calls. Use the 'GGSCI EDIT' command to prepare the parameter file. Before defining the Replicat, login to the target database and define the checkpoint table. The final step defines the Replicat, which uses the checkpoint table and is defined globally.

```
GGSCI (oltp02.oracle-ggs.com) 5> EDIT PARAMS R01SRCDB
```

```
REPLICAT R01SRCDB
ASSUMETARGETDEFS
DISCARDFILE ./dirrpt/R01SRCDB.dsc, purge
USERID ggs_admin@TGTDB, PASSWORD oracle
MAP scott.*, TARGET scott.*;
```

```
GGSCI (oltp02.oracle-ggs.com) 1> DBLOGIN USERID ggs_admin, PASSWORD oracle
Successfully logged into database.

GGSCI (oltp02.oracle-ggs.com) 2> ADD CHECKPOINTTABLE

No checkpoint table specified. Using GLOBALS specification
(ggs_admin.chkpt)...

Successfully created checkpoint table ggs_admin.chkpt.

GGSCI (oltp02.oracle-ggs.com) 3>
```

```
GGSCI (oltp02.oracle-ggs.com) 3> ADD REPLICAT R01SRCDB, EXTTRAIL ./dirdat/sb
REPLICAT added.

GGSCI (oltp02.oracle-ggs.com) 4>
```

Starting the Replicat

Start and verify the Replicat process. The 'INFO ALL' command indicates the status is RUNNING.

```
GGSCI (oltp02.oracle-ggs.com) 9> START REPLICAT *

Sending START request to MANAGER ...
REPLICAT R01SRCDB starting

GGSCI (oltp02.oracle-ggs.com) 10> INFO ALL

Program     Status      Group       Lag at Chkpt  Time Since Chkpt

MANAGER     RUNNING
REPLICAT    RUNNING     R01SRCDB    00:00:00      00:00:02

GGSCI (oltp02.oracle-ggs.com) 11>
```

Insert Data and Run Statistic Report

Test the data movement by inserting on the source database.

```
SQL> INSERT INTO scott.dept VALUES (50, 'GG', 'DUBAI');

1 row created.

SQL> COMMIT;

Commit complete.

SQL>
```

Verify the data is inserted into the target database.

```
SQL> SELECT * FROM scott.dept;

    DEPTNO DNAME          LOC
---------- -------------- -------------
        10 ACCOUNTING     NEW YORK
        20 RESEARCH       DALLAS
        30 SALES          CHICAGO
        40 OPERATIONS     BOSTON
        50 GG             DUBAI

SQL>
```

Also, use the 'GGSCI STATS' command to display statistics for INSERT, UPDATE and DELETE DML operations.

```
GGSCI (oltp02.oracle-ggs.com) 7> STATS R01SRCDB
```

```
Sending STATS request to REPLICAT R01SRCDB ...

Start of Statistics at 2015-05-03 23:47:52.

Replicating from SCOTT.DEPT to SCOTT.DEPT:

*** Total statistics since 2015-05-03 23:42:59 ***
        Total inserts                                   1.00
        Total updates                                   0.00
        Total deletes                                   0.00
        Total discards                                  0.00
        Total operations                                1.00

*** Daily statistics since 2015-05-03 23:42:59 ***
        Total inserts                                   1.00
        Total updates                                   0.00
        Total deletes                                   0.00
        Total discards                                  0.00
        Total operations                                1.00

*** Hourly statistics since 2015-05-03 23:42:59 ***
        Total inserts                                   1.00
        Total updates                                   0.00
        Total deletes                                   0.00
        Total discards                                  0.00
        Total operations                                1.00

*** Latest statistics since 2015-05-03 23:42:59 ***
        Total inserts                                   1.00
        Total updates                                   0.00
        Total deletes                                   0.00
        Total discards                                  0.00
        Total operations                                1.00

End of Statistics.

GGSCI (oltp02.oracle-ggs.com) 8>
```

Deploying Integrated Capture on a Downstream System

The following sequence of steps prepares the source database (SRCDB) and the Logmining Database system (mdbs) for an integrated capture deployment. The source database performs a redo transport to the downstream database in preparation for performing a real-time integrated capture.

Prior to starting the deployment of the integrated capture, configure the Logmining database system listener and verify the database is reachable from the source database using the TNSPING utility.

```
[oracle@oltp01 admin]$ tnsping mdbs

TNS Ping Utility for Linux: Version 12.1.0.2.0 - Production on 08-MAY-2015
17:20:45

Copyright (c) 1997, 2014, Oracle.  All rights reserved.

Used parameter files:

Used TNSNAMES adapter to resolve the alias
Attempting to contact (DESCRIPTION = (ADDRESS = (PROTOCOL = TCP)(HOST =
oltp02.oracle-ggs.com)(PORT = 1521)) (CONNECT_DATA = (SERVER = DEDICATED)
(SERVICE_NAME = mdbs.oracle-ggs.com)))
OK (10 msec)
[oracle@oltp01 admin]$
```

Prepare the Source Database

The integrated capture employs the Streams Pool Memory of the System Global Area (SGA). Allocate an adequate size; The recommended value setting is 700MB. Query the current Stream Pool Size and change it to meet the recommended minimum. When the SGA is dynamically allocated, the Stream Pool Size is an auto-tuned component and the size is based on the current workload.

```
SQL> SELECT NAME, BYTES
  2  FROM   v$sgainfo;
NAME                                BYTES
-------------------------------- ----------
Fixed SGA Size                     2289016
Redo Buffers                       4235264
Buffer Cache Size                  159383552
Shared Pool Size                   138412032
Large Pool Size                    8388608
Java Pool Size                     4194304
Streams Pool Size                  4194304
Shared IO Pool Size                4194304
Data Transfer Cache Size           0
Granule Size                       4194304
Maximum SGA Size                   413372416
NAME                                BYTES
-------------------------------- ----------
Startup overhead in Shared Pool    113301824
Free SGA Memory Available          92274688

13 rows selected.

SQL> ALTER SYSTEM SET streams_pool_size=700M SCOPE=BOTH;

System altered.

SQL>
```

Prepare the Downstream Database

The downstream Logmining Database system must operate on the archive log mode. The following SQL steps enable the archive log mode and supplemental logging required by the Oracle GoldenGate capture. A new parameter introduced in database 11.2.0.4 is 'ENABLE_GOLDENGATE_REPLICATION.' The parameter default value is 'FALASE', enable the use of XStream API by setting the parameter value to 'TRUE.'

```
SQL> SHUTDOWN IMMEDIATE
Database closed.
Database dismounted.
ORACLE instance shut down.
SQL> STARTUP MOUNT
ORACLE instance started.

Total System Global Area  1269366784 bytes
Fixed Size                   2287912 bytes
Variable Size              855639768 bytes
Database Buffers           402653184 bytes
Redo Buffers                 8785920 bytes
Database mounted.
SQL> ALTER DATABASE ARCHIVELOG;

Database altered.

SQL> ALTER DATABASE ADD SUPPLEMENTAL LOG DATA;

Database altered.

SQL> ALTER DATABASE FORCE LOGGING;

Database altered.

SQL> ALTER DATABASE OPEN;

Database altered.

SQL> ALTER SYSTEM SWITCH LOGFILE;

System altered.

SQL> SELECT log_mode, force_logging, supplemental_log_data_min
  2  FROM   v$database;

LOG_MODE     FORCE_LOGGING                           SUPPLEME
------------ --------------------------------------- --------
ARCHIVELOG   YES                                     YES

SQL> ALTER SYSTEM SET enable_goldengate_replication=TRUE SCOPE=BOTH;

System altered.

SQL>
```

Create the Password Files

Use the Oracle utility 'orapwd' to create the password files. The source and target password files must match. For a specific Oracle GoldenGate capture, it's mandatory to use the 'IGNORECASE=Y' option to ignore the password case sensitivity.

```
[oracle@oltp01 dbs]$ cd $ORACLE_HOME/dbs
[oracle@oltp01 dbs]$ orapwd file=orapwSRCDB password=oracle_4U ignorecase=Y
entries=10 force=y
[oracle@oltp01 dbs]$

[oracle@oltp02 ~]$ cd $ORACLE_HOME/dbs
[oracle@oltp02 dbs]$ orapwd file=orapwmdbs password=oracle_4U ignorecase=Y
entries=10 force=y
[oracle@oltp02 dbs]$
```

Configure Redo Transport of the Source Database

Use the database parameter 'LOG_ARCHIVE_DEST_2' to enable the source database to ship the transaction logs to the downstream Logmining Database. For the real-time redo transport, specify the 'SYNC' option. Specify the connect string of the downstream database for the 'SERVICE' attribute. Then, enable the destination using the 'SQL ALTER' command.

```
SQL> ALTER SYSTEM SET
  2  LOG_ARCHIVE_DEST_2='SERVICE=mdbs LGWR SYNC NOREGISTER
  3  VALID_FOR=(ONLINE_LOGFILES,PRIMARY_ROLE) REOPEN=15
  4  DB_UNIQUE_NAME=mdbs';

System altered.

SQL> ALTER SYSTEM SET LOG_ARCHIVE_DEST_STATE_2=ENABLE;

System altered.

SQL>
```

Specify the Data Guard Configuration

Add the source and downstream Logmining Database using the database parameters 'LOG_ARCHIVE_CONFIG.'

```
SQL> ALTER SYSTEM SET
  2  LOG_ARCHIVE_CONFIG='DG_CONFIG=(SRCDB, mdbs)';

System altered.

SQL>
```

Determine the Source Database Redo Log Files

This step is needed when configuring the downstream Logmining Database standby redo log groups. The best practice is to create one additional standby redo log group of the same size.

```
SQL> SELECT group#, bytes/1024/1024 bytes
  2  FROM   v$log;

    GROUP#      BYTES
---------- ----------
         1         50
         2         50
         3         50

SQL>
```

Based on the above query result, the downstream Logmining Database needs (4) standby redo log groups — each the size of 50M.

Configure the Directory Structure

Create the following directory structures for the archive, redo, and standby files.

```
[oracle@oltp02 dbs]$ mkdir -p /u01/app/oracle/oradata/mdbs/arch
[oracle@oltp02 dbs]$ mkdir -p /u01/app/oracle/oradata/mdbs/redo
[oracle@oltp02 dbs]$ mkdir -p /u01/app/oracle/oradata/mdbs/standby
```

Configure Downstream Archive locations

The downstream Logmining Database is configured to receive and archive locally and to create the standby redo data. Enable the destinations using the SQL ALTER command.

```
SQL> ALTER SYSTEM SET
  2  log_archive_dest_1='LOCATION=/u01/app/oracle/oradata/mdbs/arch
  3  VALID_FOR=(ONLINE_LOGFILE,PRIMARY_ROLE)';

System altered.

SQL> ALTER SYSTEM SET
  2  log_archive_dest_2='LOCATION=/u01/app/oracle/oradata/mdbs/standby
  3  VALID_FOR=(STANDBY_LOGFILE,ALL_ROLES)';

System altered.

SQL> ALTER SYSTEM SET log_archive_dest_state_1='ENABLE';

System altered.
```

```
SQL> ALTER SYSTEM SET log_archive_dest_state_2='ENABLE';

System altered.

SQL>
```

Specify the Data Guard Configuration

Add the source and downstream Logmining Database using the database parameters 'LOG_ARCHIVE_CONFIG.'

```
SQL> ALTER SYSTEM SET
  2  LOG_ARCHIVE_CONFIG='DG_CONFIG=(SRCDB, mdbs)';

System altered.

SQL>
```

Create the Standby Redo Log Files

The last configuration step of the downstream Logmining Database is creating the standby redo log files. Refer to "Determine the Source Database Redo Log Files" to determine the number and size of standby redo log files, which is calculated as:

- The number of standby redo log file groups is the number of redo log groups in the source database, plus one: 1 + 3 = 4.
- The size of the standby redo log file is at least the same size as the source redo log files: 50MB.

```
SQL> ALTER DATABASE ADD STANDBY LOGFILE GROUP 4
  2  '/u01/app/oracle/oradata/mdbs/redo/stdby1.log' SIZE 50M;

Database altered.

SQL> ALTER DATABASE ADD STANDBY LOGFILE GROUP 5
  2  '/u01/app/oracle/oradata/mdbs/redo/stdby2.log' SIZE 50M;

Database altered.

SQL> ALTER DATABASE ADD STANDBY LOGFILE GROUP 6
  2  '/u01/app/oracle/oradata/mdbs/redo/stdby3.log' SIZE 50M;

Database altered.

SQL> ALTER DATABASE ADD STANDBY LOGFILE GROUP 7
  2  '/u01/app/oracle/oradata/mdbs/redo/stdby4.log' SIZE 50M;

Database altered.

SQL>
```

Create Database Users for GoldenGate

Database users are needed by Oracle GoldenGate to perform a capture on the source and delivery on the target database. The following illustrates creating and granting a user on the source and downstream Logmining Database.

- Source Database User

```
SQL> CREATE TABLESPACE ggs_dat;

Tablespace created.

SQL> ALTER DATABASE FORCE LOGGING;

Database altered.

SQL> GRANT DBA TO ggs_admin IDENTIFIED BY oracle;

Grant succeeded.

SQL> ALTER USER ggs_admin DEFAULT TABLESPACE ggs_dat
  2                       QUOTA UNLIMITED ON ggs_dat;

User altered.

SQL>
```

- Downstream Logmining Database User

```
SQL> CREATE TABLESPACE ggs_dat;

Tablespace created.

SQL> GRANT DBA TO ggs_admin IDENTIFIED BY oracle;

Grant succeeded.

SQL> ALTER USER ggs_admin DEFAULT TABLESPACE ggs_dat
  2                       QUOTA UNLIMITED ON ggs_dat;

User altered.

SQL> BEGIN
  2     DBMS_GOLDENGATE_AUTH.GRANT_ADMIN_PRIVILEGE
  3          (grantee=>'GGS_ADMIN',
  4           privilege_type=>'capture',
  5           grant_select_privileges=>true,
  6           do_grants=>TRUE);
  7  END;
  8  /

PL/SQL procedure successfully completed.

SQL>
```

Database Connections Using Oracle GoldenGate

Perform database connections using Oracle GoldenGate. For integrated capture on a downstream deployment, it requires concurrently connecting to the source and Logmining Databases.

- Login to the source database. Use the 'DBLOGIN' command to login to the database.

```
[oracle@oltp01 oggcore_1]$ ./ggsci

Oracle GoldenGate Command Interpreter for Oracle
Version 12.1.2.0.0 17185003 OGGCORE_12.1.2.0.0_PLATFORMS_130924.1316_FBO
Linux, x64, 64bit (optimized), Oracle 12c on Sep 25 2013 02:33:54
Operating system character set identified as UTF-8.

Copyright (C) 1995, 2013, Oracle and/or its affiliates. All rights
reserved.


GGSCI (oltp01.oracle-ggs.com) 1> DBLOGIN USERID ggs_admin@srcdb,
PASSWORD oracle
Successfully logged into database.

GGSCI (oltp01.oracle-ggs.com) 2>
```

- Login to the Downstream Logmining Database. Use the 'MINING DBLOGIN' command to login to the database.

```
[oracle@oltp02 oggcore_1]$ ./ggsci

Oracle GoldenGate Command Interpreter for Oracle
Version 12.1.2.0.0 17185003 OGGCORE_12.1.2.0.0_PLATFORMS_130924.1316_FBO
Linux, x64, 64bit (optimized), Oracle 12c on Sep 25 2013 02:33:54
Operating system character set identified as UTF-8.

Copyright (C) 1995, 2013, Oracle and/or its affiliates. All rights
reserved.

GGSCI (oltp02.oracle-ggs.com) 2> MININGDBLOGIN USERID ggs_admin@mdbs,
PASSWORD oracle
Successfully logged into mining database.

GGSCI (oltp02.oracle-ggs.com) 3>
```

Register the Integrated Capture

The Integrated Capture must be registered with the database. Login to the source and the Logmining Databases to perform the Extract registration.

```
[oracle@oltp02 oggcore_2]$ ./ggsci
```

```
Oracle GoldenGate Command Interpreter for Oracle
Version 12.1.2.1.2 20133048 20078949_FBO
Linux, x64, 64bit (optimized), Oracle 12c on Apr 17 2015 03:22:09
Operating system character set identified as UTF-8.

Copyright (C) 1995, 2015, Oracle and/or its affiliates. All rights reserved.


GGSCI (oltp02.oracle-ggs.com) 1> DBLOGIN USERID ggs_admin@srcdb, PASSWORD
oracle
Successfully logged into database.

GGSCI (oltp02.oracle-ggs.com as ggs_admin@SRCDB) 2> MININGDBLOGIN USERID
ggs_admin@mdbs, PASSWORD oracle
Successfully logged into mining database.

GGSCI (oltp02.oracle-ggs.com as ggs_admin@SRCDB) 3> REGISTER EXTRACT EASRCDB
DATABASE
Extract EASRCDB successfully registered with database at SCN 2678787.


GGSCI (oltp02.oracle-ggs.com as ggs_admin@SRCDB) 4>
```

Verify that the integrated capture has been successfully registered with the Logmining Database. Query the database dictionary view 'DBA_CAPTURE.'

```
SQL> SELECT capture_name, client_name, purpose
  2  FROM   dba_capture;

CAPTURE_NAMN       CLIENT_NAME                    PURPOSE
-----------------  ---------------------------    -----------------
OGG$CAP_EASRCDB    EASRCDB                        GoldenGate Capture
OGG$CAP_EXY        EXY                            GoldenGate Capture

SQL>
```

Prepare and Define the Primary Integrated Capture

To enable the integrated capture, use the GoldenGate parameter 'TRANSLOGOPTIONS' with the following options: 'MININGUSER' specifies the database user of the Logmining Database. The 'INTEGERATEDPARAMS' specifies the SGA memory size and the real-time logs mining is enabled by the option 'downstream_real_time_mine' to Y. When defining an integrated capture, specify the option 'INTEGRATED TRANLOG' of the 'ADD EXTRACT' command. Associate the local trail './dirdat/ia' with the integrated capture using the 'ADD EXTTRAIL' command.

```
GGSCI (oltp02.oracle-ggs.com) 1> EDIT PARAMS EASRCDB
```

```
EXTRACT EASRCDB
USERID ggs_admin@srcdb PASSWORD oracle
```

```
TRANSLOGOPTIONS MININGUSER ggs_admin@mdbs MININGPASSWORD oracle
TRANSLOGOPTIONS INTEGERATEDPARAMS (max_sga_size 256,
downstream_real_time_mine Y)
EXTTRAIL ./dirdat/ia
TABLE scott.*;
```

```
GGSCI (oltp02.oracle-ggs.com) 2> ADD EXTRACT EASRCDB, INTEGRATED TRANLOG,
BEGIN NOW
EXTRACT added.

GGSCI (oltp02.oracle-ggs.com) 3> ADD EXTTRAIL ./dirdat/ia, EXTRACT EASRCDB,
MEGABYTES 15
EXTTRAIL added.

GGSCI (oltp02.oracle-ggs.com) 4>
```

Prepare and Define the Secondary Capture

As per Oracle GoldenGate best practices suggests, define a Secondary Extract (data pump). The Extract sends data to the Oracle GoldenGate instance specified by the combination of parameters 'RMTHOST' and 'MGRPORT.'

```
GGSCI (oltp02.oracle-ggs.com) 4> EDIT PARAMS PASRCDB
```

```
EXTRACT PASRCDB
USERID ggs_admin@srcdb, PASSWORD oracle
RMTHOST 192.168.1.78, MGRPORT 7809
RMTTRAIL ./dirdat/ib
PASSTHRU
TABLE scott.*;
```

```
GGSCI (oltp02.oracle-ggs.com) 13> ADD EXTRACT PASRCDB, EXTTRAILSOURCE
./dirdat/ib
EXTRACT added.

GGSCI (oltp02.oracle-ggs.com) 14> ADD RMTTRAIL ./dirdat/ib, EXTRACT PASRCDB,
MEGABYTES 15
RMTTRAIL added.

GGSCI (oltp02.oracle-ggs.com) 15>
```

Starting the Extracts

The next step is to start the Extracts 'EASRCDB' (Integrated Capture Extract) and the data pump (PASRCDB).

```
GGSCI (oltp02.oracle-ggs.com) 6> START EXTRACT *

Sending START request to MANAGER ...
EXTRACT EASRCDB starting
```

```
Sending START request to MANAGER ...
EXTRACT PASRCDB starting

GGSCI (oltp02.oracle-ggs.com) 7> INFO ALL

Program     Status      Group       Lag at Chkpt  Time Since Chkpt

MANAGER     RUNNING
EXTRACT     RUNNING     EASRCDB     unknown       00:00:09
EXTRACT     RUNNING     PASRCDB     00:00:00      00:00:00

GGSCI (oltp02.oracle-ggs.com) 8>
```

Prepare and Define the Replicat

The Replicat is defined in the same way of classic capture. Since there's no transformation, the Replicat RASRCDB uses the parameter 'ASSUMETARGETDEFS.' The MAP statement uses the schema-level rather than specifying the table-level for identifying the list of target objects.

```
GGSCI (oltp02.oracle-ggs.com) 3> EDIT PARAMS RASRCDB
```

```
REPLICAT RASRCDB
ASSUMETARGETDEFS
DISCARDFILE ./dirrpt/RASRCDB.dsc, purge
USERID ggs_admin@TGTDB, PASSWORD oracle
MAP scott.*, TARGET scott.*;
```

```
GGSCI (oltp02.oracle-ggs.com) 5> ADD REPLICAT RASRCDB, EXTTRAIL ./dirdat/ib
REPLICAT added.

GGSCI (oltp02.oracle-ggs.com) 6>
```

Starting the Replicat

Starting the Replicat, the 'INFO ALL' command displays the status of the Replicat RASRCDB.

```
GGSCI (oltp02.oracle-ggs.com) 16> START RASRCDB

Sending START request to MANAGER ...
REPLICAT RASRCDB starting

GGSCI (oltp02.oracle-ggs.com) 17> INFO ALL

Program     Status      Group       Lag at Chkpt  Time Since Chkpt

MANAGER     RUNNING
REPLICAT    RUNNING     RASRCDB     00:00:00      00:00:00

GGSCI (oltp02.oracle-ggs.com) 18>
```

Insert Data and View Statistics Report

Login to the source database. Insert data and view the statistics. The database insert is transformed into the format Logical Change Record (LCR), processed, passed, and processed by the integrated capture.

```
GGSCI (oltp02.oracle-ggs.com) 6> stats EASRCDB
```

```
Sending STATS request to EXTRACT EASRCDB ...

Start of Statistics at 2015-05-08 18:24:47.

Output to ./dirdat/ia:

Extracting from SCOTT.DEPT to SCOTT.DEPT:

*** Total statistics since 2015-05-08 18:24:29 ***
    Total inserts                                   1.00
    Total updates                                   0.00
    Total deletes                                   0.00
    Total discards                                  0.00
    Total operations                                1.00

*** Daily statistics since 2015-05-08 18:24:29 ***
    Total inserts                                   1.00
    Total updates                                   0.00
    Total deletes                                   0.00
    Total discards                                  0.00
    Total operations                                1.00

*** Hourly statistics since 2015-05-08 18:24:29 ***
    Total inserts                                   1.00
    Total updates                                   0.00
    Total deletes                                   0.00
    Total discards                                  0.00
    Total operations                                1.00

*** Latest statistics since 2015-05-08 18:24:29 ***
    Total inserts                                   1.00
    Total updates                                   0.00
    Total deletes                                   0.00
    Total discards                                  0.00
    Total operations                                1.00

End of Statistics.

GGSCI (oltp02.oracle-ggs.com) 7>
```

Migration from a Classic to Integrated Capture

A classic capture can be upgraded to an integrated capture. It's also possible to downgrade an integrated capture to a classic capture. Since classic and integrated captures may co-exist, this feature minimizes the impact (if any) of upgrading to an integrated capture by gradually migrating one schema or set of tables at a time.

Use the steps below to migrate the Extract:

1. Stop the Classic Capture Extract
2. Register the Extract with the Logmining Database
3. Alter the Extract for migration (to classic or integrated)

The following 'GGSCI' commands downgrade (migrate from integrated to classic) the extract then upgrades it again (from classic to integrated).

```
GGSCI (oltp01.oracle-ggs.com) 9> STOP EXTRACT E01SRCDB

Sending STOP request to EXTRACT E01SRCDB ...
Request processed.

GGSCI (oltp01.oracle-ggs.com) 10> DBLOGIN USERID ggs_admin, PASSWORD oracle
Successfully logged into database.

GGSCI (oltp01.oracle-ggs.com) 13> ALTER EXTRACT E01SRCDB, DOWNGRADE
INTEGRATED TRANLOG
Extract E01SRCDB successfully downgraded from integrated capture.

GGSCI (oltp01.oracle-ggs.com) 14> ALTER EXTRACT E01SRCDB, UPGRADE INTEGRATED
TRANLOG
Extract E01SRCDB successfully upgraded to integrated capture.

GGSCI (oltp01.oracle-ggs.com) 15>
```

Restrictions, Limitations, and Patches

Though an integrated capture removes the major limitations found with a classic capture, the following restrictions and limitations should be taken into consideration when using an integrated capture.

- When the Logmining Database name is alphanumeric, the 'GGSCI REGISTER' command fails with error message 'OCI 40,044.'

- When using an integrated capture with Oracle Database 11.2.0.3, apply Oracle database patch 14551959 to enable data types support.

- 'SECUREFILE LOBs' are captured from the redo log only when the LOBs are not compressed, encrypted, or de-duplicated and stored out-of-row. Otherwise, they are captured from the source table.

- Integrated Capture does not support the following data types:

ANYDATASET
ANYTYPE
BFILE
MLSLABEL
ORDDICOM
TIMEZONE_ABBR
URITYPE/UROWID

Deploying Intermediate Systems Instances

The use of Oracle GoldenGate intermediate system extends Oracle GoldenGate scalability and enhances the source and the target systems performance by moving and consolidating the transformation and the application functions into the intermediate system. In a highly secured distributed database environment, the intermediate system operates externally and does not connect to the source and target systems as illustrated in Figure 10-7, where data is tunneled through the firewalls.

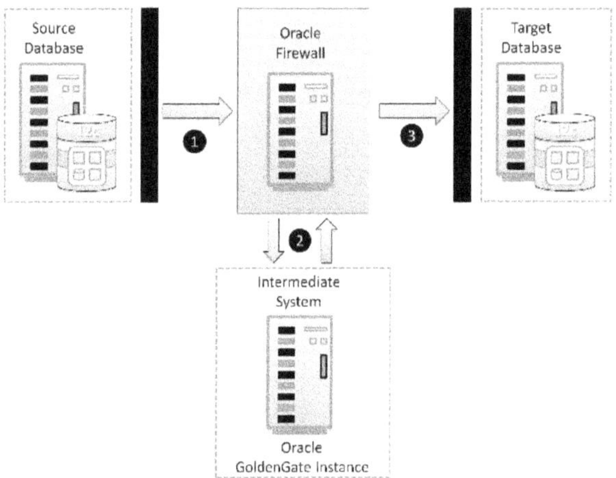

Figure 10-7: Oracle GoldenGate Intermediate System

Figure 10-7 depicts the architecture of a secured distributed environment where firewalls and ports restrictions apply. The Oracle GoldenGate Intermediate System manager processes parameter files must be configured to use an open range of ports specified by the parameter 'PORT' and 'DYNAMICPORTLIST.'

There are (3) options for deploying Oracle GoldenGate instance as an intermediate system.

- No-Database Intermediate System
- Database Intermediate System
- Cascade Topology Intermediate System

No-Database Intermediate System

The *No-Database* option is the most commonly deployed Oracle GoldenGate instance for an intermediate system. It only requires the Oracle Database software installation. The intermediate system continuously receives the stream of trail files shipped by the Primary or Secondary Extract. Through Oracle SQLNET, the Oracle GoldenGate intermediate system instance connects to the source and target databases. This type of intermediate system is suitable when database access is not required for data transformation, where data transformation is strictly performed using Oracle GoldenGate functions without the need to reference the database. Figure 10-8 shows the components for no-database intermediate system performing data transformation using Oracle GoldenGate functions.

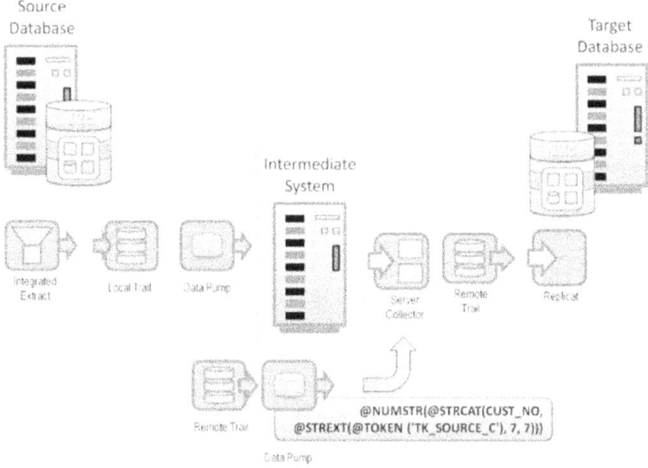

Figure 10-8: No-Database Intermediate System

Database Intermediate System

The *Database* option is applicable to a secured environment operated by independent but related groups. The source database Oracle GoldenGate instance forwards trails to the intermediate system. The intermediate system logs in to its dedicated database for table lookup queries and data transformation. The intermediate database schemas do not store transactional data. Rather, they store the application's lookup tables to translate coded values and form the rows expected by the target database tables.

Figure 10-9 shows database an intermediate system performing data transformation using SQL queries.

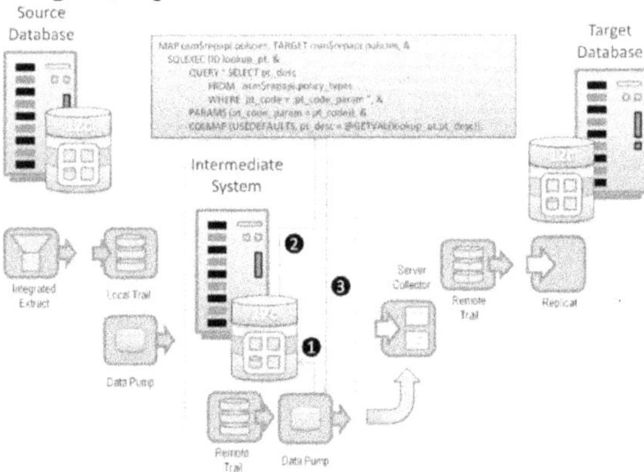

Figure 10-9: Database Intermediate System

Cascade Topology Intermediate System

The *Cascade* option is designed for a large-complex data warehouse environment, where tightly-coupled Oracle GoldenGate instances of intermediate systems are configured between the source and target databases. This type of deployment further promotes scalability by separating the processing across the Oracle GoldenGate instances. For example, the data transformation is performed by intermediate system 'A' and data delivery is performed by intermediate system 'B'. The set of cascaded Oracle GoldenGate instances may be a combination of No-Database and Database Oracle GoldenGate intermediate system instances. Figure 10-10 shows the cascade topology intermediate system.

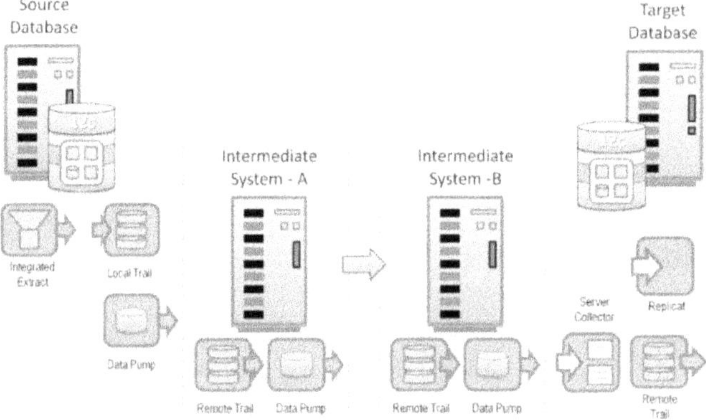

Figure 10-10: Cascade Topology Intermediate System

Deploying No-Database Intermediate System

This section deploys a *No-Database* Intermediate System. The trails received from the source GoldenGate instance are subjected to various data transformations using Oracle GoldenGate functions. The data transformation dynamically changes the ENAME column value to upper case enforced by the target database using the CHECK constraint.

```
SQL> ALTER TABLE scott.emp ADD CONSTRAINT ENAME_UPC
  2  CHECK(ename=upper(ename));

Table altered.

SQL>
```

The deployment is based on the processes workflow depicted by Figure 10-8.

Prepare and Define the Primary Extract

Prepare the Primary Extract parameter file, which is the Extract defined to perform a capture from the online redo log file and write it to the local trail.

```
GGSCI (source1.precisetrace.com) 2> EDIT PARAMS E01S1C1
```

```
EXTRACT E01S1C1
SETENV (ORACLE_SID=S1C1)
SETENV (ORACLE_HOME="/u01/app/oracle/product/12.1.0/dbhome_1")
SETENV (NLS_LANG=AMERICAN_AMERICA.AL32UTF8)
USERID ggs_admin, PASSWORD oracle SYSDBA
RMTHOST 192.168.1.70, MGRPORT 7810
RMTTRAIL ./dirdat/sb
DISCARDFILE ./dirrpt/E01S1C1.dsc, PURGE
TABLE scott.*;
```

```
GGSCI (source1.precisetrace.com) 5> ADD EXTRACT E01S1C1, TRANLOG, BEGIN NOW
EXTRACT added.

GGSCI (source1.precisetrace.com) 6> ADD EXTTRAIL ./dirdat/sb, EXTRACT
E01S1C1, MEGABYTES 15
EXTTRAIL added.

GGSCI (source1.precisetrace.com) 7>
```

Prepare and Define Level-1 Secondary Extract

Level-1 Secondary Extract forwards the local trail from the source system to the intermediate system. Prepare the Level-1 Secondary Extract parameter file, which is the extract defined to perform a capture from the local trail and write it to the intermediate system remote trail.

```
GGSCI (source1.precisetrace.com) 16> EDIT PARAMS P01S1C1
```

```
EXTRACT P01S1C1
USERID ggs_admin@S1C1, PASSWORD oracle
RMTHOST 192.168.1.70, MGRPORT 7810
RMTTRAIL ./dirdat/si
PASSTHRU
TABLE scott.*;
```

```
GGSCI (source1.precisetrace.com) 8> ADD EXTRACT P01S1C1, EXTTRAILSOURCE
./dirdat/sb
EXTRACT added.

GGSCI (source1.precisetrace.com) 10> ADD RMTTRAIL /dirdat/si, EXTRACT
P01S1C1, MEGABYTES 15
RMTTRAIL added.

GGSCI (source1.precisetrace.com) 11>
```

Prepare and Define Level-2 Intermediate System Secondary Extract

Level-2 Secondary Extract forwards the level-1 remote trail stored at the intermediate system to the target system. Prepare the Level-2 Secondary Extract parameter file, which is the extract defined to perform read from the level-1 remote trail and write it to the target remote trail. The Oracle GoldenGate intermediate system instance is composed of the manager process, remote trail, and the data pump only.

```
GGSCI (t2c1.precisetrace.com) 5> EDIT PARAMS P02S1C1
```

```
EXTRACT P02S1C1
USERID ggs_admin@T1C1, PASSWORD oracle
RMTHOST 192.168.1.152, MGRPORT 7809
RMTTRAIL ./dirdat/tb
PASSTHRU
TABLE scott.*;
```

```
GGSCI (t2c1.precisetrace.com) 3> ADD EXTRACT P02S1C1, EXTTRAILSOURCE
./dirdat/si
EXTRACT added.

GGSCI (t2c1.precisetrace.com) 4> ADD RMTTRAIL ./dirdat/tb, EXTRACT P02S1C1,
MEGABYTES 15
RMTTRAIL added.

GGSCI (t2c1.precisetrace.com) 5>
```

Prepare and Define the Replicat

Prepare the Replicat parameter file. The Replicat reads the remote trail then applies the transaction using the target database native SQL calls. Another option of delivery is to configure the Replicat local to the intermediate system instance. Connect remotely via SQLNET to the target database for applying the transactions.

```
GGSCI (target1.precisetrace.com) 2> EDIT PARAMS R01S1C1
```

```
REPLICAT R01S1C1
ASSUMETARGETDEFS
DISCARDFILE ./dirrpt/R01S1C1.dsc, purge
USERID ggs_admin@T1C1, PASSWORD oracle
MAP scott.*, TARGET scott.*;
```

```
GGSCI (target1.precisetrace.com) 1> DBLOGIN USERID ggs_admin, PASSWORD
oracle
Successfully logged into database.

GGSCI (target1.precisetrace.com) 2> ADD CHECKPOINTTABLE

No checkpoint table specified. Using GLOBALS specification
(ggs_admin.chkpttab)...

Successfully created checkpoint table ggs_admin.chkpttab.

GGSCI (target1.precisetrace.com) 3>
```

```
GGSCI (target1.precisetrace.com) 3> ADD REPLICAT R01S1C1, EXTTRAIL
./dirdat/tb
REPLICAT added.


GGSCI (target1.precisetrace.com) 4>
```

Starting Extracts and Replicat

The last step is to start all of the Extracts and Replicat. Begin by starting the Primary & Secondary Extract (data pump)...

```
GGSCI (source1.precisetrace.com) 3> START *

Sending START request to MANAGER ...
EXTRACT E01S1C1 starting

Sending START request to MANAGER ...
EXTRACT P01S1C1 starting

GGSCI (source1.precisetrace.com) 4> INFO ALL

Program     Status      Group       Lag at Chkpt  Time Since Chkpt
```

```
MANAGER     RUNNING
EXTRACT     RUNNING     E01S1C1     00:00:25     00:00:03
EXTRACT     RUNNING     P01S1C1     00:00:00     00:00:23

GGSCI (source1.precisetrace.com) 5>
```

Then, start the intermediate system Secondary Extract (data pump) …

```
GGSCI (t2c1.precisetrace.com) 21> START *

Sending START request to MANAGER ...
EXTRACT P02S1C1 starting


GGSCI (t2c1.precisetrace.com) 22> INFO ALL

Program     Status      Group       Lag at Chkpt  Time Since Chkpt

MANAGER     RUNNING
EXTRACT     RUNNING     P02S1C1     00:00:00      00:00:39


GGSCI (t2c1.precisetrace.com) 23>
```

Lastly, start the Replicat on the target system…

```
GGSCI (target1.precisetrace.com) 9> START *

Sending START request to MANAGER ...
REPLICAT R01S1C1 starting


GGSCI (target1.precisetrace.com) 10> INFO ALL

Program     Status      Group       Lag at Chkpt  Time Since Chkpt

MANAGER     RUNNING
REPLICAT    RUNNING     R01S1C1     00:00:00      00:00:02


GGSCI (target1.precisetrace.com) 11>
```

Insert Data and Verify Statistics

On the source database, perform the following INSERT statement.

```
SQL> INSERT INTO scott.dept
  2  VALUES (60, 'ODI', 'RESTON');

1 row created.

SQL> COMMIT;
```

On the target database, perform the following SELECT statement to verify the row has been added to the target database.

```
SQL> SELECT * FROM scott.dept;
    DEPTNO  DNAME                 LOC
----------  --------------        -------------
        10  ACCOUNTING            NEW YORK
        20  RESEARCH              DALLAS
        30  SALES                 CHICAGO
        40  OPERATIONS            BOSTON
        50  GG                    DUBAI
        60  ODI                   RESTON

6 rows selected.
SQL>
```

Another option is to display Extract and Replicat statistics. The following statement displays the Replicat Statistics and comprehensive DML statistics.

```
GGSCI (target1.precisetrace.com) 3> STATS R01S1C1

Sending STATS request to REPLICAT R01S1C1 ...

Start of Statistics at 2015-05-11 01:14:45.

Replicating from SCOTT.DEPT to SCOTT.DEPT:

*** Total statistics since 2015-05-11 01:09:11 ***
    Total inserts                                    2.00
    Total updates                                    0.00
    Total deletes                                    0.00
    Total discards                                   0.00
    Total operations                                 2.00

*** Daily statistics since 2015-05-11 01:09:11 ***
    Total inserts                                    2.00
    Total updates                                    0.00
    Total deletes                                    0.00
    Total discards                                   0.00
    Total operations                                 2.00

*** Hourly statistics since 2015-05-11 01:09:11 ***
    Total inserts                                    2.00
    Total updates                                    0.00
    Total deletes                                    0.00
    Total discards                                   0.00
    Total operations                                 2.00

*** Latest statistics since 2015-05-11 01:09:11 ***
    Total inserts                                    2.00
    Total updates                                    0.00
    Total deletes                                    0.00
    Total discards                                   0.00
    Total operations                                 2.00
End of Statistics.

GGSCI (target1.precisetrace.com) 4>
```

Data Definition Language Replications

In addition to replication of DML transactions, Oracle GoldenGate supports the replication of Data Definition Language (DDL) statements. This feature enables a dynamic in-house development team to rollout changes to a database objects definition by means of parameters and options for fine grain control and filtering of DDL statements from the source to one or more target databases.

By default, the Primary Extract has the DDL synchronization disabled, where as the Replicat has the DDL replication enabled. The Extract DDL synchronization is explicitly activated by the inclusion of the DDL parameter in the same parameter file for DML synchronization. The Secondary Extract (data pump) applies 'PASSTHRU,' and the Replicat applies 'ASSUMETARGETDETFS' parameters. DDL statements are limited to a length of 2MB. Larger statements are skipped by the Extract.

Filtering in which DDL statements are replicated is done by extending the Extract or Replicat DDL parameter to include conditions that must be stratified to capture the corresponding DDL statements. The conditions are evaluated using the 'AND' logical operator for the options as operands.

Supported Database Object Types

Oracle GoldenGate supports DDL statements replication of the major database object types. These are the objects types commonly utilized by the database applications.

- Tables
- Indexes
- Clusters
- Packages
- Procedures
- Synonyms
- Triggers
- Types
- Views
- Materialized Views
- Database Users
- Tablespaces
- Roles

Oracle Database 12c has 44 object types, only subsets of them are supported.

```
SQL> SELECT unique object_type
   2 FROM   dba_objects
   3 ORDER BY 1;
```

Activating DDL Statements Replication

For Oracle Database 12c, none of the steps below are required. However, Oracle Database 10g and Oracle Database 11g activation of DDL statements replication requires executing the following sequence of steps.

Disable the Database's Recyclebin Support

```
SQL> ALTER SYSTEM SET recyclebin=off SCOPE=SPFILE;

System altered.

SQL> STARTUP FORCE
ORACLE instance started.

Total System Global Area           1068937216 bytes
Fixed Size                            2296576 bytes
Variable Size                       973079808 bytes
Database Buffers                     88080384 bytes
Redo Buffers                          5480448 bytes
Database mounted.
Database opened.
SQL>
```

Create DDL Statements Replication Tables Support

Navigate to the Oracle GoldenGate instance software location. Execute the scripts 'maker_setup.sql and ddl_setup.sql.' When prompted, enter the Oracle GoldenGate database schema. Upon successful completion, it creates the following tables:

- GGS_MARKER
- GGS_DDL_RULES
- GGS_DDL_RULES_LOG
- GGS_DDL_HIST_ALT
- GGS_DDL_HIST

```
SQL> @marker_setup.sql

Marker setup script

You will be prompted for the name of a schema for the Oracle GoldenGate
database objects.
NOTE: The schema must be created prior to running this script.
NOTE: Stop all DDL replication before starting this installation.

Enter Oracle GoldenGate schema name:ggs_admin
```

```
Marker setup table script complete, running verification script...
Please enter the name of a schema for the GoldenGate database objects:
Setting schema name to GGS_ADMIN

MARKER TABLE
------------------------------
OK

MARKER SEQUENCE
------------------------------
OK

Script complete.
SQL>
```

```
SQL> @ddl_setup.sql

Oracle GoldenGate DDL Replication setup script

Verifying that current user has privileges to install DDL Replication...

You will be prompted for the name of a schema for the Oracle GoldenGate
database objects.
NOTE: For an Oracle 10g source, the system recycle bin must be disabled. For
Oracle 11g and later, it can be enabled.
NOTE: The schema must be created prior to running this script.
NOTE: Stop all DDL replication before starting this installation.

Enter Oracle GoldenGate schema name:ggs_admin

Working, please wait ...
Spooling to file ddl_setup_spool.txt

Checking for sessions that are holding locks on Oracle Golden Gate metadata
tables ...

Check complete.

Using GGS_ADMIN as a Oracle GoldenGate schema name.

Working, please wait ...

DDL replication setup script complete, running verification script...
Please enter the name of a schema for the GoldenGate database objects:
Setting schema name to GGS_ADMIN

CLEAR_TRACE STATUS:

Line/pos   Error
---------- -----------------------------------------------------------------
No errors  No errors

LOCATION OF DDL TRACE FILE
--------------------------------------------------------------------------------
/u01/app/oracle/diag/rdbms/s1c1/S1C1/trace/ggs_ddl_trace.log
```

```
Analyzing installation status...

VERSION OF DDL REPLICATION
--------------------------------------------------------------------------------
OGGCORE_12.1.2.0.0_PLATFORMS_130924.1316

STATUS OF DDL REPLICATION
--------------------------------------------------------------------------------
SUCCESSFUL installation of DDL Replication software components

Script complete.
SQL>
```

Create Database Role and Grant Privileges

Create the database role 'GGS_GGSUSER_ROLE' required for DDL statements replication. Then, grant the role to the Oracle GoldenGate database schema.

```
SQL> @role_setup.sql

GGS Role setup script

This script will drop and recreate the role GGS_GGSUSER_ROLE
To use a different role name, quit this script and then edit the params.sql
script to change the gg_role parameter to the preferred name. (Do not run
the script.)

You will be prompted for the name of a schema for the GoldenGate database
objects.
NOTE: The schema must be created prior to running this script.
NOTE: Stop all DDL replication before starting this installation.

Enter GoldenGate schema name:ggs_admin
Wrote file role_setup_set.txt

PL/SQL procedure successfully completed.


Role setup script complete

Grant this role to each user assigned to the Extract, GGSCI, and Manager
processes, by using the following SQL command:

GRANT GGS_GGSUSER_ROLE TO <loggedUser>

where <loggedUser> is the user assigned to the GoldenGate processes.

SQL> grant ggs_ggsuser_role to ggs_admin;

Grant succeeded.
```

Enable DDL Replication Support

The last step is to enable DDL statement replication support and pin the package into the database shared pool area.

```
SQL> @ddl_enable.sql

Trigger altered.

SQL> @ddl_pin ggs_admin

PL/SQL procedure successfully completed.

PL/SQL procedure successfully completed.

PL/SQL procedure successfully completed.

SQL>
```

DDL Parameter Syntax and Options

By default, DDL statements replication are unconstrained. Optional conditions are applied to control and filter the replication. If the DDL parameter's options are included, the DDL statements must satisfy all conditions to be replicated. The DDL parameter has the following syntax:

```
DDL [
 { INCLUDE | EXCLUDE }

  [, MAPPED | UNMAPPED | OTHER | ALL]
  [, OPTYPE ]
  [, OBJTYPE '']
  [, OBJNAME ]
  [, INSTR '']
  [, INSTRCOMMENTS '']
  [, STAYMETADATA]
  [, EVENTACTIONS {}
]
```

Table 10-1 lists the DDL parameter's options.

DDL Option	Description
Include and/or Exclude	Identify what to include and what to exclude when performing DDL statement replication
Mapped, Unmapped, Other R and All	Applying include and exclude according to the DDL operation scope.
OpType	Applying include and exclude to specific operation types.

ObjType	Applying include and exclude to specific object types.
ObjName	Applying include and exclude to matching object name.
InStr	Applying include or exclude to DDL statements based on matching characters of the DDL string.
InstrComments	Applying include or exclude to DDL statements that contain a matching characters of string within a comment.

Table 10-1: DDL Parameter Options

Strings Replacement

The string replacement allows the replacement of a source string with another string on the target. The following example illustrates the substitution of the schema 'SCOTT' with 'GGS_ADMIN' when performing the 'CRATE TABLE DDL' statement:

```
REPLICAT R01S1C1
ASSUMETARGETDEFS
DISCARDFILE ./dirrpt/R01S1C1.dsc, purge
DDL include ALL
DDLSUBST 'SCOTT' WITH 'GGS_ADMIN'
DDLERROR DEFAULT IGNORE RETRYOP
USERID ggs_admin@T1C1, PASSWORD oracle
MAP scott.*, TARGET scott.*;

SQL> CREATE TABLE scott.cust(cust_name VARCHAR2(40) PRIMARY KEY);

Table created.

SQL>
```

Replicated on the target under the schema GGS_ADMIN.

```
SQL> DESC ggs_admin.cust
 Name                                      Null?    Type
 ----------------------------------------- -------- --------------------
 CUST_NAME                                 NOT NULL VARCHAR2(40)

SQL>
```

The Extract and the Replicat Parameters Files

The Extract parameters file may performs filtering using the object type option. Only the object of table type and index are replicated. The Replicat application of the DDL statement on the target database is unchanged. The filtering may be performed on either side.

```
EXTRACT E01S1C1
SETENV (ORACLE_SID=S1C1)
SETENV (ORACLE_HOME="/u01/app/oracle/product/12.1.0/dbhome_1")
SETENV (NLS_LANG=AMERICAN_AMERICA.AL32UTF8)
USERID ggs_admin, PASSWORD oracle
EXTTRAIL ./dirdat/sb
DDL include ALL
DISCARDFILE ./dirrpt/E01S1C1.dsc, PURGE
TABLE scott.*;
REPLICAT R01S1C1
ASSUMETARGETDEFS
DISCARDFILE ./dirrpt/R01S1C1.dsc, purge
DDL include ALL
DDLERROR DEFAULT IGNORE RETRYOP
USERID ggs_admin@T1C1, PASSWORD oracle
MAP scott.*, TARGET scott.*;
```

Replication Examples of DDL Statements

The following are examples for demonstrating DDL replication from a source to target system. The DDL statement is executed on the source database then verified on the target database.

Tables Replication

The table 'SCOTT.PROFILES' is created on the source database. Since the Extract is configured to include all types of objects, it replicates the table DDL statement on the target database.

```
SQL> CREATE TABLE scott.profiles(
  2  pname  VARCHAR2(32) PRIMARY KEY,
  3  pemail VARCHAR2(64),
  4  paddr  VARCHAR2(128));

Table created.

SQL>
```

Connect to target to verify the table has been replicated successfully.

```
SQL> DESC scott.profiles
 Name                                      Null?    Type
 ----------------------------------------- -------- ----------------
 PNAME                                     NOT NULL VARCHAR2(32)
 PEMAIL                                             VARCHAR2(64)
 PADDR                                              VARCHAR2(128)

SQL>
```

Oracle GoldenGate DDL statements replication supports Index Organized Table (IOT) and the ALTER TABLE statement.

Indexes Replication

While connected to the source database, create an index on table 'SCOTT.PROFILES' for the column 'PEMAIL'.

```
SQL> CREATE INDEX scott.pemail_idx
  2  ON scott.profiles(pemail);

Index created.

SQL>
```

Connect to the target database and verify the index has been replicated successfully.

```
SQL> SELECT index_name
  2  FROM   dba_indexes
  3  WHERE  owner='SCOTT' and table_name='PROFILES';

INDEX_NAME
----------------------------
PEMAIL_IDX
SYS_C009867

SQL>
```

Clusters Replication

The purpose of clusters is to provide an efficient mechanism to store data blocks and to enhance the data retrieval (queries). Create a cluster on the target database then verify the replication on the target.

```
SQL> CREATE CLUSTER scott.dept_no(deptno NUMBER);

Cluster created.

SQL>
```

Connect to the target database and query the data dictionary view 'DBA_CLUSTERS.'

```
SQL> SELECT cluster_name
  2  FROM   dba_clusters
  3  WHERE  owner='SCOTT';
CLUSTER_NAME
--------------------
DEPT_NO
SQL>
```

Procedures Replication

A procedure is an exactable PL/SQL code stored in the database. The following programs create a procedure called 'GETEMAIL.'

```
SQL> CREATE OR REPLACE PROCEDURE scott.getemail(Ppname   IN VARCHAR2,
                                                Ppemail OUT VARCHAR2) IS
        vpemail VARCHAR2(64);
     BEGIN
       SELECT pemail into vpemail
       FROM   scott.profiles
       WHERE  pname =ppname;
     END;
     /

Procedure created.

SQL>
```

Connect to the target database to verify it has been created successfully.

```
SQL> DESC scott.getemail
PROCEDURE scott.getemail
 Argument Name                  Type                    In/Out Default?
 ------------------------------ ----------------------- ------ --------
 PPNAME                         VARCHAR2                IN
 PPEMAIL                        VARCHAR2                OUT

SQL>
```

Synonyms Replication

From the source database create a synonym for 'SCOTT.PROFILES.'

```
SQL> CREATE PUBLIC SYNONYM profiles FOR scott.profiles;

Synonym created.

SQL>
```

Query the data dictionary view 'ALL_SYNONYMS' to verify it has been created successfully.

```
SQL> SELECT SYNONYM_NAME
     FROM   all_synonyms
     WHERE  table_owner='SCOTT' AND table_name='PROFILES';

SYNONYM_NAME
----------------------
PROFILES

SQL>
```

Views Replication

Views Replication is a result set of a query. The views enable database users to access one or more base tables through the views. Create the view 'EMP_VW_10' which stores the result set of department 10 only.

```
SQL> CREATE VIEW scott.emp_vw_90
  2  AS
  3  SELECT *
  4  FROM   scott.emp
  5  WHERE  deptno=10;

View created.

SQL>
```

Verify the view has been successfully created on the target database.

```
SQL> DESC scott.emp_vw_90
 Name                                      Null?     Type
 ----------------------------------------- -------- ----------------
 EMPNO                                     NOT NULL  NUMBER(4)
 ENAME                                               VARCHAR2(10)
 JOB                                                 VARCHAR2(9)
 MGR                                                 NUMBER(4)
 HIREDATE                                            DATE
 SAL                                                 NUMBER(7,2)
 COMM                                                NUMBER(7,2)
 DEPTNO                                              NUMBER(2)

SQL>
```

Database Users Replication

Create a new user on the source database then grant 'CREATE SESSION' to the user.

```
SQL> CREATE USER ggs2_admin IDENTIFIED BY oracle;

User created.

SQL> GRANT CREATE SESSION TO ggs2_admin;

Grant succeeded.

SQL>
```

Navigate to the target system. Connect using the database username created on the source database.

```
SQL> CONN ggs2_admin/oracle
```

```
Connected.
SQL>
```

Tablespaces Replication

Create an Oracle Managed File (OMF) tablespace 'GGS2_DAT' on the source system.

```
SQL> CREATE TABLESPACE ggs2_dat;

Tablespace created.

SQL>
```

On the target system, query the data dictionary 'DBA_TABLESPACES' to verify the tablespace has been successfully created.

```
SQL> SELECT tablespace_name
  2  FROM   dba_tablespaces;

TABLESPACE_NAME
------------------------------
SYSTEM
SYSAUX
UNDOTBS1
TEMP
USERS
GGS2_DAT

6 rows selected.

SQL>
```

Roles Replication

Create a database role 'SEL_ON_EMP' on the source database. Grant the role basic object privilege.

```
SQL> CREATE ROLE sel_on_emp;

Role created.

SQL> GRANT SELECT ON scott.emp TO sel_on_emp;

Grant succeeded.

SQL>
```

Connect to the target database. Grant the role another object privileges, which verifies the role of the DDL statement has been replicated successfully.

```
SQL> GRANT UPDATE ON scott.emp TO sel_on_emp;
Grant succeeded.
SQL>
```

Summary

This last chapter of the book has covered integration-specific techniques, normally found in large scale environments. The integration of Oracle GoldenGate with Oracle database features extends the functionalities of applications and maximizes the Oracle GoldenGate Return of Investment (ROI). Though the chapter has covered specific integration areas, Oracle GoldenGate is engineered to support highly complex infrastructures, such as ATM networks, legacy systems, and various adapters.

Since Oracle customers are using Oracle Data Guard for building their disaster recovery (DR) site, Oracle GoldenGate allows these customers to synchronize a second read-write copy from the read-only standby database. This database can be used for different projects including reports and business intelligence.

Oracle's decision of not enhancing Oracle Streams 11.2 announced following the acquisition of Oracle GoldenGate. Hence, customers should plan the migration from Oracle Streams to Oracle GoldenGate. The feature sets delivered by Oracle GoldenGate enable customers to extend their distributed applications to support maximum Heterogeneities, a key feature not available from Oracle Streams.

Oracle GoldenGate Intermediate System is designed to maximize the scalability of a complex environment consisting of a large number of targets. The intermediate system becomes the data hub for distributing data to meet the target system's requirements by performing data transformation prior to sending the data.

Oracle GoldenGate 11.2 introduced the Integrated Capture option for Oracle Database only. It eliminates installing Oracle GoldenGate on the production systems. Instead, Oracle GoldenGate is installed on a downstream system receiving the database transaction logs, performing the capture, and creating the trails for the next systems. The integrated capture option is suitable for a highly secured environment.

Data Definition Language (DDL) is useful for application with frequent changes and ad-hoc deployments. Database objects such as tablespaces, tables, indexes, users, etc. are replicated. DDL replication is flexible for enhanced security and database objects filtering.

And lastly, Oracle GoldenGate 12c is engineered to be highly integrated with advanced database features, in particular Oracle Real Application Clusters (RAC) and Oracle Data Guard (DG). Oracle GoldenGate is positioned to complement these database options and not to replace them. Adapting state-of-the-art transformation capabilities on heterogeneous environment, and it continues support for the major database vendors: Oracle, Microsoft, IBM, Teradata, HP and open source (MySQL).

Index

E

F

G

H

I

J

K

L

M

N

O

P

Q

R

S

T

U

V

W

X

Y

About the Author

Fawzi A. Alswaimil purchased and started using Oracle (Version 6) for a DOS-based operating system in 1988 during his undergraduate studies at the University of Arizona. During his studies, he adapted Liner Programming techniques using Oracle PRO*C to develop a "Rivers Flood Simulator" for his senior project. He graduated in May, 1989 with a Bachelor of Science in Engineering Mathematics.

His first job was as an Oracle DBA (1989-1994) with Oracle 7.3, he earned the Oracle Master in 1993. He worked with Oracle CASE tool (Oracle Designer) extensively and published an Oracle Designer White Paper titled "Database Reverse Engineering Using Oracle Designer." Since the release of Oracle 8, he has been working extensively with Oracle Database options and features for high-availability and scalability, including Advanced Replication, Streams, the Recovery Manager (RMAN), Real Applications Cluster (RAC), and Data Guard (DG).

Soon after the acquisition of GoldenGate Inc. by Oracle Corporation in 2009, he dedicated his focus on Oracle GoldenGate. He developed an "Oracle GoldenGate Implementer's Workshop", Oracle GoldenGate software at major Oracle customer sites, utilities for Oracle GoldenGate, and delivered the official Oracle University GoldenGate curriculums to end users. From 1995-2015, he has been teaching the majority of Oracle Technology courses at Oracle University.

On the other side of his professional career as an Oracle Database administrator, he is an advanced Oracle for .NET and Oracle Web PL/SQL toolkit developer. He developed a lightweight PL/SQL API using a PL/SQL Web toolkit used by several portal applications, products, and utilities. Developed various Oracle for .NET applications: Xplain (An Oracle Database Reverse Engineering and performance management tool), Internet Protocol Surveillance System (IPSS), Oracle GoldenGate Configuration Assistant (GGCA), Oracle GoldenGate Companion, and Oracle GoldenGate load-balancer.

www.ingramcontent.com/pod-product-compliance
Lightning Source LLC
Chambersburg PA
CBHW080335220326
41598CB00030B/4508

* 9 7 8 0 9 8 6 1 1 9 4 3 9 *